FRANK LLOYD WRIGHT
THE LOST YEARS, 1910-1922

ANTHONY ALOFSIN

FRANK LLOYD WRIGHT
THE LOST YEARS, 1910-1922

A STUDY OF INFLUENCE

THE UNIVERSITY OF CHICAGO PRESS CHICAGO AND LONDON

This publication has been supported by a grant from the Graham Foundation for Advanced Studies in the Fine Arts.

Frontispiece: Frank Lloyd Wright, c. 1909

The University of Chicago Press, Chicago 60637
The University of Chicago Press, Ltd., London
© 1993 by Anthony Alofsin
All rights reserved. Published 1993
Paperback edition 1998
Printed in the United States of America
02 01 00 99 98   2   3   4   5

ISBN: 0-226-01366-9 (cloth)
ISBN: 0-226-01504-1 (paperback)

⊗ The paper used in this publication meets the minimum requirements of the American National Standard for Information Sciences—Permanence of Paper for Printed Library Materials, ANSI Z39.48-1992.

To the memory of EBA and FBA

Contents

Acknowledgments

In the years this book was in progress I received generous assistance from several academic institutions, archives, and many individuals in America, Europe, and Japan. A grant from the University Research Institute of the University of Texas at Austin supported preparation of the book, and the university's School of Architecture provided invaluable assistance. Support from the Austro-American Fulbright Commission and the Bundesministerium für Wissenschaft und Forschung allowed for a guest professorship at the Akademie der bildenden Künste in Vienna where I began revisions to the manuscript. Otto Antonia Graf, director of the Akademie's Institut für Kunstgeschichte, stimulated my interest in the logic of Frank Lloyd Wright's geometry; Graf's work and the discourse that sprang up between us helped open my eyes to the prevalence of primary forms in art. At Harvard University, I am indebted to Eduard Sekler, my first professor and mentor, who has provided support, encouragement, and critical insight with greater consistency and for a longer time than any other of my teachers. To him and James Ackerman I owe my formation in the history of architecture. At Columbia University, the late Howard Hibbard and his colleagues on the faculty of the Department of Art History and Archaeology instilled in me the need for an open, challenging mind.

Several archives gave crucial assistance without which this work could not have been written. The Frank Lloyd Wright Foundation provided me, starting in 1984, with the first extended access to Wright's archives in over forty years. I owe a particular debt to Richard Carney, Bruce Brooks Pfeiffer, Oscar Muñoz, and Margo Stipe. The members of the Frank Lloyd Wright Fellowship—too numerous to cite individually—graciously shared their lives, work, and friendship with me. And while I benefited from their direct experience with Frank Lloyd Wright and his wife, Olgivanna, I formed my own independent assessments and critical perspective.

In the early research phases, Nicholas Olsberg of the Canadian Centre for Architecture and Gene Waddell of the Getty Center for the History of Art and the Humanities facilitated my work. Wim de Wit of the Chicago Historical Society provided generous access to the manuscript collections in the society's Charles F. Murphy Architectural Study Center. At the University of Utah, the staff of the Special Collections and Peter Goss, of the School of Architecture, made available the Taylor Woolley papers and photographs from the Woolley Collection. Shonnie Finnegan and Jack Quinan facilitated my access to the Wright–Darwin D. Martin papers at the State University of New York at Buffalo. The Northwest Architectural Archives of the University of Minnesota provided important documents. C. Ford Peatross, curator of architecture, design, and engineering collections at the Library of Congress, assisted my study of newly accessioned and unpublished drawings by Frank Lloyd Wright. Alan Seaburg, curator of manuscripts at the Andover-Harvard Theological Library, provided material from the William Norman Guthrie Collection. Meg Klinkow and Elaine Harrington of the Frank Lloyd Wright Home and Studio provided research material and helpful suggestions. Domino's Center for Architecture and Design also assisted my research.

Several friends and colleagues in Vienna shared their insights and experience with me. Paul Asenbaum not only opened his extensive collections of Austrian art and furniture but shared with me his prodigious knowledge of art and architecture. Christian Witt-Dörring, curator of decorative arts at the Museum für angewandte Kunst, assisted me in the use of his institutions' archives, collections, and library, and we had many thought-provoking discussions. Additional assistance and insight came from Almut Krapf, of the Institut für Kunstgeschichte, Akademie der bildenden Künste; Dr. Michael Krapf, curator of Baroque painting, Österreichische Galerie; and Dr. Gabriele Helke, Kunsthistorisches Museum. Dr. Eva Erblich, Österreichische Nationalbibliothek, and Dr. Marian Bisanz-Prakken, Albertina Collection of Graphic Arts, aided my research.

I received rich insights from the readers of the manuscript—two who were anonymous, and two who were not, Elaine and Kevin Harrington. Several scholars made invaluable comments and suggestions, including William Marlin, Narciso Menocal, Jack Quinan, Robert Sweeney, and David Van Zanten. The late Edgar Kaufmann, Jr., shared his insights with me and, writing with grace, set a standard of inquiry I have emulated. Others who assisted my work in numerous ways were Betty Sue Flowers, Christiane Collins, Jelle de Boer, Robert Bruegmann, Barbara Elsner, Jutta and Wolfgang Fischer, William Griffith, Elizabeth Wright Ingraham, Paul Kruty, Maya Moran, Nina Nedeljkov, Anne Nissen, Francesco Passanti. In addition there are several individuals I gratefully acknowledge in the notes of this book. I owe a special thanks to Masaaki Sekiya for his assistance and to Naibo Akashi for permission to reproduce illustrations from thelate Dr. Nobumichi Akashi's *Kyu Teikoku Hoteruno Jisshoteki Kenkyu* (Frank Lloyd Wright in Imperial Hotel), the definitive recording of the Imperial Hotel prior to its destruction in 1968. Masami Tanigawa, who pioneered studies of Wright in Japan, generously allowed me to reprint his illustrations. Other authors, archives, photographers, and publishers who generously provided many of the illustrations for this book are cited separately in the photographic credits.

In Austin, I benefited from many discussions with Christopher Long. For preparation of the manuscript and illustrations I am grateful to Tracy Hall Smith, Patricia Tierney Alofsin, and Katie Kosut. Dana Norman's photographic skills were invaluable in the preparation of illustrations.

Finally, I owe a special thanks to Karen Wilson and John McCudden—without their help this work would not have reached its present development.

We are all prisoners of a rigid conception of what is important and what is not. We anxiously follow what we suppose to be important, while what we suppose to be unimportant wages guerrilla warfare behind our backs, transforming the world without our knowledge and eventually mounting a surprise attack on us.—Milan Kundera, *The Book of Laughter and Forgetting*

Introduction

The influence of Frank Lloyd Wright on young European architects has always been one of the major conventions in the history of modernism. The source of Wright's influence has been attributed to his famous books *Ausgeführte Bauten und Entwürfe von Frank Lloyd Wright* (1911) and *Frank Lloyd Wright: Ausgeführte Bauten* (1910–11), published by the Wasmuth Verlag in Berlin. The story of Wright's influence is repeated in almost every standard history of modern architecture. Henry-Russell Hitchcock's appraisal, written in 1932, typifies the conventional form this story takes: "The Wasmuth publications of Wright's work in 1910 and 1911 for which Kuno Francke and Werner Hegeman [*sic*] were chiefly responsible made Wright's work more familiar to Europeans than to his own compatriots."[1] The standard survey text, *Gardner's Art Through the Ages* repeated the story, with slight variations, in several of its editions. The version published in 1970 is typical: "Discerning clients commissioned his works, but his reputation grew more rapidly in Europe, especially Holland and Germany, than in America. The publication in Berlin in 1910 of a portfolio of Wright's work hastened destruction of the dying Art Nouveau and stimulated younger men to turn in the new direction."[2]

My purpose here is to show that the standard assertions about the influence of the Wasmuth publications were part of an elaborate misunderstanding by historians and architects; that the historical record of Wright's experience of Europe is far more complex than was previously believed; that contact with Europe in 1909–11 had a greater impact on Wright than he had on European architecture; and that Wright's work from 1910 until the early 1920s had a richness which has not yet been understood.

This study challenges previous opinions that have become myths in the history of modern architecture. Research for this radically new view rests on complete access to Wright's archives in 1984–85, the first such access in forty years, and to the extraordinary letters between Wright and his client in Buffalo, Darwin D. Martin.[3] The uncovering of the complex and contradictory events of Wright's life and work, revealed from these archival studies, gives depth to the lost years of Wright's career from 1909 to around 1922. While the period has been considered lost in terms of our understanding of Wright's work, it was rich in creative development, regardless of the fact that Wright built far fewer buildings in the decade after 1910 than in the previous decade.[4] I present one aspect of that period: Europe's impact on Wright's artistic development. The complementary study of Wright's influence in Europe will follow.[5]

The initial myth about Wright and influence arises from the fact that historians and architects have tended to repeat received views about Wright and his relationship to Europe. His designs, published in Germany, are said to have provided immediate models for modern European architecture. For instance, Walter Gropius and Adolf Meyer's 1914 Werkbund Pavilion in Cologne is used as an example of the influence of

1. City National Bank and Hotel, Mason City, Iowa, 1911 (*Western Architect,* December 1911).

2. Walter Gropius and Adolf Meyer, Werkbund Pavilion, Cologne, view from interior court, c. 1914 (Busch-Reisinger Museum, BRM-GA 6.3).

Wright's City National Bank in Mason City, Iowa (figs. 1, 2). But the example of Wright's work used to illustrate this influence does not come from the Wasmuth publications. The image, reproduced by Vincent Scully, comes from the *Western Architect* of 1911.[6] It actually shows the shop facades in front of a hotel attached to the bank. And there is no indication that Gropius and Meyer knew the magazine. In the Wasmuth plates Wright gave more emphasis to the bank than the hotel, and the internal disposition of rooms in both parts is quite different from the great open hall of the Werkbund Pavilion (fig. 3). Fur-

3. City National Bank and Hotel, Mason City, Iowa (published in Wasmuth monograph, *Ausgeführte Bauten und Entwürfe von Frank Lloyd Wright,* pl. XLIXa, 1911).

4. Walter Gropius and Adolf Meyer, Werkbund Pavilion, Cologne, front view, c. 1914 (Busch-Reisinger Museum, BRM-GA 6.2).

thermore, the illustration used to show Wright's influence is a view from the interior court; the front facade (fig. 4) resembles Wright's hotel even less. The claimed "influence" by Wright occurs only through a simple visual analogy. Using such assertions, one historian has passed the myth of influence to another in a series of historical explanations that has lasted for sixty years without anyone examining the evidence for such claims. The lineage extended from one generation of historians to the next: from Nikolaus Pevsner to Henry-Russell Hitchcock, Sigfried Giedion, Vincent Scully, and those who followed.[7]

Wright's writings, archives, and collateral documents show, however, that the reception of his work in Europe was incidental to his own purpose of creating a primer for a new American architecture. The publication of the *Ausgeführte Bauten und Entwürfe*, in two folio volumes, and the small book of photographs and plans, *Ausgeführte Bauten*, which Wright referred to as a *Sonderheft* (special edition), were vanity printings that were fraught with problems. Finances and difficulties with his publisher in Berlin actually limited the distribution of the folios to 100 copies reserved for European sale out of a projected total of 1,250. The *Sonderheft* was more available, with 3,900 copies of an inferior first edition designated for European distribution. Wright ultimately sought to sell his own copies of both publications by mail order in the United States. The dates and availability of these publications have never been correctly reported. The monograph appeared in 1911, not 1910, with Wright receiving the first volume in June and the second volume in December. An initial run of the European edition of the *Sonderheft* was printed in November 1910, but the American edition was printed in 1911 and did not arrive in Chicago until November 1912. And the availability of the Wasmuth publications to Europeans was later in 1911 and 1912 than has previously been supposed. Except for one brief review in 1913, there was virtually no critical response in Germany to Wright's work as a result of the publications.[8]

A second myth about Wright's influence in Europe concerns the existence of an exhibition in 1910 that popularized his work. While such major figures of the Modern Movement as Walter Gropius and Mies van der Rohe stated that they saw an "exhibition" of Wright's drawings in Berlin, there is no documentary evidence to support their claims. Their memories of an exhibition may have been the product of the repeated stories associated with the Wasmuth publications' importance. Instead of a public exhibition of Wright's work, there was a lecture presented by Bruno Möhring, the distinguished German architect, to a club of Berlin architects in February 1911 at which some of Wright's drawings were on display.

Möhring turns out to be critical in unraveling a third myth, that Harvard professor Kuno Francke was Wright's connection to the Wasmuth publishing empire. Wright thought that Francke suggested his project to Wasmuth, and historians have subsequently repeated Wright's version. However, Wright was never sure that Francke provided the important contacts with Wasmuth. It is more likely that Möhring, who had attempted to visit Wright in America and was an editor and author for the Wasmuth Verlag, prepared the way for Wright's access to German publishing.

A fourth myth has arisen from the few discussions that claim Europe influenced Wright.[9] Wright was influenced by Europe, but not in the ways that historians have assumed. Some writers have noted briefly a similarity between Wright's designs for furniture and objects and those of his European contemporaries.[10] But the connections between them were far more significant than the superficial resemblances: he shared with the artists and architects of the Secession movements a belief in "pure forms" as the source of cultural rebirth. This belief led artists to search for models of modern design in the art and architecture of ancient, exotic, and primitive cultures. In addition to discovering a common bond with his contemporaries, in 1910, at the age of forty-two, Wright saw for the first time the monuments of Western architecture, the traditions of European vernacular building, and the great capitals of Europe: London, Berlin, Paris, and Vienna. Wright's visit to Vienna rejuvenated his work. There he found examples of cubic, figural sculpture that allowed him to end his own search for the geometric representation of the human figure. He adapted these sculptures for his own major works of the decade: Midway Gardens and the Imperial Hotel.

Wright also saw systems of ornamental design, based on the rotation of simple geometric forms, that confirmed and extended his own methods of composition. The geometric aesthetic used by the architects and artists of the Viennese Secession in designs for total environments paralleled his own work. Although he had utilized rotated shapes and the circle and square in his compositions before 1909, after his return to America he began to use the rotated forms of geometry to unite his designs of furniture, chinaware, light fixtures, and windows into more integrated compositions than he had previously achieved. Beginning with experimental designs of ornament in 1911, Wright developed a system of rotating geometric forms that increasingly became one of his principal methods of design. This system eventually involved a fundamental alteration in his basic design process that has not been previously recognized: Wright transferred the asymmetry in his ornaments to his plans. A new dynamic visual diagonality entered his planning process, and the primary forms of geometry—circles, ellipses, triangles—eventually became plan motifs. These joined the square, the major element in rectilinear designs, to form a basic mode of design that Wright relied on for the rest of his career. At the same time, these basic elements of geometry existed in Wright's mind not purely as formalistic objects but as symbols of societal and universal meaning.

A fifth myth about Frank Lloyd Wright concerns how Maya architecture influenced him. This myth does not take into account that Wright's European experience stimulated his broad interest in exotic architecture. Vincent Scully has perceptively pointed out Wright's extraordinary ability to "condense" the work of other architects into a "new unity."[11] Suggesting that this central issue has been absent from Wright studies, Scully suggests a lineage from one building to another that is rooted in similarities between Wright's buildings and, among other sources, Maya architecture. The historian maintains that, as early as 1889, the influence of the Maya can be traced through Bruce Price's house at Tuxedo Park to Wright's own house in Oak Park and onward to Wright's Winslow House of 1893. However, these examples of influence provide no explanation of how and why Wright might have used such motifs. Although Wright had a latent interest in exotic architecture from childhood, his experiences in Europe provided the turning point at which he began self-consciously to experiment with exotic motifs. Wright saw that the artists of the Secession had been searching for original and pure sources of art in the exotic motifs of Egypt, the ancient Near East, and the Orient. The motifs of the Maya parallel in form similar motifs found in ancient Egypt and Mesopotamia. Without necessarily understanding the complex attitudes of the Secessionists towards exotic and primitivist motifs, Wright launched his own studies. When he returned to America, he explored throughout the 1910s and early 1920s a series of designs in which he transformed the motifs of the Secession and the forms of Maya architecture and other primal cultures into the expression of his own search for the origins of architecture.

Wright's articulation, in the introduction to his Wasmuth monograph, of the necessity of searching for the origins of architecture was one of the first expressions of European influence on him. He also articulated a theory of "pure form" in his essay *The Japanese Print,* published in 1912.[12] Identifying with tradition, Wright claimed that geometry had cosmic meaning, and that its use as the means of ordering design connected man to the cosmos. Pure forms were the forms of art and architecture that were linked to the basic traditions of a culture, yet avoided the blatant imitation of historical motifs. If a culture used forms that expressed its values and ideals, its individuals would be integrated into social life. When integrated into social life, the individual could stand in closer harmony to the cos-

mos. In this idealistic and romantic view, architecture could provide the means of harmony between the individual, society, and the universe.

A final myth revolves around the standard views of Wright's life and work and the relationship of his art to his view of society. These views consider that after 1910 Wright's work went into decline, and he retreated into an aestheticism that lacked social purpose. Although Frank Lloyd Wright may be the most internationally recognized name among American architects, a definitive biography coordinating his life with his work has not yet been written, more than thirty years after his death. Recent biographies have filled in some gaps, and forthcoming research will provide an increased understanding of Wright's work.[13] For his early work until 1909, which has been most celebrated and studied, we still rely on standard works published in the 1940s and the 1950s. Grant Manson's classic *Frank Lloyd Wright, the First Golden Age,* in particular, still stands, but Manson implied that a pinnacle of creative activity was reached in the Prairie Style houses around 1909 and that decline followed.[14] The period from 1910 to the public adulation of Wright in the late 1930s, when Wright designed Fallingwater and the Johnson Wax Administration Building, has been neglected, and the works produced by Wright during that period have frequently been denigrated as decadent or inferior to those that preceded them; or critics have maintained that his career was at a standstill during that time.[15] Hitchcock initially saw the work of the 1910s and early 1920s as decadent in its explosion of ornament, and claimed Wright had been spoiled by rich clients.[16] Actually, Wright's work simply did not fit into Hitchcock's perception of the International Style. By the time of *In the Nature of Materials,* his pioneering study published in 1942, Hitchcock described some of Wright's buildings of the 1910s as less elegant than preceding work, with interiors characterized by a "heaviness" that was less delicate than in his earlier work. This pejorative stylistic assessment stuck; presumably, "light" architecture was the true modern architecture of floating planes and dematerialized mass.[17] Other writers asserted that in this decline Wright was so beset with personal problems that he retreated into a personal aesthetic that was without social implication for his work.[18]

These simple oppositions between Wright's life and his work, or between his role as artist and his role as social critic, are inadequate; what we find is a complex duality in a man who appears personally full of contradictions. However, the utopian dream of culture and society unified through art was at the core of Wright's hopes for a democratic America. His theories of form became inseparable from his social theories of a Whitman-esque land that championed the individual.

Wright's view of individualism was also strongly affected by his European experience, especially when he encountered the call for a new morality propounded in the writings of Ellen Key, the Swedish feminist. Her ideas had an equally strong effect on Mamah Borthwick Cheney, who had left her family to travel with Wright to Europe. Key wrote early in the century that the only valid bond between men and women is based on equality and love, and that hope for social change lies in the education of youth. Her ideas enriched Wright's vision of a new social order and provided the moral justification for his abandonment of his family to pursue with Mamah Cheney a life unbounded by convention. Immediately upon his return from Europe, Wright, as co-author, and Cheney, as translator, had Key's books published in America.[19]

My point of view in this study results from observations about the role of influence in the visual arts. Despite fresh ways of looking at history that have developed over the last twenty years, assessing influence still remains the cornerstone for analyzing the history of art. The art historian's common practice is to assume that, if B looks like A, then A has influenced B. Every standard history of art contains hundreds of examples of influence. Behind this practice is the assumption that, if the influences on an artist can be determined, we have either linked the artist to a tradition or discovered sources of information about the forces that produced his or her work. Influences are often passed off as explanations of meaning, yet they rarely explain how or why an artist creates or how an artist assimilates, copies, imitates, or transforms the work of other artists. Such an approach to history often depends on superficial resemblances and neglects exploring any mechanism for the transferral and transformation of ideas as well as issues of creative process and social meaning. The attributed influence of Wright's hotel and bank in Mason City on the Gropius and Meyer Werkbund Pavilion in Cologne exemplifies the use of visual analogy. This assertion of influence is characteristic of how the influence of Wright's Wasmuth folios on the early pioneers of modern architecture has been proposed exclusively by the drawing of visual analogies between his designs and the work of other European modernists.

The reliance on visual analogy is also a symptom of the broad intellectual issue of the problematics of influence. In clinging to a belief in the existence of objective truth, some historians rely too much on establishing influences and thus avoid many important questions about the meaning of objects. What is the relationship of the object to an individual's taste, habits, and intentions? What are the meanings of an object outside the context of authorship or location? What do we say about an object—building, sculpture, or painting—whose maker is anonymous and whose cultural context is only a subject of conjecture?

In literary criticism, simplistic assumptions of influence have been challenged by works such as Harold Bloom's *The Anxiety of Influence*.[20] However, despite serious critical inquiry into the nature of influence, it remains a problematic concept because it is difficult to prove or disprove. How are we to say definitively that the "important" work of a major architect has more influence than the unidentified buildings of unrecognized architects? One answer is to believe the words of artists, that, indeed, they were influenced by the work of other artists. But can we deny the impact of seeing or experiencing a building or work of art that is unconsciously recorded in the mind and manifests itself later? Does seeing an illustration of a building in a magazine or in the plates of a folio constitute influence? What actually is influence? The etymology of the word indicates a flowing in, but what flows out? The domain of these inquiries is the realm of the creative process itself, a process that continues to defy understanding because the vehicle of our understanding—the human mind—is also the vehicle of creative force.

The basic method of the historian dependent on influence is linear reasoning. History moves in lines that are usually straight, for instance, from Cézanne to Picasso, or occasionally branching, as from Caravaggio to a school of his followers. The linear approach also allows for dead ends, or truncated limbs, such as the "end" of Art Nouveau. This linearity provides units of time that allow us to grasp information about diverse figures and developments, yet too often historians assert that a linear description is the Truth.

Since the late nineteenth century, unique processes have been at work that further challenge our concepts of traditional imitation and originality. Walter Benjamin brought attention to the impact of mechanical reproduction on the concept of originality.[21] As the late Reyner Banham pointed out, during the Modern Movement for the first time in history forms were copied from photographs rather than originating from personal inspection or measured drawings.[22] While Banham was referring to the Europeans' borrowing of American industrial prototypes as the imagery of the International Style, his observation applies to Wright's designs: they were often transmitted visually through photographs and idealized drawings without being physically experienced.

Historians often use linear reasoning to pursue "problems" that can be defined as considerations of complex events in simplified terms. The historiography of modern architecture consists largely of problems upon which the historian grinds his axe. Establishing the continuity of a tradition is one such problem. Some historians assert that the traditions of the true, legitimate, modern American architecture were derailed by the foreign influences of the Modern Movement imported from Europe in the 1930s and 1940s, and that they were victoriously reestablished with a revival of nineteenth-century shingle-style architecture and the classicism of postmodernism in the 1970s and 1980s.[23] Many of these historians also believe that classicism never vanished but lay latent in the work of architects—regardless of the physical appearance of their work or overt opposition to classical canons—waiting only to be discovered by the historian himself.[24]

The problem of the continuity of classicism has been applied to Frank Lloyd Wright along with a large set of other linear histories. Hitchcock was the first to see an academic phase in Wright's work, which in turn has led others to assert, for instance, that underneath Wright's attachment to nature and organicism is a classicist core.[25] In discussing Wright's designs, the classicist historian points to the symmetrical plan of the Imperial Hotel or Midway Gardens as a reversion to Beaux Arts principles.[26] Linked with the classical traditions of realism, Wright's "true" classicism reemerges when his architecture becomes the representation of nature itself.[27] By this reasoning, a terrace that resembles a mushroom, as in the resort and club designed for Huntington Hartford, is a not a visual metaphor but a representation of a mushroom. Wright's adaption of courtyard schemes for house designs after his visit to Italy in 1910 are seen only as a confirmation of his latent classicism. Because he is the most important American architect, Wright's tendencies, therefore, confirm that the true American architecture is rooted in classicism.

Wright, however, vehemently objected to the vocabulary of classicism. Certainly there are visual analogies between the walled courtyard of an Italian villa and the designs for Wright's Allen House and Cutten House, but we can also see the oriental courtyard as an element in the Coonley House, in the project for the McCormicks, and in Wright's own home, Taliesin (figs.

20, 101, 102). As for the Italian landscape, who can spend a day in Italy without feeling its effects? The Beaux Arts classicism that had swallowed the American movement led by Louis Sullivan was still a burden to Wright, and its practitioners remained an enemy camp. Rather than providing him with direct models or inspiration, Wright's experience of Italy was more subtle, romantic, and not limited to didactic lessons. As of 1910, the weight of classicism in America still inhibited the flowering of the architecture of democracy that Sullivan and his followers sought.

Another problem that preoccupies the historians who rely on influence is the question of Wright's role in the development of the Modern Movement. One view, which the architect himself helped to shape, consists of seeing Wright as the sole source of modern architecture in Europe.[28] Wright then becomes a unique originator from whom the lineage of modern architecture springs. Conversely, when other writers invert Wright's role as the originator of modern architecture and turn it inside out, he is presented as an artistic thief who has never been successfully caught. The historian with this claim sees Wright as "borrowing" his designs from the works of other architects instead of originating his own. He is said to have adapted forms of Japanese architecture and motifs from Japanese wood-block prints. Or his plans for domestic residences sprang from English architects such as Voysey or Lutyens. Or Wright lifted motifs of Maya architecture for his designs, as at the A. D. German Cold Storage Warehouse or the Hollyhock House for Aline Barnsdall. Again, the underlying assumption is a simple, linear expression of artistic influence: architecture consists of a compilation of motifs from existing sources, a compilation that Wright tried to hide.

The tendency to knock the arrogant genius off his pedestal has also been the central problem of most recent biographies of Wright. Robert Twombly's seminal work was biased by the need to correct uncritical adulation of Wright. Brendan Gill went to extremes in his biography to portray Wright as fraudulent, deceitful, and contemptuous of other people.[29] Such linear approaches tend to present biography and the history of art and architecture in reductive and simplistic terms.

The point of view of this book differs from a traditional approach to the history of art and architecture. Rather than trace a line which begins at one point and concludes at another, with a resulting truth, I hope to sketch a mesh or netting as an image of the complex events that describe creative processes and historical events. Where the cords of the netting are tied into knots, we can see an analogy to the complex strands that tie together Wright's work and life. The strands themselves are intertwined so that a complex view of artistic and biographical events occurs. Instead of seeing Wright as simply a self-indulgent egotist when he advocates his own iconoclastic life as a model for others, we can observe complex motivations which include his own claim that he is sacrificing himself for the good of others.

Contradictions further confound the conventional ways of seeing the facts of historical events. Instead of producing an immediate response in Germany, Wright's work there had less impact in the 1910s than in the 1920s and 1930s, when debates about Wright's work occurred under very different conditions. Instead of providing final answers, some factual accounts of Wright's experiences in Europe may remain forever incomplete. While primary research has revealed new documents and facts, it has also uncovered fragments of information and holes in our knowledge that may never be filled. Throughout his career, Wright saved copies of letters he wrote and those he received, but he wrote only a few letters from Europe.[30] Wright traveled in secrecy, and for highly personal reasons he may have later avoided documenting this period because it contained tragic and painful memories. And some letters and documents may have been burned or destroyed. Furthermore, Wright carefully avoided acknowledging any influence on his work from other architects. This varying availability of documentary materials has also required shifts of methodology. A host of documents provides evidence of Wright's "influence" in Europe through the Wasmuth publications, so that the documents create a factual history of their own, which I interpret. Fewer documents exist to show Europe's "influence" on Wright, so that evidence comes from whatever documents exist, retrospective and word-of-mouth accounts, careful study of original drawings, and analyses of the objects made during the period. Whenever I could find letters and documents, I have woven them into the accounts here, juxtaposing them with Wright's version of events and the recollections of others.

Seeing Wright's work and life as knots in a net also reveals discontinuities that reflect life itself. Events appear as discontinuous or shifted in time: Wright appears to have begun understanding the Secessionists' belief in primitivism and the symbols of ancient form at a time when the members of the movement had moved on to explore the possibilities of their own traditions and artistic sources in classicism and vernacular folk art.

Finally, the nonlinear approach attempted here allows hidden and unexpected linkages to occur. While we could expect that Wright, as an inheritor of the ideas of Emerson and Whitman, would seek to find a symbolism for his vision of a true American architecture, we would not necessarily expect him to choose ancient and universal symbols as the language of his architecture.

In addition to the problematics of influence, the central concepts underlying this investigation involve the migration, assimilation, translation and convergence of forms. These concepts motivated much of the seminal research of Rudolf Wittkower, who, in his last lectures, examined the flow of ideas between Europe and the Near East, including Mesopotamia and Egypt, and between Europe and the Orient, including China, India, and the world of Islam.[31] Two antagonistic theories complete the conceptual framework of these exchanges: the idea of the diffusion of ideas and forms, and the idea of autonomous, independent creation. As Wittkower noted, diffusionism has been developed into a "universally accepted technique of research." However, he added, "The test of diffusionism lies, of course, in the proof of the existence of historical roads of migration, transmission, and dissemination."[32] This study is an attempt to investigate some of those roads.

In order to avoid facile assumptions of influence, I rely in this study on the concepts of diffusion and parallelism. As Wittkower indicated, diffusion implies a traceable mechanism for the dissemination of ideas that at the same time guarantees no simple causal relationships. Parallelism acknowledges the appearance throughout time and space of similar forms of expression, particularly artistic motifs, that occur in cultures which have had virtually no mutual contact. The appearance of the "key" motif in the art of ancient Greece, Japan, and among the Maya of Central America, is one example of parallelism. The rationalist rarely ventures an explanation for this phenomenon; the positivist has faith in "facts"; the mythologist believes in a universal realm of symbolic form. Despite the absence of definitive explanations, a fundamental premise of this study is that parallel forms have arisen in various cultures throughout time. Wright and his European contemporaries shared this belief, and it provided a fundamental bond between them.

Ultimately, by following a complex view of life and art, we can begin to see Wright not as an artist in retreat or merely as an arrogant social critic; he emerges as an artist with an extraordinary ability to synthesize and transform the work of others while focusing his artistry in a vision of an ideal society.

There never was exterior influence upon my work, either foreign or native, other than that of Lieber
Meister, Dankmar Adler and John Roebling, Whitman, and Emerson, and the great poets worldwide.
My work is original not only in fact but in spiritual fiber. No practice by any European architect to this
day has influenced mine in the least.—Frank Lloyd Wright (1957) [1]

1   Points of Departure: Wright Before 1909

Frank Lloyd Wright himself confirmed a myth about the origins of his architecture by stating that no European architect
had influenced his work in any way. Insisting on this up to end
of his life, Wright wanted us to believe that his originality and
creativity were independent of European culture. But the insistence of his defense suggests the presence of a deep anxiety
about influence—an anxiety imbedded in a search for his own
artistic identity. At other points in time, Wright also wanted to
confirm speculation that, if there had been any influence, it had
been one-way: he had influenced modern architecture in Europe—it had never influenced him. Despite his denials, during
the early phases of his career the traditions of European architecture and its modern developments had surrounded Wright;
they worked on him even as he sought to find a true American
architecture.

The context of Wright's departure to Europe in 1909 provides a background for examining the unexplored ways that
Europe influenced Wright and for seeing an adventure that
transformed his life and his work. What did he know of the Europe that awaited him? How after fifteen years had his independent, successful practice come to a close? And what were the
personal motivations that caused him to openly defy the social
conventions of family life and abandon his wife and children?
These questions help us to examine the myths of influence surrounding Wright, and that examination indicates that he knew
more about the art and architecture of Germany, Great Britain,
and Austria than he ever acknowledged.

Although Wright's early career matured within the rich cultural ambience of Chicago, it took place without any direct
experience of the models of Western architecture that had generated either American architecture or contemporary developments abroad. Because he had not yet traveled, his experiences
remained second-hand and were obtained through the adaptations of European styles of architecture around him, through
the cultural exchanges of international fairs, through accounts
of others who had visited or studied in Europe, or through the
various international journals that he and his colleagues read.
Nevertheless, Wright took part in an interchange of ideas between America and Europe before World War I that was far
richer than has even been suspected. Our understanding of this
interchange places Wright in an international context rather
than isolating him as a regional architect. Europe had called to
Wright as a source of inspiration long before he was able to
answer with a visit. Ultimately, influence would flow in both
directions.

Wright's View of Europe before 1909

European architecture had formed the cultural legacy of America, a legacy that architects sought to assimilate in the search
for a distinctive American architecture. Architects who were
trained in American schools generally were taught with European methods, and the European Grand Tour of monuments
still held the appeal of a sought-after dream for those architects

who could afford to follow it. Wright had been an exception. He had been reluctant to study abroad, and, at the age of forty-two, had never been to Europe.

From his "Lieber Meister" Louis Sullivan, Wright absorbed the view that the influence of classicism was destroying the possibilities of a true American architecture. The architecture of the Great White City, embodied in the Chicago Columbian Exposition of 1893, was equated with the Ecole des Beaux-Arts, and the Ecole became the proxy for Europe as a whole. Edward C. Waller, Wright's friend and client, and Daniel H. Burnham, a preeminent force in American architecture and a civic leader of Chicago, had offered Wright the opportunity to study for four years at the Ecole and two years in Rome.[2] With such study would come the promise of influence and prosperity, with Burnham's powerful backing. Wright, delighted and embarrassed by the offer, declined, saying that the classical style was uncreative and a flight from the struggle to create a national architecture, a flight from "what I see as *ours* in our country, to what can't belong to me, no, I mean *us*."[3] Although Wright would travel to the Orient in 1905, he had forsaken a significant opportunity in favor of his principles.[4] His bias against the architecture of the Ecole des Beaux-Arts deepened, but he nevertheless must have been curious about the experience of confronting the monuments of Western architecture.

Wright gave as a reason for finally visiting Europe the opportunity to oversee the German publication of his built work in a small book of photographs and drawings, *Frank Lloyd Wright: Ausgeführte Bauten,* and a sumptuous monograph on his buildings and projects, *Ausgeführte Bauten und Entwürfe von Frank Lloyd Wright.* But in many ways Germany had come to Wright long before his venture abroad. In addition to their presence in Milwaukee and other cities in Minnesota, German architects were prominent in Chicago. German culture, newspapers, and cafés were a part of Chicago culture.

Chicago's German Culture

After the failure of the revolution in Germany in 1848–49, a tide of German immigration flowed into Chicago, producing a profoundly significant cultural presence. Wright would have been surrounded by contemporary images of Germany. Newspapers in Chicago thoroughly reported events in Germany. Exploits of the German military were covered in detail, while notice of visiting foreigners in Germany received attention: An-

drew Carnegie, the industrialist, joked with the Kaiser at Kiel, and Joseph Pulitzer, the publisher, had retired temporarily to Berlin. In 1900, over 13 percent of the Chicago population was German, and the huge waves of German immigration spawned such extensive economic success that almost one-third of the businesses in the city were run by Germans.[5] The city was a natural stopping point for German visitors because of its large German population. Some of Wright's clients, such as Fred C. Robie, were of German ancestry.[6] In fact, three of Wright's collaborators, the sculptor Richard Bock, the furniture maker and interior designer George Niedecken, and the building contractor Paul F. P. Mueller were German.

The German presence pervaded the architectural profession, resulting in Chicago's becoming different from other major American cities through the presence of its many German-educated architects.[7] They formed the largest ethnic group in the profession, adding an intellectual component directly connected to the mainstream of German architecture. This mainstream traced its flow from Karl Friedrich Schinkel (1781–1841), the greatest nineteenth-century neoclassicist architect in Europe, whose impact was felt on Frederick Baumann, the first German-born architect who came to Chicago. Baumann translated an oration for Schinkel's birthday in 1869 and increased Americans' awareness of the seminal Bauakademie, Schinkel's architectural school built in Berlin between 1831 and 1835. Baumann's work and that of his contemporaries and followers demonstrated the call to rational function that lay beneath the *palazzo*-style vocabulary that Schinkel popularized. The pursuit of rationality and its expression in building became paramount for the successive generations of Chicago architects who developed tall buildings.

Wright began his Chicago apprenticeship in a German ambience. Dankmar Adler, Wright's employer when he worked for the firm of Adler and Sullivan from 1887 to 1893, was one of the members of the second generation of German-born Chicago architects. He had moved to Chicago in 1861 and, before his partnership with Louis Sullivan, worked in a style that was similar to the style of contemporary architecture in Berlin in the 1870s: a severe, post-and-beam, neo-Renaissance mode that was informed by the use of structural frames. Louis Sullivan's role as chief draftsman for buildings, such as the Borden Block, confirms his involvement with the *palazzo* style that had its theoretical sources in the work of Schinkel.[8] From Adler and Sullivan, Wright would have absorbed a receptivity to a German interest in functionalism—an interest in efficiency and the formal expression of a building's purpose; and tectonics—the expression of building structure.

The German presence came to Wright not only through his work with Adler and Sullivan but directly into his studio through apprentices who had studied with Nathan Clifford Ricker at the University of Illinois.[9] Having visited the Bauakademie in Berlin to study its library and teaching methods, Ricker used German architectural theories in the teaching of design and translated several treatises that were then circulated in manuscript among his students. Apprentices in Wright's Oak Park studio who had received training under Ricker included Walter Burley Griffin, William Drummond, and Harry Robinson.

The dissemination of German ideas was also apparent in the other offices of Chicago practitioners active in the first decade of the twentieth century. They included George W. Maher, who had come from the office of Joseph Lyman Silsbee, as Wright had, in 1887; Bruno Paul, who systematically followed the German and Austrian Secession; and Richard E. Schmidt, who was born and trained in Germany and designed, with Hugh M. G. Garden, the Madlener House in Chicago (1901–2), a building modeled on the cubic houses of Schinkel's followers. Also, the work of the firm of Hill and Woltersdorf revealed their interest in the functionalist ideas in Germany that were inspiring the young designers there.[10]

A fundamental current of rationality in Chicago's architecture emanated from the German school of Schinkel and its views of expressing building structure. These ideas fed the sources of Chicago's emerging commercial architecture. The architects who had inherited Schinkel's ideas, through their training in Germany or at the University of Illinois, were in a position to unite the clarity of the Gothic style and the order of classicism, the two basic models and poles of architectural theory in the nineteenth century.

French ideas and training at the Ecole des Beaux-Arts was, of course, the other major factor in Chicago architecture. Although Wright had spurned a French architectural education, he found common ground between German theory, with its rational expression of structure, and the emphasis on structure enunciated by his principal source of architectural theory, Eugène Emmanuel Viollet-le-Duc. From the writings of Viollet-le-Duc Wright saw that Gothic architecture contained a rational approach that was worth studying.[11] An interest in the rational expression of building structure, shared by French and German theorists in the nineteenth century, was a major source for the development of modern architecture in the twentieth century. Wright inherited both French and German traditions of rationalism.

The Wasmuth Venture

The opportunity to see Germany firsthand came unexpectedly when the great publishing house of Ernst Wasmuth made an offer in 1908 for Wright to come to Berlin and publish his work.[12] Wright's account of the Wasmuth commission needs to be considered cautiously. He assumed the offer had come through the intervention of Kuno Francke.[13] German-born, Francke was a professor at Harvard and played a significant role in promoting cultural exchanges between Germany and America.[14] As Wright recounted the story, when Francke and his wife visited Oak Park, Francke told him, "Your life will be wasted here, do come to Germany. . . . My people are groping, only superficially, for what I see you doing organically: your people are not ready for you. But my people are ready for you. They will reward you. Fifty years, at least, will pass before your people will be ready for you."[15] After four or five months, according to Wright, Francke went back to Germany. And Wright received a proposal from the Wasmuth Verlag, "the greatest art publishing house in the world," offering to publish his entire work if he would come and supervise.

The Wasmuth Verlag had been founded in 1871, and by the time of its incorporation in 1903 it not only produced books on architecture but sold art as well.[16] Wasmuth's subjects included archaeology, architecture, art, crafts, costumes, and ornament. The press was publisher of the crafts collection of the Imperial Arts and Crafts Museum of Berlin and publisher to the Imperial Prussian Government. It published important architectural periodicals that were familiar to Wright's European contemporaries and even to Chicago architects and designers: *Architektur des XX Jahrhunderts, Berliner Architekturwelt, Charakteristische Details von ausgeführten Bauwerken, Der Städtebau,* and the *Wasmuths Monatshefte.* Wasmuth also sold lithographs, heliographs—reproductions that came from hand or high-speed presses—and photographs. By 1904 the firm had 150 people on its staff and had won fifteen prize medals for its work.

Francke, the man always identified in standard histories of modern architecture as the link to Wasmuth, was for part of his life the most distinguished Germanist in America, a scholar, poet, and student of American culture.[17] His dreams of cultural exchange between the United States and Germany took the form of his founding a museum of Germanic art at Harvard in November 1903, later known as the Busch-Reisinger Museum. His efforts were part of an optimistic movement whose followers believed that a familiarity with national cultures would create greater understanding between countries.[18]

When Francke met Wright, he may have seen the presentation of Wright's work in Germany as an excellent vehicle of cultural exchange, with Wright's architecture as a representation of American culture. Wright's exposure in Germany, therefore, would have completed an exchange between two national cultures through the medium of architecture and provided an example of cultural and political progressivism in America that would see its demise in the war years.

How Francke came to know Frank Lloyd Wright is not clear.[19] They probably met in the first week of February 1908, when Francke was lecturing in Chicago.[20] Francke did return for a visit to Germany that summer, but there is no indication that he contacted Wasmuth or discussed Wright with German colleagues.[21] Despite Francke's admiration of Wright, no continuing relationship developed between the two men. Francke did not mention Wright in his autobiography, and he made no reference to Wright when he returned to Chicago in the summer of 1914.[22] Thus, while Wright assumed that Francke made the initial suggestion to the Wasmuth Verlag for publication of Wright's work, he never knew that with certainty.

Contrary to myth, there was another, more direct connection to the Wasmuth publishing empire that Wright had apparently forgotten: Bruno Möhring, a leading conservative architect in Berlin (fig. 5). Möhring had come to St. Louis in 1904 to direct the general organization of the German exhibition at the Louisiana Purchase Exposition.

In addition to having a major architecture practice, Möhring was also a city planner, writer, and an editor of the *Berliner Architekturwelt,* the journal that sponsored the series of special publications, or *Sonderhefte,* in which Wright's book of photographs, *Ausgeführte Bauten,* would appear.[23] In 1902 Möhring's own designs had appeared as the second volume of the *Sonderhefte* in the series. He was also an editor of the *Wasmuths Monatshefte,* and his buildings and projects appeared in it along with those of other contemporary German architects; both periodicals were enterprises of the Wasmuth Verlag. He was, then, well known in Berlin and an associate of Wright's future publisher, the Ernst Wasmuth Verlag.

Furthermore, during his visit to the United States Möhring visited Wright's studio in the spring of 1904.[24] This distin-

5. Bruno Möhring, portrait, c. 1915–1920 (Berlinische Galerie, Collection of Photography).

guished architect sought out Wright in Oak Park, yet Wright, absent from his studio, apparently never knew that Möhring had come to visit him and see his architecture. Although he did not meet Wright, Möhring had direct contact with Wright's work as a result of his visit and could have later informed the Wasmuth publishing empire about Wright.[25]

The St. Louis World's Fair of 1904

The fair that brought Möhring to America also brought Frank Lloyd Wright to St. Louis. There has been no question about the significant influence of the Columbian Exhibition of 1893 on American culture in general, and on architecture in particular, but the St. Louis World's Fair of 1904 had a strong impact on the country that historians have overlooked. In a last-gasp effort, St. Louis was trying to rival Chicago as a gateway to the West. By having a fair to celebrate the centennial of the Louisiana Purchase, it hoped to attract Americans on their way westward. The St. Louis Fair exposed Wright to developments in the opposite direction—to Europe—in advance of his going there.[26] After visiting the fair, Wright recommended it to members of his studio in Oak Park as "a liberal experience"; he was so impressed with the German installation that he gave one of his draftsmen train fare to see it.[27] Besides providing Wright with a sense of developments in Europe, the fair gave him a glimpse of work in Germany and Austria and a taste of the exotic culture of Japan.[28]

Presenting a point of cultural tangency between America and Europe, the exhibition presented the latest examples of European architecture.[29] At the St. Louis Fair Wright could have experienced a sampler of German culture directly imported by its most noted artists and architects and by its captains of industry and commerce. The comprehensive display grouped exhibitions into categories of science, industry, and technology, and contained works by the leading German architects, artists, and craftsmen.[30]

The exhibitions at St. Louis synopsized contemporary German architecture and interior design just before the visible development of a German avant garde in architecture as represented by Peter Behrens's Turbine Hall (1908–9) and Walter Gropius and Adolf Meyer's Fagus Shoe-Last Factory at Alfeld (1911). Deutsches Haus, the main location for exhibits, was an eclectic assemblage of parts of historical buildings, with construction supervised by Bruno Schmitz, that attempted to present the true national architecture and history of Germany.[31] The building, which had an academic plan, was symmetrically arranged around an entry hall, with wings flanking main exhibition rooms and a terrace with veranda. Although it is doubtful that Wright would have approved of its historicizing pose, the building's contents could have given the "liberal experience" he noted.

The leading figure associated with the German pavilion was the venerable Bruno Möhring. In addition to supervising construction of the pavilion's honor court and exhibition hall, Möhring exhibited his own work and oversaw the design of displays.[32] Wright did not know that the architectural interiors he saw in the German pavilion were by someone not only interested in his own work but in a position to promote him in Germany.

The presence of other architects' designs reinforced Wright's exposure to Europe. The drawings of fourteen architects hung alongside those of Möhring, including drawings by Joseph Maria Olbrich, whose exhibited works were second in number to Möhring's.[33] Olbrich, an Austrian, had designed the Secession Building in Vienna in 1897–8, the major exhibition space for the movement that had rebelled against academic art, and then had been lured from Vienna to Darmstadt in 1899. Wright, who tried to visit Olbrich in Europe ten years later, compared himself to Olbrich and to no other European architect. In St. Louis, Olbrich exhibited "architectonic sketches," drawings, perspectives, and prints in the architecture section; he also designed a courtyard and six rooms of a summer residence for the arts and crafts display (fig. 6). In the industrial section, Olbrich showed designs for seating, embroidery, and carpets. Of the significant architects whose work he saw at St. Louis, Wright alluded only to Olbrich in his later writings.

However, among a group of lesser-known architects exhibited in St. Louis was Peter Behrens, a rising star in Germany and director of the arts and crafts school at Düsseldorf. Behrens's designs provided an important transition between the Viennese Secession that Olbrich brought to Darmstadt and the industrial aesthetic that would soon dominate functional industrial design in Germany. It was during the period of working in Behrens's office that Walter Gropius and Mies van der Rohe claimed to have been influenced by an exhibition of Wright's work. Behrens's work, therefore, is an important reference point for comparing Wright's work to that of his peers in Europe.

In St. Louis Behrens showed designs for the official German catalogue of the exhibition.[34] They consisted of striking graphics in the current *Jugendstil* mode that boxed text with frames, marked paragraph headings with frames and glyphs, and made use of colored inks for printing; in the section for books and newspapers, Behrens had additional graphic designs. Wright would also have seen in the interior decoration section Behrens's spatial arrangements of furniture for a salon whose overall artistic direction was supervised by Möhring.

Behrens's display of work occurred while he was in the process of making the transition from artist to designer. His reading room for the State Library in Düsseldorf, disassembled and reerected, complete with furniture, wall hangings, and general decor, demonstrated his increasing involvement with architectural ensembles (fig. 7). Behrens's cubic lamps for reading

6. Joseph Maria Olbrich, fountain court, St. Louis Exposition, 1904
(*Deutsches Kunstgewerbe in St. Louis 1904*).

tables closely resembled Wright's own lamps, designed around 1904, for the William E. Martin House and for Unity Temple, which was designed the following year (fig. 8). This visual similarity immediately raises the fundamental issue of influence: was Wright "influenced" by what he saw, imitating the forms he encountered, or was he working in parallel with developments in Europe? If Wright was "influenced" by Behrens, then how can we explain the similarity between Behrens's designs and Wright's lamps for the Larkin Building, which was designed in 1903, before the St. Louis Fair, and completed in 1906? While he could have noticed a visual similarity between Behrens's work in the lights of the reading room and his own Unity Temple, Wright probably did not realize that he was seeing in Behrens's work the impact of the Dutch theory of design funneled through the architect and theosophist J. L. Mathieu Lau-

weriks, whom Behrens had brought to Düsseldorf as a teacher; the parallels between Wright's designs and German and Dutch work that used the square as a central motif of a design system are so important that we will examine them later in detail.

As a prelude to Wright's own visit to Europe, the fair would have exposed him not only to Germany's architects but also to its artists. Six years later he would purchase prints, generally of romantic landscapes, by some of the *Jugendstil* and Secession artists who exhibited in St. Louis.[35]

Reflecting the international scope of interest in the Arts and Crafts movement, the work of a number of German collective workshops was included in the Palace of Fine Arts. These groups produced etchings, embroidery, lithography, and bookmaking, which fascinated Wright. Displays ranged from examples of hand techniques to the latest technological innova-

7. Peter Behrens, reconstruction of reading room for the State Library in Düsseldorf, St. Louis Exposition, 1904 (*Deutsches Kunstgewerbe in St. Louis 1904*).

8. Unity Temple, Oak Park, Illinois, interior, designed 1905 (TAL).

tions in printing. Wright had explored typography and book design with his and W. H. Winslow's printing of *The House Beautiful* in 1896–97, and his intense interest in the presentation of his own work carried over to his German publications.[36]

Even Wright's future publishing firm, Ernst Wasmuth, had its own exhibits (fig. 9). Wasmuth was at the fair, like other firms, to promote its various publications.[37] Publishers, artists, and architects exhibited their work along with all the products of commerce and industry to convey German culture. Germany, however, was not the only imperial power to demonstrate its achievements.

Austrian artists also exhibited at the St. Louis Fair.[38] Josef Hoffmann, Gustav Klimt's colleague and a founder of the Wiener Werkstätte, had designed an exhibit largely devoted to the work of Klimt, the outstanding figure of the Viennese Seces-

sion.[39] Because of internal politics between rival groups in the Secession, the plans for the Klimt room were canceled, foreclosing any possibility for a complete exhibition of the best work of the Austrian Secession movement. Hoffmann, however, designed a room for the Vienna School of Arts and Crafts that was built. Executed predominantly in black and white, it included display cases, lecterns, tables, and carpets. These would have been among the first examples of the artifacts of the Vienna Secession exhibited in America (fig. 10).

Wright's exposure to contemporary work in Germany and Austria was complemented by his exposure to art and architecture from Holland. That country's exhibit included the work of Hendrik Petrus Berlage, the leader of Dutch modern architecture. He would eventually be a key figure in promoting Wright in Europe and in understanding Wright's influence on Europe—the complementary history to our study here.[40] Drawings of Berlage's Beurs, the stock exchange that had just opened in 1903 in Amsterdam, were exhibited in St. Louis.[41]

The international exchange of ideas at the fair was reinforced by the fact that while Americans, such as Wright, journeyed to St. Louis, the fair gave Europeans a reason to visit America. Dr. Paul Cohn, editor of the prominent Viennese newspaper *Die Zeit*, went to the fair in St. Louis and also traveled to Springfield, Illinois. In an example of the complex, interlocking connections between Wright and Europe, Cohn attended a party at the home of Susan Dana Lawrence, the client whose lavish residence in Springfield Wright had just completed in 1904.[42] Cohn, therefore, had an opportunity to see one of Wright's most accomplished designs. In sum, the St. Louis Louisiana Purchase Exhibition served its function as a fair that brought the cultures of the world closer together at a time when late nineteenth-century modes of transportation and communication still prevailed. For Frank Lloyd Wright, the fair provided a glimpse of the latest artistic developments in Europe.

Travel and Journals: News From Abroad

In the first decade of the twentieth century the transmission of ideas and images from Europe to America was far more extensive than has been imagined. Wright's colleagues supplemented the experience of exhibitions and world's fairs by traveling and studying in Europe. En route to study vernacular architecture in Scandinavia, William Gray Purcell, a young architect who worked in Louis Sullivan's office, visited Berlage in Amsterdam in 1906.[43] Berlage apparently first heard of Wright from Purcell; certainly Wright would have been mentioned by Purcell in any discussion of developments of the "New School of the Middle West." George M. Niedecken, the Milwaukee furniture and interior designer, studied in London, Berlin, and Paris, and his designs of the early 1900s have Parisian and Austrian decorative motifs.[44] Niedecken's design for a glass and wrought-iron portico, drawn in 1900, shows his direct importation of the Art Nouveau of Hector Guimard's Paris Metro stations.[45] His furniture design for Wright's Avery Coonley House shows around 1909 that the motif of the square within a square had already been absorbed into his current design vocabulary (fig. 11).

Newspapers and journals supplemented travelers' accounts, private photographs, and fairs. The journals were a particularly important and regular source of information about the other European currents in modern architecture.[46] Wright and his

9. Bruno Möhring, entry to Wasmuth Verlag exhibit, St. Louis Exposition, 1904 (*Deutsches Kunstgewerbe in St. Louis 1904*).

10. Josef Hoffmann, Austrian exhibit, St. Louis Exposition, 1904 (*Dekorative Kunst 8*, 1905).

11. George Mann Niedecken, American, 1878–1945. Presentation Drawing: perspective rendering of desk for rear guest room, Avery Coonley House, Riverside, Illinois, ink and watercolor on tracing paper, c. 1907, 27.9 × 39.4 cm (Gift of Mr. and Mrs. James W. Howlett, 1990.41, photograph courtesy of The Art Institute of Chicago).

12. Joseph Maria Olbrich, exhibition poster for the opening of the Vienna Secession (*The Studio* 16, 1899).

contemporaries subscribed to both American and foreign periodicals. German-language publications were available within Wright's circle: Niedecken maintained runs of periodicals that featured Secessionist architecture.[47] Colleagues such as the German-born sculptor Richard Bock could translate articles Wright might want to read.[48] Wright himself apparently had a run of the *Wasmuths Monatshefte*.[49] Even the principles of modern architecture could be studied: the theory of Otto Wagner, the mentor of the Viennese school, could be read in Nathan Ricker's abridged translation of *Moderne Architektur,* published in the *Brickbuilder* in 1901, only five years after its original publication.[50]

Wright's other foreign sources included *The Studio,* a journal that disseminated the art and architecture of Great Britain and the Continent to the international Arts and Crafts movement.[51] Wright's son, Lloyd, recalled that copies of the journal could be found in Wright's office and drafting studios.[52] Published in London, *The Studio* allowed architects to follow the opening of the Vienna Secession in 1899, when the journal reviewed the first exhibition in the Secession's new building designed by Olbrich.[53] In addition to a highly laudatory text, it included an

illustration of a portion of a poster of Olbrich's Secession Building (fig. 12).[54] The small but boldly graphic image showed the upper part of the building entry. The Secession motif of bands of alternating squares was clearly visible as were two great piers between which sat a massive sphere. There were also handcrafted objects that demonstrated the range of Secession designers and their basic design motifs, most notably the square within a square, which served as a monogram of the Secession.[55] This was the same motif that Niedecken had used on the Coonley furniture. It was also the same motif that Wright knew before his travels to Europe; after 1910, it increasingly became his own graphic signature.

The art revival in Austria was the subject of an entire special edition of *The Studio* in 1906 that included the work of Secessionists Koloman Moser, Hoffmann, Olbrich, Wagner, and

Klimt.[56] The introduction to the issue asserted that there was much of general value to be gained from the new "Austrian Revival" as seen in the issue's essays and illustrations of painting, sculpture, architecture, and decorative arts. Ludwig Hevesi's "Modern Painting in Austria" would have given Wright a brief synopsis of the history of Austrian painting and introduced him to the founders of the Secession, who formally started their activities in April 1897. Carl Moll received high praise as a founder first of the Secession and then of the "New Secession"—a term used to describe a group that formed around Klimt—and as a person having a "crucial role in modeling the art life of Vienna."[57]

In the 1906 issue on Austria's art revival Wright could have learned of another source of art that interested him, the Society of Reproductive Art. It maintained that graphic arts had a pre-eminent role in "the modern style."[58] Artists whose work was produced by the society executed prints that Wright bought during his European travels.

The special issue of *The Studio* in 1906 would have also pro-vided Wright with another opportunity to learn more about modern Austrian architecture. Hugo Haberfeld's essay, "The Architectural Revival in Austria," drew attention to the first appearance of Wagner's publication, *Moderne Architektur,* as the beginnings of modern architecture in Austria. Haberfeld noted that Wagner's book was first greeted with scorn but then a younger generation of Austrian architects rallied around its innovative stance.[59]

Wright would have seen the work of Olbrich in *The Studio* and would have read about the importance of Josef Hoffmann and the Wiener Werkstätte. Olbrich's work would have been seen again by Wright in the periodical's illustrations of the fountain for the German exhibition at the St. Louis Exposition, a garden villa, and the design of a dining room in the house of the chaplain-in-ordinary to his patron, the grand duke of Hesse.[60] Haberfeld's essay mentioned Hoffmann's buildings, be-gun in 1900 for a villa colony on the "Hohe Warte," a plateau in hilly country at the outskirts of Vienna. Carl Moll lived in the colony, and the area was the subject of a print by Moll that

13. C. F. A. Voysey, Broadleys, Lake Windermere (*The Studio* 16, 1899).

14. River Forest Tennis Club, River Forest, Illinois, 1898, demolished (S).

Wright later bought. The colony's houses were situated within gardens, and the gardens were integrated into the designs of the houses—an integration that Wright had been pursuing in his designs, such as those for the Darwin D. Martin and Coonley houses. Haberfeld mentioned Hoffmann's workmen's hotel at Kladno of 1902, and Hoffmann's sanatorium at Purkersdorf near Vienna was extensively illustrated; Wright later confirmed that he knew the building from *The Studio*.[61] *The Studio* issue of 1906 also featured color and monochrome illustrations of the work of the Wiener Werkstätte, including a bedroom designed by Koloman Moser, designs by Otto Prutscher, and a boudoir by Joseph Urban.[62]

Not only did *The Studio* carefully cover the Secession movements on the Continent, it later explored diverse vernacular expressions in a special series of books that reflected the efforts of Europeans to search in primitive sources for connections to native traditions.[63] In addition, *The Studio Year-Book of Decorative Art,* which provided, as of 1906, an organized means of surveying the latest designs for artifacts and crafts, reproduced illustrations of the work of British, Dutch, German, and Austrian designers.[64]

In other British international journals, including the *International Studio, Academy Architect,* and *The Architectural Review,* readers could see illustrations of Great Britain's leading architects and designers, such as Charles F. A. Voysey, Edwin L. Lutyens, and Charles Rennie Mackintosh and Margaret McDonald-Mackintosh, his wife and collaborator, of Glasgow. German-language periodicals, *Dekorative Kunst* and *Moderne Bauformen,* which were available and eagerly read by Wright's

German-American contemporaries, would also have informed Wright about work in Austria, Germany, and other "new art" movements. Despite their diverse styles, the artists from Great Britain, Germany, and Austria all had at least some of their roots in the Arts and Crafts movement.

Arts and Crafts: An International Style

In the rare instances when a writer—either a historian or architect—has considered Europe's influence on Wright, the writer has turned to the similarities between Wright's designs and the work of various British and European Arts and Crafts architects who are seen as direct influences on Wright. These assertions of influence tend to characterize our received views, but an analysis of such assertions shows the complexity of proving influence and the care required in making such attributions. In order to assess whether these architects influenced Wright, we must look at the available vehicles of this influence. Unless Wright saw photographs of buildings prior to publication, photographs taken by others, or heard travel accounts, he could only have known about such buildings from their being published. While a complete assessment is unnecessary here, a few examples of the chronology of publication will help us correct some previous claims about European influence on Wright.

Voysey's "Broadleys" near Lake Windermere, England, has been cited as a clue to Wright's use of a hipped roof over continuous windows at his River Forest Tennis Club of 1898 (figs. 13, 14).[65] However, Broadleys, designed in that same year, was published in *The Studio* in 1899, one year after Wright designed and built the tennis club.[66] Unless he had some other source, it seems unlikely that Voysey's Broadleys directly influenced Wright's design.

Similarly, Lutyens' Deanery Garden has been suggested as an influence on Wright's Heurtley House (figs., 15, 16).[67] But Deanery Garden, designed in 1899 and finished in 1901, was apparently first published in 1903 in the English magazine *Country Life*.[68] Wright's Heurtley House in Oak Park was built in 1902. Thus, it is doubtful Wright could have directly borrowed the *parti* of Deanery Garden. The first American publication of Lutyen's work was in September 1909, just prior to Wright's departure for Europe.[69]

Because of the visual similarity of the furniture designed by the two men, it is also tempting to assume that Charles Rennie Mackintosh's work influenced Wright.[70] Although he forged important links with the Viennese Secession, Mackintosh saw his work published less widely than did Lutyens or Voysey.[71] *The Studio* drew attention to his successful early work in 1897. Wright could have heard of Mackintosh from other architects.[72] In 1904 the *American Architect and Building News* published Mackintosh's house for an art-lover, designed as an entry to a limited competition in Darmstadt; it was, however, the only example of his work published in America during the decade.[73]

It is reasonable to assume that Wright would have known of his leading contemporaries in Europe, but these few examples show how carefully we should proceed before claiming influence.[74] Illustrations of some of the latest European architecture were available to Wright before 1910, but precisely how they

15. Edwin Lutyens, Deanery Gardens, steps to orchard (*Country Life* 13, 1903).

16. Arthur Heurtley House, Oak Park, Illinois, 1902 (S).

affected him and his evolving style for the prairies of the West is a complex issue. While the pages of *The Studio* provided illustrations of decorated objects whose motifs were transferable to architectural forms and surfaces, the similarity between Wright's designs and the motifs of the Viennese designers raises again questions of influence. Otto Prutscher's textile designs, executed by J. Backhausen & Sons of Vienna, resemble some of Wright's designs, and Prutscher's designs for cigarette and card cases, and pocket books in leather, paralleled Wright's designs for windows, rugs, and graphics—rectilinear geometry dominated all these objects (figs. 17, 18).[75] But was Wright influenced by the Viennese designs? Was their work somehow influenced by him? Or was there a common bond and approach that lead them to similar solutions? To answer these questions requires an analysis that extends beyond the visual analogy of one motif to another or one building to another. Certainly, Wright's work was influenced by the Arts and Crafts movement, but the route of that influence is not simple.

The matrix of artistic ideas that surrounded Wright before his travels to Europe had been enriched by the international development of the Arts and Crafts movement. It provided a powerful impetus to his principles and designs. From ideas that had been evolving in England since the late 1830s, the Chicago Arts and Crafts movement had transformed its British models into a distinctive regional development.[76] Chicagoans' interest took definitive shape when the Chicago Arts and Crafts Society was formed at Hull House in October 1897. The premise of the society and the settlement house was that life could be enriched through handcrafts. Hull House provided a platform for debates on the arts, crafts, and society, and was the location for Wright's seminal speech, "The Art and Craft of the Machine" in 1901.[77]

The Arts and Crafts movement in Chicago had broad support from the overlapping memberships of the Chicago Arts and Crafts Society, a group of architects called the Eighteen, to which Wright belonged, and the Chicago Architectural Club, to which Wright did not belong. The Arts and Crafts movement, however, did not represent immutable ideas and absolute agreement among its adherents. The traditional objections to machine production had been modified even by William Morris himself so that the machine began to be seen as a liberator of labor. A significant role for the machine implied that the products of machine technology should reflect their processes of manufacturing. Materials were to express their true nature, and machines were to express theirs. Consequently, in a "Machine Age" the rectilinear cutting beds of milling machines and gang saws were destined to produce simple, planar, rectilinear shapes.

These were also distinctions that made the Chicago Arts and Crafts movement different from its English models. The English movement preferred handcrafts over machine-made detail and machine-made ornament. The international movement had been more an ethos than a style, and stylistic similarities were restricted to a shared simplicity of design. In Chicago, the ethos allowed for directions that were either conservative, tending toward English models, or progressive, with tendencies that emphasized eclecticism and the transformation of motifs. The results ranged from the work of Wright and his followers, such as Walter Burley Griffin, to Howard Van Doren Shaw, an architect who drew on a variety of stylistic sources. Following the precedents of Morris, Lutyens, Voysey, A. H. Mackmurdo, and Charles Rennie Mackintosh, Chicago architects defined their own direction.

From the Arts and Crafts movement Wright absorbed the fundamental principles of simplicity and community. Simplicity in design provided an antidote to moribund historicizing forms and allowed for the truthful expression of materials and machine technology. The Arts and Crafts propositions about the role of the machine as the liberator of labor provided a justification rather than a primary motivation for Wright's aesthetic for rectilinear designs. In a similar way the Arts and Crafts goal of integrating the everyday life of communities into a harmonious relationship with nature reinforced Wright's views of true American architecture as a democratic architecture, with nature and the individual forming a harmonious community.

The Arts and Crafts movement was part of a flow of ideas between Great Britain and the Continent that provided an international context for the development of Wright's earlier work. The spread of the Arts and Crafts ethos was evident when the eighth exhibition of the Secession in Vienna, in 1900, included work from Charles Robert Ashbee's Guild of Handicraft, the designs of the Scots Charles Rennie Mackintosh and Margaret

17. Otto Pruscher, carpet design, executed by J. Backhausen, Vienna (*The Art Revival in Austria,* 1906).

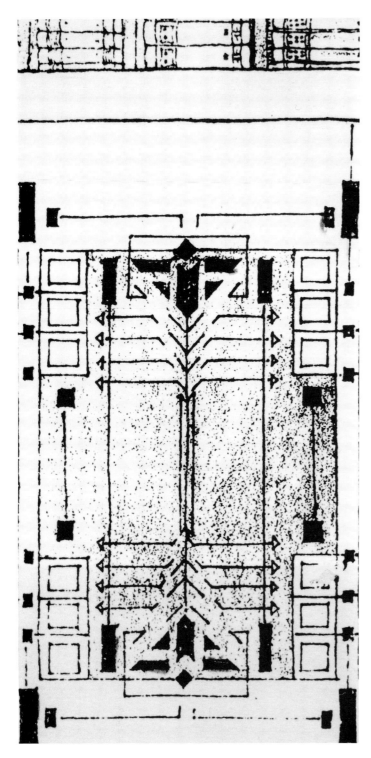

18. Frank Lloyd Wright, detail of rug design, Harley Bradley House, Kankakee, Illinois, c. 1900 (*W,* pl. 22).

Macdonald-Mackintosh, and exhibitions by the Belgian Henry Van de Velde from his Maison Moderne in Paris.[78] This international venue was accomplished through the initiative of Josef Hoffmann, who dedicated the exhibition to European applied arts and crafts and consequently cemented the Austro-Anglo connection. Hoffmann brought the Mackintoshes to Vienna, where they designed a music room for Fritz Wärndorfer. Gustav Klimt saw a flowery garment painted by Margaret Macdonald-Mackintosh and painted one for the kneeling woman in *The Kiss,* one of his major works. The Mackintoshes became friends with Otto Wagner. Thus, Charles Rennie Mackintosh and his rectilinear designs with square motifs became known in Vienna.

Through journals and the St. Louis World's Fair Wright indirectly witnessed these European developments as they were quickly concluding. The Deutsche Werkbund, founded in 1907, added an emphasis on commercialism that ultimately helped deflate the artistic emphasis of the Secession movements. By the time Wright reached Europe, the various strains of arts and crafts from England and the Jugendstil from Germany, Austria, and Holland had been assimilated and were already declining.

Aside from getting a glimpse of European developments through international fairs and literary sources, the only way for Wright to grasp fully the art and architecture of Europe was to see the work firsthand. Three factors besides the offer from the Wasmuth Verlag to publish his work contributed to Wright's decision to go to Europe: the encouragement of Charles Robert Ashbee to visit Europe, a hiatus in his practice, and domestic strife.

Ashbee

Charles Robert Ashbee, the architect who was a leader of the Arts and Crafts movement on the international scene, became one of Wright's friends and wrote the Introduction to Wright's *Sonderheft,* published by the Wasmuth Verlag (fig. 19). They had met in 1900 when Ashbee was on a lecture tour to promote England's National Trust.[79] Ashbee had invited Wright to visit England in 1901, but Wright declined.[80]

When, in December 1908, Ashbee returned to stay with the Wrights in Oak Park, he again invited Wright to Europe—first to Sicily to see the Villa San Giorgio at Taormina that Ashbee was constructing and then to Ashbee's home in England.[81] In the first extant mention of what became the Wasmuth venture, Wright replied at Christmas 1908, with some hope of going, since he had some "German business" to pursue.[82] But this hope was immediately delayed, despite the "great temptation" of the visit, because Wright's work had piled up unexpectedly:

Two bank buildings, a hotel and some residence work in Mason City to the tune of about twenty-five thousand pounds,—and the Lexington—a wilderness of small apartments, costing some hundred thousand pounds:—all on the boards here now for continuous attention. Add to this a number of fine residences in different parts of the country and you will see that I must make hay while the sun shines, particularly as this year has been a lean one.[83]

Despite the burst of professional activity during a slow year, Wright added a premonition of trouble in his personal life: "No temptation to 'desert' was ever so difficult to resist as this one from you and I shall only postpone the visit—surely I shall join you in England within a year."[84]

Professional Travails

The gloom that Wright experienced in 1908 came at the end of fifteen years of independent and increasingly successful professional practice. He was seen as a predominantly local architect who was developing a national exposure through the domestic publications of his work, but the revolution that he had brought to American domestic architecture had not been recognized, and he was virtually unknown in Europe. He had executed over 130 designs for buildings and objects out of over 450 projects.[85] He had synthesized the images of traditional architecture, particularly the Arts and Crafts movement and the spirit of Japanese architecture, into a distinct aesthetic. He had seen that a liberation of the spatial dimension of architecture, the freeing of space to allow movement through a house from interior to exterior, had experiential and sociological implications. He had begun to perceive that the opening of rooms and their connection to the outside world, allowing freedom of movement, was associated with both the liberation of the individual and with the bonding of the individual to nature.

Part of Wright's success emanated from his own theories, his design process, and the metaphorical relationship between the two. His work had been first extensively and thoroughly published by his friend Robert C. Spencer, Jr., in 1900; Spencer was so imbued with Wright's designs that he made the layout of the text and illustrations of his article in the *Architectural Review* resemble the symmetrical and rectilinear geometries of Wright's building plans.[86] Another summary of Wright's work had appeared in 1908, and while the quality of photographic repro-

19. Charles Robert Ashbee, portrait by Frank Lloyd Wright, c. 1900.

ductions disappointed Wright, the opportunity allowed him to publish a major theoretical statement, "In the Cause of Architecture"—the first in a series using a similar title.[87] There he summarized the six principles characteristic of his concept of organic architecture: measure art by simplicity and repose; make as many styles of houses as styles of people; let a building grow out of its site and harmonize with its surroundings; harmonize, or "conventionalize," colors with their surroundings, as in nature—soft warm colors are optimistic and wholesome; reveal the nature of materials; and build for character rather than according to the prevailing styles. The statement of principles gained considerably by having Wright's work alongside it to demonstrate his design theory put into practice.

The success of Wright's designs was rooted in his satisfying a pressing social problem, the articulation of the burgeoning suburb with an imagery that its middle-class occupants found comforting. The articulation had two fundamental images. One was the long, low-slung sheltering roof of his residences articulated in the metaphor of the prairie. As Richard Guy Wilson has succinctly pointed out, it "served as a metaphor offering the promise of a new society and a new art, freed from stultified Old World and East Coast traditions."[88] Like Walt Whitman, Wright and his mentor, Louis Sullivan, believed that a new man would come from the western prairies. Theirs was a vision of an architecture of democracy, a democracy lodged in the middle class. Known by various names as the Chicago school, New School of the Middle West, or simply Western, a native school had evolved to build this vision.

The second image was the hearth, whose protruding vertical chimney punctuated the horizontality of the prairie roof. Values of the community were developed in the home, and Wright's domestic architecture symbolized the values of the nuclear family. Both for his own family with its six children and the families of his clients, the hearth was the psychological center of his buildings.

Wright amalgamated this theory and practice to create innovations in domestic architecture, but his numerous commissions seemed to to have left him fatigued and foreboding. A crisis of mid-life confronted the forty-one-year-old architect. The lean year of 1908 combined with a creative and emotional exhaustion that Wright acknowledged in his *Autobiography:*

Weary, I was losing grip on my work and even my interest in it. Every day of every week and far into the night of nearly every day, Sunday included, I had "added tired to tired" and added it again and yet again as I had been trained to do . . . as a boy. Continuously thrilled by the effort but now it seemed to leave me up against a dead wall. I could see no way out. Because I did not know what I wanted I wanted to go away. Why not go to Germany and prepare the material for the Wasmuth Monograph? . . . I looked longingly in that direction.[89]

20. Project for Harold McCormick, c. 1907 (*W*, pl. 58a).

21. Darwin D. Martin, portrait, April 1908 (SUNYB).

along with the McCormick design, appeared only as plates in the Wasmuth monograph.[91]

Personal Travails

Wright's creative fatigue and professional disappointment had begun to combine with a deep personal struggle. In December 1908 he revealed his professional and personal problems to Darwin D. Martin, a man who would play a critical role in Wright's return from Europe and his subsequent career (fig. 21).[92] Martin, a wealthy executive of the Larkin Company, was the client for whom Wright had designed a house in 1902 in Buffalo, and he was instrumental in the commission of one of Wright's major buildings, the Larkin Company Administration Building of 1904. When Wright returned from Europe, he would turn to Martin for help. A devout Christian Scientist, Martin would use his friendship, moral fervor, and money to affect Wright, and theirs became one of the great relationships of this century between architect and client. The initial revelation of Wright's dilemma occurred when he wrote to Martin to decline an invitation for him and his wife, Catherine, to visit:

This year has been a great disappointment so far as opportunity to work is concerned and the future is not especially encouraging from any present outlook. . . . In my own life there is much that is complex, at least. Life is not the simple thing it should be if within myself I could find the harmony that you have found.[93]

The disharmony in Wright's life, however, had grown into a crisis: he had fallen in love with Mamah Borthwick Cheney. Wright had designed a house for her and her husband, Edwin H. Cheney, in Oak Park in 1903. She had a strong interest in literature and was more highly educated than many of her peers, having graduated from the University of Michigan at Ann Arbor with a bachelor of arts degree and then earning a master of arts degree (fig. 22).[94] She had been head of the public library at Port Huron, Michigan, where she met Cheney, her future husband. He pursued her, despite rebuffs, and was reported to have "literally carried [her] off into matrimony."[95] He became president of the Wagner Electric Manufacturing Company and the Fuel Engineering Company of Chicago, and was, thus, like some of Wright's other clients, an entrepreneur in fields relating to engineering.[96] The Wrights and the Cheneys had shared a social life in Oak Park. Mamah Cheney and Catherine Wright even belonged to the same civic organizations. But around 1907 an attraction between Wright and Mamah Cheney evolved

This condition was exacerbated by the demise of a project for Harold F. McCormick, heir to the farm machinery fortune, in Lake Forest, Illinois.[90] Composed in plan of a series of shifted wings surrounding open-ended courts, it was the largest residence Wright had designed, the most elaborate, and most free of bilateral symmetry (fig. 20). After considerable development of the design, however, Mrs. McCormick rejected it apparently in favor of a more conventional estate in an Italianate mode designed by Charles A. Platt. More than half of Wright's other designs were also relegated to the status of unexecuted projects, including the Horseshoe Inn, in Estes Park, Colorado; a planned community for Bitter Root Valley in Montana; and the Lexington Terrace Apartments in Chicago—the three projects,

into a love affair, and by 1909 Catherine Tobin Wright knew she was losing the devotion of her husband.[97] With Wright and Cheney's love came the inevitable tension within their own families. For Wright the pressure began to disintegrate his home:

Everything, personal or otherwise, bore heavily upon me. Domesticity most of all. What I wanted I did not know. I loved my children. I loved my home. A true home is the finest ideal of man, and yet—well, to gain freedom I asked for a divorce.[98]

Catherine Wright asked that he wait a year before it was granted, but after a year she refused to allow the divorce.[99] Wright's desire to "desert," which he had described privately, became more intense, and he decided to take matters into his own hands. He began making plans to leave his work and his family and travel to Europe.

His office had to be closed and plans had to be made for finishing projects and accepting new work while he was away.[100] Despite the assertions of historians that Wright, in the midst of a hurried departure, left his practice to a stranger, he tried to arrange for a competent architect to assume his business; he offered the responsibility to recent employees, Barry Byrne and Marion Mahony, but both refused.[101] He also contacted the firm of William G. Purcell and George E. Elmslie to take over.[102] Wright traveled to Minneapolis to persuade Purcell in person to take over his Chicago office.[103] Purcell wrote in retrospect: "[Wright] spent an hour trying to persuade me to come to Chicago—move my family down and take over his business for two years while he 'went to Germany.' George G. E[lmslie] was to carry on our Minneapolis office—I could look after Chicago office of P & E Sat[urday] and Sunday."[104] Purcell replied to Wright's offer that it would be too difficult to look after both his and Wright's offices, particularly since most of Purcell and Elmslie's work was in Minneapolis at the time. Isabel Roberts, Wright's secretary, later wrote to Purcell, after Wright left for Germany, to acknowledge Purcell's refusal and to announce the alternative found by Wright: "You will be interested in knowing that Mr. H. V. Von Holst, a Chicago architect whom you may know, has taken charge of this office and we think the work will be cared for nicely during Mr. Wright's absence."[105]

Hermann Von Holst had studied architecture at the Massachusetts Institute of Technology, and was credited with designing in the arts and crafts style as well as in a shingle style that hugged the landscape and provided an organic affinity that may have drawn Wright to him.[106] Wright claimed in his *Autobiogra-*

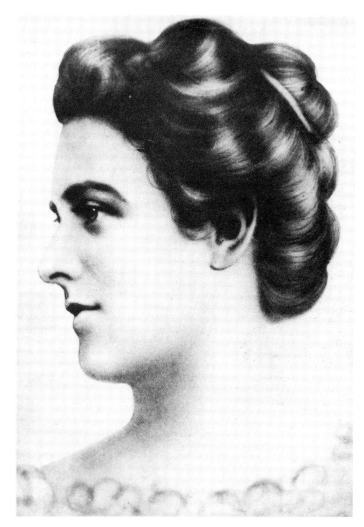

22. Mamah Borthwick Cheney, portrait, 1909 (*CDT*, 1909).

phy that he and Von Holst had only recently met, but Von Holst had an office in Steinway Hall, as Wright had had for several years, and Von Holst had designed an octagonal barn at the Hillside Home School that belonged to Wright's aunts near Spring Green, Wisconsin.[107]

On 22 September 1909 in Oak Park Von Holst and Wright signed a detailed five-page contract for the conveyance of Wright's office to Von Holst.[108] For his staff, Von Holst utilized two of Wright's former employees, Marion Mahony, whom he would have known while both were students at MIT, and Walter Burley Griffin, Mahony's future husband, regardless of the fact that relations between Wright and most of his former draftsmen had soured because he resented their competing with him and imitating his work.[109] Attached to the contract was a list of "actual and prospective" projects in Wright's office at the date of conveyance. The document provided a list of projects that were to be turned over to Von Holst, their status, and the terms by which revenues and expenses would be credited while Wright was in Europe.[110]

The contract also tacitly acknowledged Wright's established professional stature in comparison to Von Holst's. It favored Wright in the payment of commissions and percentages for work that arrived as a result of Wright's reputation and for any work that he would design. At the same time the contract provided safeguards for Von Holst in the collection of fees, safeguards he would eventually use to his advantage.

With his business affairs in order, Wright broke the news of his departure to Darwin Martin in Buffalo. In a letter concern-ing a bill for a gardener's cottage that Wright had designed for Martin's property, he described his plans and announced a "spiritual adventure":

Let the bill rendered cause you no emotion. If it is more than you think it worth amend it as you wish and send what it may be, or, noth-ing,—to the office,—the matter is not worth any agony. I am leaving the office to its own devices, deserting my wife and children for one year, in search of a spiritual adventure, hoping it will be no worse.[111]

Wright confirmed his friendship with Martin and his family and wrote that "You will probably not hear from me again."[112] There was no mention of Mrs. Cheney, who would accompany him to Europe.

On 20 September 1909, Wright left Oak Park and boarded a train for Chicago on the first segment of his journey to Europe.

I had always loved old Germany, Goethe, Schiller, Nietzsche, Bach—the great architect who happened

to choose music for his form—Beethoven and Strauss. And Munich! This beloved company—were they

not old Germany? And Vienna! Vienna had always appealed to my imagination. Paris? Never.

—Frank Lloyd Wright (1932) [1]

2   Wright in Europe

Consistent with his denial of architectural influence, Frank Lloyd Wright claimed that Europe's influence on him before 1909 was limited to the music and literature of Romanticism. German writers and Austrian composers, their capitals of Munich and Vienna—not historical architecture—interested him. Paris was outside consideration because it was the seat of the Ecole des Beaux-Arts and the classicism he loathed. Wright expressed no interest in modern developments, yet he arrived in Europe in 1909 at a critical time in the development of modernism. Various Secession movements, artists' collectives, and new schools were calling for attitudes and images that broke with the past. Stultified academies and artistic dogma were under siege. A revolt was occurring in art, literature, and criticism. An interest in iconoclastic life-styles emerged, often fueled by contrary political points of view, from socialism to utopianism. Idealism was reflected in communal artistic efforts to form collective studios. At the same time, despair and melancholy drove the art of some individuals. In this era the study of the psyche—stimulated by Freud and his colleagues—spread. The subject of extensive scholarly investigation, these changes have been explained often by historians as phenomena of the fin de siècle, but they are full of rich contradictions that play a major role in the history of modernism.

A fervor pervaded Europe that linked art and society. In Vienna a group of rebels dedicated themselves to a *Ver Sacrum*, a sacred spring, an offering of the firstlings of spiritual rebirth with the founding of their own Secession in 1897. Its motto, composed by the journalist and critic Ludwig Hevesi, was "To every era its art: to art its freedom." [2] Fundamental to this statement was the modernist belief in the *zeitgeist*, the spirit of an age reflected in its art, which presupposes a spirituality in art itself. Implicit in the minds of rebellious artists was the supposition that the rebirth of art was integral with changes in society: new forms in art required new forms of a mass society and, conversely, new democratic and socialist societies required their own distinctive expressions of art. The view that class structure needed restructuring apparently motivated Hermann Bahr, the poet and "herald" of the Secession: he took working-class people on tours of the Secession Building to show them they could be proud of their own handcrafts. The admirers of the Secession, however, were increasingly middle-class.

Among the diverse groups pursuing reforms in art were those in the forefront of creating the Modern Movement in architecture. The Modern Movement in Germany had just been launched through the work of Peter Behrens and the German Werkbund in 1907. Despite the fact that August Perret had initiated the movement's emphasis on structure and concrete, France greeted the tectonic expression of his Théatre des Champs Elysées with outrage for being too Germanic in appearance. Antonio Gaudí was carrying out romantic and rationalist experiments in Barcelona. Filippo Marinetti announced the rhetoric of Italian Futurism in *Le Figaro* in February 1909.

Into this frenzy of modernism sailed Frank Lloyd Wright in October 1909, at a pivotal moment in the history of modern architecture when the burgeoning Modern Movement began to overwhelm traditional practitioners who thought their work was modern because it was contemporary.[3] Wright may have been oblivious to contemporary architecture once he reached Europe. Or, if he did perceive some of the modern developments around him, he could make his own work seem independent and original by denying any knowledge of these developments. In this case Wright could give the impression that if he knew nothing of the Modern Movement, he could not be influenced by it.

Wright was also reticent about how his experiences in Europe affected him personally. Defying social convention, in search of refuge, love, and spiritual sustenance, he wanted his activities to remain unknown to the world. Secrecy was necessary in order to avoid scandal. With the exception of a few comments in his autobiographical writings, Wright covered his tracks. No journal or passport exists to mark his comings and goings, and only a few extant letters indicate his motivations and plans.[4] The full details of where he went, what and whom he saw, may never be known.

It is clear, however, that when Wright began to travel in Europe, he had the opportunity to see firsthand the great monuments of Roman, medieval, and Gothic architecture and contemporary art and design. He saw the capitals of Europe—London, Berlin, Vienna, and Paris—and he saw the cities en route to the capitals as well as vernacular buildings of the countryside in Tuscany, Bavaria, and the valley of the Rhine. He could also see craft objects, furniture, murals, textiles, and sculpture that he could previously have known only from illustrations. What he saw provided the artistic inspiration that allowed his practice to enter a rich, experimental period upon his return from Europe. He even found moral support for his future in the writings of Ellen Key, the Swedish feminist, who argued for relationships sanctioned by love, not marriage, and for the liberation of children.

Departure

Travel abroad had glamour and notoriety in 1910. Newspapers had copious advertisements for the shipping lines that crossed the Atlantic. Those people who desired more visibility than Wright did often had their names published in the papers prior to their European departures; the foreign exploits of famous people were covered diligently by American reporters. Wright and Mamah Cheney, however, were intent on avoiding pub-

licity. Wright's explanation for his departure was that he had an opportunity to publish his work in Germany. No mention was made publicly that he was leaving with Mamah Cheney, but both Catherine Wright and Edwin Cheney, as well as their mutual friends, knew of the lovers' plans. Mamah Cheney had left her husband in Oak Park on 28 June 1909 and taken her two children to Boulder, Colorado, to spend time with a pregnant friend. The friend died after childbirth in early October, and Mamah sent for her husband to pick up their children. When he arrived, she had departed. There are no documents to indicate if she and Wright communicated while he arranged his affairs in the summer and fall. They met apparently in October, after Wright's departure from Oak Park on 20 September, staying in New York City at the Plaza Hotel. While the precise date of their sailing has not been determined, they arrived in Berlin in late October or the very beginning of November 1909.

Berlin

Relief from the domestic strife in Oak Park did not last long. A reporter from the *Chicago Daily Tribune* making the rounds of hotels to note visitors' names discovered on 7 November 1909 that "Frank Lloyd Wright and Wife" had registered at the sumptuous Hotel Adlon in Berlin but had left three days earlier.[5] Knowing or finding out from his editors that Catherine Wright had stayed in Oak Park, the reporter broke the cover of the lovers. In Chicago, the *Tribune* trumpeted on its front page that the couple had deserted their families, and that Frank Lloyd Wright had made "an affinity tangle . . . unparalleled even in the checkered history of soul mating."[6] The newspaper reported that Catherine Wright had alleged that Mamah was a "vampire" who caused Wright to flee. Wright was portrayed in the reports as strange and cryptic, yet a victim of infatuation and caught in a moral crisis. On the one hand, his wife was quoted as saying, "I have lived my life with a strange man. Only a few of his friends are able to understand him."[7] On the other hand, Catherine Wright reiterated the belief that her husband would come to his senses and return to her, and that his actions stood outside the conventions of others. After all, he was no mere man, but an artist: "There should not be the same moral gate for all of us. The idea that such should be seems inexorable, but it is not justice."[8]

Other reports appeared in Chicago about the runaway couple.[9] The humiliation was lavish and extreme: Mamah Cheney's picture was published, and Wright's behavior was attributed to

23. Hotel Adlon, Berlin, c. 1910 (*Hotel Adlon*).

his being spoiled as a child. He was further described as a somewhat mad artist, an outlaw, flaunting conventional social behavior; she was his temptress. Implicit in these diatribes was the
judgment that such people should be cast out of decent society.

In order to throw reporters and any other pursuers off his
track, Wright announced in Berlin that the couple was off to Japan. He and Mamah Cheney then dropped out of sight. Sub-
merged in secrecy, they left almost no traces, and the date of
their departure from Berlin is unknown. Although Wright
signed a contract with the firm of Ernst Wasmuth, his Berlin
publisher, on 24 November, there is no further evidence of his
whereabouts until January 1910, by which time he was in Paris.
The ambience he would have experienced during his travels,
the key cultural events, can be deduced only from fragmentary
references in his letters and contemporary sources.

In Berlin Wright and Cheney had stayed in the heart of the
city until their discovery. The Hotel Adlon, one of Berlin's new-
est, designed by Gause and Leibnitz (1905–7), was at the
southeast corner of Pariser Platz, thus, at the end of Unter den
Linden, Berlin's main boulevard (figs. 23, 24).[10] The accommodations chosen by Wright were sumptuous: sponsored by Kaiser Wilhelm, the hotel was described as "half dwelling and half
monument" and was compared at its opening in 1907 to the
halls of Venetian palaces and royal palaces of Bavaria.[11] Its location allowed Wright and Cheney easy access through the Bran-
denburg Gate to the Tiergarten, Berlin's great park at one end of
the Unter den Linden. The first-class hotel provided them luxu-
rious accommodations: a fine restaurant, garden, palm court,
and the convenience of an international travel bureau.

The city was full of the culture of art and architecture. To
move through Berlin was to see its history. Museums complemented the numerous art galleries. Several of those museums
contained not only the treasures of Western painting but the
artifacts of ancient cultures and the "primitive" art that would

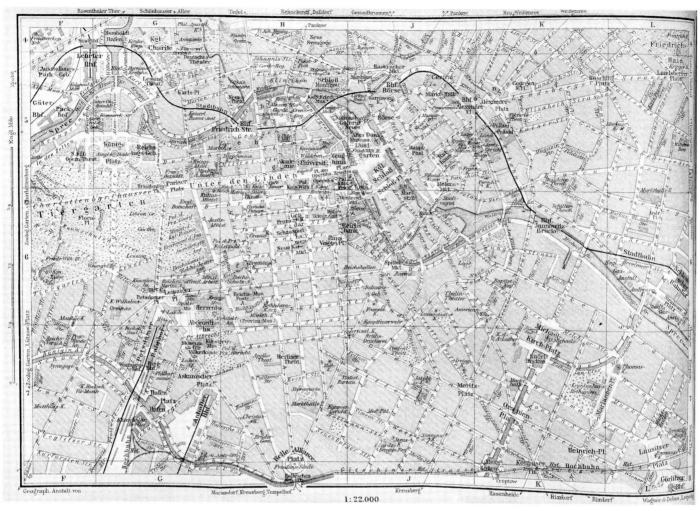

24. Plan, Berlin, c. 1910 (Baedeker, *Northern Germany, as far as the Bavarian and Austrian frontiers*).

become important to Wright as demonstrations of the exotic origins of architecture. The ideas Wright gained from these sources became a central part of his experience in Europe and would be developed in his introduction for his Wasmuth monograph.

Regular exhibitions supplemented the museums and were found at the Academy of Art in Pariser Platz, close to Wright and Cheney's hotel; at the Union of Berlin Artists at the Künstlerhaus; and at the Berlin Secession on the Kurfürstendamm in Charlottenburg. Also, the large, annual Greater Berlin Art Exhibition was held in the Exhibition Park from the end of April until the end of September.[12]

Wright and Cheney visited Germany at the pinnacle of a rich cultural exchange between America and Europe, an exchange that would be damaged by World War I. One special example of that exchange occurred in 1910 through an exhibition that Wright certainly would have known about: the Universal City Planning Exhibition, the first exhibition to deal exclusively with city planning. Confirming the enthusiastic interest Germany had for American developments, it provided a cultural bridge between the two countries, and between Chicago and Berlin in particular.[13] The exhibition included the work of such architects as Bruno Möhring and provided a major stimulus for the planning profession.[14] Wasmuth, Wright's publisher, issued a guide to the exhibition in 1910 and, subsequently, a two-volume report on the results, edited by Werner Hegemann, who was primarily responsible for the exhibition and who had included much material on American city planning.[15] The entire event was important for America and Germany, and the interest in American planning was confirmed the following year, 1911, when Wasmuth published Hegemann's *Der Neue Bebauungsplan für Chicago* (The New Development Plan for Chicago).[16] Berlin and Chicago were comparable, Hegemann stated, because both had grown so rapidly during the last half-century, in contrast to European cities that had developed slowly over time.

How the Universal City Planning Exhibition may have affected Wright's own ideas on city planning is unclear, if it affected them at all. The event, which emphasized a comparison of Berlin to Chicago and the German interest in American city planning, did not transmit specific influences but provided a testament to the receptivity to American ideas in Germany that encouraged Möhring and the firm of Ernst Wasmuth to take an interest in Wright's work. It also reinforced the strong American interest in German planning developments, art, architecture, and Germanic culture in general.

The American presence in Berlin was also felt through the ongoing efforts of cultural exchange fostered by Kuno Francke, who was supposedly Wright's connection to the Wasmuth enterprise. He organized an exhibition of American art at the Akademie der Künste, and the same show was exhibited in Munich from April through May in 1910.[17] Yet, there is no indication that Wright made any contact with Francke.

Reciprocally, German art was amply available for American visitors. Besides the traditional artists represented in museums, Karl Baedeker's guide to Berlin pointed out artists who were considered to have led the recent counterhistorical movements, such as Max Liebermann, leader of the Munich Secession, and Walter Leistikow, who had exhibited at the St. Louis Fair and had been instrumental in the Secession in Berlin until his death in 1908; Wright and Cheney bought wood-block prints by both artists.[18] Since 1902 the movement to counter the historicist styles had developed through the work of sculptors and painters, among whom were Otto Eckman, Bruno Paul, Emil Orlik, and Peter Behrens.[19] They and others were leading the developments that had particular importance for the design of crafts and household artifacts. Behrens, whose work had been exhibited in the St. Louis Fair, was now the in-house designer of the industrial giant Allgemeine Elektricitäts Gesellschaft, the AEG. Paralleling Wright's ambitions to create the total built environment, or *Gesamtkunstwerk,* Behrens was in the process of designing everything from factories to desk lamps.

It is important to emphasize that Wright made almost no mention of contemporary German architectural developments in any of his major statements. The nineteenth-century architectural monuments of Karl Friedrich Schinkel appear to be the only buildings in and around Berlin that Wright noted. In one of his few references to architecture in Europe, Wright reported that Schinkel's work thrilled him.[20] Seeing Schinkel's work gave Wright the opportunity to experience a principal source for many of the German-trained architects in Chicago. In Berlin, at the opposite end of the Unter den Linden, was Schinkel's Altes Museum, which Wright and Cheney could have easily walked to from the Hotel Adlon, passing Schinkel's New Guard House en route. Potsdam, a location of important work by Schinkel, also particularly impressed Wright.[21] On the other hand, Wright made no mention of the Turbine Hall that Behrens had designed in the Berlin suburb of Moabit for the AEG even though the opening in October 1909 was the most significant architectural event of the year.[22] Wright made no mention of Behrens, or of Behren's studio, the most progressive in Berlin, which in 1910 provided work for three major figures in modern architecture: Walter Gropius, Mies van der Rohe, and Charles Edouard Jeanneret (later Le Corbusier).[23] When Wright passed through Berlin in 1910, what did he know of them, and what did they know of him?

Wright's "Exhibition" in Berlin

It is tempting to imagine that the young architects who worked for various times in Behrens's office met Wright, but close scrutiny of the dates involved shows that neither Mies nor Jeanneret was in Behrens's office while Wright was in Berlin.[24] This temptation is fostered by one of the claims in the myth of Wright's influence on Europeans: that an exhibition was held in Berlin around 1910 that introduced Wright's work. Reiterating Mies's recollections made some thirty years after the event that "there came to Berlin the exhibition of the work of Frank Lloyd Wright," historians have repeated—without any documentary evidence—the story of the existence of an exhibition until it has become a canonical account in histories of modern architecture.[25] Mies went on to say that through some extraordinary force, Wright's "influence was strongly felt even when it was not actually visible."[26] Gropius gave, through his biographer, his own version of an exhibition, but it too lacked any substantiation, and he may have confused it with a later exhibition by Wright in 1931.[27]

Wright also visited the nearby ancient castles along the Rhine Valley. From the description he gave in July 1910, he appeared to have had delightful travels along the Rhine from Cologne to Coblenz.[54] The romantic, picturesque valley would have evoked for Wright the castles of fairy tales and romantic fables that he read as a child. Germany's romantic castles on the Rhine, Schinkel's neoclassical buildings in Potsdam, and Olbrich's Wedding Tower in Darmstadt interested Wright, but he made no reference to living architects in any of his writings.

Paris—A First Visit

While there are no documents to confirm Wright's whereabouts from early November through December 1909, collateral evidence shows that he and Mamah Cheney were in Paris by mid-January 1910.[55] Although Wright later claimed that Paris had never appealed to his imagination, he made two trips to the City of Light, one at the beginning of his European sojourn, the other at the end. Accounts by Wright's sons Lloyd and John and a letter from Wright's twelve-year-old daughter Frances confirm the first trip. Because she was studying French landmarks in her Oak Park school, Frances wrote to her father to ask all about Paris and added that she was relieved he had just missed the disastrous record floods that had made the Seine go over its banks.[56] Wright had witnessed the results of the inundations that caused buildings to collapse, streets to cave in, and incomplete sections of the subway system to be destroyed that winter.[57]

The natural disaster that Wright encountered in Paris oc-

31.   Joseph Maria Olbrich, Wedding Tower on the Matildenhöhe, entry detail, Darmstadt, 1905–8 (author).

mantic ambience of the ancient town.[94] Fiesole lay five miles to the northeast of Florence and could be reached in three-quarters of an hour by electric tram, the first of its kind in Europe (fig. 38).[95] On the way to the town Wright and Cheney passed by the Badia di Fiesole, which had been famous as a rallying point of the humanists of the Platonic academy in the time of Lorenzo the Magnificent and was now a school. Fiesole itself had Etruscan origins and, as recounted in popular con-

temporary histories, was "ever the centre of Italian and democratic discontent against Rome and her Senate" until it was forced to surrender to the Romans under Julius Caesar.[96]

A place with ancient origins, the town had been historically the stronghold of independent rebels. It was here in a lofty aerie called the Villa Belvedere that rebellious Wright and Cheney found temporary safety from a prying public. Wright recognized the place as sanctuary:

39. Villino Belvedere, contemporary view of corner entry, 1990 (author).

40. Villino Belvedere, view from side entry, Taylor Woolley photograph, 1910 (UUL).

41. Villino Belvedere, garden, Taylor Woolley photographer, 1910 (UUL).

she gave him two dictionaries—the tools of her trade as translator—as mementos when he left.

Wright recalled in his *Autobiography* the walks in their garden around a pool sheltered by the arbor of roses, and hikes over undulating hills, through fields of poppies, towards Vallombrosa, into the midst of pine forests, spending the night in an inn, then returning along the old, dusty Roman road.[101]

42. Lloyd Wright at Villino Belvedere, Taylor Woolley photographer, 1910 (UUL).

How many souls seeking release from real or fancied domestic woes have sheltered on the slopes below Fiesole! I, too, now sought shelter there in companionship with her who, by force of rebellion as by way of love was then implicated with me.

Walking hand in hand together up the hill road from Firenze to the older town, all along the way in sight and scent of roses, by day. Walking arm in arm up the same old road at night, listening to the nightingale in the deep shadows of the moonlit wood—trying hard to hear the song in the deeps of life. So many Pilgrimages we made to reach the small solid door framed in the solid white blank wall with massive green door opening toward the narrow Via Verdi itself. Entering, closing the medieval door on the world outside to find a wood fire burning in the small grate. Estero in her white apron, smiling, waiting to surprise Signora and Signore with the incomparable little dinner: the perfect roast fowl, mellow wine, the caramel custard—beyond all roasts or wines or caramels ever made, I remember.[97]

Located on the Viale Giuseppe Verdi, a narrow road leading from the southeast corner of the piazza, their rented house sat at a fork on the road (fig. 39).[98] The lower floor, entered from the walled garden, provided a temporary studio with drawing tables (figs. 40–43). Its walls were covered with drawings in various stages of completion for the Wasmuth plates. The upper floor, entered from the higher fork, provided parlor and living accommodations. From their windows Wright and Cheney had sweeping views of Florence over the precipice of the hill below.

While living in the Villino Belvedere, Cheney studied Swedish and Italian and translated Key's works, which were later published in Chicago.[99] Aside from Wright's accounts, little else is known of her activities. Woolley described Mamah as "one of the loveliest women I ever knew."[100] The affection was mutual;

43. Villino Belvedere, interior view, Taylor Woolley photographer, 1910 (UUL).

They toured not only through hills and fields but through art galleries and buildings:

Together again tired out, sitting on benches in the galleries of Europe, saturated with plastic beauty, beauty in buildings, beauty in sculpture, beauty in paintings, until no Chiesa however rare and no further beckoning work of human hands waylay us anymore.
Faithful comrade!
A dream? In realization ended? No. Woven, a golden thread in the human pattern of the precious fabric that is life: her life built into the house of houses. So far as may be known—forever![102]

What better way to make these romantic visions permanent than for Wright and Cheney to have their own villino. He set about designing the ideal, if modest, studio home for artists. It could have been intended for a future return or as a means of capturing the dream of the moment. For his design Wright took advantage of the Mediterranean tradition of the walled garden, which characterized Villino Belvedere.

Two sets of drawings of Wright's villino were made: a pair of studies for the elevations and four studies in perspective.[103]

Woolley retained the elevations and plans, which had a forecourt and entry hall that opened onto the courtyard garden, the living quarters on one side, and Wright's office on the other. This was the embryonic design concept for Wright and Cheney's house, Taliesin, which he would build in Wisconsin in 1911. One elevation study combined a flat roof with a partially pitched roof, the other elevation had a roof with low-pitched gables and arched entryway (figs. 44, 45). The flat-roofed scheme took precedence, and it was developed into two pairs of perspectives. In one pair Wright tried out the entry on the right, in the other pair he tested the entry on the left.[104] Both pairs retained elements of Italian vernacular architecture: a small, shuttered window opening onto the street; topiary (on the balcony of the second floor); and a special element, panels of sculpture in several locations over doors and windows. This use of sculpture and its integration into architecture became increasingly significant for Wright.

But the designs were fantasies. Despite these idealized visions of home and studio and the rapturous views, the spiritual

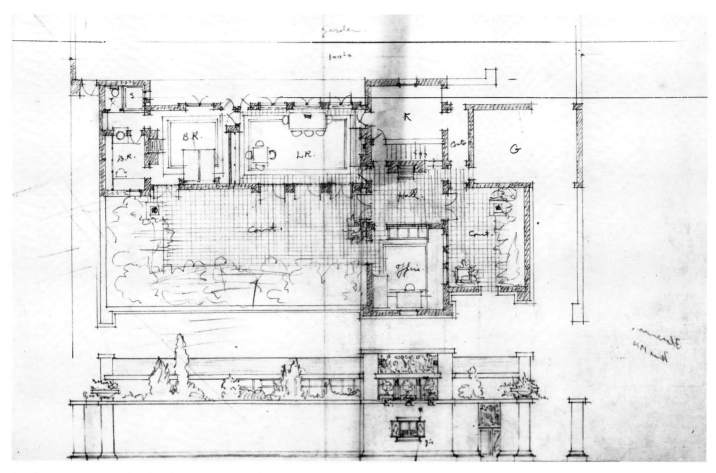

44. Fiesole studio, project, flat-roof study with plan and elevation, 1910 (UUL).

adventure had its frustrations and emotional difficulties. Rancor with his former employees, particularly Walter Burley Griffin, caused conflict and distrust. In June, Wright composed a letter from Fiesole to Griffin to deal with a rumor that Griffin was unhappy with Japanese wood-block prints that Wright had provided for him.[105] Also, soon after getting settled in Florence, Wright had to confess his adultery to his friend Charles Robert Ashbee. In late March, Wright had explained that he had not come to visit the Ashbees in Chelsea because he was with a woman, not his wife, with whom he had been in love "for some years."[106] Despite the revelation of his infidelity, Wright hoped that the Ashbees would not give up their friendship.

As Guthrie had predicted, Wright had become torn between concern for his family and the pursuit of his own needs. On the one hand, he was aware that his daughter Catherine was having a difficult time adjusting to the scandal of his abandonment and that his wife had received from the Ashbees an invitation for Catherine to visit them in England.[107] On the other hand, the pain and challenge of the spiritual adventure preoccupied his thoughts. In a plaintive, pained and poetic tone Wright explained to Ashbee:

I wanted to square my *life* with *myself.* I want to do this now more than anything else. I want to *live* true as I would *build* true, and in the light I have tried to do this thing. Advice has been of little use. The necessary light must come from within. Life is *living* and living only brings the light. . . .[108]

Using words he had written to Darwin Martin prior to his departure, Wright gave the ordering of life and soul the metaphor of geometry, a metaphor that would have an expanding meaning for the architect.

During the summer, thoughts of his family continued, and Wright began plans for a return to America. By early July 1910,

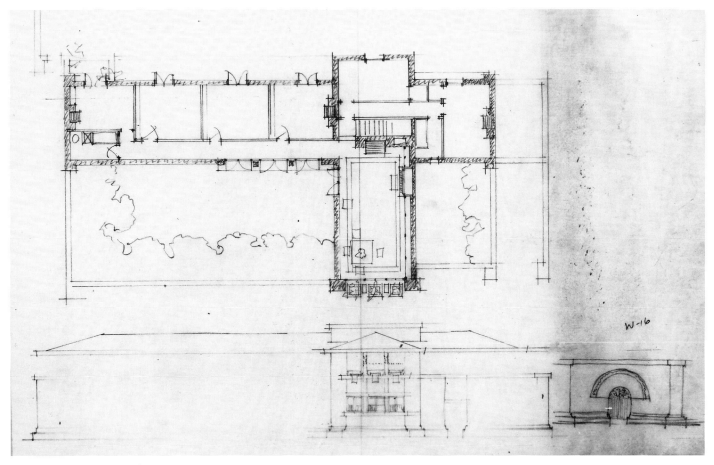

45. Fiesole studio, project, low-pitched roof study with plan and elevation, 1910 (UUL).

Wright thought he had resolved his guilt and struggle about returning to his family. He wrote to Ashbee:

The fight has been fought—I am going back to Oak Park to pick up the thread of my work and in some degree of my life where I snapped it. I am going to work among the ruins—not as any woman's husband but as the father of the children—to do what I can for them. And I shall come to see you on my way—early in September. My contract with Wasmuth in Berlin will keep me until then.[109]

Despite his moral anguish, Wright continued to absorb the life in Italy around him, complete preparations for the Wasmuth publications, and travel. He reported to Ashbee on his Tuscan experiences:

I have been very busy here in this little eyrie on the brow of the mountain above Fiesole—overlooking the pink and white, Florence spreading in the valley of the Arno below—the whole fertile bosom of the earth seemingly lying in the drifting mists or shining clear and marvelous in the Italian sunshine—opalescent—iridescent. I have poked into the unassuming corners where this wondrous brood of Florentines—painters, sculptors, sculptor painters and painter sculptor architects worked. I declare you cannot tell here; there was no line drawn,—between mediums.[110]

Clearly, the beauty of nature and the perception of a time when the artisan and artist were one and the arts formed an indivisible cultural whole appealed to Wright. His direct experience of Western culture was further reinforced by his reading of the standard works of travel literature and art criticism:

I have read Howells, Ruskin and Vasari on Florence . . . and in my travels I have been surprised to find that European culture in the fine arts worth considering except the Gothic of the Middle Ages is but a lesser light lit from the Italian flames of the 12th, 13th & 14th, 15th centuries—an afterglow in the 16th.[111]

46. Harley Bradley House, interior (lithograph published in the Wasmuth monograph, pl. 22, 1911).

Meanwhile, Woolley, who was then traveling in Germany, telegrammed Wright from Berlin to say that he had been to see Wasmuth, where unspecified troubles were preventing any chance of an early completion of the publications. Wright had been out of Fiesole between 8 July and 20 July when the telegram arrived, but upon his return answered Woolley about the status of the project.[112] By this time all the plates were finished except one of the Harley Bradley House which Wright stated that he himself would retrace (figs. 46, 47).[113] In addition, the photographs sent from America for the *Sonderheft* had been forwarded to Berlin; but of the fifty sent, only thirty were good enough to use. Wright replied that he understood the problems with Wasmuth, that the delays were tedious, and that he had suspicions about Otto Dorn, the German editor at Wasmuth: "but these Dutchmen [*sic*] move slowly and this particular Herr Dorn is a smooth party I am persuaded. I shall be in England September 10 [1910]."[114]

In answering Woolley, Wright also inadvertently indicated

one way his European adventure was being financed: by the sale of Japanese prints, prior to his departure, to Sallie Casey Thayer, a wealthy widow from Kansas City, Kansas, who had been frequenting the Chicago art scene.[115] Her anticipated payments to Wright would allow him to give more funds to Woolley if he needed them in Paris.[116] This sale had been supplemented by a loan from client Francis Little for which Wright had used Japanese prints as collateral.

Plans proceeded for Wright's visit to England.[117] Wright's funds were shrinking, and he was growing impatient with the idyllic life. His frustration with Wasmuth also was mounting because of problems with production: the pace of producing the monograph and the picture book was too slow for Wright, and he objected to someone besides himself writing the monograph introduction.[118]

We have always thought that publishing the monograph was Wasmuth's main intention, but Wright's description of the venture shows that Wasmuth's original interest had been to produce a book of pictures as a photographic essay on Wright's work for their series of special publications, or *Sonderhefte*, with Wasmuth retaining ownership. Wright had proposed an additional book, a monograph that would be the graphic ideal of his work. The book of photographs would be of the actual built work, and both books would appear simultaneously as a pair. For the monograph, seventy-three buildings were to be illustrated in one hundred plates; twelve proofs had been pulled, but printing of the better projects had not yet been finished. Wright blamed the slowness of the publishing house, but the tardy arrival of the photographs for his *Sonderheft* had interfered with Wasmuth's publishing schedule, and the books would not be available until the beginning of January 1911. Frustrated at the delays, Wright contemplated finding a new publisher, "but," as he wrote to Ashbee, "they are doing a little

better and I will wait with what patience I can command."[119] At this moment, the pursuit of his work became increasingly intertwined with the resolution of his personal dilemmas:

I suppose I will have to "bide their time" however. They are now two months behind agreement, with the work. I am so much in haste because I need the moral support the work in beautiful dress and strong form would give me in the scramble to my feet that lies just ahead. My position is one I cannot see in perspective as another sees it. I have not the angle or—I fear the elevation but I am going to do what I can.[120]

With the end of the sojourn in sight, Wright grew anxious to confront the reality that faced Cheney and him. He continued in his letter to Ashbee that:

The little Villino Belvedere here is a charming little place—with its tiny enclosed garden hanging out over the valley—but my work and life in it draw toward a close—There is something good in this life

47. Harley Bradley House, interior (photograph published in the *Sonderheft,* 1910–11).

here that I dare hope may not be lost,—that out of it will come something of greater strength and deeper understanding which will leave all who are touched by it, better, richer—truer,—but is it a vain hope? The "cruelty" of its basis in other hearts clutches at mine when I see its bearings—as I see it now—eventually—Its price must be paid. . . .[121]

A sense of isolation and loneliness appears to enter as well: "Outside the house on the corner in Oak Park—since I left there a year ago—the twentieth of next September I have written only my mother—one letter to Guthrie and to you—drop me a line soon. . . ."[122]

Five weeks remained to contemplate the return home. Before his departure from Europe, however, Wright journeyed to Vienna, a city he admired.

Vienna

The precise dates of Wright's travels between Fiesole, Berlin, the valleys of Germany, and Vienna may never be firmly established. In the summer, while in and out of Fiesole, Wright traveled in Bavaria, near the Tirol mountains west of Vienna, to see the Passion play at Oberammergau, the famous dramatization of the story of Christ's suffering and death.[123] Wright and Cheney could have continued to Vienna by train (fig. 48). Furthermore, the summer months were a logical time for their visit—the work on the Wasmuth monograph was substantially complete, the couple had been reunited in Fiesole—but there is no indication that a visit at some other time was not possible. Wright left no official trace in Vienna; the archives of the city's *Meldezettel* have no records of his visit.[124] Up to now, only speculation has linked Wright and the artists of the Secession. There is evidence, however, that confirms a journey to Vienna in the last moments of its cultural power as the capital of the Austro-Hungarian Empire.[125]

It is important to keep in mind that Wright encountered the influence of the art and architecture of the Secession movement after it had reached its apex; his adaptation of the ideas at the end of the movement creates a displacement in historical time rather than a set of simultaneous developments. The pinnacle of the Austrian Secession had occurred in the early part of the decade, with the fourteenth exhibition of the Secession honoring Beethoven in April 1902. The Secession had split apart in 1905, with fourteen or fifteen members seceding to form a group around Gustav Klimt.[126]

In 1910 the maelstrom of politics, art, music, literature, theater, and the sciences of the mind were reaching an explosive intensity in the imperial capital of two million inhabitants.[127] In January, Giacomo Puccini's *Tosca* opened at the royal opera, and Edmund Eysler's *Der unsterbliche Lump* premiered in October.[128] In the Salon Heller an art exhibition of Arnold Schönberg's was held. He also was teaching at the Vienna Music Academy, while the composer Alban Berg was writing his string quartet Opus 3 and Mahler worked on his tenth symphony. Hermann Bahr, whose words had inspired the artists in Darmstadt, opened his *Lustspiel* in three acts. The Vienna and International Psychoanalytic Unions were founded. Also, an immense exhibition of art, craft, and artifacts was held at the Museum for Art and Industry.[129]

The great building program of the Ringstrasse had been completed. Citizens were traveling on the best streetcar system in Europe. The building of the French Embassy was celebrated. Adolf Loos's design for the firm of tailors, Goldman and Salatsch, was under construction, and the "Urania" exhibition building and planetarium had just been completed.

The city was an international meeting place. President Theodore Roosevelt visited on 15 and 16 April, and in May 1910 a major international congress on low-cost housing was held at the Museum for Art and Industry.[130] The congress included the latest developments in city and town planning from Germany, Denmark, Great Britain, and other countries. Models of housing from Holland by M. P. de Clerq, as well as the "Vanderbilt Tenements" in New York City were included.[131]

The general interests of the Viennese extended from the urban scale to the small-scale artifact of humble origin. The same museum that held the colossal exhibition on low-cost housing also exhibited folk art, crafts, and textiles from Sweden.[132] Woven fabrics were of particular interest, and most came from craft collectives and cottage industries.

Into the city of these artistic activities came Frank Lloyd Wright, probably with Mamah Cheney, whose facility with German must have made their visit easier. Regardless of when he came, the city left a powerful impression through its art and buildings, as seen from scattered references by Wright, letters he wrote, and the effect it had on his own designs.[133]

The rebellious architects of the Secession movement, trained in the school of their master, Otto Wagner, had been extremely active since 1897, when Olbrich's Secession Building had opened for the exhibitions of its members (figs. 49, 50). Wright now had the opportunity to see in person the building by the architect to whom he had been compared.

Initially the Secession Building had been ridiculed as ap-

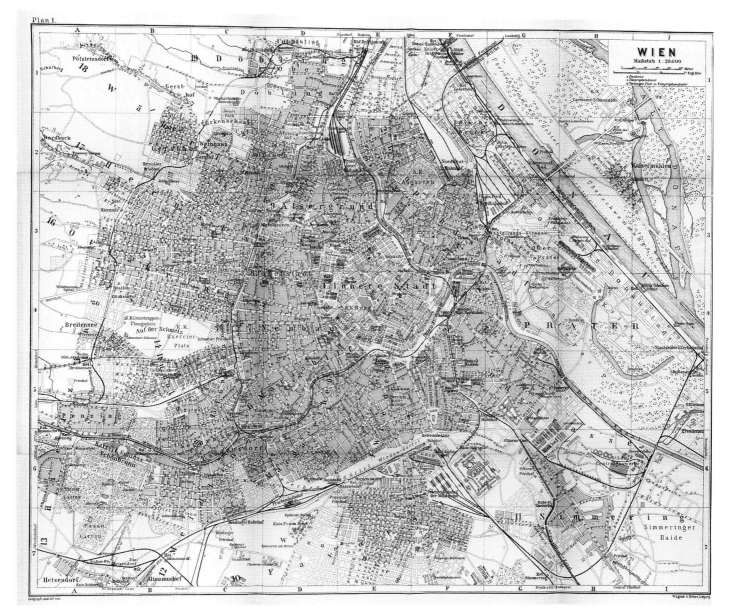

48. Plan of Vienna, c. 1910 (Baedeker, *Austria-Hungary including Dalmatia and Bosnia*).

pearing oriental and foreign. It was called Egyptian, Assyrian, Indian, and Spanish, but six months after its opening it had become an object of Viennese pride.[134] By 1910 it was still identified in Baedeker's guide as "a curious building in an Assyrian-Egyptian style."[135] The popular description was not far off the mark; the building's images derived from the exotic origins of architecture in the ancient Near East, the entry itself being in the form of an Egyptian hieroglyph representing the entry to the underworld of the gods. Such images were seminal for the Secessionists and became so for Wright.[136] The rear of the building was an immediate recollection of ancient Egypt; it was in the form of a pylon and had a painted frieze of Egyptian figures. Olbrich himself compared the experience of the building to standing "alone before the unfinished temple at Segesta," where he realized why he disliked the absence of "warmth" and "heart" in the buildings around him in Vienna.[137]

In one of the problematic assertions of Europe influencing Wright, Scully has cited the Secession Building as the "model" for Wright's Unity Temple and his Larkin Building, with the motif of the spheres on the piers of the Larkin Building resembling the gilt laurel dome at the entry of the Secession Building.[138] But, as in the historian's claim about the "influence" of Olbrich's Studio Building on Wright, the assertion of visual similarities lacks an explanation of how or why Wright might have used the building as a model for his own designs. He already had formal precedents for the Larkin Building and Unity Temple in his own project for the Abraham Lincoln Center in Chicago. Although the Secession Building's massing, its recessed blind panels, its square, sectioned moldings, and its overhanging eaves seemed suitable for concrete construction, it was built of brick with a thick cement stucco. Wright's Unity Temple, built of poured concrete, had more "truth" because its method of construction better expressed its square, heavy massing. As for the

49. Joseph Maria Olbrich, Secession Building, entry with Olbrich's poster at entry door, Vienna, 1898 (Bildarchiv, ÖNB).

globes at the Larkin Building, a recent monograph shows that the Larkin globes were not derived from the Secession's "Golden Cabbage" but from a terrestrial globe.[139]

However, like Olbrich's Studio Building, the Secession Building presented to Wright a symbolism that had no parallel in America and a sampler of the expressive means of the Secession artists and architects: the square, the recessed plane, and the exoticism of ancient architecture. Despite the massive, abstract presence in America of the architecture of Henry Hobson Richardson, the emotive force of Frank Furness, and the lyricism of Louis Sullivan's floral ornament, no such architecture existed in the United States. Wright's own symbolism had been in some instances more abstract, and in others more literally figurative.

In Vienna, Wright was in the ambience of Otto Wagner, the mentor of Olbrich and his peers and the most revered modern architect in Vienna.[140] Wagner stood in relation to his followers as Sullivan stood to Wright and his contemporaries, but Wagner contributed to shaping a city through his municipal transportation system in ways of which Sullivan had never dreamed. Although Wagner had been denied several major public commissions, his architecture and planning could be seen in his rapid transit stations, bridges, apartment houses, and in the central Postal Savings Bank, built in its first phase between 1904 and 1906. Whether Wright met Wagner is unknown, but Wright at least spoke highly of him and knew him well enough to have his address three years later when Wright's son John considered studying in Vienna.[141] Wagner, at the age of seventy, was at the end of his career as a practitioner and a teacher at the Vienna Academy of Fine Arts, one of the few schools where Wright considered the principles of a new architecture could be pursued. Before he stopped teaching entirely, however, he acknowledged Wright's work in 1911 as it appeared in the Wasmuth *Sonderheft*, telling his students, "Gentlemen, today I have something special. This man knows more than I do."[142] Wagner was especially impressed with the Larkin Building and Unity Temple.

While in Vienna Wright also apparently met some of the distinguished architects who had studied under Otto Wagner, including Josef Hoffmann, the driving force of the Wiener Werkstätte.[143] Wright probably saw the showrooms of the Werkstätte, replete with the objects he had previously seen illustrated in *The Studio*; while there he apparently bought a rug that resembled his carpet design for the Avery Coonley House in Riverside, Illinois.[144]

In addition to seeing the Secession Building and Wiener

Werkstätte, Wright would have seen the Kunstschau building in which the Klimt group had held its own exhibitions after its split with the Secession; its architecture embodied ancient motifs and sculptural treatments Wright later used. Designed as a temporary pavilion in 1907 by Josef Hoffmann and built in 1908, the building was a subject of much attention (fig. 51).[145] The first Kunstschau exhibition of 1908 had focused on Viennese art. The second, in 1909, was an international exhibition featuring the work of Munch and Van Gogh, as well as arts and crafts architects, Charles Rennie Mackintosh, C. F. A. Voysey, and Wright's friend Charles Robert Ashbee. It also included the sculpture of the German Franz Metzner, Hoffmann's colleague, who was considered by some art critics as even more important than Gustav Klimt.[146] Wright met Metzner, and the meeting became instrumental in Wright's development of "conventionalization," a current theory of abstracting nature for artistic purposes.[147]

The second Kunstschau exhibition closed before Wright's arrival, but talk about it must have persisted. Despite the artistic success of the pavilion complex, demolition had begun on it, but remains of the building were probably still visible in 1910.[148] The building provided a powerful link between the architecture of the Secession and Wright's work upon his return to America: its sculptures were the models for Wright's figures at Midway Gardens.

Finally, Wright had contact with the work of Gustav Klimt, the leading artistic personality of the Secession, whom he greatly admired. There is no confirmation that Wright met the artist, who spent his summers outside Vienna, but Wright reported later that the exposure to Klimt or his art had "refreshed" him.[149] Klimt's work in 1910 was visible in a number of international exhibitions: the Ninth Biennale in Venice; the German Künstlerbund in Prague; and the exhibition "Drawing Arts" in Berlin.[150] Locally, his work could be seen at the Galerie Miethke, whose director was Carl Moll.[151] In addition to his role as cultural impresario, Moll was a cofounder of the Secession, its president in 1900–1901, and an important collaborator in it until his departure with the Klimt group in 1905.[152] Eight of Klimt's paintings,

50. Secession Building, Vienna, 1899 (Kunstbibliothek, Berlin).

51. Josef Hoffmann, Kunstschau Building, front facade, Vienna, 1908 (*Der Architekt* 14, 1908).

principally landscapes, were on sale, and a ninth was exhibited from a private collection; drawings on the walls and in the windows of the gallery complemented the paintings.[153]

The regenerative power of Klimt's work so impressed Wright that he later obtained two important and rare folios of Klimt's wood-block work, *Das Werk von Gustav Klimt* and *Gustav Klimt, Fünfundzwanzig Handzeichnungen*.[154] In addition, he later received as a gift and owned for many years Klimt's *Alte Frau*, a dark, foreboding painting thought by Klimt scholars to have been lost (fig. 52).[155]

Whether Wright met Moll, or saw the art at the Galerie Miethke, remains unconfirmed. Wright's purchase of Moll's print *Hohe Warte in Wien*, however, implied that Wright may have known that the residences of some key members of the Vienna Secession were located near the depicted scene (fig. 53). Moll's winter scene was a view of the elegant quarter on a hill at the northern outskirts of Vienna where he and Koloman Moser, another Secession member, lived in houses that were part of a showcase of designs by Josef Hoffmann.[156] In itself the print, which had been exhibited that year at the Museum for Art and Industry, links Wright to the Secession.[157]

The print, among others in Wright's collections, however, apparently provided a souvenir rather than an artistic inspiration for him. Wright took the more abstract motifs of Viennese art and architecture as expressed in ornament, absorbed them, and transformed them into his own work upon his return to America. Before he could begin this new experimental phase of his work, however, he had to prepare himself for the demands of conventional morality in America.

Return Preparations

Having concluded his travels in the summer of 1910, Wright made plans to return alone to America; Mamah Cheney stayed in Europe.[158] Wright spent early September in Berlin, consulting with his publisher. He then traveled to Campden and stayed with the Ashbees.[159] At this time, Wright asked Charles Robert Ashbee to write the Introduction to the *Sonderheft,* partly out of friendship and partly because he considered Ashbee one of the most distinguished British architects.[160] But when Wright returned to London, he became angry and disappointed at what Ashbee had written in his introductory text.[161] In a series of letters written later in September, each man accused the other of having a grandiose case of "individualism," but more crucial for Wright were some of Ashbee's assertions about Wright's archi-

52. Gustav Klimt, *Die Alte Frau*, 1909, formerly in the collection of Frank Lloyd Wright (Fischer Fine Art, London).

53. Carl Moll, *Hohe Warte in Wien*, 1903, from Frank Lloyd Wright's collection of Secessionist prints (TAL).

tecture.[162] Ashbee lauded Wright's efforts "to master the machine and use it at all costs and find the forms and treatment it may render without abuse of tradition."[163] On the other hand, he saw Wright's designs as too severe and appropriate only for the prairies of America. He intended to introduce Wright's built works to Europe as coming from an architect whose principles, but not his style, should be followed. Ashbee's most offensive statement, however, was the assertion that Wright was influenced by Japanese architecture.[164]

Smarting from the implication that he copied Japanese art or even that he used it as a literal source for his work, Wright claimed that he had "digested" Japanese art rather than adapted it. To set the record straight he insisted that Ashbee change his text:

My conscience troubles me—Do not say that I deny that my love for Japanese art has influenced me—I admit that it has but claim to have digested it—Do not accuse me of trying to "adapt Japanese forms" however, *that is a false accusation and against my very religion.* Say it more *truthfully* even if it does mean saying it a little more *gently.* W.

Please forward immediately all the proofs that may have arrived before my letter to Wasmuth cuts them off and oblige yours. FLW.[165]

Ashbee did not alter his text to suit Wright's wishes, and Wright ultimately excised Ashbee's comments about his adaptation of Japanese forms from the English version of the Introduction. Only the German version of Ashbee's Introduction included the full text; the English text, as censored by Wright, was included with the American edition of the *Sonderheft,* and an edited version appeared in an article in 1913, but the full English edition was never published (see Appendix B).[166]

The disagreement temporarily cooled their friendship, but Wright eventually made amends for his "selfishness and absurdity."[167] Ashbee later visited Wright, and their friendship survived.

The Results

By mid-September 1910, Wright's first journey to Europe was at its end. The received notions of Europe's influence in Wright or Wright's influence in Europe have been put forward outside of any biographical context. Yet, the impact of Europe on his art was bound up with his personal experiences. The year abroad had provided an escape from a difficult personal family situation, had allowed him to summarize in a systematic way his own architectural ideas through the Wasmuth publications, and to encounter, through Cheney's translations, the feminist ideology of Ellen Key. Berlin had been a place of frustration where he transacted business with his publisher; Paris, a brief interlude; Italy, his refuge; Vienna, his touchstone.

The most immediate demonstrable result of his travels was the collation of his work in a graphic format for the monograph that was unparalleled by the publications of any contemporary American or European architect. He had assembled a version of a book of photographs of built work that would become his *Sonderheft.* He had seen the capitals of Europe and some of the latest modern architecture in them. In the countryside, he experienced vernacular buildings and landscapes, whose images were the subject of prints he bought by *Jugendstil* and Secession artists. He had confronted in person aspects of the historical legacy of Western architecture and had begun to write about his reactions to it for his Wasmuth Introduction. And yet Wright's "spiritual adventure" was incomplete. Before he could fully reveal how Europe had affected his work he had to face a return to his family, to translate his experience into his art, and to fit his principles into an unconventional life. His explorations of the lessons of Europe would take place in the midst of intense strife.

I believe that true life—and life is living—can only be realized as God intended—where one's thought, feeling, and act *square* with each other—or where one has the hope at least and makes the struggle to square one's *self* with one's life—and failing in this endeavor—then to square one's life with one's self.—Frank Lloyd Wright (1910)[1]

3   Squaring the Self with Life: Return from Europe

By using a metaphor that related geometry to personal harmony— "to square my life with myself"—Wright introduced a theme that became increasingly important to him artistically and personally. This theme was more metaphorical than literal. Although the square had been critical to Wright's design processes before 1910, after his travels in Europe his further manipulations of the square would add a new dimension to his ornament, and he would develop the forms of primary geometry into shapes that he believed could represent the aspirations and values of a society.

Establishing the context of Wright's return from Europe is critical in understanding how his life and art were linked. It is through this complex linkage that Europe's influence on Wright is revealed. A period of emotional strain, financial struggle, and frustration would intervene prior to the recommencement of his practice and the distribution of his publications. In describing to Darwin D. Martin his efforts to integrate his life with the world around him, Frank Lloyd Wright chose a metaphor, the making of a square and the ordering of a life, that linked his personal struggle with artistic creation.[2] The making of squares was central to his method of design, but Wright appeared unsure if these linkages occurred through divine purpose; in rereading his prose he crossed out in his letter the words "as God intended." Yet, whether the intention is divine or mortal, to

square one's self with one's life means allowing thoughts and feelings to become integrated into a whole so that the inner being is in harmony with one's outer conditions. To square life with the self, on the other hand, implies adjusting the outer conditions to fit the inner self. These adjustments of social demands and personal identity often oppose each other. Wright seems to have been better at changing his life to fit his self than at doing the converse. He seems increasingly, in fact, to have been interested in changing more than his own life: his life and work show a remarkable effort to make American society as a whole mirror the image of self he created.

Wright was not, however, the total egoist that some have painted him to be. He suffered from the rift with his family. Upon his return from Europe in 1910, Wright needed to square himself with what he had left behind. Identified as an adulterer who had abandoned his family, he needed to adjust to a future without his wife and children, to reconcile their sense of loss with his own feelings of guilt, feelings he had expressed in his letters from Europe and shortly after his return. But Wright also had to make a number of practical adjustments in the external world. He had to provide pragmatically for his family's independence and generally to square his finances with his plans. He had to resolve a complex web of debts, to reestablish his architectural practice, and to assure the publication of his work. Finally Wright needed to change his outer circumstances to fit himself for a new domestic life with Mamah Borthwick Cheney; their life together required a refuge that resulted in the building of Taliesin, in Wisconsin, and in a public defense of their principles of open love.

The context for Wright's efforts to adjust his life to his private self had become a public issue even before his return from Europe. Early in August 1910 the *Chicago Daily Tribune* reported that the infatuation between Wright and Mamah Cheney had ended, that their "spiritual hegira" was over, and that she had returned briefly to Oak Park to pick up her two children and had gone into seclusion.[3] None of this was true, yet the article refreshed the public with details of the couple's elopement and stated that, with the demise of the scandalous relationship, Catherine Wright would now go to Berlin with her children and join her husband (fig. 54). The newspaper described Wright as an "architectural genius":

His bungalows and churches have given him an international reputation. Occasional freakish styles have caused comment. One residence he planned is built about a large tree. Another house which attracted attention was one without windows. In his own residence the architect also carried out his peculiar ideas, one of which was to design his wife's gowns. He also allowed his children to select their own names at the age of 6 years.[4]

Edwin Cheney refused to confirm that his wife had returned because she had not, and he had no idea if she would. He was reported to be furious with Wright, and he also was obliged to contradict his own mother, who had been quoted as saying that he would not forgive his wife.[5]

A second report in September 1910 announced Wright's imminent return and included a portrait of Mamah with a caption that she and Wright had been forgiven by their respective families.[6] Using language that mirrored Wright's own words, Catherine Wright stated that her husband had "completed a course of study of the architectural world abroad—one of the reasons for which he went to Europe—and is coming home to square himself with the public, his creditors and his family."[7]

Contrary to rumors that he had returned earlier, Wright actually arrived in America on board the SS *Bleucher* on Thursday, 6 October 1910, after a year abroad.[8] His appearance in Oak Park allowed another public iteration of his scandalous behavior—his return on 8 October made front-page news.[9] The *Chicago Daily Tribune* simply confirmed that Mamah Cheney had not returned to Oak Park and reported—again erroneously—that Lloyd Wright had arrived in New York with his fa-

ther but had not gone to Oak Park. The newspaper also stated that Catherine Wright's faith in her husband's return had never wavered, and that their children were delighted to see their absent father. Upon his arrival, Wright refused to give a statement to the press. Instead, Catherine relayed a message that the situation was "nobody's business, that his coming home is his own affair in which no one has the right to meddle."[10]

The press persisted in giving reports of Wright's arrival and created the image of a dandy who shirked responsibility for his actions. An unnamed source said that Wright's appearance was improved by a touch of gray at the temples, that his hair was "'bobbed' " so that it hung over his collar, and that he wore on arrival "a rough English tweed suit, knickerbockers, leather leggings, and an unmistakably English walking-hat of gray."[11] Another observer stated that after leaving the train station Wright waited in a taxicab for forty minutes, until dark, before telling the driver to go to his residence.[12] The day after his return, Wright was verbally attacked from the pulpit of the First Presbyterian Church in Oak Park: his desertion of his family for another woman was the sign that "a man has lost all sense of morality and religion and is damnably to be blamed."[13] While his character was debated, Wright's former status in the press as "an architectural genius" was now attributed to his "bizarre" style.[14]

Wright's personal conflict, the need to defend himself against the public, and some indication of the results of his travels were apparent in one of his first conversations after arriving in Oak Park. He spoke about his dilemma to his former client, William E. Martin, who passed on to his brother Darwin in Buffalo how Wright saw his actions affecting others, including his family and William R. Heath, another former client in Buffalo: "I admit I have done wrong, but I am not sorry for myself. I am only sorry for my family, my children and my clients. Your poor brother [Darwin] and Mr. Heath, they must have had to swallow humble pie in large quantities for my misdoings."[15] William Martin also briefly described Wright's reactions to Europe and the status of his publications: "He is enthusiastic about Europe and Germany in particular. Says his books are well along and the foreword was written by the foremost English Architect."[16]

Mamah Borthwick Cheney

Squaring his life with the truth of his relationship with Mamah Cheney was difficult. Instead of finding himself metaphorically

54. Catherine Tobin Wright, 1908 (Frank Lloyd Wright Home and Studio H&S H182).

in a square, Wright, his wife, and his lover formed a triangle that was falling apart. Mamah Cheney had stayed behind in Europe, and Wright kept her location and their plans secret. He returned to live with his family in the house and studio on Forest Avenue in Oak Park, but he had no intention of staying with them. Within a short period of time after his return, he made it clear to his wife, Catherine, that their marriage would not continue. The experiment he and Mamah Cheney had carried out in Europe had met with success, and their life together was to continue. Wright asked again for a divorce, but Catherine refused, holding on to a futile hope that he would emotionally return to her or, less likely, that she would maintain some contact with or control over Wright as long as they were married. Wright never returned emotionally, as far as we know, but Catherine did not allow their divorce until twelve years later, in 1922.

Faced with this impasse, Wright decided to convert his studio into living quarters, have his family move into his studio after it was converted, remodel the house as a rental apartment to provide income for his family, and then rent their former house.[17] He planned to move to a town house on Goethe Street in Chicago that he designed for himself (fig. 55). For all these changes, Wright desperately needed money. But in order to obtain money, he had to lie about his relationship with Mamah Cheney and convince Darwin Martin, his principal financial backer and one of the few people with whom he had communicated while in Europe, that he had ended his relationship with her.

While trying to suggest to Darwin Martin that Mamah Cheney was independent of him, Wright gave the first indication of her whereabouts in Europe and provided a description of her activities as a teacher and translator:

the unfortunate woman in this case is making her way herself—with German pupils in English—and she is now official translator of Ellen Key's—a Swedish writers [sic], works,—which keeps the wolf from the door. I understand she is to have her children with her also, which will be a good thing all around and eventually may be easier for her than it is just now. I do not wish you to repeat this to anyone as of course you will not.[18]

In another effort to claim he had broken off his relationship with Mamah Cheney, Wright nevertheless ambiguously implied that he was still obligated to her:

I have left the woman you have in mind, to make her future plans as though I were dead. She would assure you that anything between us

55. Studio residence for Wright, Goethe Street, Chicago, 1911 (TAL 1113.004).

would be impossible. She could not understand that you could think so. I cannot help feeling an obligation to a woman who owing to my cooperation has no friends! What would you think of me if I did not have such a feeling?[19]

Wright was now obliged to lead a double life, a life of denying his love for Mamah Cheney while planning his future around her. Wright's caution—his mixture of denial and protection—continued for almost a year, to counter Darwin Martin's suspicions and his exhortations for Wright to return to Catherine. But Wright had to have Martin's financial support to provide desperately needed living expenses for himself and his family and funds to remodel his studio in Oak Park, plan a new house in Chicago, and restart his practice.

Restarting a Practice

At the same time that Wright tried to square his personal life with his needs, he attempted to put order in his professional life so that he could explore new experimental designs stimulated by his visit to Europe. The only way to find financial stability was to reopen an office. His efforts to resume his practice began when he tried to assume the business that he had left with Herman Von Holst. Dealings with Von Holst quickly soured, and Wright had no ongoing work to resume.[20] He then attempted to collect revenues from his practice through William R. Heath, who, in addition to being a former client, was the legal council for the Larkin Company. But the situation for receiving proceeds from Von Holst was not immediately promising. As Wright informed Darwin Martin: "My practice will yield me nothing for months and months—the statement [from Herman Von Holst] sent to Heath is uncollectable except the work in his hands and if that goes through he will pay me when it is finished a year or two from now."[21]

For the interim, Martin suggested the unthinkable—that Wright consider working for another firm until he was established. He reassured Wright that he would still have clients even after the scandal of his departure "now that he is better qualified by European travel and study, to do stronger work than before."[22]

For other prospects Martin recommended that Wright consider designing, at Martin's expense, a building for the Tuskegee Institute, a place that hundreds of influential people visited annually.[23] Martin assured Wright that the atmosphere would be receptive to his architecture: "Their latest architecture was done by a Boston Tech graduate of color, the teacher of architecture

at Tuskegee is a good deal more in sympathy with your work than some of your avowed imitators, because it is more decent and consistent."[24] And finally Martin attempted to provide Wright with some work on the Martin's own house in Buffalo: a trunk room for the northwest corner of the second floor and alterations to the landing windows and piers to allow more light into the stairway, alterations for which Martin would pay Wright.

In a display of desperation, while attempting a legal resolution of the conflict about his practice, Wright went after any projects that were loosely associated with Von Holst. Wright asked Martin to intervene in a large commission that Von Holst was preparing for Childe Harold Wills of Detroit.[25] Wright mistakenly thought that Wills and Martin were friends and that Wills admired Martin's house in Buffalo.[26] Wright disapproved of designs by the Von Holst firm: "I have seen the plans and it is a crime to waste an opportunity like this on stuff so weak."[27] It was a bold move on Wright's part; Marion Mahony, designing for Von Holst, had started the design for Wills as early as December 1909, and Wright was trying to snatch the job from her and Von Holst.[28] Wright abandoned his interest in the Wills project, but a set of the drawings, hitherto unknown, found their way to Taylor Woolley, Wright's former assistant in Italy.[29]

Despite the false start with the Wills project, there was some progress with the prospects for architectural jobs later in November, 1910. Wright intended to write "my young man from Chicago to take him on," as an assistant, but it was too soon for that. This may have been Edward Sanderson, a young, unknown architect who soon became Wright's office manager. Wright had a potential commission for a small house in Winnetka, Illinois, but before taking on an employee for this or other projects, he had to settle at least some of his pressing debts.[30]

Martin continued to give Wright practical advice. He suggested that Wright pursue the design of an exhibition pavilion for the Universal Portland Cement Company.[31] Remaining sympathetic but practical, Martin further insisted in December 1910 that Wright pursue jobs, regardless of small size, and of publishing contracts, until Wright could sell his books and some of his Japanese print collection appeared.[32] Martin passed on a letter from another potential client, although without positive results.[33] Without being aware of Wright's disagreement with Walter Burley Griffin over Japanese prints and his resentment of Griffin's independent practice, Martin also recommended that Wright contact Griffin to see if he had any work that he could pass on to Wright.

By early December 1910, Wright claimed that his practice had become very busy, and he informed Martin that "A house burned down here day before yesterday and the owners [sic]—[Walter] Gerdt [sic] has employed me to rebuild it."[34]

The prospects for small commissions added momentum to Wright's first public work after his return, his exhibition pavilion at the Cement Show in New York City. This show, held from 14 December through 20 December 1910, was the first exhibition in New York to feature the use of cement as building material.[35] Wright had little time to arrange the commission before the opening date, but his earlier work for the Universal Portland Cement Company—a pavilion at the Pan American Exposition in Buffalo in 1901—may have helped him to obtain the job on short notice.[36]

The exhibition was intended to be an annual event and had come about as a result of a general interest in the fireproof qualities of cement and its increased use in houses and buildings by architects, builders and prospective home owners. Further impetus for the show came from the improvement of building techniques and recent interest in concrete for homes in suburban districts of New York. People were also interested in concrete's damp-proof qualities, and its use for architectural ornament, including, even, garden furniture.[37]

Wright had arrived too late to exhibit drawings or a model of his own concrete building, Unity Temple, and his cast concrete sculpture, but his pavilion created a striking presence. As seen in its publication in the American edition of the *Sonderheft*, it consisted of a raised, open-air sitting platform flanked on two sides with low walls on which stood Wright's characteristic shallow urns (fig. 151). A bench was placed in front of a high back wall. In front of the bench was a platform with two abstract cruciform sculptures. With plants in front of the platform, the object took on the appearance of an altar. The strangeness of this image and the articulation of its ornament presaged the exotic developments that became a focus of Wright's work in the next few years.

Wright informed Martin in January 1911 about the positive reaction to his pavilion at the cement show: "The cement people I designed the booth for say it was the finest thing at the Madison Square Garden show and now propose to build a concrete home on Sheridan Drive—to promote construction—so you see I haven't lost the touch."[38]

The ongoing effort to square his work with his self occurred in the midst of an optimistic—and sometimes overenthusiastic—assessment of his progress. Wright told Martin that he

was now very busy working sixteen hours a day.[39] Although his affairs with Von Holst were not yet in order, his projects supervised by or associated with the Von Holst office were completed.

In addition to five or six small projects, the most important work in the office was a house for Sherman Booth, a new client who also became Wright's lawyer.[40] The design was for a house on a site of hills and ravines in Glencoe, Illinois (fig. 56). Sketches were due in March. It would have a similar program and be on a scale with the Coonley House, the largest and most lavish house he had executed and the one he had praised above his others. Furthermore, the Booths were "Nice clients."[41]

By spring of 1911, Wright perceived the Sherman Booth House as a commission to salvage his career. It was one of seven projects Wright designed for Booth within the next two years, most of which focused on providing the town of Glencoe with public amenities, such as a town hall and art gallery. Wright later designed a general plan for a housing complex for Ravine Bluffs in Glencoe. But in all these designs ambition outpaced the pocketbook; only six houses, a sculpture in concrete, a bridge, and Booth's own house, built on a vastly reduced second scheme, were constructed by 1915 when the professional relationship with Booth began to dissolve.[42]

Enthusiasm and financial profit were not easily reconciled. For the moment Wright had only one person to help him and had decided not to rehire any other former employees, except for Taylor Woolley. As Wright informed Woolley: "I am working day and night myself—I will not try any of the old guard again I think. A. McArthur wanted to come in but I hesitate to begin the old game again in the old way."[43] Wright hesitated because he wanted to break with the old pattern of the studio in Oak Park and because he now saw his former employees imitating his work. While Albert McArthur had worked briefly for Wright starting in 1907 and was the son of a former client, Wright associated him with many of his other employees—such as John Van Bergen, William Drummond, Walter Burley Griffin, Marion Mahony—who had now become his young competitors.[44] The problem of trust weighed on Wright's mind, as he indicated to Woolley: "Van [sic] Holst turned on me and would do nothing—our affairs are now in the hands of a third person—all the architects about here are inimical [?]—nothing to expect of them or of those whom I once regarded as my own architectural family—but that is natural and not a total loss."[45]

In early July, Wright's conflict with Von Holst was settled after seven months of legal negotiation. If there had been any

56. Sherman Booth House, first scheme, Glencoe, Illinois, 1911 (TAL 1118.001).

friendship between the two men, their business relation had ended it. The resolution provides much information about the confusing status of Wright's projects just before his departure and during his stay in Europe. It also helps clarify long-standing problems of attribution about who worked on various projects and when the work was carried out. The accounting of Von Holst's expenses showed additional work for other clients not turned over in the contract of 22 September 1909. Furthermore, it indicated work that Von Holst completed, which had been started before Wright's departure, the revenues received from clients, and how Von Holst credited Wright for commissions. It also settled questions about the amount of work Von Holst and Marion Mahony performed on Wright's behalf (Appendix B).[46]

The final financial tally, after collection of fees from clients, showed that Von Holst owed Wright only $108.29.[47] Von Holst had tended to Wright's various clients, supervised the completion of houses, including the Frederick Robie House, and stood by as Wright lost his hold on the Joshua G. Melson House, which Wright had indicated in his 1909 contract as "work under construction."[48] Von Holst, with Marion Mahony as his chief designer, was able to develop the design of the E. P. Irving House, which Wright had described in 1909 as "work in hand," and design and build the Robert Mueller House and the J. H. Amberg House, which had previously been listed as "probable and prospective."[49] Von Holst and Mahony also found work of their own that had not been included in the 1909 contract.[50] Wright obtained a pittance in profit, but at least most of his cli-

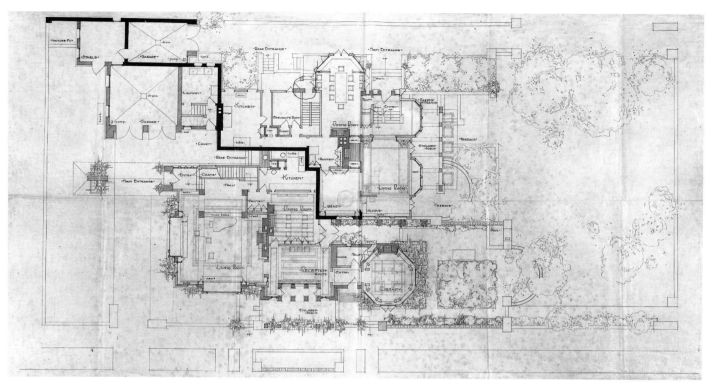

57. Plan for remodeling, Wright Home and Studio, Oak Park, 1911 (TAL 1125.007).

ents had received service and his unfinished work had been supervised.

By the end of the summer of 1911, preparations had begun for the conversion of Wright's home into a rental apartment and the studio into living quarters for his family (fig. 57). It was reported on 8 September that Wright was dividing his house and studio in Oak Park "to protect his soul."[51] While maintaining an office in Chicago at Orchestra Hall, Wright sought additional help in his practice and transferred Taylor Woolley from Chicago to Hillside, Wisconsin, where Wright increasingly spent his time supervising his own new home, Taliesin.[52]

By the end of December 1911 Wright could sense that his practice had actually augmented. Darwin Martin remained one of Wright's major financial backers. No doubt adverse newspaper articles and provincial attitudes discouraged some previous clients and some potential clients, but Martin reassured Wright that clients would be supportive of him.[53] Despite the scandals that had enveloped Wright and Mamah Cheney, some clients returned, and new clients commissioned work.[54]

Foremost among those who returned to Wright in 1911 were Avery and Queene Ferry Coonley in Riverside, Illinois. For them he designed a gardener's cottage, a kindergarten, a greenhouse, and a "playhouse," but only the playhouse and the gardener's cottage were built. The playhouse was actually used as a coeducational school run by Mrs. Coonley, whose interest in education mirrored Wright's (figs. 58, 59).[55]

Wright also had new clients and associations, in addition to Sherman Booth. With Francis Sullivan, a Canadian who may have been briefly in the Oak Park studio during 1907, Wright began a series of collaborations in Canada.[56] Their efforts resulted in a lasting friendship and the building of the Banff Park Pavilion for the Banff National Bank in Alberta. An even more important client and associate was Arthur Richards, a Milwaukee contractor, who commissioned a series of projects beginning in 1911, from a hotel remodeling in Madison to the Lake Geneva Inn in Geneva, Wisconsin, and eventually Wright's most elaborate system of prefabricated housing, the American Ready-Cut System.[57] Richards may also have been Wright's link to other projects in Milwaukee. There were, in addition, other clients who commissioned projects that were not built.

The augmentation of Wright's practice continued into the new year of 1912 and intertwined with his effort to disseminate his Wasmuth publications. By February, Wright had obtained the services of Edward Sanderson as manager of his office in Orchestra Hall in Chicago.[58] By early April, Wright hoped for financial relief by selling his Wasmuth publications, but, as he wrote Martin, in one of his perpetual pleas for money, "even my books are not yet wholly released. So I am totally caught."[59]

At Martin's insistence Wright reported his expenditures on the alterations of the Oak Park residence and his daily expenses in Wisconsin, which included board for his draftsmen, a sum that could have equalled five to six salaries.[60] In order to satisfy further Martin's interest in his financial condition—an interest based on humanitarian and practical considerations—Wright had Edward Sanderson describe for Martin projects on the drawing boards in Wright's office and prospective jobs as of April 1912. Sanderson sent a list that amounted to a rare accounting of Wright's work, including clients, locations, and budgets of current and future projects.[61] Despite the probable exaggeration of the budgets for these projects, and the certainty that not all of them would be built, the list of projects shows that an office had begun to emerge even though it was susceptible to fluctuations in activity.

By the summer of 1912 Wright's professional life seemed to have settled down to waiting for revenues from his publications and proceeding with designs of projects in hand. Sanderson re-

58. Coonley Playhouse, exterior, Riverside, Illinois, 1912.

mained in the Chicago office, and Wright brought draftsmen to Taliesin in Wisconsin where they worked and received room and board. Wilhelm Bernhard, one of the draftsmen, was skilled enough as an architect to engage in town planning; he submitted a planning scheme for the competition to develop a typical quarter section on the outskirts of Chicago, for which Wright also entered a noncompetitive scheme.[62] William R. Gibb was another draftsman.[63] They were accompanied, at least briefly, by a third draftsman named Fucher, of whom only his name is known. In mid-July, 1912, however, Wright wrote to Woolley, who had temporarily returned home to Utah, to indicate that the pace of work had leveled off and that his services were not immediately needed:

Dear Wooley [sic]—Take your time—enjoy yourself. There is no especial hurry. All well here—place quite transformed—Bernhard and Gibbs here. Fucher went back some weeks ago. Madison Hotel laid aside for the time being—Glad your mother is recovered—as ever, Frank Lloyd Wright.[64]

Darwin Martin and Finances

Wright's efforts to resurrect his practice occurred in the midst of pressing debts and difficulties with his publications. Just as Guthrie had predicted, all Wright's interconnected problems challenged his ability to create. He owed money to his publisher in Berlin, the Ernst Wasmuth Verlag. His monograph and picture book, or *Sonderheft*, were printings for which he was obligated to pay in installments. Wright wanted to obtain the highest quality reproductions of his work and to control its distribution; Wasmuth wanted not to lose money on the publications. To judge from the number of copies to be printed, the *Sonderheft* would be ten times more available than the monograph; the low price of the *Sonderheft* was set for mass distribution, and the high price of the portfolio for a more expensive taste. Wright described anticipated revenues of $20,000 for 1,000 copies of the monograph and $20,000 for 10,000 copies of the *Sonderheft*:

When the payments are made, I am the owner of one thousand copies of the Monograph to be sold at $37.50 in America. There is little doubt but that it will bring me $20,000, inside of eighteen months. In addition to this there is a *Sonderheft* of 116 pages containing photographs, the preface to which has been written by C. R. Ashbee, F.R.I.B.A. and 10,000 copies of this are being printed. Two dollars per copy goes to me, which I have every reason to believe good for $20,000 or more. . . . There is a likelihood, also, that the publication will exceed the figures I

give. There are eighty thousand architects in America, besides the layman, students and draftsmen in the work.[65]

Wright also owed money to Francis Little, the client for whom he had previously designed a house in Peoria, Illinois. Wright's debt of $9,000 that he had used to finance his European trip with Mamah Cheney as well as his Wasmuth publications was compounded by the fact that Wright also owed Little the designs of a second house to be built outside of Minneapolis.[66] For the loan from Little, Wright had used his collection of Japanese wood-block prints as collateral, and he would continue utilizing the prints, either selling them, or collateralizing them for future loans, to finance the publications.

Darwin Martin was once again Wright's principal source of support. Shortly after his return from Europe in 1910, Wright had asked him for money. In response to Wright's request, Martin replied that he understood Wright's Japanese print collection had been inventoried before his trip to Europe, that Wright had realized $10,000 from the sale of Japanese prints, and that the remaining inventory was worth $53,000.[67] If the report were accurate, Martin suggested, Wright should have no financial worries.[68] With this comment Martin directed a subtle, moralizing critique at Wright: in effect, he told him that if he needed money, he should find it the same way he had financed his escapade in Europe.

After Martin refused him, Wright turned to John D. Larkin, Martin's employer and Wright's former client as president and treasurer of the Larkin Company. Wright needed the loan to pay off an unnamed creditor—Francis Little, his client—to whom he had given a selection of Japanese prints as security for the initial payment of his "German publication"; to pay Wasmuth; to redesign his "expensive studio" in Oak Park into expanded living quarters for his family; and to make a separate property that could provide a rental income.[69] He did not want to make a quick sale of prints but to dispose of them gradually.[70] He offered to reinforce his appeal by going personally to see Larkin in Buffalo, but Larkin still refused.

Martin helped Wright in many ways, but he also felt free to criticize his behavior. He declared that the improvements to the house in Oak Park were an overly ambitious and ill-timed effort that would flaunt his activities to the Oak Park community, especially considering the public shock that his departure had created.[71] Even though Martin had initially welcomed Wright back as a prodigal son, he also believed that Wright, lacking humility, was insufficiently sorry for deserting his family.[72] A de-

59. Coonley Playhouse, interior, Riverside, Illinois.

vout Christian Scientist, Martin continued to assume the role of protector of Wright's distraught family and of a sympathetic but self-righteous guide to the wayward Wright. Martin was willing to help Wright if Wright was willing to help himself and if he assumed responsibility for his wife and children.

Wright finally began to express responsibilty for the suffering he had caused, as he continued to press for money.[73] He wrote to Martin again that his family was in great need, and that the first payment to Wasmuth was "due November 25 or thereabouts—the second part of the Monograph . . . due in

March."[74] A critical moment in Wright's publishing venture had arrived.

Wasmuth

The great folios, to which so much influence on modern architecture has been attributed, almost failed to appear because of financial and production disputes with the Wasmuth Verlag. In early November of 1910, after printing 4,000 copies of the *Sonderheft* for distribution in America, the publisher sent Wright three advance copies, demanded payment for the picture book, and announced that the monograph, too, was ready except for the text, which Wright had promised to provide.[75] Wright borrowed $2,500 from Martin to pay Wasmuth, but Wright claimed Wasmuth's agent in New York would not accept the funds.[76] More to the point were Wright's reservations about the publisher, which would eventually delay the monograph and *Sonderheft* and put their completion in jeopardy. Wright decided that he would pay Wasmuth only after the the publisher had met certain stipulations concerning the monograph. Wasmuth had to stop printing extra copies of the monograph to cover their expenses for covers that contained the folio plates; Wasmuth had already printed 250 copies over which Wright had no control.[77] Under the existing terms of his contract, Wright was afraid that additional casing costs would reduce his profit from the *Sonderheft*.[78] Furthermore, his revenues would also be reduced because he had to pay for 1,000 copies of the English translation of the Introduction for the monograph at an undetermined cost.[79]

Wright also wanted Wasmuth to print "the Work" immediately and at the same time return the "pirated" copies to Wright.[80] From Wright's point of view arrangements for receiving the *Sonderheft* were in order. He had taken a copy to the customshouse depot in New York City in order to confirm that no duty would be required when he imported it.[81] But he worried that if he did not send Wasmuth $1,000 immediately, Wasmuth would drop the project and further printing of the *Sonderheft* and the monograph would cease.[82]

Martin followed these developments closely—he had a financial and personal interest in their resolution.[83] He made Wright summarize a complicated payment schedule, which required some payments immediately, others when the work was ready in Germany, and final payments upon the books' arrival in New York.[84] In addition to concerning himself with Wright's financial situation, Martin also resumed his questioning about Wright's domestic situation. Martin feared that if he loaned Wright more money, Mamah Cheney would have access to funds before Catherine Wright and the Wrights' children would:[85]

For all I know to the contrary you may feel and be deeply indebted or rather obligated to an unfortunate woman, not your wife. None of us including yourself know the effect of a sudden pull at your heartstrings upon your pursestrings. Hence, I want to protect you (and incidentally your family's prior claim and not forgetting my own) from yourself.[86]

Martin's response combined paternalism, moral rectitude, and self-interest. His own claim involved not only money but his

stature in the community as sponsor of an errant genius. He felt a sincere friendship for Wright and was willing to help him, but only on the condition that Wright co-sign a note with his wife, Catherine Wright, so that she would be included in the arrangements. "Hold tight to her apron strings," Martin advised Wright.[87]

Concerning the "pull" of Mamah Cheney that Martin mentioned, Wright deceived Martin by denying again the depth of his involvement, stating that if he were subject to it, he obviously would not be in Chicago.[88] To counter Martin's suspicions, Wright tried to show progress in getting his publications into print by sending a proof copy of the *Sonderheft*. "There are mistakes in it," Wright noted, "but it is well done. I think I will accept it."[89] With the work in hand, he planned to take it to a German lawyer to copyright it.

Martin pursued the situation with Wright's German publisher. He wanted to know if Wright had sent Wasmuth the text for the monograph, and if so, when.[90] Wright was still in the middle of revising it after receiving editorial comments from his cousin in New York.[91] This text was to be Wright's Introduction for the Wasmuth folios and his major theoretical statement of architectural historicism, expressing his hopes for the future of architecture and an implicit program for his own future work. Consequently, he was taking great care with it.[92]

More problematic than progress on the Introduction was Wasmuth's request for the remittance due for the *Sonderheft*. If Wright paid for the *Sonderheft*, the first part of the monograph would follow as soon as the text was printed. In the meantime, Wright had lost his original contract with Wasmuth and realized that he had negotiated no written arrangements for the *Sonderheft*.[93]

After a series of tactical and business errors and confusions, all progress with the publishing venture collapsed.[94] Wright decided that the quality of the *Sonderheft*, which he had previously described as "fine," did not meet his expectations. He had high standards for the reproduction of his work, and he decided that Wasmuth had printed the illustrations cheaply and that they did not rise above the quality of the murky pictures which had appeared in the 1908 publication of his work in the *Architectural Record*. When he informed Wasmuth that he was rejecting the edition, Wasmuth stopped printing the monograph and halted the entire project. Wright informed Martin of the setback: "I have bad news from Wasmuth—He has laid down on the Monograph until I take up the *Sonderheft* —but I will not take it—He has skinned it to the point where it is no better

60. RMS *Lusitania,* broadside view (Bain Collection, LC, USZ62-61939).

than the *Record* was and I won't have it—We will fight it out."[95]

In light of the dispute with Wasmuth, Wright informed Martin of his plans for the funds in hand. He also elaborated on additional problems with his text for the monograph and with the errors he had discovered in the monograph itself, including misidentified plates:

I am holding $1800.00 of the money you contributed to drop on Wasmuth when he sees a light. The situation there is very bad and getting daily worse—they can make nothing of my text [for the monograph]—they say. They have made serious mistakes also in two of the plates of the Monograph. I have rejected the *Sonderheft* totally, as they skinned it to death. I have prepared and have ready a complete dummy with photographs ready for a revised edition of the work which they can have when they come to time. My efforts in dealing with Consul have only proved abortive. I have spent $54.00 in cablegrams to Wasmuth. I could straighten the thing out in two hours personally. . . .[96]

In early January of 1911 Wright decided that a face-to-face confrontation with Ernst Wasmuth in Berlin was necessary, and he began preparations for a second trip to Germany to negotiate a new contract. Wright dutifully informed Martin, who advised Wright that if he planned to return to Berlin, he should take his wife with him.[97] Although he may have been genuinely disappointed in the quality of Wasmuth's work, the flap with the publisher also provided an important pretext for a mission that Wright kept to himself: he intended to bring back Mamah Cheney from Germany to America.[98] Once more Wright deceived Martin to pursue his love with Mamah.

Wright's second trip to Germany, a journey that he never mentioned in his autobiographies or elsewhere, took place in even greater secrecy than his first voyage, and the details of his travels are even fewer. Leaving behind his estranged wife, he departed from New York for Europe on the *Lusitania* on 16 January 1911 or shortly thereafter (fig. 60). A few days later, while on board, Wright wrote Martin that his family would be relieved that he had left them:[99] "I think my going at this time if it has any particular effect on the fortunes of 'Wright' family can have a good effect—for reasons no one need care about. I think Catherine feels as I do about that."[100]

At this time Wright felt some personal relief in the prospect of ameliorating his financial condition by making further sales of Japanese prints. Sallie Casey Thayer, the art patron from Kansas City who had financed part of his first European journey by buying prints, planned to purchase additional prints worth approximately $10,075, and an unidentified man would

8. Sonderheft der
Architektur des
XX. Jahrhunderts

Frank Lloyd Wright

Chicago

Verlegt bei Ernst Wasmuth A.-G., Berlin
1911

Diese deutsche Ausgabe ist nur in Europa verkäuflich.

61. Cover, *Frank Lloyd Wright, Chicago,* 1911, European edition of the *Sonderheft.*

still was worried that when people learned of his departure, another scandal might erupt again in the newspapers.[103] Despite his personal apprehension, Wright hoped to take advantage of the shock of his unannounced arrival in Berlin to clear up all the problems with his pubisher. He informed Martin: "I am going to be a total surprise party at Wasmuth's and as I have a good case when I am on the ground I expect to have the matter [of the publications] straightened out without much more than a loud noise. I will let you know."[104]

Wright took along for his visit to Wasmuth a revised dummy for the *Sonderheft* that he had designed in Oak Park. Wright had changed the format of the first edition, added photographs, including an illustration of the exhibition pavilion for the Universal Portland Cement Company, and updated the catalogue of his work. This revision clarifies the mystery about different editions of the *Sonderheft:* the *Sonderheft* that Wright took with him to Germany was different from the first version and resulted in the confusing situation of two picture books ultimately appearing, one for an American audience, the other for sale only in Europe.

Wright's negotiations with the Ernst Wasmuth Verlag succeeded, and by 13 February 1911, Wright had revised his contract.[105] With these agreements, Wright hoped to achieve both of his objectives: high quality and maximum control of distribution. The memorandum of agreement was in two parts, one dealing with the *Sonderheft,* the other with the monograph. Both appeared to work to Wright's advantage.

The agreement for the *Sonderheft* determined two distinct editions: a European edition consisting of the original edition of 4,000 Wright had rejected, with 3,900 copies belonging to Wasmuth and 100 copies to Wright; and an American edition, enlarged through the addition of forty-five illustrations, which would be Wright's property. The European edition would be marked "For Sale in Europe Only." Wasmuth agreed not to sell the European edition until one month after he had printed a American edition of 5,000 copies and delivered them to Wright in Chicago.

The European edition appeared as *Frank Lloyd Wright, Chicago.* As the eighth *Sonderheft* of the series, *Architektur des XX. Jahrhunderts* (Architecture of the Twentieth Century), it would comprise 113 pages with a total of 148 illustrations, including a color plate of a drawing of Unity Temple (fig. 61).

The American edition of 141 pages and 193 illustrations curiously retained its German title and would be published as *Frank Lloyd Wright, Ausgeführte Bauten* (fig. 62). Wright con-

buy $3,000 worth, thus leaving two-thirds of Wright's collection intact. Among the few people Wright had informed about his trip was his lawyer and client, Sherman Booth, to whom Wright confided that he was returning to Berlin to arrange his affairs with his publisher and that he had brought along with him his Glencoe building plot to work on. Wright, however, was too seasick to work while on board.[101]

Wright planned to arrive in London where he anticipated staying for several days with Charles Ashbee and attending an auction of Japanese prints, probably held by Sotheby's.[102] In spite of the financial assistance that came from selling prints, he

tinued to call it the *Sonderheft*, but eventually it became popularly known as "the little Wasmuth" in contrast to the big folios of the monograph. It would include ultimately 163 halftone pictures, a colored frontispiece, and "tail piece," all made according to Wright's instructions. Wright insisted on superior workmanship, and that the same cover paper used for the covers of the monograph be used for the American edition. Both editions carried Charles Robert Ashbee's introduction translated into German.[106] Wright would later fold into the American edition an expurgated English translation of Ashbee's text that he paid for himself.

Regardless of the previous tallies, the revised contract now definitively established that the total number of copies for both editions of the *Sonderheft* was 9,000 with Wasmuth's 3,900 for sale in Europe and 5,100 copies for Wright to sell in America.

As for the monograph, Wright became exclusive owner of all copies with his purchase of the copies Wasmuth had printed for his own use. The revised contract did not specify the total number of monographs to be printed, but the total run would have been 1,275 copies. This included the 250 copies that Wasmuth had already printed to cover its cost and the 25 special copies of the monograph that Wright had ordered to be printed on Japan paper and bound in half-leather as a deluxe edition for his special friends and clients.[107] Wright granted Wasmuth a license to sell his work and provided stipulations for purchase prices. From his holdings, Wright conveyed 100 copies to Wasmuth, without folio covers, that were to be marked "For sale in Europe only" and to be sold by Wasmuth.[108] Although Wright reported later that Wasmuth sold about 52 monographs prior to publication, it appears that initially Wasmuth would have had less than 200 copies of the monograph to distribute, and as few as 100 copies. Upon these low numbers, the entire myth of the Wasmuth folios' influence on European architecture has been based.

Having concluded his negotiations with Wasmuth, Wright was impatient to depart for America.[109] There are no details on the reunion between Wright and Mamah Cheney. She may have accompanied him on the return voyage, but there is no evidence to confirm the date of her return. By 3 April 1911, Wright had arrived in Oak Park from Germany a second time.[110] Without any reference to returning with Mamah, Wright wired Darwin Martin of his successful negotiations with Wasmuth and brought up a new financial issue—the need for money to finance a vaguely defined real-estate transaction involving his mother, Anna Lloyd Wright:

62. Cover, *Frank Lloyd Wright: Ausgeführte Bauten,* American edition of the *Sonderheft.*

Successful throughout / new contract and letter mailed you today / money ready if needed but may I use it to help my mother out of tight real estate situation closing Saturday / will then pay May first / have paid Wasmuth three thousand and Maas [the folio supplier] five hundred / wire please / gratefully yours / Wright.[111]

Martin sent congratulations to Wright from Boston where he and his wife had gone for instruction at the mother church of Christian Science.[112] Martin confirmed that the 1 May payment date would be satisfactory, but he made no comment about Anna Lloyd Wright's "tight real estate situation."

Following the pattern of obligatory accountability to Martin,

Wright soon gave additional details of his return from Germany and a description of his expenses.[113] Wright had planned to sail on 7 March 1911, but was delayed "with customary German slowness" until Wasmuth had prepared copies of the monograph, the final proofs of the text, and half-tone proofs of the *Sonderheft* for Wright to take with him.[114] Wright told Martin that the financial problem with Little was finally resolved: Little had written "a nice letter" indicating that he would buy $2,000 worth of prints and some additional items in Wright's collection.[115] Wright still needed more time to pay off his note to Martin and hoped—unrealistically—that by 1 June he would have sold enough books to cover the debt.

Within the first six months after his return from Europe in October 1910, Frank Lloyd Wright had wrestled with and partially resolved a number of practical, professional, and personal issues. He had lived through the direct focus of a public scandal, assured the publication of the books that codified his architecture, and retrieved some Japanese prints while he sold others to raise cash and pay debts. He also had resolved many of the difficulties with his German publisher and reestablished his architectural practice. All of this "squaring" of his life, however,

took place within the private context of his domestic and personal struggles, and those were not easily resolved. Despite his financial reprieve and professional hopes, by April 1911 the "spiritual adventure" of Wright's emotional life, the dilemma of the man in the triangle had not improved:

The situation here has not changed radically for better or worse, everything in relation to it is from within, whatever the outcome may be, you may be sure, it is the truth that is sought—not *a* truth but *the* truth.[116]

In his search for "*the* truth" Wright also began to articulate the social agenda for his work and to elaborate his theories of architecture. This articulation was another attempt to square the life around him with his own inner vision. As he made public his principles of architecture, the social vision they presented began to take form through books, buildings, and public pronouncements. In the context of restarting his practice and the settling of his domestic problems, the first lessons of his trips to Europe began to unfold as Wright's image of himself changed from oppressed iconoclast to visionary prophet.

After Louis Sullivan, [Wright] is the most important of American Secessionists and is so recognized by the leading Secessionists abroad.—Harriet Monroe (1914)[1]

4 The Lessons of Europe

What did Frank Lloyd Wright learn from his experiences in Europe? The answers to this question have been obscured by the assumption that it was Wright who taught Europe while Europe made little impact on him. Although Harriet Monroe, editor of *Poetry, a Magazine of Verse,* had the prescience to recognize that Europeans saw Wright as America's premier Secessionist, her view has long been forgotten.[2] Wright's role as a foreign influence on European modern architecture evolved into a mythology that portrayed him as the American mentor of young European architects of the Modern Movement. As I mentioned, this view is supported by visual analogies that rely on transitivity: if A resembles B, then B has influenced A.

To distinguish more clearly how forms and ideas change over time it is necessary to provide examples from a point in time or critical event and compare those with examples that occur afterwards. In Wright's case, that point in time is 1910, the event is his travels in Europe, and the detailed comparisons of his work before and after are explored through analyses in the subsequent chapters of this book. What we see is not a simplistic proof of influence in terms of a linear analogy but differences in quality and aesthetic effect. Some aspects of Wright's European experience reinforced what he had known before, other aspects independently added new insights as he shifted from the Prairie-house period into an experimental phase of work. The pattern that emerges results from a complex interplay of numerous factors, some identifiable through documentary sources and the overt statements of the artist, and some

that are elusive, undocumented, and unconscious. We have already seen how this pattern was laced with paradox: Wright grew up in a culture descended from Europe, but he had no firsthand knowledge of it. He maintained that his work developed autonomously, but he was highly aware of European developments through publications, exhibitions, and the work and ideas of other Americans. The reputation of his Wasmuth publications was attributed to their influence on Europeans, but Wright intended them for an American audience.

Despite the problematics of proving influence, there have been some attempts to consider how Europe influenced Wright, but these assertions also rely on visual analogies that follow linear logic in which Wright borrowed motifs from other artists. An instance of these assertions is Wright's use of the circle as an ornamental motif, found in the Coonley Playhouse windows. The use of the circle did mark a turning point in his work, but the change was not the simple result of any direct influence of a European artist on his work. In his designs for the Coonley Playhouse, the use of the circle in the windows came after the initial design drawings, in 1912.[3] Avery Coonley confirmed to Wright that a balloon scheme for the playhouse windows under the eaves was "charming," but Wright's design for a "confetti" of abstract festive streamers was not successful.[4] Three sets of windows were executed. One set was a horizontal series located at the clerestory of the playhouse. They were placed in a linear sequence and visually connected by horizontal leading.[5] A second set was for niches and various locations along the walls; these

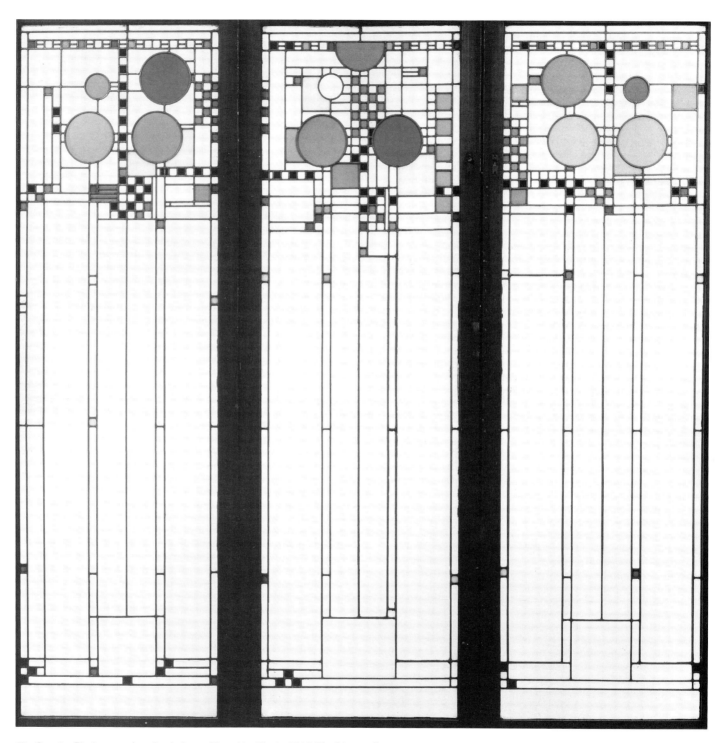

63. Coonley Playhouse, triptych windows, Riverside, Illinois, 1912 (The Metropolitan
Museum of Art; Purchase, 1967, Edward C. Moore, Jr., Gift and Edgar J. Kaufmann Charitable
Foundation, 67.231.1–3).

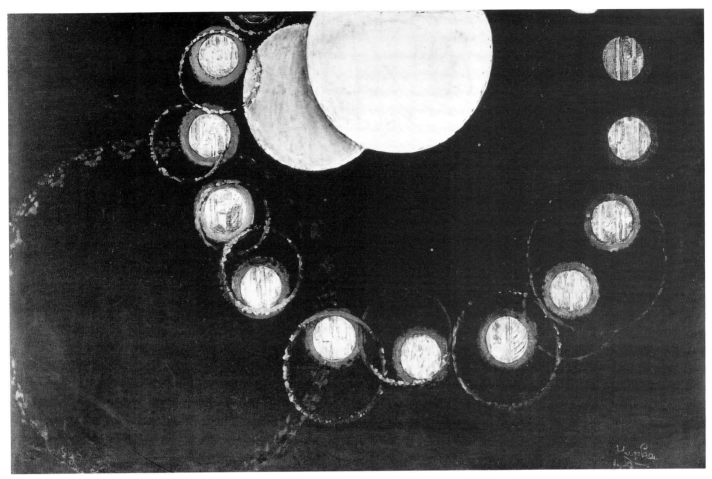

64. František Kupka, *The First Step,* 1910–13? (date on painting 1909), oil on canvas, 32¾″ × 51″ (Collection, The Museum of Modern Art, New York. Hillman Periodicals Fund).

included triadic combinations of small and large windows. The third set constituted a grand triptych that provided the visual focal point of the playhouse.[6] At the top of the triptych panels were bright colors of red, yellow, blue, and green, and white circles amid fields of colored squares; the lower two-thirds consisted of more open frameworks (fig. 63).

These circular designs have generated considerable speculation about the influence of European artists on Wright. Hanks and Toher summarized the attributions by various critics, including themselves, who assert that French sources—Robert Delaunay and František Kupka—"must have" influenced Wright (fig. 64).[7] Tselos stated that in the Coonley Playhouse and Midway Gardens murals Wright brought back the motif from Paris, where he had been preceded in the use of the circle by Kupka and Roger de la Fresnaye.[8] Kaufmann cited Wright's circles as exactly contemporary with work by Kupka and Delaunay. Parisian "influence" was also attributed to Wright's murals at the Midway Gardens.[9] Hanks and Toher mention the circle motif used in the tea and coffee service designed by Jutta Sika, as if these too might be an influence on Wright (figs. 65, 66).[10]

Calling the windows a "*kindersymphony,*" Wright casually explained the source of the imagery as his observation of a parade that had balloons, American flags, and confetti.[11] The circle conveniently expressed a lighthearted and festive image—a symphony for children—as if school occurred in a continuous party. Wright had been fond of balloons; he had filled his childrens' Oak Park playroom with them for celebrations.

In addition to these assertions, other sources could be proposed as influences on Wright's design motifs. Joseph Olbrich designed china that used simple motifs of triangles that resembled Wright's designs. Koloman Moser might have provided a source that has not been mentioned previously by critics. He designed plates with motifs of squares that resembled Wright's chinaware at Midway Gardens with its border of squares (figs. 67, 68). Peter Behrens's lamps, exhibited in a dining room at the St. Louis Fair in 1904, resembled Wright's light fixtures at Unity Temple. The murals of Behrens's display room have motifs that are similar to the pier capitals at Wright's church, and Behrens's rugs could easily have fit into a number of Wright's domestic interiors (figs. 69, 70).

But these observations of influence raise questions. We do not know if Wright knew specifically of the Moser plates or Behrens lamps. Did Wright see Sika's work before his travels to Europe when it was published in *The Studio Year-Book of Decorative Art*?[12] Did he also know the tea-service design by Theresa Trethan published along with Sika's but not mentioned by critics?[13] Did he see Sika's tea set when it was published earlier in 1902 in *Das Interieur*? Did Wright know it from the workshop salesroom of the Wiener Werkstätte? How can we confirm that these were the models for Wright's china designs for the Imperial Hotel?

At least it is certain that, regardless of when he saw the work of Olbrich, Behrens, and Sika, only after his visit to Vienna did Wright extensively use the motif of the circle as ornament, first for window designs and then for china, as seen in his plates, cups, and saucers for the Midway Gardens and Imperial Hotel. But fundamental questions remain about the traditional assumptions. What was the mechanism of influence? None is suggested. Where and when did Wright see the works of these artists? No evidence is presented. Furthermore, there is no indication that Wright had any awareness of avant-garde developments in French art at this time; instead, there are clear indications that, except for his interest in the Petit Palais and the airplanes at Bourget airport, Wright was more concerned with personal problems than delving into the Paris art scene. Why would Wright be interested in the circle? Why did Wright use the circle as a major motif only after 1910? What was the meaning of the motif? And what were the fundamental bonds that Wright and his contemporaries shared?

Wright learned far more from Europe than speculations about influence would lead us to assume. These lessons manifested themselves tangibly in his art through explorations of primitivist sources, innovations in sculpture, the intensification of his ornament, and complex new iconographic programs for his architecture. Less tangible, but as important, was Wright's view of himself, his art, and society. A reformer by family background and temperament, Wright returned from Europe a crusader more dedicated than ever to connecting his architecture to its role in American society. Education became his bridge be-

66. Imperial Hotel China service, originally manufactured c. 1922 (Fischer Fine Art, London).

67. School of Koloman Moser, plate, 1901–2. ceramic, ¾"h. × 9¹¹⁄₁₆" diameter
(Collection, The Museum of Modern Art, New York. Estee and Joseph Lauder Fund).

68. Midway Gardens, glazed ceramic plate, Chicago, 1914.

69. Peter Behrens, dining room for the "Moderne Wohnräume" exhibition, 1902 (*DKuD*, 1902–3).

70. Coonley House, living room, Riverside, Illinois, c. 1907.

tween art and society. Wright believed that architecture had the power to change society, but for this to occur people needed a proper education. To him, education was the preparing of individuals for ethical and responsible lives, not simple academic learning found in schools. Only an educated public could understand how architecture could express the true, natural values of a society. The architect was obligated to take up the role of educator, a role that required the vision of prophet and poet.

Wright expressed this European lesson of a new devotion to education as soon as he returned to Oak Park in October 1910. There he gave a clue to Europe's influence on him when he told William Martin that his goal in life was the education of youth. As Martin relayed the news of Wright's return to his brother Darwin, he stated, "He is as charming as ever when he wants to be nice. Says his work in life will be to educate children."[14] The teaching of children became part of Wright's preoccupation with the role of education in a democracy and the search for purity—an uncontaminated authenticity and truth—in the structures of society and in its visual language. He began to see his own architecture, including his Wasmuth publications, as vehicles for educating Americans to appreciate American values.

A search for purity characterized what Wright had absorbed from his European experiences. A pure society would be cleansed of hypocrisy: marriage would be based on love, not obligation, women would be free to pursue their own identities, and children would be educated to retain their innate sensitivity to the world. In Europe, Wright had found support for his concept of pure structures of society in the ideas of Ellen Key, the Swedish feminist who advocated a return to the beginnings of moral obligation and whose work Wright and Cheney would promote. At the same time, Wright began to pursue a pure art that would be the expressive vehicle of a pure society. Pure artistic forms were to be found in a study of the ancient origins of human habitation still present in the cultures of exotic and primitive peoples. The abstraction and simplicity of the work in those cultures could purify modern art. This idealistic—and naive—search for purity in architecture and human relations became his goal. That search is first described in his Introduction to the Wasmuth folios.

The Wasmuth Introduction

Wright's first seminal statement on architecture after his return from Europe was the Introduction to the Wasmuth monograph. Simply titled "Studies and Executed Buildings by Frank Lloyd Wright," it amounted to a major position paper. Although it was dated May 1910, Florence, in the German version and June 1910, Florence, Italy, in the American edition, Wright did not finish it until December 1910, two months after his return to America.[15] Sensing its significance, Wright needed time to reflect on its content, and he spent much effort perfecting the text. By the time he finished, he had described his perception of the maladies of modern architecture and proposed the sources for their cure. The essay summarized aspects of his direct contact with Europe and dealt with several complex and interconnected issues: historicism; education—true and false; the definition of organic architecture; the sources of true architecture in primitive and non-Western cultures; the modern American challenge; and a self-critical analysis of his own architecture.

Wright developed these themes with a circular rather than linear organization, returning at various times to the negative

impact of the Renaissance while calling for a democratic American architecture and the study of primitive cultures. His writing style added to the poetic richness of the text but also to its density. The publisher in Berlin had great difficulty in translating the text into German, and the resulting translation was somewhat garbled. Consequently, the circularity and opacity of Wright's Introduction have contributed to its being either misunderstood or ignored.[16]

Despite its obscurity, this theoretical statement is a fundamental expression of Europe's impact on Wright. His trip during 1909–10 allowed him to speak with the authority of his own experience. Until his journey to Europe, his experience of this legacy came only secondhand, from literary sources—books, periodicals, and illustrations; from the opinions of others; and from American adaptations of European models. But now he had seen with his own eyes the sources of what he described as purity and corruption in architecture.

In striking out to find an architecture that liberated itself from European precedent, Wright was obliged to reconcile the indigenous and unique character of America with the great traditions of European architecture rooted in classicism and its various rebirths. An architect could rant against the influence of the Ecole des Beaux-Arts in America and its retarding effect on American developments, yet if he wanted to refute or transform those effects, he ultimately had to confront the cultural impact, principles, and values represented by the historical forms upon which America relied. Wright's Introduction to the Wasmuth monograph provided an opportunity for his own resolution with the problems posed by historicism and for the announcement of a new program based on preclassical, nonclassical, and non-Western traditions of architecture.

By beginning his Introduction with a reference to his latest theoretical statements that had appeared in *Architectural Record* in 1908, Wright set the stage for his essay to be a continuation of some earlier ideas and a revision of others in response to his studies in Europe.[17] His first investigation in the Wasmuth Introduction was the Renaissance as it was expressed by the sculptors, painters, and architects of Florence. Wright saw clearly that a unity had existed between art and culture: sculptors were painters, painters were architects, and architects were sculptors, which resulted in a total artistic environment where artists expressed the spirit of their age because, "No line was drawn between the arts and their epoch."[18]

The historical developments of the Renaissance were codified in official ("professional") and academic ("good school") architecture, but neither revealed the truth. The essence of architecture, according to Wright, lay in the native traditions of a people: "the true basis for any serious study of the art of architecture is in those indigenous structures, the more humble buildings everywhere, which are to architecture what folk-lore is to literature or folk-songs are to music, and with which architects were seldom concerned." Indigenous architecture, as opposed to official monuments executed in imported styles, was significant because it revealed the characteristic traits of a country, its national spirit, the quality of its environment, and the "habits of life of the people." In these qualities were to be found a transcendent experience, a "joy in living" that exceeded analysis and formula. In establishing a basic analogy between life and nature, Wright compared this joy to the way a flower turns towards the sun. Although organized by the rational order of nature, the flower is unconcerned with the geometric structure of its petals or the mechanics of its movements.

The important lesson of Italy as the cradle of the Renaissance was not to be found in its classical vocabulary but in the realization that its architecture captured "joy in living" by integrating color and ornament into a rich landscape of rocks, slopes, and trees. Ignoring the cultural implications of urban architecture, Wright asserted that this integration of form with the landscape did not come about through style, but by buildings themselves lying "close to the earth." Indigenous peoples made buildings according to their needs and fitted their buildings "with native feeling" into the environments they knew and understood, resulting in "buildings that grew as folk-lore and folk-song grew." Italy's gift was its embodiment of this process through principles that Wright believed were more important to study than were "academic" attempts at creating beauty. According to Wright, however, the process was subverted when the forms of the Italian Renaissance were copied by other countries that should have developed their own indigenous cultural expressions. In his view, the style of the Renaissance had spread like a disease, obliterating the art of the Middle Ages. As it passed to France, Germany, and England through a series of stylistic modifications, this historical legacy became banal, boring, and extravagant.

At the outset of his essay, then, Wright acknowledged the synthesis of the arts as they occurred in the Italian Renaissance, yet he castigated mere imitation of Renaissance forms. He established, as a corrective, essential themes for the program of his own architecture: the study of indigenous architecture as the democratic embodiment of a people and the integration of form with its environment in a manner harmonious with nature.

The themes of the wisdom of the primitive and the necessity for harmony with nature placed Wright within fundamental intellectual currents that ran throughout nineteenth-century aesthetic and philosophical discussion. One of those currents was the pursuit of primitivism as an antidote to a moribund historicity. Primitive man lived close to the earth in harmony with nature and uncorrupted by consciousness of styles—a romantic observation that had long been pointed to in Europe as a source of spiritual rebirth. If rationalism could unite intellect and beauty, as proponents of Gothicism had maintained, then the primitivist search reaches even deeper into spiritual origins.

Although primitivism apparently had always interested Wright, only after 1910 did he begin extensively to explore and adapt originary forms for his own architecture. Claiming to be on a search for the spiritual qualities of form, Wright consciously equated symbolic and social values with specific forms, thus revealing a new self-consciousness that places the architect in the realm of the artist. In doing this Wright defined a new role for himself as an artist who reveals reality to the world: "The artist makes this revelation to us through deeper insight. His power to visualize conceptions being greater than our own, a flash of truth stimulates us, and we have a vision of harmonies not understood to-day though perhaps to-morrow."

With these words Wright announced in his Wasmuth Introduction his individual emergence from his roles as architect and social critic to that of the artist whose insight allows visualizations of the future. By acknowledging that these visions may be misunderstood, Wright hinted for the first time at another new role—that of the artist as prophet—which he would assume publicly and upon which he elaborated in his subsequent writings.

Wright's vision of the role of the artist was shared by some contemporaries in Europe, particularly members of the Secession movements whom he had just encountered. The correlation between a people and its art was underscored by Otto Wagner, the mentor of the progressive architects of the Vienna Secession: "It should never be forgotten that a country's art is the measure not only of its well-being, but also first and foremost of its intelligence."[19] Attesting to a vision common to Wright and the Secessionists, the words of Herman Bahr over the communal studio at Darmstadt mirrored Wright's: "The artist will show his world which never was nor ever will be."[20] The artist, then, aspires to reveal a world outside of ordinary thought, a world of meaning beyond our understanding.

In his Wasmuth Introduction Wright questioned what impeded such a hopeful cultural and spiritual renovation. He laid the blame on problems of traditional education. By making people too "sophisticated," education refined only the intellect and inhibited the perception of spiritual values that involve reaching "for the light spiritually, as the plant does physically."[21] The corruption of styles that emanated from the Renaissance was also a result of "false education" that alienated people from nature and natural laws as it civilized them. People consequently lost the ability to distinguish between artifice or "merely curious" visual effects and profound organic beauty, with the result that "Education seems to leave modern man less able than the savage to draw the line between these qualities." Wright was, however, selectively anti-intellectual; the overtraining of the intellect prevents the soul of nature from being perceived. Yet, in the American tradition of Thoreau, Whitman, and Emerson, it was through a focusing of intellect on the rationality of nature that true education, which was "natural education" instead of "academic education," would come about.

While the emphasis on education was an idea newly articulated after Wright's return from Europe, he reiterated his long-standing views on nature. In his Wasmuth essay, he correlated education and nature by asserting that the source of true education and the hope for the future lay in returning to nature. In revealing a world beyond the ordinary, great artists achieved insights about nature by instinct, by feeling, or by divination; thus, according to Wright, "the poetry which is prophecy is not a matter to be demonstrated." Consistent with his other statements on culture and architecture, Wright maintained that knowledge of the laws of nature was embodied in the intuitive powers of the ancient and primitive cultures. The forms of nature could be analyzed for their function, the expression of their constituent materials, and the laws of structure. These analyses provide relationships of cause and effect between line, color, and form with the result that the artist has a rational means to assess his "ideas and ideals" and to "sift materials, test motives, and direct aims." According to Wright's own studies, Japanese artists, such as Hokusai and Korin, were particularly adept at finding the graphic means to reduce the "fundamental conditions" of form to simple geometry. Great art of the West, whether of Velasquez, Franz Hals, or Gothic architecture, contained the same conditions of "organic" character. And true education could bring others, who were not great artists, to a better understanding of nature.

The central pursuit in the study and research of the organic qualities of art and architecture was discovering the "soul of the thing." This "soul" was the essential character of a form, the inherent nature that integrated it into its time and place, its culture and tradition, and into the transcendent cosmic order. It was the force that characterized a pine as a pine or a willow as a willow, an "organic" building as opposed to an "inorganic" building. And it arose from certain relationships of line, form, and color that produced emotion in a "language of sentiment."

By pursuing research into the "soul of things," an artist could maintain his ideals and overturn his false education. Study of these essential qualities would lead to simplification. This simplification would become a central principle in Wright's designs as he subjected them to a method of abstraction that he defined as "conventionalization" in his subsequent writings. Although the term had been used in reference to two-dimensional design during the nineteenth century, for Wright it became a key concept. When this use of simplifying convention was combined with the "spiritual lessons that the East has the power to teach the West," Western culture would have the required highly developed forms of modern life.

In looking for sources of purity in the primal cultures of the world, Wright again connected himself to the artists of the Secession movements in Europe who carried on a similar search. Recalling the training of artists in Japan or the practice of apprenticeship in the Middle Ages, he concluded that a new education was necessary for youth, incorporating the spirit of great architecture, "the study of the nature of materials, the *nature* of the tools and processes at command, and the *nature* of the thing they are called upon to do."[22] As Wright noted, "German and Austrian art schools are getting back to these ideas."[23]

This search bound Wright and a cluster of European modernists together in the recognition of the spirit of the Gothic, the simplification of the Orient, and the ancient forms of original architecture as the antidotes to the corruption of the arts. Youth—the *Jugend* in Germany and Austria, and the "Young Man in Architecture" in America, as Wright described him— would be the champions of a new cause.

Although Wright found common ground between himself and European artists and architects, if he and other Americans were to be truly educated they would need to separate from their European roots. Americans had to find the means of representing values that were distinctly American. This nation had a special character that mixed poetry and rebellion. Whitman pointed out this character when he wrote in the Preface to

Leaves of Grass, "The Americans of all nations at any time upon the earth, have probably the fullest poetical nature. The United States themselves are essentially the greatest poem." [24] In a nation whose citizens sing the self, as did Whitman, a nation of pioneers, dreaming of freedom and privacy, individualism was a central value. Following in the tradition of Whitman, Wright claimed that "America more than any other nation presents a new architectural proposition." [25] That proposition was rooted in democracy. In Wright's terms, true education of the individual was an act of defiance that makes an individual "a rebel against his time and its laws, but never lawless." In Wright's view: "Individuality is a national ideal. Where this degenerates into petty individualism, it is but a manifestation of weakness in the human nature, and not a flaw in the ideal." [26] Americans live with greater "independence and seclusion" than other peoples. Therefore, they require greater individuality and privacy, and their architecture must express their own "character, tastes, and ideas." According to Wright, the American problem, however, was aggravated because Americans acknowledge none of their own traditions and borrow instead from a panoply of styles that rob them of their collective soul.

Education of the citizenry was the means of creating a distinctive American style. While the issues of education applied generally to the populace, architects faced specific difficulties and responsibilities. Wright believed that no schools in America trained architects to find the forms—the "organic architecture"—that were independent of historical styles. Therefore, the architect needed a new system of training. Furthermore, a new educational process was required not only for the architect but between the architect and his client. Wright wrote in his Wasmuth Introduction that the architect should educate the client, and the client in turn would educate the architect so that a distinct America character would be represented in buildings. The relationship of architect to client was, therefore, a factor in the development of style. Revealing his own answer to the perennial problem of style, Wright asserted that an organic style allowed diverse shapes of buildings, both low and tall, and various treatments, including flat and pitched roofs, rectangular, square, or vertical windows. All would be linked harmoniously because they were each a result of an individual investigation into form, material, and character.

The search for the character of harmonious color, pattern, and usefulness of a system of ornament presented itself distinctly as "the modern American opportunity." Unsure of their roots yet unburdened by stifling tradition, Americans could cre-

ate a truly democratic language of form. The American opportunity, then, was precisely the individualist's opportunity that Wright had expressed privately as the need to square one's private self with the demands of public life, or failing that, square public life with the private self.

By the conclusion of his Wasmuth essay Wright had called for education to transform society, and he had made his own peace with the traditions of historicism and their influence on him. One the one hand, he espoused a rejection of the past for the sake of a vision of the future. On the other hand, the future paradoxically lay in the resurrection of a deeper past—a past found in the very origins of human creativity. He outlined future directions as a search for ornament, sculpture, and harmonious forms that expressed the uniqueness of a nation and the universality of human culture. The experience of Europe, combined with his collaborations with Mamah Cheney, gave Wright a new focus on educating the American public, searching for a purity of social mores, and developing a purity of aesthetic means found in the "conventionalization" of form.

Educating the American Public

The theme of education was bound up with Wright's intentions for the Wasmuth publications. After completing the Introduction in December 1910 and assuring publication of the monograph and *Sonderheft* in February 1911, Wright faced the business of distributing his collected works. As he prepared to disseminate his books, he made explicit their purpose as tools of education for the youth of America. Despite historians' repeated assertions of the books' influence in Europe, the monograph and *Sonderheft* were intended not specifically for Europeans but as primers of building types for an expanding America.

Wright's goal was to reach the young architects and citizens of the New West of America, whom he wanted to guide to a new vision of life embodied in architecture. He deliberately tailored the sales of his books to the young and impressionable: "I want the young fellows to have the work—say $10.00 down and $10.00 per month for the youngsters and $25.00 down—$25.00 in three months for the grown up's [*sic*] who are hard up's [*sic*]." [27]

Wright's goal of reaching the fresh minds of architecture—the "young man" in architecture—reflected a theme first pursued by Louis Sullivan in a speech of 1900 to the Architectural League of America. [28] In order to reach his targeted audience,

Wright personally directed the effort to distribute his publications in America from early April 1911 until January 1913. At first, he relied on book dealers in Chicago and Seattle. The failure of the dealers to pay for their purchases caused Wright to advertise the books and sell them directly through the mail. Wright's office administered the system of sales, postal distribution, and bill collection.

Wright was assisted in disseminating his primers for an American architecture by Taylor Woolley, his trusted draftsman whom he asked to help sell the books in the West. To prepare Woolley for the sales campaign, Wright summarized for him the complex events that had occurred with the Wasmuth Verlag, and announced that Wasmuth had promised to send the completed work to Wright by 15 May 1911.[29] Wright's description to Woolley indicated that the *Sonderheft* was a supplement to the monograph, contrary to Wasmuth's original intention of featuring the *Sonderheft* as part of the series *Architektur des XX Jahrhunderts* (Architecture in the 20th Century).

In further explaining to Woolley how to sell the publications, Wright explicitly stated the didactic intentions behind the whole venture and further defined his audience:

Your [Woolley's] idea as to selling the work is quite right I think— It must have a chance to sell itself—Libraries—Building Contractors, Private persons with money and an interest in building—would be easier to interest perhaps than architects—the field undoubtedly is in the South & West. There is nothing in Advertising. . . . The lesser architects are more apt to buy than the bigger ones—The more important one's [sic] feel compromised to have the work of a living contemporary in their libraries—but I can't die to further sales. Schools—should prove willing and able to buy—And I think all the public libraries of all the Small [sic] towns in America should be taught the value of a copy to the young [mothers? illegible] of the neighborhood or those interested in home planning—It would have more cultural effect on their people than almost anything else that could be put on their shelves and perhaps many could be made to see it that way.[30]

Wright's intended audience was not composed of sophisticated eastern architects but rather of citizens of the South and expanding West of the United States. He hoped that the publication of his architecture would affect and shape the cultural life of people in their homes and their community centers, the schools, libraries, public buildings, and religious institutions of American towns.

Wright's primer for a new American architecture would contain a uniform set of drawings consisting of seventy-two plates and twenty-eight tissue overlays in two folio cases. The designs demonstrated a wide variety and versatility of work, from single-family houses to public buildings to multifamily dwellings, from urban to rural settings with building types ranging from a mortuary to a tennis club, and from estates for the rich to housing for factory workers.

Wright touted the two portfolios as comparable to the work of the late Joseph Maria Olbrich, the architect to whom Wright, the "Olbrich of America," had been compared in Europe.[31] Wright presented his magnum opus as above that of any other architect in Europe or America:

The finest publication of any Architect's work in any country—not excepting the work of the Austrian Architect, Olbrich—and necessary to the completeness and efficiency of the library of any American Architect who cares for the progress of his art in his own country.[32]

Fulfilling the purpose of providing Americans with a primer of democratic architecture, however, was not easily or immediately achieved. The production of the publications had been plagued with delays and problems. The complete monographs did not arrive in America until late 1911, with the first folio appearing in June and the second in December. Wright did not receive the first volume of the monograph until mid to late June 1911, and the second and final folio did not arrive until December 1911.[33] The *Sonderheft* did not appear in Chicago until November 1912. And the availability of the Wasmuth publications to Europeans was later in 1911 and 1912 than has previously been supposed.

Purity of Social Structure

The search for purity through education that Wright brought back from Europe extended beyond providing a primer of building types for a democracy to an advocacy of social reforms that struck at the core of the traditional family. Both objectives— to reform architecture and social mores—were efforts to find an idealized purity in life. The purity of architecture and the purity of social mores would substitute honesty and truth for hypocrisy and effect. Education linked these objectives. To demonstrate the effects of "true education" Wright tried to make his own life a model of an individual who risked social censure to pursue what in his eyes was an honest love. Travel to Europe had brought Wright and Cheney in contact with the ideas of Ellen Key, the Swedish feminist who wrote on love-marriage as the only moral form of intimate relationship between a woman and a man. Wright and Cheney, who resumed her maiden name of Borthwick after her divorce on 5 August

71. Ellen Key, at her home in Sweden, 1911 (Nyström-Hamilton, *Ellen Key, Her Life and Work*).

Ellen Key (fig. 71), born of Scottish ancestry, grew up in Sweden to become a strong individualist.[36] Her career was devoted to lecturing and writing on the history of Swedish civilization, the history of literature, and feminism, for which she became controversial. Her ideas were based not solely on the emancipation of women but on the liberation of the individual. Articulating the concept of "love-marriage," she stated that the only moral bonds between man and woman were based on love, not marriage, and that the only hope for the future morality of society lay in the education of youth. This liberating education began for children in kindergarten. Theirs was the birthright to create a just society. According to Key, "It is a deep psychological truth that the kingdom of heaven belongs to children."[37]

By 1910 Key had become the talk of Europe. As Key's official translator, Mamah, with Wright's assistance, was among the first to introduce the work of the radical feminist to America, where her ideas were little known. Borthwick translated treatises on the liberation of women, men, and children. The first, *The Morality of Woman and Other Essays* appeared in 1911 from Wright's friend and publisher in Chicago, Ralph Fletcher Seymour. *Love and Ethics, The Torpedo under the Ark; "Ibsen and Women"*, and *The Woman Movement* followed in 1912 (fig. 72).[38]

Key's principles on marriage and divorce and the hope she vested in the child were so significant for Wright that he reiterated them almost twenty years later in his *Autobiography*. He expressed three premises "as a means to an honest life" and a moral domain where common laws should have no jurisdiction:

First: Marriage not mutual is no better, but is worse than any other form of slavery.
Second: Only to the degree that marriage is mutual is it decent. Love is not property. To take it so is barbarous. To protect it as such is barbarism.
Three: The child is the pledge of good faith its parents give to the future of the race. There are no illegitimate children. There may be illegitimate parents—legal or illegal. . . .[39]

These beliefs in the role of education imply an underlying premise that social transformation was possible. It was, therefore, no idle remark when Wright told William Martin in 1910 that he would devote his life to the education of children. It was not a casual thought or simple pragmatism that caused Wright to try to place his German publications in the hands of the youth of America, the country's unsophisticated and unformed hope for the future. And it is not an accident that among Wright's first designs upon his return to America were a kindergarten

1911, published Key's work in America, and Key's ideas became a reply to the criticism of the two lovers who had abandoned their families.[34]

Wright's promotion of the spouses' search for true love at the expense of family stability and social acceptability can be assessed from two points of view. One viewpoint is that Wright, assuming a superiority over others because of his role as an artist, showed an outrageous arrogance in his moralizing pronouncements.[35] A second viewpoint is that Wright was accepting a burdensome role similar to that of the prophet who risks scorn to point out the hypocrisy around him. To assess accurately which viewpoint seems more feasible it is necessary to look closely at the ideas of Ellen Key, the context in which Wright and Borthwick utilized them, and their reverberation in Wright's life.

THE MORALITY OF WOMAN

AND OTHER ESSAYS

AUTHORIZED TRANSLATION FROM THE SWEDISH

OF

ELLEN KEY

BY

MAMAH BOUTON BORTHWICK

THE RALPH FLETCHER SEYMOUR CO.
FINE ARTS BUILDING
CHICAGO

72. Title page, Ellen Key, *Morality of Woman and Other Essays*, Mamah Borthwick, translator, 1911.

and a school—the "playhouse"—for Queene Ferry Coonley. Wright and Mrs. Coonley now shared an interest in education. She was also particularly interested in women's suffrage and progressive education. A follower of John Dewey, she made the playhouse into a "children's community."[40] Although she did not believe in love-marriage, this emphasis on education, particularly at the kindergarten level, made her, in terms of edu-

cation, an American in sympathy with the Swedish feminist Ellen Key.[41]

Key's insistence on the proper education of children as the prerequisite to a necessary transformation of society reinforced Wright's belief in the education of youth, a belief rooted in his family's involvement in teaching, including his mother, a former school-teacher, and aunts Jane and Nell, who operated their own school in Hillside.[42] Wright's wife, Catherine, had also been interested in children's education. She operated a kindergarten for her own and neighborhood children and encouraged her children's interests in arts and crafts.[43] After 1910 education for Wright also became imbedded in his conception of architectural practice. His studio in Oak Park had in its early years the friendly atmosphere of an atelier where more experienced architects tutored younger apprentices. But with the building of his home in Wisconsin, Wright's draftsmen both lived and worked where he lived and worked, providing a potentially more intimate situation. Although Wright maintained a distance between himself and his employees, eventually the arrangement with his apprentices evolved into a commune, and ultimately into the Taliesin Fellowship, which combined apprenticeship, building, and farming with an architectural practice.

Educating the public, however, became intertwined with Wright's justification of his own behavior. At the risk of offending the "established order" Wright called on the principles of Ellen Key in a series of dramatic public defenses of his and Mamah's behavior.[44] With the completion of Taliesin, their new home, Wright began preparations to settle permanently into the community of Spring Green, Wisconsin, by explaining publicly his behavior to the press, which once again had discovered the scandalous couple (figs. 73, 74).[45] In a series of statements issued in December 1911 to the local and Chicago press, Wright revealed Key's influence on him by criticizing traditional marriage and the family.[46] With respect to abandoning his family, Wright was reported as saying that "instead of having committed a sin he has lived up to a high ideal."[47] He explained the demise of his marriage as resulting from the union of two young people who had grown very apart after twenty years.[48] His wife had found herself as a mother devoted to her children; he had found himself as an artist:

I started out to give expression to certain ideals in architecture. I wanted to create something organic, something sound and wholesome, American in spirit and beautiful if might be. I think I have succeeded in that. In a way my buildings are my children.[49]

73. Taliesin I, Hillside, Wisconsin, c. 1911 (Iconographic Collections, State Historical Society of Wisconsin, WHI [X3] 41630).

By saying this, Wright implied that if children were the hope of the future, as Key proposed, then his hope also lay in his buildings and their ability to educate the public in a true American architecture.

Returning to Key's concept that moral behavior lay outside conventional canons, Wright stated to the press that "laws and rules are made for the average," not for those individuals with spiritual power "to see and to feel the higher and better things of life." [50] This statement obviously opened Wright to accusations of arrogantly placing himself above others. He, however, had begun to see himself as a member of the nonconformist American tradition who would pay the price for speaking against the status quo. The crises caused by his confrontations with a probing public were already threatening the social purpose of

his work to create the architecture of an American spirit: "It will be a waste of something socially precious if this thing robs me of my work. I have struggled to express something real in American architecture. I have something to give." [51]

While Wright was defending himself in public, he tried to obtain a divorce from Catherine Wright, and he issued short daily statements on his actions from 27 December to 31 December 1911. [52] In these he promoted further the principles of Ellen Key on marriage and the family. "The time is coming when people will understand what it means to say a wife is not the property of the husband and that the husband is not the property of the wife." [53] Paralleling Key's ideas in the *Morality of Woman,* Wright declared that the patriarchal family, in which the husband owns the wife and children, still held on, but

74. Taliesin I, Hillside, Wisconsin, c. 1911 (Iconographic Collections, State Historical Society of Wisconsin, WHI [X3] 41625).

would die. The "modern family" in which the wife owned the husband was no better.[54] Instead, he advocated that "marriage ought to be put on an economic basis," an unclear allusion to each partner providing for the material maintenance of the family.[55]

The scandal began to arouse not only the public but Wright's relatives in the valley outside Spring Green. Reverend Jenkin Lloyd Jones, Wright's uncle, wrote to his sister Jane that their nephew's presence was exacerbating the financial problems of the Hillside Home School.[56] Aware of the family's fears, Wright eventually had to deny any association "socially or financially" with his aunts in order "to check certain mischievous statements intended to injure the Lloyd Jones Sister's Home School."[57]

Wright's lessons in morality and pleas for sympathy were met with disapproval by the editor of the local *Weekly Home News*.[58] Contrary to Wright's view of himself, he saw the architect as an "unhonored prophet" and the couple as flaunting their outrageous behavior before God-fearing people. Furthermore, they had besmirched the Lloyd Jones family by advocating immorality and vice when the family of teachers and ministers taught respect and dignity.

Despite disapproval, the saga continued, and Wright revised his Christmas statement with comments that appeared in the *Chicago Daily Tribune* on 31 December 1911.[59] Providing previously unknown details concerning his European venture with Mamah, he gave a full public accounting of his present conditions by describing their falling in love, their waiting a year in Europe to see if the love would last, the conflict that the two husbands and two wives had experienced, and the continuity of the bond with the woman he loved.[60] Wright gave additional information about the reasons for his return to America, claiming that he had to return because the office work as he had left it in the hands of his wife was not financially supporting his family. Distorting his affairs with Von Holst, he claimed that jobs had been "unscrupulously taken from him."[61] He further informed the public that by the time he had returned from Europe he had decided to make the break; he returned only as the father of his children, not as the husband of his wife. At Taliesin, he "had gathered the remnant of his forces to fight for the life of his work."[62] He was thus making a public announcement to give courage to those "behind the curtain . . . so that honest souls may profit" by seeking happiness and integrity over legal bonds.[63] Wright summarized his basic problem as a conflict between conventional and true morality in which, for him and Mamah Borthwick, "The established order and the claims of daily companionship were pitted against the integrity of life that is the only real life."[64]

Wright replied to the local criticism, defending himself as moral, praising the "consideration and courtesy" of the community, and hoping that they would give him the benefit of their doubts.[65] While some sense of outrage continued, *The Chicago Daily Tribune* reported that his family's presence in the locality and fictitious rumors of his wealth prevented the community from any general condemnation of Wright.[66] Gradually inhabitants around Spring Green accepted the couple, although perhaps with resignation. Wright's interest in the cause of women, however, apparently continued because he designed an unknown project for a Women's Building and Neighborhood Club in Spring Green. The design, drawn by Herbert Fritz, Sr., was published on 16 July 1914 on the front page of the newspaper in Spring Green (fig. 75).[67]

The publication of the Women's Building project occurred one month before the tragic deaths of Mamah and her children at the hands of Julian Carlton, a servant who worked at Taliesin. On August 15 while Wright was in Chicago working on the Midway Gardens, Carlton set fire to the residence wing of Taliesin, locked all but one of the doors, and then hacked to death Mamah Borthwick, eight year-old Martha, and eleven year-old John as they fled. Carlton bludgeoned Fritz with an axe and murdered four others as they struggled to flee, including the draftsman Emile Brodelle, who had drawn the perspectives of

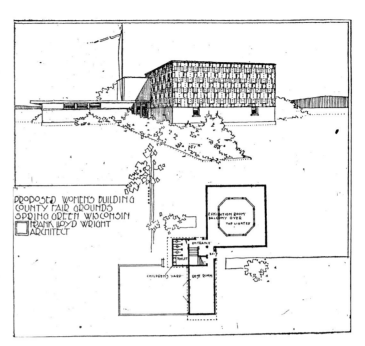

75. Design for Women's Building and Neighborhood Club, Spring Green, Wisconsin, unbuilt as designed (*Weekly Home News,* Spring Green, Wis., 16 July 1914).

Midway Gardens and the Imperial Hotel (figs. 76, 77).[68]

Some accounts imply the servant was insane, others that he had been insulted by the draftsmen at Taliesin, or that he was incited to violence by the fact of Wright and Mamah Borthwick living in sin. New evidence based partly on court transcripts may challenge all these accounts, but these have not yet been published.[69] Regardless of motivation, a profound tragedy occurred. While devastated by his loss, Wright himself rejected the suggestion that the murders were divine retribution for his iconoclastic and immoral life.

At Mamah Borthwick's funeral Wright read a portion of Goethe's "Hymn to Nature." He and Borthwick had found a copy in a Berlin bookshop and translated it.[70] In his *Autobiography* Wright described the burial:

Men from Taliesin dug the grave, near Grandfather's and Grandmother's grave. . . . The August sun was setting I remember on the familiar range of hills. Dimly, I felt coming in far-off shadows of the ages struggling to escape from subconsciousness and utter themselves. . . . Then slowly came darkness. . . . I filled the grave, staying there in the dark. It was friendly.[71]

Despite Wright's rejection of divine retribution, his personal suffering, like that of Job, may have reinforced his sense of pro-

The Chicago Sunday Tribune.
THE WORLD'S GREATEST NEWSPAPER

AUGUST 16 1914. A ★ ★ PRICE FIVE CENTS.

BATTLE COMING WHICH WILL SHOCK WORLD
Awful Crime in Wisconsin Cottage

MRS. CHENEY AND FIVE OTHERS SLAIN IN FRANK LLOYD WRIGHT BUNGALOW

NEGRO HELPER KILLS FAMILY WITH HATCHET

Architect, in Chicago, Hears of Crime and Goes to Scene.

SLAYER CAPTURED

PACKERS MAY BE INDICTED IN PRICE WAR

Federal Grand Jury to Turn Fire on Big Concerns Again.

CHARGE CONSPIRACY

LATEST WAR BULLETINS.

SUMMARY OF DAY'S WAR NEWS

FRENCH WIN FOUR TOWNS, ROUTING FOE

Commander of Fifteenth German Corps Wounded in Fight.

LINES 200 MILES LONG

MAMAH BORTHWICK

Bungalow Murder Victims.

THE DEAD.
MAMAH BORTHWICK CHENEY
JOHN BORTHWICK CHENEY, her son.
MARTHA CHENEY, her daughter.
EMIL BRODELLE, draftsman
THOMAS BRUNKER, farm laborer.
EMIL WESTON, their boy.

THE INJURED.
WILLIAM WESTON, carpenter
HERBERT FRITZ, draftsman
DAVID LINDBLOM, gardener

PRINCE AAGE OF DENMARK TELLS OF THRILLING TRIP.

DROP BOMBS IN NAMUR; GERMAN AIRMEN WOUND 5.

WEALTHY CHICAGO WOMAN COOKS FOR LONDON POOR.

WAR TRAPS 20,000 STUDENTS

76. Reports of the Taliesin tragedy, *Chicago Sunday Tribune,* 16 August 1914, p. 1.

77. Reports of the Taliesin tragedy, *Chicago Daily Tribune*, 17 August 1914, p. 7.

phetic mission. Because he assumed the moral obligation of ridding life of its false forms, his voice became that of a self-proclaimed prophet, replete with an occasional stridency and the appearance of self-righteous arrogance. Prophets are destined to suffer, and Wright would suffer as he entered a period of greater risks and larger defeats than anything he had experienced during his middle-class life in Oak Park. In Wright the roles of prophet, teacher, and visionary began to merge.

Conclusion

Instead of being merely simple influences on his work and irrelevant factors in his chaotic personal life, Wright's travels to Europe precipitated a break with his past that wove together his life and work. Mamah Borthwick had been at the center of Wright's life, but her precise impact on him requires careful observation.[72] There is no facile analogy between the independence of thought that supported their behavior and the reformulation of Wright's design ideas, but there are powerful indications that the liberation he experienced at a personal level paralleled the liberation he began to feel in his work. Although he had been in love with Mamah for years, would he have had abandoned his family without going to Europe? Where would he have turned to see his collected works appear as models for a new American architecture? Would he ever have found in America a feminist like Ellen Key whose principles coincided so well with his and Mamah's? While Wright struggled to square

the demands of his life with the nature of his self, he had begun to transform himself from a social critic and successful regional architect who had abandoned his family and practice for the sake of love, into a visionary. According to this perception, Wright represented the great American phenomenon embodied in the poems of Walt Whitman, who saw the visionary as indispensable in the evolution of American democracy. At the core of the visionary was the individualist—Whitman's "Me in the centre"—who will lead a collective society to its true constitution, one in which each person will be an individualist, as nature intends everyone to be.[73] This elevated role of visionary individualist was also heroic. As described by Thomas Carlyle, whose books Wright owned and annotated, "The Hero can be Poet, Prophet, King, Priest or what you will, according to the kind of world he finds himself born into."[74]

As Wright embraced the role of visionary for a rudely formed America, he expanded his search from purifying relations between men, women, and children to purifying forms themselves. The struggles to integrate the lessons of Europe in a search for pure form had now begun. These lessons would be manifested in sculpture and the symbolic language of ornament that would preoccupy his designs and theories. His experience of Europe paradoxically bound him to other explorers in the search for spiritual rebirth and for the pure forms found in ancient and traditional non-Western cultures, yet the lessons imbedded him more deeply into the culture of America than anyone has suspected. Europe made Wright more American than ever.

The appreciation of beauty on the part of primitive peoples, Mongolian, Indian, Arab, Egyptian, Greek and Goth was unerring. Because of this, their work is coming home to us to-day in another and truer Renaissance, to open our eyes that we may cut away the dead wood and brush aside the accumulated rubbish of centuries of false education. This Renaissance means a return to simple conventions in harmony with nature. Primarily it is a simplifying process. Then, having learned the spiritual lesson that the East has power to teach the West, we may build upon this basis the more highly developed forms our more highly developed life will need.—Frank Lloyd Wright (1910)[1]

5 A Lesson in Primitivism

When Wright identified in his Wasmuth Introduction the basis for the forms of a "highly developed life," he gave us a fundamental insight into the views common to him and his European colleagues. Entering his own primitivist phase in 1910, Wright proposed that the antidote to the decay of architecture would be found in the origins of architecture. Wright's view was shared by certain progressive artists and architects in Holland, Germany, and Austria. By stating in his Wasmuth Introduction that "German and Austrian art schools are getting back to these ideas," he could reiterate that these views were "coming home to us to-day."[2] His acknowledgment implied that he recognized that exoticism had been important to the Secessionists—the leaders of progressive schools—and that an interest in primitivism was spreading among other artists.

The artists and architects who pursued primitivism assumed that usable traces of origins of art and architecture were still to be found in the "primitive" and exotic cultures of the world.[3] Frazer's *The Golden Bough,* published in England in 1890, had been a precursor that connected primitive customs to religion and magic. Primitive architecture increasingly was associated with folkishness, nativism, and simplicity. Exotic architecture differed from the primitive by its connotations of complexity, foreignness, and a fascinating otherness. The study of both exotic and primitive architecture provided a way of rejecting decadent Western values and of replacing them with values that seemed simple and pure. Wright made little distinction between the exotic and the primitive; he generally used the

word "primitive" in his writings even when it included exotic sources. For him, this lack of distinction reflected his belief in a universality of forms in all older cultures and in those cultures' "unerring" appreciation of beauty. The "Renaissance-of-the-Primitive," as Wright later called it, provided an antidote to historicism in art; direct imitation that led to the use of historicist styles would be irrelevant when primitivist forms became the basis of art and architecture.[4] Such views as Wright's were based fundamentally on belief in the existence of a Golden Age, long lost to modern man, but still alive in the artifacts of primitive and native peoples. The works of the "noble savage" were associated with what was perceived to be the inherent goodness of vernacular and folk traditions.[5]

For Wright and his small circle of European colleagues the origins of culture existed in the architecture of the ancient Near East, the Islamic world, the Far East, and, especially for an American, the pre-Columbian world.[6] The specific sources included the cultural artifacts of the Mongolian, Indian, Arab, Egyptian, Greek, and Goth. Added to these sources were folk and vernacular arts and architecture. By studying these sources, either firsthand or through literary sources, Wright and his colleagues uncovered the systems and basic forms of art that had application to modern culture.

Before 1910 there had been some indication of Wright's latent interest in primitivism. He acknowledged one instance of this interest in exoticism when he remodeled the Rookery Building in Chicago. "I did the Rookery at the time Uncle Dan Burn-

78. Balustrade from the remodeled lobby of the Rookery Building, Chicago, 1905.

79. Owen Jones, Mauresque Ornament No. 4 (*Grammar of Ornament*, pl. 42).

ham was alive—more or less oriental. Nevertheless much is characteristic of my work at the time notwithstanding Persian motive [*sic*]."[7] The pierced metal grill of the balustrade could easily have been derived from the plates of Owen Jones's *Grammar of Ornament,* but the treatment of the newel posts and the light fixtures bears out Wright's assertion that his own rectilinear and planar aesthetic of his early period dominated (figs. 78, 79). The mural in the dining room of the Beachy House may have been an immediate response in 1906 to his trip to Japan the previous year, with the design resembling a scroll of oriental landscape.[8] The mantel over the living room fireplace at the Darwin Martin House resembles a Japanese textile in Wright's collection.[9]

Wright's travels in Europe in 1909–10 involved him in a whirl of excitement about exotic sources and primitive art. Paintings with themes of foreign lands had offered an alternative to the tradition of history painting that focused on mythological subjects. Exotic themes offered a change of subject and locale while new findings in archaeology increased the general awareness of exotic sources.[10] As excavations spread to the classical world and Mesopotamia, new discoveries excited the public's interest in the possibilities of finding both evidence of antiquity and the "truth" about the people of the Bible.[11] Egyptian art, particularly after Napoleon's campaigns, was one of those powerful forces of the exotic. Rudolph Wittkower described the important impact of Egypt on European culture:

Whether the Near East or Egypt had a greater effect on Europe is difficult to decide. Yet one thing is certain: The Egyptian influence was more sustained than the Near Eastern, lasting well into the nineteenth century. Historians underestimate that influence on European thought, whereas in many respects the Egyptian impact is as important as the classical tradition in its formative influence.[12]

By the turn of the twentieth century, European interests in both primitivism and exoticism had melded to serve a common goal: the artistic search for spiritual renewal. In progressive German and Austrian circles, young artists, the *Jugend,* led the rejection of the old and its replacement by a new order. Despite the differences of complexity, indigenous meanings, and origins

80. Spear and dance ornament (*Hohe Warte*, 3, 1906–7).

It has an inventive, heuristic character with a predilection for primitive forms.[13]

Like the Secessionists, Expressionists also found inspiration in these sources; the work of the Blaue Reiter group demonstrated the fecundity of primitive art. Wilhelm Worringer's *Abstraktion und Einfühlung* had helped stimulate a reassessment of vernacular art and of the art of nonliterate peoples, such as the tribes of Oceania and Africa.[14] According to Worringer's theories people identified or empathized with qualities of life in works of art. Classical and Renaissance art allowed people to harmonize with their world, while Byzantine, Egyptian, and Indian art exerted a sense of conflict with the material world. Although for Worringer the Gothic was the perfect compromise, artists began to feel that primitive art was more sophisticated than had been assumed. It integrated artistic expression with its medium in novel forms of representation—the grain of a painted wooden panel could become the texture of cloth. It was often composed of very flat surfaces without the use of one-point perspective (fig. 80). And the subject matter of primitive art often involved the primordial relationship of humans to nature.

The sources of study were close at hand through books and museums. Motivated to find a pure language of architecture, European artists interested in primitivism only had to look around them for literary sources of primitive and exotic culture. In Vienna, as the well-used books and folios of the city's libraries and archives show, the artists and architects frequently turned to historical reference material on the art and architecture of Mesopotamia, Egypt, and Japan. Extraordinary compilations of plates, printed in richly saturated colors, provided treatises on the history of ornament from Western and Eastern cultures. These included the folios of Racinet's *Ornement polychrome*, and Owen Jones's, *Grammar of Ornament*, a basic source for Wright.[15] First published in 1856, Jones's plates provided perhaps the best summary of comparative ornament, and its various editions were recognized internationally.[16]

Museums were major repositories of ancient art and artifacts for Viennese artists in their search for pure forms. The galleries of the Egyptian collection at the Kunsthistorisches Museum provided a treasury of the motifs of ancient art and architecture ranging from sarcophagi, with temple motifs, to symbols of religion, including the ibis and the disk of the sun-god, Horus (fig. 81).[17] On the ceiling of the Egyptian galleries decorators used the outspread wings of the ibis to complement the wallpaper, which was reused from the Egyptian installation at the Vi-

between exoticism and primitivism, they both became sources for a rejection of the recent past. Not limited to their application in graphics, painting, and sculpture, these sources could stimulate the making of architecture. Ferdinand von Feldegg, editor of *Der Architekt*, commented on the search for recurring principles in architecture:

Modern architecture creates more consciously from the inner, primal, individual source than its historical predecessors ever did. Like the other arts, modern architecture rejects the idea of constantly reviving objectively established norms, but rather strives to create new values.

81. Egyptian Galleries, Kunsthistorisches Museum, Vienna, c. 1905 (Kunsthistorisches Museum, Vienna).

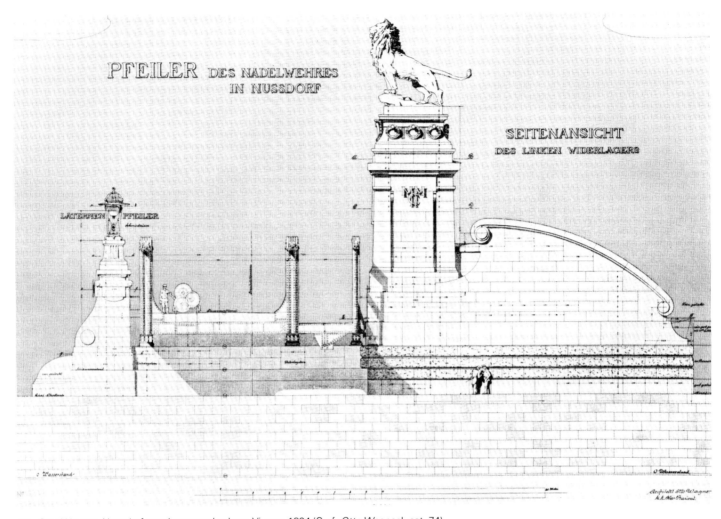

PFEILER DES NADELWEHRES IN NUSSDORF

SEITENANSICHT DES LINKEN WIDERLAGERS

LATERNEN PFEILER

82. Otto Wagner, Nussdorf gate house and pylons, Vienna, 1894 (Graf, *Otto Wagner* I, cat. 74).

enna World's Fair of 1873. In spandrels above the museum's great staircase Gustav Klimt announced the themes of Egypt and ancient Greece in the murals *Egyptian Art I* and *Art of Ancient Greece I*. Other Egyptian symbols, including the crux and mummy mask, were used in his intercolumnar painting, *Egyptian Art II*.[18] Klimt also made extensive use of archaic Greek, Assyrian, and Mycenaean motifs, particularly in emulation of gold repoussé, which had generated much excitement after the excavations of Schliemann.[19] He was sufficiently discriminating in his sources from the ancient Near East that he used for the background of his painting *Judith I* of 1901 a detail from the Assyrian palace relief of Sennacherib at Nineveh.[20] Klimt used Egyptian motifs for the freize at Palais Stoclet, begun in 1905

and completed in 1911. Responding in part to his experiences of conflict, and thoughts about death and rebirth, he drew upon Plutarch's account of the legend of Isis and Osiris, the theories of the esoteric Father Desiderius Lenz of the Beuron School, Beuronic art exhibited in Vienna, art collections, and even contemporary dance—a broad range of sources that indicates the extensive aura of Egypt and the call of the ancient world as a source for modern art.[21]

With these images from the museums' collections and illustrations from beautiful folios, it is not surprising to see the richness of Egyptian and Mesopotamian art pervade the motifs of the Secession. Otto Wagner canted the walls of his Nussdorf gatehouse for the Danube Canal (1894–98) to recall pylons of

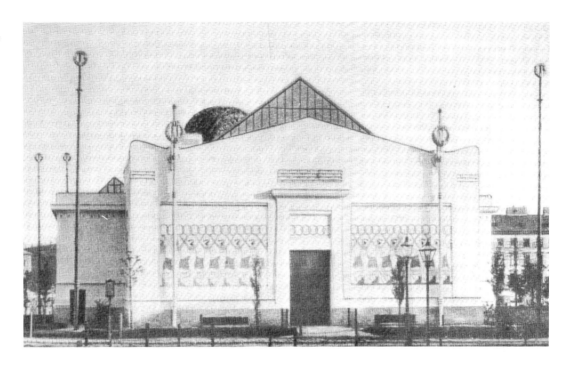

83. Koloman Moser, Secession Building, rear view, Vienna, 1897 (Kunstbibliothek Berlin).

Egyptian temples. He transformed the roaring lions on curving bases at the gatehouse into sphinxes: the lion became the head of the sphinx; the statue base and volute, its main body; and the pier with curving base in front, its paws (fig. 82). Contemporary publications made the allusions to Egypt clear.[22] The motifs of the ancient world were paramount in Olbrich's design for the Secession Building, which was noted in Baedeker's guidebook—with some curiosity—for its Egyptian and Assyrian associations.[23] Formed to resemble temple pylons, the rear facade of the building was directly inspired by Egyptian motifs as is obvious from the frieze of Egyptian figures designed by Koloman Moser (fig. 83).

Frank Lloyd Wright had his own references for primitivist sources. In the early 1880s he had made a hundred tracings from the plates of the *Grammar of Ornament* and studied Jones's "Propositions," noting that "the first five were dead right" and the next five were "equally sound."[24] These all reflected Wright's view of an organic architecture in which decoration and architecture are interrelated, architecture expresses the needs and spirit of the age, and style and beauty result from such integral expressions. Wright could also have studied Jones's discussions of design systems that used grids, compared ornaments from different cultures, and improvised upon motifs as he did with those from the plates of Gothic ornament.[25]

In addition to compendiums of comparative ornament, Wright had available numerous other sources for primary forms. Along with his collection of Japanese art and wood-block prints, Wright owned a copy of the 1896 edition of Friedrich Deneken's *Japanische Motive für Flächenverzierung*.[26] Deneken expressed an interest—widespread among European artists—in motifs as surface decorations for craft objects. The plates of blooming peonies, chrysanthemums, carp, and bamboo contained abstracted forms of nature in their purest essence. In these motifs, geometry and nature were integrated into rational and reproducible patterns that could reveal the processes by which they were designed.

Berlage's Theory

Clearly Wright was not alone in his belief in the validity of primitive, exotic, and archaic sources as a guide for modern culture. The shared interest in primitivism found in these various sources created bonds between Wright and his European colleagues. The links between Wright and a small group of Europeans indicate that, instead of finding linear explanations of influence, we discover knots of associated ideas. These ideas seem to have a life of their own, and artists interpreted them and explored them in parallel with varying degrees of contact among themselves. One knot of ideas involves the Dutch, the Germans to a limited degree, and the Viennese. In calling for the recognition of a universal order in architecture, Hendrik Petrus Berlage, the revered leader of Dutch modern architecture who had helped introduce Wright to Europe, implicitly confirmed an ideological bond between Wright and European progressives in the search for a modern architecture, while at the same time acknowledging Wright's originality (fig. 84). Commenting on the work of Wright and Sullivan as "the two greatest American architects of our time," he noted, "We Europeans have no reason to regard American architecture as inferior. On the contrary, the best work demonstrates both originality and imagination, and promises much for the future. We should accord it the high estimation that it so richly deserves."[27]

Berlage's theories emanated from a system developed in the 1890s by the young Dutch architects J. H. De Groot, J. L. M. Lauweriks, and K. P. C. De Bazel.[28] Berlage even used their studies as illustrations for his own texts: De Groot's project for a triumphal arch demonstrated quadrature, and the exercises of Lauweriks's students provided further examples. These members of the Dutch modern movement shared with Berlage basic premises: architecture has a significant role in the life of a community; the purification of architecture comes about through the rejection of historical imitation; and modern architecture can be based in a search for eternal laws.[29]

These shared beliefs help explain why the Dutch were generally interested in Wright and why it is not surprising that Wright was called the "Berlage of America" in 1912.[30] Wright did not imitate Berlage or copy his ideas, just as Berlage did not copy Wright's buildings or philosophy. Instead, they shared a basic affinity, which they eventually recognized.

Berlage summarized the principles of the Dutch school and its system of geometry for an American audience when he published a multipart article in the *Western Architect* in 1912.[31] This occurred in the year following his two-month trip to America and the same year of his seminal lectures about Wright in Europe as well as the publication of Wright's *The Japanese Print.*[32] Recalling the rationalism of Viollet-le-Duc and the historic precedents of classical and archaic cultures, Berlage described principles that paralleled the system of Frank Lloyd Wright.

The aesthetic theory of the Dutch system began with the proposition that beauty exists in a building when its elevations develop logically from the ground plan, its masses are in harmony, and its overall structure appears in its parts. The result is a unified whole that conveys a "unity in diversity"—a concept

84. H. P. Berlage at his drafting board (Nederlands Documentatiecentrum voor de Bouwkunst, Amsterdam).

that goes back as far as Greek philosophy. This beauty also exists in universal laws of nature. These laws are not arbitrary because, according to Berlage, "everything is fixed by circumstances and proportions (relations)."[33] In this view both nature and human institutions are subject to laws. Berlage pointed out that stars and planets moved in pure geometric orbits; animals, flowers, and plants had geometrical forms; and crystals had stereometric forms as did lower animals and vegetable orders seen under microscopes.

Reiterating the popular nineteenth-century tenet, Berlage asserted that nature is the fundamental guide to primary form and the source of style free of historical imitation. Wright reiterated the same idea in his theories. The beauty and harmony of nature reside in an inherent order that can be defined by the laws of mathematics. These laws provide an alternative to indulgent personal creation, which, stemming from the individualism of the Renaissance, ultimately leads to decline. A modern culture could be developed by using these laws as guides, with the result that culture could be free of the imitation of the past but tied to tradition at a basic level of aesthetic structure. Berlage stated that if art is to manifest a harmonious relationship between man and the universe, it, too, should be defined by mathematical laws. History, therefore, reveals not a succession of styles but a continuity of mathematical order as the basis for form. Pursuit of these laws as the foundation for a modern architecture makes sense because it is in line with the modern notion of art developing in conjunction with science.[34]

Paralleling Wright's concept that "Geometry is the grammar, so to speak of the form,"[35] Berlage reduced stylization and the problem of style to mean simply:

the creation of form according to geometrical laws. A facade is in truth nothing but an ornamented plane, whilst a building may be composed with a crystal, that is with a rigorously stereometrically constructed whole, or with a composition of different crystals, the deviations of which are determined by peculiar circumstances.[36]

Repeating classical antiquity's ideal of unity in diversity, Berlage pointed out that the practical deviations that arise from particular circumstances create endless opportunities for variety within a definable system. By providing geometric form in crystals, plants, and animals, nature yields up its own spirit, which unites with the "spirit of the Ancients" to create beauty.[37] Spiritual impact is the goal of architecture so that its works are a "styled part of the universe."[38] In Wright's terms, nature, embodied in geometry, shows "that precious something in ourselves which we instinctively know to be life. . . . a proof of the eternal harmony in the nature of a universe too vast and intimate and real for mere intellect to seize."[39]

While nature was the fundamental source of these principles, they were also manifested in the monuments of ancient Greece, the sublime religious architecture of the Gothic style, and the architecture of China, Japan, and Islam—all "children of the same Mother."[40] (For Wright these "children" were the architectures of the Mongolian, Indian, Arab, Egyptian, Greek, and Goth.)[41] According to Berlage, because the laws are universal they can be seen in diverse architectures, such as that of the Greeks and the medieval world, which appear diametrically opposite in their expression. The universality of the mathematical order of nature is further confirmed by its presence in cultures as different as those of the Orient and of the Arab worlds.

In the theory of universal sources, study of ancient, exotic, and primitive architecture revealed proportions and modules of design that could have modern applications. The modules had been explained in standard late-nineteenth-century texts such as Fergusson's *History of Architecture* and by Charles Chipier, who discussed the relationships between architectural proportions and chords in music. The latest investigations of scholars

had also revealed similar proportions in Persian monuments. More fundamental to Judeo-Christian traditions were the citations to systems of proportion found in the Bible, in which the dimensions of Noah's Ark were in the proportions of $1:5:30$. Order was to be found in the ratio of base to height in Egyptian pyramids, which Berlage maintained had a fixed proportion of $5:8$.

Three geometrical relationships dominated the systems that Berlage described: triangulation, the Pythagorean hexagram, and quadrature. The means of making these forms utilized the geometric rules with which both Berlage and Wright designed, providing another link between Wright and the progressive architects of Europe. Berlage presented them as proof of the long tradition of using proportion and number as the basis of design. According to Berlage, scientific investigation revealed that the art of the Middle Ages was based entirely on systems of triangles. Guarded as a secret by masons, triangulation was first used for practical purposes and later took on aesthetic meanings. Fixed proportions were established, which often were the relationship of the height of an equilateral triangle to its base, an irrational nonprime number. To prove his point, Berlage presented analytical drawings of several churches that showed triangulated compositions (fig. 85).[42] He extended such findings in medieval examples to their use as proportional systems in classical architecture. By borrowing their building types from the Romans, even the Renaissance benefited from rules that contained these systems of proportion.

The Pythagorean hexagram, the second geometric relationship, can be seen as the overlapping, in opposite orientations, of two equilateral triangles around a center, or as the addition of equilateral triangles to each side of a regular hexagon. This motif represents the intersection of two identical primary forms, or a six-pointed star. If left by itself, the motif implies a centrally planned object. If multiplied in series, it provides a structure comparable to that underlying the grids of Islamic ornament (figs. 86, 87).

The system of quadrature, which provides the third geometric relationship, evolved from replications of the square and its subdivisions into relationships between the square and the circle. Combining both allows for the definition of squares on the interior or exterior of the original square. The numerical relationships of the areas of circles to the squares and of the squares to the diagonals within them provide the ratios of rational to irrational numbers. Throughout history these relationships fascinated artists, architects, and theorists, who saw in the

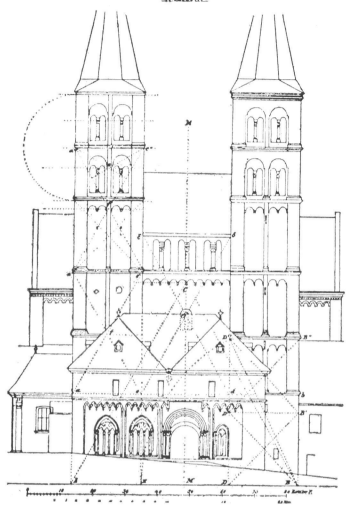

85. "Elevation of Old Church," analytical drawing of facade (*Western Architect* 18, 1912).

86. Hexagonal motif on blue glazed tile with gold paint (from Sarre, *Denkmaler persischer Baukunst*, pl. 59).

relationship of rational to irrational numbers a metaphor for the relationship of the physical to the metaphysical world.[43] Recalling the tradition of squaring the circle, Wright had used a circle within a square as his own signature as early as 1894 at the Winslow House, on the prospectus that announced the opening of his Oak Park studio in 1898, and at the entry of the studio (fig. 88).[44]

Quadrature, like triangulation or the Pythagorean hexagram,

exemplified a systematic approach to design that could be defined by laws. Berlage argued that these laws, which were sanctioned by tradition and nature, still provided the appropriate foundation for modern architecture, and from these laws new forms could be created (figs. 89, 90). As Wright stated in his Wasmuth Introduction, the abstraction of forms by the use of simple laws would be necessary to create "the highly developed forms of our more highly developed life."[45]

According to Berlage, the choice of geometrical relationships is immaterial, but its consistent use is crucial for the details and the whole to obey the same system. With that consistency, unity in diversity is created. The periods of the great styles—those of the Greek and the medieval ages—followed these premises. And the art and architecture of Japan, China, and the Islamic world all used these principles in the pursuit of their distinctive styles. Rather than hinder artists and architects, work with "fixed methods" provided stimulus for the imagination, the possibility of a spiritual impact, and a connection to the "spirit of the ancients."[46] In Wright's words, this connection was crucial because "the indigenous art of a people is their only prophecy and their true artists their school of anointed prophets and

87. Owen Jones, grid showing base for Moorish design (*Grammar of Ornament*, p. 73).

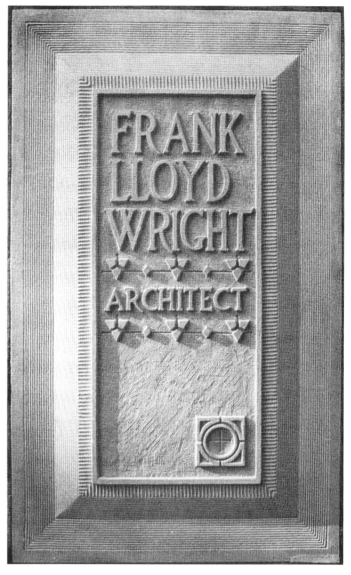

88. Wright's circle in a square signature, lower right, Oak Park Studio, 1898 (Ann Abernathy, photographer).

kings."[47] At the same time, the system provided a more scientific approach to art, called for by modern times.

Like Wright, Berlage relied on the principle that forms could be divided into parts and reunited by logical rules into a whole. The procession of division and reunion required a grid. It allowed for the generation of compositions according to a set of proportions that governed every detail. In Wright's terms, one idea provided the unity of a building so that "the differentiation of a single, certain simple form characterizes the expression of one building."[48] From the simple idea of a form, multiples could be made, with a grid providing a base for organizing the multiples.

Berlage specifically described how to proceed with the Dutch version of the method: divide the ground plan into squares (quadrates) and make a triangular grid, or lattice, for the composition of the elevation. While the grid provided a system for locating squares, it also provided a locus for rotating squares, either simply, from the horizontal to forty-five degrees, or in several rotations to make polygons. Each problem could have what Berlage called a "ground figure"—a basic module of the grid—for an endless number of alternatives.[49] From a few basic forms of geometry, endless solutions would be possible because, for each design problem, the artist could define a separate ground plan and a proportional system emanating from it. Proportions would be the key to a new modern architecture, "for in architecture as well as in organic and inorganic nature, proportions are the daughters of the science of geometry."[50] Proportions would develop from the ground figure of the grid, and, from these proportions, the massing and all ornament

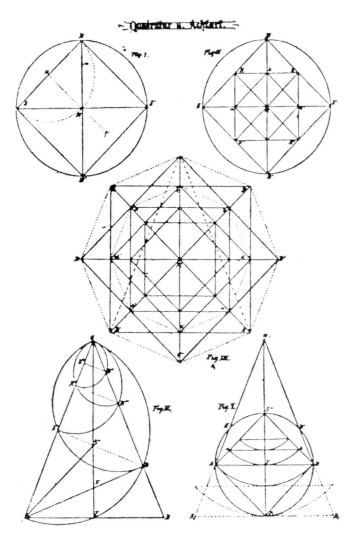

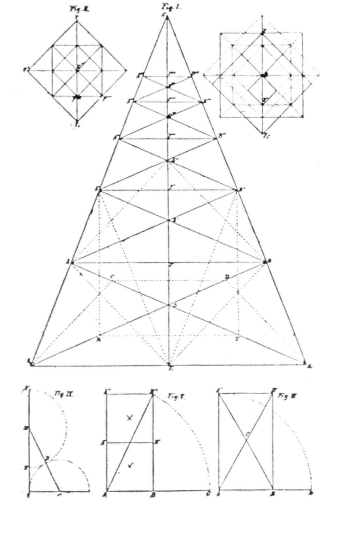

89. H. P. Berlage, diagrams of quadrature (*Western Architect* 18, 1912).

would be derived. Consequently, the same system of lines governs the most abstract conception of the plan and all the details of a building. For the modern architect, these encompass "profilation and decoration," and the design of everything, from furniture, lighting, and carving to painting, in order to achieve harmony.[51] When the architect integrates all aspects of space and form, people "will be able to speak of space-art; only then will the harmony between the whole and the details, the unity in diversity, be reestablished."[52] Berlage published photographs and the designs of the Beurs, his celebrated stock exchange in Amsterdam, as an example (fig. 91). Its facade shows a triangulated grid, the plan a square system (figs. 92, 93).

In his Wasmuth Introduction Wright expressed a similar concept of the unity of architectural form: "In a structure conceived in the organic sense, the ornamentation is conceived in the very ground plan, and is of the very constitution of the structure."[53] For Wright, the concept of ornament should be the same as the concept for a building itself. That concept would be as present in a building's plan as in its details—not added as a visual frill. According to Wright, integration of the concept of ornament into plan and detail produced variety even at the risk of harshness: "Where the warp and woof of the fabric do yield sufficient incident or variety, it is seldom patched on. Tenderness has often to be sacrificed to integrity."[54]

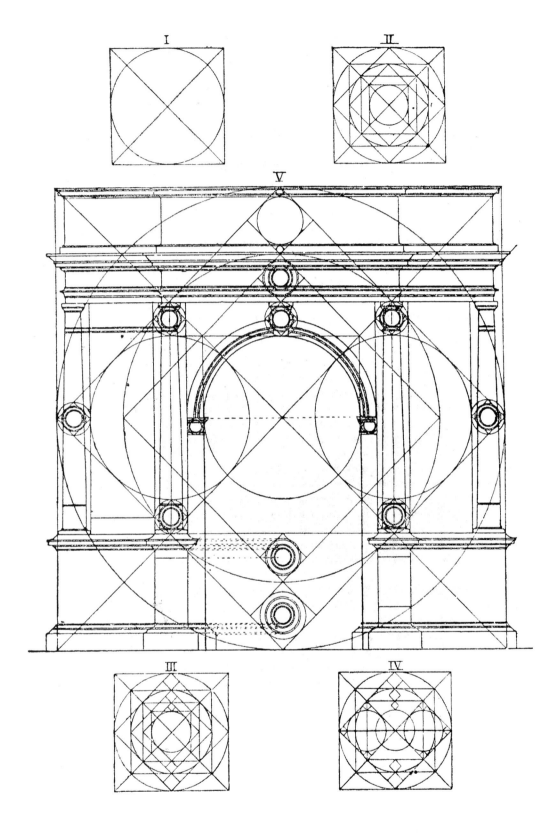

90. J. H. De Groot, design of a triumphal arch using quadrature (*Western Architect* 18, 1912).

91. H. P. Berlage, Beurs, Amsterdam, 1897–1903 (*Western Architect* 18, 1912).

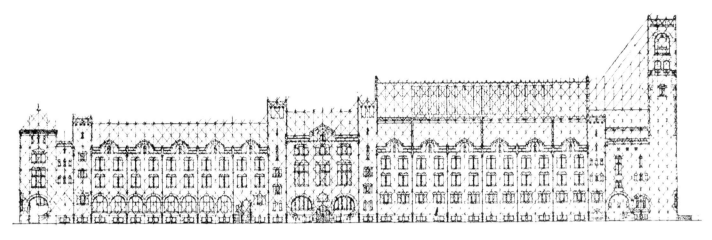

92. H. P. Berlage, grid system, facade, Beurs, Amsterdam (*Western Architect* 18, 1912).

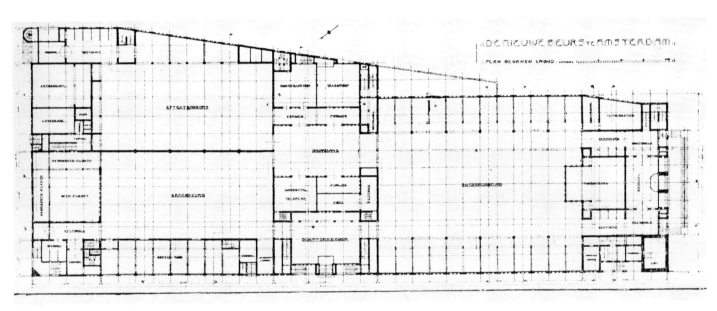

93. H. P. Berlage, grid system, plan, Beurs, Amsterdam (*Western Architect* 18, 1912).

Wright's approach also varied somewhat from the Berlagian system: Wright usually applied square instead of triangular grids for composing his elevations; he used the module of the building material to inform his system of proportion, and he made daring innovations in architectural space. He emphasized in his writings the ethos of "truth to material"—the visual expression of the structural qualities, natural colors and textures, and methods of manufacture. A brick, a stone, a standard length of lumber, or a poured slab of concrete could provide the unit

of proportion. Consequently, the system of units that ruled the plan ruled his facades, making the system even more unified than Berlage's, and having the overall proportional system reflect the dimensions of building materials as they were manufactured (figs. 93, 94).

Despite these differences in their interpretations, Berlage's description of proportional systems paralleled Wright's concept of organic architecture. Both had roots in nineteenth-century thought, particularly the ideas of Viollet-le-Duc. Both

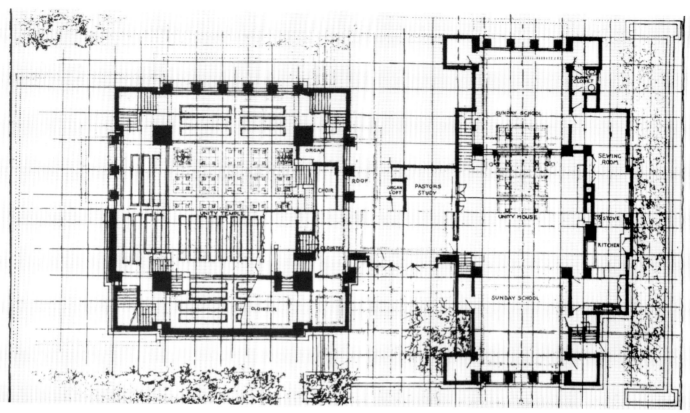

94. Plan for Unity Temple, Oak Park, Illinois, 1904–6 (*Architectural Record* 63, 1928).

95. J. L. M. Lauweriks, grid for design studies (Tummers, *J. L. Mathieu Lauweriks*).

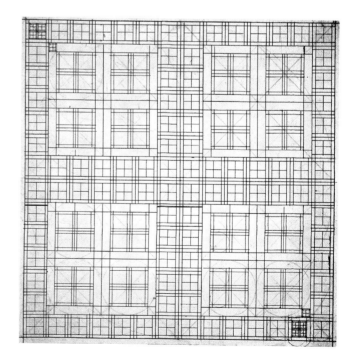

espoused an organicism in which nature and geometry provide mass, proportion, and a system of ornament, allowing unity in diversity. Both believed in the total work of art, a building for which an architect designs all the elements and objects. The desired results of the system proposed by Wright and Berlage would be the harmony and beauty of a truly spatial art in which the design of all objects emanates from a unified system of proportion expressed in simple geometric shapes. Their system would follow a rational process that links design method with logic of structure and materials. The forms of the system would mediate between spiritual and social meanings. In Berlage's terms the result would be a "new community art"; for Wright it would be the conventionalized, democratic architecture of America.

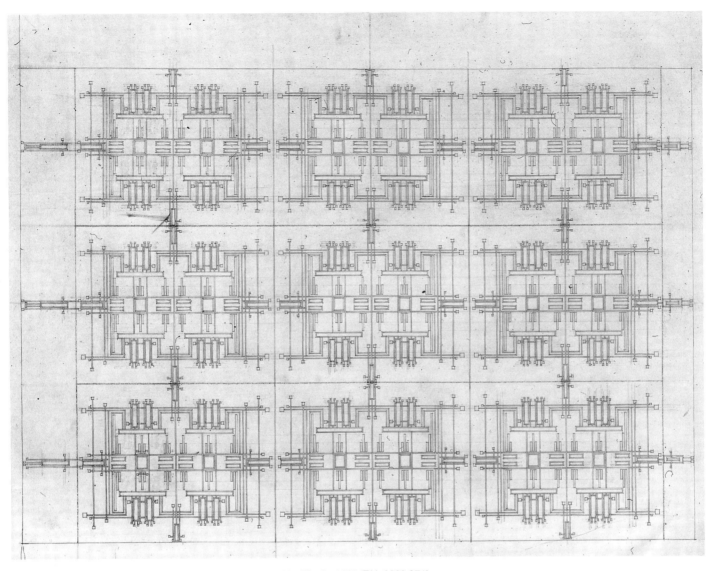

96. Wright's grid for mural design at Coonley House, Riverside, Illinois, 1908 (TAL 0803.071).

Lauweriks and the Spread of the System

Despite the universality of these laws, Berlage felt that they needed to be studied and understood. He warned that knowledge of the science of proportion did not make an artist: "Inartistic persons can do *nothing* with this method—artists *everything*—on condition, however, that they will be its masters, not its slaves."[55] Mastering required learning these principles which had been handed down from generation to generation through apprenticeship and guilds and finally schools.

Lauweriks took the lead as a teacher. In his teaching and his own designs he relied on the use of an underlying grid to provide a matrix for defining forms. Simple rules of geometry—the arithmetic of architecture—allowed for the orderly creation of circles, squares, and triangles, the basic primary forms. By multiplying, adding, and subtracting combinations of these forms, an architect could achieve immense variety (fig. 95).

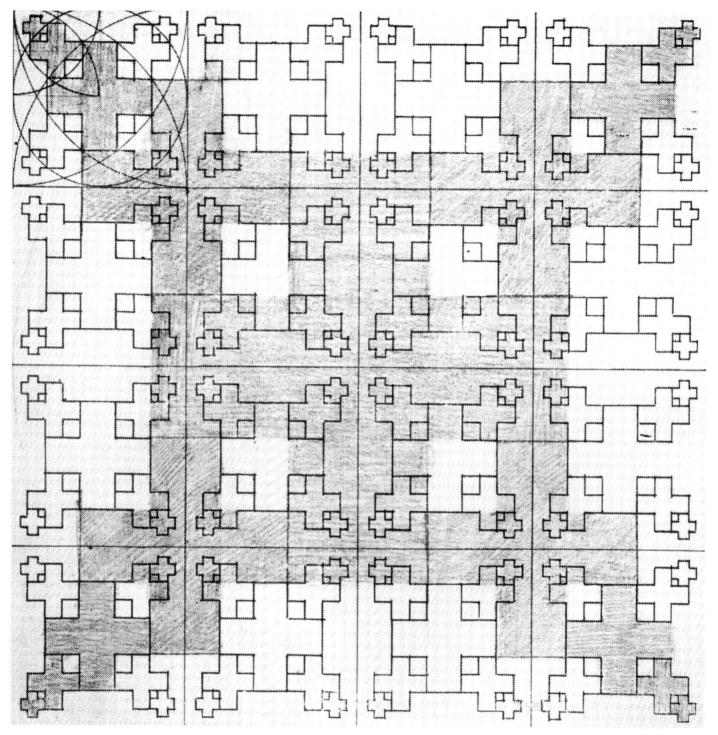

97. J. L. M. Lauweriks, grid for design studies (Tummers, *J. L. Mathieu Lauweriks*).

Wright used a similar system. His wall murals for the Coonley House could have been generated from Lauweriks's grid (fig. 96). The comparison between the two systems is even more striking when Lauweriks's motifs are compared with Wright's. The glass building-blocks that Wright designed for the Luxfer Prism Company in 1897 provide an ideal comparison; one of Wright's forty-one prism designs is nearly identical to the "prisms" produced in the upper left corner of Lauweriks's grid (figs. 97, 98).[56] Both prisms are produced by the same methods of design, using a grid that allows for all the means of composition common to Wright's design process: axiality, replication, addition and subtraction of elements, and rotation.

The Dutch theory of ancient sources as the basis for modern architecture was codified into an educational program that moved to Germany. According to Berlage the spread of the system had started "in Holland, and through Holland's influence in Germany, this principle has been more widely applied."[57] From Berlage and his associates in Holland the system was passed to Peter Behrens in Germany. In 1904 Behrens had just left the Darmstadt commune to head the Düsseldorf arts and crafts school. Behrens, emerging from the shadow cast by Olbrich, used simple geometric shapes, at the height of his Secessionist phase, in the composition of his ornament.[58] He had begun to transform himself into an architect capable of designing a total environment. The unity in diversity offered by the Dutch system apparently appealed to him, and he selected Lauweriks to teach at the school and formally bring the system to Germany.[59] While in Düsseldorf, Lauweriks had the opportunity to reach the youth who were coming under the impact of Behrens, including Adolf Meyer, the future partner of Walter Gropius (fig. 99).

The clarity, rationality, simplicity, and perhaps even the cosmological basis for Lauweriks's system may have stimulated Behrens's advocacy of it as a teaching method. Behrens's interest in the system was immediately reflected in his own work, some of which could be seen in America at the Louisiana Purchase Exposition in St. Louis in the same year he appointed Lauweriks (figs. 7, 69).[60]

The connection between Lauweriks and Behrens exemplifies the complex parallelism of ideas that was evolving between Wright and his European contemporaries. If Wright saw Behrens's work when it was exhibited at the St. Louis Exposition, he would have also seen, in part, the latest Dutch theories that were being emulated in Germany. However, the success of these ideas in Germany was short-lived. The system as it applied to

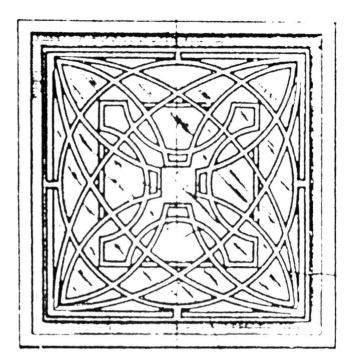

98. Frank Lloyd Wright, Luxfer prism, U.S. patent no. 27, 977 (courtesy of Otto Graf).

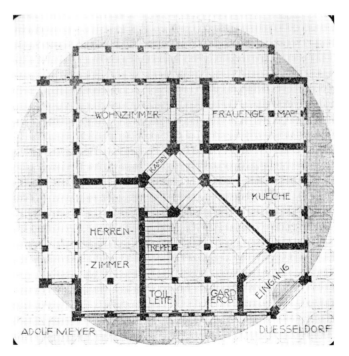

99. Adolf Meyer, plan of a modern house using Lauweriks' design system, (*Western Architect* 18, 1912).

total design, which integrated structure and ornament, soon came to a dead end as the German designers quickly left behind ornament for an emphasis on function.

The ornament of "pure forms" that Wright described as fundamental to his work, however, retained its role as the essential vocabulary of the artists and architects of the Viennese Secession. While Lauweriks had officially brought the system to Germany in 1904, the Dutch had begun as early as the 1890s to open the eyes of Austrian artists and architects to mystical forms, showing their own theosophical associations with the square.[61]

In Europe, Wright witnessed this interest in primitivism and exoticism and the belief in youth as the hope of the future. In both traditional and modern architecture, he saw the potentialities of developing abstract, geometric motifs for powerful symbolic and aesthetic purposes, motifs that surpassed those of his own previous work and the floral abstractions of his mentor, Louis Sullivan.

After his direct experience of Europe, when he saw that the artists of the Secession movements had tapped these sources in their own search for a purity that rejected historical imitation, Wright began new formal experiments in geometry that revitalized his architecture and gave him a powerful set of iconographic symbols. His experiences in Europe also stimulated his own latent interest in primitivism which combined with his ambitions to change society by elevating its culture through art and the education of its youth. In the writings that immediately followed his Introduction to the Wasmuth monograph Wright elaborated his views on primitivism while he transformed the contemporary notion of conventionalization into his own theory of abstraction.

Wright's Theory of Conventionalization

Wright inherited and transformed the concept of conventionalization as it had been frequently used during the nineteenth century.[62] Not only did an English line develop through Jones and Morris but so did a French lineage through Viollet-le-Duc and Victore Ruprich-Robert, whose *Flore Ornamentale* appeared in 1866. Wright's immediate architectural forefathers—H. H. Richardson, Louis Sullivan, J. Lyman Silsbee, and John Wellborn Root—interpreted the ideas of conventionalization from these lineages, and their work formed part of Wright's background. The underlying premise of conventionalization was that the highest form of art was not making something look real

but the representation of it in pure geometric forms. Conventionalization was the means of abstracting nature into its pure geometric forms. Designers of decorative arts and architectural details often used the concept of conventionalization for flat, two-dimensional design; for example, a flower could be conventionalized as a design for textiles. Implied in this design process was the discovery of universal laws. As Owen Jones described the process in proposition 13 of his *Grammar of Ornament*:

Flowers or other natural objects should not be used as ornaments, but [as] conventional representations founded upon them sufficiently suggestive to convey the intended image to the mind, without destroying the unity of the object they are intended to decorate. *Universally obeyed in the best periods of Art, equally violated when Art declines.*[63]

If the laws of structure were universal, then they could be found throughout a variety of cultures, including non-Western or "pagan" cultures, a principal reason that Ruskin condemned conventionalization as leading to "Hindoo depravity."[64] It was this depravity that Wright and others saw as the untainted sources for a rebirth of architecture. Owen Jones suspected that the rebirth of architecture could come about through the transformation of ornament which conventionalization made possible. According to Jones, "a new style of ornament may be produced independently of a new style of architecture; and, moreover, . . . it would be one of the readiest means of arriving at a new style [of architecture]."[65] Jones thought the key would be in finding a new expression of structure—"a new termination to a means of support."[66]

Wright seemed to be the only architect to grasp and fully develop the implications of this idea. While most designers saw conventionalization as a means of abstracting nature into two-dimensional surface designs and ornament, Wright, after his travels in Europe in 1910, differed from his contemporaries in his use of conventionalization by associating a formal aesthetic process with its cultural and social implications. Moving far beyond his mentor, Louis Sullivan, Wright extended the formal implications of conventionalization into three dimensions by seeing that it could link all parts of a building and guide the design development of plan, section, and facade to form an integral whole. Furthermore, Wright associated the simplification resulting from abstraction with a vision of social transformation. The purification of form through conventionalization was analogous to the purification of society through the definition of its essential values. Wright made conventionalization—his version of abstraction—a link between art and society. In doing this he was a quintessential modernist.

After his travels in Europe, Wright saw that the exotic, primitive, and classical worlds—not just forms of nature—incorporated the process of conventionalization. He described this process in the art of the Egyptians and the Greeks in *The Japanese Print:*

Egypt thus knew the lotus, and translated the flower to the dignified stone forms of her architecture. Such was the lotus conventionalized. Greece knew and idealized the acanthus in stone translations. Thus was the acanthus conventionalized.[67]

If the lotus had been merely literally represented—"plucked . . . as it grew"—the translated stone forms would be dead.[68] But the Egyptian artist passed the form along "through a rarefying spiritual process" that transmitted the "natural character" of the form, which gave the lotus permanent meaning. Wright saw this process as analogous to the means by which ancient and oriental civilizations inculcated a sense of order and appreciation of beauty in their citizens:

As the Egyptians took the lotus, the Greek the acanthus, and the Japanese every natural thing on earth, and as we may adapt to our highest use in our own way a natural flower or thing—so civilization must take the natural man to fit him for his place in this great piece of architecture we call the social state.[69]

This sense of "idealized, conventionalized" harmony and the perception of culture would come only to those with the "prophetic artist eye."[70] Literal representation, as embodied in Naturalism, was the "established order"; abstraction, as achieved by conventionalization, was Wright's means of overthrowing it.

Just as conventionalization had distinct implications for two-dimensional design in the nineteenth century, conventionality had a particular usage at the turn of the twentieth century with nuances that have since changed. Berlage implied in his essay on "Art and Community" that the term connoted a generally understood set of beliefs more than conformity to norms. He correlated metaphysics and conventionality:

only a general ideal leads to spiritual harmony, to spiritual organization. Of this all religions give evidence, because a religion without conventionality cannot exist. The reflection of such a spiritual dogma is equally an organized or conventional art, that is, a style.[71]

Berlage reinforced his viewpoint by citing Scheffler, the German art critic who asserted that "All art in so far as she will be a lan-

guage of the soul, has to take recourse in conventionality."[72] Conventionality provided the grounds for an essentialist belief in the spirituality of art and for the existence of style as an inherent quality of objects in contrast to styles as a repertoire of visual representations.

Recognizing that Secessionist artists and their schools in Germany and Austria were interested in conventionalization helped catalyze Wright's formulation of a system of ornament and a process of design that he hoped could express the true character of a culture. Only with simplified abstract forms could the architect provide an architecture that did not replicate the past. The presence of these forms, in turn, provided the ennobling of a culture and the opportunity for social change, or as Wright wrote in *The Japanese Print:*

All the wisdom of science, the cunning of politics, and the prayers of religion can but stand and wait for the revelation—awaiting at the hands of the artist "conventionalization," that free expression of life-principle which shall make our social living beautiful because organically true.[73]

Wright's experiments were no mere exercises in aesthetic indulgence for its own sake, but were an attempt, as part of his espoused theory, to find the true conventionalized forms of a culture. He believed that the discovery of these forms and their representation in architecture could transform the society of that culture and create a harmony between a society's institutions and its individuals. Wright searched for harmony not only in architecture but also in social structures, such as marriage. Just as an individual must find the forms that express his individualism, Wright felt that a people must find the forms that collectively express its cultural identity:

So the indigenous art of a people is their only prophecy and their true artists their school of anointed prophets and kings. . . . Our own art is the only light by which this conventionalizing process we call "civilization" may eventually make its institutions harmonious with the fairest conditions of our individual and social life.[74]

Paradoxically, at the root of indigenous forms is a common symbolic and visual language that unites various peoples into the collectivity of humanity, yet allows for variations that express the differences between cultures. In Wright's terms the search for an appropriate language translates into a quest for the forms that express a democracy. At the same time, this search is an ancient quest that involves questions of the relationship of spirit to matter, the individual to the collective, and the individual to the cosmos.

Among all arts, Japanese art was Wright's ideal model for providing a guide to conventionalized form that represented social values.[75] The Japanese recognized geometry and structure in nature. According to Wright, the Japanese artist was able naturally to grasp the underlying structure of a form, to analyze its geometry, and, by sensing its symbolic meaning, to obtain the "secret of getting to the hidden core of reality" (fig. 100).[76] Wright's conviction of the presence of these underlying structures was confirmed by his own graphic analyses of Japanese wood-block prints.[77] He explained that the beauty of a flower arose:

because in its geometry and in its sensuous qualities it is an embodiment and significant expression of that precious something in ourselves which we instinctively know to be life . . . a proof of the eternal harmony in the nature of a universe too vast and intimate and real for mere intellect to seize.[78]

By structure, he meant "primarily the pure form, an organization in a very definite manner of parts or elements into a larger unity—a vital whole."[79]

Structure, according to Wright, was arranged, fashioned, or grouped to "build" the idea, thus giving an idea its "reasonableness," or rationality.[80] Consequently, from the interdependence of structure and geometry emerged a deep resonant, essential force that Wright called "spell power":

Geometry is the grammar, so to speak of the form. It is its architectural principle. But there is a psychic correlation between the geometry of form and our associated ideas which constitutes its symbolic value. There resides a certain "spell power" in any geometric form which seems more or less a mystery, and is, as we say, the soul of the thing.[81]

Identifying the correlatives of primary forms in geometry, Wright then identified their symbolic meanings: "human ideas, moods, and sentiments—as for instance: the circle, infinity; the triangle, structural unity; the spire, aspiration; the spiral, organic process; and the square, integrity."[82]

Wright's ideas about the spell power of the circle, triangle, square, and spire are necessary to understand his subsequent architectural experiments. Easily attacked for lacking empirical proof, associations of form with metaphysical meaning have nonetheless a long tradition in cultures around the world. Connections of the metaphysical with the physical world had been part of the appeal of Japonism that had such a strong impact on Viennese artists as well as on Wright.[83]

The aesthetics of the Japanese emphasized the essential reality of an underlying structure by "stringent simplification" and "elimination of the insignificant."[84] This process of simplification dramatized the subject and formed the basis of conventionalization:

To dramatize is always to conventionalize; to conventionalize is, in a sense, to simplify; and so these drawings are all conventional patterns subtly geometrical, imbued at the same time with symbolic value, this symbolism honestly built upon a mathematical basis, as the woof of the weave is built upon the warp.[85]

Wright's theory of conventionalizing and simplifying form had significant aesthetic consequences. He related the essence of form that revealed reality's core to Plato's conception of the "eternal idea of the thing."[86] The theory of conventionalization also implied that the rendering of shade and shadow in simplified form—at least in two-dimensional designs—is unnecessary. The great Western tradition of chiaroscuro was, therefore, irrelevant, and three-dimensional surfaces were to be rendered only to show their depth of relief. Color, used as a flat field, could provide "charm," with connotations more of magic than of allure. Color could also serve as "a means of emphasizing and differentiating the forms themselves, at the same time that it is an element of the pattern."[87]

According to Wright, conventionalization is a process that had occurred in literature as well as art. In contrast to the stylized realism of Rossetti, Wright cited the conventionalizing tendency of a prose epic or verse tale by Morris or of Spenser's *Faerie Queene*—examples that reflected Wright's love of myth and the Arthurian mystique.

In its ultimate manifestation the conventionalization of nature expressed a civilization itself, and in elaborating this concept Wright transformed an aesthetic credo into a social program. When an artist conventionalized native forms and traditions, the artist became a political force. Modern people had to find their own true cultural conditions. The artist who conventionalized form would become a giver of laws and social reforms:

Real civilization means for us a right conventionalizing of our original state of nature. Just such conventionalizing as the true artist imposes on natural forms. The law giver and reformer of social customs must have, however, the artist soul, the artist eye in directing this process, if the light of the race is not to go out. So, art is not alone the expression, but in turn must be the great conservator and transmitter of finer sensibilities of a people.[88]

100. Sengai, *The Universe,* Japanese Zen painting (Idemitsu Museum of Art, Tokyo).

Wright stated that for those who could grasp its meaning art was capable of bringing a "coercion to bear upon the material of human conduct."[89] The raw material for these changes lay in the nature of a people as they discovered their native art. People of "primitive" cultures had retained a connection to their native art.

In describing the social force inherent in conventionalization, Wright implied that he saw himself as an anointed prophet or king. He was the artist whose quest for the true forms—"the in-

digenous art"—of America would express the harmony of the individual in society.

Wright's own home, Taliesin, embodied in spirit a mythic past, individuality, and a quest for origins, but in its physical expression it relied on the language of the Prairie school era (fig. 101). In building his home and studio Wright articulated his perception of "indigenous art" by combining the stories of his own Welsh heritage with the old myths of the poet Taliesin while at

101. Taliesin I, Hillside, Wisconsin, 1912.

the same time providing an immediate shelter for himself and Mamah Borthwick.[90] Wright recognized archaic and timeless qualities in the Taliesin myth: "The story of Taliesin, after all, is old: old as the human spirit. These ancient figures were traces of that spirit, left behind in the human process as Time went on its way. . . . But they were only the story within the story: ancient comment on the New."[91]

The saga of Taliesin combines memories of a historical poet of the sixth century with the myths that later grew up around him. The myths focused on the classical concept of the change-ling, a magical being who changes form in response to the occasion and whose domain encompasses all realms of worldly experience. Wright had literary sources for the Taliesin myth. He stated that he had read Lady Charlotte Guest's *Mabinogion*, which collected the Taliesin myth in prose.[92] Guest popularized the literal meaning of Taliesin as the "shining brow" of the poet, and her work generated widespread popular editions.[93] Wright took the literal, popular meaning of the name to describe the site of his home, the "shining brow" of the hill in the valley of his ancestors in Wisconsin.

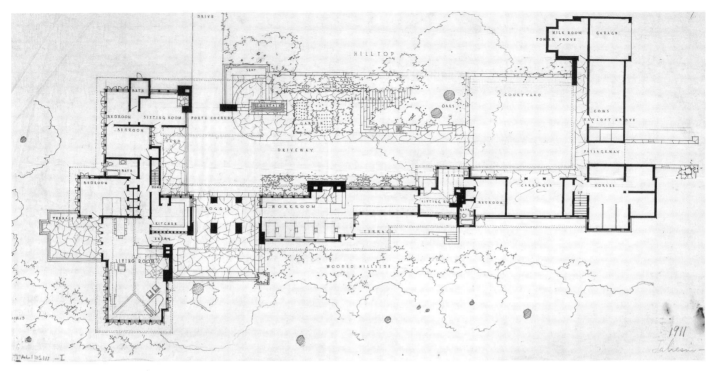

102. Taliesin I, plan, 1912 (TAL 1104.013).

Wright was also probably aware of the association of Taliesin with the political struggle for a Welsh national identity, since a copy of Arthur Granville Bradley's *Owen Glyndwr and the Last Struggle for Welsh Independence* was in the library of Wright's aunts' Hillside Home School.[94] Wright may have associated the historical battles of Welsh warriors, who fought for freedom and were traditionaly celebrated by the poet Taliesin, with his conception of the struggle for a true American architecture.[95]

Equally important to Wright's vision of the Taliesin myth was Richard Hovey's *Taliesin, A Masque,* a copy of which Wright inscribed in February 1908.[96] Hovey's version cast Taliesin, the poet, in the role of the archetypal artist whose personal quest represents a collective need for spiritual salvation.

For Wright, the symbolism of the myth of Taliesin conveyed a meaning of continual transformation that paralleled the dramatic personal change he experienced as his life in Oak Park unraveled around 1910. Like the shape-changing classical figures in the Taliesin myth, he had to transform his way of life as he adapted to personal and professional pressures.[97] His interest in the Taliesin myths with their roots in the artistic visions of Richard Hovey and the nineteenth-century romantic revival of a

Welsh Renaissance was part of Wright's efforts to go back to his own roots, and it coincided with the manifestation of his interest in American Indian, Maya, Japanese, and other non-Western cultures. As an abode derived from the inspiration of myth, Taliesin became archetypal, as bound to the traditions of architecture as it was incorporated into the brow of the hill.

Paradoxically, while Wright sought to express mythic origins at Taliesin, the architectural vocabulary he used adhered conservatively to the medium of his Prairie school period. His materials were stucco and local stone, and his wall and roof articulations, his details, moldings, and ornament were similar to those he had used before he went to Europe. Conservative in expression, these materials recalled the basic and classic traditions of architecture itself.

Only in the plan of Taliesin was there a hint of profound change (fig. 102). Shifting around the edges of the hill, Taliesin contained a new asymmetry that would eventually affect his entire design process. While there are no simplistic correlations between architecture and its symbolic content, it does appear that at Taliesin this shifting asymmetry represented a transformation of the symbols of domestic life. One entered Taliesin into a living room, across which shot a diagonal view towards the windowed corner and the airy sky beyond—the hearth was behind the visitor and off the main axes of the room. If one can judge from the experience of the current version of the living room, a visitor would have felt lofted up over the hill and into the air. This sense of a floating, pure, abstracted nature, a nature beyond the limits of a room, replaced the hearth—the symbol of domesticated family unity—as the focus of the living space at Taliesin. Similarly, in his own life, the unitary vision of family life in Oak Park, with its axial focus on the centralized hearth, had been replaced by a more abstract process of creativity, a search that thrust Wright diagonally off the path of conformity into a quest for new form. It was at Taliesin, his mythic fortress dedicated to artistic change, that Wright sought to develop a vocabulary of originary forms from a series of experiments using primitive and exotic sources.

Wright's interest in primitive sources as a font of social and spiritual renewal was shared by Reverend William Norman Guthrie, his confidant and client and one of the few people with whom Wright communicated while he was in Europe in 1909–10. Guthrie could almost be speaking for Wright in his comments on mysticism and primitivism in his *Offices of Mystical Religion*.[98] According to Guthrie, in modern life incomprehension blocked the path to genius and made efforts at spirit development "useless." Under these conditions, Guthrie asked: "Why not go back to the common primitive and then go forward to recover the psychological realities and the ethnic special emphasis which the creative genius once brought so hopefully into history as a saving enthusiasm and wisdom!"[99] Guthrie's route to origins would take the path that lead to sacred mysteries:

So I go back to Eleusis. I go back further to Mithras; the sunlike man-god who emerged from Persian myths before Zarathustra's time. I strive to understand Adonis, Lord of the Phoenician-Greek world. Or-

pheus carries me from Hellas to Egypt, where I study Osiris, his great Queen Isis, and his son avenger-Horus. Well and good. But the results of all this study are extremely difficult to bring together into contemporaneous context.[100]

Not only did Guthrie identify the font of original forms that fascinated Wright, but he also identified the central problem in their application, the synthesis of archaic and ancient ideas for application to the modern world. The synthesis required the transformation of realistic representations into abstractions, or what Wright called conventionalization.

Guthrie's views about ancient sources of Greece and Egypt paralleled Wright's receptivity to the indigenous forms of other cultures and the art of the primitive and the exotic. This receptivity also provided a bond with his European contemporaries who believed that primitivism contained a purity of form that the modern world could emulate. One of Wright's lessons from Europe, manifested after 1910, was the confirmation of primitivism as a source of modern art. This realization had been stimulated by encountering the creative forces of European artists and architects and recognizing their shared interest in Japonism and other exoticisms. Rather than forming a simple linear progression of influences, these forces combined to make a network of ideas that moved in several directions simultaneously.

Wright and his European colleagues tried to use conventionalization as a means of abstracting form to find a symbolic language that broke with historicism and represented the most idealistic values of a culture. In addition to the Dutch, the artists and architects of the Viennese Secession were Wright's closest collaborators in this search. Their shared sources were to be found in the primary forms of ancient, primitive, and exotic architecture. A "Renaissance-of-the-Primitive" was their goal, a modern spiritual rebirth, with two basic subjects of exploration: the human figure and the primary forms that referred to the origins of human habitation.

As for the conventionalizing of the flesh, it was my suggestion and a thing I have tried to do many times before and long ago—a desire intensified by my visit to Metzner—a desire I worked at with Bock as he knows—a desire which is imperfectly attained in the present figures—an old motif of mine which I suggested to you and helped you by criticism to realize upon—to a certain extent. I am not satisfied yet, however, with that "extent."—Frank Lloyd Wright (1915)[1]

6   A Lesson in Figural Sculpture: "Conventionalizing the Flesh"

With these words to Alfonso Iannelli, his sculptor at Midway Gardens, Frank Lloyd Wright acknowledged meeting Franz Metzner, a leading sculptor in Austria and Germany, and thereby made his only reference to the direct impact of a Secession artist on his work. Metzner's abstracting the figure into cubic geometry was a way of breaking with traditions of realism and recalling the archaic past. In mentioning Metzner, Wright came as close as he could to admitting that a living artist had influenced him, and his words provide a missing connection between Wright and Europe. The link between Wright and Metzner was their desire to "conventionalize" the human figure. For Wright "conventionalization," as he had explained in *The Japanese Print*, was a process of abstracting form which produced a visual expression of the essential values and aspirations of a society. The "conventionalizing of the flesh" was his effort to integrate the human figure into the geometric schema that defined every aspect of his designs. He had attempted this conventionalization in earlier work, as at the Larkin Building, but never fully succeeded. For Wright and Metzner, primary forms were the means of finding archaic origins. The results for both artists were innovative experiments in the geometric representation of the human figure that paralleled cubism as it was just emerging from the work of Braque and Picasso in Paris.

As Wright indicated, the contact with Metzner and his work stimulated a solution to the integration of sculpture and architecture. Indeed, Metzner's work and the work of his former student Emilie Simandl provided the figural types for Wright's own sculpture after 1910. Wright's sculptures at Midway Gardens, built in 1913–14, confirmed the direct link to Vienna and provided a symbolic program that neither the public nor historians have addressed. Part of the expressive power of the sculptures arose from Wright's putting into practice theories that related art and architecture to their roles in society.

The Precursors: Metzner and Simandl

Franz Metzner (1870–1919) was a German sculptor who had strong ties to the Viennese Secession.[2] He was so esteemed that he had his own gallery in the Secession's twentieth exhibition in 1904 (fig. 103).[3] He had taught figure modeling from 1903 to 1906 at the School of Arts and Crafts in Vienna with Josef Hoffmann and Koloman Moser and had worked on Hoffmann's Palais Stoclet in Brussels starting in 1905.[4] When Klimt and the group around him split from the Secession in 1905, Metzner left with them. Wright could have seen Metzner's sculpture published extensively in the *Deutsche Kunst und Dekoration* in 1907 in an article on architect Bruno Schmitz's Haus Rheingold, a restaurant in Berlin filled with dramatic decor.[5] While Metz-

103. Franz Metzner, age 33, at his Vienna residence (Pötzl-Malikova, *Metzner*).

tionalizing the figure, amplifying it, and now and then compressing it into unwonted spaces, but always with a pattern so essentially decorative and touch so sure that one is compelled to recognize his authority."[6] Taft added that, despite the power and variety of Metzner's inventions, "there is no effect of lawlessness, or riotous excess. Bronze and stone and wooden panels are treated according to the demands of the materials and the severe requirements of architecture." In Taft's positive assessment Metzner's artistic strengths involved conventionalization, disciplined invention, and the use of materials in harmony with the nature and the architectural demands of their subjects.

In 1910 Metzner was working on a variety of projects, including conventionalized cubistic figures for the Völkerschlacht monument in Leipzig (fig. 104).[7] Designed by Bruno Schmitz, who had also created a war monument in Indianapolis, the monument in Leipzig commemorated the German victories of October 1813 over Napoleon and his allied forces. In the crypt dedicated to fallen soldiers, Metzner made sculptures of armor-laden soldiers, returning warriors, and colossal figures representing Courage, Religious Faith, Self-Sacrifice and National Strength.[8] For the timeless character these qualities demanded, Metzner went beyond the archaism of the classical world to the ancient cultures of Egypt and Assyria; they provided the monumental scale and sense of solidity required. Paralleling Wright's yearning for a time when the arts were amalgamated, Metzner approached the monument not as a mere imitation of archaic forms but as a creation that recalled the original sources of all art. As a contemporary critic noted about Metzner's work:

We think of the Parthenon, of Assyria, of Egypt and feel at the same time that the apparent archaism of this art is not an artificial imitation of primitive effects, but, a creation arising from the original source of all art, a return to the principles of those times when the individual disciplines were not distinct from one another, but when architecture dictated the style for all.[9]

When visiting Mamah Cheney in Leipzig, Wright could hardly have avoided seeing the huge monument in its final stages of construction. Located on the outskirts of Leipzig, it was dedicated in 1912 and boosted Metzner's fame.[10]

In 1910 Metzner's work was also exhibited at the Berlin Secession and at the Galerie Miethke in Vienna, along with the work of Gustav Klimt. The sculptor maintained an atelier in Berlin-Wilmersdorf, but also spent much time in Vienna. Whether Wright met him in Berlin or Vienna is unclear, but meet him he did, and Metzner's figural sculptures and those of his student Emilie Simandl became sources for Wright.[11]

ner's figures conveyed the pathos of the Wagnerian legend of the Rheingold, the sculptures had sinewy and elongated features and lacked geometric abstraction. Perhaps Wright saw Haus Rheingold when staying in Berlin in late 1909 or early 1910—there is no evidence of a visit to the restaurant—but he would not yet have seen Metzner's geometric style.

Metzner's work was known to the American architects and craftsmen who followed the Continental modes in the first decade of the twentieth century. Some of the interest that Metzner held for Wright can be deduced from the comments of Lorado Taft, sculptor and critic. Taft noted the "weird and strikingly original effects" that Metzner obtained at Haus Rheingold: "He uses the human body as others employ plant forms, conven-

104. Franz Metzner, sculptor, Völkerschlacht monument, view of sculptures in crypt, Leipzig, 1908–13 (Pötzl-Malikova, *Metzner*).

During his visit to Vienna in 1910 Wright could easily have seen Metzner's great figures under the eaves of the Zacherl House, adjacent to the Stephansplatz in the historic center of the city. Jože Plečnik, one of Otto Wagner's most gifted students, had designed the building as an office and residence for the industrial magnate Johannes Zacherl (fig. 105).[12] While trying to break with the Secessionist tendencies inculcated by Wagner, Plečnik still relied, at the Zacherl House, on the use of symbols that referred to ancient sources for a rebirth of art and architecture. The building recalled the numinous qualities associated with ancient Egypt by using a facade sheathed in polished stone, which, in terms of Wagner's ideology, represented the perfection of Egyptian art.[13] Plečnik's rectilinear layout of

the stone pattern, however, created a soaring verticality to the building that he needed to terminate visually. He accomplished this termination and provided a transition from the vertical wall surface to the building cornice by placing Metzner's cubic figures under the eaves.[14] These sculptures were Atlantae, figures of men, like the classical Atlas, used in place of columns to support entablatures. Vienna had several examples of Atlantae bearing heavy loads, the best of which were the works of Fischer Von Ehrlach, the Baroque architect. But Metzner's Atlantae were an innovation in representation.

Except in the case of Rodin and of Georg Minne, sculpture in Europe at the turn of the century had been dominated by repetitive work from the academies. A rupture with this tired

105. Franz Metzner, sculptor; Jože Plečnik, architect, Zacherl House, general view, Vienna, 1905 (*Der Architekt* 12, 1906).

106. Franz Metzner, sculptor, detail of Atlantae, Zacherl House, Vienna, 1905 (*Der Architekt* 12, 1906).

style was made by the Secession sculptors.[15] Max Klinger, whose completion of a monument to Beethoven had been the focus of the fourteenth exhibition of the Secession in 1902, was in the forefront of breaking with academic sculpture. Othmar Schimkowitz made the sculpture at the top of Otto Wagner's Ionic Building in Vienna, where crouching figures hold their hands to their mouths as if crying out to announce the new architecture.[16] Schimkowitz's Nikes, portraying Victory in archaic costumes, are also at the top corners of Wagner's Postal Savings Bank. Collectively, the new sculptors differed from the academics in espousing the idea of renewal and in rejecting the imitation of realistic historical models. Consequently, their work had a more poignant symbolic content than that of their conservative colleagues and with that symbolism came a new search for form.

Metzner was a leader of the new sculptors. He intended to have figural sculptures convey human emotion in ways achieved by few other sculptors, and his abstraction of the human figure into cubistic forms of geometry was totally innovative. His understanding of the need for having one language apply to architecture and sculpture produced his Atlantae figures. He had exhibited them at the twentieth exhibition of the Viennese Secession in 1904. There Metzner showed them in a group surrounding a crouching figure, *Erde* (Earth).[17] Familiar with Metzner's work, Plečnik had the Atlantae cast in pebbledash, the material of Vienna's sidewalk borders, and, around 1906, placed them under the eaves of the Zacherl House (fig. 106).[18] The dark brooding figures had the iconographic function of supporting the eaves of the building on their shoulders, and

Wall," on center with the house's entry (fig. 108).[33] Named after Tennyson's poem about man's metaphysical understanding of God, the figure has been the subject of various interpretations.[34] The sculpture is a female nude that emerges from a crystalline base. In her right hand she holds a fragment which appears to have been part of the abstracted floral form rising in front of her. The abstracted forms are the conventionalized forms of nature. Yet the human figure resists conventionalization by retaining its traditionally modeled realistic features. The figure also retains the normative proportions that had been standards of Western art from the Gothic through the Symbolist movements. Human beings and nature retain a duality. If Wright could resolve this duality with one formal language, then he could symbolize an underlying unity of man and nature—his goal for organic architecture.

The figure at the Dana House had been executed by Richard Bock, a sculptor who had dual traditions and dual allegiances. Born in Germany, he grew up in German neighborhoods of Chicago, and studied in Berlin, as well as at the Ecole des Beaux-Arts in Paris. He generated his own designs for sculpture, and also executed the designs of others, including leading Chicago architects as well as the younger generation associated with the school of the New West. Bock's work with Wright began in the winter of 1897 with his sculptures for Wright's Heller House in Chicago. He became Wright's friend and a member of the group of craftsmen who executed much of the architect's early work.

Bock's sculptures for Wright were loaded with sentimentality. The sculpture under the eaves of the Heller House falls into a saccharine figural style that characterizes much of Bock's work.[35] He derived the design of the sculptures from Wright's own graphic designs of the late 1890s, which display his own adherence to stylizations of the late nineteenth century.[36]

Wright's inability to integrate the human figure into a purely geometric format is clear in the relief panels at the Larkin Company Administration Building in Buffalo.[37] During the construction of the building in 1904, Wright located the relief "Aurora" on the east wall of the annex lobby as part of a program representing the rewards of virtuous labor and the idealistic ambitions of the Larkin Company (fig. 109).[38] A winged Nike with a radiant halo holds a wreath and a globe in outstretched hands in an emblematic representation of the victory of commerce throughout the world. The wings and the body are conventionalized, that is, abstracted into primary geometric shapes of cubes, trapezoids, and rectangles. But the arms and head of the Nike are realistic. The dichotomy between the geometric and

108. Wright and Richard Bock, "Flower in the Crannied Wall," sculpture, Dana House, Springfield, Illinois, 1904 (S).

109. Wright and Richard Bock, "Aurora," relief sculpture, Larkin Building, Buffalo, 1904 (*S*).

110. Nike of Samothrace at upper gallery level of Larkin Building, Buffalo, 1904 (S).

was caught in the academic realism of his training. At the Larkin Building, the putti that appear to support the globes on the massive piers at the front and back of the building were anemic and wispy compared even to any standard chubby sculptures of amorous young boys.[40] Similarly the figures in the relief of the fountain at the Dana House are overwrought with sentimentality.[41] Bock's "John Lloyd Wright as Goldenrod," a free-standing figure of Wright's four-year-old son with butterfly wings, is amusing but static in its symmetrical pose.[42]

Wright's early taste in sculpture was not immune to sentimentality and to an eclecticism that was at odds with his theories of unified design. He had an interest in certain classical sculptures because he could see them as original points of departure. As he observed in the *Japanese Print,* "The Venus, the Victory, classics living in our hearts today, and a long list of noble peers, are true sculpture. But the slavish making of literature has cursed both painter and sculptor."[43] The Venus de Milo and the Nike of Samothrace, classic figures from the fourth century of Greek culture, were syntheses of known types, not imitations. The Nike and other winged sculptures reappeared in several of Wright's interiors, including Brown's Bookstore in Chicago and the upper gallery level of the Larkin Building (fig. 110).[44] Wright was also fond of winged figures on globes, a typical theme in late nineteenth-century academic sculpture; he had one in his Oak Park Studio, and they appear in plates of the Wasmuth folios.[45] He also placed, or allowed to be placed, in other interiors a surprising variety of sculptures, some of which appear trivial in comparison to classical sculptures.[46]

Although he included the sculptures in his early buildings, he also appeared to be ambivalent about them. The inclusion of the naturalistic figure could be awkward by not fitting into his idealized architectural spaces: a large-breasted portrait bust in his Oak Park studio, which was so visible in one of the illustrations in the European edition of the *Sonderheft,* had been painted out by Wright in the American edition (figs. 111, 112). In the American edition he published a photograph showing a small model of Michelangelo's *David* at the Dana House. But in the Wasmuth folio plate traced from the photograph, Wright replaced the figurative sculpture with a conventionalized form, a faceted crystal that resembles the base of the "Flower in the Crannied Wall." The replacement of the realistic forms of figures with the pure forms of geometry seems to confirm Wright's own awareness that the classically modeled figure was at odds with the dominating rectilinear schema of everything else around it.

realistic forms ruins the consistency of the conception and makes the figure appear as if she is inserted into a stiffly starched gown. Wright and Bock's reliefs for the fountains at the exterior entries of the Larkin Building also confront the same formal dilemma as they extol other virtues of labor, freedom, and commerce.[39] Although the costumes of the figures have been conventionalized, their exposed arms and faces remain modeled.

When left on his own to execute independent work, Bock

111. Portrait bust, Wright's Oak Park Studio (*Frank Lloyd Wright, Chicago,* 1911, European edition of the *Sonderheft,* p. 90).

112. Wright's Oak Park Studio, altered illustration (*Frank Lloyd Wright, Ausgeführte Bauten,* American edition, p. 108).

As for the Nike, despite the original's intrinsic beauty, the winged figure was no more integrated into Wright's interiors than any object of academic realism. Wright was not content with the coexistence of realistic human figures and geometric schema of the Renaissance that he had seen in Florence. He was intent on the total design of interiors and exteriors through the use of a single, consistent vocabulary. Classical sculptures must have jarred the consistency of interiors for which every detail from rug to chair to art glass was intended to be composed of the same formal language as floors, walls, and roofs. Wright's tendency after 1910 was to exclude realistic sculpture and to provide his own conventionalized versions of the human figure.[47]

Midway Gardens: Background

Wright's designs for Midway Gardens in Chicago provided the opportunity to correct the incongruity between sculpture and his buildings. In addition, the project was a tribute to the German population in Chicago who traditionally loved beer gardens and music. The project also gave Wright the chance to utilize any visits to European pleasure gardens in his work and to recall his own previous designs for fairs and amusement parks.[48]

The commission for Midway Gardens appeared suddenly in the fall of 1913. Wright's assignment was to design a multipurpose entertainment complex with a winter garden and a summer garden. The location had been the site of the Sans Souci casino and pavilion at the foot of the Columbian Exposition's Midway, a parkway over one hundred feet wide and a mile long that linked two of Chicago's largest parks. The front of the building would be along Cottage Grove Avenue south of 60th Street, with entries at the corners through belvederes. The prime mover behind Midway Gardens was Edward C. Waller, Jr., son of Edward Waller, Wright's friend and client.[49] For the Midway Gar-

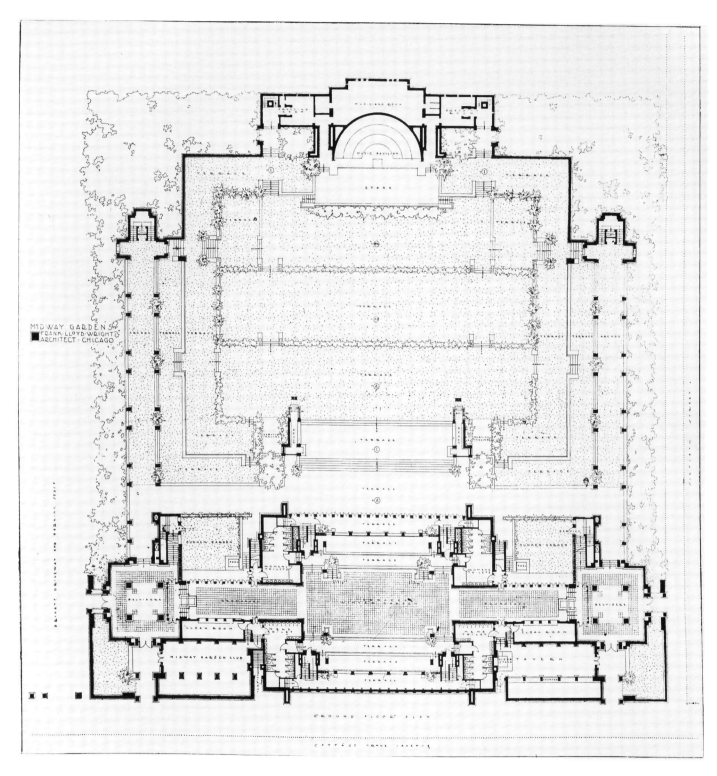

113. Plan of Midway Gardens, Chicago, Illinois, 1913–14 (Wijdeveld, *Life Work*).

dens project the younger Waller enlisted the financial support of Oscar J. Friedman, a Hyde Park florist, and the enthusiasm of Charles H. Matthews, an amateur musician and close friend.[50] Waller was one of the few people, including Wright's mother, Darwin Martin, and William Norman Guthrie, to whom Wright had written while in Europe.[51] The young developer was involved in real estate, and felt that to counter the barrenness of Chicago's "wilderness of smoky dens, car-tracks, and saloons," the citizens needed a handsome garden resort where they could congregate, listen to good music, eat, and dance.[52] Waller had in mind an outdoor garden—a summer garden—similar to the small parks around Munich where German families enjoyed themselves. Matthews, who had studied conducting in Germany and Austria, suggested a German concert garden.[53] To make the operation financially successful, a winter garden was proposed as a hall for dancing and dining. The enterprise would feature sophisticated music and entertainment year-round, with a full orchestra in the summer garden alternating with a dance band in the winter garden. The presence of a bar would make the venture "surefire as to money," but local proponents of prohibition later put a damper on drinking.[54]

With receipt of the commission, Wright's "spirits soared."[55] According to his son John, one day Wright entered his Chicago office and within an hour drew on one sheet of paper all the plans, sections, elevations, and perspectives necessary for the development of the design. Although this drawing does not seem to have survived, the story indicates that Wright conceived of the design totally in his imagination, forming the interior and exterior spaces in relationship to the building's program.[56] Drawings in Wright's archive show, however, that there were various studies that preceded this impressive feat witnessed by his son.[57]

The program for the Gardens provided a context for Wright's experiments in conventionalization. A unique mix of highbrow and popular attractions provided the justification for Wright to abstract forms into symbolic representations of a rich American culture. The space for activities included a casino, concert hall, formal dining area, private club, and outdoor pavilions for sophisticated music lovers and high society, and informal dining and a public bar for less fancy tastes, all with a background of dance music or serious classical concerts.[58] For all these activities a large complex measuring three hundred feet square was required, for which Wright settled on a symmetrical scheme consisting of a main pavilion connecting with wings to an open summer garden (figs. 28, 113). The main pavilion contained the winter garden with its three-story hall, a private club, and a tavern (fig. 114). Diners could eat on the balconies that surrounded the hall and dance on the main floor. For outside eating and dancing, the framing wings of the summer garden contained five levels of terraces. Dining and musical performances could occur simultaneously as concertgoers could proceed to sit directly in front of the bandshell. Located opposite the restaurant of the winter garden and across from the summer garden, the bandshell was separated from diners, dancers, and listeners by a narrow pool.

The interior and exterior areas flowed into each other so smoothly from winter garden to summer garden that a visitor could almost dance from one to the other. Space flowed up as well as out: visitors could walk onto the roofs, which were turned into terraces and gardens, and observe the spectacle below them.

Beset with financial and labor problems, construction of the project was both frantic and exhilarating, but Midway Gardens became for Wright a subject of delight and fantasy that he described at uncharacteristic length in his *Autobiography*.[59] According to Wright, the color, light, music, and movement required for this festive environment were to be found through judicious use of the tales of the *Arabian Nights:* "Aladdin and his wonderful lamp had fascinated me as a boy. But by now I knew the enchanting young Arabian was really just a symbol for creative desire, his lamp intended for another symbol—imagination."[60]

Wright described himself as Aladdin, Edward Waller, Jr., as the genie, and a host of others as "the slaves of the lamp."[61] Principal among these were Paul F. P. Mueller, the contractor who had built Wright's other major projects, Wright's son John, who acted as site supervisor, and Alfonso Iannelli, a young sculptor who had studied with Gutzon Borglum.[62] Lloyd and John Wright had met the sculptor in California earlier in 1913 and brought him to the attention of their father.[63] Additional "slaves" included Richard Bock, who prepared reliefs for the four corner stair-towers in the winter garden, and Ezio Orlandi, who made the molds and castings of Wright's and Iannelli's sculpture.[64]

Iannelli's first direct contact with the work of Frank Lloyd Wright came in September 1913 when John Wright asked Iannelli to design figural reliefs to go under the eaves of the Coonley Playhouse.[65] In February 1914, with Midway Gardens under construction, John asked Iannelli in Los Angeles to come to Chicago for two to three months to work on the models of

114. View of interior, winter garden, Midway Gardens, 1914 (TAL 1401.039).

sculpture for the "concert garden"; the completion deadline was now 10 June 1914.[66] Iannelli headed to Chicago and by late May 1914, when he had engaged Orlandi to cast the sculpture and ornament, work proceeded.[67] The concrete work was done at the site in a plant supervised by Iannelli. Nearly a hundred figures and many hundreds of panels were required.[68] These sculptures represented a summation of Wright's three-dimensional exploration of the human figure that was never surpassed in his subsequent work.

The Sculpture at Midway

The concrete sculptures at Midway have been referred to generally as Sprites, but there were varieties of Sprites, and Wright actually named the sculptures according to their physical and symbolic attributes. In addition to Sprites he designed with Iannelli relief and free-standing sculptures named Cube, Octagon, Triangle, Sphere, and Totem Pole. Demonstrating his theories

of conventionalization, Wright could experiment with the sculpture's ability to contain the "spell power" of geometry and to represent the social and cultural program embodied at Midway Gardens.

Wright's program focused on the mixing of high and popular culture. To accomplish this mix, Midway Gardens had to be more than a beer garden and become a place of refinement, music, art, and pleasure. Revealing once again his belief in the didactic power of architecture, Wright hoped to make Chicagoans more sophisticated by experiencing an environment that integrated the arts. Commenting on his intentions for his designs at Midway, Wright noted in his *Autobiography:*

Fortunately, human beings are really childlike in the best sense when directly appealed to by simple, strong forms and pure, bright color. Chicago was not sophisticated. Chicago was still unspoiled. So probably all this could go straight to the Chicago heart if it would.

Meantime the straight line, square, triangle and circle I had learned to play with in Kindergarten were set to work in this developing sense

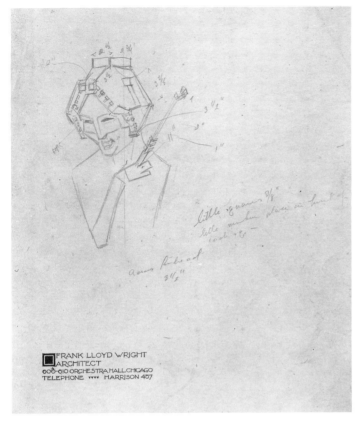

115. Sketch, female Sprite, Midway Gardens, 1914 (TAL 1401.074).

116. "Maiden of the Mud" (Sprite), Midway Gardens, 1914.

of abstraction, by now my habit, to characterize the architecture, painting and sculpture of Midway Gardens.[69]

Sculpture played a principal role in this program. And Wright knew precisely the appropriate symbols to present the required iconography—the sculpture he had seen in Europe in 1910. Moving far beyond the moralistic paternalism of the Larkin sculptures, Wright's sculptures now served the joyful program of the Gardens and also, like Midway Gardens itself, symbolized, with their platonic solids, the essential attributes of architecture, painting, and sculpture. The unity of the arts at Midway Gardens was analogous to the sculptural program at the Kunstschau, which represented the unity of arts in the figures of painting, sculpture, and architecture.

At the same time that Wright's sculptures were the symbols of the Gardens, they had deeper and more universal meanings recalling Wright's symbolic interpretations in which the circle stood for infinity, the triangle for structural unity, the square

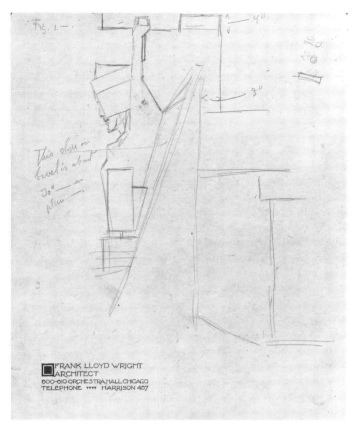

117. Sketch for Winged Sprite, Midway Gardens, 1914 (TAL. 1401.075).

for integrity.[70] To these Wright added associations of primal female and male forces. Wright's desire to associate the geometry of the sculptures with symbolic qualities was literally confirmed when he later explained to Iannelli:

They [the sketches] were practically as above—each figure holding aloft the form characterized with little of [sic] similar forms, rising in some cases, depending in others. The square and octagon masculine—the sphere and triangle feminine—each figure to partake in treatment of the form characterized?[71]

The early sketches to which Wright referred showed the characteristics of each figure in two dimensions. One sketch was of a female holding an object in her right hand (fig. 115). This sketch was conventionalized through a series of drawings into a prismatic treatment of the entire figure that resulted in dimensioned drawings for modeling. Maquettes, or study models, were made, and then full-size models were made for casting.[72] This figure became a Sprite with a smiling face of slanted features (probably designed by Iannelli), a downward inclined

118. Winged Sprite with cube over head, Midway Gardens, 1914.

and turned head, crossed arms, and scepter (fig. 116). This Sprite was called the Maiden of the Mud—an ungeometric, but appropriately amusing name—who, after installation in the Gardens, surveyed the writhing crowds dancing below her.

The second early sketch was for the Winged Sprite that held a cube over its head (fig. 117).[73] The sketch of the Winged Sprite was conventionalized into a full frontal figure with geometricized wings, given precise dimensions and cast in multiples (fig. 118).[74] This figure, as we will see, was loaded with iconographic meaning.

The large number of other Sprites resembled the Maiden of the Mud but had more solemn faces and no scepters (fig. 119).[75] After casting, the Maiden of the Mud, the Winged Sprite, and the other Sprites were located throughout the Gardens where their silhouettes often articulated the skyline or flanked important features of the building.[76]

Other sculptures represented attributes of geometry to which Wright had attached symbolic and metaphysical meanings. Cube was a conventionalized figure who held his attribute, tilted at an angle, in his right hand (fig. 120). The inclined head of the figure gives an impression that, in examining the cube he holds, he contemplates not only his name but geometry itself.

Octagon, another conventionalized male figure, similarly contemplates his own attribute transformed into a three-dimensional polyhedron (fig. 121).[77] He appears to study the faceted polyhedron in his left arm and the faceted, spherical forms that emanate from it. He rises out of a base of polyhedra of different sizes. After casting, he was placed in the hall of the winter garden.

The figure Triangle was the least symmetrical of the conventionalized sculptures, and it shows more of Iannelli's intervention (fig. 122).[78] Here the triangle is translated into a pyramid's three dimensions. The faceted female figure holds a large version of her attribute in her right hand, a smaller one in her left, and is flanked by stacks of pyramids.

The one anomaly in this program of conventionalized sculpture is the figure Sphere (fig. 123). She also seems to have been more Iannelli's creation than Wright's, with Iannelli signing a sketch for the design in March 1914.[79] The sinewy figure was the only sculpture to resist conventionalization, a fact that proved ironic, since the model for the sculpture later became John Lloyd Wright's wife. Nevertheless, a comparison of the majority of the Midway sculptures with Wright's earlier sculpture shows the total geometrization of the figure that had eluded him before his travels to Europe.

119. Sprite with solemn face, Midway Gardens, 1914.

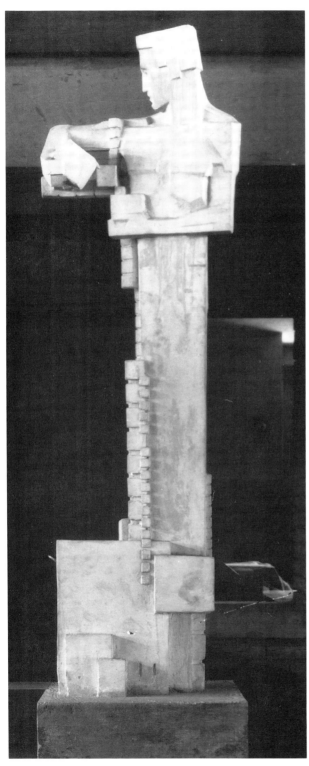

120. "Cube" in winter garden, Midway Gardens, 1914.

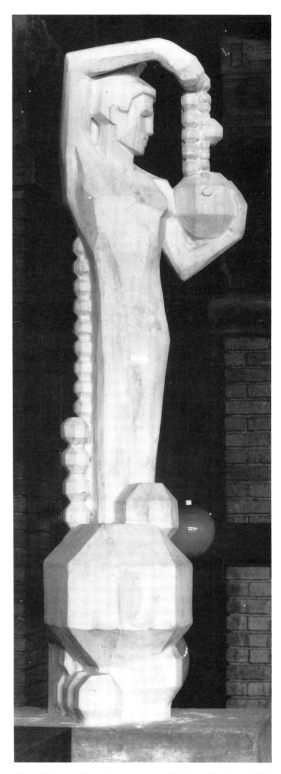

121. "Octagon" in winter garden, Midway Gardens, 1914.

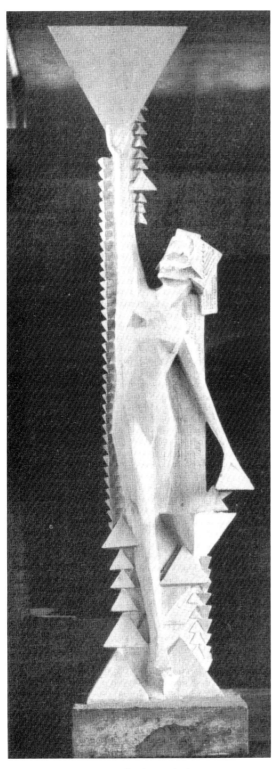

122. "Triangle," Midway Gardens, 1914.

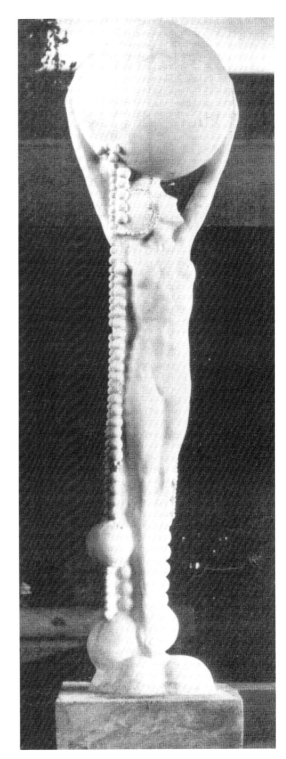

123. "Sphere," Midway Gardens, 1914 (*International Studio* 55, 1915).

124. "Totem Pole" in summer garden, Midway Gardens, 1914.

Wright also designed composite figures. He created Totem Pole, a figure that relied on symbolic geometry and attributes generally associated with American Indians. The sculpture consisted of a figure attached to a vertically projecting shaft that served as a lighting fixture (fig. 124).[80] Using attributes of Cube and a Sprite, Wright conventionalized the shaft into alternating squares of blue and gold with smaller squares of white and orange, interspersed along the length of the front side of Totem Pole. Light bulbs were inserted into the rear face of the shaft, and it was used prominently in the summer garden along with other geometric light fixtures of Wright's design.

Altogether, the attributes of the Midway sculptures could be related directly to the program of the Gardens, providing themes appropriate to laughter, dancing, music, eating, the visual splendor and fun of the Gardens.[81] With Totem Pole, Wright symbolized the theme of fruition and plenty through the use of a geometricized cornucopia, transforming the traditional meaning of a totem pole as a symbol of family lineage. In the figure's hands were two overflowing cubic containers, holding "fruits," which were painted red, orange, blue, black, and white.[82] The result was the creation of a figure of Plenty, an iconographic symbol. This delight in the fruits of life recalled the "joy of living" that Wright had seen as a goal of art.

But the program of sculpture had another iconographic purpose as well: embodied in the symbolism of geometry, the sculpure can also be seen to comment on the making of architecture itself. By making his sculptures the physical manifestation of "spell power," Wright translated into three dimensions the two-dimensional primary forms of circle, square, and triangle. He reiterated the themes of these three shapes by drawing on one of his development sketches a circle, triangle, and square.[83] Wright's sculptures—Cube, Octagon, Triangle, and to a lesser degree, Sphere—appear to contemplate platonic forms of geometry itself—the same forms from which architecture is constructed.

The sculptures at Midway Gardens therefore resonate with many associations. In this context, the Maiden of the Mud with her scepter represents not only a Bacchanalian overseer but also the presence of a magic, numinous force that activates the elements of geometry. She could both cast spells over the joy-seeking visitors of the Midway Gardens and animate the life of form itself. The Sprites share in this duality of delight and seriousness. While Sprites can be seen as playful, at times their posture appears votive, adding a solemn dimension that places them in a long tradition of frontal figural representations of the

125. Solemn Sprite with crossed arms, Midway Gardens, 1914.

126. *Mater Dolorosa,* thirteenth Century, height 129 centimeters (Hispanic Society of America, D90).

127. Winged Sprite with cube, Midway Gardens, 1914.

female with crossed arms (fig. 125). These range from the Mater Dolorosa of the thirteenth century to figures with crossed arms on sepulchers (fig. 126).

In a symbolic interpretation of the sculpture, the Winged Sprite holding the iconic cube over its head becomes the representation of the art of architecture itself (fig. 127). In the design of both Emilie Simandl's sculpture "Architecture" at the Kunst-

schau and Wright's sculpture at Midway Gardens the cube is a platonic iconographic symbol—a "primary form"—associated with architecture. Wright's Winged Sprite also recalls Atlas, the bearer of the heavens, and the central figure on the tomb of Michelangelo at Santa Croce in Florence (fig. 128).[84] Within the context of his own development, Wright's sculpture is the fulfillment of his first use of the human figure with a square held

128. Vasari, designer, with collaborating artists, tomb of Michelangelo, Santa Croce, Florence, 1570 (La Basilica di Santa Croce).

over the figure's head—his graphic design on the title page of *The House Beautiful* of 1896.[85] There, the traditional representation of the body and the platonic shape exist as two different worlds. At Midway Gardens, eighteen years later, body and conceptual realization are part of the same world.

With the realization of these conventionalized sculptures Wright could now jettison all Nikes and winged academic sculptures. He had found a means for conventionalizing every part of the sculpture with results that can be compared with Simandl's sculpture at the Kunstschau Pavilion (figs. 129, 130). Here was a direct link that confirmed one of Europe's lessons.

Not only can the figure of the Winged Sprite be seen as the representation of architecture but also as the symbol of the architect, the bringer of geometry. And Midway, as Wright de-

129. Emilie Simandl, "Architecture," Kunstschau
Pavilion, Vienna, 1908 (*Der Architekt* 14, 1908).

scribed it, became a place of the architect's mastery: "Here in
Midway Gardens painting and sculpture were to be bidden
again to their original offices in architecture, where they belonged. The architect, himself, was here again master of them
all together making no secret of it whatever."[86] This symbolic
purpose recalled the role of the American architect as creator
and poet for his country. At Midway Gardens, Wright privately
acknowledged this exalted role of the architect by providing a
special outside viewing box. Perhaps it was just another place to
sit for visitors, but for Wright it was the place from which the
architect—the master of form and poet-priest of a new society—could view the events transpiring in the summer garden.[87]

The Reception of Conventionalization
at Midway Gardens

For Frank Lloyd Wright, Midway Gardens had been a major
opportunity to evoke "spell power" in physical form. The Gardens officially opened, unfinished, on 27 June 1914, the day before Archduke Franz Ferdinand of Austria was assassinated,
precipitating World War I.[88] Although in September John Lloyd
Wright wrote Iannelli in Los Angeles that work at Midway Gar-

dens was "practically complete," in actuality the work was never
finished according to Wright's designs.[89] The reception by public and critics gives some indication of how effective he had
been in his experiments in conventionalization.

Wright said in his *Autobiography* that the whole environment was a magical synthesis of the essential qualities found in
the pure sources of architecture, which connected Egypt, the
Maya, and Japan:

In a scene unforgettable to all who attended, the architectural scheme
and color, form, light and sound had come alive. Thousands of beauti-
fully dressed women and tuxedoed men thronged the scene. And this
scene came upon the beholders as a magic spell. All there moved and
spoke as if in a dream. They believed it must be one. Yes, Chicago mar-
veled, acclaimed, approved. And Chicago came back and did the same,
marveling again and again and again. To many it was all Egyptian. Mayan to some, very Japanese to others.[90]

Overall, the furniture, sculpture, and reliefs at Midway Gardens were examples of Wright's most successful efforts to create
a total work of art that represented the true culture of America.
Ironically, the distinguishing features of this expression of American culture arose from the multiplicity of its exotic and oriental associations, just as the identity of America is defined by its
multiple races and ethnic groups. By providing this distinct iconography with his ornament, Wright hoped to elevate the so-
phistication of ordinary citizens, to educate them and to delight
them at the same time.

Favorable local reception of Midway Gardens first appeared
in a reporter's account just prior to the opening.[91] He lauded
Wright for having the courage to design such a building and
praised the clients for having the courage to risk spending the
money involved. To the anonymous visitor the Gardens was
"the finest thing of the kind in this country at least, if not in
Europe to boot," a place appropriate to the best of music and
dance, a place destined for success.[92]

The innovative use of concrete in the construction of Midway Gardens was not lost on the building industry. The trade
journal *Rock Products and Building Materials* extolled the opportunities of using concrete as a decorative material and alerted
cement-block manufacturers and concrete workers to the extraordinary potential for industry of the new craft.[93] The author
of the journal article pointed out that the Gardens in concept
were modeled after "gardens of Germany and other Continental
European countries," but its architecture is "purely and originally American."[94]

The artistic issues presented by Midway Gardens were ad-

130. Sprite, Midway Gardens, 1914.

dressed in Henry Blackman Sell's review, "Interpretation, Not Style," in the *International Studio*.[95] According to Sell, the Gardens brought together for the first time in many years art, architecture, painting, and sculpture from the same mind. The delight and fun emanating from this unity of the arts also raised for a discerning critic some pressing questions: how to create "Style" in architecture instead of selecting from among already existing styles, and how to appropriately represent contemporary life in art and architecture.

The critic deduced these issues directly from Wright's most recent installment of "In the Cause of Architecture," which appeared in the *Architectural Record* in 1914.[96] Providing insight into the theories that supported Wright's work at the Gardens, Sell relayed to the public the architect's views that style is the external manifestation of an inner order that makes ornament; and ornament, for Wright, embodied the conception of a design—"decoration" is only an aspect of style.[97] As reported by Sell, Wright believed that style was an expression of the spirit of the age, signified by "the machine," combined with the best traditions of architecture.[98]

In Wright's opinion, the linking of style to representation had been stimulated by cubist art in the Armory Show that had traveled from New York and been seen in Chicago from March through April of 1913.[99] Including among its art three works by Braque and eight by Picasso, the show had caused a furor.[100] Sell recounted that a local art critic had asked Wright, "Hasn't your work rather cubistic sympathies?" Wright replied, "What do you mean by 'cubistic?' If you refer to the fact that the work is a form of natural design rather than natural imitation, I might plead guilty."[101] Wright explained that natural design was an interpretation of nature that avoided the imitations historically central to realism. Not only was the core of realism an imitation that often missed the essence of things, the architectural imagery of realism had traditionally been classical architecture. Realism, then, took on the same inimical role as classical architecture, which in its latest manifestation in America, was inhibiting what Wright considered the development of an independent American architecture. "Natural design" was design codified by conventionalization, the "expression of spirit in terms of pure design." Conventionalization required discovering a "new" nature that united culture and its appropriate forms through processes of abstraction. Wright was searching for a release from the old idea of the imitation of nature, from the moribund icons of classicism, and from the realism associated with it. Natural design—the abstraction of form into geometry in a manner analogous to the order of nature—contained in its essence universal elements of human experience. At Midway Gardens, Wright explained, he had searched for "elemental chords of harmony in line, in colour or in modulation of surfaces."[102] These "chords" produced subtle patterns which, in turn, induced in those who experienced them a sympathy with eternal forces, "the joys and sorrows of all ages."[103] Ultimately, in Wright's new work, the old order of realism yielded.[104]

Sell's article in the *International Studio* was the direct catalyst for the unpleasant dispute between Wright and Iannelli over their respective roles in designing the Midway sculptures.[105] Wright received credit for the entire design, with the exception of a polychrome mural above the cigarette counter, designed and executed by his son John. The Sprites were identified as "designed by Frank Lloyd Wright, executed by A. Janelli," an affront to Iannelli, whose name was not only misspelled but who was demoted from artist to mere craftsman, while he, in fact, had collaborated on the designs of most of the sculptures. It was during the effort to resolve the disagreement that Wright made clear his intentions behind the Midway sculptures and their direct links to the proto-cubist experiments of Franz Metzner.

In May 1915, Iannelli objected to his role being publicly cited as that of "a mere executive."[106] He claimed that he had achieved for the first time "an idea never before accomplished . . . that is, the usage of architectural form through the human figure . . . and which offers the only solution to the problem of the adaptability of sculpture to architecture, where one is the outgrowth of the other."[107]

Wright could not accept this presumption on Iannelli's part and replied by asking if Iannelli recalled the thumbnail sketches he had made at Taliesin and brought to Chicago. Wright then mentioned his efforts in the "conventionalizing of the flesh . . . a desire intensified by my visit to Metzner" (Appendix B).[108] Wright maintained that he did not intend to omit Iannelli's con-

tribution, and he admitted that if Iannelli had not executed the sculptures as well as he had, the work would have been "not so sympathetic in detail or so successful in expression."[109] From Wright's point of view the proper attribution was, "the ideas are mine—their 'expression' yours," with Wright identified as architect and Iannelli as sculptor, and that the matter should be of no interest to anyone but themselves.[110] Wright continued to protest, however; to claim "that the scheme and nature of the sculpture at the Midway is yours and not mine is as astonishing to me as it is absurd."[111]

While the architect and sculptor argued and the public thrilled to the music of Max Bendix and, later, the dancing of Anna Pavlova, the financial condition of the Gardens steadily deteriorated. Midway Gardens had lacked sufficient capital at the outset, and its owners were never able to pay its construction costs. The building went into receivership in 1916, starting a decline that eventually culminated with its being completely torn down in 1929.[112]

Despite the dispute with Iannelli and the eventual destruction of the Gardens, Wright had launched a new representation of the human figure. His sculptures were integral elements in the most extensive and imaginative public building that he had achieved up to that time. In his first major public building after he came back from Europe, he had made a triumphant return to architecture after a series of personal scandals. Entering his primitivist phase, he had begun to transform the formal language that he shared with the Secessionists into his own symbolic vocabulary. For Wright, abstracting the human figure had been an obvious means of finding the ancient roots of form. Abstracting nonfigural forms that represent the origins of culture became at the same time an equally challenging and rich subject for his experiments. This lesson of Europe and its subsequent developments preoccupied Wright for the rest of the decade.

Italy was indebted to Greece, Greece to Egypt and Egypt to—? As a consequence of all this procession, see how the beam that bore the poet-builder's message to humanity down the ages has been short circuited by modern science. But only for the time being—until the true significance of the mother-art comes again clear.—Frank Lloyd Wright (1957)[1]

7 A Lesson in Primary Forms

For Frank Lloyd Wright, the great lineage of architecture that extended from prehistory to Egypt, Greece, and Italy had been temporarily halted. The spiritual message transmitted by architects—the "poet-builders" of society—was no longer conveyed to humanity. When Wright returned from Europe in 1910, he believed, however, that architecture's true significance could be conveyed once again through a purified language of form, a view Wright shared with his progressive European contemporaries. As we saw earlier, in Wright's theoretical writings the forms of this language were the circle, square, and triangle, to which Wright attributed meanings of infinity, integrity, and structural unity. Because these motifs could symbolize timeless values, Wright saw them as the visual correlative to moral principles.

Conventionalization—Wright's theory of abstraction—applied both to Wright's architecture and to his social program. He associated social mores with a purified expression of art. A people could tap their fundamental values by going back to their native roots through a process of simplification—all that was false would be cast off, and the pure, basic values of society would remain. In the America of Emersonian and Whitmanesque ideas that Wright inherited, these values would be individualism, the pursuit of private liberty coupled with a responsibility for the collective good, and a rebellion against conformity. Wright had attempted with Mamah Borthwick to define a set of modern mores, based on love-marriage and progressive education, and to disseminate them through the writings of

Ellen Key. His Wasmuth publications were a summation of his previous efforts to find an uplifting democratic American architecture. The reduction of social principles to their basic values paralleled an abstraction of architecture into its basic shapes, stripped of superfluous historical additions. As he described it, reform of the social structure was dependant on conventionalization. In Wright's view, society required conventionalized forms in order to express its own values:

All the wisdom of science, and cunning of politics and the prayers of religion can but stand and wait for the revelation—awaiting at the hands of the artist['s] "conventionalization," that free expression of life-principle which shall make our social living beautiful because organically true.[2]

While Wright was learning how to conventionalize the human figure, he began to explore another lesson of Europe: abstracting the symbols of human habitation itself in a search for the purified architectural vocabulary of a true American architecture. Wright had written in his Wasmuth Introduction of 1910 that his preceding work had not fully lived up to his expectations in revitalizing architecture. He explained that although his designs had style, repose, unity of idea, and simplicity, they had, in his opinion, the shortcoming of not being "highly developed in detail."[3] This shortcoming came about because of "self-imposed limitations" and a "lack of intricate enrichment."[4] For Wright "developed detail" and "enrichment" implied the full exploration of the inherent qualities of a design

153

in which every part was abstracted and made an integral part of the whole, with nothing extraneous added and nothing literally imitative of nature.

Wright's perception of his shortcomings centered on the problem of defining an appropriate language of ornament for the modern industrial world. He hoped that conventionalization would create that appropriate language. He called the new ornament "Machine Age Ornament" because it would be produced by and responsive to the processes of industrial production.[5] The making of this new ornament would involve an ongoing search for an expression of the meaningful symbolic forms of a culture and for the technology that produces those forms.

During his Prairie Style period, Wright had used the square, the circle, and the polygon as the basis of his work. He created them by the simple manipulation of his drawing tools—compass, straight edge, and triangle. Wright had given an essential view of his concept of Euclidean geometry prior to his departure for Europe when he replied to Russell Sturgis, the critic who found the Larkin Building's "bare, square forms . . . so impossible."

I confess to a love for a clean arras; the cube I find comforting; the sphere inspiring. In the opposition of the circle and the square I find motives for architectural themes with all the sentiment of Shakespeare's "Romeo and Juliet": combining these with the octagon I find sufficient materials for symphonic development. I can marry these forms in various ways without adulterating them, but I love them pure, strong, and undefiled. The ellipse I despise; and so do I despise all perverted, equivocal versions of these pure forms.[6]

Until 1910, Wright used geometric forms statically in symmetrical arrangements. He appended one form to another when he designed, and his skillful use of the square in his plans had been a factor in his successful and distinctive architectural practice. Wright, felt, however, before he left for Europe that his work in general had become fatigued: "The absorbing, consuming phase of my experience as an architect ended about 1909. I had almost reached my fortieth year. Weary, I was losing grip on my work and even my interest in it."[7]

After Wright's European experiences in 1909–10, he developed a system of creating ornament with a rich formal complexity that had not previously been central to his work. No revolution in Wright's work occurred, as it had around 1900 when he codified the distinct expression of the Prairie Style period, but his experiences in Europe helped catalyze a series of experimental designs that focused on the development of his

ornament. He incorporated motifs using circles, square within squares, and triangles, that reinvigorated his use of geometry in addition to integrating sculpture more successfully into his architecture than ever before.

The language of the new system of ornament would paradoxically rely on the most ancient systems of basic forms to which architecture had traditionally been indebted for its ornament. As Wright, Berlage, and the Vienna Secessionists had claimed, these conventionalized forms were to be found in the ornament of primitive, exotic, folk, and vernacular cultures. The ornament of these cultures provided the unitary modules required in theories of primitivism to actualize ancient, but still valid, systems of proportion.

The visual representation of the origins of culture was the set of "pure" forms of the circle, square, and triangle noted by Wright. They are so basic that we can call them "primary." Recurring in the earliest artifacts of human creation, primary forms had provided the basic patterns of ornament common to the art and architecture of diverse exotic and primitive cultures. In Western European traditions the use of primary forms had been a basic part of the unwritten legacy in art and architecture that had been passed from master to apprentice until the end of the nineteenth century.[8]

A plate from *Japanische Motive für Flächenverzierung,* a reference source in Wright's library, shows how ornament can be dissected into primary forms. In "Spade Pattern with Hishi Flowers" the "spade pattern" consists of a figure (which here contains a flower) that can be graphically reduced to the tangential intersection of four circles; the ground of the motif is a circle inscribed from the mid-point between points of tangency (fig. 131). The points of tangency also define an implied square that is rotated about its regular axis. In effect, the structure of the motif contains a basic relationship between the circle and square. This provides the repeatable unit of the pattern that consists of a circle with the overlapped portions of four other circles. The entire field of the pattern is made by multiplying the units into a series of overlapping circles. Reversing the process of this analysis describes the rudimentary means by which the ornament was made.

The unit of a circle with overlapped circles and the series of these motifs found in the spade pattern provide one example of a pattern that exists in various cultures; it can be seen in ancient Egyptian designs as well as in Wright's own Luxfer prism designs (figs. 132, 98).[9] Otto Graf has demonstrated the persistence of the motif of the circle with overlapping circles from the

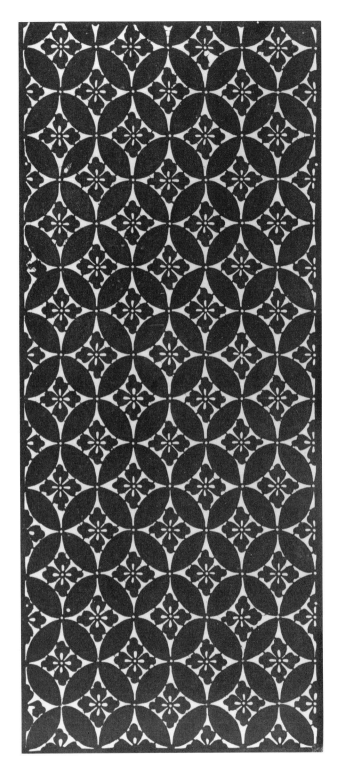 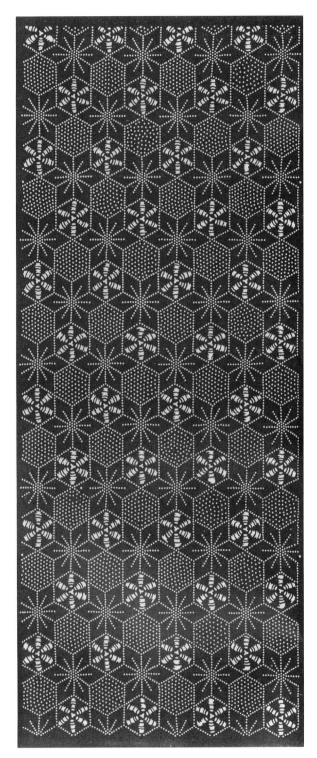

131. Spade pattern with Hishi flowers (*left*), star pattern with snow flowers (*right*) (Friedrich Deneken,
Japanische Motive für Flächenverzierung, pl. 80).

132. Egyptian ornament no. 7, "Circle of Isis" at upper right (Owen Jones, *Grammar of Ornament,* pl. X).

earliest evidence at the ancient site of Çatal Hüyük in Mesopotamia (c. 6500 B.C.E.) to the art of many cultures worldwide.[10] He calls the motif the Circle of Isis because he identifies it with Egyptian representations of the disk of the sun that the goddess Isis holds over her head.[11] A family of forms can be generated from this motif, and Graf attempts to derive from it basic, recurrent forms of architecture and art, from the individual column and the plan of temples to Wright's own architecture. The motif is significant because, instead of being merely a decoration applied to a surface, it is a basic pattern with a historical legacy that has contemporary application (figs. 133, 134). It was the kind of generative idea that Wright, the school of Berlage, and the school of Wagner believed could generate the total work of art. Designing with a motif that governs plan and detail allows the integration of ornament and architecture.

The Circle of Isis—the structure of overlapping circles—is only one motif that emanated from the origins of civilization. In addition to the primary forms of the circle, square, and triangle, several basic formal motifs are made through geometric rotations: the circle within a square, one square within another square, and circles overlapping around a central point. As we

133. Byzantine ornament, "Circle of Isis" on lower left of plate (August Racinet, *L'ornement polychrome*, pl. XXXIII).

134. Franz and Hubert Gessner, interior with "Circle of Isis" motif in project for buildings of the First Lower Austrian Worker Cooperative Union, Vienna (*Hohe Warte* II, 1905–6).

saw in Berlage's theory, the circle within a square can be subdivided to form polygons, the square within a square can be rotated and replicated to create a series of squares within squares, and overlapping circles can be grouped around centers or rolled out in linear arrangements (fig. 135).

The rotated square is formed by drawing a circle from the center of the square with a radius extending from the center to the corner (fig. 135, Ia). The projection of perpendicular lines from the center of the square through the midpoints of the sides determines the location of the corners of a second square. When these points are connected, a rotated square appears (fig. 135, Ib).[12] The rotations of a square form the tradition of quadrature—the processes of making squares or determining areas—which has often been associated with Greek theory and medieval and Gothic architectural practice. But such uses of the square go back to Neolithic times.

The rotation of the square also provides the means of making another primary form, the square within a square (fig. 135 Va). This motif is formed when a second square is rotated within the first square so that its sides are parallel to those of the first square. The process can be repeated indefinitely so that a series of squares appears, one within another, with each square having one-half the area of the previous square. The effect of the series is analogous to the layering of planes, one within another (fig. 135 VIa,b). In this version the primary form can be called a *multiple frame,* and the planes of the frame can be seen as layers. All these circumscriptions, rotations, and superimpositions seem to proceed in a rational, orderly way, just as nature, according to Wright, Berlage, and their colleagues, is orderly and rational.

The shared interest in these motifs provided one of the fundamental bonds between Wright and his small circle of European colleagues. Underlying their common beliefs was a shared language of forms: Wright, Otto Wagner (the leading architectural mentor in Vienna), and the Secessionists used the same formal vocabulary. In exploring these motifs in their own work they sought to associate an idealized purity found in the origins of culture with a new, modern life.

During the early formation and development of Wright's architecture for the New West, a school had formed under Otto Wagner in Vienna that attempted to break with the historicism of the nineteenth century and its architecture of styles. The break that Wagner led came through synthesizing the architectural traditions of the square, circle, and triangle into a burst of innovative and imaginative design solutions. This synthesis be-

gan after 1894, when Wagner became professor at the Vienna Academy of Fine Arts, peaked within ten years and then gradually declined. Unlike Lauweriks, who codified a system of composition but had limited success in the realizations of his own designs, Wagner and his students used their version of the system with dramatic aesthetic results.

Wagner's earliest buildings, which still used the motifs of Renaissance architecture, had underlying their traditional ornament primary forms that relied on the simplification found in ancient sources. The apartment house he designed on the Schottenring in 1877 had the pure forms of triangles in its facade, on the paving tiles of its floors, and in the simplified black-and-white color schemes that Wagner knew from Japanese designs exhibited at the World Exposition in Vienna of 1873.[13] As Wagner dissolved his learned vocabulary of classical forms into the floral style of the 1880s and early 1890s, the motifs of the square and triangle became accentuated. The floral style coincided with the establishment of the Vienna Secession in 1897, with primary forms becoming dominant motifs. In the austere and abstract phase of Wagner's work that began in the early 1900s, primary forms became the exclusive language of his architecture.

After Wright's encounter with Secessionist art and architecture in Europe, a rejuvenation occurred in his work that can be seen by comparing his work before and after his experience in Europe. The complex design programs at Midway Gardens and the Imperial Hotel confirm that after he returned from Europe his ornament reached a degree of development that he had never before achieved. While he developed his ornament, he attempted the difficult feat of having architecture represent both his vision of the true values for modern society and his ideas about the true forms for architecture—those that referred to the origins of culture itself.

Wright and the Secessionists apparently associated primary forms with symbols derived from sacred architecture. They associated a purity of origin with these symbols because the symbols, arising at the beginnings of civilization, were not imitations of previous forms. Wright and his colleagues reasoned that, if artists and architects designed with primordial and primitive forms, they would have the purity for which they were searching—true expression was their goal. This search was a basic aspect of the development of modernism in which artists attempted to correlate spiritual issues with physical forms.[14] Were these unsubstantiated, romantic associations a yearning for a long-vanished idyllic past, or did they have a basis in fact?

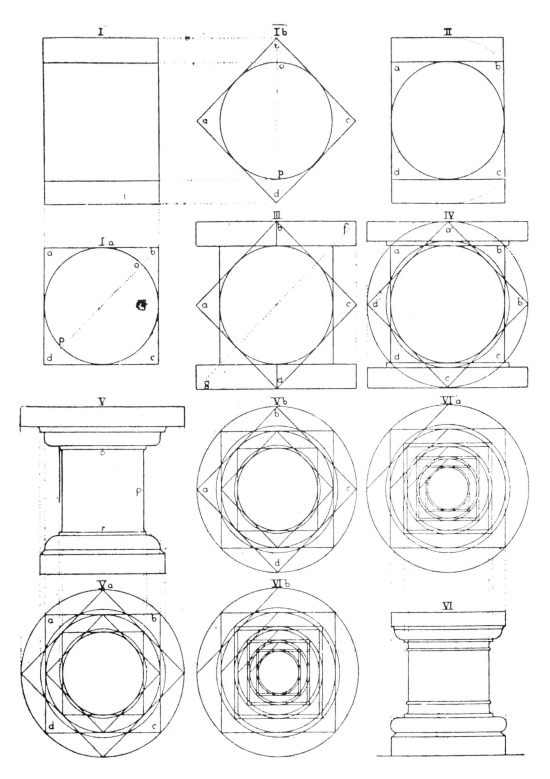

135. H. P. Berlage, systematic construction using circle and square (*Western Architect* 18, 1912).

136. Circular stone foundations of tombs (tholoi), Arpachiyah, TT 7–10 (*Iraq* 2, part 1, 1935).

137. Fragment, Eye Temple sanctuary, Brak, Syria, Uruk and Jamdat Nasr period (*Iraq* 9, 1947).

To explore this question it is necessary to consider the modern archaeological evidence of primary forms, their diversity and near universality, how they can be associated with the origins of human habitation, and finally how Wright and the Secessionists attempted to represent them in a modern language of form.

The Circle

Instead of being the rectilinear house of trees, described as the "primitive hut" of classical theory, the first habitation, beyond the cave, may have been in the shape of a circle, as seen in the stone foundations for tombs at Arpachiyah in present-day Iraq (fig. 136).[15] The layout of a circular dwelling plan was simple: the desired area could outlined by a compass consisting of a string or sinew and a fixed point. Circular objects could be made from cut sections of cylinders of rolled clay. Circular imprints could be made by sticks and stones and even the human heel, when rotated on the ground.

Besides providing floor plans, circles in Neolithic buildings were used as symbols. The circle played a role in cult worship, symbolizing the eye in a frieze with gold bands at the Eye Temple sanctuary at Brak, in Syria (fig. 137).[16] Hundreds of idols with pierced eye-circles were deposited within the temple, yet the practices there remain mysteries. Circles were also used as poly-chromed cones imbedded in the walls of the sanctuary between niches to form diamond-shaped patterns.[17] On the inner facade of the Column Hall at Uruk, the Sumerian city on the Euphrates, cone patterns were combined congruently with the other motifs of the temple, the triangle and the recessed panel.[18] In a use that confirms it as a sacred symbol, the circle was identified with the sun-god, Shamash, as seen in neo-Sumerian stele (fig. 138).

Circles appear in the earliest art of Egypt in the seventh millennium B.C.E.[19] The Egyptians combined the disk of the sun-god with their own conventionalization of the scarab beetle and the ball of dung it rolled. Symbolizing the sun god Khepera, this motif of the scarab with the flat disk found widespread use as a talisman, ornament, and symbol of resurrection on mummies.

The circle had a long and diverse legacy as a symbolic form in art. In Western traditions its use as an animating motif can be seen richly developed at Hadrian's Villa (fig. 139). The circle was a primary form for work of fine mosaic inlay, as seen in the interlocking motif, or *guilloche*, for a cathedral ambo at Ravello that dates from 1272 (fig. 140). Both the circle and the guilloche were still part of the repertory of standard Beaux-Arts architecture as seen in the Petit Palais, which Wright visited on his Paris trip in 1910 (figs. 141, 142). In the work of the Viennese Secession artists the circle became a primary form of importance, particularly as a two-dimensional motif for graphic designs and artifacts.[20] Its straightforward use ranged from craft objects of the Wiener Werkstätte, to the ornamental pattern of a heating grill, to a portion of the interior of the Secession Building itself (figs. 143–144).

Before 1910, Frank Lloyd Wright's use of geometry made the "Circle of Isis" inherent in his design process (fig. 145). But he did not exploit the motif as an ornament, and he often suppressed the circle as a major building element, preferring to use the square and octagon in his designs. He used half-circles in ground plans largely as secondary features, such as the driveways and gardens seen at the Coonley House, the Darwin D. Martin House, and the William E. Martin House. The semicircle appeared as bays at the Winslow House, in a breakfast nook of the Dana House, and as the plan of porches at the Tomek

138. Stele of sun god Shamash, Susa, late 3d millennium B.C.E., excavated 1898; collection, Louvre (*Encyclopédie photographique*).

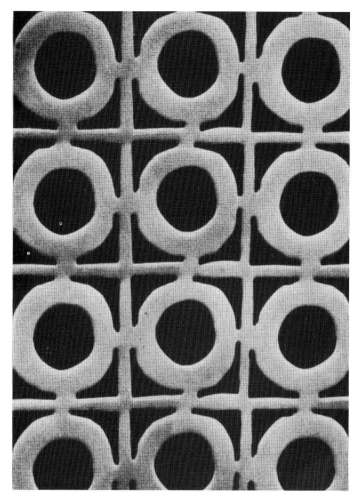

143. Richard Riemerschmid, heating grill (*Moderne Bauformen* 10, 1911).

power such forms contain. After Wright used circles at the Coonley Playhouse in 1912, he made the circle a major motif the following year at the Midway Gardens. He included the circle as balloons in perspective drawings, and he used it in his cabaret murals, where it could suggest the bubbles in sparkling drinks.[22] In the mural that surrounded the cigar stand, Wright showed how effectively he could use the circle and an underlying grid to integrate structure and geometry (fig. 146). In the mural, circles appear to be floating, with some circles passing above or beneath others.[23] Where circles overlap, the color of the overlaps is altered, implying the translucence and the interaction of different hues. This floating effect of lightness and randomness is countered, however, by a carefully and rigidly controlled grid (fig. 147). The random rhythm of the floating circles contrasts with the rhythms of the grid itself—an "aesthetic skeleton," as Wright described the function of geometry.[24] The result is a highly disciplined and rational order that lies hidden beneath images that appear free and floating.[25]

The visual dynamism of the composition arises from the underlying tension between control and apparent randomness. This pair of mural drawings provides an example of how the "reasonableness" of structure—Wright's term for rationality that he articulated in *The Japanese Print*—allows for the emergence of the "spell power" of geometry.[26] The spell power of the circle at Midway Gardens can be seen to represent the delight, gaiety, and pleasure Wright hoped people would experience there.

House. Wright used partial circles as arched entries at the Devin House and as an arch over the fireplace at the Heller House. The exceptions to using circles and semicircles for secondary features occurred when Wright made them the plan forms for the Municipal Boat House for Lake Mendota, near Madison, Wisconsin (1893), and for the projected amusement parks at Wolf Lake, Indiana (1895)—an imaginative integration of water, galleries, and festivities—and at the Cheltenham Beach Resort (1899).[21]

After his return from Europe, Wright began to make the circle the subject of his ornament. This development occurred after he saw the ornamental and symbolic uses of the circle in the hands of the artists of the Secession. The motif of the circle fit into the context of Wright's ideas of pure form and the spell

The Square

Archaeological evidence of the origins of the square extends back at least to the plans of the dwellings and artifacts at Çatal Hüyük of the sixth and seventh millenniums (fig. 148). Like other primary forms, the square has tectonic and symbolic meanings. Egyptian monuments indicate a long legacy in temple architecture in which the square could be considered an element in a grid used for the construction of rectilinear plans and even figural sculpture.[27] Use of the square allowed for the systematic repetition of a module in design and construction. Symbolic associations with the square are found in a variety of cultures. The square has been symbolically associated with quaternity—four elements, four seasons, four stages of life, four points of the compass, all of which are brought into relationships of order and stability. In Japan, ancient Greece, and in Christian theology it was seen as a symbol of earth. In Chinese

138. Stele of sun god Shamash, Susa, late 3d millennium B.C.E., excavated 1898; collection, Louvre (*Encyclopédie photographique*).

139. Hadrian's Villa, Tivoli,
A.D. 125–135 (author).

140. Guilloche pattern on the
Ambo, San Pantaleone Cathedral,
executed by Nicola da Foggia,
Ravello, 1272 (author).

141. Luxfer prism, Petit Palais,
Charles Girault, architect, Paris,
1900 (author).

142. Guilloche pattern on
floor, Petit Palais, Charles Girault
architect, Paris, 1900 (author).

143. Richard Riemerschmid, heating grill (*Moderne Bauformen* 10, 1911).

House. Wright used partial circles as arched entries at the Devin House and as an arch over the fireplace at the Heller House. The exceptions to using circles and semicircles for secondary features occurred when Wright made them the plan forms for the Municipal Boat House for Lake Mendota, near Madison, Wisconsin (1893), and for the projected amusement parks at Wolf Lake, Indiana (1895)—an imaginative integration of water, galleries, and festivities—and at the Cheltenham Beach Resort (1899).[21]

After his return from Europe, Wright began to make the circle the subject of his ornament. This development occurred after he saw the ornamental and symbolic uses of the circle in the hands of the artists of the Secession. The motif of the circle fit into the context of Wright's ideas of pure form and the spell power such forms contain. After Wright used circles at the Coonley Playhouse in 1912, he made the circle a major motif the following year at the Midway Gardens. He included the circle as balloons in perspective drawings, and he used it in his cabaret murals, where it could suggest the bubbles in sparkling drinks.[22] In the mural that surrounded the cigar stand, Wright showed how effectively he could use the circle and an underlying grid to integrate structure and geometry (fig. 146). In the mural, circles appear to be floating, with some circles passing above or beneath others.[23] Where circles overlap, the color of the overlaps is altered, implying the translucence and the interaction of different hues. This floating effect of lightness and randomness is countered, however, by a carefully and rigidly controlled grid (fig. 147). The random rhythm of the floating circles contrasts with the rhythms of the grid itself—an "aesthetic skeleton," as Wright described the function of geometry.[24] The result is a highly disciplined and rational order that lies hidden beneath images that appear free and floating.[25]

The visual dynamism of the composition arises from the underlying tension between control and apparent randomness. This pair of mural drawings provides an example of how the "reasonableness" of structure—Wright's term for rationality that he articulated in *The Japanese Print*—allows for the emergence of the "spell power" of geometry.[26] The spell power of the circle at Midway Gardens can be seen to represent the delight, gaiety, and pleasure Wright hoped people would experience there.

The Square

Archaeological evidence of the origins of the square extends back at least to the plans of the dwellings and artifacts at Çatal Hüyük of the sixth and seventh millenniums (fig. 148). Like other primary forms, the square has tectonic and symbolic meanings. Egyptian monuments indicate a long legacy in temple architecture in which the square could be considered an element in a grid used for the construction of rectilinear plans and even figural sculpture.[27] Use of the square allowed for the systematic repetition of a module in design and construction. Symbolic associations with the square are found in a variety of cultures. The square has been symbolically associated with quaternity—four elements, four seasons, four stages of life, four points of the compass, all of which are brought into relationships of order and stability. In Japan, ancient Greece, and in Christian theology it was seen as a symbol of earth. In Chinese

144. Joseph Maria Olbrich, interior, Secession Building, Vienna, 1899 (*Catalogue 10th Exhibition of the Vienna Secession,* 1899).

and Hindu traditions the square was associated with the earth and the feminine character, in contrast to the masculine character of the circle and triangle. In Egyptian hieroglyphs the square signified achievement; the square-shaped spiral, materialized energy.[28]

Used on everything from building surfaces to craft objects, the square became a signature of the Secession. Josef Hoffmann was so closely associated with the square that he was nicknamed "Quadratl Hoffmann."[29] It was a principal motif for the craft objects of the Wiener Werkstätte, which Hoffmann directed. Other architects and artists used the square as an articulating motif and translated it into a cube (fig. 149). Koloman Moser, the brilliant graphic artist, made the square a central motif of many of his designs, particularly in the pages of *Ver Sacrum,* the artistic and literary journal that heralded a sacred spring of cultural renewal. The journal's pages suddenly ex-

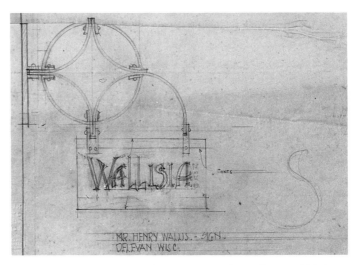

145. Sign for the Henry Wallis Gatehouse, with Circle of Isis motif, Lake Delevan, Wisconsin, 1901 (TAL 0109.001).

plode with the motif beginning in 1902 in the borders of advertisements (fig. 150).[30] Olbrich used the square at the Secession Building in Vienna. There, its "unity" provided great "diversity" as a compositional element available for division and subdivision, for example, in the building's windows. The square was also the articulating motif of the ornamental bands on the surface of Olbrich's own house in Darmstadt. In his Secessionist phase, Behrens employed the motif to articulate buildings and utilitarian objects.

By the time he completed the Wasmuth folios, Wright had begun using the square exclusively as his signature or monogram; his earlier use of the square as a signature was rare, and the circle and cross inscribed in a square became imbedded in the building fabric itself.[31] He also had it embossed onto the

146. Mural surrounding the cigar stand, Midway Gardens, 1914 (Wijdeweld, *Life Work*).

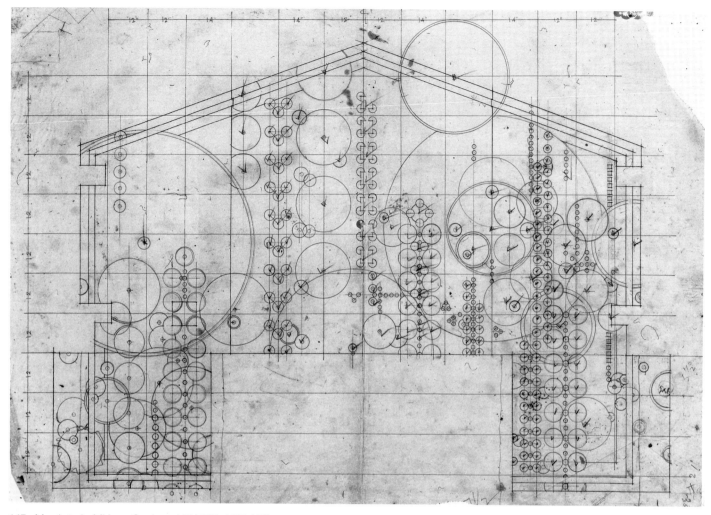

147. Mural study, Midway Gardens, 1914 (TAL 1401.115).

folio plates of his Wasmuth monograph. He soon signed the drawings for the Coonley Kindergarten with the square.[32] Later, Wright even re-signed drawings made before 1910 with the square signature.[33]

Although the Wasmuth folios show that the square was the most prominent compositional element of Wright's building plans until 1910, after that time he used the square and its rotated permutations increasingly to articulate the surface of his designs, bringing the square as the plan figure of a building into the detail of its parts with greater intensity than before.[34] Wright's first design upon returning from Europe in 1910, the exhibition pavilion for the Portland Cement Company, provided the opportunity to experiment with the square as it had

been used by the artists of the Secession to articulate planar surfaces (fig. 151).[35] Coming immediately after his return from Europe, this design was the sole new project that Wright published in the American edition of his *Sonderheft*.[36]

In the design, the cruciform piers of the freestanding bench, partly abstract and vaguely anthropomorphic, were a transition between a two-dimensional figure, analogous to the designs of the Luxfer Prism, and a conventionalized human figure. On the other hand, the bands of alternating light and dark squares, like mosaic strips, provided clear, vibrant, linear elements to terminate the planar surfaces. Rectangular panels with the same square motif provided the articulation of the flat concrete surfaces.

CATAL HÜYÜK
BUILDING LEVEL VII

LEVEL VII

148. Square plans, Çatal Hüyük, level VII, sixth and seventh millennia (*Anatolian Studies,* 14).

149. *Lower left,* G. Roth, exhibition object for a munitions factory (*Der Architekt* 3, 1897).

150. Koloman Moser, design of borders for poem by Arno Holz (*Ver Sacrum* 4, 1899).

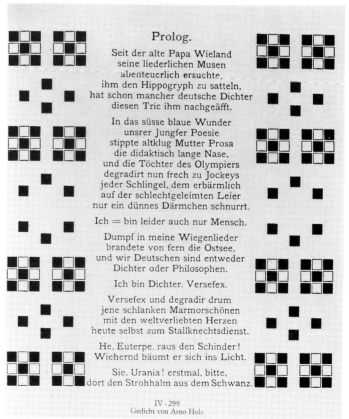

Prolog.

Seit der alte Papa Wieland
seine liederlichen Musen
abenteuerlich ersuchte,
ihm den Hippogryph zu satteln,
hat schon mancher deutsche Dichter
diesen Tric ihm nachgeäfft.

In das süsse blaue Wunder
unsrer Jungfer Poesie
stippte altklug Mutter Prosa
die didaktisch lange Nase,
und die Töchter des Olympiers
degradirt nun frech zu Jockeys
jeder Schlingel, dem erbärmlich
auf der schlechtgeleimten Leier
nur ein dünnes Därmchen schnurrt.

Ich = bin leider auch nur Mensch.

Dumpf in meine Wiegenlieder
brandete von fern die Ostsee,
und wir Deutschen sind entweder
Dichter oder Philosophen.

Ich bin Dichter. Versefex.

Versefex und degradir drum
jene schlanken Marmorschönen
mit den weltverliebten Herzen
heute selbst zum Stallknechtsdienst.

He. Euterpe, raus den Schinder!
Wiehernd bäumt er sich ins Licht.

Sie. Urania! erstmal, bitte,
dort den Strohhalm aus dem Schwanz.

IV - 299
Gedicht von Arno Holz

151. Universal Portland Cement Company exhibition pavilion, 1910 (*S*, American edition).

Moving from the transitional cruciform sculptures at the Portland Cement pavilion, Wright developed his ideas about the use of the square. At Midway Gardens he featured the square and its three-dimensional form, the cube. Wright wanted such conventionalized forms not only to have "spell power"—the ability to create a magical effect and to convey a message about contemporary culture—but to represent the means by which they were made. When an ornament represented its method of modern production, it qualified as "Machine Age Ornament" (fig. 152).[37] The title implied that because the forms were created as a result of mechanized production that used contemporary materials in a rational response to their physical properties, they were appropriate to the modern age.[38] Precision, replication, sharp edges, and flat surfaces were characteristic of the fast-moving cutter heads of mechanical milling machines, and, therefore, were an expression of the "nature of the means of production" that Wright had described in his theoretical writings. Replication of forms, as seen in many of the decorative elements at Midway Gardens, suggests that machines could produce quantities of decorative details with precision and control and that smooth planar surfaces were the most appropriate expression of the dynamics of the power tool. Furthermore, these ornaments were of the Machine Age because they expressed the "nature of materials."[39] In this case, simple, solid, cubic forms were appropriate to concrete, which could be cast into molds without undercuts. Finally, the square and cube were appropriate modern forms because, as "pure" forms, they were free of the classical imitations and eclectic styles that had

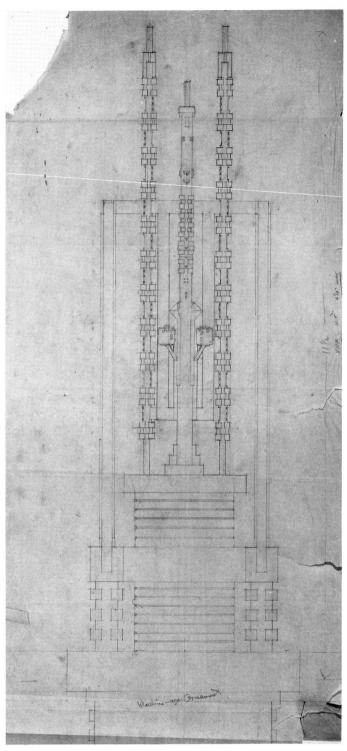

152. "Totem pole," with note "Machine Age Ornament," Midway Gardens, 1914 (TAL 1401.014).

infected architecture throughout the nineteenth century and into the twentieth.

The Rotated Square

The square, used as a primary form applicable to design methods and cultural symbols, could be easily transformed into other primary forms—platonic solids, the motifs of the rotated square, the square within a square, and the multiple frame. Simply to draw the diagonals of a square turns the square into four triangles, as we see in designs from Çatal Hüyük.[40] In its simplest version these crossed diagonals within a square form the plan of a pyramid. Clusters of such squares placed in lines produce the effect of bands of squares rotated at a forty-five degree angle to the horizon. A field of these motifs produce a lattice, or rotated grid, a motif which occurs in many cultures over time.[41]

The history of Western architecture in Europe confirmed the legacy of the rotated square. Socrates used the making of a square, with another square rotated inside it, as a didactic tool in his dialogue with Meno about the nature of learning and virtue.[42] The rotated square was found throughout Greco-Roman culture (fig. 153). During his travels Wright had seen the motif sanctioned by tradition in architecture that he admired. He was surrounded by examples of the square in rotation in architecture of the Italian Middle Ages, including the facade of the baptistery at the Duomo in Florence, the central aisle of S. Miniato al Monte (on the hill above his first residence in Florence), and the facade of the Badia Fiesolana (on the way to his villino in Fiesole). Wright could also see the rotated square in contemporary use, as in the complex floor patterns at the Petit Palais in Paris (figs. 154, 155).

The Wagner school carried on the traditions of the rotated square. Otto Wagner himself used it in his apartment house at 23 Schottenring as the motif of interior door moldings and the ceiling of a corridor (fig. 156). Olbrich gave the rotated square prominence at the Matildenhöhe in Darmstadt by locating it below the crest of the grand duke of Hesse at the entry of the tower that celebrated the grand duke's wedding (fig. 31). As the motifs of the Secession spread throughout Europe, the rotated square could be seen in work executed as far from Vienna as Finland (fig. 157).

Wright had occasionally used the rotated square as a motif before 1910 but had not fully exploited its potential. He combined it with the circle for one of his Luxfer prism designs.[43] It also appeared on an elevation drawing for the Harry E. Brown House.[44] The rotated square present in the plans for his remodeling of his aunts' Hillside Home School of 1902, published in the Wasmuth monograph, gives a good idea of the compositional potential of this simple configuration.[45] A square in the floor pattern of the assembly room provided the reference around which a second square was rotated (fig. 158). A person would sense this rotated square by the presence of a double-height vertical space formed by the balcony on the gallery level above. At the gallery level, a rotated square, formed by the low walls of the balcony, fits within the larger square defined with the room walls themselves. The square of the plan is in turn framed within a square made by the eaves of the roof lines, which is itself crossed by diagonals that define the roof pitch.[46] Consistent with Wright's design principles at this time,

153. Detail, Pompeian Ornament No. 3 (Owen Jones, *Grammar of Ornament,* pl. 25).

154. Baptistery of San Giovanni, facade of white and green Prato marble, executed in 11–12th centuries, Florence (author).

however, the rotated square was an additive element, inserted into the composition, or, in the case of the angular balconies of the art and science rooms, appended to the rectilinear plan.[47] In Europe, Wright had seen the prevalence of the square as he had used it—as a basic unit of composition—but he had also seen the immense expressive potentialities for articulating the surface art by rotating the square through the processes of quadrature.

After his return from Europe, the rotated square became a central motif in Wright's work. In its simplest form, Wright added the motif to the new, low wall in front of his Oak Park house during its remodeling around 1911 (fig. 159).[48] He used the rotated square in his design for the Ravine Bluffs Bridge, commissioned by Wright's lawyer, Sherman Booth, and built

in 1915, in a series of polychromed reliefs on the side of the bridge.[49] Each relief was composed of a square with a superimposed cross. The cross had been formed by first rotating the square and then by subtracting triangular areas from the rotated square to reveal the cross.

Square within a Square

The motif of the square within a square, which derives from the rotated square, typically contains the multiple references of other primary forms. It expresses structure and the symbolic meanings associated with ancient religious architecture. The motif's complexity can also be increased by translating it from one material to another: from concentric recessed panels of mud

155. Stairwell floor, Petit Palais, Paris, 1900 (author).

156. Otto Wagner, apartment building, 23 Schottenring, Vienna, 1877 (Graf, *Otto Wagner,* 3).

bricks to stone coffers. In addition, it can represent a building
plan. Seen on a large scale, the square within a square is the
plan of the stepped pyramids of Zoser and the Bent pyramid at
Seneferu in Egypt, and it becomes highly visible when projected
into three dimensions (figs. 160, 161.)[50]

 The motif of the square within a square was known to generations of architects. From early quasi-archaeological investigations, artists could see the transformation of ancient motifs
into the classical forms of antiquity. Recall Herodotus's observation that for the art of Rome one only need look back to Egypt.
The plates of Desgodetz's *Les Edifices Antiques de Rome* (1682,
1779) were available to the Viennese in the library of the Academy of Fine Arts, and provided clear views of the dome of the
Pantheon that showed how the coffers of the Pantheon were
analogous in plan to stepped pyramids in Egypt (fig. 162).[51]
However, the procedure of making a square within a square to
produce layered planes is so basic that it appears in cultures
around the world, for example, in the stupas of India and the
temples of China and Japan. Even the plans of pre-Columbian
temples, massed as a series of stepped pyramids, had bases that
formed the familiar motif of the square within a square, as seen
in Temple II at Tikal, published in 1911 by the Austrian photographer and Mayanist Teobert Maler (fig. 163).[52] Furthermore, throughout Western painting, the motif of the square
within a square persists.[53]

 Artists and architects in Vienna used the square within a
square with immense variety. Transforming typical molded
panels, Wagner used the motif in 1882 for the stucco panels of
the interiors of an apartment house on Stadiongasse and at the
central office building of the Austrian Länderbank.[54] It was a
feature of his Postal Savings Bank, where it is found, among
other places, on the ceiling of the main entry, on the boardroom
walls, and on the underside of the cornice at the top of the
building.[55] Hoffmann used the motif on the floor at his Purkers-

158. Hillside Home School, interior assembly room, Hillside, Wisconsin (State Historical Society of Wisconsin, WHI [X3] 23643).

159. Rotated square on low wall in front of Wright Home, Oak Park, c. 1911 (author).

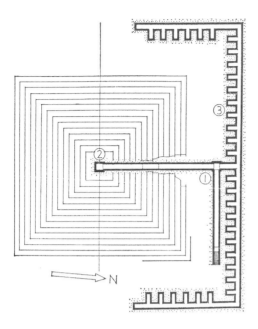

160. Plan, the Layer pyramid of Zawiyet el-Aryan, Egypt, 2d dynasty (Dows Dunham, *Zawlyet El-Aryan: The Cemeteries Adjacent to the Layer Pyramid,* Museum of Fine Arts, Boston, 1978).

dorf Sanatorium in 1904 (fig. 164).[56] In one of his many studies for the Zacherl House, Plečnik had tried using the square within a square as the motif of the facade. Although he finally used a different system, the square within a square was replicated in the published plans of the building in 1906 (fig. 165). The motif of the square within a square found frequent use in furniture and objects of the Wiener Werkstätte (fig. 166). Hoffmann even used the pattern for glassware, and Adolf Loos, the critic of the Secessionists, turned the motif into the coffered ceiling of the American Bar off the Kärntnerstrasse, completed in 1909.[57]

Wright knew the square-within-a-square motif not only from Secessionist sources but also from black laquerware he had bought in Japan in 1905. The laquerware service included a tray, tray server, and soup bowls with covers that were all marked with a red square with a gold outline. Wright apparently used the motif on his personal stationery that may date to 1902 and 1903.[58]

Wright could also see close at hand the square within a square in the Kabuki actor prints, which he loved, collected, and merchandised. As Wright noted about the actor Ichikawa Danjurō, whose showpiece *Shibaraku* (Wait a Moment) Wright loved:

161. Gateway to stepped pyramid enclosure, Saqqara, Egypt, 3d dynasty (Edwards, *Pyramids of Egypt*).

162. Section through Pantheon, Rome, from Antoine Desgodetz (*Les Edifices Antiques de Rome*, 2d ed., Paris, 1682).

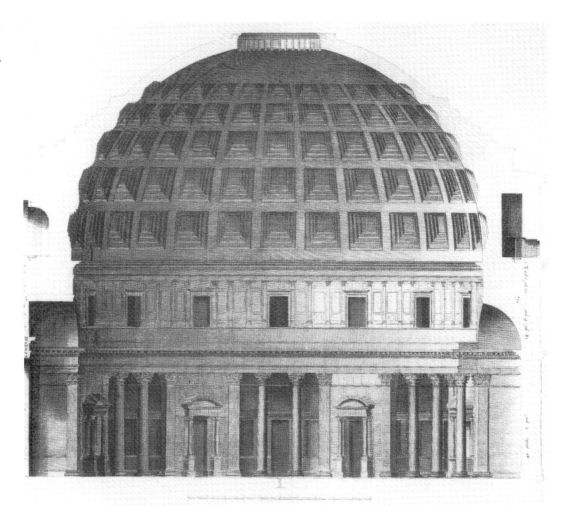

163. Teobert Maler, plan, Tikal, Temple I (Memoirs, Peabody Museum of Archaeology and Ethnology 5, 1911).

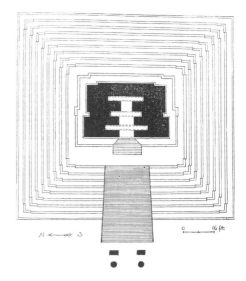

You many never fail to recognize Danjurō in all the various drawings by Shunshō and other artists that he inspired, and you may recognize others when you have made their acquaintance. But the means by which this was accomplished are so slight that the convention is scarcely disturbed, and no realism taints the result.[59]

One of these subtle means of recognition was the *mon*, or heraldic badge, of the Ichikawa family of actors, a square within a square. The key to a character's identity is an abstraction, not a realistic representation. The motif appeared frequently in woodblock prints.[60] The Viennese also collected such prints because of their intense interest in Japonism from as early as the 1870s.[61]

164. Josef Hoffmann, Hall, Purkersdorf Sanitarium (Eduard F. Sekler, *Joseph Hoffmann*, © 1982 Residenz Verlag, Salzburg and Wien, p. 71, fig. 81, Johanna Feigl, photographer).

At one time or another Wright owned several examples, among them a print by Shunkō, *The Red Danjurō*, whose red robes have the square-within-a-square motif (fig. 167).[62]

Before his trip to Europe Wright had used the motif sparingly. Such uses were exceptions, however, in a body of work that had utilized the unframed square as an ornamental motif largely restricted to the art glass of windows and piers, as at Unity Temple.

After 1910, when Wright returned from Europe, the dual currents of Secessionist art and oriental tradition formed a torrential flow in which the square within a square and other motifs were used by him interchangeably and regardless of their precise cultural affiliations. The square within a square found increasing use in Wright's designs for ornament and details. It was present in the earliest sketches of the Coonley Kindergarten and was developed there as a sun screen in the flat overhanging eaves.[63] At Midway Gardens, the motif was more extensively developed than in any previous work. It was used to form the checkerboard panels, described in one drawing as the "characteristic detail of the Building," and on the surfaces of columns (fig. 168).[64]

The Multiple Frame

Closely related to the square within a square was the multiple frame. It could be used two-dimensionally for its graphic quality or three-dimensionally as a layering of planes that produces a recessed panel or series of recessed panels (fig. 169). In creating nests of frames, the motif could be complete and enclosed, or open on one side.

The multiple-frame panel shared the symbolic and tectonic duality of the other forms. In mud-brick architecture the mass of the wall carried the loads, and the higher the wall the thicker it needed to be. In temples, staggering the rows of bricks as they were laid became a primary means of articulating the relentless flatness of the surface and a way of eliminating excess building material. Corbeling of the bricks resulted in forms ranging from a simple groove, to a recessed panel, to multiple recessed panels and frames. This multiple framing in the depth of the wall could also create a crenelated niche, a place for the sacred or ritual object.

The recession of the wall plane into crenelated niches appears in the ground plans of the most ancient sites excavated by archaeologists. Over time the multiple frame became the basic

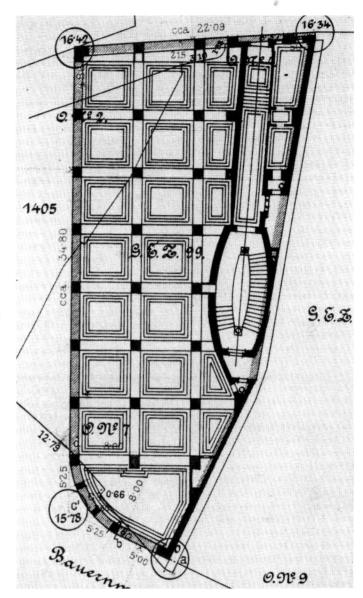

165. Jože Plečnik, plan, Zacherl House, Vienna, 1906 (*Der Architekt*, 12, 1906, pl 11).

representation of the sacred temple facade itself. The iconography became so standard that it was used for three-dimensional clay models of temples, as seen in a model from the second millennium in Ashur.[65] The niches appear at Tepe Gawra on the level with major architectural remains and at Uruk in the White Temple and in the Eannu precinct, where it appears in a temple plan for Level XIII (fig. 170).[66]

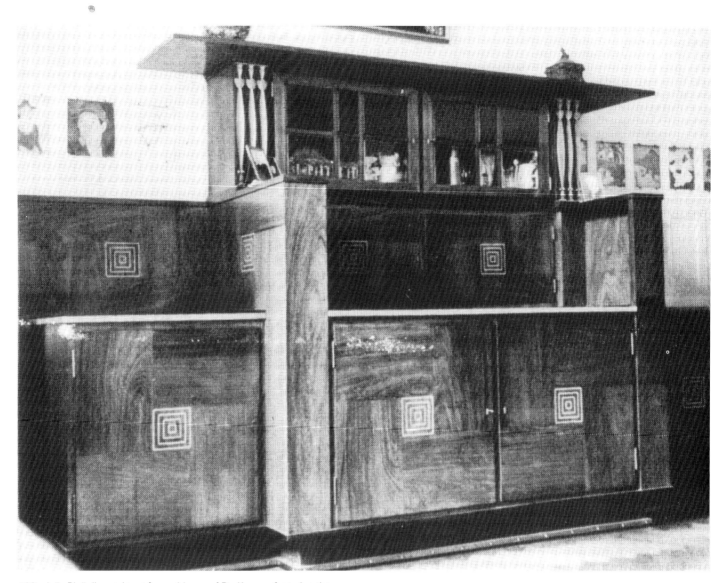

166. Jože Plečnik, credenza for residence of Dr. Knauer, featuring the
motif of the square within square (Prelovsek, *Josef Plečnik. Wiener Arbeiten von 1896 bis 1914*).

167. Shunkō, "The actor Ichikawa Monnosuko 2nd in the Shibaraku role," c. 1789 (The Metropolitan Museum of Art, Rogers Fund, 1922).

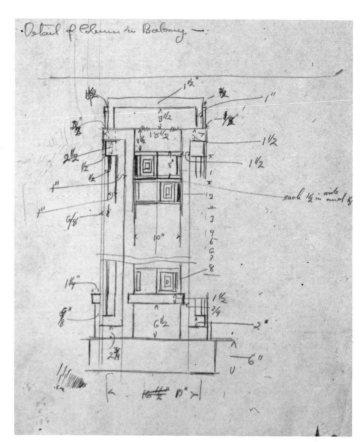

168. Detail of a square within a square motif, Midway Gardens, Chicago, 1914 (TAL 1401.085).

The motif, expanded into broader recessed panels, was a dominant feature of the ziggurat in Ur at the time of the third dynasty (fig. 171). The identification of the multiple frame with the temple front was incorporated into the neo-Sumerian stele of the sun god Shamash (fig. 138).[67] Illuminated by a flaming disk, the god sits on a representation of the temple as he holds out the insignia of power to an approaching worshiper. The same use of the motif follows about two hundred years later in a historically important and celebrated work of art, the *Code of Hammurabi*, where the law-giving king of Babylonia sits on the symbol of his temple.[68]

In its symbolic and tectonic meanings the recessed panel of Mesopotamian and Egyptian temples paralleled the *Talud-Tablero* system of talus and entablature that formed the recessed panels found in Maya architecture. In Mesoamerican culture, the system developed in Teotihuacan between 300 and 100 B.C.E. and had the most pronounced effect of any architectonic

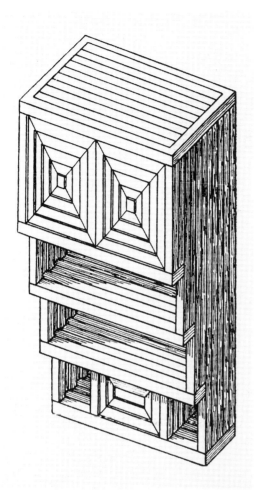

169. Wall cabinet using J. L. M. Lauweriks' design system, 1910 (Lauweriks, *Aus der Praxis der Knaben-und Mädchenarbeit,* vol. 1, 1910).

element on other regions of the Maya territory.[69] The sloping *talud* (talus) supported a vertical *tablero* (panel).[70] The great panels on the Temple of Kukulkan in Chichén Itzá are variants of the tablero; there are fifty-two on each side of the pyramid (figs. 172, 173). Integral with the cosmological program of the temple, they recede in size as they ascend the pyramid to provide an exaggerated illusionistic increase in height.

The physical evidence of the continuity of the multiple frame and its sacred symbolism from the ancient Near East to Egypt could be seen in museums during the formative years of the Secession and when Wright visited Europe. In the Kunsthistorisches Museum in Vienna, which acted as visual reference library for Secessionist artists, the sarcophagus of King Nesschutefnut of Memphis, c. 350 B.C.E., was incised on its lower sides with the multiple frames of the Mesopotamian temple, transformed into the iconography of the funereal mastaba (fig. 174).[71] In the same gallery were further examples of the motif on a relief from the temple of King Psammetich II and on the altar for a cult figure from the time of Sety I.

Like the square, the multiple frame and the recessed panel became signs of the Secession from around 1900. The representation of the temple in rituals of death survived to represent the house of the living; the motif, associated with Egypt, became widespread as an ornament for furniture, objects, and for building facades (figs. 175, 176). The walls of Olbrich's Secession Building had contained the recessed panel as a principal motif, using it in its most elemental form as recessed bands, laid in long strips along the sides of the building.

The fully developed motif, however, occurred in Hoffmann's work before it appeared in Olbrich's. Hoffmann claimed it as "his invention" as early as 1902.[72] By 1903 the Wiener Werk-

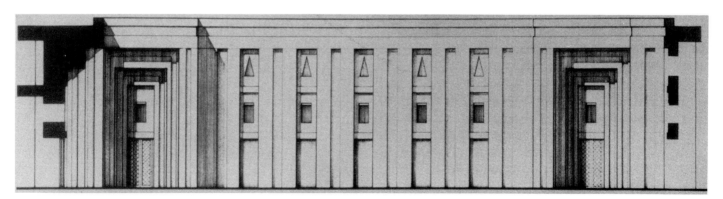

170. Recessed wall planes, entry palace, "Building with Four Columns," Uruk (Heinrich, *Die Temple und Heiligtümer*).

171. Crenelated niche, detail, ziggurat in
Ur, time of Warad-sin of Larsa, 1834–1823
B.C.E. (Orthmann, *Der Alte Orient*).

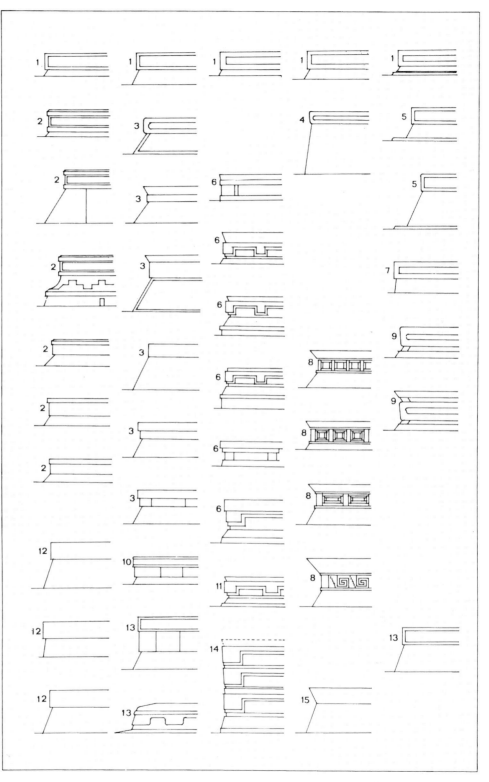

172. Tablero systems in Mesoamerican
architecture (Gendrop, *Architektur der
Hochkulteren Mittelamerikas*).

173. Tablero, Kukulkan, Chichén Itzá (author).

174. Sarcophagus of King Nesschutefnut of Memphis, c. 350 B.C. Kunsthistorisches Museum (author).

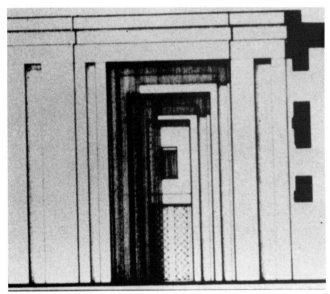

175. Entry palace detail, Uruk (Heinrich, *Die Tempel und Heiligtümer*).

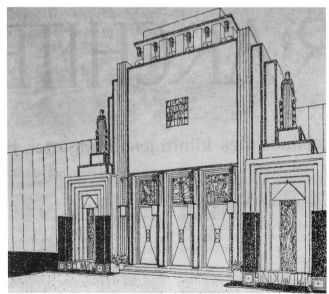

176. Robert Mallet-Stevens, "Exposition du Commerce De Luxe" (*Der Architekt* 20, 1914–15).

177. Wiener Werkstätte, interior view, Vienna, 1904 (*DKuD*, 1904/05).

178. Joseph Maria Olbrich, Wedding Tower gable, Darmstadt (author).

stätte had many examples of the multiple frame. A view of the interior of the Werkstätte showroom in 1904 indicates how the motif fit into an ensemble of objects using primary forms, including the circle, square, and rotated square (fig. 177). These Wright could have seen in his visit to the showroom. The motif of the multiple frame was also an important means of articulating the walls of the Kunstschau Pavilion of 1908. The inner courts used the motif, and the main entry, below Simandl's sculpture, consisted of a series of recessive planes. Wright might have seen these wall treatments before the pavilion was fully demolished.[73]

At Olbrich's communal studio in Darmstadt, which Wright visited, the layering of planes in recession revealed the depth of the inner structure of the wall. The canted mass of the walls— signs of the Egyptian pylon—were peeled back in layers to their basic tectonic function, as if to relate the modern form to its ancient origins, a theme which was reinforced by Olbrich's

treatment of the entry. The top of the wedding tower, which contained bells, used the developed motif in brick, which was glazed blue, an exotic recollection of the waters of the Nile or of the Assyrian tiles of the Ishtar Gate.[74] The shaft of the tower, on which sat a clock face, was composed of rough brick masonry and pierced by openings for windows. At the base of the tower, which was built, like the studio, of stucco over masonry, Olbrich returned to the motif of the recessed plane: layers of the wall plane receded to reveal the depth of the wall and an elongated, rectangular window (figs. 178, 179).[75]

Wright had used the multiple frame very little before 1909. It occurs in his study for the copper roof of the Harvey P. Sutton House and in the Emma Martin House of 1901 (fig. 180).[76] Wright also used the multiple-frame motif as a relief panel in the Larkin Building in Buffalo in 1904–5.[77]

After 1910, when Wright saw the layering of planes in the work of the Viennese, he made the multiple frame central to his

179. Joseph Maria Olbrich, Wedding Tower, window detail, Darmstadt (author).

ornament. It immediately appears in the revised drawings for the Wasmuth folios for the Coonley House and the McCormick project; for both houses, the motif is used as a representation of water in the ponds.[78]

Wright also used the motif of the multiple frame in his project for a new office building for the *San Francisco Call* newspaper (fig. 181).[79] In the midst of reviving his practice, Wright obtained this commission in 1913 from John D. Spreckels through the architect Harrison Albright, for whom his son John was working.[80] Although it was not realized, the project for the *Call* epitomized Wright's visionary pursuit of the tall building he sought to erect throughout his career.[81]

In the *Call* project Wright articulated major motifs used by Secession artists and architects: the square, multiple frames, and conventionalized sculpture (fig. 182).[82] He composed the main entry as a series of receding planes that accentuated the depth of the entry, a device precisely analogous to Olbrich's design for the entry to the Wedding Tower at Darmstadt and Hoffmann's treatment of entries at the Kunstschau Pavilion.[83] From

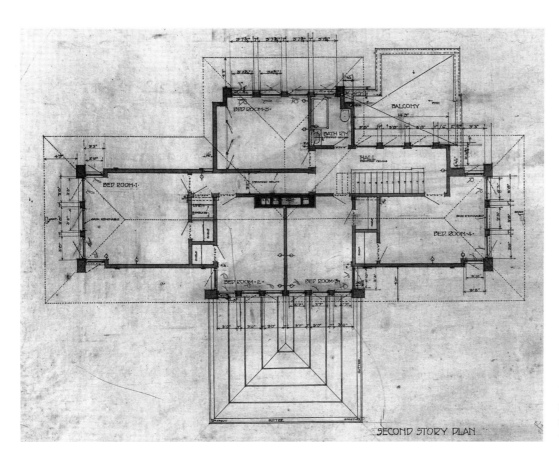

180. Harvey P. Sutton House, scheme no. 3, second-story plan showing roof above first floor, 1905 (TAL 0710.005).

181. *Call* Building, model, exhibited at the Art Institute of Chicago, 1914 (TAL1500.011).

182. *Call* Building, model detail, 1911 (author, Collection TAL).

the outset, sculptures were intended to flank the entry. In one study these sculptures are abstract, rectilinear forms, but when the model of the building was constructed for exhibition in Chicago in 1914 the sculptures were clearly the conventionalized human figures developed at Midway Gardens from the precedents of Metzner and Emilie Simandl (figs. 51, 129, 300).[84] Finally, the motif of the square itself is announced by three deeply set windows above the entry.

The Triangle

The triangle, the third basic primary form, is an ancient symbol which can be traced back to its use to symbolize fertility and the sacred temple. In ancient cultures, where mud-brick construction was used, a triangle sitting on its base was a logical window form because it could be built by the corbeling of mud bricks. This avoided the use of the post-and-lintel system of wood or stone that was required for rectangular or square windows. At the same time, when inverted, the motif was associated with fertility, as represented by the Venus figures, whose pelvises were consistently shaped in pronounced triangles.[85] The triangle had also appeared as a symbolic form in a Neo-

183. Ornamental wall painting from Catal Hüyük, Anatolia, level VII, early neolithic, before c. 6000 B.C.E. (Mellink and Filip, *Frühe Stufen*).

lithic wall mural in Anatolia before 6000 B.C.E., thus making it one of the earliest extant images created by human hands (fig. 183).[86]

Combining its tectonic use and symbolic meanings, the triangle became a pierced opening in the sacred buildings of Mesopotamian culture. At Tepe Gawra, in the earliest known habitations of the ancient Near East, the triangular window appeared in temples (fig. 184).[87] In the Anu ziggurat in Uruk, the triangular window was used, transferred into alabaster, on the temple front. It was used as a sacred element in cult houses of the Tepe Gawra type of the Uruk period. And it was a principal motif of the White Temple itself at Uruk, where the windows were placed high above a recessed panel and below a frieze. At Uruk, the motif also appears in the Stone Temple in the Eannu precinct; in the inner court of the Entry Palace, or "Building with Four Columns"; in the Column Hall, phase IV, where it appears in low relief as incised lines—an example of the representation in its minimal form (fig. 170).[88]

The triangular window also appeared in combination with the crenelated niche as a complete temple representation, an iconography occurring both on the facade and on pottery that represented the same temple (fig. 185).[89] The complete temple representation also proliferated as recorded in the impressions of cylinder seals (the small incised ceramic devices used for sealing documents) from the ancient Near East. One such seal

of the Jamdat-Nasr period shows the sacred herd approaching the temple, represented symbolically by the triangular windows and crenelated niche (fig. 186).[90] Through time, the triangle persisted as a symbolic representation in the altars of fired clay in Assyria and ultimately in Egyptian temples.[91]

184. Tepe Gawra, Level VIIIb (Speiser, *Excavations at Tepe Gawra*, vol. 1, 1935, pl. 22).

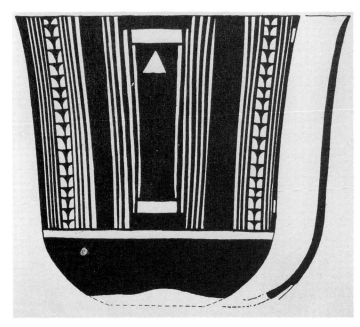

185. Pottery fragment, with representation of temple front, level XIII, Central Temple Complex, Tepe Gawra (Tobler, *Excavations at Tepe Gawra,* pl. 130, no. 204).

From Egyptian, archaic, and even folk sources, the triangle became a motif of the Secessionists in Vienna.[92] Joseph Urban used the triangle in the interior of a dining room (fig. 187).[93] The triangle was also widely utilized for tablecloths or other graphic designs (fig. 188). Hoffmann's teapot design of 1910/ 1911 for the Wiener Werkstätte uses the triangle for its patterns, as does his fabric pattern "Montezuma"; the title itself links the design to the exoticism of pre-Colombian Mesoamerica, another source of originary forms.[94] Reinforcing the Secessionist interest in exotic origins and primary forms, Klimt used the triangle in his *Beethoven Frieze* of 1902 where it closely resembled a *mon,* or crest, in Japanese art (fig. 189). The triangle also appears in the details of his painting *Three Ages of Life* of 1905, where it is treated like the fish-scale pattern of Japanese textiles.

The triangle, the pure form least evident in Wright's design process before 1910, gradually became more prominent in his vocabulary after his return from Europe. At Midway Gardens, this symbol of structural unity was used as the plan configuration of the cast cement flower-holders for the belvederes of the Gardens.[95] It also was used for the designs of door panels and windows, and it appeared more frequently in combination with other primary shapes.[96] Yet if the triangle was made at a large scale for a floor plan, its geometry produced angular corners that could be awkward to use in a dwelling. Only after Wright

186. Cylinder seal, sacred temple with rows of horned animals, Jamdat Nasr period (Collection of the Pierpont Morgan Library).

187. Josef Urban, dining room interior, mahogany with mother of pearl, c. 1906 (*The Art Revival in Austria,* 1906).

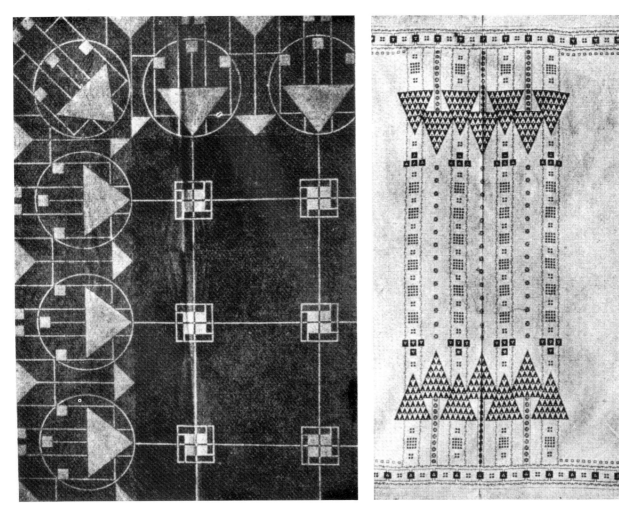

188. Marcel Kammerer, left, and W. Truneček, tablecloths with triangles (*The Studio Yearbook*, 1907).

began rotating geometric forms at irregular intervals in the 1910s did the triangle become central to his ornament, and only later in the 1920s did it become important in the development of polygonal plan forms. As Wright discovered with his design for the Steel Cathedral of 1926, an entirely different organization was necessary when the triangle, or forms derived from it, was used for ground plans.[97]

Combinations in Vienna

In the designs of the Secessionists, combinations of primary forms provided a variety of expressive means that allowed both the development of symbolic programs and the integration of several motifs into unified compositions. Otto Pruscher used triangles and squares for the motifs of his design for a crypt (fig. 190). In addition to his designs that used the square alone, Moser provided in *Ver Sacrum* a tour de force of combined motifs.[98] Two of Wagner's former students, Emil Hoppe and Otto Schöntal, produced a beautiful ensemble of motifs for the facades of their project for a synagogue in Trieste (fig. 191). Leopold Bauer's design for a rug for the interior of the Austrian exhibition in St. Louis in 1904, combined the motifs of squares, triangles, and circles with great freedom; he even transformed the corners of the recessed squares into swirls, a motif appearing in Mycenaean art that was used on the mosaic urns in front of Olbrich's Secession Building.

189. Japanese *mon,* upper left; Japanese textile pattern of fish scales, upper right; Gustav Klimt, *Beethoven Frieze,* detail, 1902, lower left; Gustav Klimt, *Three Ages of Life,* detail, 1905, below right (*Verborgene Impressionen*).

Olbrich had been highly imaginative in using primary forms to create a complex symbolic program that had no equivalent in American architecture. Wright saw an example of Olbrich's work at the Ernst Ludwig House in the Matildenhöhe complex at Darmstadt, where Olbrich combined figural sculpture with primary motifs of interlocking circles, triangles, recessive wall planes, and the rotated square. The sculptures related more to Symbolist images than Metzner's geometric style. Primal figures of man and woman, personified as "Strength" and "Beauty," representing the polarities of male and female energy, flanked the door of the communal studio. In addition to the colossal figures of Strength and Beauty, a pair of black Nikes with folded wings at the corner of the door frames implied that victory awaited those who rose to the challenge of creation (fig. 192). Even though the Nike was a favorite sculpture of Wright's, these figures differed from any he had used.

In back of the sculptures and around the doors were primary forms of overlapping circles and dazzling gilt triangles on an earth-colored ground, an ensemble that signified entrance into the cosmic domain of art.[99] More freely abstracted than Wright's ornament, the circles, overlapping in groups of three, were glazed in white, and each circle contained three gilt spheres. The clusters and the triangles surrounding them were contained within amorphous vegetal forms linked to each other by branch-like bands. Over these were a double row of roundels, glazed with white swirls to represent stars. And above the rows of stars was a quotation from Hermann Bahr, the inspiring polemicist of the Secession for whom Olbrich had designed a house in Vienna:

The artist reveals a world which never was nor ever will be his.[100]

These words echoed those that surrounded the winged figure in the circular window in the entry hall of the Secession Building in Vienna: "The Artist shows his own world: the Beauty that was born with him, that was not before and will never come after."[101]

In effect, the ensemble created a cosmology, with earth and nature below and the heavens above. The artist's role within that universe was to reveal the higher realm of being, an aspiration mirrored in Wright's phrase that "the indigenous art of a people is their only prophecy and their true artists their school of anointed prophets and kings."[102]

Olbrich combined primary forms at the entry of the Wedding Tower on the Matildenhöhe, which Wright could have inspected. Framing the entry were bands of gold mosaics and

190. Otto Pruscher, design for a crypt, 1905 (*Der Architekt* 11, 1905).

double rows of interlocking circles filled with white squares. When these bands were seen from a distance with the steps in front, they formed a series of receding frames—the ancient motif of the multiple frame—into which the entry appeared deeply set. The entry gate was a cast-iron screen at whose center was the crest of Ernst Ludwig. The upper part of the door was composed of cast-iron frames joined by gilt spheres. The lower portion contained four metal-paneled sheets on which were laid

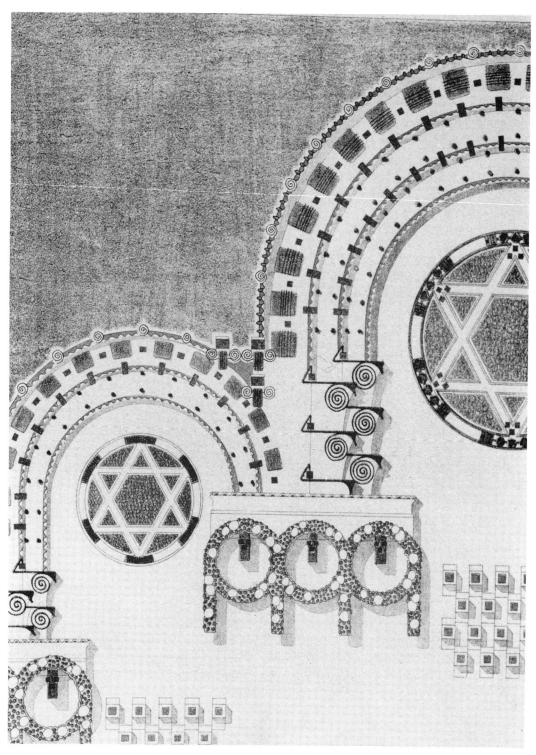

191. Emil Hoppe and Otto Schöntal, competition project for a synagogue in Trieste, facade detail, 1903–4 (*Der Architekt* 11, 1905).

192. Joseph Maria Olbrich, Ernst Ludwig Haus, entry detail, Darmstadt, 1901 (author).

four gilt hemispheres flanking a square rotated ninety degrees about its normal axis. The entry resembled a jeweled, medieval book cover, an artifact that craftsmen of the Secession often emulated in their work. The tower, as a whole, was an unparalleled monument to matrimony.

Wright's Ensembles

At Midway Gardens, Wright created a scenario analogous to the Matildenhöhe complex and combined the primary motifs of geometry into the most complex symbolic program thus far attempted in his practice. It was his reply to the late Olbrich, his competitor from the Secession. The sculpture program contained the figural representations of geometry—Wright's version of the Kunstschau representations of sculpture, painting,

and architecture—but the great piers that marked the corners of the winter garden were the ultimate abstract representations of geometry (fig. 28). These piers, seen in the section drawings of the building, were the vertical elements that contrasted with the long horizontal facade of the Gardens; they provided a dramatic silhouette to the building and acted as beacons to attract the public.[103] If they had been completed as Wright intended, they would have had "finials" consisting of the primary forms of square, circle, and triangle dangling in multicolored swags and garlands.

Wright studied the placement of the combined motifs of the pier finials in elevation and perspective to test how they would be seen from below (fig. 193). He had intended the fully developed cement piers to have at their tops hanging chains of spheres, cubes, and pyramids that would be colored red, white,

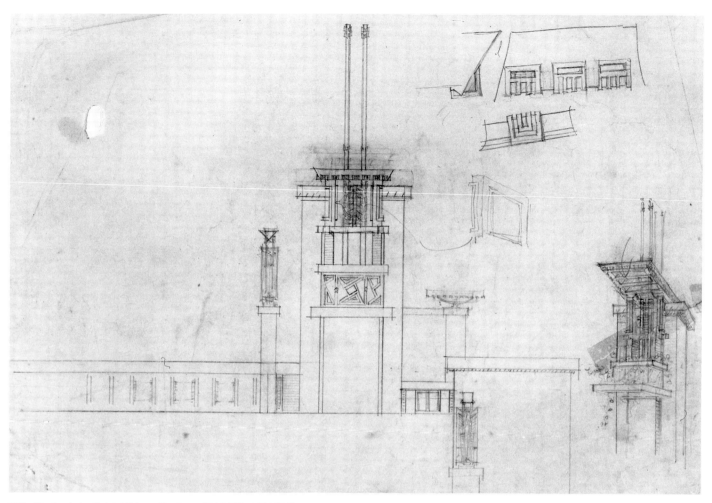

193. Study of pier finial, Midway Gardens, 1914 (TAL 1401.080).

orange, blue, and gold.[104] To prevent these necklaces from fluttering in the wind, solid lead balls were to be attached to the tips. Below the lead orb was a horizontal cement shelf from which five dangling strings of soft cast-copper spheres, cubes, and pyramids were suspended, announcing abstractly the iconographic program of geometry at the Gardens (fig. 194). Much to Wright's regret, these ornaments were never added (fig. 281).

Combinations of geometric motifs were used throughout the ornamental program at Midway Gardens, from tableware to door panels. Wright had seen in the work of the Secessionists an expressive range of everyday objects that did not exist in America. Upon his return, he embarked on the design of the most complete ensembles of furnishings in his career. By pushing further the concept of the *Gesamtkunstwerk*—the total work

of art—from the domestic to the public realm, he began to find the "intricate enrichment" of ornament he had not achieved in his earlier work.

For the first time, Wright designed table settings to complete the kind of total environment he had attempted earlier at the Coonley House. At Midway Gardens, there were three alternate designs of dining ensembles, including dinnerware, furniture, and light fixtures. In one table grouping for the summer garden, the triangle and circle are featured as main themes, with the triangle contained in a band extending along the center of the round chair-back. The motif is reinforced by its appearance on the tablecloth and by the use of crossed, welded steel rods for the framework of the chair. Both the seat and back are circles, and globes or solid circles dangle from the planters, in-

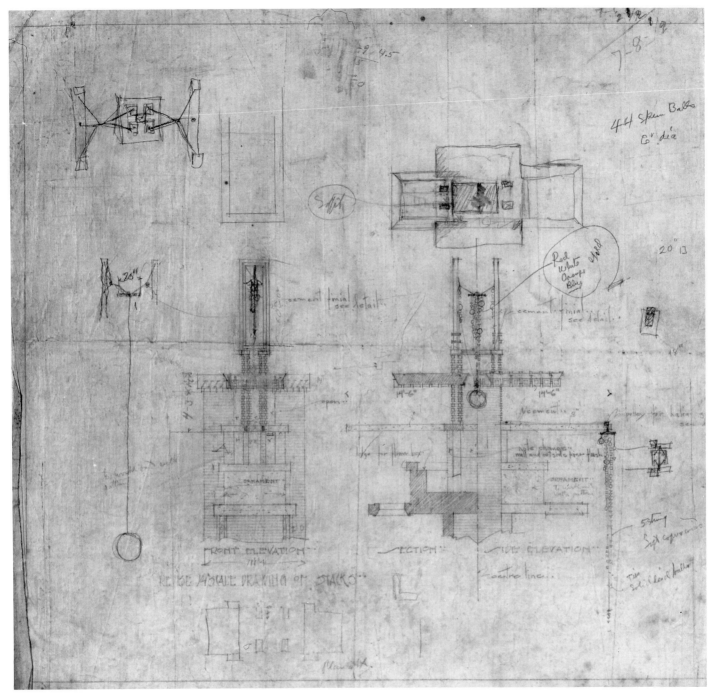

194. Detail of pier finials with swags of colored geometric solids, Midway Gardens, 1914 (TAL 1401.082).

195. Table setting and furniture, Midway Gardens, 1914 (TAL 1401.006).

196. Hexagonal chairs in special guest box, Imperial Hotel, Tokyo, 1916–22 (*IH*).

tertwined with vines, nearby.[105] The square makes its presence felt in the rectilinear forms of a lamp fixture near the table and in the checkerboard pattern that covers parts of the cubes at the base of the fixture.

The use of primary forms allowed Wright to make variations of the table settings with accompanying lamps and chairs. In one of these studies, straight-backed, slatted chairs have squares and triangles for principal motifs (fig. 195).[106] The polygonal shade of the lamp, the edge treatments of the plates and napkins, and the angled, inset panel of the chair reinforce the prevalence of organizing motifs. In his design drawing, Wright emphasized the role of the motifs—a square, subdivided into four squares, filled with a circle, triangle, and further subdivisions into squares—by inserting them into the floor patterns. From this study, Wright's lamp and china were made.[107] Wright turned the motif of the square into a monogram for the china of the Midway Gardens: a series of simple checks placed at wide intervals along the edges of the plates, cups, and saucers. Recalling the parallel use of a shared language, this design resembled that of china previously designed by Moser (figs. 67,

68).[108] Whether Wright knew of Moser's plates is not known. Rather than representing an instance of confirmed influence, the existence of two similar plates provides another example of parallel development.

Imperial Hotel—Primary and Combined Forms

Along with the Midway Gardens, the Imperial Hotel provided a laboratory for Wright's inventions in ornament. Initially conceived simultaneously with Midway Gardens, the commission for the Imperial Hotel provided a major testing ground for Wright's new experiments in ornament. The hotel, designed for foreign visitors to Tokyo, was the most complex and challenging commission of his life. In addition to guest rooms, the hotel had public and private dining rooms, parlors, promenades, galleries, a cabaret, an auditorium, a banquet hall, and even a library and a tea balcony. Using primary forms, Wright designed dining room furniture with polygonal shapes that were consistent with geometric patterns of the whole. Dining-room chairs and side chairs both used the hexagon, with every element of

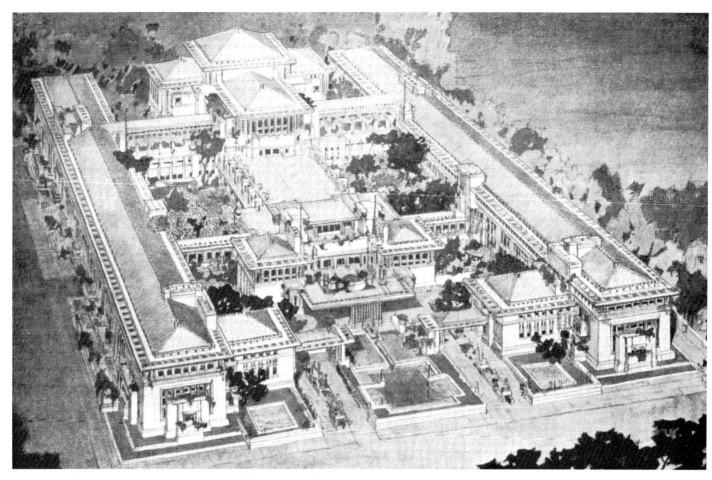

197. Imperial Hotel, perspective, Tokyo, 1916–22 (Wijdeweld, *Life Work*).

the chair angled to maintain the formal consistency (fig. 196).[109] Cups and saucers designed for the main dining room and cabaret used circular motifs that were analogous to the circular patterns of the Midway Gardens murals.[110]

However, it was difficult for Wright to complete all of his designs. Because of several interruptions, building the hotel would take almost ten years to finish from Wright's first involvement in 1913 (fig. 197). Despite a series of delays and setbacks, during which his competence was questioned and natural disasters slowed construction, Wright proceeded to make a vast number of ornamented designs based on similar themes. His output of developed details was massive because, given the project's imperial sponsorship, he had an unlimited labor force to execute his designs and a relatively unlimited supply of the soft *oya* stone for a building material. The design process for the hotel was extremely complicated, with five phases of design for the central pavilion alone.[111]

The dozens of beautiful studies among the some 850 extant drawings in the Taliesin archives for the Imperial Hotel reveal the full range of Wright's ornamental ensembles, in which he used primary forms alone and in combinations. These designs for the building show how Wright absorbed the lessons of primary forms, combined his own design process with the vernacular methods of Japanese architecture, and produced a richness that had no parallel in Europe or elsewhere. All the fundamental motifs of geometry are present in the drawings, ranging from simple expressions to dazzling complexities drawn as full-scale details.

The circle proliferated as an ornamental motif at the Imperial Hotel (fig. 198). As at Midway Gardens, Wright associated

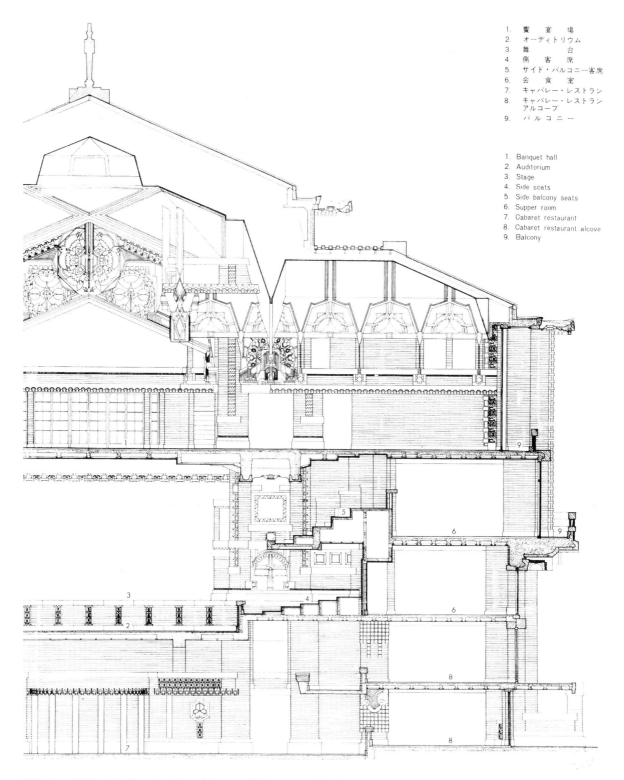

1. 饗 宴 場
2. オーディトリウム
3. 舞 台
4. 側 客 席
5. サイド・バルコニー客席
6. 会 食 室
7. キャバレー・レストラン
8. キャバレー・レストラン
   アルコープ
9. バ ル コ ニ ー

1. Banquet hall
2. Auditorium
3. Stage
4. Side seats
5. Side balcony seats
6. Supper room
7. Cabaret restaurant
8. Cabaret restaurant alcove
9. Balcony

198. Imperial Hotel, half-section through banquet hall, measured drawing, 1968 (*IH*).

199. Oya sculpture of piled spheres, Imperial Hotel, 1916–22 (*IH*).

it with a bubbly, festive atmosphere, and he designed a series of panels using circles, whole and overlapped, for the stone piers of the hotel's cabaret and for oya sculpture (fig. 199). Wright could use the circle motif simply, as in his design of the perforated panel of a screen (fig. 200).[112] He also used it complexly, as in the study of a detail in which the repetition of semicircles within circles and overlapping shapes activates the interstitial areas and creates an illusion of one plane hovering above another. This complexity was increased by three-dimensional effects obtained by deeply recessing elements to create shadows. Circles were inscribed in squares, the rotations of which dictated the shape and placement of truncated triangles that formed peripheral bands (fig. 201).[113]

The square was almost too simple to exist by itself. It was absorbed into the motif of the square within a square, and incorporated into numerous complex designs (fig. 202). The triangle was also used as a motif, but again rarely on its own, except in the design of a wastebasket and cuspidor.[114] More often it was subsumed into more elaborate schemes involving rotated elements, or it was defined as the result of overlapping, or used to demarcate the boundaries of patterns.

A small sampling of the rotated square includes its use in a series of reliefs and in multiple rotations that produced interior crosses.[115] The complexity available from combining the rotated square and accentuating its subdivisions is seen, for example, in a drawing for a copper soffit of a beam in the hotel's theater and on the balcony of the promenade (figs. 203, 204).[116] A series of rug designs used the rotated device combined with other motifs (fig. 205).[117]

At the Imperial Hotel, the square within a square, the easily recognized *mon* of the Ichikawa clan, was a motif that had leaped continents—from Europe and America—to return home to Japan. Wright used the motif in its entirety, or in parts with quadrants suppressed. The motif of the square within a square was used on sides of blocks that formed columns, perforated like open fretwork, in the lobby; in another use on a column, it was extended from one side of a block to another (fig. 206).[118]

Wright used the multiple frame as part of matrices that included circles and, at a larger scale, to articulate an alcove between the lobby and a lounge (fig. 207).[119] He also used the multiple frame as a linear fret, thus transforming the pattern's purpose as a surround (fig. 208). One way of creating this motif was to divide a closed series of multiple frames, or a square within a square, in half. Wright could then use the halves independently. For a rug for a small bedroom in the hotel, Wright

200. Perforated screen with
circle motif, Imperial Hotel,
dated 15 February 1921
(TAL 1509.099).

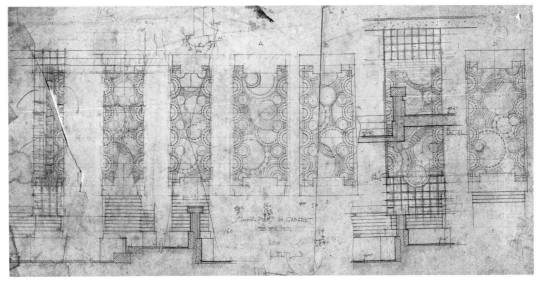

201. Circle inscribed in square,
soffit of promenade balcony,
Imperial Hotel, 1916–22
(TAL 1509.520).

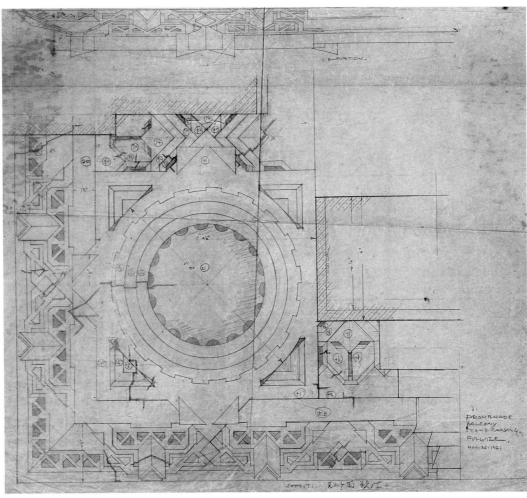

202. Column detail, dining room, Imperial Hotel, 1916–22 (*IH*).

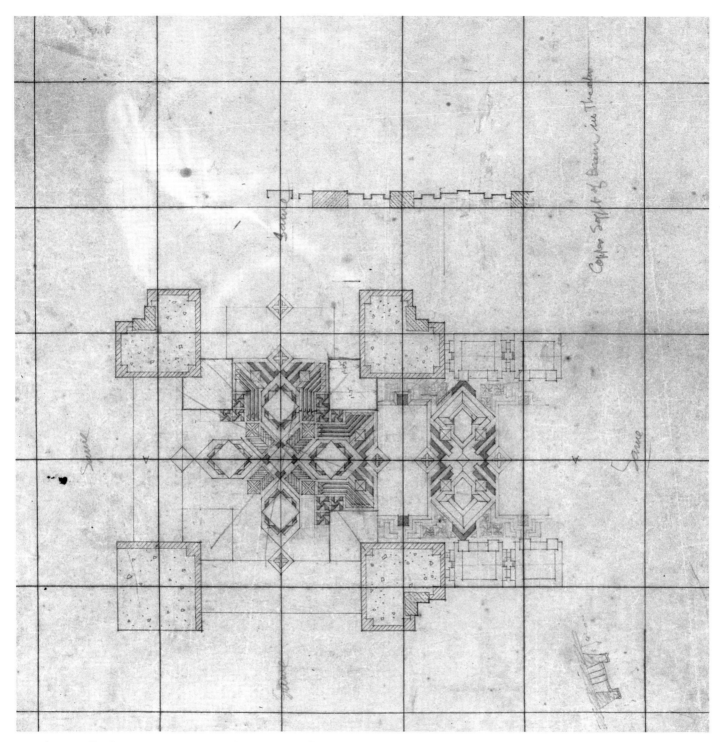

203. Copper soffit of beam in theater, Imperial Hotel, 1916–22 (TAL 1509.006).

204. Rotated square, detail at promenade gallery, Imperial Hotel, 1916–22 (*IH*).

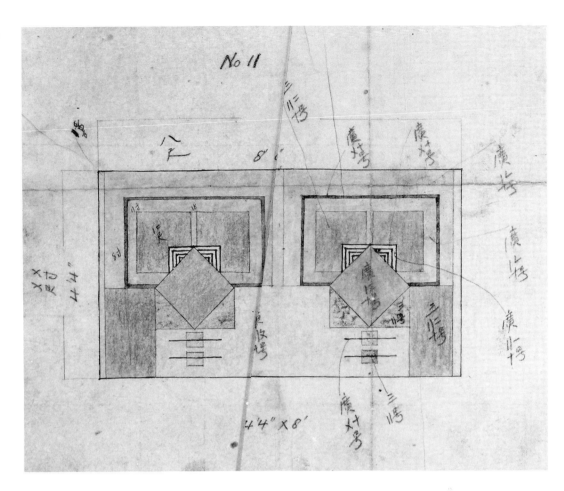

divided a full square of recessed frames into halves and turned each half to face in opposite directions (fig. 209). Using patterns unexplored by the artists of the Secession, Wright also elongated the frame as a fret, deformed it with protrusions, and bent it around corners to create a continuity of surface (fig. 210).[120] This fret became a new motif in his repertory. It can be seen in his work over the next thirty years, his use of it ranging from the two-dimensional design of flat surfaces to the three-dimensional staggering of wood siding.

The multiple frame was so important that Wright used it as the articulating device and basic aesthetic for his first scheme for the Imperial Hotel in 1913. In this first design Wright experimented with primary forms to define a new modern Japanese architecture (fig. 211). He defined the roof—always one of the most iconic aspects of his architecture—as layers of planes, stacked in receding sizes with the ends turned up as a variation from the conventional treatment of multiple framing.[121] He also made the walls of the hotel flat, taut planes reminiscent of the aesthetics of the Viennese Josef Hoffmann.[122]

Never before recognized for its connections to the forms of the Viennese Secession or primary forms, the first scheme for the Imperial Hotel helps justify Wright as "the most important of America's Secessionists."[123] The main pavilion at the rear repeats the motif of multiple frames, and the visual activity of these layered planes is contrasted, as in Hoffmann's exhibition pavilion in Rome, with broad, unarticulated wall surfaces (figs. 212–14).[124] The section drawings of this first scheme show the layering motif and how it could be superimposed on the traditional roof systems that used layers of ceramic tiles.

In effect, Wright intended to provide his Japanese clients with the latest developments from Europe, translated into an oriental idiom of massing and detail and constructed of poured concrete. But Wright later decided to abandon the aesthetic of layered planes and flat walls as too progressive and too de-

206. Square-within-a-square motif, detail, central hall lobby, Imperial Hotel, 1916–22 (*IH*).

207. Multiple frame, alcove between lobby and lounge, Imperial Hotel, 1916–22 (*IH*).

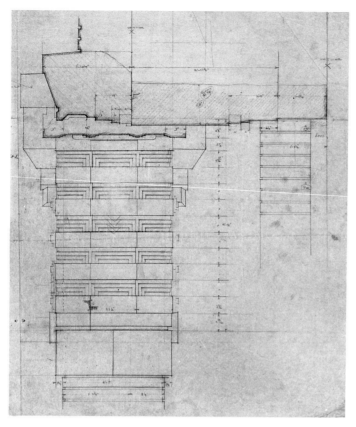

208. Multiple frame as linear fret, Imperial Hotel, 1916–22 (TAL 1509.486).

manding of Japan's limited building technology. He kept the plan, but recast the exterior in favor of a more literal adaptation of Japanese forms.[125] If he had continued with his first scheme, the abstraction implied in the use of flat multiple planes would have made the Imperial Hotel an international example of modernity. Although the motif of the multiple frame was universal and found in Japanese art, the spareness and flat planarity of Wright's wall surfaces would have conflicted with the indigenous forms of Japanese architecture.

Although Wright often made a primary form the generative theme of a design, he combined primary forms to produce the dense texture that defined much of the atmosphere of the hotel. The result was an extraordinary series of designs that completely surpassed the complexity of his earlier ornament. The high points, Wright's designs for carved oya panels in the banquet room, showed the expressive power of combining motifs of circles and squares (figs. 215, 216). Wright designed eight relief panels, which were grouped in pairs and flanked the massive piers in the banquet hall. The center of the design consists of layers of squares within squares. Multiple framing descends straight down and at angles from the central element. The background is made of layers of elements: the upper layer, contained within a partial circle, consists of overlapping circles, hexagons, and triangles; a lower layer, emerging at the edge of the design, restates the motif of the multiple frame and semicircular band-

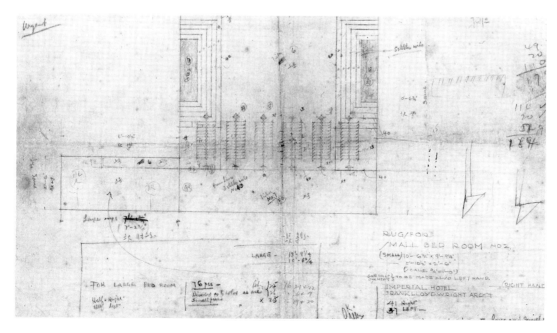

209. Multiple frame as motif for rug design, Imperial Hotel, 1916–22 (TAL 1509.032).

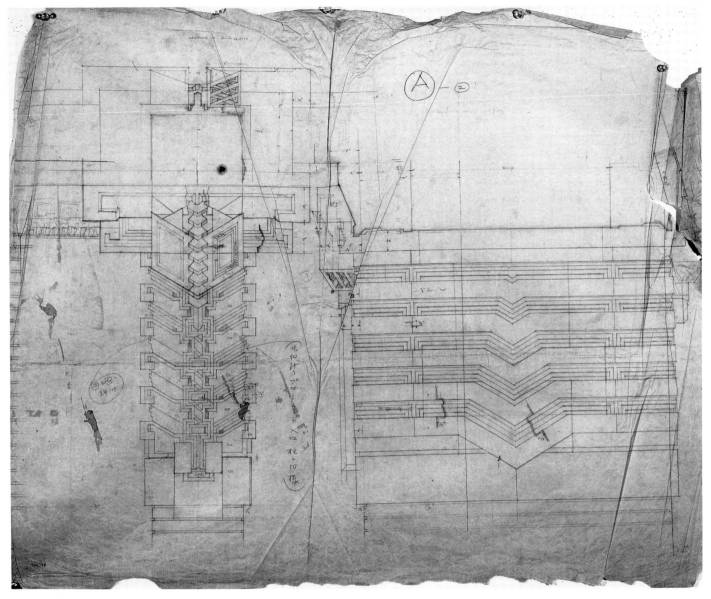

210. Multiple frame as elongated fret, Imperial Hotel, 1916–22 (TAL 1509.198).

ing. Fully abstract in their conventionalization, these designs contained the spell power of geometry. People associated the designs with peacocks—the central element can be seen as the body of the peacock, the circular design behind as its fan—and the banquet hall became known as the *Kujaku-No-Ma,* or Peacock Room. Pulling together vertical and horizontal surfaces, Wright developed a variation of the peacock design for rugs for the hotel (fig. 217). These were apparently woven in China, but never received at the hotel. Despite the virtuosity of these designs, they formed part of the overall program of ornament at the hotel. The circular forms related them to the mandala designs on the ceiling beams of the banquet hall, to the circles carved in reliefs, and to the spheres used as sculpture (fig. 218).

Having seen how Wright used primary forms at the Imperial

211. Perspective, Imperial Hotel, first scheme, 1913 (TAL 1509.003).

212. Perspective elevation of front, Imperial Hotel, first scheme, 1913 (TAL 1409.016).

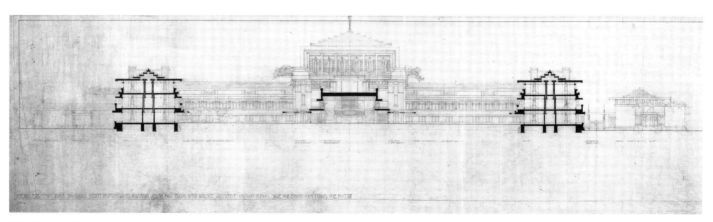

213. Section/elevation, Imperial Hotel, first scheme, 1913 (TAL 1409.031).

214. Josef Hoffmann, Austrian Pavilion, Rome, 1910–11 (*Der Architekt* 17, 1911).

Hotel to unify a variety of designs, we can reconsider the questions underlying this study: Was the symbolism associated with primary forms based on fact or on romanticized idealizations? And how effective were these visual symbols in achieving the reform of social life sought by Wright?

Archaeological material indicates that there is some factual basis for associating simplified geometry with the origins of material culture. A materialist might explain the occurrence of primary forms in different cultures as a result of people having similar materials and technology. Using only a measuring stick and a string for a compass, and sand, mud, stone, and wood as materials, pyramids could be created and temple walls could be articulated with recessed planes. A spiritualist might explain the persistence of these forms as manifestations of a collective unconscious. No longer tenable, however, is the view that only contact with an advanced culture can introduce such forms to an inferior, primitive culture. Regardless of whether one accepts a materialist or cosmological explanation, or a diffusionist or antidiffusionist perspective, the motifs appear through time in diverse cultures from Mesopotamia, to Egypt, to the Orient, to Mesoamerica.

In answering the question about the romanticizing of primary forms we must assume that an idealization of forms took place. After all, Wright and the Secessionists were artists, not archaeologists, and their intentions were to associate new forms with old, not to replicate them or to literally recreate the conditions under which they occurred. The evidence of design in nature, not historicist imitation, was the central issue. Josef A. Lux, the Viennese critic, summed up the problem in his analysis of the ambitions of the Secession:

It is not a question of excavating an old temple, but of breaking away from stereotype, of recognizing and making visible the basic principles of purpose and materials known to earlier cultures. The relationship, therefore, is not historical but teleological. We must bring to light these timeless, autonomous, and immanent basic principles, to which modern plastic art (*Raumkunst*) again pays honor . . . not out of the rubble of centuries, but out of our own souls.[126]

In the work of the Viennese, the motifs of the square within a square, the multiple frame, and recessed panel appear to be more than mere decoration. For the artists of the Secession, the importance of such motifs seems to derive from their metaphysical meanings.[127] By associating these motifs with structure,

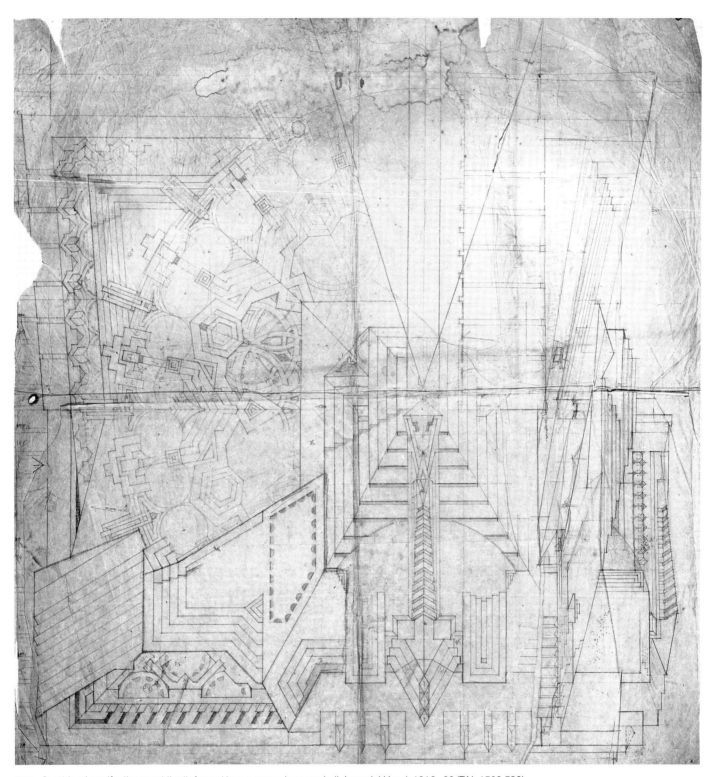

215. Combined motifs, "peacock" relief panel in oya stone, banquet hall, Imperial Hotel, 1916–22 (TAL 1509.530).

216. Combined motifs, "peacock" relief panel in oya stone, banquet hall, Imperial Hotel (*IH*).

217. Carpet design with "peacock" motif, Imperial Hotel (Wijdeweld, *Life Work*).

218. Banquet Hall, Imperial Hotel, c. 1922.

artists could symbolize the making of architecture itself. By associating them with sacred architecture, they could symbolize the origins of culture with forms untainted by historicist imitation. Despite such high aspirations, it is difficult to establish how seriously artists and architects took these associations and how well they understood them. Although Wright was probably unaware of the complex underpinnings for the convic-

tions of the Viennese, he appeared to take the meanings of such forms seriously. For him, seeing the motifs of the recessed plane and the multiple frame reinforced his own beliefs in the power of geometry and stimulated his experiments in ornament. These motifs appear to resonate for Wright because they had the power of symbols.

In responding to the question of how, or whether, primary

forms could affect contemporary society, we confront the problem of the relationship of symbols to their social meanings. Although I have suggested general associations with these motifs, different cultures may have dramatically different symbolic associations. The same motif of a triangle, for instance, may appear in folk art as well as Neolithic art with vastly different symbolic meanings to its makers. The forms persist through time, but their associations may change, making questions of interpretation complex. Furthermore, explanations of cause and effect are too simple to provide a basis for the correlation of changes in art with changes in society.

While answers to such basic issues lead to other questions, it would appear that we have some answers about the bond between Frank Lloyd Wright and his European colleagues. Wright and the artists of the Secession seemed to share an ardent interest in spiritual rebirth, in a sacred spring that witnessed the rejection of moribund values, and in a movement towards abstraction and away from naturalism. Sharing a formal language, symbolic associations, and common design processes joined Wright and the Secessionists. When he saw firsthand the artistic developments of the Secession, he found an additional confirmation—one more lesson from Europe that allowed long-standing interests to emerge with a new purpose and vigor. Understanding the bond between Wright and Europe allows us to see how Wright differed and how he went beyond the Secessionists. With this realization, a new way of seeing Wright's work in this period emerges: inspired by Europe and entering his own primitivist phase, he intensified the iconography of his ornament in a pursuit of the primal origins of architecture itself.

I remember how as a boy, primitive American architecture—Toltec, Aztec, Mayan, Inca—stirred my wonder, excited my wishful admiration. I wished I might someday have money enough to go to Mexico, Guatemala and Peru to join in excavating those long slumbering remains of lost cultures; mighty, primitive abstractions of man's nature . . .—Frank Lloyd Wright (1957)[1]

8   A Lesson in Iconography

One unexpected lesson of Wright's European experience was an awakening of his dormant interest in the original architecture of the Americas. As he admitted, this interest had existed since he was a young boy. But how did this indigenous architecture influence him? What were his intentions in using primitive motifs? What were their underlying meanings? The pursuit of these questions provides some insight into the designs catalyzed by Wright's travels in Europe, the influences on the architect, and his goal of transforming the social order in an ongoing search for a truly American architecture.

A clear understanding of the primitivism that emerged in Wright's work after his travels to Europe has never been a factor in the perception of Wright's designs of the 1910s and early 1920s. Wright relied for some of his buildings and projects on the Prairie Style with little innovation, but he made others the subject of experiments. Hitchcock disparaged Wright's work of this period as being stylistically "heavy" and lacking coherence.[2] Critics who have written about Wright's exotic interests have emphasized pre-Columbian architecture as the source of motifs for his buildings after 1910.[3] Some historians have even tried to trace an exotic strand in his work back to the 1880s.[4] Most historians cite the A. D. German Warehouse, the Bogk House, and the Hollyhock House as examples of Maya influence. But until now, Maya influence and the experimental quality of Wright's work have not been understood.

Wright's aesthetic experiments in ornament combined with an interest in ancient and non-Western cultures that extended throughout the decade of the 1910s and into the early 1920s to create the primitivist phase of his work. Frazer's *The Golden Bough*, which began to be published in 1890, had been an early precursor to developments that came to fruition for Wright after his travels in Europe. Fundamental to these formal developments were Wright's associations of aesthetic, mystical, and social forces with the geometric elements of his designs. Paralleling the beliefs of the Secessionists, Wright's theory of architecture held that the social and artistic functions of design were inseparable, and that form and meaning were indivisible. Wright and the Secessionists, who used similar primary forms, associated ancient and primitive sources of art and architecture with purity.

These beliefs belonged to the tradition that a Golden Age existed in which a culture's architecture expressed the true values of its people. In a Golden Age there could be noble savages whose connections to nature brought an innocence that had been lost to modern people. In Wright's and the Secessionists' views, if these ancient sources became tools in the hands of prophetic and revolutionary artists and architects, then modern culture might have some hope of finding its own purity and truth while retaining some connection with man's basic creative urges.

Instead of being simple influences, the forms associated with the pure origins of Mesoamerican architecture and sculpture became for Wright part of a universal language. This language existed throughout primitive and exotic cultures worldwide and even in the exemplars of Western architecture. As he had stated in *The Japanese Print*, Wright believed that a "spell power" existed in primary forms, which allowed the creation of an iconography that had cultural significance. An artist could take indigenous forms with received meanings and transform them to represent contemporary social values in what Wright later called "emulation. . . . [not] imitation" of tradition.[5] Simplification and abstraction through conventionalization were the means of converting the universality of a motif into a particular expression. Conventionalization, according to Wright, had the power ultimately to create the true architecture of a culture. It provided the tool for abstraction by which Wright interchanged, exchanged, and transformed motifs composed of primary forms.

Could Wright have entered this primitivist phase in his work without going to Europe? There is no absolute answer to this question. However, only after his return from Europe in 1910 does any primitivism, including pre-Colombian references, become central to his work. This occurred after Wright saw firsthand in Europe that the Secessionists had absorbed the lessons of simplification contained in ancient architecture. Primitivism allowed a movement from—but not total rejection of—his earlier Prairie Style houses. Entering his own primitivist phase, Wright began to surpass his European contemporaries by creating motifs that were unexplored by his peers. Although he recognized their interest in primary forms, as manifested in their interest in Japanese art, Wright thought his European colleagues still had much to learn. He wrote in *The Japanese Print:* "The German and Austrian Secession movement owes [the influence of Japanese art] a large debt of gratitude. Yet the in-

219. Plaster casts of Maya buildings at Labna and Uxmal, World's Columbian Exposition, Chicago 1893 (*The World's Colombian Exposition Reproduced; . . . The World's Fair Chicago, 1893,* reprinted in Weisberg, *Art Quarterly* 30, 1967).

220. Plaster cast of portal vault of the House of the Governor, Uxmal, World's Columbian Exposition, Chicago 1893 (*The World's Colombian Exposition Reproduced; . . . The World's Fair Chicago, 1893*, reprinted in Weisberg, *Art Quarterly* 30, 1967).

fluence of this art is still young. The German mind has only recently awakened to its significance, and proceeds now with characteristic thoroughness to ends only half discerned."[6] Wright sought to speed up the learning process by focusing, during the 1910s, on the evolution of his ornament and not on a search for new planning principles. His language of ornament took on a tectonic expression that had no parallel in Europe. It became more three-dimensional, while the Secessionists tended to pursue an art of the surface. Although he continued some of the idioms and methods that characterized his Prairie Style period, he experimented throughout the 1910s until his final return from Japan in 1922.

The basic concept that defines Wright's experiments in primitivism is paradoxical: he tried to define a specifically American iconography by searching for universal sources. This approach includes using and transforming the motifs of primary forms found in many other cultures. Grasping the duality of Wright's work, we can begin to understand the complex creativity of this period.

Sources of Influence

There were numerous sources available to Wright for studying the art and architecture of the Americas. These sources pro-

vided Wright with the cultural context and images he needed in defining his iconography. The scope ranged from the popularly available John L. Stephens's *Incidents of Travel in Central America, Chiapas, & Yucatan,* first published in 1841 with drawings by Frederick Catherwood, to the casts of Maya buildings displayed at the Chicago Columbian Exposition in 1893, to Teobert Maler's stunning exhibition of photographs of ruins in Guatemala, and to the Field Museum in Chicago (figs. 219, 220).[7] Even Viollet-le-Duc, Wright's favorite architectural theorist, had written on the "Antiquités américaines," the subject of his introductory essay to the 1863 edition of Charnay's *Cités et ruines américaines . . . ,*[8] but it is doubtful that Wright absorbed this work since he did not read French.

The works of Stephens and Catherwood, of Charnay, and the Chicago Exposition are the sources to which historians have often turned in establishing the traces of Maya influence in Wright's architecture. But they have never asked why references to Maya architecture appear so dramatically in his designs after 1910. Could he have been inspired by a direct confrontation with the ancient monuments and ruins? Wright's son Lloyd even told the story that his father went to the Yucatan—the location of many major Maya sites—during the 1910s.[9] But this account lacks documentary confirmation, and the dates of a visit do not fit into the chronology of Wright's travels during the decade. Without such a visit, the context that emerges is a complex one and, until now, has not correlated Wright's emerging primitivism and his perceptions of primitivism in Europe. Also, many sources for Wright's primitivist architecture have been unexamined. And until now, no study has been done that examines the various meanings of the motifs or how they were created.

The problem of establishing Maya influence on Wright's work can be exemplified in a study of the fret, or key, motif. Tselos cited the fret as found in the facade of the House of Governors at Uxmal as an influence on Wright (fig. 221).[10] Perhaps the architect saw this motif in Stephens's *Incidents of Travel,* or elsewhere. Tselos argues that the Maya motif influenced Wright's use of the fret for his graphic signature in various publications

and for the entry to Taliesin West, which was begun in 1937 (fig. 222).

As soon as we consider Owen Jones's discussion of the fret, however, we realize that reading the fret only as an example of Maya influence is too narrow. As I pointed out earlier, Jones's *Grammar of Ornament* provided a common source of comparative ornament for Wright and his European contemporaries. Jones begins his examination of the fret in Greek sources and provides lineal and parallel developments of the motif that include its appearance in Arabian, Moorish, Celtic, and Maya architecture. Wright's insignia is analogous to the frets shown in Jones's plate of Pompeian ornament or in examples eight and twenty-two in his plate of Greek ornament (figs. 223, 224). Wright, however, alters the limitation of the band as a horizon-

221. Uxmal, House of the Governor (*Art and Archaeology* 1, 1915).

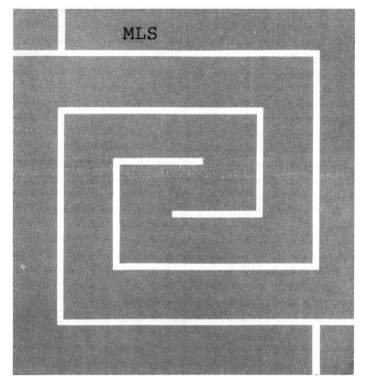

222. Frank Lloyd Wright monogram printed as a mailing label (TAL).

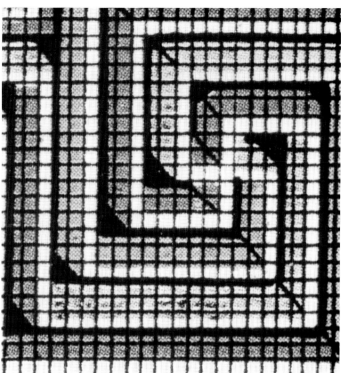

223. Pompeian fret, detail, no. 3 (Owen Jones, *Grammar of Ornament*, pl. 25).

tal strip by reversing the figure and ground relationships of the forms and by adding linking elements that extend vertically. The vertical lines imply that the motifs could be assembled to form a field. While Jones's observations on the cultural contact between various cultures were limited by the available ethnology, he clearly proposed here, and throughout his *Grammar,* the common occurrence of similar motifs in widely disparate cultures of archaic, primitive, and even Western civilization, at least through the Renaissance (figs. 225–28). He did not reduce motifs to singular meanings, and he could identify differences in development that allowed for the parallel evolution of a motif: Celtic interlacing differed from Moorish interlacing by the Celtic design having curved terminations where the Moorish had intersections of diagonal lines; the Chinese fret was "less perfect" than the Greek fret because it lacked regularity, was elongated in a continuous band as a meander, and was used discontinuously as fragments.

Instead of seeing Wright as influenced by the Maya fret alone, we can see him reflecting both Maya motifs and the universal set to which the motif belongs. The fret is part of a series of mo-

tifs that are originary forms found in ancient, exotic, and primitive cultures. If we look at the problem from this perspective, we can replace the standard critical reliance on influence as a one-to-one visual correspondence with a complex overlay of similar and dissimilar elements, rich in source and association, that are available to the artist.

The complexity of the web of forces that entangled Wright is underscored by his knowledge of another overlooked source of pre-Colombian influence: the font of motifs of the Maya world exhibited in the Panama-California Exposition in San Diego.[11] In January 1915, before his dispute with Wright, Alfonso Iannelli took Wright to the Maya exhibition at the exposition. He introduced Wright to Alice Klauber, a painter who would become associated with the Southwest school, and she gave Wright a collection of photographs of the Maya exhibits.[12] This cache of photographs has not surfaced, so we cannot know precisely Wright's reference material. The exposition, however, was amply documented in the journal *Art and Archaeology.*[13]

The themes of the Panama-California Exposition clearly coincided with Wright's awakened interest in primitivism and

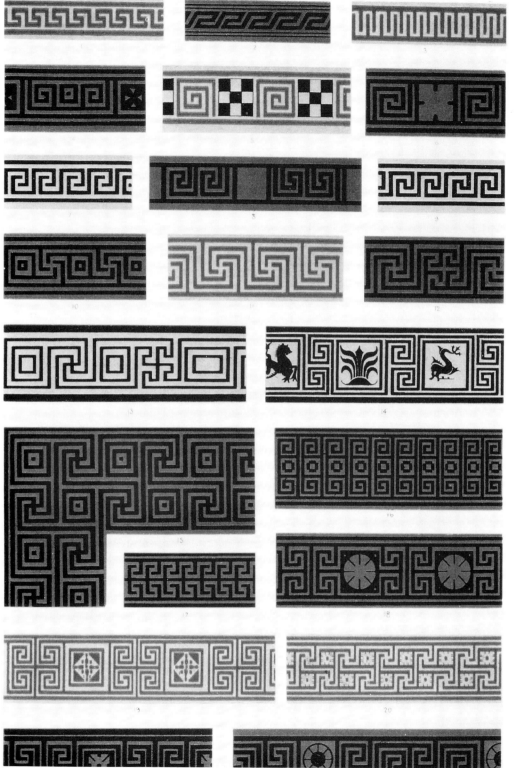

224. Greek frets (Owen Jones, *Grammar of Ornament*, pl. 15).

225. Greek fret resembling a guilloche (Owen Jones, *Grammar of Ornament*, p. 35).

226. Yucatan fret (Owen Jones, *Grammar of Ornament*, p. 35).

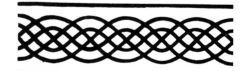

227. Arabian, Mauresque, and Celtic frets (Owen Jones, *Grammar of Ornament*, p. 35).

228. Chinese fret (Owen Jones, *Grammar of Ornament*, p. 35).

help clarify why he may have identified the Maya as the original Americans. The exposition emphasized the history of man in the early stages of development, with a particular emphasis on native American culture. Illustrated in the exposition was the "highest achievement of aboriginal American—the work of the Maya race."[14] Housed in the California building, the exhibits of Maya art and architecture were extensive and intended to show the "golden age of the ancient race."[15]

The objects representing the Maya in the California building ranged from casts of sculptures at Palenque to hieroglyphs to a series of frescoes depicting six of the most important cities of ancient Central America (fig. 229).[16] Of particular note were the architectural models—these alone would have provided Wright with a trove of motifs and building masses which he could transform into his own iconography. The buildings represented by the models were cited as the greatest achievements of Central America. The emphasis placed on these models around 1915 gives some indication of how the buildings were seen by Wright's contemporaries: "El Castillo," the Temple of Kukulkan at Chichén Itzá, was a "design . . . of exceptionally high order, indicating great progress in architecture"; "The Palace" or "House of the Governors" at Uxmal was described as the "last

229. Carlos Vierrà, fresco of Chichén Itzá, Panama-California Exposition, 1915 (*Art and Archaeology* 2, 1915).

230. Model, "El Castillo," Chichén Itzá, Panama-California Exposition, 1915 (*Art and Archaeology* 2, 1915).

word in the building art in Ancient America"[17] (figs. 230, 231).

The attitude of archaeologists, according to the magazine, was that all aboriginal people of Central America and North America were part of one "American Indian Race." They formed one identity and were not descended, as some fantastical theories would have it, from Egypt or the Orient. Comparisons were frequently made between Maya art and that of North American Indians.[18] Maya artists were admirable because they "tell of human dignity and divinity—tell in a way that was perfectly naive and honest, of their belief in the efficacy of ritual, symbolic ornamentation, gorgeous vesture in dealing with divinity—tell of profound veneration for life and life forces, even though enshrined in bird or beast."[19]

In other words, the contemporary view of the Maya held them as the peaceful embodiment of humane qualities and artistic richness. Their art and religion were inseparable, provid-

ing what Wright had described as the source of a new language of form. Although different linguistic groups had begun to be recognized among widely dispersed tribes, the Maya became the collective representatives of the American Indian race. Representing all North American Indians, they become a symbol of the original Americans, a position that Wright adopted in his subsequent designs of the 1910s.

If Wright perceived that the Maya embodied all Indian cultures, his view was reinforced by his long-standing interest in North American Indians particularly. Indian themes, represented naturalistically, had been part of Wright's designs. He had used the imagery of American Indians in the murals of his bedroom in Oak Park and in other designs before 1910.[20] However, they took on a new importance as a source of artistic renewal in Wright's primitivist phase. In his *Offices of Mystical Religion*, Reverend Guthrie, Wright's friend and alter ego dur-

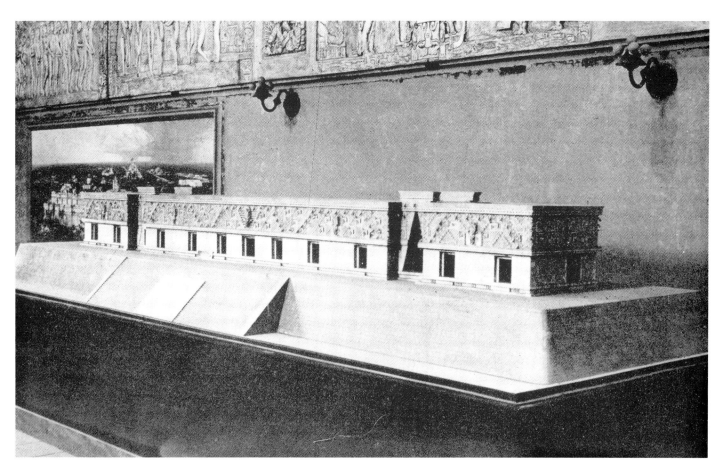

231. Model, "The Palace," Uxmal, Panama-California Exposition, 1915 (*Art and Archaeology* 2, 1915).

232. Kehl Dance Academy, perspective, project for Madison, Wisconsin, 1912 (Wijdeweld, *Life Work*).

ing his personal crises of the 1910s, expressed attitudes about the Indians that could have stood for those of Wright.[21] According to Guthrie, new inspiration for the purification of modern culture could be found in the Hako, a North American Indian ritual for the rebirth of the soul. An explanation of the ritual, including the role of sacred objects and music, had been published in 1904 in the *Annual Report of the Bureau of American Ethnology*.[22] Although the version of the ceremony was that of the Pawnee Indians, it had broad usage among many tribes. The ceremony had two central purposes: "to benefit individuals by bringing them the promise of children, life, and abundance; and to establish bonds between two distinct tribes."[23] The betterment of the individual and the society was accomplished through the use of sacred objects in a complex two-part ritual ceremony.[24]

The ritual of the Hako had particular appeal because its symbols were "ethnically American." Summing up the relevance of Indian culture for contemporary American life but connecting Indian rites to those of ancient and primitive cultures, Guthrie observed that these rituals made the ideas, symbols, and ceremonies of the Egyptians, Persians, Greeks, and Hebraic culture more appealing and understandable, while at the same time allowing a break with those same old world traditions.[25] The beauty of the Hako, as it was described, its cosmic purpose, and the devotion expressed by its songs, which were transcribed, could affect Americans searching for true and pure roots of life.

Guthrie's search for the pure sources of religions and their true American expression directly paralleled Wright's search for an American architecture and an American individualistic lifestyle. Guthrie's ideas, expressed in his books, many of which

Wright owned, provided a spiritual context for the architect's artistic investigations.[26]

An American Iconography

Having established a context for Frank Lloyd Wright's search for an American iconography, we can reexamine the pre-Columbian influences on him as references both to the aboriginal American culture and to universal motifs. The experiments in primitivism that Wright undertook in his Portland Cement Pavilion, *Call* Building, Midway Gardens, and the Imperial Hotel occur also among his designs for buildings and projects that have been particularly singled out as showing Maya influence. One of those ventures was a project for the Kehl Dance Academy in Madison, Wisconsin (fig. 232).[27] The design was executed in the late spring or summer of 1914 for Professor Frederick W. Kehl, the leading dance-master in Madison, who had also taught dancing at the Hillside Home School of Wright's aunts. For the academy, Wright initially designed a building containing a banquet hall, reception parlor, and auditorium for seven hundred people. In a subsequent plan, he replaced the parlor and banquet hall with a candy store and flower shop

on the ground floor, and a three-bedroom apartment on the mezzanine.

Gabriel Weisberg has proposed the perspective of this scheme as Wright's earliest developed pre-Columbian design because it recalls elements of the Temple of Tulum, published in Catherwood's *Views of Ancient Monuments* (fig. 233).[28] Common elements are described as pillars, a serpentine zig-zag motif at corner posts, and wedge-shaped stones recalling Indian feathers. Weisberg cites a "maze device" between the piers of the second floor of Wright's scheme as analogous to the volute motif of the Maya fret combined with coiled serpents found in the western range of the Nunnery at Uxmal and partially recast in plaster at Chicago's Columbian Exposition in 1893 (fig. 219).

In addition to any superficial visual analogies to Maya architecture, the ornamental motifs of the perspective of the Kehl Dance Academy have multiple references. They are experiments in Wright's development of primary forms within the context of his established design methods and his use of a universal symbolic language. In the subsequent examples I will try to show that whenever Wright used a Maya motif he was referring to more than the Maya.

The examples of Maya influence were not part of Wright's

233. Frederick Catherwood, Temple of Tulum (reprinted in Weisberg, *Art Quarterly* 30, 1967).

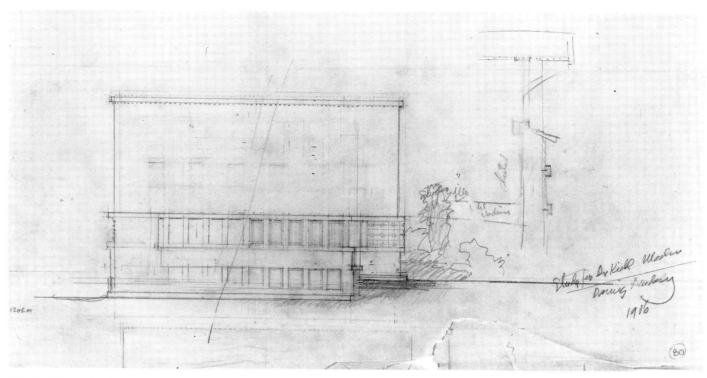

234. Kehl Dance Academy, elevation, Madison, Wisconsin, 1912 (TAL 1205.001).

early designs for the dance school (fig. 234). The earliest elevation shows a simpler blank attic and an ornamental motif around the mezzanine level of clusters of squares, resembling the ornament of the Coonley House.[29] The preparatory study for this perspective does not include a "maze device."[30] As Wright subsequently developed the scheme, he began at the mezzanine level to wrap the wall plane around the corner, his long-established design strategy for reinforcing the continuity of planar surfaces. The slanted planes between the piers, which are purported to resemble the Maya maze motif, are not actually frets but the primary form of the square within a square, split in half. Here Wright divided the panels by piers as he had done in numerous variants in Midway Gardens. At the clerestory level above the mezzanine, the windows are set within multiple frames, and the treatment of the corners of the attic is an example of the multiple frame used in turning a corner. The flag-like elements flanking the mezzanine windows consist of alternating rows of bare light-bulbs, a device similar to the lighting fixtures at Midway Gardens. The posts in front of the attic, described by the historian as representations of symbolic serpent coils,[31] can be seen similarly as restatements of the wrapping plane treatment of the corners of the mezzanine.

The motifs of the square within a square and the multiple frame of the Kehl Dance Academy are also, however, signs in a language of forms found in the ancient architecture of many cultures, including the pre-Columbian. As we saw earlier, these motifs were used by the Viennese Secessionists and now by Wright (fig. 107). Despite the commonality of appearance with pre-Columbian architecture, the entire design could have been generated with the basic motifs of the multiple frame and the square within a square. Instead of being an example of simple influence, the design occurs in the context of Wright's other contemporary designs in which the architect avoided literal references of naturalism and promoted abstraction through the transformation of primary forms.

A. D. German Warehouse

A second example of multiple reference—a literal, visual reference to pre-Columbian motifs combined with Wright's use of a family of archetypal forms—is the Albert Dell German Cold Storage Warehouse in Richland Center, Wisconsin, the town of

232   CHAPTER EIGHT

Wright's birth (fig. 235).[32] Designed around 1915 and under construction from July 1917 to July 1920, it was built with poured concrete floors, masonry walls, and cast concrete. Intended to house wholesale supplies of sugar, cement, and other commodities, the building was never fully completed because construction costs far exceeded the client's budget.[33]

To begin with Tselos's observations, the warehouse has been cited as an example of Maya influence on Wright and compared as a "direct match" to the Temple of Three Lintels and the Red House (known also as Chichenchob or the Prison) at Chichén Itzá (fig. 236).[34] The warehouse, Temple of Three Lintels, and the Red House all have blank walls, three openings, and decorated friezes, but there are also numerous formal differences between the warehouse and these possible Maya influences. While some Maya buildings, such as the Temple of the Frescoes at Tulum in the Yucatan, corbel outward in their attic zones, as does the warehouse, most of those with slanting attics cant inward.[35] The motifs of the frieze of the Temple of Three Lintels are sets of stone columns between sections of perforated lattice in a rhythmic alteration.[36] But the German Warehouse frieze is made of primary forms and is based on a regular grid filled with a pattern of four elements each of which is derived from a basic square.[37] On the top cornice the square is transformed into a square within a square that is subdivided into quarters, as clearly seen in a working drawing of an elevation (fig. 237).[38] Also, the cornice intended to be above the entry is composed of the multiple frames used in bands, punctuated with a square within a square at each end, and accented at the bottom of the bands by a row of triangles. This cornice sits on the capitals of four columns with cast integral patterns that can be seen as the tectonic expression of the loads they are carrying. These motifs of a square within a square and multiple frames are found in a variety of cultures far distant from the Maya. Once again, an entire composition could be generated from primary forms.

At the same time, multiple references apply to the German Warehouse. The principal sculptural ornaments can be seen as derived from masks of the rain-god Chac, as seen at the Red House. Wright located those conventionalized faces at the corners of the warehouse, where he placed protruding brackets, analogous to Maya hooked tongues, to hold flagstaffs.[39] This combination of abstraction from primary forms and the transformation of Maya references complicates any simple analogy between the warehouse design and specific Maya buildings and supports the need to rely on multiple references in interpreting Wright's design.[40]

In addition to exploring primary forms and Maya references, Wright pursued his interest in the building construction technology of precast concrete, which affected the formal expression of the building. Such rectilinear shapes without undercuts all required relatively simple forms, and the casting, which was done on site, could use the cement purchased at wholesale by the client. Indeed, every ornament of the building is appropriate to the technology of concrete casting. In this light, the A. D. German Warehouse demonstrates the nature of the technology of its materials as much as it displays exoticism. As an alternative to seeing the warehouse strictly as a derivation from Maya buildings such as the Red House, it can be seen as an experiment in the basic motifs of the multiple frame and recessed panel, as the expression of the nature of materials, and as a search for an abstract, generalized primitivism. The question remains, however, of why Frank Lloyd Wright would design a stylized Maya building in the small town of Richland Center, Wisconsin, for a wholesale grocer. A direct reference to the indigenous Indians of Wisconsin is possible but unlikely, since they built no temples. Here, the popular conflation of the Maya with North American Indians appears. Instead of seeing North American Indians as having moved across Asia over the Bering Straits and then descended from the north, Wright may have thought, like many of his contemporaries, that they had ascended from the south or that they had contact with indigenous cultures of Mesoamerica. The references at the German Warehouse then would be generalized to the aboriginal Americans, the Maya who represented the collective Indian race. The project then becomes a marker in Wright's effort to define an iconography of American culture, one that refers to the original Americans in a language of form found in many cultures.[41]

The Barnsdall House

The commission from Aline Barnsdall for a complex of buildings in Los Angeles provided a major opportunity to experiment with a vital American iconography (fig. 238).[42] Wright had first met Barnsdall in Chicago after the Taliesin tragedy; on one of his stops in California on the way to Japan, he renewed his acquaintance with this wealthy enthusiast of the little-theater movement. She wanted Wright to design her own residence, an experimental theater, a movie theater, terraced housing, studios, and shops on a hill that she had bought in Hollywood. Wright designed her home, Hollyhock House, around an open

235. A. D. German Cold Storage Warehouse, Richland Center, Wisconsin,
designed c. 1915 (TAL 1504.001).

236. Temple of Three Lintels,
Chichén Itzá, Yucatan, Mexico
(Heyden and Gendrop,
*Pre-Columbian Architecture
of Mesoamerica*).

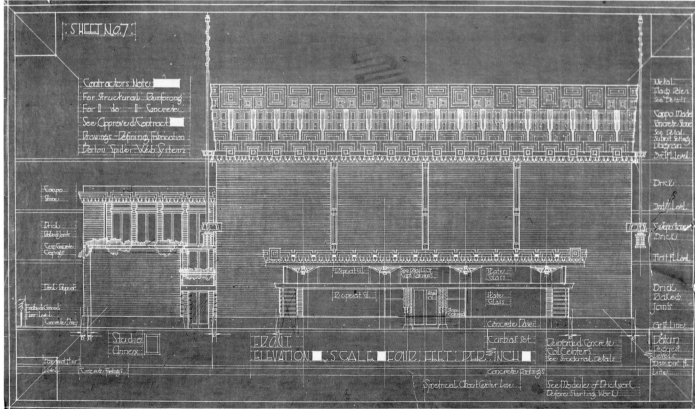

237. A. D. German Cold Storage Warehouse, elevation working drawing, 1915 (TAL 1504.008).

238. Hollyhock House, perspective view, Los Angeles, 1917–20 (Wijdeweld, *Life Work*).

239. Hollyhock House, exterior view of living room, Los Angeles, c. 1920 (Wijdeweld, *Life Work*).

240. Temple of the Tigers, view from southwest, Chichén Itzá, Yucatan, Mexico, c. 975/1200 (Willey, *Das Alte Amerika*).

courtyard that could be used as an open-air theater, with the audience watching performances in the courtyard from roofs of the building's wings. The early studies for the Hollyhock House show little resemblance to Maya forms but instead a stylistic evolution from pyramidal roofs and bare planar walls to a transitional design that combined steep, pitched roofs and a flat roof with canted attic. This was followed by a later scheme showing all the attics having canted sides.[43] Construction began in 1916, but relations between client and architect were full of conflict. Their clash of egos and Wright's lengthy absences ultimately alienated him from the project. Only Barnsdall's residence and two other houses were built, and Wright's designs were compromised.

As built, the canted attics dominated the massing of the house (fig. 239). Their presence and the building's proportions have prompted assertions that the hood-like attic is derived from Maya architecture. Tselos has described one influence on the Hollyhock House as the Temple of the Tigers at Chichén Itzá.[44] Scully has pointed to Structure 33 at Yaxchitlan as another influence (figs. 240, 241).[45] Although simplifying academic writing for popular taste, Ingle has repeated Scully's assertion.[46]

Multiple readings are required to interpret the Hollyhock House and to see how Wright interchanged and exchanged motifs. Before examining these processes of appropriating or transforming forms, we must first make more precise any reference to Maya architecture. Although the Hollyhock House's sloping

241. Structure 33, Yaxchitlan, Chiapas, Mexico, reconstruction, c. 757 (Willey, *Das Alte Amerika*).

attic bears an obvious similarity to Maya buildings, the analogies cited by historians are among the least successful attributions of Maya influence. The Temple of the Tigers, located at one corner of the great ball court at Chichén Itzá, has upper sides that do not slope but rise straight. Similarly, Structure 33 at Yaxchitlan is more dominated by its perforated, straight-sided roof comb than by the canted frieze below it. Numerous other examples would provide more convincing visual analogies between the Hollyhock House and Maya architecture than these examples. Sitting on platforms of steps, temples with heavy piers supporting a sloping attic without roof-combs are widespread. Temple buildings at "The Palace" at Palenque are merely one set of models for sloping roof-attics above huge, solid piers of masonry (figs. 242, 243). Stephens published a drawing of one of these buildings in his *Incidents of Travel* that shows an inclined attic and frieze with cornice above a temple building supported by massive piers.

But were the forms of the Hollyhock House actually derived from any explicit Maya model? The exterior stairs of the court at the Hollyhock House are analogous to the temple stairs of Maya ceremonial temples, but on a vastly reduced scale. The court of Hollyhock House recalls the quadrangle of the ball courts of the Maya, but it also shares the Mediterranean tradition of the enclosed courtyard, which Wright had begun using in other houses during the 1910s.[47]

While generally referring to Maya prototypes, the origins of such roof forms of stone are found in earlier precedents of canted roofs made of thatch (fig. 244). These structures are so basic that we could see them as the "primitive huts" identified in traditional architectural theory as the originary sources of architecture in a variety of cultures (fig. 245). From this perspective, the massing of the Hollyhock House can be seen as a reference to the building typology of the primordial shelter.

In addition to recalling originary qualities in its massing, Wright used primary forms as the ornament of Hollyhock House. The multiple frame motif, absent in the Barnsdall residence as built, is visible in a more developed study that defines the courtyard scheme of the house and its projected wings; the house sits on a base consisting of stacked, receding planes—the square within a square motif raised into three dimensions. Wright used the square within a square motif as the design for the pond (as in the McCormick project) and as an extension of the central living area (fig. 246). Furthermore, utilizing the interchangeable character of primary forms, he placed at the be-

242. "The Palace," Palenque, Chiapas, Mexico, view from southwest, c. 600–900 (Willey, *Das Alte Amerika*).

243. East courtyard at "The Palace" of Palenque, Chiapas, Mexico (John L. Stephens, *Incidents of Travel*).

244. Reconstruction of Piedras Negras, Guatemala, Structure K-5 3d.

ginning of the entry pergola and in trim detail a motif that both represents the corbeling of a Maya arch and doubles as a fret. Wright, however, turned the motif upside down. By doing this he both affirmed and denied its meaning while establishing a subtle minor formal theme in his design.

Recalling Wright's tendency to merge forms of Mesoamerican and North American Indian cultures, we can find other readings for the Hollyhock House. Wright's son Lloyd suggested that his father had conceived the house as reflecting the character of the culture of American Indians of the Southwest, as "a mesa silhouette, terrace on terrace, characterized and developed by Pueblo Indians."[48] Associations of the forms of Maya therefore become subtly overlaid with those of North American Indians.

As at the German Warehouse, the multiple references of the Hollyhock House are augmented by considering the role of building materials and their tectonic expression in the massing of the house. Consistent with one of his long-standing interests, Wright intended that the building be constructed of poured concrete.[49] The solidity of a structure of poured concrete would have altered the experience of the building, made it even more primal, and given Wright an occasion to use one of his favorite building materials on a large scale. Unfortunately, when the house was built, conventional wood framing, hollow structural tile, and stucco were used throughout.[50] Concrete was used only to cast the principle ornamental motif of the Barnsdall residence—a conventionalized hollyhock, from which the house received its name (fig. 247). Nevertheless, Wright's intention of using concrete for the monolithic massing of the building reflects his interests in both technology and iconography.

The Barnsdall Theater Projects

The link between Wright's search for an American iconography and primitivist forms and motifs is reinforced in his drawings and models for the experimental theater at the Barnsdall complex on Olive Hill in Los Angeles. Testing various motifs in a project that had several design phases from 1915 to at least 1920, Wright developed two basic alternative schemes for the theater, one with cubic massing, the other with polygonal massing over the main theater space. When he later had them published, the square-topped scheme was identified as the "first plan" and the octagon-topped scheme as the "second plan."[51]

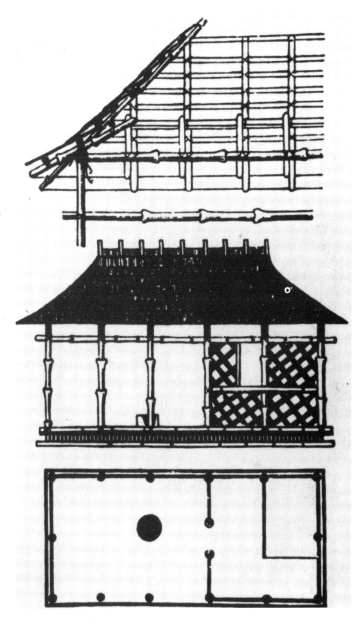

245. Indian hut from Trinidad, 1851 (Gottfried Semper, *Der Stil in den technischen und tectonischen Künsten, oder praktische Aesthetik, 1860– 1863*).

Models were made of both schemes and various versions were studied (figs. 248–50).[52]

Historians have claimed that the theater projects were influenced by Maya buildings at Chichén Itzá and Uxmal.[53] Tselos compared a rendering of the Barnsdall square-topped theater project with a view of a building described as located at the east

STUDY FOR BARNSDALL DWELLING

246. Hollyhock House, pond with square-within-a-square motif, residence
of Aline Barnsdall, Los Angeles, 1917–20 (TAL 1705.002).

247. Conventionalized Hollyhock sculpture at Hollyhock House (author).

end of the Nunnery at Chichén Itzá (fig. 251).[54] The raised lintel and continuous molding above the doorway in that building is cited as the influence on Wright's raised lintel and continuous framing for an exit to a balcony at the theater.

Once again, the simple visual analogy is an inadequate interpretation. Wright's treatment of molding to accentuate the continuity of wall surfaces is consistent with his design methods as early as 1895—Tselos even reproduced an elevation of Wright's studio of 1895 without acknowledging the motif's role as the sign of surface continuity. The lower walls of the square-topped project have few, if any, Maya references. The interpenetrating cubes of the lower massing, instead, have blank surfaces, articulated by continuous bands of ornament (fig. 252).[55] These bands are set vertically away from the corners of the building mass as a means of denying the termination of the corner—one of Wright's distinctive modes of plastic expression developed in his work before 1910.[56] At the upper level of the frieze, however, Wright transformed his earlier practices by turning the bandings into moldings consisting of multiple frames. Here his approach is similar to the developed designs of multiple frames for the Kehl Dance Academy. In using this device he is, in effect, relying on his earlier work as a model while replicating a motif that also appears in the ornament of the Imperial Hotel.[57] Furthermore, the drawing identified in Wright's hand as the "original sketch" of the theater and its associated buildings also shows the motif of the multiple surround on the facade of the central building (fig. 253).[58]

In considering Maya influence on the theater projects, historians have omitted an obvious fact: Maya architecture provides no models for polygonal roof forms. The octagonal-topped scheme and Wright's use of the octagon plan came from his

248. Theater project for Aline Barnsdall, octagon-topped version, 1917–20 (TAL 2005.003).

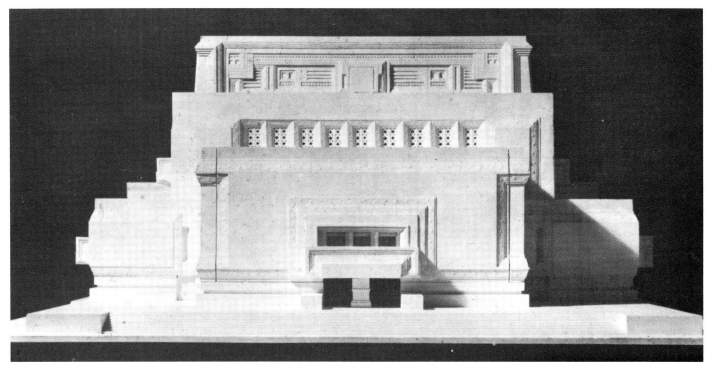

249. Theater project for Aline Barnsdall, model, square-topped version, 1917–20 (Wijdeweld, *Life Work*).

250. Theater project for Aline Barnsdall, model, top portion, octagon-topped version, 1917–20 (author; TAL, Spring Green).

251. East end of Nunnery, Chichén Itzá, Yucatan, Mexico (author).

own long-standing interest in the ability of polygonal forms to emphasize central spaces. The interest in the basic strategy of rotation that defines a polygon is confirmed by a small sketch of one square rotated within another found in Wright's prelimi-nary drawing for the theater complex.[59] It is an example of pri-mary forms being used to generate a building plan.

In addition to experimenting with massing and primary forms, Wright continued in the Barnsdall theater projects to explore conventionalized sculpture, doubling the associa-tions of the Maya with North American Indians. In the square-topped version of the theater, he incorporated symmetrical, frontal figures, each with a conventionalized headdress and wings composed of feathers expressed as linear and grooved elements (fig. 254). The sculptures' importance is underscored

by their appearance in the drawings used to construct the model (fig. 255).[60] Wright intended them for the upper area of the side interior, and he used three-dimensional representations of these figures prominently in the interiors on pedestals in front of the stage.[61] He even tried adding conventionalized sculpture on the perimeter wall on the main mass of the build-ing (fig. 256). Related to the figures at the Midway Gardens and the Imperial Hotel, these sculptures were nearly identical to the sculptures he had placed at the entry of the project for the *Call* Building and would become prototypes for the sculptures of Indians in Wisconsin that he called Nakoma and Nakomis in 1926 (figs. 300, 305).[62]

For the octagonally-topped scheme Wright also added con-ventionalized sculpture on the upper frieze. The extant portion

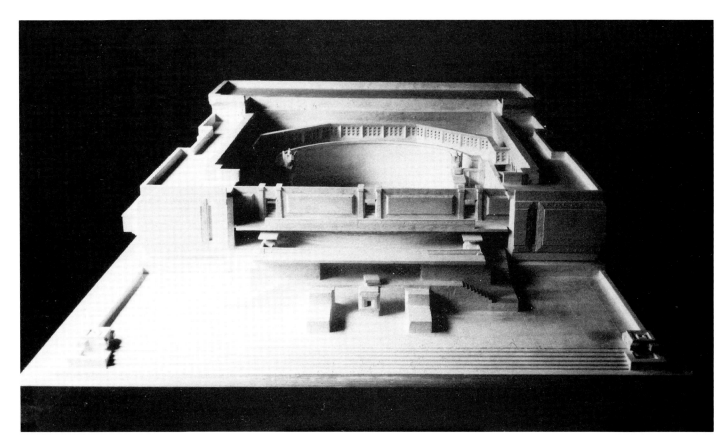

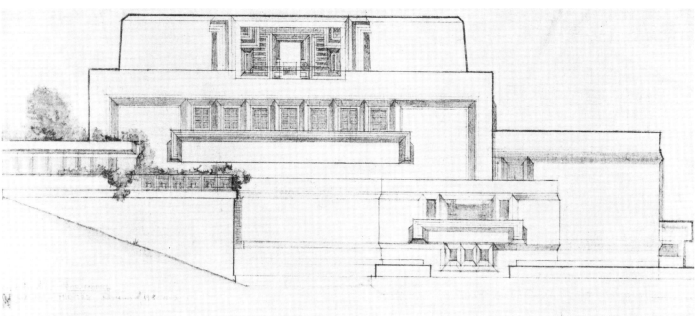

252. Theater project for Aline Barnsdall, elevation drawing for model, and model, 1917–20 (Wijdeweld, *Life Work*).

253. Theater project for Aline Barnsdall, original sketch, 1917–20 (TAL 1705.001).

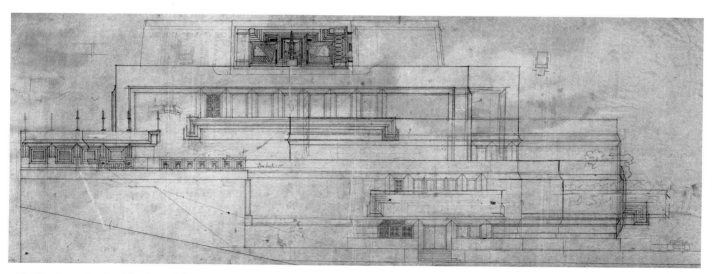

254. Theater project for Aline Barnsdall, square-topped scheme, detail of relief sculpture, 1917–20 (TAL 2005.005).

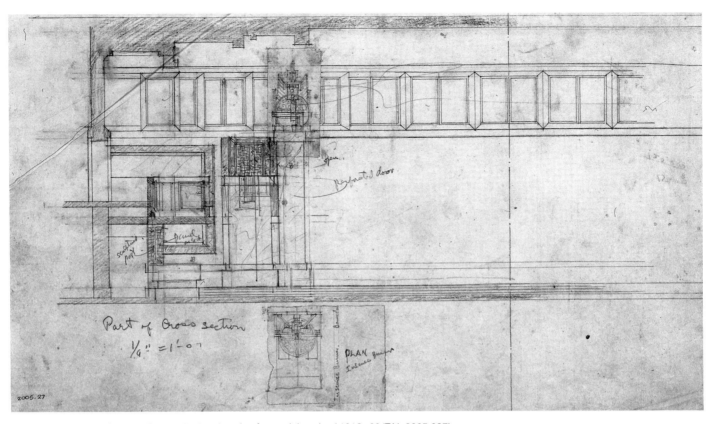

Part of Cross section
1/8" = 1'-0"

PLAN

2005.27

255. Theater project for Aline Barnsdall, site elevation for model, revised 1918–20 (TAL 2005.027).

256. Theater project for Aline Barnsdall, model, upper portion of octagonal scheme, 1917–20 (author; coll. TAL, Spring Green).

257. Frederick C. Bogk House, general view, Milwaukee, 1916 (TAL 1602.010).

of the model shows blocks with striated diagonal grooves that recall patterns found on Aztec pottery, but they also introduce a diagonal dynamism that counters the horizontality of all other abstract motifs.[63] These sculptures are another example of how Wright intertwined elements from Mesoamerican cultures with figures of North American Indians.

The Bogk House

Wright's search for an American iconography continued at the Bogk House, where conventionalized winged figures provided a major sculptural motif on the exterior of the building.[64] Built for Mr. and Mrs. Frederick C. Bogk in 1916, the two-story house was constructed of Roman brick, had a square plan, and was located on a city lot in Milwaukee (fig. 257).[65] Mrs. Bogk commissioned Wright after visiting her friend Queene Ferry Coonley.[66]

On the street facade under the eaves and on the exterior of the sun porch Wright showed how far he had moved from realism to geometric abstraction and how his work differed from Secessionist designs. Before 1910, Wright's Indian murals were literal representations. After his return from Europe in 1910, he

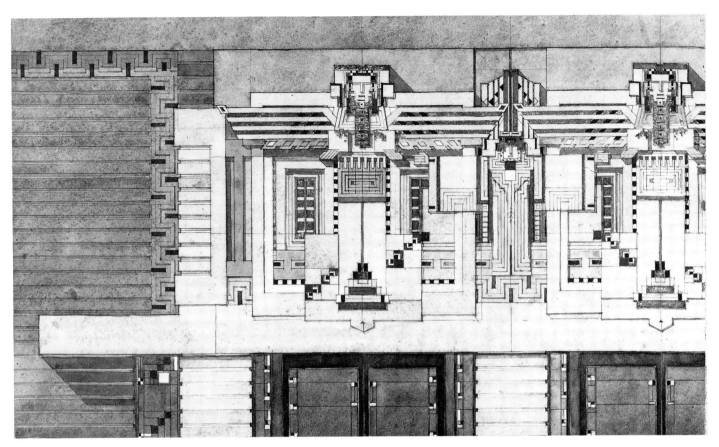

258. Rendered detail of stone lintel, Bogk House, Milwaukee (LC, no. 887810.4).

259. Maya breechcloth, Yucatan, Mexico (Reprinted from *The Ancient Maya*, 4th ed. by Sylvanus G. Morley and George W. Brainerd; rev. by Robert J. Sherer with the permission of the publishers, Stanford University Press. © 1946, 1947, 1956, 1983 by the Board of Trustees of the Leland Stanford Junior University).

transformed the realistic representation of the American Indian into abstractions that took on a generic identity with primitive man and with the aboriginal inhabitants of the continent. These figures were now in a totally geometric style that allowed sculpture to merge with the forms of buildings and create an organic whole. A sketch of the elevation for the Bogk House faintly shows, above the detailing of the windows, the blocking in of four figures in relief on a ledge.[67] Wright developed the designs in a series of extraordinary renderings in watercolor, gouache, and shimmering, metal-flaked paint (fig. 258). These sculptures became frontal, symmetrical, winged sculptural reliefs. The

250   CHAPTER EIGHT

chins of the figures have geometric forms that represent necklaces or beards. The arms are represented as outstretched wings, composed of bands of feathers in alternating gold and beige with diagonal flecks of black and red markings and white borders at the wing tips. The remainder of the torso is absorbed into a rectilinear massing: a stylized "corset" flap at the waist with bands of black and white checks suspended from them. When the figures were cast in concrete, however, the features were simplified.[68]

The sculptures at the Bogk House have been cited as another example of pre-Columbian influence, combining Aztec and Maya motifs. The head has been compared to that of an Aztec goddess of agriculture; the sculptural "Ex" to a loincloth or breechcloth worn by male figures on Maya stelae (fig. 259); the wings and recessed patterns to the frieze of the Nunnery at Uxmal (fig. 260); the diamond-shaped blocks to the overhanging plane of the Temple of the Dwarf at Uxmal; and the rectangular units, or corbeling, at the lower "legs" of the sculpture are compared to the arch at Labna, a cast of which appeared at the Columbian Exposition of 1893.[69]

Each of these assertions can be examined on the basis of visual evidence, and some similarities can be established, with varying degrees of success. Reference to an Aztec goddess of agriculture expands the associations of the sculpture and supports Wright's acknowledged interest in the Aztec culture. For the

Aztecs, feathers took on a range of symbolic meanings on standards, shields, and costumes as insignia of the Aztec military aristocracy.[70] The feathered serpent, a major emblem, represented a concept, not a deity, and was symbolized by a rattlesnake covered with quetzal feathers instead of scales. As was the case with the distinct cultural meanings of many symbolic forms, Wright may not have known of these specific symbolic associations—the general identification with primitivism itself is what interested him. References to the Maya breechcloth ornament, with its stylized scarf or ceremonial beard and abstracted lower torso, suggest a resemblance to parts of the Bogk sculpture, but, unlike Wright's sculptures, the breechcloth ornament has no wings.

The comparison of Wright's Bogk House sculpture to a detail of the frieze at the Nunnery of Uxmal is less impressive: the historian has apparently confused the raised corbeling motif of the facade with wings. This ensemble, including the head at its center, bears little resemblance to the Bogk sculpture. The "skeleton-stepped pyramid or corbeled arch" at the lower body and under the beard is not only the motif of a corbeled arch in section, but also the motif of the multiple frame. The configuration is so basic that it appears as the plan of Egyptian pyramids as well as pyramids of the Maya and in ornament ranging from works of the Wiener Werkstätte to Wright's Barnsdall House and theater designs.

260. Detail from frieze, east range, The Nunnery, Uxmal, Mexico, c. 600/900 (Proskouriakoff, *Album of Maya Architecture*).

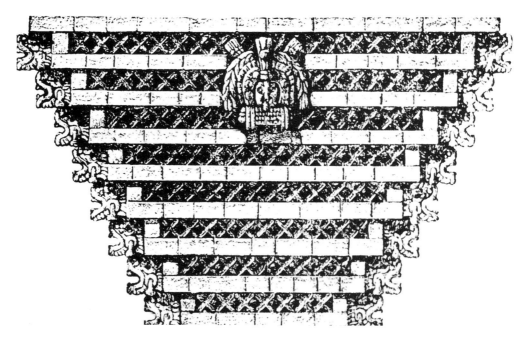

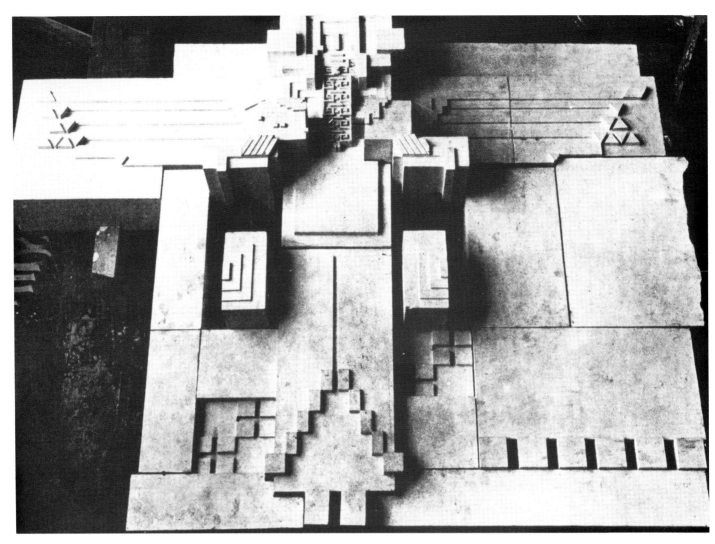

261. F. C. Bogk House sculpture, section of frieze in cast concrete, Milwaukee, 1916 (Wijdeweld, *Life Work*).

A much more obvious, but previously overlooked, potential reference for the Bogk sculpture appears in sculptural figures of Hochob, published in Herbert J. Spinden's *A Study of Maya Art* (figs. 261, 262).[71] Appearing in 1913 in a memoir of the Peabody Museum of American Archaeology and Ethnology, the plates and text could have provided a convenient primer for Wright. Frontal, symmetrical figures are located at the corners of the principal building. Each figure has a geometricized breastplate and an abstracted lower torso separated by a lattice. If a headdress, ceremonial beard, and wings are added, the sculpture would indeed closely resemble Wright's Bogk sculptures. Wright, however, would have taken the wings from other sources.

While the Bogk House sculptures suggest associations with Maya and Aztec models, they also recall, like other projects of the 1910s, Wright's interest in American Indians and in forms that appear in other non-Western cultures. At the Bogk House, Wright continued his efforts to create a mythology of the American Indian. His interest in representations of deities of Indians of the American Southwest are recalled in the facial features of the four large figures. They are composed of rectilinear masses, and their bonnet-shaped headdresses are reminiscent of Hopi

262. Hochob, entry facade, Campeche, Mexico, c. 600–900 (Spinden, *A Study of Maya Art*).

Indian ceremonial headdresses. At the same time, a figure with oriental associations appears in the Bogk House sculptural frieze. Wright had considered having the large sculptures alternate with smaller conventionalized figures.[72] In these designs, the wings in the large figures resemble the hanging sleeves of an outstretched kimono. Contained on each sleeve is the *mon* of the Ichikawa family of Japanese actors, which is also the motif of the square within a square (fig. 167). The body itself of the shorter figure is composed of multiple frames of recessed planes. The smaller figures differed by having tall headdresses and wing extensions that are more square than those of the bigger sculptures. While not executed, these smaller figures add to the "universal" references of the sculptures. Associations with Mesoamerica, Amerindian cultures, and abstract motifs of primary forms show that Wright used the universality of basic forms in the specific cultural context of America.

Japanese Projects

Just as he interchanged motifs between cultures in North and Mesoamerica, Wright exchanged motifs between the West and the East. In his buildings and projects in Japan, he carried his interest in primitivism back to one of its sources. His work there allowed for the interchange and exchange of motifs that linked his own designs in disparate contexts and connected them to a common set of motifs. Including the monumental Imperial Hotel, Wright designed a total of twelve projects for Japan, of which seven were executed to various degrees of completion.[73] He used the idiom of his earlier Prairie Style houses in some designs while experimenting with more exotic motifs in others that had been catalyzed by his European experiences. Of the smaller-scaled built designs, the Tazaemon Yamamura House and the project for a cinema in Tokyo's Ginza demonstrate the multiple readings that arise from Wright's use of primary forms and the exchanging of motifs between cultures.

Wright designed the Yamamura House for the president of a saki brewery in 1918, but it was completed in early 1924 after Wright had left Japan (fig. 263). The architect made preliminary sketches and turned the work over to Arata Endo, his trusted assistant at the Imperial Hotel.[74] Because of its canted roof forms, the Yamamura House has been cited in particular as "Wright's most impressive, abstracted Mayan pyramid."[75] The Yamamura House could be compared to such buildings as the Maya Temple of the Sun at Palenque that Wright might have

263. Tazaemon Yamamura House, model, Ashiya, Japan, designed 1918, built 1924 (Tanigawa, *Measured Drawings*).

known from Charnay's *Ancient Cities of the New World*, or to images of Temple I, photographed by Maudslay in the 1880s and published by Maler and Tozzer in 1911 (fig. 264).[76] In spite of these visual analogies the question remains of why Wright would have emulated a Maya form when in Japan he was surrounded by indigenous roof forms of similar shape.

One possible explanation is that Wright was honoring Japan with a gift of what he perceived as the noblest forms of the architecture of the Americas. The architect was reported to have stated that "Japanese art and architecture are respectable as presented, therefore I decorated the Imperial Hotel with ancient American art and Mayan decoration."[77] One great ancient culture then deserves the tribute of another ancient culture. Consistent with views at the time, Wright apparently saw the Maya

as the "mother civilization" of Mesoamerica.[78] He brought the symbols of the originary culture of the Americas as a tribute to the originary culture of Japan.

To this interpretation of tribute can be added several associations. Japanese folk architecture is an obvious reference for the Yamamura House. Its roof resembles thatched forms Wright would have known from houses seen during travels he made in the countryside or from houses illustrated in Morse's pioneering and well-known *Japanese Homes and Their Surroundings* (fig. 265).[79] Not only was the steeply pitched roof a native form, but Japanese multistoried houses had series of pent roofs.[80] Although the cultural contexts for roofs of Japanese folk architecture and Maya buildings are different, the roofs are similar in form because they are made of similar natural materials and

264. Temple of the Sun, Palenque (*Art and Architecture,* 1, 1914).

265. Traditional roof shapes in a house near Mororan, Yezo, Japan, c. 1886 (Morse, *Japanese Homes*).

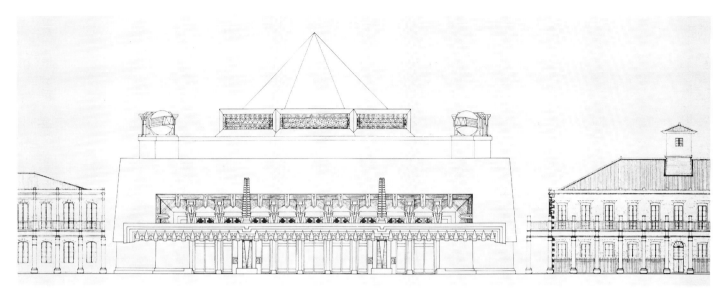

266. Cinema (or theater) for the Ginza, front elevation, Tokyo c. 1917–22 (Tanigawa, *Measured Drawings*).

have the same purpose of shelter. Wright retains the association of the primitive hut with the image of the roof, but he transforms the material of roof in a manner that is analogous to that of the canted roof at the Hollyhock House, a design contemporaneous with the Yamamura House.[81] The result is a linkage between the Orient, Mesoamerica, and North America.

In the context of Wright's other contemporary designs, the Yamamura House becomes an experiment in generalized primitivism and an example of reverence for tradition. Assertions that Wright's primitive designs derive from a specific source miss his search during this period for a set of universal forms. In observing this search, we see a paradox emerging: Wright uses similar forms that may have different cultural and social meanings.

The complex layering of Wright's iconography is visible in his project for a cinema for the Ginza, Tokyo's first westernized quarter, center for the latest western fashions, and theater district (fig. 266). Little is known of the circumstances of the project, but its form, function, and approximate date link it to a series of designs for theaters and interior spatial studies of polygonal forms, including Aline Barnsdall's theater projects as well as the theater and studies for polygonal ceiling and roofs at the Imperial Hotel.[82] Consistently relying on primary forms, Wright used an octagon inserted within a square for his plan of the Ginza project. He projected a pyramidal roof from the octagon, creating a centralized space below. How a centralized space could be used as a cinema is unclear; the plan is more conducive to performances for theater in the round, raising the question of whether the project was actually for a cinema or for Wright's own conception of theatrical performances based on traditional Japanese theater.[83]

Tanigawa's measured drawings of the model of the Ginza project show how effectively Wright interchanged and exchanged motifs between his projects for different cultural contexts. The transferral of motifs was possible because the primary abstract character of the forms allowed Wright to use the same design processes for different sites and building programs. In the Ginza project, the patterns of winged frontal figures recall the figures at the Barnsdall Theater project (fig. 267). The low treatment of the entry recalls Wright's German Warehouse design, and the pyramids placed over squares and surrounded by multiple frames are analogous to the key motif at the warehouse entry (fig. 235). Above the entry is a pierced screen of cast concrete blocks, a motif that Wright would use later at the Millard House in 1923. The tall, tapered three-dimensional sculptures above the entries can be seen as conventionalized pagodas, used in gardens, or as forms of nature, such as an oriental pine, which makes them analogous to the conventionalized hollyhock at the Barnsdall residence.

All these forms, however, are ambiguous. Like the Bogk House reliefs, the sculptural reliefs of the frieze along the front facade have symmetrical, grooved striations that conflate wings

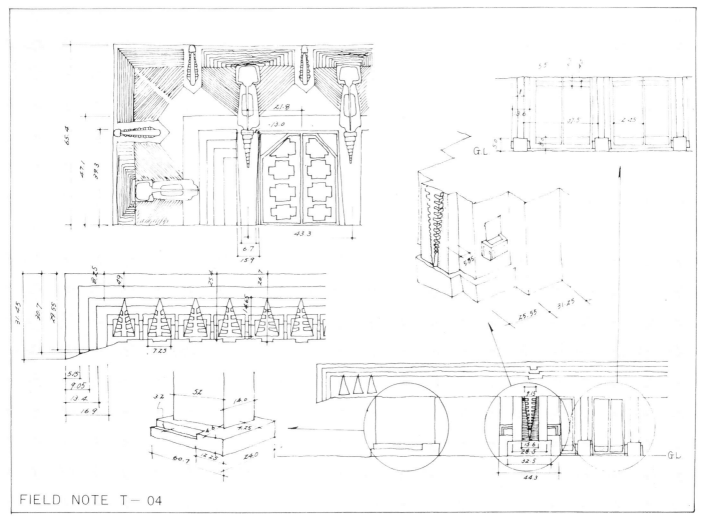

FIELD NOTE T-04

267. Cinema (or theater) for the Ginza, details, Tokyo (Tanigawa, *Measured Drawings,* field note T-04).

and background surface, and a body composed of head, torso with arms, and tapering legs. The lower "torso" even has a series of rectangular blocks—a corbeling motif turned upside down. But the featureless face is so abstract that it denies obvious associations with figural representation. Wright's sculptures now reach such a degree of abstraction that they hover between nonobjective form and figural representation.

The ambiguity between pure abstraction and representation is also present on the globes that mark the upper four courses of the project (figs. 268, 269). Recalling Wright's use of the globe at the Larkin Building, these spheres are cradled by pairs of forms—linked by inclined bandings—that appear both as

abstract winged figures and as architectonic representations. The figures have grooved, angled elements, or wings, similar to the sculptural reliefs at the Barnsdall Theater project (fig. 256). They also recall the piling up of rectangular, layered masses that Wright used for the planters at the entry to the Unity Temple and even, in microcosm, the tall piers of the Larkin Building. These associations do not imply that Wright was consciously or deliberately referring to any specific building in his work, but they indicate that in his process of design he accumulated and assembled architectural ideas with an extraordinary consistency and that he subjected his designs to a rigorous abstraction.

A LESSON IN ICONOGRAPHY   257

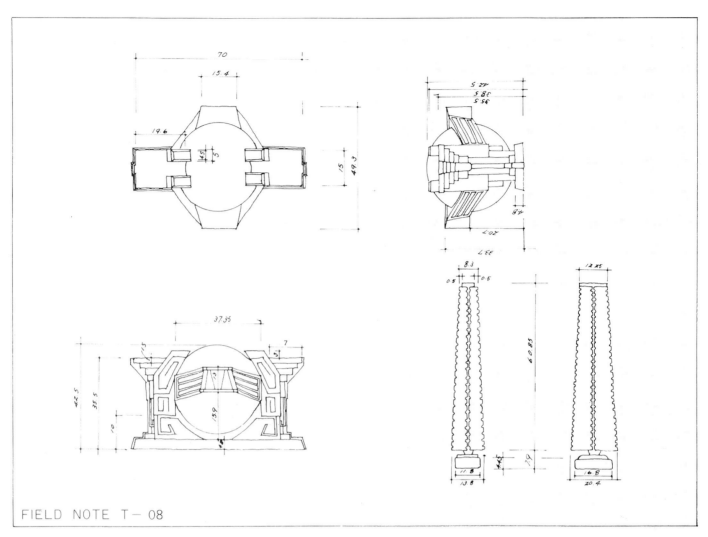

FIELD NOTE T— 08

268. Cinema (or theater) for the Ginza, globe detail, Tokyo (Tanigawa, *Measured Drawings,* field note T-08).

Conclusion

My analysis of motifs from Wright's primitivist designs begun after his return from Europe in 1910 has extended from Maya architecture and American Indians to forms and motifs found in the Orient. The patterns of ornament, sculptures, and geometric motifs of these buildings and projects recur in Wright's other experimental buildings of the period. The melding of various sources demonstrates Wright's consistent search for an abstract, universal exoticism that both presented the unique nature of a culture's tradition and incorporated motifs from other cultures, including the "culture" of Wright's own architecture.

At the same time, Wright's approach was consistent with his intention, as articulated in his Wasmuth essay, of creating a true American architecture: he believed that the original architecture of a culture should provide the sources for "the organically true" forms of that culture, and that once found, they would transform the lives of the members of that culture.[84] The doubled nature of primary forms—their cultural and transcultural significance—allowed Wright to interchange the motifs within a specific context and to exchange them in different contexts, resulting in a rich ambiguity.

Multiple readings of Wright's buildings are necessary to understand fully Wright's primitivism and to unravel the knot of influence. One reading comes from recognizing that Wright associated the true architecture of a culture with its originary forms. Aboriginal American architecture provided the basis of a true American architecture, and indigenous, traditional Japanese architecture provided the basis of a true Japanese architecture. A second reading arises from exploring the metaphorical meanings of forms that appear nearly universal. The forms that represent these meanings are primal forms appearing at a fundamental level in architecture across culture and time: the earth mound heaved up as a canted mass, the recessed panel originally formed from mud brick, the triangle symbolizing fertility, and the circle representing the sun.[85] The forms persist and are widespread, independent of the distinct social, religious, and symbolic meanings attached to them. A third reading recognizes that these ornamental patterns are integrated into a rational system of design based on a rectilinear grid and are often

the subject of Wright's interest in technology and materials. The grid creates a pattern of squares of its own, so that ornament, as it fits into the grid, is part of a rational system linked to the building process itself and to the expression of the nature of materials.

Wright's primitivism extended the conventionalization of the human figure to ornament, and to the conventionalization of building mass itself. All Wright's references were intended to be deliberately generalized in an effort not to quote but to transform. For Wright, the transformation of form becomes more important than its referential qualities. As he himself wrote in his Wasmuth monograph essay: "Any attempt to use forms borrowed from other times and conditions must end . . . with total loss of inherent relation to the soul life of the people."[86]

Throughout Wright's experiments with primitivist sources his focus was on transformation of form. As he explored

269. Cinema (or theater) for the Ginza, model, front view, Tokyo (Tanigawa, *Measured Drawings*).

the variations of motifs in what he called his "developing sense of abstraction," he set the stage for the dramatic changes in his compositions that began to develop by the mid-1910s.

Travel to Europe, not the passage of time, had been the proximate factor in the development of Wright's art. His experiences there provided nodes of connection in the web that defined the influences on his work. After his return from Europe, when Wright began his primitivist experiments, another development occurred: he began to explore new expressions of the rotated square. He transformed it by combining it with other elements, by overlaying several rotated forms, by suppressing parts of the overlapped areas, and, eventually, by rotating the square at angles other than forty-five degrees. As he replicated and rotated primary forms, he broke down the rigid system of symmetry of his ornament, and a new dynamic diagonality entered his work. After 1910, the rotation of primary forms became a design principle in itself that set him apart from his European contemporaries. Exploring methods untouched by the Secessionists even at their creative apex, Wright developed this dynamic diagonality into a system that eventually became a major design mode throughout the rest of his career.

So, in design, that element which we call structure is primarily the pure form, as arranged or fashioned and grouped to "build" the Idea; an idea, which must always persuade us of its reasonableness. Geometry is the grammar, so to speak, of the form. It is its architectural principle. But there is a psychic correlation between geometry of form and our associated ideas which constitute its symbolic value.—Frank Lloyd Wright (1912)[1]

9   A Lesson in Diagonality

One of the catalyzing effects of travel abroad was a new development in Wright's design process that occurred as he explored the geometric grammar of form and its association with symbolism. After 1910, as Wright moved forward with his experiments in primitivism and explorations of ornament, a new force developed in his architecture: a dynamic diagonality that allowed for fresh asymmetrical compositions. The forces of "spell power" latent in the circle, square, and triangle that Wright developed became a tool in his exploration of primitivism and an element in the creative catharsis he experienced in the 1910s. The square, its rotation, and its translation into dynamic compositions became a means of artistic expression he pursued at the Imperial Hotel throughout the decade. Wright began to turn, to implode, and, ultimately, to explode the square. These processes created the "intricate enrichment" he had sought in his abstract and figural ornament and that he had described in the Wasmuth monograph essay as needed in his work.[2] They reflected the lessons of quadrature—the ancient tradition of rotating the square—and the symbolic power of primary forms that Wright had seen in Europe. In subjecting primary forms to rotations that made them dynamic, Wright began to transform the character of traditional motifs. In pursuing these developments he absorbed and moved beyond the influence of his European colleagues.

Before 1910, axiality, additive processes, and grids provided a range and variety of design methods that Wright honed to acuity. When the compass swung around a point to mark the placement of a wing or arm of a building, it marked a regular shift from an axis, a partial circular movement, usually an arc of ninety degrees. Regularity also produced a dominance of bilateral symmetry in Wright's compositions, a condition that many late nineteenth-century theorists described generally as a basic parallel between nature and art.[3] One side mirrored another in a clear expression of the orderly process of additive and axial composition. Even where there were L-shaped plans or polygonal appendages to a plan that indicated an overall asymmetry, local symmetries were present.

The regularity and order that arose from the processes of addition and axial rotations around pivot points also provided, to some degree, predictability. For instance, each panel in the windows of the dining room at the Robie House of 1906–10, if considered alone, has asymmetrical elements. The same conditions applies to the windows of the Harley Bradley House (figs. 270, 271). However, Wright used these designs in pairs, making the mullion of a window frame a center line around which two such panels are placed. The effect was ultimately symmetrical even though each symmetrical pair contained local asymmetries.[4]

The square had been the predominant module in Wright's system before 1910. While the square can be rotated, it can also be divided diagonally into two triangles along a common hypotenuse. After 1910, as Wright manipulated the square, he began to stop its rotation before it reached a regular interval, positioning it at an angle between the horizontal and ninety de-

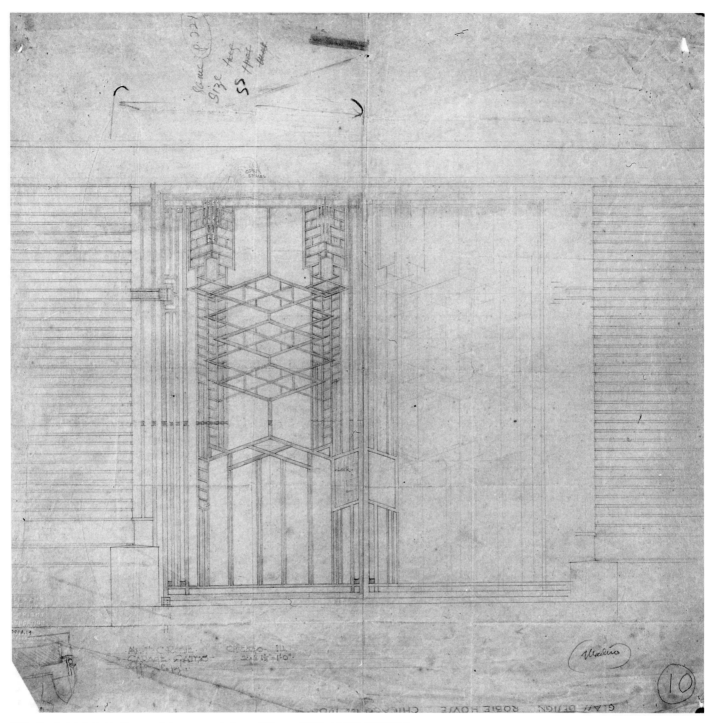

270. Frederick C. Robie House, dining room windows, Chicago, 1909–10 (TAL 0908.014).

grees. By stopping the rotation before a regular interval, he introduced a diagonality that created a visual tension with little precedent in his previous work. Although Wright had used the trapezoid in designs of his art-glass windows to create angular effects, these were only details in generally symmetrical compositions.

A hint of the potentialities of asymmetric diagonality is visible at the Coonley House of 1907–9. One example is the band of light screens along the edges of the living-room ceiling, which counters the angular treatment of the moldings and planes above them (fig. 272).[5] Another diagonality is visible in Wright's design of a bronze plate intended as a kind of monogram and compass for the terrace. The diagonality comes from the compass points that Wright superimposed over a rotated square (fig. 273).

Historians have discussed the role of diagonality in the overall context of Wright's work. Banham, among others, pointed to Wright's visit to the desert of Southern California in 1922 as a liberation from axial symmetry, the right angle, and centralized spaces.[6] Referring to Banham's earlier observations, Levine has postulated the appearance of the diagonal in plan in Wright's early work, starting with the Cooper House of 1887 and reemerging explicitly in his work in 1921, after the interim "regression" of his plans of the Midway Gardens and the Imperial Hotel.[7]

While a break does occur in Wright's work and life around 1922, the rise of *explicit* diagonal planning had its roots in the formal experiments in ornament that he began in 1910 and that were stimulated by his experience in Europe. Only after his return from Europe in 1910, when he began intensifying the exploration of ornament, does a dynamic diagonality appear central to his design process. Wright's drawings and buildings of the period show the process at work, a process which had its beginnings in Wright's apprenticeship under Louis Sullivan in the early 1880s.

Sullivan's Matrix of Ornament

Sullivan's *A System of Architectural Ornament* defines the design process that had helped form Wright's methods.[8] The plates in this collection show not only a method of composition but a complete metaphysical association of form and symbol (fig. 274). This approach similarly characterized Wright's own statements in the 1910s that identified primary forms with symbolic values. Sullivan developed sequential designs using basic

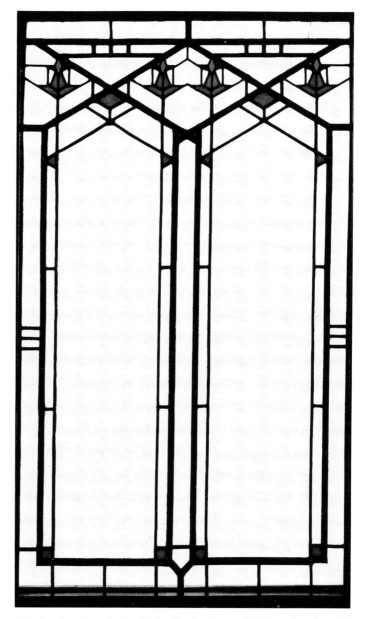

271. Leaded glass window, Harley Bradley House, Kankakee, Illinois, 1900 (Fischer Fine Art, London).

geometric shapes located in matrices (fig. 275). These basic shapes were the equivalent of primary forms, to which Sullivan attached his own vision of organicism as he equated spirit and matter.[9] According to Sullivan, the use of axes and the development of forms were "to be taken from the realms of the transcendental and brought into physical, tangible, even psychic

272. Coonley House, ceiling detail of living room, Riverside, Illinois, 1908 (TAL 0803.031).

reality." By geometric rules, Sullivan abstracted, step by step, a natural element—a "seed germ"—into an architectural element. The result was a floral ornament that became the prominent aspect of Sullivan's iconography and a unique contribution to American architecture. It was under this system—using grids, matrices, and geometric rules—that Wright himself learned to design ornament. Yet Wright pushed his ornament through to an abstraction and three-dimensionality that Sullivan never sought or achieved.

Diagonality at Midway Gardens

Wright began to develop asymmetric and dynamic diagonality while designing the ornament at Midway Gardens. The potentialities of this new use of diagonality can be seen in a design for a pair of relief panels at the Gardens (fig. 276). In the right panel, a void extending from upper left to lower right is demarcated by truncated triangles in the diagonally opposite corners. These angles are simply formed by the use of a thirty-sixty-degree triangle. In the left panel, the repeated use of the triangle at regular intervals shows the creation of a family of smaller, similar triangles. The diagonal lines are replicated in parallel, but Wright added horizontal returns to counter the diagonal thrust of the composition. This countermove creates a visual tension between forces and counterforces. In this way Wright

enriched the panel with the simplest of means. Other designs at Midway Gardens show a design development that uses his earlier techniques of diagonality.[10]

Wright called this new diagonality "Dancing Glass" (figs. 277, 278).[11] The motif, cast into concrete panels, was used for the Garden's railings along the arcade balcony, the belvedere balcony, and the roof gardens of the main building (fig. 279).[12] "Dancing Glass" could also be combined with other primary forms, such as diagonal arrangements of squares, multiple frames—whole and halved—and rotated double squares linked to form a linear pattern. Such combinations were seen in the frieze above the entry pavilions of the Gardens (fig. 280).[13] The motif consisted of a layering of elements: squares were overlaid by halved multiple frames which, in turn, were overlaid by the partial rectangles made from doubled squares. When panels were placed in series, the partial rectangles were completed to unify the entire series into a three-dimensional running fret. With the development of this motif Wright added his own version of the fret to an ancient language of ornament, an innovation that had no parallel in the work of his European colleagues.

The complete repertory of diagonally oriented compositions, primary forms, and even conventionalized sculpture was present in the extraordinary towers at the front facade of the Midway Gardens. Wright covered the towers with layered planes of recessed panels, multiple frames wrapping around the edges of

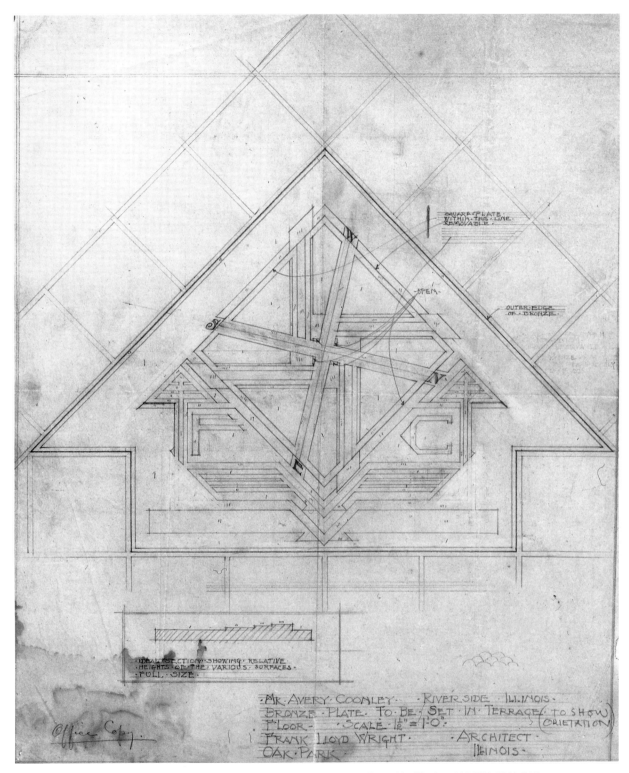

273. Coonley House, bronze floor plate with initials "A," "C" and north arrow, Riverside, Illinois, 1908 (TAL 0803.042).

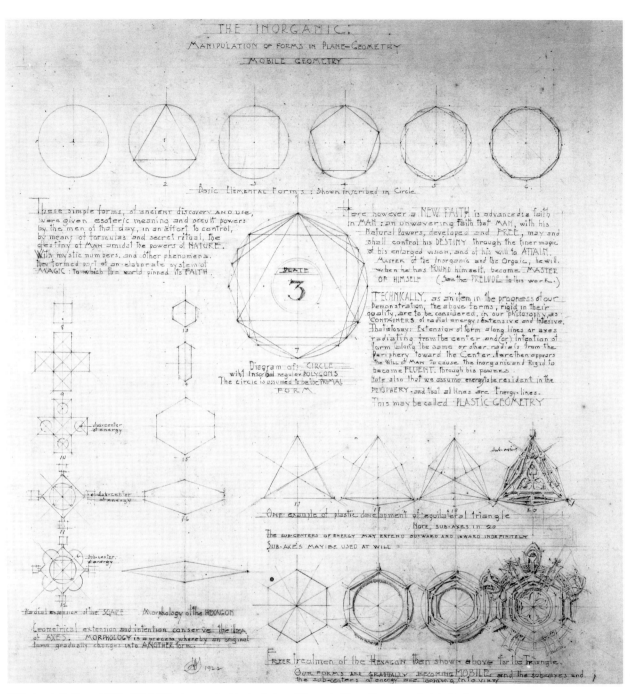

274. Louis Sullivan, 1856–1924, "The Inorganic: Manipulation of Forms in Plane-Geometry," plate 3 of *A System of Ornament*, pencil on Strathmore paper, 1922, 57.7 × 73.5 cm (Commissioned by The Art Institute of Chicago, 1988.15.3; photograph courtesy of The Art Institute of Chicago).

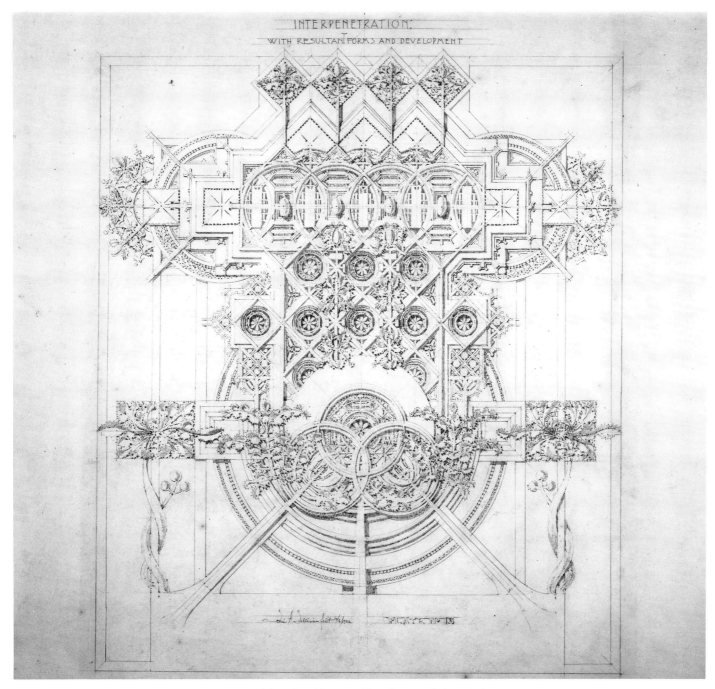

275. Louis Sullivan, 1856–1924, "Interpenetration: with Resultant Forms and Development," plate 13 of *A System of Ornament,* pencil on Strathmore paper, 1922, 57.7 × 73.5 cm (Commissioned by The Art Institute of Chicago, 1988.15.13; photograph courtesy of The Art Institute of Chicago).

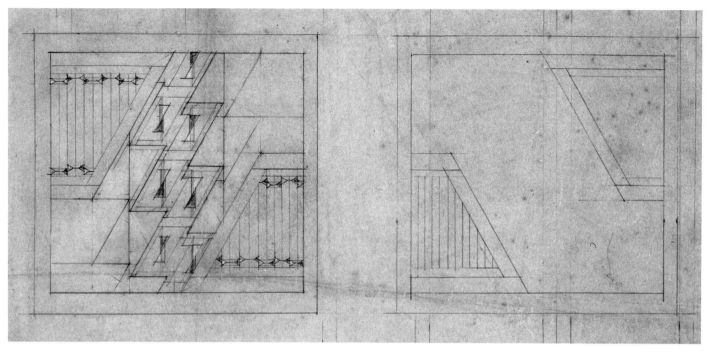

276. Relief panels, Midway Gardens, Chicago, 1914 (TAL 1401.068).

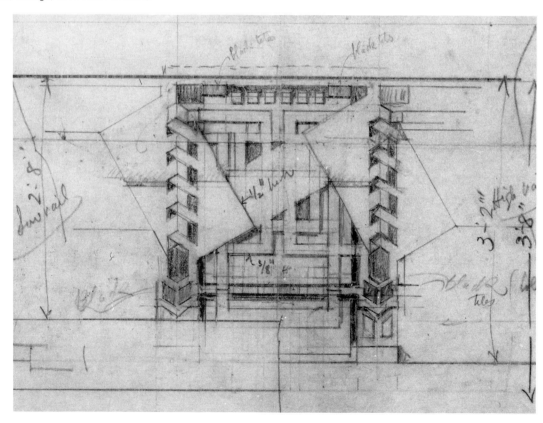

277. ''Dancing Glass'' motif for railing panel, detail, Midway Gardens, Chicago, 1914 (TAL 1401.081).

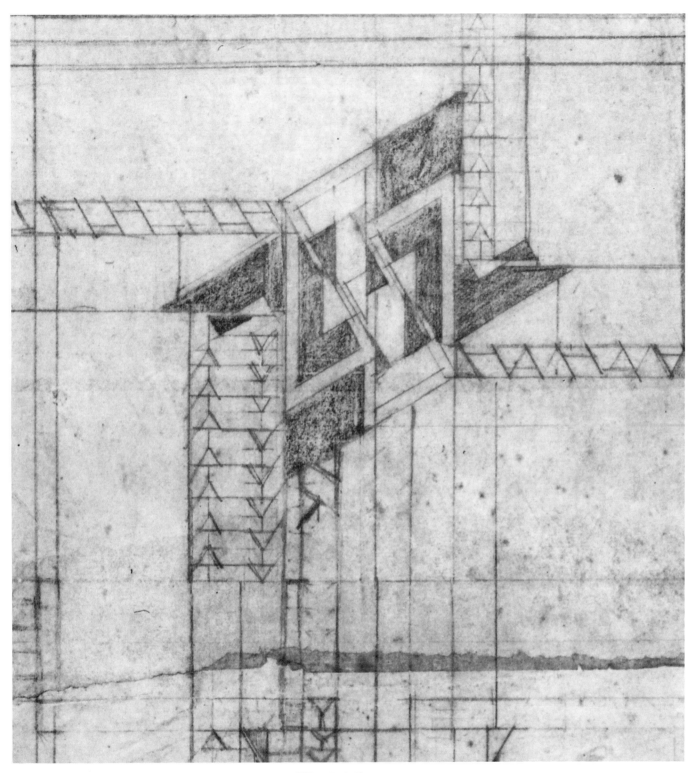

278. "Dancing Glass" detail, Midway Gardens, Chicago, 1914 (TAL 1401.015).

279. "Dancing Glass" motif, view at sunken garden, Midway Gardens, Chicago, c. 1914.

the flat moldings, and, at the lower center, rotated panels that introduced an asymmetrical diagonality (fig. 281).[14] These were the elements from whose top frames, or "finials," Wright had intended to dangle the primary forms of sphere, pyramid, and cube. The complexity and richness of the ensemble provided the overall exotic effect of the Gardens. Commenting on the visitors' associations from Maya to Egypt to Japan, Wright described its impact as "strange to all. It awakened a sense of mystery and romance in the beholder."[15]

Diagonality at the Imperial Hotel

The dynamic diagonality that had begun at Midway Gardens found an achievement at the Imperial Hotel unparalleled in Wright's previous work. By 1914 Wright had begun to develop a complex system of ornament that outstripped the design methods of the Secessionists. Not only were his results richer, they were more three-dimensional. The design drawings of something as modest as a floor plate show Wright's process of creat-

280. "Dancing Glass" motif in panels at pavilion entry, Midway Gardens, Chicago, c. 1914.

281. Pier with "Dancing Glass" motif at center and frames for finial above, Midway Gardens, Chicago, c. 1914.

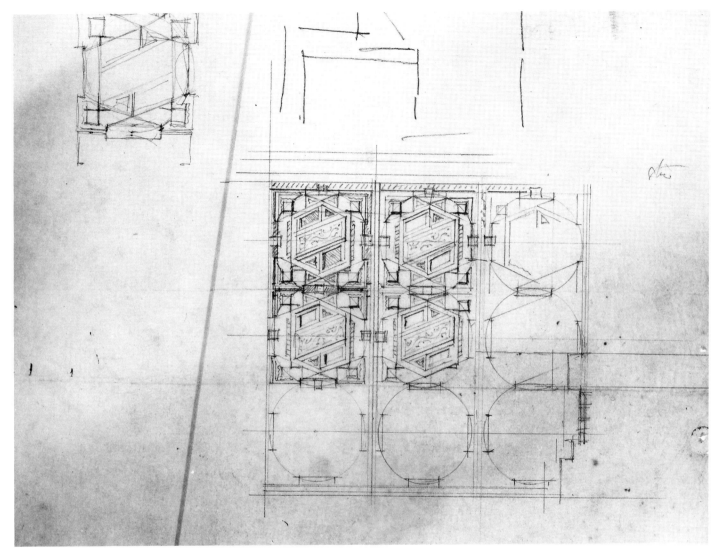

282. Imperial Hotel, study for floor plate, 1917–22 (LC).

ing diagonality and how much more complex it was than the Secessionist's use of the circle and square. Wright started with the basic idea of a unit, which he sketched at the upper left of the drawing (fig. 282).[16] It has as its central focus a hexagon, but it also contains a diagonal element thrust between the figure's lower left and upper right. The border around the figure has squares at its corners, rectangles with pyramidal extensions at top and bottom, and rectangular notches at its sides.

To the right of the sketch for the unit, Wright diagrammed a portion of the unit to study the problem of how the adjoining corners would meet. He provided a linear space between the units to keep the doubling of squares at the corners from cramping the design. This was a traditional problem encountered by any architect designing a coffered eave.

Wright then made a group of nine units to form a matrix—comparable to one of Sullivan's—that shows the process of design from sketch to full development. The units in Wright's design can be described diagrammatically:

G	F	E
H	I	D
A	B	C

The basic structure of a square with inscribed circle appears in the lower left of the matrix (A). Notches, added to each side, provide the possibility of reversing the figure and ground between the circle and its pendentives. This unit is repeated in the unit to its right (B) and in the lower right corner where Wright studied the joint of the edge of the unit (C). Following the periphery of the matrix, in the center unit in the far right column (D), an inscribed circle reveals the beginnings of the central figure. From points of tangency between the circle and notches, Wright drew diagonal lines. The result is a clear visual emphasis on the diagonal movement between lower left and upper right.

In the unit at the upper right corner (E), the hexagonal figure is completed to form a flattened, elongated, irregular polygon. Since this figure is symmetrical around only its horizontal axis, an inequality is introduced into the composition. This inequality creates the dynamism of the pattern. The visual tension of the pattern is increased by the imposition within the irregular hexagon of a regular hexagon; its beginnings are sketched in this unit. Elaboration of the peripheral squares and the identification of triangular, interstitial spaces are also begun here.

Wright next developed the pattern in the center unit of the top row (F). The regular hexagon now appears to dominate the figure, but within it the theme of diagonality is expressed, like a leitmotif, as trapezoids. While the regularity of the hexagon appears to dominate, creating an overall symmetry to the pattern, the original flattened figure lies recessed, subtly contrasting with the major element.

After developing these units in a sequential and systematic way, Wright used the remaining three units to develop the pattern with interstitial triangles, recesses, and trapezoids (G, H, I). These manipulations of shape and depth result in the play of textures and shadows. They also allow alternative ways of joining the corner squares to the figure, which also contribute to the dynamism of Wright's ornament. In this simple, nine-unit repeat, smooth and rough textures coexist. Within symmetry, regularity and irregularity are present.

Another set of drawings for floor plates at the Imperial Hotel shows how effective Wright's rotational system could be in producing a visually dynamic diagonality (fig. 283). Each plate was fitted with tabs and slots to make an interlocking group. The plates were intended to be cast in bronze and laid in groups of four. To make the design, Wright took a square at whose periphery he drew a border. Within the incised area Wright ro-

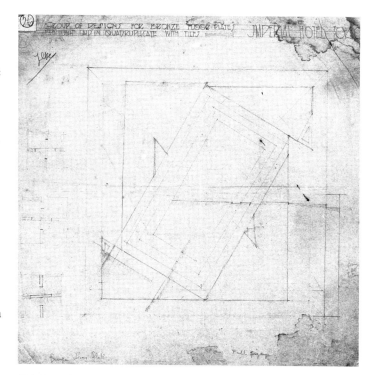

283. Imperial Hotel, study for bronze floor plate, 1917–22 (TAL 1509.095).

tated a rectangle at 60 degrees from horizontal. This angular rotation was the prime generator of successive motifs. Within the rectangle, Wright inscribed additional borders, one within another. The rotation generated similar triangles at the intersections of the main rectangle with the peripheral border.

Two interesting results occur. One is that the borders can be moved up and down to create layers of planes. From this layering of planes, Wright creates visual tension with the design. The second interesting effect originates in the "ears" attached to the mid-points of the long sides of the primary rectangle. These "ears" are not right triangles, but oblique triangles, and the line that would connect their shortest sides across the rectangle subtly introduces a diagonal into the composition. In effect, Wright sets up a rule of parallelism—that every line has a parallel—but he introduces the diagonal without any parallel line to it. The diagonal acts as a counterpoint to the rule. Thus, the static state possible from the rotation of rectangles, with their inscribed triangles, becomes dynamic.

The other floor-plate designs in this series also show the expressive design potentialities of these processes. In one study

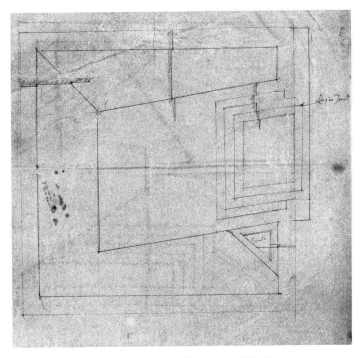

284. Imperial Hotel, study for bronze floor plate, 1917–22
(TAL 1509.096).

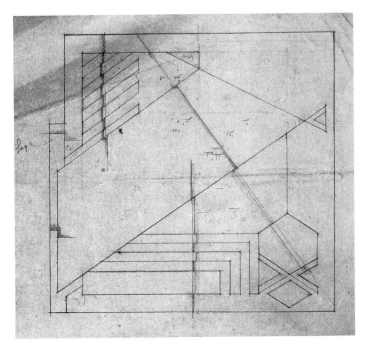

285. Imperial Hotel, study for bronze floor plate, 1917–22
(TAL 1509.098).

the rotated rectangle itself, now a parallelogram, becomes the diagonal force (fig. 284).[17] In another study Wright turns the parallelogram into a trapezoid (fig. 285).[18] He introduces into the corner of this design an additional basic shape, the hexagon, which exerts a strong visual weight because of its regularity and thus counters the unstable quality of the trapezoid. The hexagon, in turn, is juxtaposed with a flattened parallelogram, or diamond. In this complicated serial process of design, Wright transforms his compositional devices from rectangles to parallelograms to hexagons.

The working out of this rotational system, using the combination of diagonality and primary forms, produced an overwhelming variety of ornament in the Imperial Hotel. The patterned block at the hotel became analogous to the "Dancing Glass" motif used at the Midway Gardens; the two are similar variations on the theme of diagonality (fig. 286).[19] But with the opportunity to explore hundreds of variations at the hotel, the ornament became denser than that of the Gardens.

Asymmetrically composed designs with dynamic diagonality became major features at the Imperial Hotel.[20] When Wright incorporated primary forms and his dynamic diagonality with the tectonic expression of the building, the results were dramatic. The bronze lanterns above the promenade, at the intersection of ceiling rafters and massive piers, consist of a pierced grill of concentric semicircles placed within a triangle (figs. 287, 288). The descending corner of the triangle is removed to accommodate the asymmetrical composition of layered planes carved out of oya. The shifting diagonals of the lantern design visually impel forms against each other as if they were worlds in collision. These worlds could be seen metaphorically as the realms of symmetry and asymmetry, Cartesian and non-Cartesian universes, or even the metaphysical realms of Eastern and Western cultures.

Wright also moved beyond the Secessionists and even his own murals at Midway Gardens in the extraordinary series of polychromed relief carvings used as overmantels at the Imperial Hotel (fig. 289).[21] Two of the fireplace overmantels, located in a parlor called the "Treasure Room," synthesize Wright's accomplishment in combining primary forms and asymmetric diagonality (figs. 290, 291).[22] In pursuing his concept of a total work of art, Wright even combined different media, incorporating polychrome murals within a frame of carved oya. The fireplace on the north side contained in its mural portion the primary forms of circle, square, and triangle. Working like a painter, Wright built up the composition in transparent layers, super-

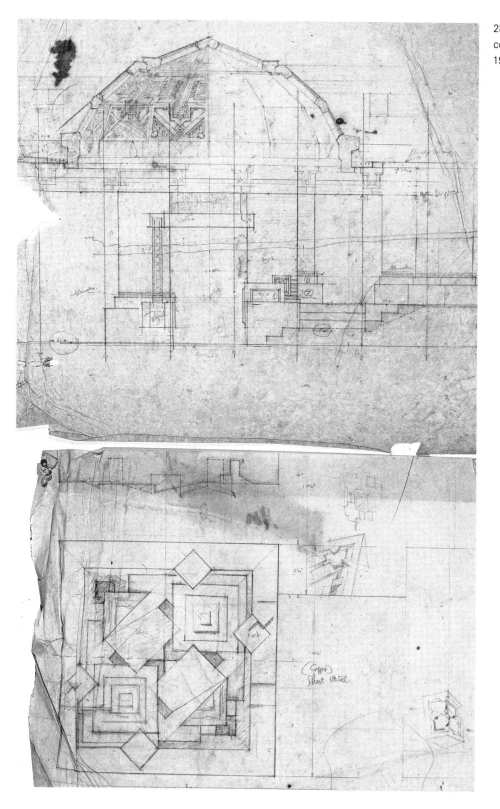

286. Imperial Hotel, block pattern in
copper sheet metal (lower);
1917–22 (TAL 1509.125).

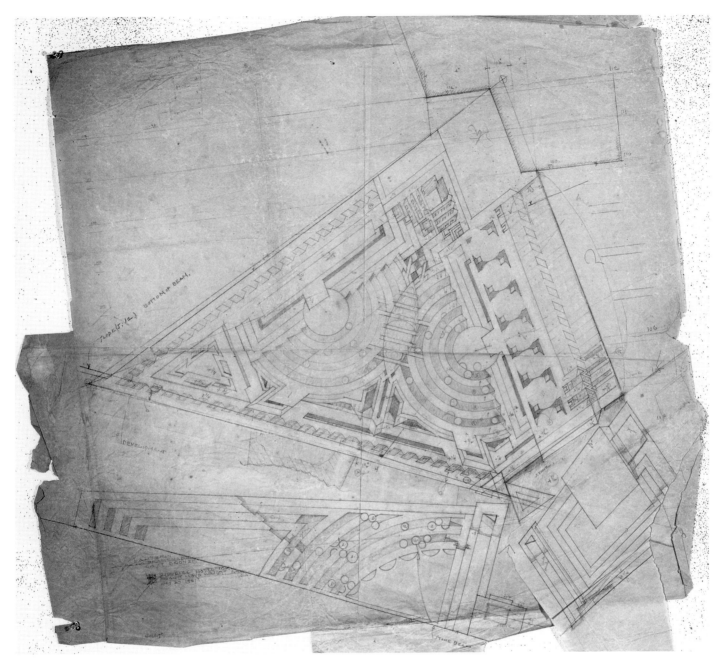

287. Imperial Hotel, bronze lantern for promenade, 1917–22 (TAL 1509.519).

imposing one system over another. He organized the entire asymmetrical composition in terms of visual contrasts between a basic diagonal laid across the composition and rectilinear and circular elements organized orthogonally. Out of the two-dimensional, polychromed surface rises its three-dimensional representation in carved oya. Its deep relief carving contrasts with the flatness of the mural as well as restating its rhomboids and diagonal thrust. Revealing his mastery of composition, Wright made the fireplace on the south side of the Treasure Room a variation on the themes of the north fireplace. This

288. Imperial Hotel, bronze lantern for promenade, 1917–22 (*IH*).

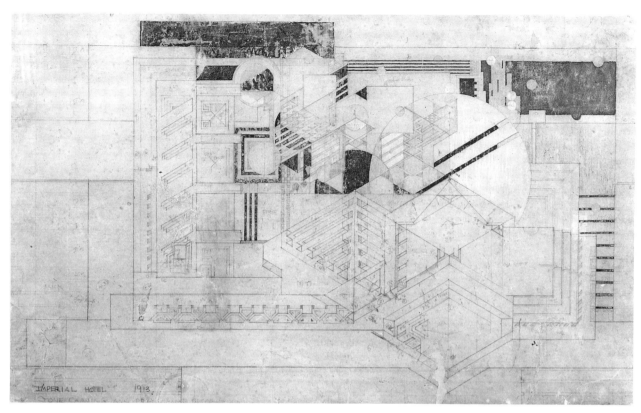

289. Imperial Hotel, design for relief carving of overmantel, 1917–22 (TAL 1509.004).

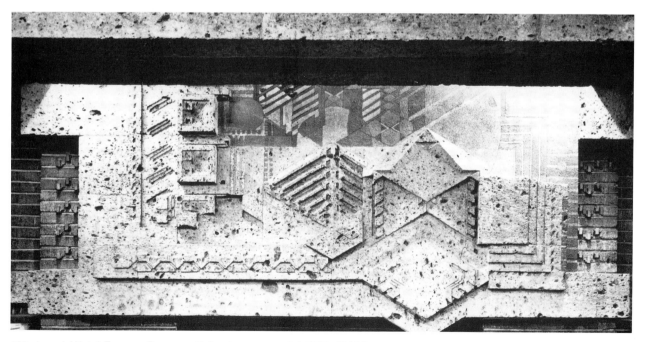

290. Imperial Hotel, Treasure Room, south fireplace overmantel, 1917–22 (*IH*).

291. Imperial Hotel, Treasure Room, north fireplace overmantel, 1917–22 (*IH*).

variation, which emphasizes more the motif of the multiple frame, is evidence of the concept that Berlage had described as "unity in diversity."

With the manifestation of diagonality as a dynamic force, a new expressive means of design expanded Wright's vocabulary of ornament and rigid symmetry began to disappear from his compositions, ultimately giving the plans themselves an asymmetrical, open quality. This dynamism was at the core of his creative rejuvenation and added to the "intricate enrichment" of his ornament. A mode of composition entered his designs that had no parallels in Europe or America; in exploring myriad permutations of geometric patterns, he had moved beyond the Secessionists, even to extremes to which he would never return. In pursuing his experiments, Wright began to move diagonality and asymmetrical composition from ornament to plan as he created entire programs of his American iconography.

Diagonality in Plan

The potentialities of Wright's diagonality and non-square plans were evident as early as 1921 in his design for a shrine and compound for Albert M. Johnson in Death Valley, California (fig. 292). A 1922 design for a desert residence and studio compound of Wright's own also showed the new tendencies. The use of polygonal forms and diagonal planning proliferated in numerous projects, ranging from the "Little Dipper" (a kindergarten for Aline Barnsdall), to the development of the Doheny ranch in the Hollywood Hills (a vast project of which little is known), to designs for a family barge and lake cabins for a speculative resort on Lake Tahoe of 1922 (figs. 293, 294).

Wright used dynamic diagonality in his plan for the Nakoma Country Club in a program that demonstrated his evolving American iconography. The 1923 commission provided an opportunity to explore his interest both in discovering a true American vocabulary based on aboriginal sources and in the new dynamism that came from introducing diagonal elements in his plans. Located in a suburb of Madison, Wisconsin, the country club had indigenous Indians for its theme.[23] Wright's project featured as its main social space a fifty-foot-high conventionalized tepee. However, like many of Wright's projects of the period, his designs for the country club were not executed: costs, a changing board of directors, and Wright's declining personal reputation were apparent factors in the failure of the project.

Recalling his attempts in his earlier primitivist designs to explore a true American architecture, Wright combined attri-

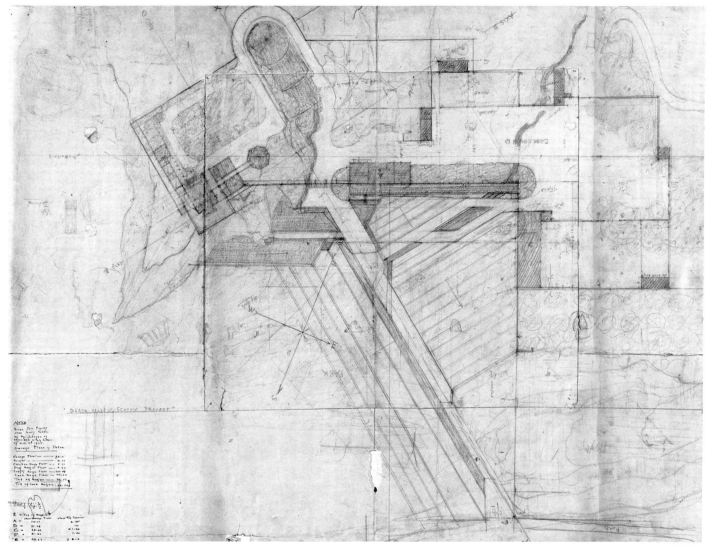

292. Albert M. Johnson compound and shrine, plan, Death Valley, California, 1921 (TAL 2306.002).

butes of various cultures in his designs for the Nakoma Country Club. The Chippewa word "Nakoma" was the name for an
area that had been originally inhabited by the Algonquin and
later became a summer campground for the Winnebago Indians. While the interior of the tepee was to include animal symbols of the Winnebago clans and other Indian characters, the
country club included an octagonal tea pavilion, whose shape
Mary Jane Hamilton has identified as a reference to the Japanese
tea ritual.[24] Even the great tepee had a conflated identity: on
some drawings Wright called it a wigwam, a hut which has a
very different structure of curving poles, instead of the conical

shape of a tepee. Recognizing in the design an Indian village of
"wigwams," the local newspaper described the clubhouse as
"the most unique building of its kind in America."[25]

The plan of the country club shows that Wright utilized the
new dynamic diagonality that had originated in his ornament
(fig. 295). Adding one form to another, he still used units composed of squares, doubles squares, and polygonal forms, as had
been his practice from the outset of his career, but these were
now oriented around diagonal axes. By extending the plan into
the landscape, Wright made the tepees move in and out of a
frontal plane when seen in elevation. This animated the whole

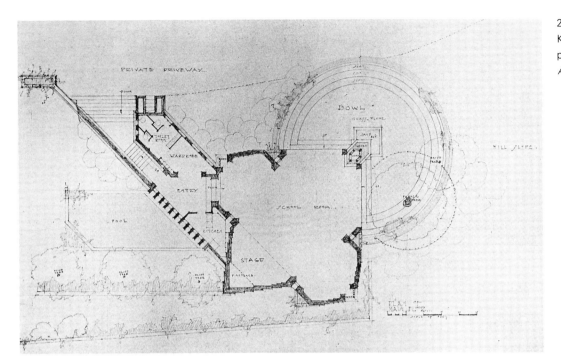

293. "Little Dipper,"
Kindergarten for Aline Barnsdall,
plan, Los Angeles, 1921 (De Fries,
Aus Dem Lebenswerke).

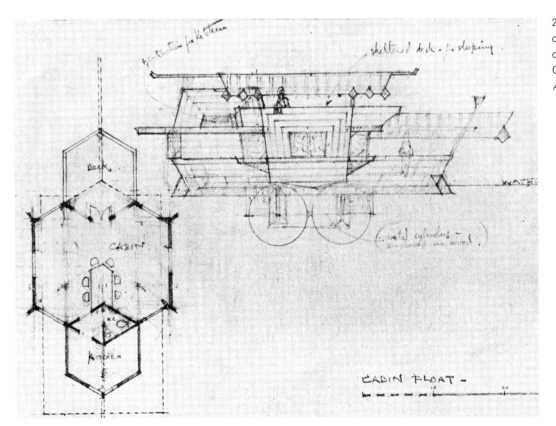

294. Lake Tahoe summer
colony, perspective rendering
of floating cabin, Lake Tahoe.
California, 1922 (De Fries,
Aus Dem Lebenswerke).

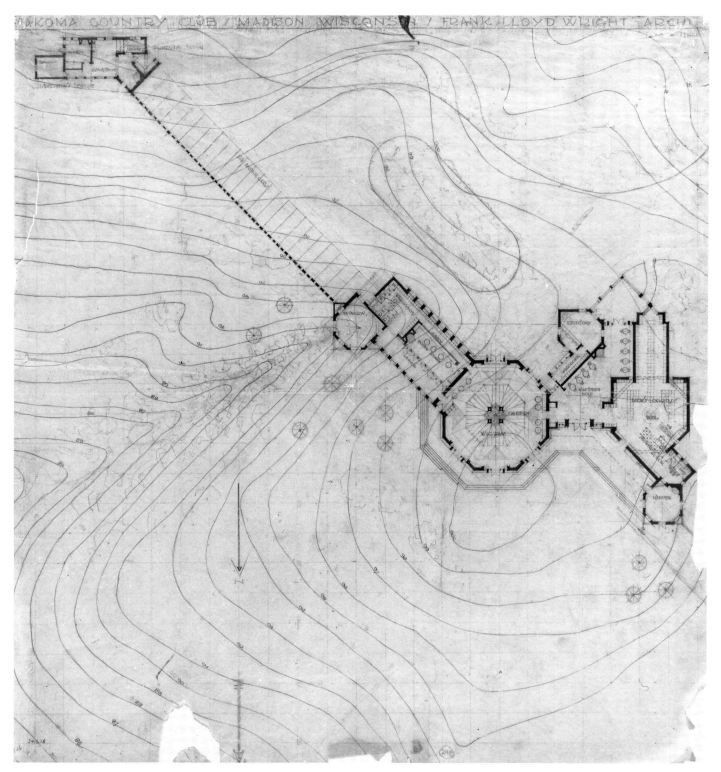

295. Nakoma Country Club, plan, Madison, Wisconsin, 1924 (TAL 2403.028).

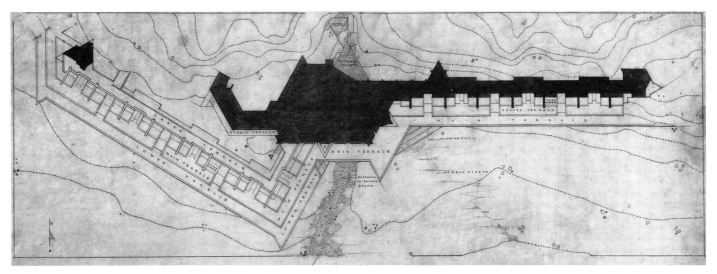

296. San Marcos in the Desert, resort hotel for Dr. Alexander Chandler, plan, Chandler, Arizona, 1928 (TAL 2704.052).

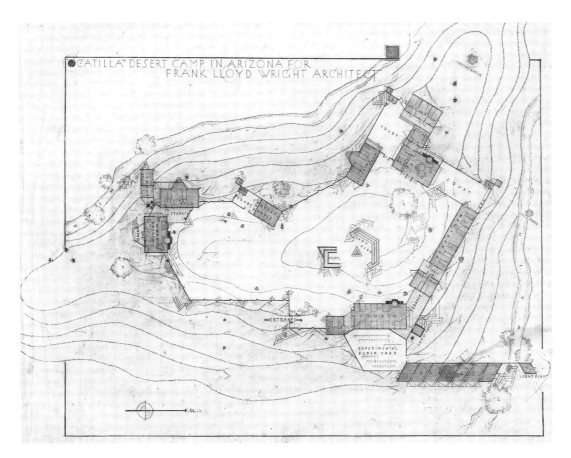

297. "Ocatilla," Frank Lloyd Wright Desert Compound and Studio, near Chandler, Arizona, 1929 (TAL 2702.004).

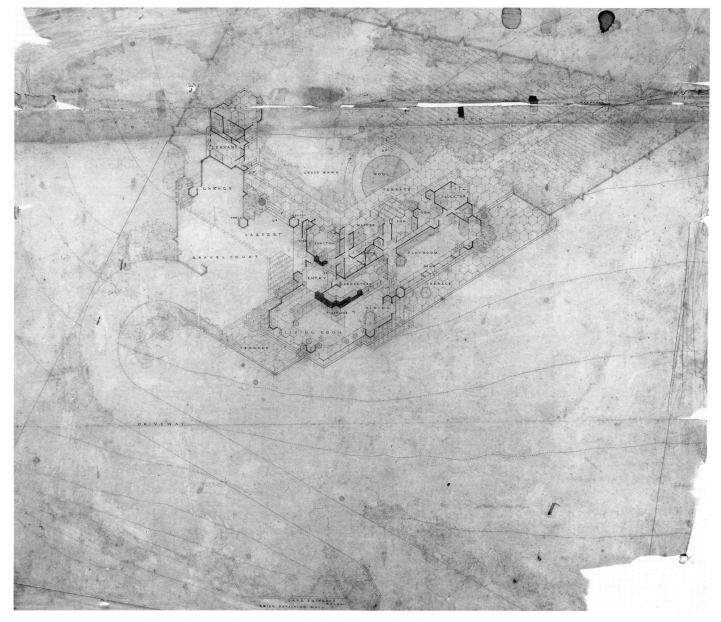

298. Paul and Jean Hanna residence, Honeycomb House, plan, Stanford, California, 1936 (TAL 3201.005).

composition in a picturesque effect that a symmetrical plan would not have allowed.

More fundamental than the visual effect was the fact that diagonal plans facilitated Wright's use of polygons as the units of his compositions. Polygonal forms and diagonal planning freed him to use the triangle as the plan generator for the central unit for San Marcos in the Desert, a resort hotel and real-estate de-

velopment in Chandler, Arizona, designed in 1929 but never built (fig. 296). He also used the triangle in plan for the detached houses at the development, including those for Owen D. Young and for Ralph and Wellington Cudney. Rotational planning was also used for tourist cabins for the San Marcos Water Gardens project of 1929. The freedom from axial symmetry in Wright's "Ocatilla" Desert Camp—a temporary headquarters built in 1928 near Chandler, for Wright and his assistants—allowed for a plan that responded to the nature of its site, climate, and surrounding vegetation (fig. 297). Taliesin West in Arizona and Wright's project for the redevelopment of the Hillside Home School into the studios of the Frank Lloyd Wright Fellowship were further developments in the 1930s. The exploration of diagonality lead to Wright's increasing use of non-rectilinear units, resulting ultimately in such designs as his "Honeycomb" plan with hexagonal units for the Hanna House of 1936 (fig. 298).

Planning with diagonality, rotated shapes of triangles, and, later, circles became a principal means of design for Frank Lloyd Wright. Rectilinear composition had been present from the outset of his career; rotational geometry, with its "spell power" of circle, triangle, square, and dynamic diagonality, received its creative impetus from the lessons of Europe. However, during the period of 1911–22, Wright worked simultaneously with two modes of design. One mode looked back to the houses designed for the prairies of the New West, the successful Prairie style. In the retrospective mode Wright maintained a style that he and his draftsmen could produce with relative ease. Since the language of that style was familiar, the design, details of construction, and the specifications for a building were easily drawn up, with the general result of creating a financially economical design. The most elaborate houses designed in the retrospective mode, however—such as the project for Arthur E. Cutten of 1911 and the house for Henry J. Allen of 1916—varied from the style of the Prairie period.[26] Their designs tended

to incorporate enclosed courtyards, a Mediterranean feature not present in Wright's early period but one which he first used in the unbuilt project of his own villino in Fiesole. Even some of the houses designed in the retrospective mode, such as the Bogk House, provided an opportunity for the experimental aesthetics that fascinated Wright.

Inspired by Europe, Wright developed the rotational mode by expanding dynamic diagonality from ornament to plan. In addition to using his mode of dynamic diagonality, Wright tended to engage the landscape in his later projects more than he did in earlier designs; he increasingly preferred dramatic, irregular topography to flat lots. As a result of these tendencies, the plans of the later designs tended towards asymmetry and away from rigid, bilateral dispositions, reflecting the general direction in Wright's planning techniques.

These two systems became the basic modes of design for the rest of Wright's career. Working as he had in the 1910s with two modes of design, Wright maintained in the 1920s both a system of diagonal planning with rotated shapes and a rectilinear system of design, using either where the method of construction, economy, and the site demanded it. The projects using the new asymmetrical diagonality occurred as Wright entered a new phase of his life and work, a phase demarcated by his final return from Japan in 1922. While some of the lessons of Europe, such as designing on the diagonal, stayed with Wright for the rest of his career, others, including conventionalized sculpture and his primitivist experiments, ended during the 1920s as Wright assimilated the influences around him.

No practice by any European architect to this day has influenced mine in the least.

—Frank Lloyd Wright (1957)[1]

10 Continuities and Discontinuities

Although he had acknowledged Olbrich as his competitor and Metzner as a fellow artist who could "conventionalize the flesh," Wright continued to the end of his life to insist that no European architect had influenced his work in the least. The preceding study of influence suggests, however, that Europe had at least as much impact on Wright as he had on it; an affinity existed between Wright and a small group of artists and architects who had comprised the rebellious Secessionist movements; and Wright emerged in the 1910s as a primitivist. These developments occurred beyond the diffusion of ideas available through Wright's Wasmuth publications, and they suggest a new way of seeing Wright's work in the 1910s. Wright and his European "co-workers," as he later called them, tended to believe in the prophetic role of the arts, in analogies between art, nature, and society. To them the slavish imitation of either nature or historical legacy led to decay. Wright and the Secessionists shared a similar design process, a common language of pure, primary forms, and a belief that the renewal of society was to be found in the purifying of its art.

For Wright, abstraction—through the methods of conventionalization—was the means of expressing the innate architectural identity of a culture and of dethroning realism. Wright identified the specific sources of architectural purity in the indigenous buildings of native, primitive, and exotic cultures. He associated their abstractions with an "unerring" sense of beauty.[2] The existence of these sources confirmed his belief in a universal power and order that could be harnessed to shape the forms

of society itself. These views were based on a belief that essences exist. Many late twentieth-century critics may consider this viewpoint naive, but, at the time, it was a powerful current in the development of modernism.

Wright's European ventures in 1909 and 1910 marked significant developments in his life and work. His contact with the traditions of Western architecture and the innovations of the Secession artists had rejuvenated his work. He had, through great struggle, brought out nearly complete publications of his work, and had tried distributing them to the American audience that he hoped to educate. He and Mamah Borthwick had found an ally in Ellen Key, whose writings on the morality of human relationships had bolstered a short and tragic love. He had intensified the design of his ornament, using what he perceived as a universal language of primary forms. He had developed a theory of geometric abstraction based on conventionalization. He had integrated sculpture into schemes for the total design of buildings that surpassed his earlier works. Continually testing and pushing developments to extremes, he had developed a diagonality in ornament, which eventually moved from motif to plan, providing a mode of composition for his designs that had no parallels in Europe or America.

By 1922, Frank Lloyd Wright had absorbed the lessons of Europe. By the time his labors were finished at the Imperial Hotel in 1922, his work had reached a point of synthesis. After his return from Japan, some of his aesthetic experiments ended but other modes of composition continued. Many of the influences—feminism, Secessionist design, and primitivism—of the previous twelve years turned out to be ironic and paradoxical.

Personal Changes

At a personal level, Wright experienced both losses and gains. Dates rarely provide rigid boundaries in the development of an artist's work and life, but 1922 serves to divide two quite different periods in the architect's life. On 1 August 1922, Wright returned to the United States after what would be his last trip to Japan. Wright's mother died in February 1923, and Louis Sullivan died in April 1924; Wright thereby lost two persons who had been of great importance in his life. The great Kanto earthquake leveled much of Tokyo on 1 September 1923, the date of the Imperial Hotel's official opening.[3] Ironically, this calamity had positive effects for Wright. In the midst of the city's destruction the hotel survived largely intact, proving, according to Wright, the validity of his structural system. Perhaps more than any other event, including the publication of his works in Europe, this attention in the international press suddenly introduced Wright's name around the world as the architect of a building that seemed to defy the acts of nature itself.[4]

The end of one cycle and the beginning of another in Wright's personal life began shortly after his return from Japan, when he obtained a divorce from his wife, Catherine, in November 1922, after thirteen years of separation. Wright had spent eight tumultuous years with Miriam Noel, much of that time in Japan. By the end of their time in Japan, instead of parting from Noel, he chose to marry her, in November 1923.[5] Wright asserted in his *Autobiography* that the marriage was an effort to rescue their relationship, but the results were disastrous: "Marriage resulted in ruin for both. Instead of improving with marriage, as I had hoped, our relationship became worse."[6]

Wright's marriage contradicted the lessons in unconventional morality, articulated by Ellen Key, in which Wright and Mamah Borthwick had found courage and strength. Paradoxically, he tried by a most conventional means—marriage—to create an equality that did not exist. Although initially Noel had appeared to be an independent fellow artist and advocate of the honest pursuit of conviction regardless of social disapproval, she became, according to Wright, dependent and psychologically unbalanced. That was Wright's view; we have no account from Noel. Regardless of blame, she and Wright could not elevate their relationship to be a public model of moral love as Wright and Mamah Borthwick had done—they were mired in

their personal discord. We will never know Wright's motivations for staying with her. Perhaps he felt empathy for her emotional problems. Perhaps he lacked the strength to pursue a "spiritual adventure" alone. Nevertheless, in marrying Miriam Noel, Wright confronted the conflict between the proposition of a moral life as the basis for transformation of the self and society, and the difficulties of integrating those moral principles into the flawed lives of human beings. After Wright and Noel's marriage in 1923, separation soon followed. Wright spent much of the 1920s in efforts to extricate himself from his second marriage and from Noel's attempts to seek revenge for his falling in love with another woman, Olgivanna Lazovich Hinzenberg, whom he had met one year after the marriage to Noel. Hinzenburg would eventually become his third wife.[7]

Wright and the Secession

The ironies that permeated Wright's personal life characterize the connection between Wright and the artists of the Secession movements. Although a basic link between Wright and Europe in 1910 was a belief in primitivism and its implications for the social meaning of pure forms, Wright's direct contact with the Secession occurred long after the movement's peak, precisely when its artists' interest in universal forms was receding in favor of attempts to reconsider the traditions of their Central European culture. Around 1905 artists and critics began in Vienna to discuss whether classicism could be totally rejected and whether abstraction and primitivism had limited application as the basis for a new art. This discussion resulted in an effort to reconcile prehistory with a new, modern approach by grafting prehistory onto classical form. The need for this reconciliation had been adumbrated in the writings of Otto Wagner. Some architects consequently began to reexamine classical architecture and adapt it to modern needs. These efforts were one of the factors that contributed to a revival of interest in the Biedermeier style, which itself was a bourgeois adaptation of classicism that had been popular a hundred years earlier. In 1910, the work of Otto Wagner himself showed tendencies opposite to the exuberant primitivism that Wright had begun to pursue. For example, Wagner, who had entered the late phase of his work, designed with primary forms but in a spare and austere mode, as in his building on Döblergasse that contained his own apartment and office. This sobriety contrasted with the animism of Wright's emerging primitivist designs. Wagner's students were moving in several directions. Some continued to use primary

299. Lajos Kozma, crematorium project, Budapest, c. 1909 (*Der Architekt* 15, 1909).

forms as the basis of their designs. Lajos Kozma's 1909 project for a crematorium exemplifies an architectural ensemble whose constituent parts are circles, squares, and triangles (fig. 299). Others combined primary forms with explorations of a classicist vocabulary.

An even more fundamental difference between Wright and the Secessionists can be seen from the appearance in Europe of two views of primitivism. One view concentrated on the ancient Near East and on prehistory, providing a focus for a mystical sense of deep artistic will. Articulated as *Kunstwollen* by Alois Riegl, the curator of textiles at the Vienna Museum of Arts and Industry,[8] this view characterized the orientation of Olbrich in Vienna and that of his comrades in Darmstadt. The Olbrichian strain of mystical form, however, faded in Austria. In Germany the search for cultural rebirth in nationalist imagery stimulated an interest in medievalism and a passion for the *Ur*, the origin of culture, in which the German race was seen to be central. This medievalism combined with folk tendencies and increased with dramatic intensity as the cataclysm of World War I approached.

Folk art provided a second primitivism. Although a general interest in folk art was a common element for artists interested in pure sources, it also allowed that interest to break down along national lines, a development that was especially important for

Central Europeans. Folk art brought them close to their own origins through the concept of a *Heimatstil* and associations with feudal or premedieval life. This distinguished the Austrian interest from the French, whose artists, centered in Paris, preferred the primitivism of African folk and religious art.

Around 1903, when the work of Josef Hoffmann, cofounder of the Wiener Werkstätte, had combined Austrian and English vernacular, the interest in folk traditions among the Austrians had peaked and led to the famous split in the Secession between internationalists, who believed in more objective cultural forms, and nationalists, who adhered to folk ideas and local traditions.[9] This split mirrored a fundamental schism in the Modern Movement that was fully played out in the 1920s between regional and vernacular idioms and international ones. The results of the domination of the internationalists over the nationalists had profound consequences for modern culture that historians are still examining as the twentieth century comes to a close.

Differences between the branches of modernism were insignificant to Wright, just as distinctions among different primitivisms were unimportant to him. He did not distinguish between exoticism, with its connotations of complexity, foreignness, and strangeness, from primitivism, with its associations of simplicity, folkishness, and nativeness. Although around 1910 mystical primitivism had waned with the death of Olbrich, its represen-

300. *Call* Building with sculpture at entry, San Francisco, 1911, reconstruction drawing (author and Katie Kosut).

tations of primitivist motifs in primary forms were still to be seen in the furniture and crafts of the Werkstätte, in architecture that used ancient motives, such as the square within a square, and in a few special examples of geometricized sculpture. Wright picked up what the Austrians had left behind: the abstract and purist phase of their interests in the spiritual qualities of primitive art.

As an outsider, Wright had little interest in Central European vernacular architecture. His taste in art, as reflected in his print collection, favored landscapes over buildings, especially those landscapes reminiscent of his ancestral home in Wisconsin. His interest was in an American vernacular, but since one had not yet emerged, he felt obliged to invent it. Consequently,

his interest turned more to the aboriginal architecture of the Americas: that of American Indians and their ancestors to the south, the Maya.

While the Secessionists looked to their own roots in vernacular and classical architecture, Wright pursued his interest in primitivism throughout the 1910s. Motivated by his European travels, he launched his own explorations of primitivism through the invention of symbolic programs of design independent of his clients' needs. No material has been uncovered to associate the specific imagery of the A. D. German Warehouse in Wisconsin, for instance, with the client's professional and personal requirements. The wholesale grocer's cold-storage warehouse had an identity that had little to do with its immediate context. A similar case held for the figural sculpture at the Bogk House. The Bogks received the beginnings of a new American iconography regardless of whether they wanted it, needed it, or understood the meanings of their house's sculpture. In both cases, the buildings' iconography referred to origins of architecture and to an idealized future in which Wright imagined that the architect would build with a true American vocabulary.

Figural Sculpture—Continuity

Conventionalized figural sculpture was one lesson of Europe that Wright explored throughout the 1910s. Conventionalized figures flanked the entries of the *Call* Building as it appeared in model and in drawings. They were visible when Wright exhibited the model of the building at the Art Institute in 1914, but they were later removed (fig. 300). In his project for a cinema in San Diego of c. 1915, Wright included conventionalized sculpture (fig. 301).[10] There he provided the two sculptures, derived directly from the Midway Gardens' Totem Pole figures and used the iconography of geometry in a self-referential way, as he had at Midway. The entry doors feature the rotated square. The conventionalized figures hold offerings represented as cubes against the rotated matrix of the upper facade.

Showing how conventionalization of the human figure could be universally applied, Wright transferred his process to the Orient. Conventionalized sculpture, transformed from Midway Gardens prototypes, appeared at the Imperial Hotel in Tokyo. Consistent with his precept of utilizing the indigenous forms of a culture, Wright took the symbolic cornucopia, held in the hands of the Totem Pole figure at Midway Gardens, and rotated the cubes to remove associations with offerings (figs. 302, 303).[11]

301. Project for cinema, detail, San Diego, c. 1915 (TAL 0517.02).

302. "Totem Pole," detail, Midway Gardens, 1914 (Onderdonk, *The Ferro Concrete Style*).

In one example he also angled the features of the face, thus orientalizing the figure's appearance. After being carved in oya, the figures were placed at opposite sides of the pond in front of the hotel entry and in an inner-court garden. Once again, they hold the primary forms of geometry, two cubes with a rotated square incised on their surfaces. For the interior of the hotel, Wright also designed two conventionalized figures that he labeled as fiddlers and that were to be carved for a private dining room. He even used a conventionalized sculpture to crown the peak of the pitched roof over the banquet hall, thus marking the skyline with a sculpture at the highest point of the building.[12]

During the mid-1910s Wright applied his geometric representation of the human figure to graphic as well as architectural designs. In a study for a poster of an exhibition of Japanese wood-block prints held in Tokyo, he drew a modest geisha with a fan raised to her face (fig. 304).[13] Both the fan and robe were conventionalized into the regularity of linear, geometric forms. Wright thrust these elements at a diagonal to create a dyna-

303. Conventionalized figural sculpture, Imperial Hotel, 1917–22.

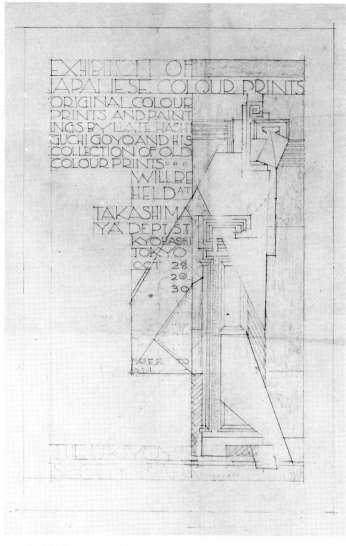

304. Exhibition poster, Ukiyoye Society, Frank Lloyd Wright, c. 1921 (LC).

mism in the composition and to suggest the obeisant bowing of the courtesan. Here, Wright created a totality of integrated parts: human figure, material form, and the natural elements of earth, air, and fire, represented as areas of green, blue, and orange.

Wright's last example of the conventionalized figure occurred around 1926 in his sculpture at the gateway to Nakoma, the residential suburb near the site of his Nakoma Country Club project outside Madison, Wisconsin.[14] Reflecting the developer's interest in having the suburb associated with Indians

and with Wright's project for the country club, Wright designed a sixteen-foot-high sculpture of the Indian woman "Nakoma," with a child at her side, and an eighteen-foot-high sculpture of a male Indian warrior, "Nakomis" (fig. 305). The two sculptures were to face each other, as features of two wide reflecting pools that would mark an entry to the Nakoma suburb.

Consistent with his practice of combining motifs to find a cultural composite, Wright joined together attributes from disparate tribes. As Hamilton has pointed out, he took his themes from various sources: the name "Nakoma" is mentioned in

305. Indian sculpture "Nakoma"
(right) and "Nakomis," originally
designed c. 1926 (TAL and Hubbard
Associates, *Nakoma, Nakomis.
Winnebago Indian Memorials*).

Longfellow's poem *Hiawatha;* Wright's reference to Nakomis's taking his bow to the sun is associated not with the Winnebago Indians but the Indians of the American Southwest; and the feather bonnets and blankets are garments not of the Indians formerly around Madison but of the plains Indians.[15]

While Wright may well have known of the colossal Indian sculpture *Black Hawk,* created by Lorado Taft for an artists' colony near Oregon, Illinois, he turned to his own previous experiments of 1911–14 in representing the human figure and adapted one of them for Nakomis.[16] Instead of pursuing any

formal innovation, the architect used the forms he had developed more than ten years earlier at the entry to the *Call* Building and at Midway Gardens. For Nakoma, Wright used circles, as he had in his sculpture Sphere at Midway Gardens, but he had more success in integrating the motif into the figure. Where at Midway Gardens Iannelli had not fully conventionalized the female figure when he executed its design, Wright made every element of Nakoma consist of spheres or parts of spheres.

Wright's symbolic associations with conventionalized sculpture, however, had changed dramatically in the previous decade. In place of idealized associations of infinity, integrity, and structural unity with the circle, square, and triangle, Wright identified the sculpture with stereotypical roles based on gender. He described the warrior:

Nakomis "rectilinear" dominant above a gleaming plateau teaching his young son to take the bow to the sun God. Nakomis represents the objective, aggressive, dramatic, principle in Nature."[17]

And the Indian woman:

Nakoma "curvilinear," submissive above a receptive basin, her brimming bowls and children symbolic of domestic virtue. Into this sunken basin flows the water from the plateau symbol. The humble figure of Nakoma is set facing her warrior chieftain. The proud figure of Nakomis is set facing Nakoma but slightly to one side in dignified preoccupation with his official "rite": his duty to posterity. [18]

The submissive, humble female bowing before the aggressive male embodiment of Nature conveys the startling change of attitude toward relationships that had transpired in the period of time that began with Wright defending himself and Mamah Borthwick as champions of male and female equality. No more eloquent statement could attest to Wright's personal transformation after the loss of Borthwick and through the disruption and anguish of his failed relationship and doomed marriage with Miriam Noel. His apparent turn from feminism may have occurred much earlier—his attitudes towards his wives require an investigation beyond the scope of this study. But with these sculptures of Nakomis and Nakoma, Wright virtually ended his explorations in representing the human figure.[19] He gave increasing emphasis to his long-standing interest in technology and materials, allowing it priority over figural representation. Commenting in 1931, he stated, "I feel the human figure as a medium of human expression has been overdone. I would like to see more plantlike structures and less bad anatomy in pattern."[20]

Wright's experiments in the "conventionalization of the flesh" had lasted briefly and then played out. The sculptures of Indians for the gateway to Nakoma in 1926, demonstrated the repetition of a design process developed at Midway Gardens and used at the Imperial Hotel. The representation of the figure had ceased being an important part of his work, as if once he had found the solution to the integration of the figure into architecture, the problem was no longer of interest. Underlying the end of sculpture were problems with the general reception to the sculpture and the concept of conventionalization itself.

Problems of Conventionalization

Contemporary taste did not support easily the primitivist aesthetic involved in conventionalized sculpture. To recall the predominant attitude toward a burgeoning modernism, we need only turn briefly to the comments by Lorado Taft in his lectures presented at the Art Institute in Chicago in 1917. Taft was a Francophile, educated at the Ecole des Beaux-Arts, and his predilections represented the values of many sophisticated American artists and critics. His heroes in France were the predecessors of Rodin; his ideal in America, Augustus Saint-Gaudens. He ridiculed the sculpture of Matisse and Brancusi, labeling them and their supporting critics as "shadowy personalities" and "aliens in France" who were perverting the great academic lineage of French sculpture.[21]

According to Taft, perversion was not restricted to the French modernists. In Germany, he detected an archaism that was "part of the white man's burden: examples of perverted orient art" that were "symptomatic" of what was wrong with German tendencies.[22] While Taft had praised some of Franz Metzner's work, he also attacked it as fantastic, absurd, grotesque, and enigmatic. The perpetrator of "such ugliness" merited attention only because he was a leading personality in German sculpture, imitated by "half the young sculptors of Germany."[23] According to Taft, Metzner's figure, *Bust of a Lady*, indicated that "he seems to have fallen under some weird oriental influence," with the result that "all other sculptural qualities have fled," the victims of the sacrifice of decorum to *Massgefühl*, or mass feeling.[24]

The experiments in conventionalizing the human figure by Metzner and Simandl, which had been models for Wright, ended before Wright began his own experiments in abstraction. After 1910, Metzner's work moved from geometrization back to roundly modeled figures, which he sculpted until he died in 1919. Simandl continued to vacillate between experimental cubic figures and sentimental figurines of mothers and children. These traditional figures satisfied bourgeois taste; stern cubic figures were too exotic for conservative collectors. The rise and the fall of Metzner and Simandl's work had occurred in parallel with the experiments that Picasso and Braque were conducting in Paris. Picasso and Braque pushed forward to create the well-known successive developments of cubism; Metzner and Simandl's reversions marked the end of the Secession's brief experiments in sculpture.[25]

By the time of his lectures in 1917, Taft perceived the latest vogue among the younger American sculptors to be an archaism based on Greek art. This phenomenon resulted from the importation of the style by graduates of the American Academy in Rome, with Paul Manship its leading exponent.[26] Wright's work fit nowhere; devoid of classicistic tendencies, it was neither based in archaism nor related to the nationalist grafting of primitivist tradition onto a classical inheritance that had preoccupied Central Europeans. Neither did it correspond to the resurgent medievalism in Germany nor to the reductive tendencies toward functionalism that began to emerge there and which eliminated sculpture entirely from architecture.

Underlying these divergences were problems with the very concept of conventionalization, which associated metaphysical and social values with art. The concept of conventionalization as an idealistic social tool to make art square with life had its own severe limits, as William Norman Guthrie pointed out to Wright in 1916:

My Dear Zealot, You need me—that's why I'm sorriest. We need each other. I need you—because I get aesthetic renewal from you—& this city is a sore tax. For God's sake do art—& don't trouble your soul to reform society. Its "conventionalization" you cannot assist in projecting. Just as Luther could not recommend marriage to ascetics after marrying a nun—with double breach of vows, so you cannot speak effectively for a larger & more stringent [ethical code] because [of the] truer constriction of matrimony. So do architecture & thank God—buy beautiful asiatic things & make a huge percentage & carry your every increased load like the man you are, magnanimous & delightful at least to me if none else! . . . Always write[.] The best & most enthusiastic wishes—call these prayers if you like—for you my aesthetic Don Quixote in the social field.
Your friend, W. N. Guthrie.[27]

Even at the cosmological level the premise on which conventionalization rests—underlying analogies between the macrocosm of nature and the microcosm of human society—is open to question. Despite Berlage's assertions that stars and planets move in pure geometric orbits, reinforcing the constancy of geometry in the universe, we now know that their orbits are not pure but eccentric. Advanced physics tells us that the laws of the universe are not easily codified and that chaos has patterns which we can barely perceive. Furthermore, the analogy between nature and art is more of an ideal aspiration than an achievable goal.

Regardless of not being fully appreciated by critics and regardless of inherent weaknesses with its premises, conventionalization in sculpture guided Wright until he had fully explored its formal expression. Having made sculpture as abstract as he

could, he abandoned any conceptual interest in the figure. At the same time, however, he continued to explore his concept of ornament in terms of new construction methods and in terms of the architectural plan itself.

Ornament in Textile Blocks

Pursuing his search for a vocabulary of ornament expressed in primary forms, Wright sought to transform the richness of Japanese oya stone into a building material that could be mass-produced. That material took the form of a textile-block construction system, and its development marks the end of Wright's experiments in exoticism and primitivism. Beginning in 1919, Wright began to explore the casting of individual blocks as an alternative to monolithic slabs. Rather than produce a whole element to make a single unit, as in the monolithic casting of concrete, he devised a system to reproduce the unit in multiples to make the whole.[28] In doing this, Wright faced the dilemma of creating mechanically in America the patterns that his unlimited Japanese labor force had cut by hand from oya. Wright hoped that the replicated unit, cast into molds at the building site, would provide the means for a major construction system in which the rotational geometry perfected at the Imperial Hotel could further evolve. The unit, designed to be inscribed on the surface of the unbuilt Monolith House, subsequently became the module of the individually cast block of the textile block system, a method of construction which Wright developed throughout the 1920s.

The textile block system became a means of constructing walls, composed of two-part units, tied vertically and horizontally into a structurally stable configuration by a web of steel rods (fig. 306).[29] Wright thought so highly of the system that he intended to patent it, as he had patented the Monolith system.[30] Reinforcing rods were placed in integrally cast grooves and anchored with mortar; the wall would obtain lateral stability by having wire ties, placed perpendicular to the blocks, connecting the rods; and the two-part system produced a cavity, which could provide insulation and two exposed surfaces.[31] These two surfaces allowed for the play of integral ornament and differing treatments for the exterior and interior of the building. This weaving together of structure and surface, like warp and weft, created a literal building fabric—hence Wright's naming of the process the textile block system.[32]

By 1923, when Wright had used the system for clients in California—including Charles Ennis, Samuel Freeman, Mrs.

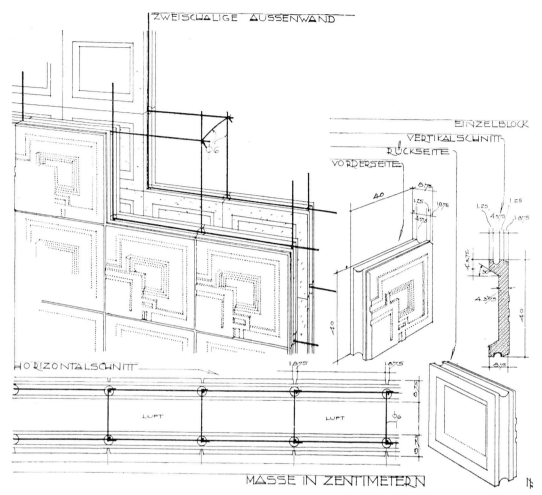

306. Textile block system, Richard Neutra, draftsman (De Fries, *Aus dem Lebenswerke*).

Alice Millard, and John Storer—the lowly, cast concrete block had achieved an unprecedented expressive force (fig. 307). The elaborate block designs showed the direct applications of the lessons in rotational geometry learned at the Imperial Hotel and, earlier, from the use of primary forms by the artists of the Secession. The rich texture of their surfaces and their massing have caused historians to cite these houses as examples of pre-Columbian influence. Tselos, for instance, cited a Maya cylinder seal as the source of the equal-armed cross in the blocks at the Millard House.[33] But there is no indication that Wright was aware of such a specific reference. The equal-armed cross has a classical Western tradition of its own as the Greek cross, and the motif was used in an identical way in the blocks of a pierced

screen in Wright's design of the Ginza theater project. These buildings reveal no more explicit Maya influence than Wright's primitivist buildings of the 1910s, with the possible exception of the Ennis House (fig. 308); Charles Ennis apparently was a "Maya enthusiast" and may have requested that the massing of his home resemble Maya architecture.[34]

While visual comparisons can be made between the California textile block houses and pre-Columbian architecture, other meanings, as in Wright's experimental buildings of the 1910s, also apply to the textile block houses. On one level, the ornamental patterns of these buildings can be analyzed as emanating from the basic shapes of geometry and motifs of origin that Wright had been developing since 1910. In developing them

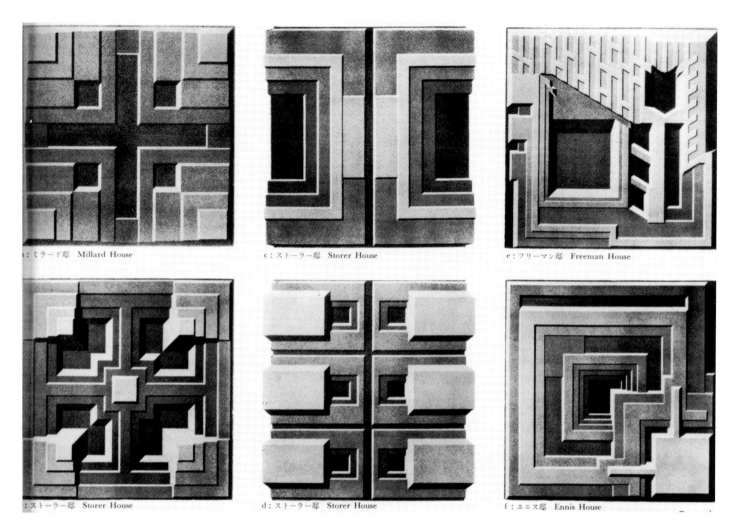

a:ミラード邸 Millard House   c:ストーラー邸 Storer House   e:フリーマン邸 Freeman House

b:ストーラー邸 Storer House   d:ストーラー邸 Storer House   f:エニス邸 Ennis House

307. Patterns of textile blocks (Sweeney and Calvo, *Space Design* 240, 1984).

Wright pursued his aesthetic interests at least as much as his interest in economic construction. Kameki Tsuchiura, Wright's draftsman from 1923 to 1925, has indicated that Wright knew the textile block system was no less expensive than conventional construction, and, in the end, he did not care: "He was an artist. He wanted to do what he wanted to do."[35]

The evolution of the textile block patterns can also be seen to have its source in the development of motifs at the Imperial Hotel and Midway Gardens; indeed, every pattern in the textile blocks has a precedent in those two buildings. A comparison of a drawing for a block pattern from the Samuel Freeman House of 1923 and blocks from the Imperial Hotel shows the literal translation of rotational pattern from oya stone to the textile

blocks (figs. 309, 310).[36] The same devices are used: recessed planes, dynamic diagonality, and rendering to indicate planar depth and angle.[37]

On another level, the patterns can be seen as Wright's taking the conventionalization of motifs and fitting them to the technology of cast concrete. Wright became increasingly preoccupied with solving the technical problems of the textile block system, and this preoccupation ultimately overshadowed the experimental aspects of design. Technical demands began to dominate form; the ornamental patterns of the blocks became limited by the constraints of manufacturing on the site, and Wright encountered difficulties in providing uniform modules for door and window openings.[38] Without totally abandoning

308. Charles Ennis House, Los Angeles, California, 1924 (TAL).

the system, Wright reduced his ornamental pattern. That reduction coincided with the demise of Wright's overt pursuit of primitivist forms, the move in his design methods towards diagonality, and his realization of the difficulties in changing the architecture of a society through form alone.

Ornament in Plan

The end of Wright's incorporation of the lessons of Europe marked a major change in his method of design: the primary forms of the ornamental motif became the primary forms of the plan itself. Ending his experiments in primitivism and the representation of the human figure, Wright used the primary forms of geometry to generate and organize his buildings without strict bilateral symmetry.[39] In Wright's building plans the dominance of the square yielded to the triangle and circle, both as simple forms and as hexagons, ellipses, and segments of circles (figs. 311, 312). This transferral of primary geometry from motif to plan was combined with the new technique, developed in the 1910s, of dynamic diagonality. These developments coin-

cided with Wright's return from Japan and his experience of the desert in southern California. There, in the desert's expanse, Wright felt an ultimate freedom to pursue non-Cartesian plans and their corresponding spatial volumes. He was able to express this freedom because he had spent the previous twelve years developing the necessary vocabulary of form and perfecting dynamic diagonality in his ornament.

Wright adopted diagonality as a design tool along with rectilinear planning, and he used both throughout the rest of his career. Later, the ellipse, which he had "despised" in 1909, became a plan form of its own, with segments of it becoming the ground plans for houses. Only after 1922 and his lessening of the square as his principal compositional motif, did the triangle assume major significance in his buildings.

While Wright continued to employ diagonality in a system of rotational geometry, after 1922 he gradually ceased using the exotic and primitive motifs from which it had arisen. The linear fret, often expressed in building siding as continuous overlapping planes, became a permanent part of his architectural vocabulary. However, Wright's various experiments with textile blocks and their muted recurrence later in concrete-block houses represent the end of his primitivist ornaments; his ornament now entered its own severe phase as the International Style began to infiltrate America.

The Shift from Primitivism

There are several reasons, ranging from the possibility of creative fatigue to cultural shifts in modernism, for Wright's move in the 1920s from an interest in primitivism that had been sig-

naled by his encounter with Europe in 1910. Some of these factors are elusive because Wright never spoke or wrote about them. He may have felt that he had fully explored in formal terms all the variations of primitivist motifs in ornament that interested him. He may have been discouraged by their lack of public acceptance, coupled with the failure of the textile block system to establish any national trends in construction. Clearer than Wright's motivations, however, are the changing conditions in Europe and America in which Wright's work of the 1920s evolved.

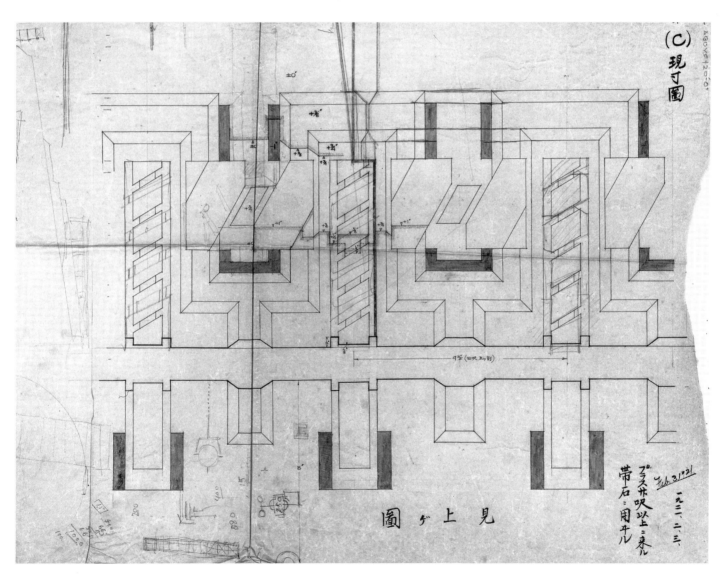

309. Imperial Hotel, block pattern of belt stone carving, 1917–22 (TAL 1509.231).

Modernism in art and architecture became more narrowly defined in the early 1920s than it had been in the 1910s. As William Rubin has noted, in the first decades of the twentieth century the meaning of primitive art changed and its scope was reduced, as "primitive art" became identified with tribal objects in a "strictly modernist interpretation" in the visual arts.[40] Strict modernist definitions also took hold of architecture. By 1922, the rise of a new dominant architectural aesthetic in Europe,

the austere vocabulary of the *neue Sachlichkeit,* coincided with the end of Wright's experiments in primitivism. Mysticism and exoticism were at an end. There seemed little place for them in the realities of Europe that followed World War I. By 1922, both the ancient sources and the expressionist forms as a basis for modern architecture were rejected by the emerging protagonists of the Modern Movement in favor of objective form. Although it had never fully disappeared in modernist architec-

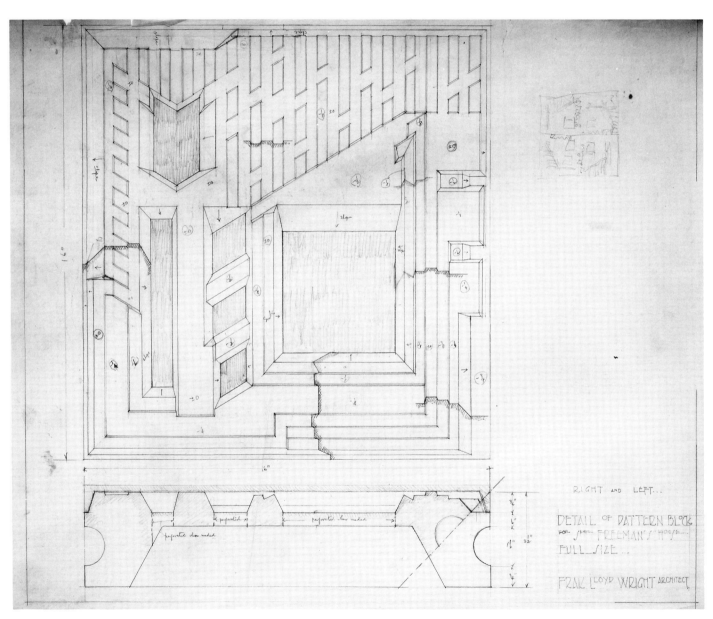

310. Freeman House, textile block, Los Angeles, 1923 (LC no. 12416).

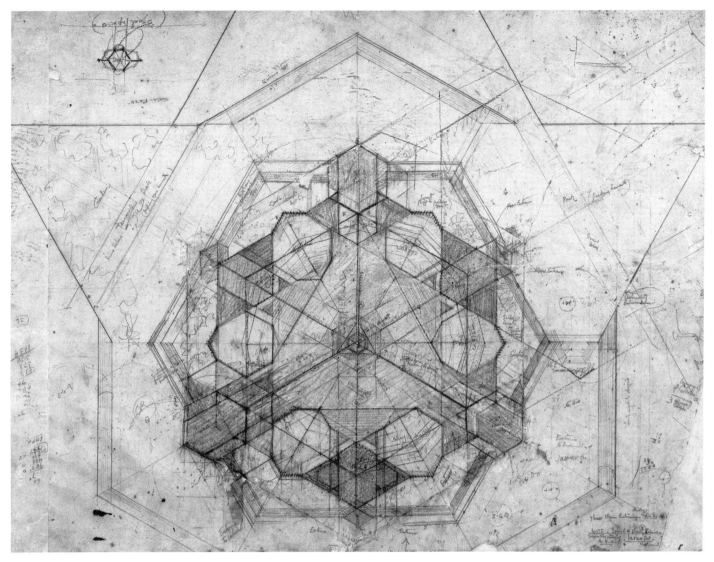

311. Steel Cathedral, project for Rev. William Norman Guthrie, plan, New York, 1926 (TAL 2602.002).

ture—even in socialist housing[41]—ornament became a bête noire in the rhetoric of the Modern Movement. Critics used reductive arguments to castigate ornament: it was too costly (which was true under the conditions in Europe and during the Depression); it had no contemporary cultural meaning; and, more fundamentally, it was associated (like the pitched roof) with the traditions of classicism and with nineteenth-century eclectic historicism generally.

Wright responded to European developments, which he knew from publications and continuing contact with European architects, by eliminating richly textured ornament from his buildings. He also felt compelled to respond to these developments in writing. The aesthetic of the New Objectivity was the formal, planar language called later in America the International Style. Assuming that his Wasmuth publications had reached a large audience and that publications of the early and mid-1920s had further spread his ideas, Wright believed he had influenced this style, and by the later 1920s he reacted both as a critic, attacking the writings of Le Corbusier, and as a designer with his own version of austere architecture, as in his 1929 apartment-building project for Elizabeth Noble (fig. 313).[42] Ornamental motifs did not disappear entirely from Wright's work, however; they moved from surface design to the plan concept of the design itself.

Wright's experimental work of the 1910s and early 1920s had placed him in an ironic position: his work followed the exotic primitivism of the Secession movements but preceded the Art Deco movement in the United States. Absorbing the *art moderne* that had centered in Paris in the mid-1920s, Art Deco picked up primitivist tendencies that had evolved from the 1910s and transformed them into a unique phenomenon: America's own

moderne in which the "depth" of the spiritual was transformed into the light airiness of a jazz culture. Aztec, Maya, and American Indian motifs were revived as styles that had little to do with the interest in a return to origins that had preoccupied Wright and the Secessionists. With several projects remaining unbuilt and his work published more in Europe than in America, Wright's primitivist designs were ignored instead of becoming models for American modernism in the 1920s. He provided an American iconography that no one pursued, with the exception of his son Lloyd.[43]

Another factor in Wright's movement away from primitivist

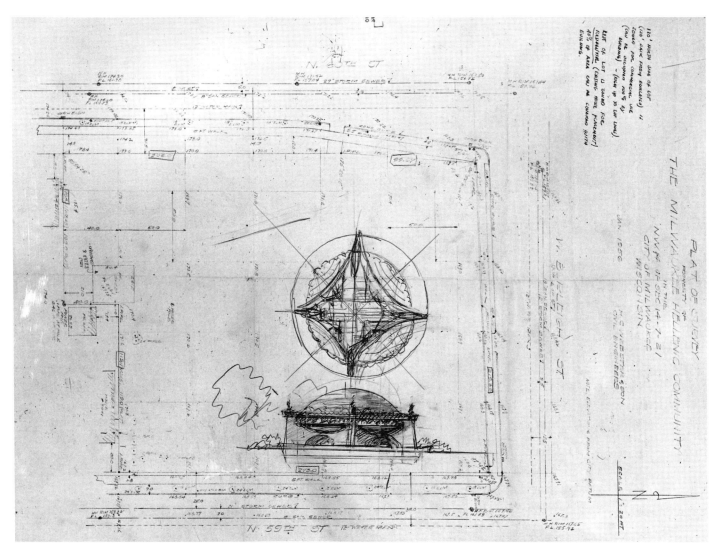

312. Annunciation Greek Orthodox Church, plan, Wauwatosa, Wisconsin, 1956 (TAL 5611.018).

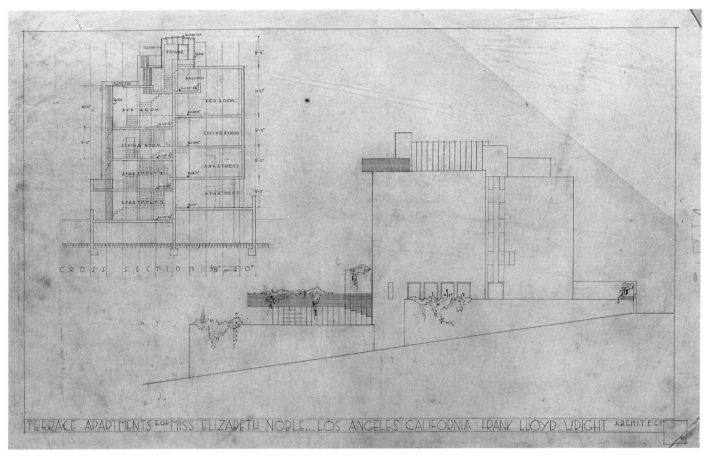

313. Elizabeth Noble Apartment Building, section and side elevation, Los Angeles, 1929 (TAL 2903.015).

ornament may have been his realization that the motifs, in the end, did not contain sufficient symbolic power to represent modern values. The motifs of origin, sought as the pure sources that would recreate meaning in architectural form, had long been stripped of their power of sacred representation. As Walter Benjamin described it, such forms had traveled a route from magic to ritual to a secular domain.[44] When people no longer believed that multiple frames symbolized the numinous power of the temple front, the image was emptied of its sacred content. It thus became truly foreign, that is, evocative of another country that existed nowhere in the present and only vaguely in the past. The efforts of artists, including Frank Lloyd Wright, to achieve meaningful symbolic form could be achieved only when a structure of belief existed and when form had affective power to engage that structure. But in the absence of any collective belief and understanding, the symbol becomes hollowed by imita-

tion and replication. Its meanings are arbitrary, its associations subjective. Thus, in America, architects in the later 1920s invigorated Art Deco architecture with the iconography of Egypt and the ancient Near East; once-sacred motifs became elements of style and fashion, flashing, colorful, and vibrant, but void of their numinous meanings as origins of forms. Rudolf Wittkower observed this problem in reference to symbols when he wrote, "Our lives are fenced in by rituals sunk down to the level of conventions."[45] Meanings of primary forms have become so transformed as to be inverted: the iconography of the temple front became the facade of the market, embodied now in the multinational corporation. Without recognizing the original sources of their forms, postmodernists in the mid-1970s and 1980s replicated the motifs of multiple surrounds, layered planes, recessed triangles, believing they were referring exclusively to the architects of the Viennese Secession.

The end of Frank Lloyd Wright's experiments in primitivism may have been hastened by his perception that an incongruity existed between the motifs of origin and the materiality that American culture perceived as symbolically meaningful. Within the context of this incompatibility, Wright's figural sculpture ceased to be important, and innovative ornamental patterns diminished in his work. As for the fate of his primitivist ornament, the pinnacle had been the Imperial Hotel. Never again would Wright design such a complex fabric of ornament.

Persistence of the Primitive

Although Wright's expression of primitivism began to diminish in his architecture, he maintained an interest in the pure sources of architecture that continued from the 1910s throughout the rest of his life. Adding to his library of sources, he obtained a series of books, published by the Wasmuth Verlag, that documented, in a brief but scholarly manner, exotic sources from around the world. At least seven volumes of the Orbis Pictus series were at Wright's studio at Taliesin, among which were Walter Lehmann's *Altmexikanische Kunstgeschichte,* with illustrations of sculpture and architecture, and Otto Weber's *Die Kunst der Hethiter,* with illustrations of what were then considered Hittite sculpture, reliefs, and cylinder seals. Other volumes covered Japanese wood-block prints, Asiatic sculpture, and Indian and Islamic architecture.[46] Though these volumes were published after Wright's exotic designs of the 1910s, from about 1922 to 1925, his possession of them confirms his continuing interest in the sense of beauty found in ancient cultures.

The interest in the primitive and the exotic persisted, even when it was not a motivating factor in Wright's architecture. Years later he would write about his early interests:

As for the Incas, the Mayans, even the Japanese—all were to me but splendid confirmation. . . . At that early day I was thrilled by Mayan, Inca and Egyptian remains, loved Byzantine. The Persian fire-domed, fire-backed structures were beautiful to me. But never anything Greek except the sculpture and the Greek vase—the reward of their persistence in search of the elegant solution. My search was more for the exception that went to prove the rule, than for the rule itself.[47]

Wright reiterated the theme of the universal human character of the forms of origin when he rebuffed a suggestion that one culture made better magazine "copy" than another.[48] Responding to British architect Alfred C. Bossom's promotion of Maya architecture as a model for the American skyscrapers, Wright stated that such a suggestion was misguided:

Poor Bossom is an incorrigible ass—He offers Mexico to copy as better "copy." It has not entered his consciousness yet that architecture is essentially *human* and its origins and affects a matter of human character and heart. In that respect we are no nearer Maya than Egyptian or any other primitive race.[49]

Egypt and the land of the Maya persisted as spiritual loci long after Wright abandoned experiments with their forms. The cultures of the past figuratively spoke of a release from materiality, just as did nature in its most majestic, uncorrupted forms. Looking at the Badlands of South Dakota in 1935, Wright associated the natural landscape with primitivism: "What I saw gave me an indescribable sense of mysterious otherwhere—a distant architecture, ethereal, touched, only touched with a sense of Egyptian, Mayan drift and silhouette."[50]

In 1938, when writing in *Architecture and Modern Life* about the role of nature in linking man to architecture, Wright cited the sources of architecture as "splendid examples: Mayan, Egyptian, Greek, Byzantine, Persian, Gothic, Indian, Chinese, Japanese."[51] They were the testament of "man in possession of his earth," a cosmological location that was constantly challenged by science replacing art, and money and machines disturbing primordial social relationships. These Western social forces, of course, had been evolving for almost five hundred years in Europe and, when transferred to foreign lands, had already whittled away many of the established values of exotic cultures.

One of the most revealing statements about Wright's continuing interest in primitivism and his perception of the limits of the pre-Columbian world as a primitivist source came in the early 1950s. In a rare venture into academic dialogue Wright responded to Dimitri Tselos's statements about exotic influences on the architect's work. Wright acknowledged that no ancient model could fit into the machine age of technological modernism:

Had I not loved and comprehended pre-Columbian architecture as the primitive basis of world-architecture, I could not now build as I build with understanding of all architecture. Only with that understanding could I have shaped my buildings as they are. Yet, of all ancient buildings, wherever they may stand or whatever their time, is there one of them suitable to stand here and now in the midst of our time, our American, our machine-age technique? Not one.[52]

Of course, providing models of buildings that stood "in the midst of our time, our American, our machine-age technique" had been the goal of Wright's Wasmuth publications. These too met a paradoxical end.

The Fate of the Wasmuth Publications

While I have tried to show how Europe had a profound influence on Wright in the 1910s, the influence of his Wasmuth publications on Europeans is a complex story. Ironically, contrary to what modernist historians have said, Wright's impact on Europe was more important in the 1920s, during critical debates on modernism, than in the 1910s. Only with the appearance of his work in Dutch publications, initiated by the architect Hendrik Berlage and followed by the overt copying of his designs, did the perception of the accomplishment of the Wasmuth monograph become widespread. German architects came to visit Wright at Taliesin; Wright's monograph was republished by Wasmuth in 1924—without Wright's permission.[53] Being aware of this European interest, Wright played off the Germans against the Dutch.[54] In the midst of this competition the first French publication of his work appeared.[55]

The subsequent reception of the Wasmuth publications turned out to be rather disappointing for Wright. From his point of view, the publications added to his European reputation but played almost no role in his career in America. He saw the work in the monograph and *Sonderheft* imitated, but the principles ignored or misunderstood. Towards the end of his life, he recounted in an interview his disappointment about the progress made towards the expression of a true American architecture:

I think that the effects have been sought and multiplied and the "why" of the effect, the real cause at the center of the life of the thing, seems to have languished. If honest seekers once mastered the inner principle, infinite variety would result. No one would have to copy anyone else. My great disappointment—it always is—is to find, instead of emulation, what I see as a wave of imitation.[56]

Wright also wrote briefly in 1957, two years before his death, in a short introduction to the reprint edition of the folios, about the fate of the Wasmuth monograph:[57]

[The monograph was] temporarily stored below ground-level at Taliesin, previous to arrangements for distribution. The entire portion of the edition meant for America was consumed in the fire destroying the first Taliesin. . . . Smoke rose from the smoldering mass below grade for several days. So America saw little of this original publication in German unless imported. But one whole copy only and about one half of another stays at Taliesin with me.[58]

Before his death, however, an old dissatisfaction surfaced: Wright had never liked the plates traced from renderings by Marion Mahony. He felt the foliage overpowered the buildings in her drawings. And in a final purgation of his ambivalent feelings he tore up the plates of his copy of the monograph, the *Ausgeführte Bauten und Entwürfe von Frank Lloyd Wright*.[59] Some copies, however, of the American edition of the *Sonderheft* survived the fire of 1914, their pages and covers stained from time and moisture. Only loose plates of the Wasmuth monograph that survived the Taliesin fires remain in Wright's archives.

Wright's Achievement

The Wasmuth monograph and the *Sonderheft* have become the misunderstood icons of the myth of Wright's influence in Europe and the key to Europe's influence on Wright. This study has tried to show that Wright absorbed and transformed the artistic influences of Europe without suffering creative blockages of anxiety. Just as he had assimilated the styles of American architecture at the turn of the century, by 1922 Wright had absorbed the lessons of Europe and moved on.[60] He had redefined his artistic self in terms of those lessons. And this resolution was so complete that Wright tended to deny it had ever occurred. This denial was reinforced by his perception, after 1922, of his influence in Europe, which was manifest in the 1920s.

Wright had dealt with the problem of influence by absorbing the motifs of the Secession and transforming them into his own medium. His absorption and transformation of the Viennese developments reveals an aspect of his creativity that has been little understood: he was a master interpreter. He could recognize the brilliance of fundamental architectural solutions and had the ability to test, accept, and reject a tremendous range of artistic ideas from other sources. Despite differences between Wright's motivations and those of the Secessionists, an affinity developed between them. Misunderstanding itself can lead to creativity. As Rudolf Wittkower noted, "Misinterpretation is the real secret of the vitality of European cosmopolitanism in the arts," an observation that could also apply to American artistic vitality.[61]

Wright's heightened sensitivity to being "influenced" was clear in his many denials of influence. His reproach to Charles Ashbee for the suggestion that Wright was influenced by Japanese art—"a false accusation and against my very religion"— was only one of several denials.[62] The process by which these sources were absorbed cannot be described by the vague term "influence" or by the specific term "imitation." Wright claimed to have "digested" his sources.[63] He himself suggested a way out of the problematics of influence: not imitation, but emulation and transformation.

The fundamental difficulty in proving artistic influence is that similar ideas may appear simultaneously throughout many cultures. There are no single sources or simple, linear pathways. Just as the motifs of the Secession were cross-fertilized with English arts and crafts, major and minor works by significant and insignificant European artists were available to Americans and Europeans through magazines. Accounts by word of mouth and the images of photography complicate the pathways of influence. Usually, superficial examples of influence provide no mechanism of transmission or theory of explanation. Can influence be proved? Can it be disproved? Explorations of questions about the transformation of ideas, the existence of contradictions, and the role of misunderstanding may be more fruitful for understanding an artist's creative processes than facile assertions of influence. Wright's creative processes may be far more informative than a search for influences alone. These processes become more vibrant when we see them as part of a net, nodes in a fabric composed of many tied strands, implying multiple meanings.

Experimentation freed Wright to resolve his own problems of influence. Could he have pursued these developments without having gone to Europe in 1909? We will never know absolutely, but it is difficult to imagine any other set of circumstances that could have so profoundly affected his work.

Wright could not, however, enact the reform of society at the pace he developed as an artist. The lessons of morality—articulated so well by Ellen Key—that Wright wanted to demonstrate in his life had been difficult to put into practice. Although he could not integrate a sense of equality into his relationship with Miriam Noel, in his life and work he continued to pursue the principles of social reform based on the education of youth. In his writings and lectures, Wright continued to speak "to the young man in architecture." His efforts took fruition in the formation of his own school, conceived in the late 1920s with Olgivanna, whom he married in 1928, and the school developed in the early 1930s as the Taliesin Fellowship, a legacy that continues.

What are we to make of Wright's ambition to change people's lives, to preach to them of liberated relationships based on love rather than social obligation, and to tout the architect as the governor of society and the fabricator of the forms that represent collective values? Were these ambitions merely the grandiosity of an egocentric and selfish individual, compulsively seeking to impose his own will? Is there not a great irony in Wright championing individualism, yet validating the manifestations of individualism by his own norms? How can a champion of the democratic ideal apply a standard of values to others' self-expression? Perhaps hubris haunts Wright's work and ideas, and his ambitions are bound by an inescapable paradox. However, from the perspective of the late twentieth century, as we look back to ideas formulated in the intellectual climate of the late nineteenth century, we may also see that Wright had a modernist yearning for the artist to lead and transform society. He saw the architect in the role of poet, priest, and social reformer. To Wright, the artist was a rebel whose efforts should continue regardless of personal defeat and social rejection. He saw art not as an end in itself but as a means of touching humanity, not just the single soul of an individual. While some people disparage as a relic of modernist culture the idea of the transformative power of art, others may see that history continually reminds us of the time when artists and architects aspired to lead society. In this view the historian has no higher goal than to recall potentialities of human life.

Despite disappointments and tragedy, Wright's conviction of the architect as reformer persisted long after his mystical associations with "spell power" diminished. No return to pure form had been possible; he discovered instead that a true American architecture cannot be static but must be a perpetual effort to distinguish itself from the European roots to which it is bound. His vision of a free society was tested by personal struggle; nevertheless, the quest for an ideal society and its appropriate forms continued. After the tumult of the 1910s and early 1920s Wright continued to believe that architecture could provide the means of social change through buildings, books, and education. Midway Gardens had briefly elevated the culture of ordinary citizens. The Imperial Hotel had provided a bridge between tradition and the demands of a modern world. Like a seeker of the Grail and the artists of the Secession, Frank Lloyd Wright had entered a search for a world that, in the words of Herman Bahr, "never was nor ever will be his." But in that search Wright found aspects of his artistic and moral self. Europe, in 1910, had brought Wright inspiration for that search.

Appendix A: Chronology

All dates and events have been established from documentary sources cited in the main text and notes. This chronology covers only the period under study here. It is intended to be a guide to significant events in these years of Wright's career, and it is not complete.

2 December 1908 • Wright confirms professional and private struggles to Darwin D. Martin.

3 January 1909 • Although Wright's work is piled up, he writes to Charles R. Ashbee of the temptation to "desert" Oak Park.

28 June 1909 • Mamah Borthwick Cheney leaves her husband in Oak Park.

16 September 1909 • Wright informs Martin that he is leaving his wife and children.

20 September 1909 • Leaves Oak Park.

22 September 1909 • Date of signature on contract with Herman Von Holst to take over Wright's architectural practice.

October 1909 • Wright and Mamah Cheney sail for Europe. AEG Turbine Factory, designed by Peter Behrens, opens in Berlin; sketches had been started in 1908.

7 November 1909 • Wright and Mamah Cheney discovered in Berlin at Hotel Adlon.

24 November 1909 • Wright signs contract with Wasmuth Verlag; original document no longer extant.

c.22 January 1910 • Wright in Paris sees the disastrous conditions of the floods. Wright and Mamah Cheney temporarily part company in Paris; she travels to Sweden, meets Ellen Key, and returns to teach languages at the University of Leipzig. She remains in Leipzig until late spring or early summer.

16 February 1910 • Bruno Möhring lectures on Wright's work and shows drawings to the *Vereinigung Berliner Architeckten*.

31 March 1910 • Wright, settled into Florence at Villino "Fortuna," writes Ashbee on "squaring" life with the self.

1 May 1910 • William Norman Guthrie writes to Wright, summarizes his personal dilemma, and advises him to give up the relationship with Mamah Cheney.

Late spring–early summer 1910. • Wright visits Paris, meets his son Lloyd; during late spring or early summer both stay at the Ritz Hotel. After the departure of Lloyd, Wright travels to Leipzig and returns with Mamah Cheney to Fiesole.

10 June 1910 • By early summer Wright and Mamah Cheney are in Fiesole; Wright drafts bitter letter to Walter Burley Griffin; the letter is not sent.

16 June 1910 • Letter of recommendation for Taylor Woolley, from Fiesole.

8 July 1910 • Wright informs Ashbee of plans to return to Oak Park; Wright absent from Fiesole between 8 July and 20 July.

20 July 1910 • Woolley informed by Wright about the Wasmuth project: all plates finished, except for Harley Bradley House; photographs of *Sonderheft* sent to Berlin in June; only 30 of 50 photographs are acceptable.

24 July 1910 • Wright, in Fiesole, informs Ashbee at length about the Wasmuth project: twelve proofs of the monograph have been pulled; the complete publication is to consist of 73 buildings in 100 plates and to be printed in 1,000 copies.

Summer 1910 • Wright visits Oberammergau and sees the Passion play; visit to Vienna probably occurs during this period.

August 1910 • Travel in Europe, itinerary undocumented or not extant.

1 September 1910 • Wright's planned arrival in Berlin.

10 September 1910 • Wright's planned departure from Berlin.

[26] September 1910 • Ashbee informed by Wright in London of disagreement about introduction for *Sonderheft;* Wright en route to board S.S. *Bluecher.*

6 October 1910 • Wright returns to New York City on the SS *Bluecher.*

8 October 1910 • Wright returns to Oak Park.

10 October 1910 • William E. Martin writes to brother Darwin confirming Wright's return.

21 October 1910 • Wright informs John D. Larkin of anticipated press runs: 10,000 copies of the *Sonderheft*, with preface by C. R. Ashbee, 116 pages; and 1,000 copies of monograph at $37.50 per copy.

3 November 1910 • Wasmuth informs Wright 4,000 copies of the *Sonderheft* are ready for sending to America; monograph "nearly ready."

15 November 1910 • Wasmuth installment payment due; second payment due March 1911. Wright is in New York City for Universal Portland Cement Company, to see sisters, cousin, and Tiffany's. Walter Gerdt's house burns, and Wright has an opportunity for remodeling it.

19 November 1910 • Accounting of Wasmuth debt.

20 November 1910 • Wright returns to the Chicago area.

22 November 1910 • Wright, in Chicago, has approved the last proofs of the first folio of 50 plates of the Wasmuth monograph.

23 November 1910 • Wright owes Francis Little sketches for Little's new house in Wayzata, Minnesota.

30 December 1910 • Wasmuth stops production on the monograph.

January 1911 • Only one man in Wright's office. Wright describes the Sherman Booth House as a major commission similar in scale to the Coonley House. Albert McArthur wants to return to work for Wright, but Wright refuses to hire most of his previous employees.

13 January 1911 • With publication of the first edition, the *Sonderheft* is available in Europe. Wright rejects first edition of the *Sonderheft*, prepares entire new dummy for publication, and plans for visit to Berlin, a second trip—previously unknown—to Europe.

16 January 1911 • Wright sets sail for Liverpool on H.M.S. *Lusitania* on second trip to Europe.

January 1911 • Wright arrives in London; forgoes stay with C. R. Ashbee.

18 January 1911 • Wright reports there are fifty-eight German subscribers to the monograph before publication.

21 January 1911 • Wright on board H.M.S. *Lusitania*; site of Sherman Booth House, Glencoe, Illinois, under consideration; Wright takes plot plan to Germany.

13 February 1911 • Wright, in Berlin, revises his contract with Wasmuth (see Appendix B). Totals for the publications: Wasmuth monograph, 1,275, with 100–200 for European distribution; American edition of *Sonderheft*, 5,100 copies; European edition of *Sonderheft*, 3,900 copies.

3 April 1911 • Wright returns to the United States by this date; becomes involved with the acquisition of property allegedly for a cottage for his mother near Spring Green, Wisconsin.

6 April 1911 • Suggestion from Wright for Woolley to look for work in California.

10 April 1911 • Anna Lloyd Wright buys the land for Taliesin: 31.561 acres for $2,274.88 from Joseph and Justina Rieder.

12 April 1911 • Wasmuth sells 52 copies of monograph to German architects before publication.

22 April [1911] • Wright discusses sale of Wasmuth publications with Woolley: only 650 monographs for sale at $50; 58 sold by subscription in Germany; number varies slightly from other reports.

1 May 1911 • Delivery of monograph and *Sonderheft* due in Chicago as per agreement of 13 February 1911.

June 1911 • Publications in transit to Chicago.

9 June 1911 • 40 copies of monograph sold in United States, probably by subscription. Only the first folio is available; complete edition still in transit.

7 July 1911 • Arbitration of contract with Von Holst settled; Wright to receive $108.29.

5 August 1911 • Mamah Borthwick Cheney granted a divorce from Edwin Cheney.

31 August 1911 • Wright wires Woolley in San Diego to come to Chicago to work at regular salary.

12 September 1911 • Wright wires Woolley from Taliesin to come and work with him.

16 October 1911 • Gookin informs Wright of possibility of commission for Imperial Hotel; contact established with Aisaku Haiyashi.

7 December 1911 • By this date Wright's office is at 605 Orchestra Hall, Chicago; second volume of monograph now ready for distribution to booksellers Robert Hentschel, Seattle, and George Dittke, Chicago.

21 December 1911 • Prairie School architects and former employees Francis B. Byrne and Andrew Willatzen request second volume of monograph.

Late December 1911 • Wright defends his behavior publicly in Spring Green; promulgates principles of Ellen Key in his defense of love without marriage.

January 1912 • John Lloyd Wright, living with his brother Lloyd, at work in San Diego for Harrison Albright; Dutch review of the *Sonderheft*, European edition.

22 February 1912 • Edward Sanderson is now Wright's office manager in Chicago.

30 March 1912 • H. P. Berlage lectures on "New American Architecture" at the Swiss Society of Engineers and Architects, Zurich.

18 April 1912 • Book sales lagging; Wright still has personal debt of $6,000.

23 April 1912 • Complaints from dealers G. Broes Van Dort Co. and J. H. Jansen on condition of *Sonderheft*, indicating availability of the publication.

23 April 1912 • The following projects are on the drawing boards in Wright's office: Edward Shroeder House, Milwaukee; E. Esbenshade House, Milwaukee; Sherman Booth House, Glencoe, Illinois; rebuilding of the Coonley Stable in Riverside, Illinois; Madison Hotel, Madison, Wisconsin; and Lake Geneva Hotel, Lake Geneva, Wisconsin. The Herbert Angster House in Lake Bluff, Illinois, is under completion, and the first sketches have been approved by Harry S. Adams for his house in Oak Park. Potential jobs are two houses similar in scale to the Schroeder House, and a building for the Milwaukee Athletic Club.

1 May 1912 • H. Shugio writes to Wright.

16 July 1912 • Office staff at Taliesin: Wilhelm Bernhard and William R. Gibb. Woolley's arrival pending; Madison Hotel project temporarily laid aside.

August 1912 • Berlage publishes first installment of "Art and Community" in *Western Architect*; subsequent installments in September and October 1912.

1 September 1912 • Announcement of the dissolution of the partnership between Wright and Edward Sanderson.

14 September 1912 • H. P. Berlage publishes first installment of lecture series on Wright in *Schweizerische Bauzeitung*.

2 October 1912 • Avery Coonley approves balloon scheme for playhouse windows, makes suggestions for a frieze but notes the "confetti" design is not successful.

11 October 1912 • Beginning of advertising campaign for the *Sonderheft* in magazines with inquiry to *The Brickbuilder*; inquiries to *Architectural Record* and *Architectural Review* (Boston) to follow shortly.

29 October 1912 • Harry Robinson has returned to Wright's office as manager.

12 November 1912 • Further confirmation of the arrival of the *Sonderheft* in Chicago.

5 December 1912 • Ill-fated contract with E. H. Hart, Chicago, to distribute monograph as exclusive agent in Chicago.

17 December 1912 • Wright in New York, prepares another letter of recommendation for Woolley.

20 December 1912 • A. Kroch, book dealer in Chicago, is selling the rejected European edition of the *Sonderheft* at reduced price.

January 1913 • Taliesin I published in the *Architectural Record*.

10 January 1913 • *Sonderheft* and monograph in distribution in America.

11 January 1913 • Wright leaves with Mamah Borthwick for second trip to Japan after almost six months of contact about the commission for the Imperial Hotel. Misses boat and spends two-week delay in California.

6 February 1913 • Opportunity for Wright to advertise in special issue of *Arts and Decoration*, planned for the New York Armory Show.

26 February 1913 • Article in *Japan Advertiser* noting Wright's arrival in Tokyo.

24 March 1913–19 April 1913 • International Exhibition of Modern Art (the 1913 Armory Show) on view at the Art Institute of Chicago.

30 March 1913 • John Lloyd Wright, from office of Harrison Albright in Los Angeles, writes to Otto Wagner, asking to study with him in Vienna.

May 1913 • Wright returns to United States. Walter Curt Behrendt reviews the *Sonderheft* in *Kunst und Künstler*.

6 May 1913–11 June 1913 • Wright exhibits work at the twenty-sixth annual exhibition of the Chicago Architectural Club, held at the Art Institute of Chicago.

14 July 1913 • Wright states that he plans to hire only people willing to make a commitment to the office, such as Austrians and Germans trained under apprenticeship system.

19 August 1913 • Imperial Hotel plan in progress; "Ground question" still unsettled.

9 September 1913 • 30 acres of land added to the south side of Taliesin. Purchased by Anna Lloyd Wright from Andrew T. and Jane Porter, her son-in-law and daughter, for $1,342.20 plus $1,657 in an outstanding mortgage.

19 September 1913 • Staff at Wright's Chicago office: sons, John and Lloyd, and Harry Robinson. Offices at 600–610 Orchestra Hall. John Lloyd Wright proposes work for Alfonso Iannelli; commission for sculpture under eaves at Coonley Playhouse soon follows.

25 September 1913 • First mortgage on Taliesin, the previous Rieder parcel, for $3,000 (paid off 30 July 1918).

20 January 1914 • Barry Byrne responds to Wright concerning Wright's enmity with former employees, particularly Walter Burley Griffin.

February 1914 • Wright completes final design for Midway Gardens; subsequent changes made during a frantic construction schedule.

12 February 1914 • Alfonso Iannelli requested to provide models of Midway Gardens.

27 April 1914 • By this date Wright maintains an office in Orchestra Hall, room 810, in Chicago; has contact with Francis Little.

30 March 1914 • Wright wires Taylor Woolley in Salt Lake City for assistance in preparing an exhibition of Wright's work done since the spring of 1911 for the annual exhibition of the Chicago Architectural Club, held at the Art Institute of Chicago.

9 April 1914 • Scheduled opening of twenty-seventh annual exhibition of the Chicago Architectural Club.

Late spring / early summer • Wright designs new dance academy for Frederick W. Kehl in Madison, Wisconsin.

27 June 1914 • Midway Gardens officially opens; construction incomplete.

16 July 1914 • Wright's design for a Women's Building and Neighborhood Club in Spring Green is published in the *Weekly Home News*.

10 August 1914 • Start of gap in communication between Wright and Darwin D. Martin.

10 August 1914 • Application signed for copyright of design for a United States Embassy in Tokyo; approved 15 August 1914.

15 August 1914 • Fire and murders at Taliesin.

20 October 1914 • Wright, "hard hit" by tragedy, replies to Martin.

January 1915 • Iannelli takes Wright to visit Panama-California Exposition in San Diego.

10 May 1915 • The Lloyd Jones sisters, Wright's aunts, convey the Hillside Home School to him.

1915 • Scandal with Miriam Noel; Wright hires Clarence Darrow to defend him.

30 June 1915 • Charles-Eduard Jeanneret (later Le Corbusier) writes August Perret to obtain a copy of Wright's *Sonderheft*.

Late December 1915 or January 1916 • Aisaku Hayashi, manager of the Imperial Hotel, departs for America; Wright officially appointed architect to the Imperial Hotel.*

February 1916 • Hayashi and wife at Taliesin to confirm commission of the Imperial Hotel.*

9 February 1916 • Wright invites Charles Robert Ashbee to visit Taliesin; Ashbee arrives by 25 February to see Wright and Miriam Noel.

Early spring 1916 • Antonin Raymond and wife Noémi arrive to live and work at Taliesin. They meet Hayashi and his wife. Raymond works on the American Ready Cut System.

25 March 1916 • Hayashi departs for Japan, arrives 14 April 1916.*

12 September 1916 • Agreement between Frank Lloyd Wright and John Lloyd Wright for John to take over Wright's Chicago office with pay of $125 per month. Signed by John Lloyd Wright; the starting date was 15 August 1916.

17 September 1916 • The American System for prefabricated homes is announced in an advertisement in the Chicago Tribune.

November 1916 • Draft of agreement to provide designs, plans, perspectives and details for the Arthur Richards Company's standardized System Built buildings. Draft unsigned and incomplete.

28 December 1916 • Wright departs, with Miriam Noel, for Japan on his second trip in connection with the Imperial Hotel.*

1917 • Antonin Raymond and wife leave Taliesin and return to New York.

9 January 1917 • Wright and Noel arrive in Japan.*

21 April 1917 Wright departs for United States after four months.* Set of working drawings dated 20 April 1917.

17 May 1917 • Wright arrives in the United States for a stay of about seventeen months.*

May 1917–May 1918 • Working drawings for Imperial Hotel done at Taliesin.* Numerous changes on site during construction.

26 May 1917 • Second mortgage taken on Taliesin for $12,000 (paid off 5 November 1919).

June 1917–July 1920 • A. D. German Warehouse, designed in 1915, under construction in Richland Center, Wisconsin. The building was never completed according to Wright's designs.

4 August 1917 • Wright buys Hillside Home School for $25,000; the property is mortgaged for $5,000 the same day (paid off 7 November 1919).

September 1917 • Stock subscription for the American System proposed.

12 October 1917 • Date of Wright's preface for the catalogue of his Japanese prints exhibited by the Chicago Arts Club.

November 1917 • Wright's work, including a model of the Imperial Hotel, published in Tokyo.

12 November–December 1917 • Exhibition of Wright's collection of 241 Japanese prints by the Chicago Arts Club at the Fine Arts Building, Chicago.

Late September 1918–c. end of May 1919 • Site clearing for Imperial Hotel

30 October 1918 • Wright departs on third trip to Japan for Imperial Hotel.

17 November 1918 • Wright arrives in Japan.

1918 • Wright goes to Peiping, China, to supervise weaving of his specially designed rugs for the Imperial Hotel. Visits famous monuments and treasures of China as guest of Dr. Ku Hung Ming, noted Chinese writer and secretary to the Empress Dowager.

Summer 1919 • Construction begins on Imperial Hotel.

June 1919 • Paul Mueller and son Ralph depart for Japan to work on the Imperial Hotel.[1]

18 August 1919 • Design of a Monolith House for T. P. Hardy patented, utilizing drawings prepared by Rudolph Schindler in July.

September 1919 • Wright returns to United States from Japan after a ten-month visit.

16 December 1919 • Wright departs for fourth trip to Japan.

31 December 1919 • Wright arrives upon the steamship Suwa Maru in Yokohama with Miriam Noel, and architect Antonin Raymond.

1919 • Wright receives first citation, Kenchiko Ho, from Imperial Household in Japan, conferred by Baron Okura for the Imperial Household.**

January 1920 • Wright taken ill.*

19 February 1920 • Anna Lloyd Wright departs from Vancouver to tend her son; she arrives 2 March in Yokohama. After his recovery, they are entertained by the Imperial Household in a rare expression for the secluded household.

2 March 1920 • Foundations of Imperial Hotel built.

June 1920 • After eighteen months in Japan, Wright returns to the United States at end of the month.

Late Summer 1920 • Work substantially complete on Hollyhock House and Residences A and B in Los Angeles.

November 1920 • Ralph Mueller returns from Japan to the United States.[2]

16 December 1920 • Wright's fifth departure for Japan.

28 December 1920 • Wright arrives in Japan.

8 February 1921 Letter from Wright to Raymond, confirming the rupture of their working relationship.

May 1921 • Wright returns to the United States after seventeen months in Japan.

June 1921 • Wright returns to Taliesin early in the month.

30 July 1921 • Wright's sixth departure for Japan; Miriam Noel accompanies him.

15 August 1921 • Wright arrives in Japan.

Fall 1921 • Crises at the Imperial Hotel: criticism of building design, delays, and rising costs.

16 April 1922 • Old Imperial Hotel burns to ground.

May 1922 • New board of directors named for Imperial Hotel.

22 July 1922 • Wright and Noel leave Yokohama on the President McKinley.

1 August 1922 • Wright and Noel arrive in Seattle, via Victoria, B.C., after Wright's last trip to Japan.

22 November 1922 • Divorce decree to Wright and Catherine Tobin Wright.

9 February 1923 • Anna Lloyd Wright dies.

1 September 1923 • Opening day for completed Imperial Hotel, coincides with the Great Kanto Earthquake.

Late November 1923 • Wright marries Miriam Noel.

14 April 1924 • Louis Sullivan dies. In same year Wright meets Olgivanna Lazovich Hinzenburg, who became his third wife.

Appendix B: Documents

Chapter One

This is the "Contract between Frank Lloyd Wright and Herman von Holst," signed 22 September 1909, that conveyed Wright's architectural practice to Von Holst. Five sheets with an additional sheet containing list of projects, William Gray Purcell Collection, Northwest Architectural Archives, University of Minnesota. Written in the margin on the first sheet by Purcell is "Please return to H. V. von Holst, Boca Raton, Florida. See letter May 25, 1981 to W. G. P. asking that I keep this contract."

Herman Von Holst and Frank Lloyd Wright hereby enter into agreement, as follows:

Appended hereto is a list of work actual and prospective now in Mr. Wright's office, divided into three classes, to wit: work under construction, work in hand, work probable & prospective.

Mr. Von Holst is to take over the architectural practice of Mr. Wright on the following terms. He is to assume the completion of superintendence of all work under construction and complete the plans for Zeigler and Melson for the sum of $500.00, defraying the cost of completing the Zeigler and Melson plans, but charging to Mr. Wright the actual cost in draughting time on such further details as may be necessary to complete the service on the other buildings embraced in this classification. The money for this work when due is to be paid over on collection to Mr. Wright.

The compensation for all work in hand, or probable or prospective, for which Mr. Wright has made sketches or may at Mr. Von Holst's request make sketches, is to be divided equally between them, payments to be made to Mr. Von Holst direct, he in turn to pay Mr. Wright his share from time to time as work progresses; this work to bear Mr.

Wright's name as architect, the cost of doing the work to be borne by Mr. Von Holst.

All new work for which no sketches have yet been made, but for which Mr. Wright has established precedents, or should there be time and the clients so disposed Mr. Wright may be called upon to make sketches, shall be done under the names of Von Holst and Wright as associate architects. The commissions to be equally divided between them as hereinbefore provided, Mr. Von Holst paying the cost of the work.

All work which owing to the good will of Mr. Wright's practice may come to Mr. Von Holst and for which Mr. Wright makes no sketches is to be done by Mr. Von Holst under his own name, he paying to Mr. Wright a commission of 1-1/2% of the cost of the buildings complete.

Should Mr. Von Holst ask Mr. Wright to design with him work which comes to Mr. Von Holst direct, they shall be associate architects so named on the plans, Mr. Von Holst paying to Mr. Wright a commission of 1/3 of the compensation.

The May residence and the Mason City work elsewhere where superintendence is arranged for by trips on call Von Holst is to have the compensation named, $25.00 per day and expenses for all trips he may make.

The title to drawings and specifications for all work, except that where Wright & Von Holst are associate architects, shall remain with Mr. Wright; where they are associated the title shall be held jointly by them.

It is agreed that any debts or liabilities which Mr. Wright may owe or which may be paid by Mr. Von Holst during his absence shall be deducted from the share due him from any of the work included in this contract.

Mr. Von Holst is hereby authorized to collect from the clients all compensation not otherwise specified which may be paid by them from time to time for services rendered under work embraced in this agreement. In any case in which such payments shall be made by Mr. Wright's clients in the form of a check or checks payable to Mr. Wright, Mr. Von Holst is hereby authorized as agent in fact of Mr. Wright's to endorse the name of Wright by Von Holst as such agent upon such check or checks paid upon such work as aforesaid. It is the intention that Mr. Von Holst shall have under his exclusive control at all times until division is made, as herebefore specified, all moneys which may be received for the benefit or account of Mr. Wright for work done under his agreement and that he shall be authorized to collect payments of compensation upon such work and deposit them in his own bank to his account from time to time as collected.

Mr. Von Holst shall make a division of the compensation received for the work as herein set forth from time to time as work progresses, paying over to Mr. Wright or depositing to his personal account in the Illinois Trust & Savings Bank or elsewhere as he may direct, such portion of the net collections thus received as may be due to Mr. Wright as his share of the compensation.

In the event that Mr. Wright should return from his travels prior to the completion of all the work which may have been begun or taken over by Mr. Von Holst during the absence of Mr. Wright, Mr. Von Holst shall have the right to carry on the completion of all such work as he may have started during the absence of Mr. Wright and shall also have the right to continue to make collections upon the work until all amounts due as compensation for all such work shall have been collected by Mr. Von Holst. And Mr. Von Holst from time to time as such collections are made, after the return of Mr. Wright shall divide the net amount on hand in accordance with terms of this agreement paying to the first party from time to time his share of such compensation out of the funds collected.

The relation covered by this contract and all of the rights, privileges and obligations of the parties thereunder shall continue during the absence of Mr. Wright from Chicago, and after his return in relation to all of the work started by Mr. Von Holst until it shall have been completed. In the event of the death of Mr. Wright prior to the winding up on the relationship herein formed, Mr. Von Holst shall complete all work begun by him as soon as is reasonably possible and shall pay over any moneys due to Mr. Wright to the administrator, executor, heirs or legal representatives of Mr. Wright.

In the event that any difference or differences shall arise between the parties hereto concerning the terms of this contract or the duties and obligations of each party thereunder, the same may be submitted to arbitration, each of the parties hereto choosing one arbitrator and the two then chosen choosing a third disinterested, impartial party as an umpire between them and the said three arbitrators having considered the subject matter of any such difference or controversy, and any two of them having decided the same, the decision of two out of three shall be final and binding and each party hereby agrees to observe, carry out and be bound by such decision to the same effect as if the matter had been judicially determined.

It is provided that Mr. Von Holst retain so far as is practicable the services of Mr. Wright's assistants. Mr. Wright agreeing to pay $10.00 per week of Isabel Robert's salary in consideration of the devotion of the necessary amount of time to Mr. Wright's personal affairs so long as she remain in the work, and the salary of the draughtsman T. A. Woolley so long as he is directly engaged upon work for Germany Publication; and to turn over to Mr. Von Holst the Oak Park office rent free so long as all expenses in heating, lighting and caring for the building are paid by him and it is properly protected.

(signed Frank Lloyd Wright; H. Von Holst)

Oak Park, Illinois.
September 22–1909.

STATEMENT of WORK in the
OFFICE of FRANK LLOYD WRIGHT
as turned over to
HERMAN VON HOLST, September 22–1909.

WORK UNDER CONSTRUCTION

J. K. Ingalls, House: Superintendence & few details
J. G. Melson, House: Superintendence & tracings
J. R. Zeigler: Specifications & tracings
Mrs. T. H. Gale House: Finish superintendence
Mason City Bank & Hotel: Make trips on call. Few details.
W. H. Copeland Alteration: Finish superintendence.
Hiram Baldwin: See what troubles are.
F. C. Robie, House: Finish superintendence
P. C. Stohr, Stores: Finish superintendence.
M. S. May, House: Trips on call.
S. C. Stewart, Cottage: Details.

WORK IN HAND
E. P. Irving: Sketches made, Plans to be made & superintended.
Walter Gerts, House: Working Plans.

PROBABLE & PROSPECTIVE
Mr. Amberg, Grand Rapids, House.
C. A. Brown, Hinsdale, Cottages.
Mr. Wood, Decatur, House.
Mr. Stiles, Riverside, House.
Mr. Mueller, Decatur, House.
Mr. Smith, Mobile, Cottages.
C. S. Church, Tacoma.

The following is the complete, edited, original text of Charles Robert Ashbee's Introduction to Wright's *Sonderheft*. It was published as "Eine Studie zu seiner Würdigung von C. R. Ashbee F.R.I.B.A" in both early editions of the *Sonderheft: Frank Lloyd Wright: Ausgeführte Bauten* [American edition] (Berlin: Ernst Wasmuth A.-G., 1911), 3–10, and *Frank Lloyd Wright Chicago* [European edition] (Berlin: Ernst Wasmuth A.-G., 1911), 3–10. The English version, censored by Wright, was reprinted in part in "Taliesin, the Home of Frank Lloyd Wright, and a Study of the Owner," *Western Architect* 19 (February 1913): 16–19. The essay was published in a reprint edition of the *Sonderheft, Frank Lloyd Wright: The Early Works*, foreword by Edgar Kaufmann, Jr. (New York: Horizon Press, 1968), xiii–xvi, with some of the untranslated German segments appended. Ashbee sent the copy of the manuscript that he had edited to Wright, who omitted some paragraphs. The original is at TAL. This is the complete text, including Ashbee's editorial corrections, as it appeared in Ashbee's manuscript of September 1910; included also are the paragraphs that Wright removed.

FRANK LLOYD WRIGHT: A STUDY AND AN APPRECIATION
by C. R. Ashbee. F.R.I.B.A.

In the modern development of the arts America excels in the art of Architecture, and there are few cities upon the great continent but can show some piece of good building, or an effort in that direction; it is a popular instinct. The rich man strives to mark his wealth in stone, the cities have great libraries, clubs, colleges and schools, the states vie with one another in the splendour of their state-houses. Into spheres in which with us the architect seldom penetrates, he in America leaves his mark; the office and business building has become his province.

The names of many of the leading architects in the last two generations have been well enough known in Europe: Richardson, Hunt, McKim, Mead and White; Cope and Stewardson; Day, Clipston Sturges, Carrère and Hastings, Cass Gilbert, and many others. The buildings of these men will take their place in the sequence of architectural history; the libraries at Boston, and Washington, the Statehouses of Pittsburgh and Providence, the Metropolitan Club in New York, the collegiate buildings in Philadelphia, in Cambridge, in San Francisco.

To us, who look at them with the eyes of the old world, American buildings connote four things in style. They stand first for the English tradition, whether through the "old Colonial" or more recent importation of English forms; the French "Beaux Arts" as we see it in Washington or Fifth Avenue, New York; the purely utilitarian as in that distinctly American Business Product, the "sky scraper"; and they stand lastly for what may be called the buildings of a new spirit, as we see it on the Pacific coast and in the Middle West. It is of these last as expressed by the work of Frank Lloyd Wright, that I wish specially to speak, because he first and before all other American architects, seems to embody it.

This new spirit has for us in Europe a peculiar charm and piquancy, just because we do not see in it that reflection of European forms to which we have been so long accustomed. Its characteristics are a departure from tradition, a distinctiveness of surrounding, and a consequent character of its own, a delight in new materials, and an honest use of machinery. There are features that give to the buildings of the Pacific coast a character quite distinct from the School of Chicago as the conditions are not the same, and I have been in houses on the Aroyo [sic] that appeal to me more than Lloyd Wright's; but all the men of the new spirit have these characteristics, and the work of Lloyd Wright has them fundamentally and more markedly than any of his contemporaries. This is not to be wondered at, because it has grown within its own province—the sphere of the Middle West—and is something absolutely new and original. Trained in the office of Louis Sullivan, who first gave rational character to the industrial building of Chicago, Lloyd Wright has carried the new spirit into domestic work and produced a type of building that is absolutely his own. In so doing he has given to the great city of the Prairie something she had never had before, and what is equivalent to a new architecture.

In estimating the achievement for which Wright stands, we have to consider the difficulties he had to face. With no background of tradition, with no forms about him upon which to model a style, surrounded by purely commercial conditions, and in the face of actual and fierce hostility, or the persecutions of "that little knowledge which is a dangerous thing," he carved out a manner of his own and worked out his own principles of design, before the English Arts and Crafts Movement, the German Secession, or the European Art Nouveau had in any way touched America. His Winslow House was designed in 1893, and other of his buildings in which the elements of his style are in formation, bear approximately early dates. I sum up the characteristics of his work thus: first, nobility of plan—some of Lloyd Wright's plans have the cleanness and simplicity we see in the planning of Gothic houses, or in the work of Bramante; then a fine proportion, witness the Oak Park houses with their long firm horizontal lines. Next, a feeling for mass and colour, as in the Unity Temple and the Coonley house; a fertility of resource in adapting means to ends; and lastly a determination, amounting sometimes to heroism, to master the machine and use it at all costs, in an endeavour to find the forms and treatment it may render without abuse of tradition. In a suggestive and interesting monograph which he contributed in 1908 to the "Architectural Record" of New York, entitled 'In the cause of Architecture,' Lloyd Wright laid down the principles that inspired his work. From among them I am tempted to extract the following because it is so significant of the work and what it stands for:

"Buildings, like people, must first be sincere, must be true and then withal as gracious and lovable as may be."

"Above all, integrity. The machine is the normal tool of our civilization; give it work that it can do well—nothing is of greater importance. To do this will be to formulate the new industrial ideals we need if Architecture is to be a living Art."

Here we are brought face to face with the problem of our civilization, the solution of which will determine the future of the Arts themselves. It is significant that from Chicago, quite independently of England, of France, of Germany or elsewhere, here is a voice calling, offering a solution.

"An artist's limitations are his best friends. The machine is here to stay. It is the forerunner of the Democracy that is our dearest hope. There is no more important work before the architect now than to use this normal tool of civilization to the best advantage, instead of prostituting it as he has hitherto done in reproducing with murderous ubiquity forms born of other times and other conditions, and which it can only serve to destroy."

There is greatness in this idea, and the future will I think show that, in the case of Lloyd Wright, the man's product has been worthy [of] the idea that has guided its development and in a measure inspired its creation. Out of it has come a different conception as to what constitutes a modern building.

Greatness demands its price, and this has often to be paid in a certain barrenness and sterility of detail owing to the severity of the limitations, a certain disregard of the intimate and personal things that make a building lovable in the sacrifice of tenderness for integrity. This is not so much the fault of the architect as of the conditions in which he is set to work. The machine is not yet mastered in modern life, nor is it possible for any individual, however strong, to accomplish the mastery. This is the community's need, a social need, and it is one which we feel essentially in the art of America. [Wright omitted: *It is less noticeable, no doubt, in California, where the conditions are different, where the pulse beats calmer, where the quieting touch of the Orient has come to me and where the builders and their clients have more leisure to think, but it is an American limitation, and this limitation within the confining province of the machine, is for the Arts in America a condition of existence.*]

Through the United States indeed the traditions of craftsmanship upon which the arts still professedly rest, have been broken down by mechanical power more than with us in Europe, and the American Architects, with all their greater organizing power, their combinations, and their opportunities which are supreme, have not yet devised a way of re-establishing them, of finding their equivalent, of readjusting the balance. It is to the credit of Lloyd Wright that he is the first American architect who has sought to consciously express this fact, to readjust this balance. He is thus a typical product of modern America, and of that aspect of America which is Chicago. He has its strength as well as its weakness, its romance as well as its freakishness and immaturity, its barrenness as well as its sanity, its fertility of recourse, and he has perhaps in an exaggerated degree its individualism. I use the word as Murray defines it, of self-centered conduct or feeling as a principle, and mode of life, in which the individual pursues his own ends or follows his own ideas. I do not know why this individualism takes its extremist form in Chicago. Every street, every avenue of that great-souled and generous, but at the same time brutal and remorseless city tells of this. It tells somehow of the New Englander driven westward and unrestrained, in a commercial world; of the Puritan cut adrift from his gods and from his conventions, striving to make new ones out of himself. "Striving," as Blake the Seer put it, "with systems to deliver individuals from those systems." I see this striving in the work of Lloyd Wright more than in any of his contemporaries.

The result is what has been called the style of the Middle West, and after accounting for him in his relation to Louis Sullivan, that style is more of his making than that of any other man. Destiny permits a man to strive, mocks him in his struggle, and in the end collects some of the fragments—that which was the best and most enduring—for the greater work that is to remain. Thus styles are made, and this is so of architecture before all the arts. One may pardon in a strong man a display of individualism that one cannot forgive in a weaker; what is the character in the one, becomes pettishness, or mannerism or affectation in the other; but we artists of Europe, while we appreciate and criticize the product, and while we often admire, may be forgiven when we say that in our feeling it sometimes needs to mellow. Yet whatever we may think of this individualism, and however it may win or repel us personally, it expresses for the time being a national condition. For my own part, speaking as an architect, I think this individualism as seen in Lloyd Wright's work, strong and sound to the core; there is in it a national ideal, but I do not always like it. It gives me at times the same feeling of irritation which Walt Whitman gives me, when after some supreme passage at which one's whole heart goes out, the poet tumbles over some trifle badly handled, as when, for instance in that sublimest of his songs "Come, I will make the continent indissoluble," he ends up with the words, "For you, Oh Democracy, MA FEMME!" He forgets that we are of the same flesh and blood, and have a sense of humour; that this trivial note tumbles us from the sublime, into detail that is badly done. I do not mean to insinuate by this example that Lloyd Wright's work has inconsistence of this nature; the analogy cannot of course be pressed, and the deduction applies only to my personal feeling regarding the sometimes undigested trivialities I find. I hold moreover that his work in architecture, while it merits the comparison, in greatness and unity, with Whitman's work in literature, is quite strong enough to stand a corresponding criticism of its limitations or its faults.

A comparison of the work of Lloyd Wright with modern work in England or Germany would take me too far afield; but a certain kinship is significant and may be referred to in passing. In Germany the names of Olbrich, Hoffmann, Moser, Bruno Paul, Möhring, suggest themselves. In England those of us who are sometimes called the Arts and Crafts men, Lethaby, Voysey, Lutyens, Ricardo, Wilson, Holden, Blow, Townsend, Baillie Scott. We feel that between us and him there is a kinship. We may differ vitally in our manner of expression, in our planning, in our touch, in the way we clothe our work, in our feeling for proportion, but although our problems differ essentially, we are altogether at one in our principles. We guard in common the lamp of truth. We hold equally with Lloyd Wright that structure should be self-explanatory, that iron is there for man's service, only he must learn to use it rightly and not learn to lie or cheat about it, that the forms of the ancient world, the traditions of the "Beaux Arts," and the old Colonial, even 'Greek purism' have their place, but that their place is not necessarily the Prairie. Their place may be Connecticut, or Virginia, may be the Boulevard Montparnasse, or Buckinghamshire, but for the great open spaces of the new world something else is wanted. This land, pierced by the great trunk lines of the Middle West, the new cities of the miners, the cattle-breeders, the canners and the grain exporters, the men of ideas [and] invention make a new appeal. The men who have created it, however we may view them, stand for something new, and the time is ripe for a new form to express the life they lead, or toward which they may aspire. And this life is a large life, it has given to the work of Lloyd Wright that unity of idea, that largeness which his plans and drawings reveal. I have seen it too in such buildings as the Coonley House near Chicago and the Larkin Building in Buffalo. It is the architects' business to express life and to ennoble it in the expression. Lloyd Wright has done this; and yet all the honour is not his.

To see these buildings, or think through these drawings, brings home to one how much he owes to his clients. They have felt the greatness themselves, and have themselves sought to become articulate. No one can study the simple and convincing forms of the Larkin Building in Buffalo without a feeling that bigness in business organization has called forth a corresponding mood in the architect.

[Wright omitted: *We in Europe often look with hungry eyes at the opportunities of our American colleagues, at the splendid sites, the virgin solitudes, the unmade cities, the liberal expenditure, but what we often long for most is that newer life, less bounded by the conventions and traditions which so restrict us when we begin to speak in stone and timber, in iron and concrete. And the life of an American patron—the giver of jobs—is after all a very different thing from that of the European magnate; it is much less restrained, freer, often bigger in its ideas, also it is usually more vulgar. Your American loves large rooms, immense spaces of equal temperature; he longs for concentration, for speed; he has no sense of leisure; his is splendidly extravagant of plumbing, and childishly eager to buy up all the bric a brac of Europe. With the English and German money magnate it is different. They have more rigid limitations. The wealthy Germany bourgeois has over him his Kaiser, whom he may not like, but who at least has a uniform, and represents another dimension; something outside that is larger and more brilliant, something unattainable, in colours and gold. In England it is the House of Lords that snores, and the country gentleman idea dominates the construction and decoration of the house. For an English gentleman to pay an American plumbing bill (in a large house it runs into thousands of pounds), would be an expensive vulgarity, would disorganize the domestic service, and hurt the feelings of the horses.*

With public buildings the condition is different again. Of the three countries, England is the most democratic—I use the word in Abraham Lincoln's sense—Germany the most ordered, while in America the power of the purse, and of the individual who holds it, is invariably the dominant force. And so it comes that with us in England the committees of petty shopkeepers who think in three-penny bits, have as a rule the ordering of our public buildings, with the melancholy result we so often see; in America on the other hand there is the 'boss system,' which sometimes, but not always, brings the best man to the top; while in Germany they have a more consistent tradition of public order, which expresses itself in their buildings. The psychology of these three forces in the life of the three countries necessarily leaves its mark, but in tracing the kinship between them certain common factors have to be considered.]

We artists ourselves are too apt to think that we are the discoverers of forms that come new to us. It is not so. We ourselves are but the instruments through which breathes the Over-soul, the Zeitgeist. Those rapid nervous lines, those big masses, this sense of a new proportion, this breaking away from old traditions, this monotony that results from constant mechanical repetition, this longing for individual expression as a refuge from it; we all have this in our work, and it has its psychological reason. Industrial concentration, rapid locomotion, the telephone, the electric light and the lines it demands, mechanical power which has enormously cheapened and as equally permeated certain conditions of labour, the breakdown of the old productive system, the photograph, the telegraph, the development of the press and more

particularly the illustrated press, these and many others are the influences that unconsciously move us all, and make us speak, puppets that we are, in ways we do not know, and what seems so strange to each of us individually, make us speak with a common voice. Thus again, styles are made, and the style of the 20th century can never have real quality if it does not somehow express those influences behind the life of the time.

So far Lloyd Wright has been given but little opportunity in public building, but in what he has done he has left his mark. No one can look at the Unity Temple in Oak Park, its monumental character, its frank revival of the temple form as best suited to a place of modern worship, its method of construction, solid monolith, cast in concrete, reinforced with steel strands, a construction that will last for hundreds of years after the whole suburb has passed away, without a sense that here is the new spirit, and distinctively America.

[Wright omitted: *I have purposely said but little of the internal detail in the buildings of Lloyd Wright, because it does not appear to me to be of the essence of his work, nor of what he stands for. Moreover its limitations are those of the great tool he strives to master,—the machine. We can often trace the influence of Japan, or the effort to adapt Japanese forms to American conditions, though I know that the artist himself disavows this; doubtless the touch of the East is an unconscious one, but I notice it most in his architectural drawings, and his method of appeal in presenting his buildings pictorially; these drawings for me have real charm. Pages _____ show examples of his interior detail in glass, in carpets, in stuffs and in furniture, but though this detail is always logical and consistent with the rest of his work, it does not to us in Europe make that same convincing appeal as do his buildings themselves. There is however always a fine purpose behind, and this is best expressed in the artist's own words:*

> *"to make of a building,—its environment and its equipment—a harmonious whole, a unit,—all appliances, fixtures and furniture merely as such regarded, and something to be absorbed and incorporated in the structure, to be foreseen by the architect and provided in the nature of the structure. This is the modern opportunity: to make the building, considered in itself, a harmonious work of art, true to the life and sentiment of the occupants, an artistic revelation of the means employed as well as an expression of individual character."*]

On the Romanesque churches of the old world, later generations set the mosaic, the tracery, the refinement and the culture that came with more leisure and sympathy; another century may do the same with the great experiments in architecture that America is putting forth. I have seen buildings of Lloyd Wright's that I would like to touch with the enchanted wand; not to alter their structure in plan or form, or carcass, but to clothe them with a more living and tender detail. I do not know how, and the time is not yet nor would I like to see Wright do it himself, because I do not believe he could; for thus to clothe them would mean a school of Craftsmanship that would tell of the intimate life of America, and imply a little of that quietude and poetry and scholarship which our English churches and country houses have received from the caressing hands of generations of craftsmen. Here at all events, witness these pages, the buildings are, and they are worthy of the life.

Morris said to me once, in praise of noble decoration, "we do not want it at all unless at the outset the buildings upon which we place it are noble." In the buildings of Lloyd Wright that postulate is granted.

C. R. Ashbee

Chapter Three

This document establishes the resolution of the contractual dispute between Frank Lloyd Wright and Herman Von Holst. In an opinion dated 7 July 1911, the firm of Silber, Isaacs, Silber & Woley informed the firm of Kerr & Kerr, Chicago, of the settling of the dispute between the two architects and included an accounting of work performed. (Silber, Isaacs, Silber & Woley to Kerr & Kerr. 7 July, 1911. William G. Purcell Collection, Northwest Architectural Archives, University of Minnesota.)

Chicago, July 7, 1911

Kerr & Kerr,
    Chicago.

Gentlemen:—
    In re contract between Herman von Holst and Frank Lloyd Wright.

We have conferred with Mr. von Holst in regard to the final accounting with Mr. Wright under the contract of September 22, 1909 and we enclose you herewith a complete and final account upon the matter according to the construction of the contract which Mr. von Holst believes proper and just. You will note that upon collections as they now stand there is $49.21 due from Mr. von Holst to Mr. Wright and that when the Irving and Orsinger matters are finally completed and settled it is estimated that there will be a net balance of $108.29 due from Mr. von Holst to Mr. Wright in full and final settlement of all claims and demands.

You will also note the difference in the items of actual cost and expense of draughting time on the various jobs, over the items for the similar jobs on the statement of account heretofore given Mr. Wright by Mr. von Holst. All of these items of draughting expense have been increased in the present account over the similar items in the former account, due to the fact that in arriving at the former draughting expense Mr. von Holst neglected to take into consideration the actual overhead cost and expense which entered into the draughting expense in his office on these various jobs. He has made a careful study and computation of this overhead expense and by a system of checking and computation has arrived at the conclusion that the actual overhead expense going into the draughting expense accounts to 60% of the actual draughting cost and the former items of draughting expense have therefore been increased by 60%, so that the items as they now stand express correctly the actual cost in draughting time covered by the language of the contract which recites as follows: "He is to assume the completion of the plans for Zeigler and Melson for the sum of $500.00, defraying the cost of completing the Zeigler and Melson plans, but charging to Mr. Wright the actual cost in draughting time on such further details as may be necessary to complete the service on the other buildings embraced in this classification."

You will understand however that the money paid to the draughtsmen in wages is only a portion of the actual cost in draughting time, and in addition the proportion of fixed charges such as rent, telephone, office supplies etc. must be charged in the draughting expense in order to arrive at a correct figure for such items.

If there is anything further that you wish to take up with us in reference to this account, or in reference to the contract or the construction thereof we shall be glad to see you at any time that may be convenient.
    FDS-R-
Very respectfully,
Silber, Isaacs, Silber & Woley,
Per _____

MEMORANDUM of items of the account between Herman V. von Holst and Frank Lloyd Wright, in relation to contract of September 22, 1909.

Actual cost of draughting time in relation to the following work:

Copeland,	$ 23.58
Robie,	$249.60
Stohr,	$ 32.30
Zale,	$ 40.50
Ingalls,	$185.84
Thurber Galleries,	$ 10.24
O. M. Steffins,	$ 2.18
City National Bank,	$414.68
May House,	$ 79.98
May Landscape,	$ 50.00
Coonley,	$ 22.34
Baldwin,	$ 7.04
Hardy,	$ 13.22
Total,	$1131.50

Money expended by von Holst for Wright.

Wooley, [sic] salary,	$143.33	
Miss Roberts, salary,	$ 50.00	
Cablegram,	$ 2.48	
Telephone in House,	$ 2.48	
Blueprints sent abroad,	$ 7.35	
Paid to Wright Oct. 22, 1910,	$300.00	
Trip to Grand Rapids for final acceptance,	$ 34.80	
		$ 540.76
		$1672.26

Wright's share of money received to date on the following work:

Copeland, actual amount received,	$ 8.55	
Mason City Bank, actual amount received,	$100.00	
Dwight bank clock, one half of actual amount received,	$ 15.00	
Mrs. Gale, actual amount received,	$ 23.50	
Ingalls, actual amount received,	$250.00	
Melson, actual amount received,	$150.00	
Zeigler, actual amount received,	$300.00	
Irving, 1 1/2% of general contract complete,	$336.00	
Ingwald Moe, 1/2 of total commission,	$100.00	
Total,		$1623.05

Balance still due von Holst over credits given to Wright,	$ 49.21	
Items still to be credited to Wright 1 1 /2 per cent of contract for Irving, furnishings, estimated cost of furnishings,	3500.00	
Estimated amount of Wright's proportion,	$ 52.50	

Orsinger, estimated amount of contract	$7000.00	
Estimated 1 1/2% due Wright,	$105.00	
Total estimated commissions still due Wright,	$157.50	
Less balance now due von Holst	$ 49.21	
Estimated final amount payable to Wright upon collection of Irving and Orsinger items,	$108.29	

NOTE: On the $340. credited to Mr. Wright on the Irving job, Mr. Irving declined to pay more than a total commission of $2000.00 upon the completed house exclusive of furnishings. The 1 1/2% due to Mr. Wright under the contract would therefore amount to $400.00 or one fifth of the total commission of $2000.00

In addition, Mr. Wright has already collected $500.00 on account of the Irving commission or $100 more than the 1 1/2% would amount to. Mr. von Holst however has given Mr. Wright additional credit of $340, making a total of $840.00 that Mr. Wright receives out of the $2000.00 commission on the Irving job, or 42% of the total commission instead of 20%.

On the work for Wills, A. Mueller and R. Mueller, Mr. von Holst construes the contract as not entitling Mr. Wright to any participation in the commissions because none of these jobs came to Mr. von Holst on account of the good will of Mr. Wright's practice. If however, it should be construed to entitle Mr. Wright to any participation in these commissions, Mr. von Holst has already expended more money on account of these three items of work than he has received, and there is now a deficit on account of such work. Because of Mr. von Holst's construc-

tion of the contract however, in respect to these jobs he declines to pay Mr. Wright any part of the commissions upon any of these three items of work.

This letter from Ernst Wasmuth to Frank Lloyd Wright confirms the printing of the European edition of the *Sonderheft*. (Ernst Wasmuth to FLW, 3 November 1910, ts. copy of original, SUNYB.)

Berlin W. 8, den 3 Nov. 1910.

Mr. Frank Lloyd Wright, Architect,
 Oak Park, Ill.
  458 Forrest Ave.

Dear Mr. Wright:

 We cabled you on the 1st inst. that the Sonderheft is ready and that we can send off 4000 copies for you to America. We are forwarding to you under separate cover three copies of the Sonderheft. The copies are so wet as they came from the press. The later ones will be of course of some more better condition.

 We hope this work will meet you and we ask you to kindly send your cheque for 9000 Mark as per our arrangements.

 The Monograph also is nearly ready. All what is wanting to us, is the text, which you promised to write and to forward to us. There is a necessity to have this text as otherwise you have to pay considerable duty on receipt of the work in America. We are willingly ready to write ourselves the text using some parts of Mr. Ashbee's article. Please cable us your decision.

 We further beg to draw your attention to the delivery of the portfolios. We think it is the best to instruct Mr. Mass that he is placing the portfolios to our disposal. We then put each copy of the Monograph into the portfolio so that there cannot be assessed any duty on them. If this is handled otherwise, we are quite sure, that you must pay duty for the portfolios when they are delivered to you together without the plates. Further more we would have to make a provisional cover for the work if we cannot lay them into the portfolios.

 Please favor us with your answer at your earliest convenience and oblige, dear sir.

Yours very truly,
(signed) Ernst Wasmuth,

Chapter Six

This memorandum of agreement Between Frank Lloyd Wright and E. Wasmuth, A. G., dated 13 February 1911, is the renegotiated contract between Wright and Wasmuth. (The document is a copy without signatures, SUNYB.)

Memorandum of an agreement this day entered into by E. Wasmuth, A.G. and Frank Lloyd Wright.

It is hereby agreed that the provisions of the original contract for Monograph and dated Nov. 24. 1909 be not changed.

The 250 additional copies of this Monograph which Wasmuth A.G. printed for their own benefit are to be delivered to Wright for the sum of Mk.6000 additional.

In consideration of which said Wright agrees to present Wasmuth A.G. with 100 copies, without covers, upon the conditions herein named:—All copies to be sold in Europe only. Each and every copy intended for such sale to be marked plainly by Wasmuth A.G., "For sale in Europe only." The price at which the Monograph shall be sold in Europe shall be Mk. 120. Should Wasmuth require additional copies he may purchase them of Wright at the rate of Mk. 600 for each ten copies, without covers. This provision to obtain until 200 copies shall have been sold. Further sales as may hereafter be agreed with Wright. Should any of these copies intended "for sale in Europe only" be found in the American market, Wasmuth agrees to pay to Wright Mk 250 for each and every copy so found.

Each copy of the Monograph shall be delivered to Wright with cover sheets carefully and properly attached, text inserted and all placed between covers provided by Wright and each copy carefully and separately wrapped and all packed for safe shipment to Chicago.

The cost of printing the introductory text shall be paid for by Wright at no more than actual cost to Wasmuth.

The work shall be delivered complete not later than May 1th, 1911 if possible.

Terms of payment as stated in original contract.

An edition of 25 copies on Japan paper shall be paid for at same rate as other copies. The additional cost of Japan paper over and above cost of paper otherwise used to be borne by Wright.

Regarding the Sonderheft:

The edition of 4000 copies only already printed, except 100 copies which shall belong to Wright, may be sold as the property of Wasmuth A.G. in Europe only, each copy to be plainly marked on cover by Wasmuth "For Sale in Europe Only." It is expressly agreed that this edition shall not be placed on the market until one month after second edition—5000 copies—herein after arranged for is completed and delivered to Wright at Chicago.

Wasmuth A.G. shall print an entire new edition of 5000 copies only, each copy to consist of about 150 pages of half-tones, colored Frontispiece and a tail piece, all according to Wright's instructions. Cover paper same as used for covers of Monograph made by Herr. Mass. Superior workmanship in every particular throughout guaranteed.

All copies to be packed carefully for shipment to Chicago. All shall be ready for delivery not later than May 1st. 1911. Wasmuth will pay all costs for packing, for boxes and carriage, paid to Bremen or Hamburg (free ship) for the Monograph and for the Sonderheft.

For the work complete Wright agrees to pay Mk 15000 i.e.: Mk 5000 down; Mk 5000 when work is ready for shipment; Mk 5000 after delivery. Ten copies are to be sent in advance by mail to Mr. Wright.

Should other editions of not less than 2500 copies be required they shall be ordered within three months from date of shipment and shall be produced within three months from date of order and at the rate of Mk. 5000 for each additional 2500 copies. Payments 1/2 down and balance on delivery, carriage paid to Bremen and Hamburg (free ship).

If such additional copies are ordered later than three months after shipment the above mentioned price may be changed and other agreements would have to be made.

Berlin, Germany, 13 February 1911.

ERNST WASMUTH
ARCHITEKTURVERLAG, ARCHITEKTURBUCHHANDLUNG UND KUNSTANSTALTEN A.-G.

In this letter to Alfonso Iannelli, Wright tries to resolve their dispute and cites the impact of his visit to Franz Metzner, the sculptor. (Frank Lloyd Wright to Alfonso Iannelli, 26 May 1915, Alfonso Iannelli Collection, folder 16, CHS.)

Chicago, May 26, 1915

My dear Iannelli:

Your note received—we will not quarrel about the "designs" for the geometric figures, but my work went a little further than you now imagine or suggest. Have you the little thumb nail sketches I made in my studio at Hillside and brought to Chicago? I showed them to my boys and to John and gave them to you, [added above: "with more detailed suggestions"] giving the ideas of the figures—*each*—They were practically as above—each figure holding aloft the form characterized with little of similar forms, rising in some cases, depending in others. The square and octagon masculine—the sphere and triangle feminine—each figure to partake in treatment of the form characterized? You will remember this?

You put these suggestions into the large ably and effectively but much more in detail I had to do to give the result—the architectural character I wanted as you also know.

As for the conventionalizing of the flesh, it was my suggestion and a thing I have tried to do many times before and long ago—a desire intensified by my visit to Metzner—a desire I worked at with Bock as he knows—a desire which is imperfectly attained in the present figures—an old motif of mine which I suggested to you and helped you by criticism to realize upon—to a certain extent. I am not satisfied yet, however with that "extent." In these cases, if I understand the nature of creative impulses, these works were certainly "designed" by me—they were more than executed by you.

I would have arrived at something just the same so far as "designs" went had you remained in Los Angeles, but not so sympathetic in detail or so successful in expression. The "ideas" I repeat are mine—their "expression" yours. I think those are the facts. Beethoven wrote the piece we'll say—Paderewski played it. No one can be said to have designed a thing where the idea and character of the thing has been given by another. The idea of the thing however, is modified by the "form" and inseparable from it—so the word "execution" does not suffice for that either.

These points are of little interest to anyone outside ourselves I imagine[.] But nevertheless essential to integrity of mind in relation to ones [sic] own work and they should be considered by us.

I do not want to rob myself of the co-operation of men who have the ability of expression, but so far, I have found few or perhaps none who understand the significance of the statement just made above— that noone [sic] can be said to have designed" [sic] a thing the *idea* of which has been contributed and the *character* of which has been determined by another.

Certainly I never could do so—Never have done so I trust—I hope you never will—certainly you won't if you care for my respect. But I am inclined to think this sense of "*idea* and *character*" is *rare,* and a property only of the clearest minds of great artists. Conscientiousness in this regard would rob most artists entirely of the things they stamp

with their names and not with their individuality—I dare say[.] I think that   Wright, Architect
              Iannelli, Sculptor   is nearest to a solution.
I should have put it so were it left to me, but John who had seen the original sketches and the subsequent development, put it the other way on the captions he put up to me and without giving the matter much thought I acquiesced. But now that it has come up, it is as well to thrash it out.

I do not think I can use in my work the "designs" of painters or sculptors. I can only utilize their superior technique and power of expression to help formulate my own.

This does not necessarily say that the individuality of painter and sculptor is barred from its share in the work. It may still be there—not as designer however, but as interpreter of another man's "design." Kreisler or Paderewski is essential to our enjoyment of the musical ideas of others and in it all always there is something of Paderewski and Kreisler and they are great artists.

What is the difference in our case? I see none.

    Sincerely yours,

(Signed)   Frank Lloyd Wright

Notes

Abbreviations

AI   Alfonso Iannelli

AI Coll.   Alfonso Iannelli Collection, Charles F. Murphy Architectural Study Center, Chicago Historical Society

CDT   *Chicago Daily Tribune*

CHS   Chicago Historical Society

CRA   Charles Robert Ashbee

CST   *Chicago Sunday Tribune*

CU   Columbia University, Avery Library, Department of Prints and Drawings.

DCfAD   Domino's Center for Architecture and Design.

DDM   Darwin D. Martin

DKuD   *Deutsche Kunst und Dekoration*

FLW   Frank Lloyd Wright

HUA   Harvard University Archives, Pusey Library, Cambridge, Mass.

IH   Akashi, Nobumichi (Shindo), *Kyu Teikoku Hoteruno Jisshoteki Kenkyu* [*Frank Lloyd Wright in Imperial Hotel*]. (Tokyo: Tokodo Shoten, 1972)

JAE   *Journal of Architectural Education*

JLW   John Lloyd Wright

JSAH   *Journal of the Society of Architectural Historians*

LC   Library of Congress, Architecture, Design, and Engineering Collections, Prints and Photographs Division, Washington, D.C.

M   Futagawa, Yukio, ed., and Bruce Pfeiffer, text, *Frank Lloyd Wright*, monograph, 12 vols. (Tokyo: A.D.A. Edita, 1984), noted by volume and figure number

MfaK   Museum für angewandte Kunst, Vienna, Austria

NYT   *New York Times*

ÖNB   Österreichisches National Bibliothek (Austrian National Library), Vienna, Austria

S   *Sonderheft*, American edition; *Frank Lloyd Wright: Ausgeführte Bauten*, Dover edition, 1982

SHSW   State Historical Society of Wisconsin, Iconographic Collections

ST   Stanford University Libraries, Department of Special Collections, Wright-Martin Papers (M355)

SUNYB   State University of New York at Buffalo, Darwin D. Martin Collection (MS22)

TAL   Archives of the Frank Lloyd Wright Foundation, Taliesin West, Scottsdale, Arizona

Th.-B.   Thieme, Ulrich, and Felix Becker, *Allgemeines Lexikon der bildenden Künstler von Antike bis zur Gegenwart*, 37 vols, vols. 16– 36 edited by Hans Vollmer (Leipzig: W. Engelmann, 1907–50)

TW   Taylor Woolley

UUL   University of Utah Library, Manuscripts Division, Special Collections Department, Taylor Woolley Papers, accession no. 152.

W   Wasmuth folios, *Ausgeführte Bauten und Entwürfe von Frank Lloyd Wright*, Dover edition, 1983

WEM   William E. Martin

Introduction

Unlike the work of Henry Hobson Richardson and Louis Sullivan, whose life and architecture have been subjected to scholarly scrutiny that now allows for undocumented analysis, Wright's oeuvre is still in need of pioneering research and requires careful documentation. I have therefore felt obliged to include extensive notes which serve the specialist, but which I hope will not burden the general reader. In quoting letters and documents, I have made some minor spelling corrections, but I have generally retained the original punctuation and Wright's idiosyncratic syntax.

1. Henry-Russell Hitchcock, Philip Johnson, and Lewis Mumford, *Modern Architects* (New York: Norton, for the Museum of Modern Art, 1932), 34. Hitchcock reasserted the significance of the Wasmuth publications in "Wright's Influence Abroad," *Parnassus* 12, no. 8 (1940): 12, and reiterated this assertion in his standard work, *In the Nature of Materials, The Buildings of Frank Lloyd Wright, 1887–1941* (New York: Duell, Sloan and Pearce, 1942), 59, where he referred readers to his article in *Parnassus* of the previous year. Hitchcock maintained his assessment of the publications through his last writing on the subject, "American Influence Abroad," in Edgar Kaufmann, Jr., ed., *The Rise of an American Architecture* (New York: Praeger, 1970), 3–48.

In addition to Hitchcock, Grant Carpenter Manson provided another standard text on Wright, *Frank Lloyd Wright to 1910. The First Golden Age* (New York: Van Nostrand Reinhold, 1958) hereafter cited as *Golden Age*. Manson began his research in 1938 as the subject of his dissertation at Harvard University. For Manson's early involvement with Wright, see his "The Wonderful World of Taliesin: My Twenty Years on its Fringes," *Wisconsin Magazine of History* 73, no. 1 (Autumn 1989): 33–41. Manson's pioneering work concluded with Wright's departure for Europe in 1909. The jacket of Manson's book announced two forthcoming volumes which were to summarize the conventional view. The follow-up to the *Golden Age* was to be called *The Lean, Lost Years: 1910–1935*, and the finale of Wright's career was to be covered in *The Second Golden Age: 1936 to the Present*. The publisher had added these forthcoming titles, but Manson had no intention of writing a trilogy (personal communication to author, 1 November 1990). This book picks up where Manson ended.

2. Helen Gardner, *Gardner's Art Through the Ages*, rev. 5th ed., Horst De La Croix and Richard G. Tansey, eds. (New York: Harcourt Brace Jovanovich, 1970), 738. The ninth edition (1991), 1001, gave this version of Wright's influence in Europe: "The publication of Wright's plans brought him a measure of fame in Europe, especially in Holland and Germany. The issuance of a portfolio of his work in Berlin in 1910 and an exhibition of his designs the following year hastened the death of Art Nouveau and stimulated younger architects to adopt some of his ideas about open plans and the freedom they afforded clients."

3. The collection of correspondence between Darwin D. Martin and Frank Lloyd Wright is divided, with the original materials from 1902 to 1914 in Buffalo in Special Collections, the State University of New York, Buffalo, MS22, no. 86–052 (cited hereafter as SUNYB), and material from 1915 to 1935 in the Department of Special Collections of Stanford University, M355 (cited hereafter as ST). Each collection has photocopies of the original material of the reciprocal collection. The papers include letters and other material between Darwin Martin (cited as DDM) and his brother, William E. Martin, (cited as WEM) and other individuals who will be cited by name.

The rich correspondence between Darwin D. Martin and Wright confirms Martin's pivotal role in the Wasmuth publishing venture.

4. Initial exploration of Wright's work around 1910 includes the following studies. Eduard Sekler first drew attention in 1959 to the resemblances between Wright's treatment of walls at Midway Gardens and the motifs in the early work of Gustav Klimt ("Frank Lloyd Wright zum Gedächtnis," *Der Aufbau* [Vienna] 14, no. 8 [August 1959]: 304). Edgar Kaufmann, Jr., pointed out, at the suggestion of Elizabeth Mock Kassler, that Wright's personal crises after 1910 were countered by a rich creativity and supported by a moral certainty ("Crisis and Creativity, Frank Lloyd Wright, 1904–1914," *JSAH* 25, no. 4 [December 1966]: 292–96). Kaufmann suggested ways in which Europe affected Wright that have been major themes of the research developed here.

Vincent Scully has turned his attention lately to the formal influences of European and Mesoamerican architecture on Wright with perceptive results. Beginning with his first publication on Wright to his most recent investigations of European influences, Scully's work has been important for this study. His first book on Wright was *Frank Lloyd Wright* (New York: George Braziller, 1960). His lecture at the symposium "Buell Talks on American Architecture," presented by the Temple Hoyne Buell Center for the Study of American Architecture, Columbia University, 13 April 1985, helped focus my critical attention on a number of formal issues concerning the relationships of Wright's work to that of his European contemporaries around the turn of the century.

Using primarily secondary sources, Heidi Kief-Niederwöhrmeier explored Wright's purported influence on Europe in *Frank Lloyd Wright und Europa: Architekturelemente, Naturverhältnis, Publikationen, Einflüsse* (Stuttgart: Karl Kramer Verlag, 1983). This was a revised edition of her *Der Einfluß Frank Lloyd Wrights auf die mitteleuropäische Einzelhausarchitektur* (Stuttgart: Karl Kramer Verlag, 1978).

Other scholars have made recent contributions to understanding Wright's work during his early period. Otto Antonia Graf's exploration of the underlying geometry of Wright's designs has revealed an unseen unity in his work. His *Die Kunst des Quadrats: zum Werk von Frank Lloyd Wright*, 2 vols. (Vienna: Böhlau, 1983), provides some of the most insightful formal analysis of Wright's work, particularly with respect to the Imperial Hotel. Neil Levine's "Abstraction and Representation in Modern Architecture: The International Style of Frank Lloyd Wright," *AA Files*, no. 11 (Spring 1986): 3–21, suggested a fundamental shift in Wright's representation of nature, which begins around 1922, precisely the end of Wright's international wanderings. Narciso G. Menocal has examined the role of geometry in Wright's work in "Form and Content in Frank Lloyd Wright's *Tree of Life* Window," *Elvehjem Museum of Art Bulletin* (1983–84): 18–32. Kathryn Smith has engaged in research on Wright's important client Aline Barnsdall and provided a basic chronology for Wright's travels to Japan concerning the Imperial Hotel in "Frank Lloyd Wright and the Imperial Hotel: A Postscript," *Art Bulletin* 67, no. 2 (June 1985): 296–310.

Gwendolyn Wright has provided the broad context for the domestic developments of Wright's early work in *Moralism and the Model Home: Domestic Architecture and Cultural Conflict in Chicago, 1973–1913* (Chicago: University of Chicago Press, 1980).

5. While aspects of the Wasmuth saga and the narrative of Wright's work after 1910 will be covered in this study, they provide in this book the framework for an emphasis on the artistic and social impact that the experience of Europe had on Wright from 1910 to the early 1920s. This study of influence will, in turn, act as introduction and framework for two studies to follow. The Wasmuth saga will be an investigation of the reception of ideas and include a history of the publications and their contents, their dispersal and distribution, and a view of the pathways and critical response to Wright's work over the spectrum of his career. Although the Wasmuth myths begin in 1910, a study of the actual reception to Wright's work will cover at least the next five decades and make an extended book on its own. The final work in this trilogy will be a study of the period from 1910 to 1922. This study will interweave biographical accounts of artistic transition and experiment that saw the design of major buildings of the period—the Midway Gardens in Chicago, the Imperial Hotel in Tokyo, and the Hollyhock House in Los Angeles.

6. Vincent Scully first published a severely cropped version of the Wasmuth plate of Wright's hotel in Mason City with a caption that said the hotel "is clearly the prototype of Gropius's Factory," in "Frank Lloyd Wright vs. the International Style," *Art News* 53 (March 1954): 32. Scully, however, then used a photograph of the hotel in his subsequent publication: *Modern Architecture* (New York: Braziller, 1961), 25, 26, and figs. 59–61. The image comes from the *Western Architect* of 1911 ("City National Bank of Mason City, Iowa, Frank Lloyd Wright, Architect," *Western Architect* 17 [December 1911]: 105, with illustrations following).

7. Preceding Hitchcock was Nicholas Pevsner's "Frank Lloyd Wright's Peaceful Penetration of Europe," *Architects' Journal* 89 (4 May 1939): 731–34. Additional examples of the myth of the Wasmuth influence include Siegfried Giedion, *Space, Time, and Architecture* (Cambridge: Harvard University Press, 1941), 397; Scully, "Frank Lloyd Wright vs. the International Style," 32–35; idem, *Frank Lloyd Wright*, 23.

8. Walter Curt Behrendt, review of *Frank Lloyd Wright Chicago. Achtes Sonderheft der Architektur des zwanzigsten Jahrhunderts* by Frank Lloyd Wright, *Kunst und Künstler* 11, no. 9 (May 1913): 487.

9. Vincent Scully elaborated his interest in Wright's appropriation of European architecture in his Introduction to *The Nature of Frank Lloyd Wright*, ed. Carol R. Bolon, Robert S. Nelson, and Linda Seidel (Chicago and London: University of Chicago Press, 1988), xiii–xxii.

10. David Hanks considered the connections between Wright's work and European developments in the decorative arts in David A. Hanks and Jennifer Toher, "The Decorative Designs of Frank Lloyd Wright and His European Contemporaries," in *Frank Lloyd Wright, Architectural Drawings and Decorative Art* (London: Fischer Fine Art, [1985]), 6–19); Hanks's earlier pioneering work was *The Decorative Designs of Frank Lloyd Wright* (New York: E. P. Dutton, 1979), subsequently cited as Hanks, *Decorative Designs*.

11. Scully, Introduction, *The Nature of Frank Lloyd Wright*, xviii–xxii.

12. Frank Lloyd Wright, *The Japanese Print: An Interpretation* (Chicago: The Ralph Fletcher Seymour Co., 1912; reprint ed., New York: Horizon Press, 1967).

13. Robert Twombly, *Frank Lloyd Wright: His Life and His Architecture* (New York: John Wiley & Sons, 1979), still provides the principal biographical source for a documentary discussion of Wright's work; it was essentially a republication of his *Frank Lloyd Wright: An Interpretive Biography* (New York: Harper & Row, 1973). Twombly's biographical material has been supplemented by Brendan Gill, *Many Masks, A Life of Frank Lloyd Wright* (New York: Ballantine Books, 1987). Meryle Secrest's elegant *Frank Lloyd Wright: A Biography* (New York: Knopf, 1992) has been criticized for lacking insight into Wright's architectural achievement. (See, for example, Blair Kamin's review, "Genius at the Drafting Board," *Chicago Tribune* 27 September 1992, sec. 14, p. 6.) William Marlin is working on a major, multivolume biography and has generously shared some of his original research with me.

14. See Manson, *Golden Age*, 203–13 for his assessment of the era ending in 1910.

15. H. Allen Brooks, *The Prairie School. Frank Lloyd Wright and His Midwest Contemporaries* ([Toronto and Buffalo]: University of Toronto Press, 1972; reprint ed., New York and London: W. W. Norton, 1976), subsequently cited as *Prairie School* (1976), sought in this seminal book to show how Wright's work declined after his return from Europe, and how that of his former employees and contemporaries flourished. Twombly emphasized the small number of buildings built after 1910 as evidence of Wright's life and practice being in disarray and described the period as "the first of many in-between years, the beginning of a quarter-century hiatus separating periods of staggering achievement" (*Life and Architecture*, 144).

16. Henry-Russell Hitchcock, Introduction, *Frank Lloyd Wright* (Paris: Editions "Cahier d'Art, 1928), n.p.

17. Hitchcock, *Nature of Materials*, 61, 66–69, and caption to fig. 217.

18. Kathryn Smith's assessment ("Frank Lloyd Wright, Hollyhock House, and Olive Hill, 1914–1924," *JSAH* 38, no. 1 [March 1979]: 32–33) typifies the view that Wright withdrew into the refuge of art: "With the family as a unit and institution no longer viable for him, Wright turned to a more ethereal realm for a sense of belonging and as an outlet for his architecture. Wright turned to art. . . . Alienated from his own family to a large extent and from the greater society around him, Wright sustained himself from 1914–1924 in a world that he understood and that understood him—the world of art."

19. For a study of Key's ideas and their impact on Wright immediately after his return from Europe, see Anthony Alofsin, "Taliesin: "To Fashion Worlds in Little," in Narciso Menocal, ed. *Taliesin 1911–1914*, vol. 1 of *Wright Studies* (Carbondale and Edwardsville: Southern Illinois Press, 1992): 44–65.

20. Harold Bloom, *The Anxiety of Influence: A Theory of Poetry* (New York: Oxford University Press, 1973). Assumptions of the existence of a mechanism of influence underlie not only the field of art history but literary criticism as well. Bloom proposed that the artist, in

order to define himself, claims to have no antecedent, no father, and not to have been influenced in his creativity. This theory provides a new perspective for Wright's claim to have been subject to no artistic influence, to have had, with very few exceptions, no architectural "fathers." In Bloom's terms the question could be asked: Was Wright, like Milton, incapable of suffering anxiety over influence that would creatively block him? Or did Wright, like Milton's successors, suffer but deny such suffering?

21. Walter Benjamin, "The Work of Art in the Age of Mechanical Reproduction, " in *Illuminations,* ed. Hannah Arendt (New York: Schocken Books, 1969), 217–51.

22. Reyner Banham, *A Concrete Atlantis* (Cambridge: MIT Press, 1986), 18.

23. On the role of the revival of the Shingle style as an antidote to modernism, see Vincent Scully, *The Architecture of the American Summer* (New York: Rizzoli, 1989), 3; and idem, *The Shingle Style Today; or the Historian's Revenge* (New York: George Braziller, 1974).

24. Colin Rowe took this approach to Le Corbusier in *The Mathematics of the Ideal Villa and Other Essays* (Cambridge: MIT Press, 1977).

25. Henry-Russell Hitchcock, "Frank Lloyd Wright and the 'Academic Tradition' of the Early Eighteen-Nineties," *Journal of the Warburg and Courtauld Institute* 7 (January–June 1944): 46–63.

26. Concerning the Midway Gardens and the Imperial Hotel, Neil Levine has written, "Wright's planning became more and more classical, emphasizing rectilinearity, closure, and formality" ("Frank Lloyd Wright's Diagonal Planning," in *In Search of Modern Architecture: A Tribute to Henry-Russell Hitchcock*, ed. Helen Searing [New York: Architectural History Foundation; Cambridge: MIT Press, 1982], 250). This view was reiterated by Levine, who saw it as part of Wright's return to "historical forms" ("Frank Lloyd Wright's Own Houses and His Changing Concept of Representation," in *The Nature of Frank Lloyd Wright*, 40).

27. On Italy's influence on Wright and the architect's "direct imitation of nature" as examples of Wright's classical tendencies, see Levine, "Wright's Own Houses," in *The Nature of Frank Lloyd Wright*, 21, 33–34.

28. Frank Lloyd Wright, *A Testament* (New York: Horizon Press, 1957), 205.

29. Gill's claim (*Many Masks*, 9) to having been a close friend of Wright's, thereby qualifying him for a privileged understanding, is open to question. Extensive correspondence in the Wright archives shows that Wright's most important connection to the *New Yorker* was through Alexander Woollcott, Gill's predecessor at the magazine, and there are only a few letters between Wright and Gill.

30. See Anthony Alofsin, Introduction, "Frank Lloyd Wright as a Man of Letters," *Frank Lloyd Wright: An Index to the Taliesin Correspondence*, 5 vols. (New York: Garland, 1988), vii–xii. Although Wright's drawings survived the Taliesin fire of 1914, we do not know about other letters.

31. Rudolf Wittkower, *Selected Lectures of Rudolf Wittkower: The Impact of Non-European Civilizations on the Art of the West*, Donald Martin Reynolds, comp. and ed. (Cambridge and New York: Cam-bridge University Press, 1989); subsequently cited as Wittkower, *Selected Lectures.*

32. Ibid., 6.

Chapter One

1. FLW, *A Testament*, 205.

2. FLW, *An Autobiography*, 2d ed. (New York: Duell, Sloan, and Pearce, 1943), 125–28; unless noted otherwise, subsequent citations are to this edition. Wright's friend and client Edward C. Waller introduced Wright to Burnham, shortly after the death of Burnham's partner, John Root (1850–91).

3. Ibid., 127.

4. Ibid., 194. Wright went to Japan to rest after completing the Larkin Building and the Darwin D. Martin House, both of which were in Buffalo, New York; he gave the date as 1906. Wright and his wife, Catherine, actually went to Japan in 1905 with Ward Willits and his wife, clients in Highland Park, Illinois, for whom Wright had designed a house in 1901 (Manson, *Golden Age*, 39).

5. "German Day and the Great Historical Achievement It Commemorates," Emil Mannhardt, 3 October 1909, *CST*, "Special German Day Supplement," n.p. Mannhardt was the secretary of the German Historical Society. The special supplement was issued on the day that 30,000 participants from 500 German-American societies celebrated in Chicago.

6. Donald Hoffmann, *Frank Lloyd Wright's Robie House* (New York: Dover, 1984), 3–4.

7. The exhibition on "Chicago Architecture, 1872–1922: Birth of a Metropolis," held in 1987–88, did much to firmly identify the international currents that flowed through Chicago in its formative period from the Great Fire until the international competition for the Chicago Tribune Tower. The essays that formed the catalogue of the exhibition, John Zukowsky, ed., *Chicago Architecture, 1872–1922* (Munich: Prestel Verlag and the Art Institute of Chicago, 1987), subsequently cited as *Chicago Architecture*, provide a new precision and depth of understanding of Chicago architecture and its relation to Europe. For an outstanding introduction to the German architectural ambience in Chicago, see Roula Geraniotis, "An Early German Contribution to Chicago's Modernism," in idem, 90–105.

For the impact of German architectural education in the Midwest, see Roula Geraniotis, "The University of Illinois and German Architectural Education," *JAE* 38, no. 4 (Summer 1985): 15–21.

Notes on an international conference, "American Architecture and the German Connection," held 7–8 April 1989 at Columbia University, New York City, appear in Barry Bergdoll and Richard Pommer, "Tagungen," *Kunstchronik* 42, no. 10 (October 1989): 570–74.

8. The Adler company's Borden Block (1879–80) exemplified the trend to open the surface of a building to express the structure within.

9. For Ricker (1843–1924), see Anthony Alofsin, "Tempering the Ecole: Nathan Ricker at the University of Illinois and Langford Warren at Harvard," in Gwendolyn Wright and Janet Parks, eds., *The History of History in American Schools of Architecture, 1865–1975* (Princeton:

Buell Center for the Study of American Architecture and Princeton Architectural Press, 1990), 73–88.

10. Geraniotis, "German Contribution," in *Chicago Architecture, 1872–1922*, 98–100, 102. The work of Schmidt and Hill and Woltersdorf occurred at a time when German and Austrian influences began to mingle as the Secession movements in both countries started to affect each other. Consequently, some caution should be used in distinguishing German ideas from those of other German-speaking countries.

11. Wright obtained Viollet-le-Duc's *The Habitations of Man in All Ages* and his *Dictionnaire Raisonné* from the Madison, Wisconsin, public library. Wright called the *Dictionnaire*, with its basis in a theory of rational architecture, "the only really sensible book on architecture" (FLW, *Autobiography*, 75). However, Donald Hoffmann has shown that Wright apparently confused the *Dictionnaire* with the *Entretiens sur l'architecture*, which had been translated as *Discourses on Architecture* in 1875. See Donald Hoffmann, "Frank Lloyd Wright and Viollet-le-Duc," *JSAH* 28 (October 1969): 173–83; and *Frank Lloyd Wright and Viollet-le-Duc: Organic Architecture from 1850 to 1950* (Chicago: Kelmscott Enterprises, 1986).

12. According to Nina Nedeljkov's research, based on the office history of the firm, Wasmuth was founded in 1872 by Ernst Wasmuth, Sr. (1845–97), and his brother Emil (1848–94). It was incorporated (G.M.B.H.) in 1898 and became Ernst Wasmuth A.G. in 1903 when Otto Dorn became editorial director. According to Nedeljkov, Ernst Wasmuth, Jr., died in 1904 and his nephew Ernst Wasmuth did not take over the firm until around 1913 (Nina Nedeljkov to author, personal communication, 19 March, 30 March 1990). This information conflicts with Wright's frequent personal references to Wasmuth and the letter of 3 November 1910 from Ernst Wasmuth to Wright (Appendix B). However, the letter is a copy prepared for Wright, and the signature cannot be verified. Aside from Otto Dorn, an ambiguity remains about Wright's contacts at the Verlag; Ernst Wasmuth, the nephew, may have already been a principal at the firm during Wright's venture.

13. FLW, *An Autobiography*, 161–62. In an unpublished lecture in 1951 Wright reiterated his earlier account (FLW, "Civilization without Culture," address to the Taliesin Fellowship, Taliesin West, 25 February 1951, transcription, MS 15, p. 3, TAL).

14. Because Wright assumed Francke was his connection to the European publication of his works, most historians have followed Wright's assumption and with varying degrees of accuracy repeated the connection between Wright and Francke. For example, Sigfried Giedion repeated the inaccurate assumption that when Francke met Wright in 1908 Francke was "a German exchange professor lecturing at Harvard University on aesthetics" (*Space, Time, and Architecture*, 5th ed. revised and enlarged [Cambridge, Mass: Harvard University Press, 1967], 320). Francke, however, was a naturalized American citizen and regular faculty member familiar with American conditions after more than twenty years of living in America.

Frank Lloyd Wright, Jr. (1890–1978), known as Lloyd Wright, made a similar assumption and repeated that Francke may have provided the connection to Wasmuth. In a retrospective account of the Wasmuth publishing venture, and the production of the Wasmuth publications, Lloyd Wright stated that Francke had seen some of the senior Wright's work published in Europe, and that Francke came to visit Wright at Oak Park because of the work's originality and his desire to learn more about it (Lloyd Wright to Linn Cowles, 3 February 1966, TAL).

15. FLW, *A Testament*, 84, 132; *An Autobiography*, 161–62.

16. Reichskommission, *Weltausstellung in St. Louis 1904. amtlicher Katalog*, Theodor Lewald, ed. (Berlin: George Stilke [1904]), 415); subsequently cited as *Weltausstellung St. Louis*.

17. For biographical material on Francke, see G[eorge] H[arvey] G[lenzmer], "Francke, Kuno," *Dictionary of American Biography*, 6 (New York: Charles Scribner's Sons, 1930); Francke's autobiography, *Deutsche Arbeit in Amerika* (Leipzig, 1930), cited hereafter as Francke, *Arbeit*; and the Harvard University Archives, Pusey Library, Harvard University, containers HUG1404.2, HUG1404.3, HUG1404.4, HUG1404.5, with biographical material in HUG 300; the archives are cited as HUA. Katherine Welch, Francke's granddaughter, provided the author with recollections about her grandfather (Katharine Welch to author, 30 November 1984). No family papers were in her possession, and she reiterated Wright's assumption that Francke was the appreciative connection between Wright and the Wasmuth Verlag.

Kuno Francke (1855–1930) was born in Kiel. He had a classical German academic education that led to studies in the universities of Kiel, Berlin, and Munich, at the last of which he wrote a dissertation in 1879 on Latin poetry of the twelfth and thirteenth centuries. Five years later he was asked through the auspices of his friend, Harvard history professor Ephraim Emerton, to teach German at Harvard ("Minute on the Life of Professor Kuno Francke," *Harvard University Gazette* [24 June 1931], HUA). Bernard Berenson was one of his first students in the fall of 1884. Francke adopted America and in 1891 became with considerable pride an American citizen. Harvard appointed him Professor of the History of German Culture in 1896.

18. Francke, *Arbeit*, 29–63. See Busch-Reisinger Museum, *The Busch-Reisinger Museum, Harvard University*, introduction by Charles Haxthausen (New York: Abbeville Press, 1980), 7–10, for a brief history of the museum and a catalogue of its collections. The collections of the museum were initially intended to consist of reproductions of major works of central and northern European art. Francke hoped that students of art, philology, and political and literary history would find a common ground in his museum that could contribute to a unified national spirit.

Francke's career survived the anti-German sentiment in America during the war years, and he later was considered the leading scholar of German culture in America. The circle that Wright touched to augment his grasp of culture and art included people connected to Francke. Arthur Davison Ficke, the author of some of Wright's principle sourcebooks on Japanese prints, wrote a remembrance of Francke at his death, "Recollections of Kuno Francke," *Harvard Graduates' Magazine* (June 1930).

19. Francke was at least familiar with the Midwest by the time he met Wright, and it is possible that he could have heard of Wright as

early as 1899 when he taught as a visiting professor at the University of Wisconsin in Madison, near Wright's ancestral home close to Spring Green (Francke, *Arbeit*, 36).

Later, in June, 1904, Francke was awarded the degree of Doctor of Laws from the University of Wisconsin and he presumably returned to Wisconsin to receive his degree, but there is no indication that met Wright (*New York Tribune*, 10 June 1904, n.p., in HUG1404.5, HUA).

20. Francke was on a short lecture tour speaking about "Chapters from the History of German Culture in the Fifteenth Century" and after a stop in Pittsburgh to lecture at the city's Germanic Society on 1 February 1908, he went on to Chicago, giving his first lecture on 3 February to the Germanic Society of Chicago and another on 6 February at the University of Chicago (newsclipping from *Harvard Alumni Bulletin* [19 February 1908], n.p., in HUD300, HUA). The Chicago society published a pamphlet of Francke's speech on "Methods of Municipal Administration in Medieval German Cities." Louis Guenzel was recording secretary of the society; he later bought a copy of Wright's Wasmuth portfolios.

21. Invitation for 11 August 1908 (HUG1404.5, HUA). A telegram from the office of the Prussian minister of culture asking Francke to participate in the development of a Germanic Museum at Kiel was sent to Francke on board the steamship *Bremen*, moored at Plymouth, England. Documents in the HUA indicate that Francke made frequent summer visits to Germany.

22. Francke, *Arbeit*, p. 60; *Harvard Alumni Bulletin* (13 May 1914), n.p., in HUG300, HUA. Francke had gone to Chicago to give an address at the University of Chicago in June 1914 and a dedicatory speech at the unveiling of the Goethe monument in Lincoln Park, when Wright's Midway Gardens was well on its way toward its August opening. The speech was on 9 June, the unveiling on 13 June 1914.

23. Bruno Möhring (1863–1929) was born in Königsberg in Prussia and died in Berlin. He had studied at the Technische Hochschule in Charlottenburg, and he became noted as a technical writer and particularly for his structures in iron, such as the bridge over the Rhine at Bonn, and later for his involvement in city planning (Th.-B, 1931, s.v. "Möhring, Bruno").

24. Charles E. White to Walter Wilcox, 13 May 1904, in Nancy K. Morris Smith, "Letters, 1903–1906, by Charles E. White, Jr. from the Studio of Frank Lloyd Wright," *JAE* 25 (Fall 1971): 105.

25. Because of his connections with Möhring's office, the young architect Bruno Taut might have learned of Wright around this date from photographs that Möhring may have brought back to Germany. Taut had gone to Berlin in 1904 to work for Möhring and attend his lectures; from 1904 to 1908 Taut worked for and studied with Theodor Fischer in Stuttgart, and returned to Berlin in 1908 (*Macmillan Encyclopedia*, s.v, "Taut, Bruno").

26. For general catalogues, see *The World's Fair, St. Louis, U.S.A., 1904* (St. Louis: R. A. Reid, 1902); and *Souvenir Book of the Louisiana Purchase Exposition: Day and Night Scenes* (St. Louis: Official Photographic Co., 1904). For a German view of the art at the exhibition, see Max Creutz, "Die 'Fine Arts' auf der Weltausstellung in St. Louis," *Die Kunst für Alle* 19 (1904): 568–74.

The exposition also interested Orlando Giannini, who collaborated with Wright on the execution of art glass and murals in Wright's early career. Elaine Harrington, curator of decorative arts at the Frank Lloyd Wright Home and Studio, has noted that the Home and Studio research collections indicate that Giannini exhibited designs for woven baskets in St. Louis as he had at the Chicago World's Columbian Exposition of 1893 (Elaine Harrington to Karen Wilson, 27 March 1992).

27. Charles White, Jr., to Walter Wilcox, n.d., in Smith, "Charles White Jr.," p. 107; and Brooks, *Prairie School*, 91. Wright gave Barry Byrne train money to see the exhibition.

28. European exhibitions at the fair were complemented by those from the Orient, which would have stimulated Wright's interest in the Japanese prints he had been collecting. The Japanese exhibition in the Palace of Fine Art included paintings on silk and paper, furniture, and artifacts, and Wright would have had a chance to see plans, sections, and elevation drawings of contemporary Japanese architecture, designed in a traditional mode. There were two drawings of a design for a gate with chrysanthemum decorations by Morita (Ichigoro) of Toyama, and four drawings for the S. Asano residence in Tokyo by Sasaki (Iwajiro) of Kyoto (Kwanjiuro Yamashita, *The Illustrated Catalogue of Japanese Fine Art Exhibits in the Art Palace at the Louisiana Purchase Exposition, St. Louis, Mo., U.S.A.* [Kobe: Publishing Department of Kwansai Shoshin Seiha Insatsu Goshi Kaisha, 20 May 1904]: 106–7).

29. Among the few references to the fair in relation to Wright is Hanks and Tofer, "The Decorative Designs of Frank Lloyd Wright and His European Contemporaries: 1895–1915," in *Frank Lloyd Wright: Drawings and Decorative Art* (London: Fischer Fine Art, [1985]), 14 (subsequently cited as "Wright and His European Contemporaries"). See also Narciso Menocal, "Frank Lloyd Wright and the Question of Style," *Journal of the Decorative and Propaganda Arts* 2 (Summer/Fall 1986): 10–11.

30. Even scholarly events were associated with the St. Louis World's Fair: Kuno Francke went to the fair as president of an international congress on the history of German literature (Francke, *Arbeit*, 40). The Harvard Germanic Museum also contributed gold and silver vases and similar objects to the fair, which were replicated from the Museum of Arts and Crafts in Berlin. These objects formed the centerpiece of the German arts and crafts exhibition (newspaper clipping [19 January 1904], n.p., in HUG300, HUA).

31. The major model for Deutsches Haus at the fair was the Royal Schloss in Charlottenburg (Reichskommission, *Weltausstellung St. Louis*, 101–2).

32. For Möhring's role at the exhibition, see *Deutsches Kunstgewerbe in St. Louis 1904* (Berlin: Ernst Wasmuth A.-G., 1904). In the architectural section of the Palace of Fine Arts he showed drawings for a bridge over the Syratal and a competition entry for piers of the Rhine bridge at Basel. In the Palace of Varied Industries he showed drawings and a plaster model. Möhring also arranged various sections of the exhibition, including the exhibition of German book crafts in the Palace of Liberal Arts. He supervised the artistic direction of the decoration and outfitting group in the industrial products section and arranged

the hygiene exhibition in the social economy group in the building for model educational affairs (Reichskommission, *Weltausstellung St. Louis*, 408, 411–12, 455, 504).

33. In addition to Olbrich, among those German architects exhibited in the fair, Wright would have seen the architectural drawings of Fritz Schumacher of Dresden and the color drawings by the Berlin firm of Spalding and Grenander, including their perspective drawing for Villa Kruse (*Weltausstellung St. Louis*, 411, 478).

For Olbrich (1867–1908), whom I discuss later, see Th.-B, 35 (1931), s.v. "Olbrich, Joseph"; Robert Judson Clark, "J. M. Olbrich: 1867–1908," *Architectural Design* 37 (December 1967): 562–72; idem, "Joseph Maria Olbrich and Vienna" (Ph.D. diss., Princeton University, 1973); and idem, *Macmillan Encyclopedia*, s.v. "Olbrich, Joseph."

34. Reichskommission, *Weltausstellung St. Louis*, 411, 421, 455; for the contents of the six rooms designed by Behrens see ibid., 461–63. For Behrens, see Tilmann Buddensieg, *Industriekultur. Peter Behrens und die AEG, 1907–1914* (Berlin: Mann, 1979; English edition, Cambridge, Mass.: MIT Press, 1984); and Stanford O. Anderson "Peter Behrens and the New Architecture of Germany" (Ph.D. diss., Columbia University, 1968).

35. Wright later collected the work of five artists who exhibited in St. Louis: Wilhelm Steinhausen, whose works in the Palace of Fine Arts had long, narrative titles: *Dieser nimmt die Sünder an und isset mit ihnen*, a "painted" lithograph, and *Kommt her zu mir alle, die ihr mühselig und beladen seid, Ich will euch erquicken* (Reichskommission, *Weltausstellung St. Louis*, 406); Karl Kayser-Eichberg showed *Abendsonne vor dem Gewitter* (ibid., 402); Gustav Kampmann exhibited *Eisenbahn am Abend*, an oil painting, in the Palace of Varied Industry, and a mural in oil in Olbrich's library room of the Summer Residence (ibid., 409, 463); Prof. Hans V. Volkmann, landscape painter of the Karlsruhe, exhibited his *Frühsommer* and a mural in oil (ibid., 409, 463). In the Palace of Liberal Arts, in the section on book publishers and presses, the printing house of etcher Otto Felsing exhibited copperplate etchings, monochrome prints, etchings, and printed matter (ibid., 413). In the photography section Felsing showed his specially patented, multicolored etching process; Wright later bought black and white etchings of Felsing's drawings of saints after Dürer (ibid., 415).

Wright had a penchant for landscapes. Acccording to Elaine Harrington, he had several in his Oak Park home, including a scenic oil by Chicago painter William Wendt and a pastel drawing of a field at harvest by Chicago painter and muralist Charles Corwin, whose architect brother Cecil was an early friend of Wright's. Wright also had a print of a pastel, *Thawing Ice* by Norwegian impressionist Fritz Thaulov; this may have been the same print exhibited at the 1893 fair. This aesthetic taste was typical of the time, and such a print was similar to landscapes collected by Elbert Hubbard, who founded the Roycroft collective that Wright knew (Elaine Harrington to Karen Wilson, 27 March 1992).

36. William C. Gannett, *The House Beautiful* (River Forest, Ill.: Auvergne Press, 1896–97). Wright designed the page decorations in red and black, and he and William Herman Winslow printed the book by hand in the stable Wright designed for Winslow, his first client (Robert Sweeney, *Frank Lloyd Wright: An Annotated Bibliography* [Los Angeles:

Hennessey and Ingalls, 1978], 4; the standard bibliography, subsequently cited as Sweeney, *Bibliography*).

37. Reichskommission, *Weltausstellung St. Louis*, 415.

38. *Universal Exhibition St. Louis 1904, Exhibition of Professional Schools for Arts and Crafts*, (Vienna: Imperial Royal Ministry for Public Instruction, 1904).

39. Hoffmann founded, with Carl Moll and Fritz Wärndorfer, the Wiener Werkstätte in 1903. For the definitive monograph on Hoffmann, see Eduard F. Sekler, *Josef Hoffmann: The Architectural Work* (Princeton: Princeton University Press, 1985), 288–89. On the Austrian involvement with the St. Louis Fair, see also Christian M. Nebehay, *Gustav Klimt: Dokumentation* (Vienna: Verlag der Galerie Christian Nebehay, 1969), 346–47; *Deutsche Kunst* 8 (1905): 125–28; *Deutsche Kunst und Dekoration* 15 (1904/1905): 211; and *Ver Sacrum*, special issue, *Die Wiener Secession und die Ausstellung in St. Louis* (Vienna, 1904).

40. Aside from the Wasmuth publications, Wright's work was brought to Europe from the travel accounts of Berlage, which appeared as "Neuere amerikanische Architektur," *Schweizerische Bauzeitung* 55 (14, 21, 28 September 1912): 148–50, 165–67, 178. These were the texts of three lectures that Berlage gave to the Swiss Society of Engineers and Architects; Wright had a translation, a copy of which he gave to Darwin D. Martin and which is now at SUNYB. After arriving in America in November 1911 for a two-month visit, Berlage saw Wright's work in 1911 but did not meet Wright. For Berlage's travels to America, see Giovanni Fanelli, "'Unity Within Diversity': The Architecture of Berlage," in Sergio Polano, ed., *Hendrik Petrus Berlage. Complete Works* (New York: Rizzoli International, 1988), 19, 150.

41. *Nederlandse Architectuur 1880–1930: Americana* (Zaandam: C. Huig, 1975), 18. Maya Moran kindly pointed out to me this reference to Berlage's exhibition.

42. Cohn was vice chairman of a jury for awards in the Fine Arts Building ("Socially Speaking," *The Springfield News*, 3 October 1904, cited in David M. Schele, "The 'Medium' Is the Message: Frank Lloyd Wright, Susan Dana, and the Dana-Thomas House" [typescript, 1989], 28 n. 31.)

43. Leonard K. Eaton, *American Architecture Comes of Age* (Cambridge, Mass., and London: MIT Press, 1972), 207–10; Fanelli, "Unity," in Polano, *Berlage*, 20.

44. George M. Niedecken (1878–1945) provided furnishings for many of Wright's houses. See *The Domestic Scene (1897–1927): George M. Niedecken, Interior Architect* (Milwaukee: The Milwaukee Art Museum, 1981); subsequently cited as *Niedecken*.

45. For Niedecken's Art Nouveau adaptations, see his print, inv. no. 1982.1091.5, in the collection of the Metropolitan Museum of Art, Edward Pearce Casey Fund.

46. See Hanks and Tofer, " Wright and His European Contemporaries," 6–19. For an additional study of European publications, see Paul S. Kruty, "The Influence of the European Early Modern Movement on the Architecture of the Prairie School" (M.A. Thesis, University of Wisconsin-Milwaukee, 1984).

47. *Niedecken*, 49, 50.

cluded some expurgated passages. Where copies were consulted at the Wright archives, the subsequent citation is TAL.

For the definitive monograph on Ashbee, see Allan Crawford, *C. R. Ashbee: Architect, Designer and Romantic Socialist*, (New Haven: Yale University Press, 1985).

80. A cordial relationship had developed between the Ashbee and Wright families. After the visit in 1900, Ashbee wrote to Wright in response to a letter from him of 26 February [1901]. Ashbee mentioned a possible reciprocal visit for Wright to England in June or July, and thanked Wright for copies of photographs taken during the recent visit (CRA to FLW, 2 April 1901, TAL). (Wright's letter of 26 February [1901] has not surfaced.) Wright tardily replied in January 1902 that he had not been able to go to England during the past July, of 1901, because of a lack of funds: "The year has proved neither feast nor famine, but a very modest mean, and I am still to[o] poor to come to England. I don't feel that I have grown much either,—in fact I am truly blue . . ." (FLW to CRA, 3 January 1902, "Ten Letters,'" 65).

Wright also mentioned reading Ashbee's report on the United States for the National Trust and reading an article by Ashbee in the "Review," and included with his letter "a little packet of prints" as a new year's gift (FLW to CRA, 3 January 1902, Crawford, "Ten Letters," 72 n. 8.). Crawford suggested the "Review" was *The Architectural Review* 9, (1901): 172–76, and that Wright may have seen Ashbee's name in a review of an exhibition of pianos designed by architects.

81. Crawford, "Ten Letters," 66. In anticipation of the visit during a second lecture tour in America, Wright wrote that he had seen a review of Ashbee's work, which brought up again their differences about the machine versus handicrafts; he wondered "how far apart we are now on some of the matters we used to discuss" (FLW to CRA, 24 October 1908, Ashbee Journals, TAL). Crawford suggested the "work" to which Wright referred was probably Ashbee's book *Craftsmanship in Competitive Industry*; it was published in 1908 at London and Campden, Glos.

82. [FLW to CRA], 25 December 1908, Crawford, "Ten Letters," 66 n. 11.

83. FLW to CRA, 3 January 1909, Crawford, "Ten Letters," 66. The letter was sent to Ashbee at Stanford University. The photocopy of the excerpt at TAL is dated erroneously 3 February.

The pound sterling was worth $5 in 1910, therefore the "hundred thousand pounds" Wright mentioned was equivalent to the fantastic amount of $500,000. For contemporary exchange rates, see [Karl Baedeker] *Austria-Hungary with Excursions to Cetinje, Belgrade, and Bucharest. Handbook for Travelers by Karl Baedeker.* 11th. ed. rev. (Leipzig: Karl Baedeker; London: T. Fisher Unwin; New York: Charles Scribner's Sons, 1911).

In addition to the residences in different parts of the country, there was the City National Bank Building and Park Inn Hotel in Mason City, Iowa, for James E. Blythe and J. E. E. Markley. A second bank could have been the Frank L. Smith Bank, the First National Bank of Dwight, Illinois, for which Wright had designed a second scheme dated 1905. Another job was the Lexington Terrace Apartment Building for E. C. Waller, which was not realized.

The residences for Mason City may have included a project for

Dr. G. C. Stockman and the J. G. Melson House, another project that would slip from Wright to Walter Burley Griffin, who designed the Rock Crest–Rock Glen project in Mason City in 1912. See William A. Storrer, *The Architecture of Frank Lloyd Wright. A Complete Catalog*, 2d ed. (Cambridge, Mass., and London: MIT Press, 1982) 155–56, subsequently cited as Storrer, *Catalog*; Brooks, *Prairie School*, 243–47; Jerry A. McCoy, "The Stockman House," *Frank Lloyd Wright Quarterly* 2, no. 3 (Summer 1991): 9–10. The other residences around the country could have been any of the projects listed in the holdings of TAL for the years 1908 and 1909. The majority of the buildings and projects for that year, however, centered around Chicago.

The project for the City National Bank Building and Park Inn Hotel, then, was a major project for Wright, both in financial terms and in physical scale, from the time of its conception in 1909, the year of Wright's departure from Oak Park.

84. FLW to CRA, 3 January 1909, Crawford, "Ten Letters," 66.

85. These figures are based on the lists of projects and buildings at TAL.

86. Robert C. Spencer, Jr., "The Work of Frank Lloyd Wright," *Architectural Review* (Boston) 7 (June 1900): 61–72.

87. FLW, "In the Cause of Architecture," *Architectural Record* 23 (March 1908): 155–221. With its emphasis on concepts of organic architecture, this statement surpassed Wright's observations in his 1901 lecture, "The Art and Craft of the Machine," published in *Catalogue of the Fourteenth Annual Exhibition of the Chicago Architectural Club* [Chicago: Architectural Club, 1901].

88. Wilson, "Chicago and the International Arts and Crafts Movements: Progressive and Conservative Tendencies," in *Chicago Architecture*, 217.

89. FLW, *Autobiography*, 162.

90. McCormick had expressed an interest in having Wright design a house in 1907 (Manson, *Golden Age*, 201–2).

91. Archival records at TAL indicate that during 1908 and 1909 Wright had sixteen unexecuted projects while twenty-five designs were built; they ranged from new residences to store interiors.

92. Wright was introduced to Darwin D. Martin in 1902 when William E. Martin wrote from Chicago to his brother in Buffalo to introduce "one of nature's *noblemen*" (William E. Martin to DDM, 22 October 1902, SUNYB.) William Martin was impressed with Wright's physical appearance, his high ideals, and his houses. Martin underscored Wright's strong points as the man who "would be *pleased* to design your house & further he is *the man* to build *your office*" (ibid.). In November 1902 Darwin Martin invited Wright to Buffalo. From this introduction developed a complex and profound relationship between architect and client. Jack Quinan is preparing the definitive treatment of the relationship of Martin and Wright. For a biography of Martin, see Quinan's "Frank Lloyd Wright, Darwin D. Martin, and the Creation of the Martin House." Supplement to *Prairie House Journal* (1987): 5–12; this is the edited text of a lecture given 10 April 1987, at a symposium sponsored by DCfAD at the University of Michigan, Ann Arbor, Michigan.

Darwin D. Martin (1865–1935) was a life-long employee of the Larkin Company in Buffalo, where he began work as a bookkeeper in

1879. He eventually became one of the highest-paid executives in the United States. For an introduction to Wright and the Buffalo circle, which included Darwin D. Martin, William R. Heath, and John D. Larkin, see Jack Quinan, *Frank Lloyd Wright's Larkin Building Myth and Fact* (New York: Architectural History Foundation; Cambridge, Mass.: MIT Press, 1987), 3–20.

93. FLW to DDM, 2 December 1908, SUNYB.

94. The scant biographical material available for Mamah Borthwick Cheney is found in newspaper accounts (see "Stoutly Defends Erring Husband," *CDT*, 8 November 1909, p. 7). Mamah's formal education distinguished her from her peers. She was known to have been interested in fiction, drama, and feminism, and after she moved to Chicago she became a student under Robert Herrick for a time at the University of Chicago. Her real ambition was to be a writer, but "she was so diffident of her talent that she published no original work" ("Mrs. Cheney and Five Others Slain in Frank Lloyd Bungalow," *CST*, 16 August 1914, p. 6). She had been born on 19 June 1869 in Boone, Iowa, received her bachelor of arts degree in 1892 and a master of arts in 1893, and married Edwin H. Cheney in 1899 (Sweeney, *Bibliography*, xxv n. 26).

95. "Stoutly Defends Erring Husband," *CDT*, 8 November 1909, p. 7.

96. "Leave Family; Elope to Europe," *CDT*, 7 November 1909, p. 1. For a discussion of Wright's early clients' interests in engineering, see Leonard K. Eaton, *Two Chicago Architects and Their Clients: Frank Lloyd Wright and Howard Van Doren Shaw* (Cambridge, Mass., and London: MIT Press, 1969).

97. Catherine Wright made a two-volume daybook of 1909 for her husband that shows she was struggling to keep him before January 1909. The book, which is in a private collection, contains many illustrations, poems, and epigrams with the theme of devotion to fatherhood and home (Elaine Harrington to Karen Wilson, 27 March 1992). See also Twombly, *Interpretive Biography*, 91–92; 318, n. 8.

98. FLW, *Autobiography*, 163.

99. Despite the trauma in his family life, Wright was not necessarily totally alienated from his family in 1909. Wright's son John disagreed with Manson's assertions (*Golden Age*, 211) that Wright and his wife were "totally estranged" and that his children had grown distant. In the margins of John's copy of Manson's monograph he wrote "No" and inserted a question mark in the margin, and underlined Manson's "quarrels" (John Lloyd Wright Collection, Avery Library, Columbia University).

100. Wright's departure from his office was not as casual as has been implied. Manson stated that Wright's departure "was an overnight decision" and questioned the rationality of choosing Von Holst (*Golden Age*, 212). Documentary evidence indicates much premeditation before Wright's departure to Europe.

101. Brooks, *Prairie School*, 86.

102. Wright knew George Elmslie from their early days of working at the office of J. Lyman Silsbee and Louis Sullivan (FLW, *Autobiography*, 97). Elmslie also worked for Silsbee in 1888, as did Wright, and Elmslie replaced Wright as chief draftsman for Adler and Sullivan when Wright left the firm in 1892 (FLW, *Genius and the Mobocracy* en-

larged 2d ed. [New York: Horizon Press, 1971], 93; and *Macmillan Encyclopedia*, s.v. "Purcell and Elmslie").

103. Isabel Roberts to William G. Purcell, 12 October 1909, with MS note attached by Purcell on a separate sheet. William Gray Purcell Collection, Northwest Architectural Archives, University of Minnesota.

104. Ibid.

105. Ibid.

106. See Elaine Harrington, "International Influences on Henry Hobson Richardson's Glessner House," in *Chicago Architecture, 1872–1922. Birth of a Metropolis* (Munich: Prestel Verlag, and the Art Institute of Chicago, 1987), 205; and Brooks, *Prairie School*, 86 n. 26, for biographical information on Herman Valentin Von Holst (1874–1955). He graduated from the University of Chicago in 1893, took the degree of B.S. in Architecture at MIT in 1896, and worked in the Chicago office of Shepley, Rutan, and Coolidge. He traveled in Europe in 1901, taught at the Armour Institute from 1904 to 1906. In addition to practicing architecture, he also wrote on the subject. He was the son of Hermann Von Holst (1841–1904), the first chairman of the Department of History at the University of Chicago and a distinguished expert on the American political system.

In an example of the small, interconnected circles of Wright's Chicago life, Wright's close friend Ferdinand Schevill later wrote a biographical entry on Von Holst, Sr. (*Dictionary of American Biography*, 9 [1932], s.v. "Holst, Hermann Eduard von"). Schevill succeeded Von Holst as chairman of the Department of History at the University of Chicago and was a founder of the corporation that supported Wright's work after 1928 (FLW, *A Testament*, 85).

107. For Wright's claim of having recently met Von Holst, see FLW, *Autobiography*, 164; and Brooks, *Prairie School*, 86;. Wright had offices at 1106 Steinway Hall from c. 1900 to 1907 (Manson, *Golden Age*, 215). The Von Holst office was listed at 1020 in the Fine Arts Building in 1910 (*The Lakeside Annual Directory of the City of Chicago* [Chicago: Reuben Donnelley, 1910–14], subsequently cited as *Chicago Lakeside Directory*). Concerning the addition of the barn, see Walter Creese, *The Crowning of the American Landscape: Eight Great Spaces and Their Buildings* (Princeton: Princeton University Press, 1985), 259, caption for fig. 10. The Frank Lloyd Wright Home and Studio has photographic documentation of the octagonal barn in its archives (Elaine Harrington to author, personal communication, 18 May 1992).

108. For contract, see, Appendix B.

109. See Brooks's account (*Prairie School*, 84–86) of the closing of Wright's studio in Oak Park, the dispersal of his draftsmen, and their relations with Wright. Brooks has also illuminated the key role of Wright's former employees in the operation of the office under Von Holst, particularly the role of Marion Mahony, who became resident designer for Von Holst and his partner, James Fyfe (Brooks, *Prairie School*, 149–50, and Manson, *Golden Age*, 213, for information on Mahony and Griffin).

Von Holst's studies at MIT overlapped with those of Marion Mahony and Marion Chamberlain, another Wright employee. Wright's studio employees in Oak Park have been the subject of Lisa Schrenk's research at the Frank Lloyd Wright Home and Studio.

110. The projects stipulated in the contract fell into three categories: work under construction; work in hand; and probable and prospective work, with specific required tasks noted in several instances. This list included eleven works under some phase of construction on 22 September 1909. Wright also turned over to Von Holst two projects noted as "Work in Hand," a category that indicated some phase of design development prior to construction: a house for E. P. Irving and a house for Walter Gerts of Whitehall, Michigan. There were also seven projects that were listed as "Probable & Prospective" (Wright–Von Holst Contract, 22 September 1909).

111. FLW to DDM, 16 September 1909, SUNYB. At the bottom of the letter was typed "Copy to W.E.M. 9/18/09. N.T.," indicating that William E. Martin was informed of Wright's plans two days later.

112. Ibid.

Chapter Two

1. FLW, *An Autobiography* (1932), 164.

2. For a synopsis of the Vienna Secession and the role of the art magazine *Ver Sacrum*, see Christian Nebehay, *Ver Sacrum, 1898–1903* (Vienna: Edition Tusch, 1975), 9–37; subsequently cited as Nebehay, *Ver Sacrum*.

3. Pevsner's classic work, *Pioneers of the Modern Movement* (London: Faber and Faber, 1936) remains a clear summary of the early Modern Movement. The latest edition is Nicholas Pevsner, *Pioneers of Modern Design*, rev. ed. (Harmondsworth: Penguin Books, 1975).

4. U.S. National Archives Trust Fund Board to author, 12 August 1985. A search of passport applications for the years 1906 through 1911 found no reference to the names of Frank Lloyd Wright, Mamah B. Cheney, Frank Lloyd Wright, Jr., or Taylor Woolley. U.S. citizens leaving the country were not required to have passports until 1916.

5. *CDT*, 7 November 1909, pp. 1, 4. See also *CDT*, 8 November 1909, pp. 7, 9; Twombly, *Life and Architecture*, 91–92; 317 n. 5; 318 n. 8; and Manson, *Golden Age*, 212, n. 2.

6. *CDT*, 7 November 1909; also, quoted in Twombly, *Life and Work*, 91; 317 n. 5.

7. Catherine Wright continued: "E. C. Waller, Arthur Heurtley, and Hamlin Garland—these are the men who are his friends. They know his makeup, his disposition, what he has had to contend with" (*CDT* [7 November 1909], p. 4). Heurtley was another client (Wright designed two houses for him) as well as a friend who, however, dropped his friendship with Wright after 1910.

8. Ibid.

9. "Stoutly Defends Erring Husband," *CDT*, 8 November 1909, p. 7; "Cheney Champion of Runaway Wife," ibid., 9 November 1909, p. 7.

10. [Karl Baedeker] *Berlin und Umgebung*, 16th ed. (Leipzig: Karl Baedeker, 1910), 2, 52.

11. Hedda Adlon, *Hotel Adlon, the Life and Death of a Great Hotel* (New York: Horizon Press, 1960), 2

12. Ibid., 35.

13. For the exhibition, see *Allgemein Städtebau-Ausstellung. Literatur Verzeichnis* (Berlin: Ulstein & Co. [1910?]). For the impact of the exhibition, see Rosemarie Haag Bletter, "Expressionism and the New Objectivity," *Art Journal* 43, no. 2, (1983): 108–20; and for a thorough discussion of its context, see Christiane C. Collins, "A Visionary Discipline: Werner Hegemann and the Quest for the Pragmatic Ideal," *Center. A Journal for Architecture in America* 5 (1989): 74–85; subsequently cited as Collins, "Practical Ideal."

14. Möhring also won second prize in the Greater Berlin planning competition in 1910 with economist Rudolf Eberstadt and traffic engineer Richard Peterson; it secured Möhring's reputation as a planner. See Rudolf Eberstadt, Bruno Möhring, and Richard Peterson, *Ein Programm für die Planung einer neuzeitlichen Gross-Stadt* (Berlin: Ernst Wasmuth A.G., 1910). Möhring was also a founder of the monthly journal *Stadtbaukunst* and a director of the Arbeitsgemeinschaft der Freien Deutschen Akadamien des Städtebaus (Th.-B., 25, p. 1).

15. Ernst Wasmuth, ed. *Führer durch die allgemeine Städtebau-Ausstellung in Berlin in 1910* (Berlin: [Ernst Wasmuth, A.G., 1910]), and Werner Hegemann, ed. *Der Städtebau nach den Ergebnissen der allgemeinen Städtebau-Ausstellung in Berlin*, 2 vols. (Berlin: E. Wasmuth, A.G., 1911–13).

Hegemann not only played a key role in the development of city planning, he was also in a unique position later as a commentator on Wright's work, particularly when in 1922 he became chief editor of the periodical *Wasmuth's Monatshefte für Baukunst*. The exhibition of the Greater Berlin competition had already been anticipated by American city planners in 1909. Hegemann's perspective was instructive because he had the dual exposure to developments in Germany and in America, where he studied and worked intermittently from 1904 to 1909, in 1913 on a lecture tour, and from 1916 to 1922.

16. Frederic C. Howe published a widely read article on the planning exhibition, "City Building in Germany," *Scribners' Magazine*, in 1910 (Collins, "Practical Ideal," 81). The exhibition also received attention in the United States when reports were published in September 1910 in *American City* 3 (September 1910): 120–24; ibid. 7 (September 1910): 73–92, pls. 38–55.

17. *Ausstellung amerikanischer Kunst*, Königliche Akademie der Künste in Berlin, essay by Christian Brinton, organized and edited by Kuno Francke (Berlin: F. Bruckmann, 1910); *Ausstellung amerikanischer Kunst* (Munich: n.p., 1910).

18. Baedeker, *Berlin*, 47.

19. Ibid., 48.

20. William Marlin to author, personal communication, 25 February 1987. Wright relayed his enthusiasm about Schinkel to Edward Waller, Jr. Waller was one of the few people to whom Wright wrote while he was in Europe, describing his experiences there. Unfortunately, Waller's correspondence is unavailable for research.

21. FLW to TW, 20 July 1910, UUL. Wright suggested that his draftsman Taylor Woolley make a particular effort to see Potsdam while visiting Berlin.

22. Signed sketches were dated 1908 (Buddensieg, *Industriekultur*, 273; See also Anderson, "Behrens," 473. Illustrations of the factory began to be widely published in Germany by February 1910. See, for example, Peter Behrens, "Der Turbinenhalle der A.E.G. zu Berlin," *Deutsche Techniker Zeitung* 27, no. 6 (12 February 1910): 87–90; and

idem, *Mitteilungen des Rheinischen Vereins für Denkmalpflege und Heimatschutz* 4, no. 1 (1 March 1910): 26–29. Both are cited in Buddensieg, *Industriekultur*, 273.

23. Francesco Passanti, who is conducting research on Le Corbusier after World War I, provided the author with unpublished information on Jeanneret's activities in 1910 and 1911 (cited as Passanti to author, personal communication, 26 January 1987). According to Passanti, Jeanneret began using the pseudonym Le Corbusier in 1920 when he started signing his articles in *L'Esprit Nouveau*.

24. Walter Gropius, who had come to work in the Behrens studio in late 1907, was still there during Wright's stay in Berlin (Walter Gropius, *Apollo in der Demokratie*, cited in Anderson, "Behrens," p. 470; Reginald R. Isaacs, *Walter Gropius: Der Mensch und Sein Werk*, vol. 1 [Berlin: Gebrüder Mann Verlag, 1983], 90–91). Differences over work on the Cuno House caused Gropius to consider leaving the Behrens office in March 1910. But Gropius's birthday was celebrated at the office on 18 May; he left by June (Anderson, "Behrens," 474).

Mies van der Rohe was at the Behrens studio during much of the same time. However, he had come to work for Behrens in October 1908, departed in late 1909, and returned in late 1910 (Franz Schulze, *Mies van der Rohe, A Critical Biography* [Chicago and London: University of Chicago Press, 1985], 38–41).

Jeanneret was in Berlin twice in 1910, once between 9 June and 20 June, to visit current exhibitions, and again on 18 October just prior to beginning work in the Behrens office, where he remained until April 1911. He had come from Munich to Berlin to see the Universal City Planning Exhibition and the Ton-Kalk-Cement exhibition on building materials (Francesco Passanti to author, personal communication, 26 January 1987). In Berlin during his summer visit, he also attended a reception given by Muthesius for the Werkbund Congress. He began work in the Behrens office on 1 November 1910. This new information gives greater precision to Schulze's comment (Schulze, *Mies*, 41) that Jeanneret was in Behrens's office in the second half of 1910.

25. The original source of Mies's remark is his "Tribute to Frank Lloyd Wright," *Collegiate Art Journal* 6 (1946): 41–42. Mies's questionable recollection of events thirty-five years earlier is further undermined by his conflating of an exhibition with the publication, as is apparent in the full citation of his comments: "At this moment [1910], so critical for us there came to Berlin the exhibition of the work of Frank Lloyd Wright. This comprehensive display and the extensive publication of his works enabled us really to become acquainted with the achievement of the architect. The encounter was destined to prove of great significance to the development of architecture in Europe." Möhring's presentation was only a partial display of Wright works— not "comprehensive"—and the publication was not available until the following year.

26. Van der Rohe, "Tribute," 42.

27. Isaacs stated that in 1910 Gropius and his mother attended an exhibition of one hundred drawings at the Akadamie der Künste in Berlin, with Wright present (Isaacs, *Gropius*, 1: 96). No documentation for this statement has been uncovered. In 1931, however, Wright's work was exhibited at the Berlin Academy of Fine Arts ("Frank Lloyd Wright Ausstellung in der Akademie der Künste, Berlin," *Bauwelt* 22 [2 July 1931]: 914). This latter exhibition is the only confirmed presentation of Wright's work in Germany after 1910.

28. "Beilage für Vereine. Berichte über Versammlungen und Besichtigungen," *Deutsche Bauzeitung* 44, no. 79 (1 October 1910): 641; subsequently cited as "Beilage für Vereine." Robert Sweeney generously brought this article to the attention of the author.

29. Vereinigung Berliner Architekten, *Anregungen zur Erlangung von Gross-Berlin* . . . (Berlin: A.G. Wasmuth, 1907). In 1907, after two years of discussion, the Union had joined with other groups of architects to set up the important competition for the Greater Berlin Exhibition, which opened in 1910.

30. The back matter of the *Sonderheft* (European edition) contained advertising as well as a list of the publications by Wasmuth, including the *Berliner Architekturwelt. Zeitschrift für Baukunst, Malerei und Kunstgewerbe*. It was a monthly, started in 1897, edited by Ernst Spindler and Bruno Möhring, with the cooperation of the Vereinigung Berliner Architekten.

31. The Union of Berlin Architects (Vereinigung Berliner Architekten) was formed in 1879 from the Architekten-Verein zu Berlin, to which it remained connected. The founding members included distinguished historians as well as Martin Gropius, a celebrated architect and the uncle of Walter Gropius. By 1904 the association had over two hundred members. Their winter meetings were frequent, and the topics presented were carefully recorded. Although its historical role has been little recognized, the Union was an active participant in the architectural life of Berlin and curious about developments elsewhere.

Nina Nedeljkov kindly provided me with information and source material on the Union of Berlin Architects. My brief account of the Union comes from the monograph of K. E. O. Fritsch, *Vereinigung Berliner Architekten*, (Berlin: 1905) and T. Stübben, "Aus der Geschichte des Architekten-Vereins zu Berlin," in *Hundert Jahre Architekten Verein zu Berlin, 1824–1924* (Berlin: Wilhelm Ernst and Son, 1924), 7–12, 20.

32. The report was of the ninth meeting of the Union of Berlin Architects, "Beilage für Vereine. Berichte über Versammlungen und Besichtigungen," *Deutsche Bauzeitung* 44, no. 79 (1 October 1910), p. 641: Hr. Möhring hatte im Sitzungssaal eine Anzahl Zeichnungen und Entwürfe des Architekten Frank Wright aus Chicago ausgestellt, zu denen er in kurzen Zügen einige Erläuterungen gab. Redner wies auf die Feinheit der Zeichnungen Frank Wrights, der kein Akademiker, sondern Selfmademan im wahrsten Sinne des Wortes sei, hin. Es liege Poesie in seinen Entwürfen. . . . Mr. Möhring exhibited in the meeting hall a collection of drawings and projects by the architect Frank Lloyd Wright from Chicago about which he gave a few remarks. Redner noted the refinement of the drawings of Wright, who is not an academic but a self-made man in the truest sense of the word. [He suggested] there is poetry in his designs. . . . [Trans. by author])

33. The group appears to have been active from about 1898 to 1914, and at its meetings shared information about competitions and discussed contemporary work. The group did publish material for suggestions on planning in Berlin in anticipation of the Universal Planning Exhibition.

34. Delegates of the Union of Berlin Architects in 1908 were the architects H. Hofman, H. Jansen; the government architects F. Körte, B. Möhring, R. Wolffenstein; and the private architect H. Kayser (*Bericht über den VIII. Internationalen Architekten-Kongress Wien 1908* [Vienna: Schroll, 1909]).

35. In order to impress Woolley with the appeal in Europe of the publications, Wright informed him that by "last January" [1911] there were fifty-eight German subscriptions, an encouraging number according to Wright because "no one of the subscribers has seen anything of the work" (FLW to Taylor Woolley, 22 April [1911], the Taylor Woolley Papers, Accession No. 152, Manuscripts Division, Special Collections Department, University of Utah Libraries, Salt Lake City, Utah. This collection will be referred to as UUL).

From Wright's comment it is clear that there was anticipation of his work, but architects in Europe significantly had no access to the plates of the monograph before January 1911. The arrival of the monographs in Chicago in middle or late June 1911 implies that their press run would have been finished at least six weeks prior to the arrival. The Wasmuth monograph, then, could have been available for sale in a quantity limited to Wasmuth's allotment by late April 1911. The figure of fifty-eight subscriptions varies from the figure of fifty-two given earlier to Darwin D. Martin.

36. Charles Jeanneret [Le Corbusier] to Auguste Perret, 30 [June] 1915, LC. MS 89, La Bibliothèque de la Ville, La Chaux-de-Fonds. Francesco Passanti generously provided information on Le Corbusier and a copy of Le Corbusier's letter; the original is a carbon copy in Le Corbusier's copybook. The war conditions between France and Germany prevented Perret from obtaining German architectural publications. Le Corbusier, therefore, sent Perret a letter along with a selection of books and periodicals that he, as a Swiss citizen, could still obtain. Wright's work was the first on the list: "J'ai fait venir pour vous, les maisons americaines de Lloyd Wright dont je vous avais parlé (M[arks] 2.25)" Ibid.

37. Wright stated that only around 1924 did he hear of Gropius, Mies, Walter Curt Behrendt, and later, Erich Mendelsohn, who came to visit Wright in Taliesin (FLW, *A Testament*, 84–85).

38. Ibid., 18.

39. "Quando venni in Europa nel 1909 me interessava un solo architetto: Joseph Maria Olbrich, per la sua opera a Darmstadt" ("'L'architettura' riceve F. Ll. Wright," *L'architettura* 2 [1956]: 398).

40. FLW, *A Testament*, 84.

41. Olbrich's work, *Architektur von Olbrich*, 2 vols. (Berlin: Ernst Wasmuth A.G. 1904), was published in the same series as Wright's monograph. The work was originally intended to contain six volumes with 450 plates and forty-nine inserts, to be issued in three series in thirty parts from 1901 to 1913; a third volume appeared in 1914. After publishing his architectural monograph, Wasmuth issued Olbrich's *Neue Gärten von Olbrich. Der Farbengarten aus einem Vortrag anlässlich der XVIII Hauptversammlung Deutscher Gartenkünstler*, (1905).

42. Advertising prospectus, *Ausgeführte Bauten und Entwürfe von Frank Lloyd Wright*, n.p., n.d., TAL.

43. Olbrich's works are published in the following: Joseph Maria Olbrich *Architektur von Olbrich*, 3 vols. (Berlin: Ernst Wasmuth; A.G.,

1901–14); reprinted as *Joseph Maria Olbrich. Architecture*, with texts by Peter Haiko and Bernd Krimmel and catalogue by Renate Ulmer (New York: Rizzoli, 1988), cited as *Olbrich Architecture*; Hessischen Landesmuseum, ed., *Joseph M. Olbrich. 1867–1908, Das Werk des Architekten*, (Darmstadt: Hessischen Landesmuseum, 1967), cited as *Olbrich* (1967); Ian Latham, *Joseph Maria Olbrich* (New York: Rizzoli, 1980), cited as Latham, *Olbrich*; and Bernd Krimmel and Sabine Michaelis, eds., *Joseph M. Olbrich 1867–1908* (Darmstadt: Matildenhöhe, 1983), cited as *Olbrich* (1983).

44. Latham, *Olbrich*, 50.

45. Under the patronage of the grand duke, Olbrich was able to create an ensemble that gained wide attention in Germany and Austria. Between 1900 and 1902, Olbrich designed several buildings for the colony on the Matildenhöhe: the Ernst Ludwig House, a communal studio building, and houses for himself and other members of the colony, including Ludwig Habich, J. Glückert, Veiters, and Keller, as well as a double house. Peter Behrens also designed buildings for the colony. See W. Fred, "The Artist Colony at Darmstadt," *The Studio* 24 (1902): 22–30, and idem, "The Work of Prof. J. M. Olbrich," in ibid., 91–100.

In 1904, Olbrich designed a group of three houses—a corner house, a "blue" house, and a "gray" house. But the most eye-catching for Wright would have been Olbrich's Ernst Ludwig Haus and the Wedding Tower, commemorating the grand duke's wedding in 1905 and completed after three years' work in 1908 (*Olbrich*, [1983], 222).

46. Scully, Introduction, *Nature of Frank Lloyd Wright*, xx.

47. Vincent Scully, Foreword to *Studies and Executed Buildings by Frank Lloyd Wright* (New York: Rizzoli, 1986), 7.

48. Historic photographs, such as the illustration from the festspiel *Das Zeichen* give a distorted impression of the length of the building (*Olbrich* [1983], 151; *Olbrich Architecture*, 23 and fig. 2). The building is 47.82 meters long (156.8 feet) and 12.63 meters wide (41.4 feet). For the plan, see *Olbrich Architecture*, fig. 5.

49. *Olbrich Architecture*, fig. 3.

50. Quoted in Latham, *Olbrich*, 103.

51. Fred, "Olbrich," 92.

52. Rudolph Bosselt sculpted the bronze figures (*Olbrich Architecture*, 23). For Wright's interest in winged victories and other classical sculpture, see Chapter 6. Beyond the entry, the interior of the central entrance hall was covered with allegorical murals.

53. The elevations of Olbrich's own house had a band of blue and white tiles, the motif of the square (*Macmillan Encyclopedia*, s.v. "Olbrich," 3, p. 316). Clark states that Olbrich and Hoffmann borrowed the quadrat motif from Mackintosh; I will examine the question of the motif's origins in Chapter 7.

54. FLW to TW, 20 July 1910, UUL. Wright had specific traveling advice for his draftsman Taylor Woolley, advice which he may well have gained from his own travels: see the sights of Berlin, particularly Potsdam, then descend the Rhine from Cologne to Coblenz and travel on to Paris. Wright added in the same letter, "The Rhein [*sic*] must be very lovely at this time of year."

55. William Marlin to author, personal correspondence, 14 July 1988. Marlin's information comes from a letter from Frances to FLW.

Lloyd and John Wright confirmed this information in interviews with Marlin.

56. William Marlin to author, personal correspondence, 18 October 1988. Marlin's information comes from an undated letter formerly in the possession of Wright's daughter Frances.

57. These events had been reported in American newspapers for several days until 12 February 1910. See *New York Times*, 22 January 1910, p. 1, for reports of damage from the floods; the newspaper is subsequently cited as *NYT*.

58. FLW, *An Autobiography* (1977 ed.), 392. Wright placed the event during the third week after leaving his home in Oak Park, but collateral evidence above establishes the date as January 1910, approximately twelve weeks after his departure from Oak Park. See also John Lloyd Wright, *My Father Who Is on Earth* (New York: G. P. Putnam's Sons, 1946), 56.

59. TW to Blossom Holm [Woolley's daughter], 2 July 1955. Peter Goss provided the author with a copy of this unpublished letter.

60. The publisher Eberhard von Bodenhausen wrote to Count Harry Graf Kassler, diarist and supporter of the art museum in Weimar, of Ellen Key's popularity at the turn of the century (see Hans-Ulrich Simon, ed., *Eberhard von Bodenhausen, Harry Graf Kessler: ein Briefwechsel, 1894–1918* [Marbach am Neckar: Deutschen Literaturarchiv, 1978], 50–52, 152).

In Vienna, Franz Cizek, an innovator in art education for children, acknowledged the significance of Key's work. Cizek, who was close to members of the Secession, noted the significance of Key's *Das Jahrhundert des Kindes*, 4th German ed. (Berlin: S. Fischer, 1903). See *Franz Cizek, Pionier der Kunstlerziehung (1865–1946)*, (Vienna: Museum of the City, 1985), 33.

61. TW to Blossom Holm, 2 July 1955. Wright informed Darwin D. Martin that Cheney had been making her own living, teaching German pupils in English (FLW to DDM, 22 November 1910, SUNYB). The specific length of her stay in Sweden is unknown.

62. Wright's presence in Florence is established in FLW to CRA, 31 March 1910, Ashbee Collection, TAL.

63. "After some time, in Germany, Father wired funds for me to join him in Italy. A draughtsman who had been in his employ for several years named Woolley was already there" (Lloyd Wright to Linn Cowles, 3, this and subsequent citations are to the copy at TAL). Peter Goss states that Woolley preceded Lloyd Wright by four months (Lecture, annual meeting, Society of Architectural Historians, Chicago, 1988).

64. A previous recommendation was dated June 1909, and stated that Woolley had worked for Wright for one year and was "conscientious and capable of good work" (FLW to anon., June 1909, UUL). Taylor Woolley (1884–1965) was born and died in Salt Lake City, Utah. His obituary in the UUL collection stated that he managed an office for Frank Lloyd Wright in Detroit after their return from Europe, but the location, without confirmation, is an error.

Peter Goss graciously showed me his unpublished article, "Taylor Woolley and the Preparation of Frank Lloyd Wright's Wasmuth Portfolio," and generously shared his thoughts about Woolley.

65. Lloyd Wright had enrolled in the University of Wisconsin,

as his father had done, in the fall of 1907 to study engineering and agronomy.

66. "Though this work in Italy would break into my college year of 1910, Father felt the experience would be worth it to me in more ways than one—it was indeed!" (Lloyd Wright to Linn Cowles, 4).

67. Gebhard and Von Breton, *Lloyd Wright*, 17, give Lloyd's departure date as early November 1909, but from collateral evidence this appears to be too early.

68. Lloyd Wright to Linn Cowles, 3 February 1966, TAL, 4. The exact location of the villino "Fortuna" is unknown, but, according to Elaine and Kevin Harrington, south of the Lungarno Serristori is a restaurant called The Nunnery, which may refer to the nunnery that Lloyd Wright mentioned (Elaine Harrington to Karen Wilson, 27 March 1992). Diagonally across from the restaurant is a small residence formed around a narrow courtyard, but I have not confirmed that this was Wright's residence.

69. Lloyd Wright to Linn Cowles, 4.

70. Gebhard and Von Breton, *Lloyd Wright*, 17.

71. For a discussion of the preparation of the Wasmuth plates and Wright's reliance on photographs, see H. Allan Brooks, "Frank Lloyd Wright and the Wasmuth Drawings, *Art Bulletin* 48, no. 2, (June 1966): 193–202.

72. Lloyd Wright to Linn Cowles, 4. Daniel Urrabieta y Vierge (1851–1904) was born and studied in Madrid and went to Paris in 1869 where he became an illustrator for newspapers and books. He generally signed his work "Vierge." He provided illustrations for books of Victor Hugo, a favorite of Wright's: *L'Année terrible* (1874), *Les Travailleurs de la Mer* (1876), *L'Homme qui Rit* (1877), *Quatre-vingt-treize* (1877), *Les Misérables* (1882), and *Notre Dame de Paris* (1882). See Th,-B, 34, s.v. "Vierge, Daniel." His watercolors, gouache sketches, crayon drawings, and engravings varied in stylistic presentation depending on their medium of publication. The many figural studies include humorous and satirical depictions of his subjects, and his work was not particularly architectural in character, with some exceptions, such as a view of Notre Dame.

The appeal of Vierge's work to Wright may have been in the loose character of his line drawings. Figures were often drawn with a crayon that appears to soften the surfaces of its subjects, and his line drawings frequently showed rapid, jerky movements of the pen that convey vitality to their subjects. The line quality of Vierge's etchings may have had particular appeal to Wright. The strokes of the engravings create effects of chiaroscuro and mass, yet each stroke retained its individual identity, much the way that a woodcut print retains the memory of the stroked cuts of which its image was formed.

73. Lloyd Wright to Linn Cowles, 4.

74. Hoffmann, *Robie House*, 25–26.

75. *The Studio*, among other art journals, had long used the practice of placing a tissue sheet with the artist's name over the color reproduction of artwork. The magazine included its own monogram embossed in the lower right corner of the plate.

76. Lloyd Wright stated that after one trip his father claimed to have met Brahms and was disappointed in the musician's stature (Lloyd Wright to Linn Cowles, 4). Brahms, however, had died in 1897.

77. Ibid., 5.

78. *Florence and Its Environs. Treves Handbook* (Milan: Fratelli Treves, 1902), 171.

79. Guthrie's house, designed in 1908 for construction in Sewanee, Tennessee, was built in 1909 in Wilmette, Illinois, for Wright's next client, Frank Baker (Manson, *Golden Age*, 178). Wright published the project in the Wasmuth folios as pl. LXI. He later designed Guthrie's church, St. Mark's-in-the-Bouwerie in New York City, which was not built.

80. William Norman Guthrie to FLW, 1 May 1910, TAL. Quotations in the text immediately following are from this letter.

81. Wright wrote a standing recommendation for Woolley's professional abilities from Fiesole on 16 June 1910, and stated that Woolley had worked for Wright "for something over two years." He commended Woolley for having ability, good character, and skill with the pen (FLW to TW, 16 June 1910, UUL). Wright wrote a previous recommendation for Woolley in June 1909 (UUL).

82. The details of Lloyd Wright's travels may be reliable, but the date of completion for the Wasmuth drawings is not. In the Gebhard and Von Breton account Lloyd stated (*Lloyd Wright*, 17) that the drawings were finished by early February, 1910, a date that is refuted by the correspondence between Wright and Ashbee and Wright and Woolley. Wright's correspondence with Woolley implies that Lloyd and Woolley's travels occurred later and that the entire description is skewed by a matter of months.

83. Lloyd Wright gave the date of travel as early April, and the date of meeting his father in Paris as May (Gebhard and Von Breton, *Lloyd Wright*, 17–18). Extant correspondence makes the date of April too early; May is possible, but unlikely.

84. Lloyd provided no date in his account to Linn Cowles (Lloyd Wright to Linn Cowles, 4). Internal evidence, however, concerning the completion of his role in preparing the Wasmuth plates, his travels with Woolley, and Woolley's arrival in Paris in mid-July 1910, implies that the visit occurred during the summer. No record of the date of Lloyd Wright's return has yet appeared; it would, at least, help establish the date of departure and the meeting between father and son in Paris.

Frank Lloyd Wright said that in the third week after he left his home in Oak Park he had wandered about Paris (JLW, *My Father*, 56). This date, which would be late October 1909, is inconsistent with other evidence, and may be an error in Wright's recollection. In particular, Mamah Cheney would still have been with him, thus alleviating somewhat the possibilities of a deep depression.

85. Lloyd Wright to Linn Cowles, 5.

86. Ibid.

87. Lloyd Wright had intended to go to England, but his father had insufficient funds to send him, so he returned to the United States, heading first to Chicago and then to Brookline, Massachusetts, where the Olmsted firm was located (ibid., 6). Gebhard and Von Breton add (*Lloyd Wright*, 18) that, without money to continue his education, he worked at the Harvard Herbarium. After a few months he began work as a draftsman at Olmsted and Olmsted, which was engaged on a project for the Chicago waterfront.

88. Lloyd Wright informed Narciso Menocal that he and his father had stayed at the Ritz (Narciso Menocal, interview with author, 22 August 1985, Madison, Wisconsin; subsequently cited as Menocal, Interview). The director of the Ritz informed the author that its records of visitors c. 1910 disappeared between the wars (personal communication, 19 September 1985, Paris).

89. Construction of Perret's controversial design for the Théatre des Champs Elysées began in the year following Wright's visit.

90. The design for the Petit Palais was held as a competition by decree of 18 November 1895 for the Exposition Universelle of 1900. In another example of cross-cultural flow, the Universal Exhibition was modeled on the World's Columbian Exposition of 1893 in Chicago (*Chicago Architecture*, 468). Charles Girault won first prize for the building. Construction started 15 October 1897 for an opening date of April 1900. The Petit Palais exhibited a retrospective of French art. It was built of reinforced concrete to help support the considerable weight of its dome. On 2 March 1901 it became the city's museum of fine arts, and was restored after alterations to its interior in 1935. For a discussion of the building and its collections, see Henri Lapauze, *Le Palais des Beaux-Arts de la Ville de Paris* (Paris: L. Laveur, 1910.) For illustrations, a brief history, and discussion of its art collection, see Sophie de Bussierre, *La Grande Galerie Nord. Histoire et Décor*, Petit Palais Dossier No. 3, (Paris: Musées de la Ville de Paris, 1984).

91. Menocal, Interview.

92. In the southeast stairwell, beneath the work of Puvis de Chavannes, the pattern of the floor was composed of gray and black glazed tiles. The same pattern was present on the level at the southeast corner (at ground level) between the present Galerie Zoubaloff and the Galerie Dutuit. The central square was rotated ninety degrees from the axes of the lattice, thus forming a superimposed pattern. Four hues of gray corresponded to the four layers of the pattern: one for the frame made by each square within a square, one for the cross containing the rotated central square, and one for the four corner squares; black was retained for the central rotated square itself. The same pattern was present at the southwest corner, beneath ancient stained-glass windows and the work of Pillemon and Hubert Robert.

These stairwells opened onto a double circuit of galleries, which gave access to the exterior and to an interior court. Some floors were oak parquet, set in a herringbone pattern. Where the pattern reversed direction, a rotated square was formed. Other floors had a lattice of ellipses in white, beige, ocher, pink, purple, and black tesserae similar to the elliptical pattern that Michelangelo designed for the Campodoglio in Rome. Segments of the ellipses were reversed in direction to form elongated diamonds. Color was integral to the manipulation of these forms.

93. The central rotunda, which contained the main entry and connected the two wings of the north gallery, had a different floor pattern: floral motives over designs, mostly a reflection of the ceiling plan of the vault.

94. Lloyd Wright to Linn Cowles, 6. After the work and travel were over, Wright joined Mamah Cheney in Fiesole, "where they stayed for several months" enjoying their view of Florence and the city itself.

95. Baedeker, *Italy*, 171. The electric tram to Fiesole, inaugurated

on 20 September 1890, was the first started in Europe ([Treves], *Florence*, p. 130).

Many of the 5,000 inhabitants of Fiesole itself made a living from straw plaiting, a common Florentine industry. On the piazza of the town were two inns: Albergo Aurora and Italia; a tea room was located on via San Francesco. On the piazza a one-horse carriage could be hired for the trip back to Florence. At the upper end was a monument to Victor Emmanuel and Garibaldi, an equestrian group by Calzolari finished in 1906. There was also the small Palazzo Preterio, dating from the thirteenth century, with a museum of antiquities where Etrusco-Roman monuments were placed after excavation.

Opposite the piazza towards the other end of town were Fiesole's ancient remains. The cathedral, founded in 1028, was one of the oldest and plainest in the Tuscan Romanesque style; it had been lately restored. Opposite the cathedral was an episcopal palace, Palazzo Vescovile, with a seminary for priests. Beyond it were fine views of Mugnone and an antique theater and the remains of a Roman temple. Lower down the hill on which these ruins were located were fragments of the town's ancient Etruscan wall. To the west, starting from the seminary, the Via San Francesco ascended to the old church of Sant'Alessandro, to beautiful views of the valley of Florence, and to the church of San Francesco, a Franciscan monastery that occupied the ancient Rocca, a powerful stronghold.

96. Edmund G. Gardner, *The Story of Florence* (London: J. M. Dent, 1908), 5.

97. FLW, *An Autobiography*, 164. Estero, referred to in this passage, was presumably the domestic.

98. See Peter Goss, "Wright's Fiesole Studio," *Frank Lloyd Wright Newsletter* 5, no. 1 (1982): 8. Viale Verde becomes Montececeri as the fork on Viale Verde ascends. Wright and Cheney's address at the side entry on the north side of the street is now number 6. The corner entry formerly had a heavy grape arbor which was removed during a recent remodeling.

99. According to Taylor Woolley's associate, Norman P. Hill, Woolley related in conversation that Mamah Borthwick (and Kuno Francke) influenced Wright's going to Europe (Norman P. Hill to Bruce Brooks Pfeiffer, 25 March 1984, TAL). Woolley implied that she worked with Wright, and Hill assumed she worked on the translation. This was further confirmed by the recollection of Woolley's son, Nathan.

100. Woolley lived with the couple until his departure from Italy (TW to Holm, 2 July 1955, UUL/Goss Collection).

101. Wright gave another retrospective account in a 1957 preface to the Wasmuth monograph of his life in Europe:

In Germany and Italy I lived and worked for a year. In the little Villino Belvedere of Fiesole, massive door of the villino opening directly upon the steep, narrow little Via Verdi of the ancient old Roman town on the hill above Florence—I found sanctuary. Just below the little villino spread downward to ancient Firenze the slope where so many distinguished refugees from foreign lands had found sanctuary and were still finding harbor. Most of that year—1910—I worked preparing the forthcoming publication in German, *Ausgeführte Bauten und Entwürfe*. . . . (*Buildings, Plans, and Designs*, preface and original introduction by Frank Lloyd Wright, foreword by William Wesley Peters (New York: Horizon Press, 1963)

102. FLW, *An Autobiography*, 165.

103. Prior to his sketches for the Villino Belvedere, Wright had designed two artists' studios. One was a house for an artist (F0311.001), which was published along with the plan of the Cheney House as pl. XXX in the Wasmuth monograph but was not identified in the table of contents. The other was a concrete studio for Wright's collaborator, the sculptor Richard Bock, published in the monograph as pls. LXII (a) and (b). Unless indicated otherwise, drawings cited in these notes are those at TAL and are indicated by "F" plus the accession number.

104. For the right side entry, see F1005.001 and F1005.003; for the left side, see F1005.002 and F1005.004.

105. Wright suggested that if Griffin were unhappy with the prints he collect and return them, and Wright would repay Griffin the money he spent plus 6 percent interest and 20 percent profit. This offer was made despite Wright's realization that the prints were worth more, but that was all he could then afford. Wright took Griffin's discontent as a personal wound at a time when things were not going well: "There is as anyone knows, enough at once [?] unfortunate and true in my life without going into the ill will of men I once trusted for more than is true." Wright concluded by saying that he would return on September 1 and that Griffin would have his money. Written in ire, the letter was not sent; Woolley somehow retained it in his possession. (FLW to Walter Burley Griffin, 10 June 1910, UUL. Written from Villino Belvedere, Fiesole; with addressed and unposted envelope.)

106. FLW to CRA, 31 March 1910, Ashbee Collection, TAL.

107. Bruce Brooks Pfeiffer stated that Catherine Wright was ejected from her school when the scandal with her father and Mamah Cheney became public (Pfeiffer to author, personal communication).

108. FLW to CRA, 31 March 1910, Ashbee Collection, TAL.

109. FLW to CRA, 8 July 1910, Crawford, "Ten Letters," 66–67, written from Villino Belvedere, Fiesole. Wright also mentioned that the budget received from "the office" included two items for which Ashbee required payment; Wright wrote that he enclosed a check, but, according to Ashbee's reply of 15 July 1910, it was not included.

110. FLW to CRA, 8 July 1910, Crawford, "Ten Letters," 66–67.

111. Ibid., 67. William Dean Howells (1837–1920) had written *Tuscan Cities* (Boston: Ticknor, 1886) and earlier, *Italian Journey*, 9th ed. (Boston and New York: Houghton Mifflin, 1896), but the latter omitted Florence. Ruskin's works are too familiar to need citation here. Giorgio Vasari's *Vita* had also recently been published in translation: *Lives of Seventy of the Most Eminent Painters, Sculptors and Architects*, ed. and annotated by E. H. Blashfield, E. W. Blashfield, and A. A. Hopkins, 4 vols. (New York: Scribner's Sons, 1907). Prior to his departure in 1909 Wright also read Goethe's *Letters from Italy* (William Marlin to author, personal correspondence, 29 October 1988.)

Wright also remarked that it was curious he had not heard up to that time directly of his daughter's visit. Apparently there were problems with the mails in Florence: "A letter my son wrote went to the dead letter office I learned from him the other day" (FLW to CRA, 8 July 1910. Ashbee Journals, TAL).

112. FLW to TW, 20 July 1910, UUL, written from the Villino Belvedere in Fiesole. Wright replied to Woolley, who by that time had traveled on to Paris.

113. The drawing of the Harley Bradley House (monograph, pl. XXII) was traced from a photograph that also appeared in the *Sonderheft* (American edition, 25).

114. FLW to TW, 20 July 1910, UUL. Dorn's identity is established by his name appearing in an advertisement for the *Berliner Künstlerhefte* and *Sonderhefte zu Architektur des XX, Jahrhunderts*, in *Berliner Architekturwelt*, 15 (1912): 504. He was responsible for the editorial staff.

115. For a biography of Thayer, see Carol Shankel, *Sallie Casey Thayer and Her Collection* (Lawrence, Kan.: University of Kansas Museum of Art, 1976).

116. Lloyd confirmed that Martin and Little helped finance the cost of the trip to Germany (Lloyd Wright to Linn Cowles, 6).

117. CRA to FLW, 15 July 1910, Ashbee journals, TAL. Ashbee responded to Wright's evocation of Fiesole by recalling his own stay there, and compared Florence to the wool cities of the Cotswold hills. Ashbee also informed Wright that his daughter Catherine, whose visit had been anticipated, had not yet come to England. For Ashbee in Florence, see Virginia Woolf, *Roger Fry* (1940), 71, noted in Crawford, "Ten Letters," 72 n. 18.

118. In his reply, Wright provided Ashbee with his most explicit description of the publishing venture to that date:

You know I have been engaged here in the preparation of drawings—for a representative monograph of my work. About 73 buildings are shown by plans and perspective drawings in about 100 plates. The work is in Wasmuth's hands and so far I have had 12 proofs. I am to own this work outright—and have bought it because I believe it will be profitable and there is no cleaner way for an architect to find his money than in the sale of his works in this way. I have a contract for 1000 copies. Their work is very good—lithography—I must acknowledge, but their slow movements drive me to desperation. The German mind is a ponderous affair I find. I thought of giving them up and asking you to help me find someone else but they are doing a little better and I will wait with what patience I can command. "I must be patient" is a phrase the Italians use continually—and I will adopt it. I will send you a proof or two so you may judge of the scope of the work and its character although the better things have not yet been reached. I should like your criticism too. The work is to be in portfolio—the text inserted in loose form in a pocket inside. The plates to carry thin paper cover-sheets with the plans—floor plans—printed on them. There will be some plates printed in grey on cream colored paper, some in sepia on cream—others in grey or sepia on grey paper with white tinted walls—or sky. It is rather large—they employ their largest stones—but I am sick of over-reduction and yearn for a face-full in each project. In addition to this—or rather before I undertook it—they had written me—in America for material for a Sonderheft to appear in a regular series now in publication. This material to consist wholly of photographs of actual work and plans. Some of the photographs wanted could not be obtained until a month ago and on this account I am told this portion of the work must go over to the beginning of next year. This work was their enterprise—but I counted on the two appearing together. The monograph giving the office-ideal—the architect's rendering of his vision—his scheme graphically proposed in his own manner—the Sonderheft, the photographs, of the results in brick and mortar. The article on the work was to have been written by some German in Cologne whom I do not know.

I am tempted to take this out of their hands if I can honestly do so—and give it to someone else or own this [the *Sonderheft*] too—myself—it would be more profitable I think than the monograph—and wonder what publishing house in London perhaps, or in Germany, beside Wasmuth could undertake it on short notice. Do you know of one?

(FLW to CRA, 24 July 1910, Crawford, "Ten Letters," 67–69. The letter had been returned to Wright for lack of postage.)

119. Ibid.

120. Ibid.

121. FLW to CRA, 24 July 1910, TAL. This excerpt was omitted from Crawford's publication of the letter in "Ten Letters," p. 68. Wright discussed the possibility of meeting his daughter Catherine at Ashbee's and taking her back with him in late September, but she did not go to England.

122. FLW to CRA, 24 July 1910, Ashbee Journals, in Crawford, "Ten Letters," 68–69.

123. FLW to DDM, n.d. [summer 1910], SUNYB. The event was presented only every ten years, thus Wright could have seen it only in the summer of 1910. Wright later wrote that he was moved by "the great teacher at the Passion play at Oberammergau." This letter is one of the few documents for this period in the Wright-Martin correspondence in the Buffalo collection that is not an original manuscript. The letter is a photocopy of original correspondence obtained by Darwin R. Martin, son of Darwin D. Martin, from Emma K. Martin, as indicated in a note, dated 20 June 1978, appended to the letter. The appended note states that the original letter is in the possession of Carolyn Mann Brackett. In the letter Wright stated he saw the performance "last summer," which would have placed Wright in Europe in 1910 and indicates that the letter was written after his return to America.

124. Herbert Koch, archivist in the Magistratsabteilung of the Vienna Stadt-und Landesarchiv, thoroughly searched the records of the Meldezettel, the official register of foreigners, on the author's behalf. No registration was found for Wright or Mamah Borthwick Cheney (Herbert Koch to author, 23 September, 1985; idem, 13 December 1985). The records were begun in 1910, the year of Wright's visit, and may not be complete.

125. See Chapter 6 for a discussion of Wright and Franz Metzner.

126. There are several accounts of the demise of the Secession. See, for example, Nebehay, *Ver Sacrum* (1977), 164.

127. [Karl Baedeker] *Austria-Hungary with Excursions to Cetinje, Belgrade, and Bucharest. Handbook for Travelers by Karl Baedeker*, 11th. ed. rev. (Leipzig: Karl Baedeker; London: T. Fisher Unwin; New York: Charles Scribner's Sons, 1911), 20. For a review of the literature on Vienna, see Christiane C. Collins, "Vienna 1900 and the Ideology of Gesamtkunst-werk," *Design Book Review* (Winter 1986): 28–33.

128. For a synopsis of cultural events, see *Traum und Wirklichkeit, Wien, 1870–1930*, 2d ed. (Vienna: Museum of the City of Vienna, 1985), 770–71.

129. *Ausstellung Österreichischer Kunstgewerbe 1910–1911*, K. K. Österreichisches Museum für Kunst und Industrie (Vienna: The Museum, 1910); subsequently cited as *Ausstellung Kunstgewerbe 1910–1911*. Included with the list of 2,383 items were prices. Among the artists were Gustav Klimt (p. 93), and Karl Moll (p. 96).

130. *Führer durch die Ausstellung des neusten Internationalen Wohnungskongress in Wien*, May 1910, in the K. K. Österreichisches Mu-

seum für Kunst und Industrie (Vienna: Verlag Kongresskomittee [1910]).

131. The Museum für Kunst und Industrie is now the Museum für angewandte Kunst.

132. *Ausstellung schwedischer Volkskunst und Hausindustrie*, K. K. Österreichisches Museum für Kunst und Industrie (Vienna: [The Museum], 1910).

133. The correspondence in 1915 between Wright and Alfonso Iannelli, concerning the role of sculpture at Midway Gardens and the sculptures' associations with Vienna will be discussed in Chapter 6.

134. Latham, *Olbrich*, 31–32.

135. Baedeker, *Austria* (1911), 51.

136. The hieroglyph representing the Secession Building entry has been described as the symbol of the sun conjunct with the earth. See Otto Kapfinger and Adolf Krischanitz, *Die Wiener Secession* (Vienna, Cologne, and Graz: Böhlau 1986), 1: 141.

137. "There I conceived the germ of that contempt with which I face clumsy pieces of work that are concerned with everything but with warmth, with the heart" (Joseph M. Olbrich, "Das Haus der Secession," *Der Architeckt* 5 [1899]: 5, quoted in Latham, *Olbrich*, 18).

138. Scully, Introduction, *Nature of Frank Lloyd Wright*, xix, xx.

139. Quinan's analysis shows a different development, through the work of Richard Bock (*Larkin Building*, 88–91).

140. For the definitive catalogue of the architecture of Otto Wagner (1841–1918), see Otto Antonia Graf, *Otto Wagner. Das Werk des Architekten*, vols. 1, 2 (Vienna, Cologne, Graz: Böhlau, 1985), subsequently cited as Graf, *Wagner*.

141. John Lloyd Wright to Otto Wagner, 30 March 1913, private collection. This request to study with Wagner was written in schoolboy German from the office of Harrison Albright in Los Angeles. When John asked his father's advice, Wright discouraged him from going. A translation of the text of John's letter to Wagner follows:

Mr. Otto Wagner, Architect
Vienna, Austria

Most honorable sir,

Your esteemed address I received through my father Frank Lloyd Wright, and allow me at this time to ask you if you have a position open in your highly respected house.

I am 21 years old, have a few years of practical experience in architecture and would gladly be prepared to send you drawing[s] or photographs, which will give you a sense of my abilities.

Respectfully yours,

John Lloyd Wright

March 30, 1913

142. Otto Antonia Graf, "Instructions from Imhotep? WW—Wagner from Vienna and Wright from Chicago," in *Frank Lloyd Wright, Architectural Drawings and Decorative Art*, 22. Wagner had the custom of telling his students every Monday morning about new books and periodicals. Karl Reinhart (b. 1890), who was a student of Wagner's in 1911–12 and 1912–13, was present when Wagner opened Wright's

picture book and made his assessment. Reinhart related the story to Graf. Reinhart was also the owner of a copy of the European edition of Wright's *Sonderheft* (Graf to author, personal communication, 3 May 1990).

143. William Wesley Peters, Wright's son-in-law and close associate, confirmed to the author that Wright and Hoffmann met in 1910 and for a second time in the 1937 when Wright, in Europe, was on his way to Russia (William Wesley Peters, interview with author, Scottsdale, Arizona, 12 January 1985). Sekler (*Hoffmann*, 236) cites only the later meeting and describes it occurring during Wright's return from Russia.

144. Wright also had the publications of the Vienna Werkstätte in the early 1900s (O. P. Reed, Jr., to author, personal communication).

145. See Sekler, *Hoffmann*, 322–25, for the catalogue entry and 116–20 for the textual discussion and additional illustrations. The pavilion was at the corner of Lothringerstrasse and Listztstrasse. Hoffmann designed the general plan, the entrance hall, and smaller court. A plan study was dated 28 February 1907, the first exhibition of Viennese art took place the following year, and the international exhibition was held in 1909.

146. For a brief discussion of Metzner's work, see Maria Pötzl-Malikova, ed., *Franz Metzner: ein Bildhauer der Jahrhundertwende in Berlin, Wien, Prag, Leipzig*, (Munich: Adalbert Stifter-Verein, 1977); subsequently cited as Pötzl-Malikova, *Metzner*. For the description of the second Kunstschau exhibition, see Otto Stoessl, *Die Fackel* 10, nos. 259–60 (13 July 1908), 29ff., in Pötzl-Malikova, *Metzner*, 33 n. 5.

147. See FLW to Alfonso Iannelli, 26 May 1915, Alfonso Iannelli Collection, folder 16, *CHS*, in Appendix B. I discuss Metzner and Wright's shared interest in sculpture in Chapter 6.

148. Notice was given that the building complex was to be pulled down as of 15 April 1909 (*Traum und Wirklichkeit, Wien, 1870–1930* (Vienna: Museum of the City of Vienna, 1985), 525. The Kunstschau was replaced by the Vienna Konzerthaus and the Hochschule für Musik und darstellende Kunst, but plans were not complete until May 1912 and the building only opened in October 1913. Thus, no new construction could have occurred during 1910. See *Die Kunstdenkmäler Wiens. Die Profanbauten des III. IV. und V. Bezirkes*, vol. 44 of Österreichische Kunsttopographie, Geza Hajos and Eckart Vancsa, eds. (Vienna: Verlag Anton Schroll, 1980), 87.

149. Bruce Goff to Eduard Sekler, 10 October 1976, personal communication, in Sekler, *Hoffmann*, 94, 510 n. 19: when asked about Klimt's influence, Wright told Goff: "Yes . . . he refreshed me."

150. Fritz Novotny and Johannes Dobai, *Gustav Klimt* (Salzburg: Verlag Galerie Welz [1967]), 391.

151. Christian Nebehay, *Gustav Klimt: Dokumentation* (Vienna: Verlag der Galerie Christian M. Nebehay, 1969), 519. My thanks to Christian Nebehay, who generously discussed with me Klimt's activities in 1910 (Interview, Vienna, 9 September 1985).

152. For Moll, see Jean Clair et al., *Vienne 1880–1938, L'Apocalypse Joyeuse*, (Paris: Centre Pompidou, 1986), 727.

153. Nebehay, *Klimt: Dokumentation*, 519. The paintings, with Nebehay's catalogue numbers, were: *Rot und Schwarz*, (D.158); *Blumenwiese*, (D.184?); *Familie*, (D.163); *Schloßteich* (D.167); *Schloss*

Kammer, (D.171); *Backfisch*, (D.176); *Der schwarze Federhut*, (D.168); and *Schlosspark*, (D.165); all were exhibited from a private collection.

154. One folio was heliogravures of paintings: *Das Werk von Gustav Klimt*, introductions by Hermann Bahr and Peter Altenberg (Vienna and Leipzig: Hugo Haller Kunstverlag, 1918), TAL 1123.013. Some plates, such as "Bauernhaus mit Birken" (80 X 80 cm, Gallerie Miethke, Vienna) and "Der schwarze Federnut" (79 X 63 cm, Collection Rudolf Kahler, Vienna), had as subjects the lonely landscapes that Wright preferred in the prints he bought in 1910.

The second folio was of drawings: *Gustav Klimt, Fünfundzwanzig Handzeichnungen* (Vienna: Gilhofer and Ranschurg, July 1919), TAL 1123.014.

155. Fritz Novotny and Johannes Dobai, *Gustav Klimt* (Boston: New York Graphic Society, 1968), 347, indicate an unknown location and no provenance for the painting after 1910. In a forthcoming article I will discuss how Wright obtained the *Alte Frau* through Paul T. Frankl.

156. Josef Hoffmann had designed a total of five houses on the hill, including two houses for Moll and a house for Eduard Ast, which was probably under construction in the summer of 1910. Hoffmann's first house for Carl Moll was designed and built in 1900–1901; it adjoined the house of Koloman Moser, designed by Hoffmann simultaneously with the Moll House. Hoffmann designed Moll's second house in 1906–7. Hoffmann's other designs on the Hohe Warte included houses for Dr. Hugo Henneberg (1900–1901), and Dr. Friedrich Victor Spitzer (1901–2) (Sekler, *Hoffmann*, 266–70, 316–17). Revised plans for the Eduard Ast House on the Hohe Warte, Hoffmann's last building in the group, were submitted on 19 May 1910 (Sekler, *Hoffmann*, 332); construction would have followed soon.

From the area came the name of the ephemeral revue, *Hohe Warte*, which published the program of the Wiener Werkstätte in 1905 and the work of its allied artists and craftsmen. Josef Lux directed the review, in collaboration with, among others, Hoffmann, Moser, Joseph Olbrich, and Otto Wagner. The periodical also published articles by Frank Brangwyn and Charles Rennie Mackintosh, principal representatives of the Arts and Crafts movement in Great Britain (Clair et al., *L'Apocalypse*, 756).

157. *Ausstellung Kunstgewerbe 1910–1911*, 96.

158. FLW to CRA, 24 July 1910, TAL. Returning to Fiesole, he intended to leave there on 1 September for a ten-day stay in Berlin, then spend some days with the Ashbees until he sailed for America. But Wright had not arranged passage and feared that he might have to return via Genoa.

159. Crawford, "Ten Letters," 69.

160. Ibid.

161. Wright and Ashbee also argued "over that silly old article," which Crawford has suggested was "In the Cause of Architecture," published in the *Architectural Record* in 1908. Ashbee quoted from it in his review, but the "article" possibly could refer to Ashbee's introduction itself; Wright seemed to be aware of its contents by the time he wrote to Ashbee on 26 September 1910.

162. FLW TO CRA, 26 September 1910, Crawford, "Ten Letters,"

69. Wright wrote to Ashbee on stationary from the Essex House Press, Bond St., London.

163. Charles Robert Ashbee, Introduction, quoted in Crawford, "Ten Letters," 70. Crawford provides a succinct and cogent statement of Ashbee's position in the essay to which my brief analysis refers.

164. Despite the dispute, the grounds of friendship remained intact, and Wright concluded his letter with the comment: "I may never see you again but I shall not be far away always, nevertheless. I can do anything in America far away, if you command me. As always your friend. Wright" (FLW to CRA, 26 September 1910, TAL, with punctuation added and previously unpublished).

165. FLW to CRA, 26 September 1910, quoted in Crawford, "Ten Letters," 69. Wright's request for the proofs followed in a postscript.

166. Ashbee's Introduction was published as "Eine Studie zu seiner Würdigung von C. R. Ashbee F.R.I.B.A" in both early editions of the *Sonderheft: Frank Lloyd Wright: Ausgeführte Bauten* [American edition] (Berlin: Ernst Wasmuth A.G., 1911), 3–10, and *Frank Lloyd Wright Chicago* [European edition] (Berlin: Ernst Wasmuth A.G., 1911), 3–10. The expurgated English version of the introduction was reprinted in part in "Taliesin, the Home of Frank Lloyd Wright, and a Study of the Owner," *Western Architect* 19 (February 1913): 16–19. The essay was published in a reprint edition of the *Sonderheft, Frank Lloyd Wright: The Early Work*. Foreword by Edgar Kaufmann, Jr. (New York: Horizon Press, 1968), xiii–xvi, with some of the German segments appended but untranslated.

167. FLW to CRA [9 February], 1916. Crawford has noted on the photocopy at TAL that the document is undated and may have been written earlier than the published date. When Ashbee was again lecturing in America in 1916 Wright reconciled his ideological differences by inviting Ashbee to visit Wright's home, Taliesin. "I have a desire to show you that I value and appreciate your friendship—not withstanding the painful evidence to the contrary of my ungracious manners when I visited you. I am sure you could not overlook some of my selfishness and absurdity. Whenever I think of my abuse of your friendship I am much ashamed" (Crawford, "Ten Letters" 70).

Chapter Three

1. FLW to DDM, n.d. [1910], SUNYB, photocopy of the original correspondence obtained by Darwin R. Martin from Emma K. Martin as indicated and formerly in the possession of Carolyn Mann Brackett.

2. Wright foreshadowed the theme prior to his departure for Europe when he wrote to Darwin Martin," It is difficult for me to square my life with myself, and I cannot rest until it is done or I am dead." FLW to DDM, 2 December 1908, SUNYB.

3. "Oak Park Soulmates Part," *CDT*, 3 August 1910, p. 1.

4. Ibid.

5. "Oak Park Woman Who Returns to Her Family After 'Spiritual Hegira,' " *CDT*, 3 August 1910, p. 5.; "Cheney Refuses to Tell Whether Wife Returned," *CDT*, 4 August 1910, p. 3.

6. "Oak Park Awaits Wright," *CDT*, 24 September 1910, p. 9. This second report spread a story that Wright, accompanied by his son

Lloyd, had sailed from Europe and was expected soon in Oak Park. The press had learned of Wright's return from Wright's friends, including James L. Fyfe, a Chicago architect, and Isabel Roberts, Wright's secretary. Fyfe became the partner of Herman Von Holst, the architect to whom Wright had transferred his practice prior to his departure for Europe.

7. Ibid. In addition to his undated letter to Martin written after his return from Europe, Wright wrote similar words to Charles Robert Ashbee in March 1910: "I want to square my *life* with *myself*" (FLW to CRA, 31 March 1910, Ashbee Collection, TAL).

8. *NYT*, 5 October 1910, p. 15. The *Bleucher* originated in Hamburg and left Southampton on 26 September.

9. "Wright Returns to Oak Park Wife," *CDT*, 9 October 1910, p. 1.

10. Ibid.

11. Ibid.

12. Ibid.

13. "Oak Park Pastor Upbraids Wright," *CDT*, 10 October 1910, p. 9. Rev. George M. Luccock spoke against Wright. Some sympathy for Wright came from the president of the Chicago Equal Suffrage League, Mrs. George W. Trout. She stated that the fallen and repentant man should be welcomed back to the community.

14. "Wright Returns to Oak Park Wife," *CDT*, 9 October, 1910, p. 1. The report concluded with a mention that "Wright became noted for the bizarre style of architecture he created and made popular in Oak Park."

15. WEM to DDM, 10 October 1910, SUNYB. William R. Heath (1863–1932) provided legal counsel to the Larkin Company and was one of Wright's clients in Buffalo. Heath had practiced law in Chicago, and in 1888 he married Mary Hubbard, a sister of Elbert Hubbard, cofounder of the Larkin Soap Manufacturing Company. In 1899, Heath and his wife moved to Buffalo. He became Darwin D. Martin's colleague while working for the Larkin Company and became successively a director, vice president, office manager, and legal advisor of the company. Heath knew Wright through Wright's design for the Larkin Building, and through Wright's design of Heath's own house in Buffalo (1905), a year after Darwin D. Martin's house was designed. Heath gave a speech to the Larkin Company employees on the meaning of Wright's design for the administration building; it was published as William R. Heath, "The Office Building and What It Will Bring to the Office Force," *Larkin Idea* 6 (November 1906): 10–14. Wright included Heath's house in plates XVIIa and XVIIb of the Wasmuth monograph, and he included two plans and six photographs of the Heath House in the *Sonderheft* (American edition), pp. 78–82. See Heath's obituary, "W. R. Heath is Dead; Lawyer, Churchman," *NYT*, 29 September 1932, p. 21.

16. WEM to DDM, 10 October 1910, SUNYB. The "foremost English architect" was, of course, Ashbee.

17. Later, the Oak Park property was configured to include additional apartments. The date of Wright's design for the Goethe Street town house would have been between October 1910 and late winter 1911. By spring 1911, Wright was involved with plans for building Taliesin in Wisconsin.

18. FLW to DDM, 22 November 1910, verso, SUNYB.

19. FLW to DDM, postmarked 29 November 1910, received 30 November 1910, SUNYB. This statement follows Wright's earlier assertions about his independence of Mamah Cheney. See also FLW to DDM, 22 November 1910, verso, SUNYB.

20. Martin recommended that Wright examine the status of his contract with Von Holst: "You tell me that you sold your work as it stood to Von Holst. Something depends on the nature of your contract with him as to what you sold him" (DDM to FLW, 14 October 1910, SUNYB). This is the first confirmation that a financial transaction was included with the transfer of Wright's practice to Von Holst.

21. FLW to DDM, postmarked 29 November 1910, received 30 November 1910, SUNYB.

22. DDM to FLW, 14 October 1919, SUNYB.

23. Martin had an ongoing relationship with the Tuskegee Institute and corresponded with its president, Booker T. Washington. Martin's interest in the first black college in America was typical of his liberal and humanitarian concerns.

24. DDM to FLW, 14 October 1919, SUNYB. In the text of the letter, "color" has an "s" at the end that has been crossed out.

25. FLW to DDM, 25 October 1910, SUNYB. Wright mistakenly identifies the prospective client as C. R. Wills, rather than C. H. Wills.

26. Ibid. Wright informed Martin that Wills was "contemplating a plant about as extensive as yours."

27. Ibid.

28. Work had begun as early as December 1909 on the Childe Harold Wills House, as demonstrated by a rendering perspective drawing by Mahony, illustrated in the Chicago Architectural Club *Catalogue* of 1911 as her work. Brooks indicates Marion Mahony designed the Wills House and gave 1909 as its date (Brooks, *Prairie School*, 152–54, 164). Her design, then, whichs shows how effectively she had absorbed Wright's style, was the object of Wright's scorn. For Mahony's rendering of a perspective, an interior perspective of hall, dining room, fountain and conservatory, and floor plan, see Ibid., 151, 152.

29. Martin agreed to write Wills in Detroit, despite the fact that he had never heard of him or his admiration for the Martin house. Martin added in a postscript that he could not find the name or address of Wills (DDM to FLW, 28 October 1910, SUNYB). Wright, however, had second thoughts and withdrew his request because it would have been too obvious to Wills that Wright was trying to take the job from Von Holst. If he continued, Wright suspected that Wills would lose respect for him (FLW to DDM, 30 October 1910, SUNYB). Wright gave the address of C. R. Wills, c/o Ford Motor Company, Detroit, and wrote that he thought Wills had admired the Martin House because the plans of his proposed house and the Martin House were so similar. Woolley's set of drawings for the Wills House are part of the microfilm images in the Taylor Woolley Collection, UUL.

30. FLW to DDM, 22 November 1910, verso. SUNYB.

31. FLW to DDM, date of receipt, 17 November 1910, SUNYB. In November 1910, when Wright received a loan from Martin "to expedite the 'magnum opus'" he replied that he would quickly tend to the "Cement people."

32. DDM to FLW, 1 December 1910, SUNYB.

33. Martin recommended Dr. C. H. Sample of Saginaw, Michigan, as a client.

34. FLW to DDM [4 December 1910], n.d., filed in sleeve with letter postmarked 5 December 1910, SUNYB. The Taliesin archives lists a remodeling project, project no. 1114, for Walter Gerts in River Forest, Illinois. Wright had designed a summer cottage for Gerts in 1902, and Gerts was one of the first clients to employ Wright after his return from Europe.

35. For reports on the exhibition in New York, see "The Cement Show," *NYT*, 4 December 1910, part 6, p. 11; "Cement Show Opens Tonight," ibid., 14 December 1910, p. 2; "Cement Show Packed at its Opening," ibid., 15 December 1910, p. 3; and "Cement Industry's Great Contribution to Sanitary and Economical Building," ibid., 18 December 1910, part 7, p. 2. The exhibition received a strong impetus from Chicago sources; it was under the auspices of the Cement Products Exhibition Company, at least three of whose directors were from Chicago: Edward M. Hagar, Universal Portland Cement Company, was president, Norman D. Fraser, Chicago Portland Cement Company, vice-president, and J. U. C. McDanniel, secretary-treasurer.

36. Storrer, *Catalogue*, no. 63, lists the temporary exhibition pavilion of 1901, but indicates that no plans or photographs survive.

37. The use of cement had increased from 5,650,000 barrels in 1901 to 63,300,00 barrels in 1909, a quantity that a reporter stated would make a "stone" highway twenty-five feet wide and one foot deep stretching from New York to Chicago.

38. FLW to DDM, 13 January 1911, SUNYB.

39. Ibid.

40. Ibid.

41. Ibid.

42. The Ravine Bluffs development was designed in 1915. For illustrations of some of the sculpture and the bridge, and the six houses that were built, see Storrer, *Catalogue*, nos. 185–92; M, 4:109–30; 12:67.

43. FLW to TW, 22 April [1911], UUL. Albert McArthur was listed as new in Wright's studio in 1907 and would have had limited experience with Wright by the time the latter left Oak Park in 1909. McArthur was the son of Warren McArthur, for whom Wright designed a residence in Chicago in 1892 and later supervised design of the Arizona Biltmore, with Albert McArthur. See FLW, "In the Cause of Architecture," *Architectural Record* 23 (March 1908), 164; Manson, *Golden Age*, 217; and Storrer, *Catalogue*, nos. 11–13, 221–22.

44. For the partial roster of Wright's apprentices in the Oak Park studio, see Manson, *Golden Age*, 217. See also H. Allen Brooks, *Frank Lloyd Wright and the Prairie School* (New York: George Braziller in association with the Cooper-Hewitt Museum, 1984); and David Van Zanten, *Walter Burley Griffin, Selected Designs*, (Palos Park, Ill.: Prairie School Press, 1970).

45. FLW to TW, 22 April [1911], UUL.

46. The conflict about compensation between Von Holst and Wright had to be settled by arbitration between two sets of lawyers. In an opinion dated 7 July 1911, the firm of Silber, Isaacs, Silber &

Woley informed the firm of Kerr & Kerr, Chicago, of their resolution of the dispute between the two architects and included an accounting of work performed (Silber, Isaacs, Silber & Woley to Kerr & Kerr. 7 July, 1911. William G. Purcell Collection, Northwest Architectural Archives, University of Minnesota; subsequently cited as Wright-Von Holst Contract, 1911).

47. Initially, the lawyers found that Von Holst owed Wright $49.21, but that when the "Irving and Orsinger matters" were settled, Von Holst owed Wright $108.29 as a final settlement. The amount owed Wright had been revised from previous figures, which would have been in Wright's favor. Von Holst added 60 percent of the former figures for drafting costs, which he had computed as his cost of overhead. The legal opinion refers to a section of the contract of 22 September 1909 in support of Von Holst's right to charge for overhead. The opinion also quotes the section on payment for the Ziegler and Melson houses; it erroneously listed the figure as $500, but the accounting shows $300 paid to Wright for this purpose. Thus Wright's settlement was in effect reduced by that amount (Wright-Von Holst Contract, 1911).

48. Walter Burley Griffin built the Melson House in 1912 in Mason City, Iowa. See Brooks, *Prairie School* (1976), 242–47.

49. The resolution of the contract provides a refinement to Donald Hoffmann's discussion of the concluding work on the Robie House. He stated that Wright "assigned an assistant to follow the finishing of the house; the furnishings could proceed at a relaxed and careful pace under the control of the Niedecken-Walbridge Company of Milwaukee" (Hoffmann, *Robie House*, 32). The Von Holst office was responsible for completing the house; the Niedecken-Waldbridge Company, indeed, supplied the furnishings.

50. The Von Holst-Mahony work included a project for a client named Orsinger.

51. "Wright divides home to Protect his Soul," *Examiner*, 8 September 1911, folder 12, item 9–1, ST/SUNYB.

52. From Oak Park, Wright wired Woolley, who had gone to San Diego, to come back and help with work (FLW to TW, 31 August 1911, telegram, UUL.). Shortly thereafter, Wright, back in Hillside, again wired Woolley, who had returned to Chicago, to come and work in Wisconsin. Isabel Roberts, Wright's former bookkeeper and client, would pay for Woolley's train fare (FLW to TW, 12 September 1911, telegram, UUL).

53. Wright had more support from his former clients than he has been given credit for. Brooks states: "Few of the clients he abandoned were to return [to Wright] (except for Mrs. Avery Coonley)" (Brooks, *Prairie School*, 148). But this assertion appears intended to support Brooks's argument that Wright lost professional ground after his return while his younger associates grew and flourished. During Wright's absence and despite the scandal of his elopement with Mamah Cheney, numerous clients—as confirmed by the resolved contract between Wright and Von Holst—came to the Wright office, under Von Holst's direction, for small work relating to jobs previously performed by Wright.

54. In addition to a remodeling for Walter Gerts, Wright had a commission from O. B. Balch for a house in Oak Park; Wright had

designed a shop interior for Balch's interior decorating firm, Pebbles and Balch, in 1907. For an illustration of the interior of the Pebbles and Balch shop, see Storrer, *Catalogue*, no. 131. The shop was later demolished.

55. New information on the relationship between Wright and the Coonleys appears in Theodore Turak, "Mr. Wright and Mrs. Coonley," in Richard Guy Wilson and Sidney Robinson, eds., *Modern Architecture in America* (Ames, Iowa: Iowa State University Press, 1991), 145–63. See also Robert L. Sweeney, "The Coonley Playhouse, Riverside, Illinois," *The Frank Lloyd Wright Newsletter* 1, no. 6 (November–December 1978): 2–4.

56. For Francis C. Sullivan (1882–1929), see Brooks, *Prairie School*, 272–79. A design for a railroad station in Alberta city was unexecuted.

57. The American Ready-Cut System, which is also identified as the American System-Built Homes, is the most extensive set of projects that Wright developed, comprising some 800 drawings in the Taliesin Archive. For Arthur C. Richards (1877–1955), see Mary Jane Hamilton, "The Madison Hotel," in Paul E. Sprague, ed. *Frank Lloyd Wright and Madison* (Madison: Elvehjem Museum of Art, 1990), 57–63.

58. [Edward Sanderson] to Andrew Willatzen, 22 February 1912, TAL, appears to be the first letter signed by Sanderson. Earlier correspondence concerning the publications was signed "the Office of Frank Lloyd Wright" without a personal signature. Little is known of Sanderson. He was recorded in the private listings of the Chicago directory in 1912 as an architect with a home address at 1655 Washington Boulevard, but was not listed under the classification "Architect" (*Lakeside Directory*, 1912, 1226); there was no listing for him in 1913.

59. FLW to DDM, n.d., postmarked 2 April 1912, SUNYB.

60. FLW to DDM, 18 April 1912, SUNYB.

61. Edward Sanderson to DDM, 23 April 1912, SUNYB. This letter was sent from Wright's offices at 600–610 Orchestra Hall, Chicago. The list was as follows:

Client	Location	Budget
Edward Schroeder	Milwaukee	$35,000
Mr. E. Esbenshade	Milwaukee	12,000
Herbert Angster (under completion)	Lake Bluff	8,000
Sherman Booth	Glencoe, Ill.	50–60,000
Rebuilding of Coonley Stables	[Riverside]	N.A.
Hotel Madison		275,000
Hotel	Lake Geneva	100,000
Girls School (first sketches in preparation)	Washington, D.C.	90–95,000
Mr. Adams (first sketches approved by client)	Oak Park	13,000

Future prospects:
Two houses similar in scale to the Schroeder House
Building for the Milwaukee Athletic Club $200,000–250,000.

In financial terms the largest project was the remodeling of the Hotel Madison in Madison, Wisconsin, for Arthur Richards. It was followed by the Lake Geneva Inn for Richards, which was built. Nothing is known about the project for a girls' school. The Booth House was considered ongoing as was a house for Booth's sister, the wife of the client Herbert Angster. The houses for E. Esbenshade and Edward Schroeder were not built. (The inventory at TAL gives 1911 as a date of conception of the Esbenshade and Schroeder schemes.) Although Harry S. Adams had approved sketches of his house in Oak Park, Wright would design two schemes before it was built the following year. Wright was involved with the Coonley stable because it had recently burned.

62. Wilhelm Bernhard's name first appeared in the *Lakeside Directory* in 1913 (p. 176). His occupation was that of architect, and he lived at 1356 Rosemont. He was not listed under the directory classifications of "Architect" or "Draftsman." Bernhard's scheme for the planning competition revealed a familiarity with Wrightian details, and developments of the German and Viennese Secession, as seen in the drawing "Village Square Looking East Toward Community Center." The clock tower, colors of his renderings, and the broad, flat areas of trees reveal European sources. The plan is illustrated in Alfred B. Yeomans, ed., *City Residential Land Development: Studies in Planning; Competitive Plans for Subdividing a Typical Quarter Section of Land on the Outskirts of Chicago*, Publications of the City Club of Chicago (Chicago: The University of Chicago Press, [1916]), 11. Under execution at the time of the competition plan was a similar plan by Bernhard for Lima, Ohio, the Shawnee Garden City, designed for Waldo D. Berryman (ibid.)

63. The *Lakeside Directory*, (p. 1511) listed Gibb as an architect living at 160 West Jackson Boulevard in 1911, with no business address cited. By 1913, however, Gibb's work address was given as 1528 Cullom Avenue (ibid., 506). Thus, his tenure with Wright in Wisconsin was two years at most.

64. FLW to TW, 16 July 1912, UUL.

65. FLW to John D. Larkin, 21 October 1910, SUNYB.

66. The Littles' house and stable in Peoria, Illinois, were built in 1903. Francis W. Little and his wife moved to Chicago c. 1908 and were early members of the Art Institute of Chicago, which exhibited both Wright's architectural works and his collections of Japanese prints (see Kaufmann, "Frank Lloyd Wright at the Metropolitan Museum," 27–35). Wright's house for Little at 603 Moss Avenue in Peoria was sold and enlarged by Robert C. Clark in 1909 (see Hitchcock, *Materials*: 41–42, 47, figs. 89–91). Little was an important client for Wright because he became involved with financing Wright's trip to Europe and had commissioned Wright to design a second house, "Northome" on Lake Minnetonka, Wayzata (Deephaven), Minnesota. Initial sketches were started by 1910, but the house was built between 1912 and 1914. It was conspicuously absent from the list Wright sent Martin, 23 April 1912. The house was later destroyed, but the living room has been reassembled at the Metropolitan Museum, New York. The library was reconstructed at the Allentown Art Museum in eastern Pennsylvania.

For a brief history of the Little House, with contemporary photographs, see Edgar Kaufmann, Jr., "Frank Lloyd Wright at the Metropolitan Museum" *Bulletin of the Metropolitan Museum of Art* 40 (Fall 1982): 26–35.

67. DDM to FLW, 14 October 1910, SUNYB. Wright's letter of 12 October 1910, written two days after his return to Oak Park, is not extant, but is mentioned in Martin's letter of 14 October 1910. Martin indicated that a Mr. Isham, who had been in Chicago in 1909, reported the information about Wright's print collection. Isham's identity has not been confirmed; several Ishams were listed in the Chicago directories. It is also possible that Martin referred to the distinguished artist Samuel Isham (1855–1914) of New York, who had been a member of the jury for the Buffalo Exposition of 1901 (*Who's Who, 1910–1911*, 995; *Who's Who, 1912–1913*, 1083).

68. Wright had sold 62 prints to Sallie Casey Thayer for $2,000 in 1908 (Shankel, *Thayer*, 26). He had expected to receive payments from Thayer while in Europe. The sale to her may be the one mentioned by Martin. Wright's funds from the sale to Thayer would have been exhausted, and no evidence of additional sales by Wright between 1908 and 1910 has appeared.

69. FLW to John D. Larkin, 21 October 1910, SUNYB. For a biography of John D. Larkin (1845–1926), see Jack Quinan, "Frank Lloyd Wright's Buffalo Clients," *The Frank Lloyd Wright Newsletter* 5, no. 1 (1982): 1–3. Wright anticipated rental income for his family of $120 per month. He asked to borrow $20,000 from Larkin, a loan that would be paid back in two years at 6 percent interest. With the cash, Wright proposed to pay off the first mortgage of $6,000 for the Oak Park Studio, spend $5,000 for the alterations, pay off $9,000 to Francis Little, and then sell only a minimum number of Japanese prints to pay Wasmuth for the German publications. If provided with the anticipated financing, much of which was needed to support his family, Wright would sell at most $10,000 worth of Japanese prints for his present expenses.

The text of Wright's letter to Larkin has "creditors" with the 's' canceled and 'a' inserted before the word. Although Wright used the plural form, subsequent correspondence indicates that settlement of the debt with Francis Little was the pressing issue of the moment. Wright may, however, have owed money to several people. He and his wife Catherine, for instance, had signed a note (19 July 1907) on their home and studio, to Peabody Houghteling & Company for $137.50. It was due on 19 July 1912 as the interest on the principal of "note #5" of $5,000.

Wright gave 15 November 1910 as the date for the additional payment for his publication ("The Letters of Frank Lloyd Wright, Notebook One: 1885–1916," looseleaf photocopies of correspondence, TAL).

70. Wright proposed as collateral his Oak Park studio, which would be worth $30,000 after $5,000 worth of alterations, and the Japanese print collection, which he still had in his possession and which Wright appraised at $40,000 but would be worth $95,000 if Wright could "handle it gradually" (FLW to John D. Larkin, 21 October 1910, SUNYB).

71. DDM to FLW, 28 October 1910, SUNYB.

72. DDM to FLW, 14 October 1910, SUNYB.

73. See FLW to DDM, 21 October 1910, SUNYB.

74. FLW to DDM, 30 October 1910, SUNYB. The prior date given to Larkin in a letter of 21 October was 15 March 1910.

75. Ernst Wasmuth to FLW, 3 November 1910, ts. copy of original, SUNYB. See Appendix B. The letter was sent to Wright's home at 458 Forest Avenue, Oak Park, Illinois. Wasmuth's address at the top of the letter was Berlin W. 8, with no street indicated. Although the copy indicates "signed, Ernst Wasmuth," the copy of the original has no signature. Whether a member of the firm, or Ernst Wasmuth, nephew of the founder, signed the letter remains unconfirmed. Three copies of the *Sonderheft* had been sent separately to Wright, but as Wasmuth informed Wright in awkward English "the copies are so wet as they came from the press. The later ones will be of course some more better condition." Wasmuth was impatient to receive the Introduction but the project was not close to completion: Wright had only just approved the final proofs for the first fifty plates of the monograph within the last few weeks. The text had to be included with the folios because if it and the monograph were sent to America separately, duty would have to be paid on both. Wasmuth asked for M9,000 "as per our arrangement" (ibid). This amount was equivalent to approximatelty $2,142. One German mark was equivalent to .238 United States gold dollars (*World Almanac and Encyclopedia for 1911*, 262).

Wasmuth offered to write the text, using parts of Ashbee's article for the *Sonderheft*, and asked Wright to cable his decision. The writer of the letter also suggested that his firm would insert each set of plates into portfolios, provided by a Mr. Mass (or Maas), who was apparently a supplier of the containers. This procedure would not require paying duty on both the portfolios and plates and would eliminate the need for a provisional cover for the plates. The relevant documents contain variant spellings for the name of the portfolio supplier, but it is treated in subsequent text as "Maas."

76. Martin's loan of $2,500 was to be paid back with interest in six months (DDM to FLW, 15 November 1910, carbon copy and original note signed by FLW, SUNYB). Wright had intended to deposit the $2,500 Martin had provided with R. F. Downing and Company. The company, however, claimed to be only forwarders for Wasmuth and refused to accept the funds, which Wright then felt obliged to return to the suspicious Martin. Concerning Martin's loan of $2,500 for the payment to Wasmuth, Wright returned the loan to see if he could manage without it and to avoid having Martin feel his integrity was compromised by Wright not paying his Wasmuth debt.

77. FLW to DDM, 19 postmarked November 1910, date of receipt 20 November 1910, SUNYB. Because Wright's contract stipulated that all rights and title rested wholly with him, Wasmuth, acting as Wright's agent, could sell the monograph only in Germany. Wright, however, had no copyright protection in Germany, and Wasmuth proceeded with printing an extra 250 copies.

78. Wasmuth had proposed to pay Wright 10 percent of the *Sonderheft* sales after deduction of all costs, but Wright feared that he would not make anything because of the extra casing costs. In addition, the contract made no stipulation for freight and other charges that Wright was obliged to pay along with the costs of printing the text, which he noted, "cannot be much—say M1000" (ibid).

79. Wright proposed to ask Wasmuth for a bill for the "over—costs," which Wright would pay if reasonable (FLW to DDM, postmarked 19 November 1910, date of receipt 20 November 1910, SUNYB).

80. Ibid. Wright used the term "the Work" to describe the material he took to customs in New York. The incomplete state of the monograph implies that by "Work" he meant the *Sonderheft*. Wright had left the copy by mistake on a Pullman coach on his recent return trip from New York via Buffalo, but he found it at the Pullman office in Buffalo.

81. In the copyright law of 1891 the United States recognized foreign copyrights for the first time. Domestic publishers, who were pirating foreign works, however, were protected by a clause that excepted protection for English-language texts by American authors printed overseas (Linda Greenhouse, "U.S. Printing May Lose Its Old Shield," *NYT*, 18 June 1986, p. B8).

82. FLW to DDM, postmarked 19 November 1910, date of receipt 20 November 1910, SUNYB. As Wright put it, without the funds "the work will be dropped."

83. Having loaned Wright money, Martin began to demand explanations for Wright's activities. After visiting Martin, Wright had traveled to New York City in mid-November 1910; Martin wanted to know why. He also wanted confirmation that all the $2,500 of his loan had gone to Wasmuth, and he wrote Wright that "I shall be interested in hearing of notice of shipment of THE [*sic*] magnum opus" (DDM to FLW, 17 November 1910, SUNYB. A copy of the letter was sent to WEM).

Wright answered Martin's inquiries in detail: he had gone to New York to see R. F. Downing and Company, who Wright assumed was Wasmuth's American business agent; to place manuscripts for publication with the help of his cousin who worked at *Colliers*; to visit his sister; and to see the Tiffany Company on behalf of the Universal Cement Company (FLW to DDM, postmarked 19 November 1910, date of receipt 20 November 1910, SUNYB). The cousin was Richard Lloyd Jones, who worked as a magazine editor for *Colliers* in New York from c. 1905. No specific manuscripts were mentioned; Wright may have been making general inquiries about raising money through the sale of his writings to magazines. (For comments on the relationship of the cousins and on "Westhope," the house Wright designed for his cousin in 1929 in Tulsa, Oklahoma, see Jenkin Lloyd Jones, "A House for a Cousin: The Richard Lloyd Jones House," *The Frank Lloyd Wright Newsletter* 2, no. 4 [1979]: 1–3; Storrer, *Catalogue*, no. 227.) The sister Wright mentioned was Maginel Enright; in her autobiography she later made no mention of this visit (see Maginel Wright Barney, *The Valley of the God Almighty Joneses* (New York: Appleton-Century, [1965]). Wright had promised the Universal Cement Company to visit Tiffany's despite its refusal to participate in an undefined role with the Universal Cement Company, presumably in the exhibition scheduled for December 1910 at Madison Square Garden in New York.

Martin immediately replied to Wright's description of the problems with Wasmuth. With annoyance, he first pointed out that the draft of $2,500 for the payment to Wasmuth had been returned by Wright unendorsed and, therefore, was useless (DDM to FLLW, 20 November 1910, copy, SUNYB).

This event demonstrated for Martin an example of incompetence, and, consequently, he asked for all of Wright's contracts and correspondence with Wasmuth, a statement of the debt to Francis Little, and copies of booksellers' propositions. Using Wright's payment

schedule, Martin summarized Wright's debt to Wasmuth at $4,000. Martin also wrote that, with Wright's permission, he would bring a description of the circumstances to William R. Heath. He and Heath would try to discern the legal conditions relevant to the situation and would possibly consult a German lawyer whom they knew.

84. Here is Wright's summary:

I am to pay on account of *Sonderheft* M9000
on account of Monograph M2000
This is to be sent when notified that
work is ready—I am to pay when work arrives at New York
for 25 extra copies on Japan paper—M1525.
I am to pay now Mr. Mass on contract for covers M915
when 1st part arrives at N.Y   M915
    2nd   "   "   "   "   M1830

(FLW to DDM, postmarked 19 November, SUNYB.)

85. DDM to FLW, 17 November 1910, SUNYB. A copy of the letter was sent to WEM.

86. Ibid.

87. Ibid. Martin extended his anxiety about Wright's behavior to a complaint about his architecture: he concluded his letter with the suggestion that Wright fix the ventilation at Unity Temple in Oak Park; he and his brother, William, "almost suffocated there last summer."

88. FLW to DDM, postmarked 22 November 1910; received 25 November 1910, SUNYB.

89. Ibid.

90. DDM to FLW, 21 November 1910, SUNYB. Martin acknowledged receiving a copy of Wasmuth's letter of 3 November 1910, and Wright's letter, which Wright had sent special delivery. A copy of Martin's letter was sent to WEM.

91. FLW to DDM, 22 November 1910, verso, SUNYB.

92. Wright informed Martin: "I have the text in the machine here now, rewriting in [it] according to paragraph suggestions made by my cousin on [*sic*] 'Colliers' [*sic*] when in New York" (ibid.). The cousin was probably Richard Lloyd Jones; see FLW to DDM, postmarked 19 November 1910, received 20 November 1910, SUNYB.

93. Wright discussed his contract with Martin: "My Wasmuth contract is mislaid. I will turn it up and send it but it is of little use I think as I consider the matter to block the game by trying to get all my points at this time. Let us take them up later. Please return the *Sonderheft* as I wish to send it on to Washington for copyright" (ibid.). Doggedly persevering and financially astute, Martin pointed out to Wright that he had made an inept tactical error which might severely interfere with receiving quick profits from the publications: the monograph, valued at sales of $35,000, was more lucrative, but Wright planned to import the less profitable *Sonderheft*, valued at $5,000, before bringing over the monograph. At the same time, Wright was allowed to sell the *Sonderheft* only after the monograph had been marketed (DDM to FLW, 26 November 1910, SUNYB):

You have explained to me that 100 copies of the *Sonderheft* go free with 1000 copies of the Monograph, that none of the remaining 9000 [*Sonderheften*] can be used until after the Monographs are marketed, yet your plan appears to bring over the *Sonderheft* first which does not represent a realizable sum in the immediate future. You are planning to put in $1500 of your money with $2500 you requested from me. It is evident that you should make every move in the direction of early results.

Martin estimated sales of the publications "to realize first $35,000 net for the Monograph and, second, $5000 [?] for the remaining copies of the *Sonderheft*" (ibid.).

Consequently, at the risk of delayed financial returns, Martin urged Wright to arrange a sales campaign as quickly as possibly so that he and Wright could recoup their investments. At this point, Wright's anticipated investment was $1,500 and Martin's was $2,500. Martin proceeded to ask for specific information on the "two experienced subscription book-sellers" who, according to Wright, were to handle the monograph (ibid.).

Showing the precarious state of the entire situation, Wright responded to Martin's financial advice by providing, in a garbled text, further details concerning the status of his contract:

I failed to find the contract [inserted above line: a contract and confirmatory letter that is all]—they are enclosed because attempts [*sic*] I have written the U.S. Consul at Berlin to do what he could—I think your advice would be valuable—I have acted on all you have given so far—I have no contracts yet with the men who are to sell the work but will have shortly and will send them for your approval. I am very glad of your help on this. These papers are all the contract I have. Nothing written on the *Sonderheft*—poor business on my part. (FLW to DDM, postmarked 29 November 1910, received 30 November 1910, SUNYB)

This statement follows Wright's earlier assertions about his independence of Mamah Cheney. (See FLW to DDM, 22 November 1910, verso, SUNYB). Along with the details about the Wasmuth transactions, Wright reiterated the conditions of his sad family situation.

94. In early December 1910, Martin still pursued the situation and Wright's poor business practices with Wasmuth. Having received Wright's remaining documents from Wasmuth, Martin prepared an extract of Wright's debts for the publications (DDM, 2 December 1910, extract of debts, SUNYB. The original contract, which is no longer extant, was dated 24 November 1909, the letter of confirmation 13 September 1910, and the extract of Wright's debts was based on his letter of 19 November 1910.) This accounting consisted of a more orderly statement of Wright's list of payments and due dates, and it indicated that Wright owed approximately M17,185 ($4,090), plus the cost of 1,000 copies of the English translation of his text for the monograph as well as the expenses identified in Wright's letter of 19 November (FLW to DDM, postmarked 19 November, SUNYB). Martin, however, could not make Wright's figures correspond with the Wasmuth documents, and consequently he asked Wright for a statement of what Wright had paid Wasmuth. Martin again inquired if Wright had mailed the text for the monograph and paid Maas the M915 due for the monograph cases (DDM to FLW, 3 December 1910, SUNYB).

Wright then informed Martin of a long communication from Wasmuth and promised to send Martin copies of the correspondence in a few days (FLW to DDM, n.d. [4 December 1910], filed in a sleeve with letter postmarked 5 December 1910, SUNYB. The nature of the communication from Wasmuth is unknown.) Wright's promised reply soon arrived:

I do not know why the contract figures do not tally with my figures but I will work it out as soon as I can and send you a clear statement. I have had two cablegrams from Wasmuth, and I think he is getting busy on the desired lines. The text he has by this time. I have written the consul at Berlin and cabled Wasmuth twice [?] also and things are stirring I think. (FLW to DDM, 7 December 1910, SUNYB)

Concerning the payment for the portfolio cases, Wright replied, "Yes the money has gone by cable to Mass [*sic*] . . .". Wright's optimism was premature. His business affairs were still unresolved and confused, and his debts to Wasmuth were due along with his debt to Francis Little.

95. FLW to DDM, 13 January 1911, SUNYB. Wright's rejection of the *Sonderheft* was based on the poor quality of the illustrations of his work. The "*Record*" refers to the *Architectural Record*. For the quality of reproductions of the fifty-six pages of illustrations, see FLW, "In the Cause of Architecture," *Architectural Record*, 23 (March 1908): 155–221.

96. FLW to DDM, 13 January 1911, SUNYB. One error in the production of the plates was the substitution in plate LI of a perspective rendering of the Alexander Davidson House in Buffalo (1908) for the Isabel Roberts House in River Forest, Illinois (1908) (see Storrer, *Catalogue*, nos. 149, 150 for a photographic comparison of the two houses). A second error was titling plate LXI as a dwelling for William Norman Guthrie instead for Frank J. Baker of Wilmette, Illinois.

Additional flaws included discrepancies between the table of contents and the published plates: the plan for an artist's house on plate XXX of the Cheney House, and the perspective studies of the Burton Westcott House on plates XVI and LIII are omitted from the table of contents; plate LIII omits mentioning the inclusion of a study for the Edwin Waller summer residence; plates XLVIII and LII have tissue overlays not described in the table of contents; plates LVI and LVIII are not listed in the table of contents—only their contents are described. The table of contents also lists an overlay to plate LXI that was not issued with the portfolios.

97. DDM to FLW, 18 January 1911, SUNYB.

98. No documents have yet been discovered to confirm when Mamah Cheney returned from Germany. Concerning his second trip to Europe, Wright later spoke of seeing an opening performance of *Der Rosenkavalier* (Bruce Brooks Pfeiffer to author, personal communication, 1984). The comedy for music by Richard Strauss premiered at the Dresden Court Opera on 26 January 1911, and several opera houses produced it within a few days of the premiere (*The New Grove's Dictionary of Music and Musicians*, s.v. "Strauss, Richard"). Strauss composed the opera in 1909–10 with a text by Austrian poet, dramatist, and librettist Hugo von Hofmannsthal (1874?-1929). At the performance in Dresden, Wright would have seen Biedermeyer sets designed by the Viennese Alfred Roller. It was the cultural event of the moment. Great excitement and advance publicity necessitated special trains from Berlin to Dresden.

99. FLW to DDM, 21 January [1911] SUNYB. Internal evidence indicates that Wright misdated the letter "1910." It was written on stationery with the seal of the R.M.S. *Lusitania*. Wright missed sending his letter to Martin from shore because a letter from the "consul" had arrived the morning of 16 January that put him in a hurry to depart.

100. Ibid.

101. Ibid.: "He [Booth] knows my errand." This observation establishes that negotiations to design the Booth House had begun by January 1911. The elaborate design dramatically engaged the rough terrain of its site and became an immediate precedent for the design of Wright's own home, Taliesin, in Wisconsin.

102. For Sotheby's auction activities, see *Catalogue of Japanese Prints*, 5 vols. in 1 (London: [Sotheby], 1913). Wright thought that sales of these purchases might allow him "to make my way." Reflecting a long-standing interest in Japonism, London had been awash with prints from an exhibition of Japanese arts displayed at the Japan-British Exhibition in 1910. See Office of the Imperial Japanese Government Commission to the Japanese-British Exhibition, *An Illustrated Catalogue of Japanese Old Fine Arts Displayed at the Japan-British Exhibition, London, 1910*. 2 vols. (Tokyo: Shimbi Shoin [1910]).

103. Wright was also worried that Francis Little would be apprehensive, because Wright, owing him money, did not inform him of his departure to Europe. "The only feature troublesome is what people will say—and I guess they ma be d—nd so far as that goes. If the papers should break out, which I think is doubtful, (they might be sick of the affair) Little will be frightened to death, thinking his worst fears realized . . ." (FLW to DDM, 21 January [1911], SUNYB).

Wright intended to pay Little $4,000 by 5 March 1911 with funds received from the sale of Japanese prints. Wright's anticipated sales were with Clarence Buckingham, the art patron, connoisseur, and dealer of Japanese prints in Chicago. Wright enclosed in his letter to Martin an order, however, for Buckingham to turn the $4,000 over on 15 February to Martin, who could pay Little if necessary, in Wright's absence. Martin noted in the margin of this letter from Wright that the note was due 10 March 1911, and that the order had been returned personally to Wright on 28 March 1911 (marginalia of FLW to DDM, 21 January [1911], misdated "1910," SUNYB: "due 3/10/11" and "Ret'd to FLW personally 4/28/11").

104. FLW to DDM, 21 January [1911], SUNYB.

105. See Appendix B for the text of the agreement.

106. The contract also provided the following financial arrangements:1. Provisions for packing and delivery state that the *Sonderheft* was due not later than 1 May 1911. Wasmuth would pay for all packing and shipping costs for both monograph and the *Sonderheft* to Bremen or Hamburg (free ship).

2. Financial arrangements for the second edition of the *Sonderheft* called for a total cost of M15,000, with M5,000 down and M5,000 paid when the work was ready for shipment. M5,000 was to be paid after delivery. Ten copies of the second edition would be sent by mail to Wright in advance of the complete run.

3. Stipulations for reissue of the *Sonderheft* required a minimum order of 2,500 copies to be placed within three months after the first printing of the second edition had been shipped to Wright. The reissued edition was to be produced within three months from the order date. The rate would be M5,000 per 2,500 copies with a down payment of half the total charges and the balance due on delivery. If orders were placed after three months, the price would be subject to change.

107. FLW to DDM, 19 November 1910 postmark, 20 November 1910, date of receipt, SUNYB. The twenty-five copies on Japan paper were a special reserve whose rarity was insured by their limited number. Wright gave Martin and Little the standard edition of the monograph, and retained the special copies. I will explore the ownership and dissemination of these special copies in a study of the reception of the Wasmuth monographs and Wright's influence in Europe.

108. The author has found no indication of the stamp "For sale in Europe only" on copies of the monograph.

109. The precise date of Wright's return has not been determined. There were several ships leaving Germany for New York that would have returned Wright to America by the end of March or the beginning of April 1911. The SS *Diamant* had departed 8 March from Hamburg and arrived in New York on 26 March; it may have been the ship Wright had intended to take. The SS *Standard* had left Hamburg on 11 March and was expected in New York on 27 March 1911; a faster ship was the SS *Amerika*, which had left Hamburg on 18 March and was due in New York on 27 March. The SS *Roon* had also left Bremen on 18 March and arrived in New York on Wednesday, 29 March. If Wright had arrived on it, he would have had enough time to return to Oak Park and send Martin a telegram. ("Shipping and Mails," *NYT*, 27 March 1911, p. 13; ibid., 30 March 1911, p. , 8; and ibid., 2 April 1911, p. 15.)

110. The first evidence of Wright's return is a night-letter telegram, sent on Easter Sunday, FLW to DDM, 3 April 1911, SUNYB.

111. Ibid.

112. In the margin of Wright's night letter of 3 April 1911 Martin noted that he had replied to Wright by wire on 5 April 1911.

113. FLW to DDM, 12 April 1911, SUNYB.

114. Ibid.

115. Ibid. Assuming that Little had demanded Wright's draft for funds from Martin, Wright thanked Martin for covering the debt to Little, but added that he might need an extension until June for the note of $2,500.

116. Ibid.

Chapter Four

1. Harriet Monroe, "The Orient an Influence on the Architecture of Wright," *CDT*, 12 April 1914, section 8, p. 8; subsequently cited as Monroe, "The Orient an Influence," 1914.

2. Monroe was not alone in seeing Wright as a Secessionist. He was included in those "who, even if they are not admittedly exponents of the Secessionists of Europe, are secessionists at heart, and in terms of their own convictions and ideals—Louis Sullivan, Frank Lloyd Wright and Walter Burley Griffin" (C. Matlack Price, "Secessionist Architecture in America," *Arts and Decoration* 3 [December 1912]: 52).

3. Wright's initial design varied from the building as it was executed. In the first place he intended to use in the window glass designs similar to his earlier work; this is obvious in the use of a rotated lattice pattern in F1109.004 or the flattened diamonds combined with trapezoid patterns in F1108.012. Secondly, he intended the main kindergarten room, which contained a stage, to be five bays wide; it was built to a width of three. (Compare F1108.007 with Storrer, *Catalogue*, 174, for the Coonley Playhouse as built.) For additional comments on the Coonley Playhouse, see Hanks, *Decorative Designs*, 111–13; idem, *Frank Lloyd Wright: Preserving an Architectural Heritage* (New York: E. P. Dutton, 1989), 75; and Kaufmann, *Wright at the Metropolitan*, 24, 25.

4. Avery Coonley to FLW, 2 October 1912, TAL.

5. The original windows are in the collection of Domino's Center for Architecture and Design (Hanks, *Preserving an Architectural Heritage*, 76–79, 81). One of the original niche triptychs is in the collection of the Art Institute of Chicago (*Chicago Architecture*, 450, cat. no. 183, pls. 50, 51).

6. The triptych was eventually purchased by the Metropolitan Museum of Art. For a brief discussion of the windows, see Kaufmann, *Wright at the Metropolitan*, 24–25.

7. Hanks and Toher, "Wright and his European Contemporaries," 16–19. According to Hanks, the Coonley Playhouse windows were "among the first nonobjective geometric designs executed by Wright upon his return from Europe, where he must have been influenced by the avant-garde work of such artists as Robert Delaunay and Frantisek [sic] Kupka" (Hanks, *Preserving an Architectural Heritage*, 75); Hanks included a similar assessment in his pioneering book on Wright's decorative arts: "Although derived from different sources, Wright's design relates visually to nonobjective experiments in European painting at the time, such as the paintings of Francis Picabia and Frank [sic] Kupka" (Hanks, *Decorative Designs* , 111).

8. Dimitri Tselos, "Frank Lloyd Wright and World Architecture." *JSAH* 28, no. 1 (March 1969): 63–65.

9. Edgar Kaufmann, Jr., "Frank Lloyd Wright and the Fine Arts," *Perspecta* 8 (1963): 40, cited in Hanks and Toher, "Wright and His European Contemporaries," 17.

10. Hanks and Toher, "Wright and His European Contemporaries," 17 and fig. 32. Hanks uses an illustration of a tea and coffee service in the collection of the Österreichische Museum für angewandte Kunst, Vienna. The authors also claim that Wright's sculpture at Midway Gardens "shows Wright's interest in Cubism" (ibid.).

11. Hanks, *Decorative Designs*, 112.

12. *The Studio Year-Book of Decorative Art* (London: The Studio, 1907): 222. See also *Traum und Wirklichkeit*, 377, catalogue no. 13/5/13.

13. *The Studio Year-Book of Decorative Art* (London: The Studio, 1907), 222. Trethan used dark overlapping circles on a white ground for her tea service. She featured the circle but used the triangle as a motif for other designs. Sika also used dark overlapping circles on a white ground for a tea service. Designed for the Wiener Werkstätte in 1901/1902, the coffee and tea service had been published in the magazine *Das Interieur* in 1902, and both Trethan's and Sika's work had been executed by the Vienna porcelain manufacturer, Josef Böck.

14. WEM to DDM, 10 October 1910. SUNYB.

15. The introduction and list of plates for the European edition consisted of 31 pages, the American edition had 27 pages. Sweeney states that Ralph Fletcher Seymour printed the English introduction in Chicago (Sweeney, *Bibliography*, 16).

16. For a dismissive critique of Wright's monograph essay, see Vincent Scully, Foreword to *Studies and Executed Buildings by Frank Lloyd Wright* (New York: Rizzoli, 1986): 5–6. Scully finds the essay unconvincing, unimpressive, and virtuous only for its "intransigence" in declaring an International Style. While Scully is on strong ground in pointing out the nineteenth-century roots of Wright's views on eclecticism, he misses Wright's call for a new and pure architecture based on indigenous art and exotic sources. Furthermore, Scully asserts that it was difficult to believe that by 1910 Wright had not read Loos's essay *Ornament und Verbrechen*, published in 1908. Frank Lloyd Wright, however, did not read German. Unless someone personally translated the text for him, it would have been unavailable—no English translation had been published at that time.

17. Wright's most recent significant theoretical statement was "In the Cause of Architecture," *Architectural Record* 23 (March 1908): 155–221. Kaufmann and Raeburn, however, cite as Wright's reference "The Arts and Craft of the Machine" (1901) (*Frank Lloyd Wright: Writings and Buildings* [New York: Horizon Press, 1960; reprint ed., New York: Meridian Books, 1974], 84).

18. FLW, Introduction, *Ausgeführte Bauten und Entwürfe*, n.p; cited as Wasmuth Introduction. Unless noted otherwise, subsequent quotations are from this source.

19. Otto Wagner, *Modern Architecture* 3d ed., Malgrave trans., 114–15.

20. "Seine Welt Zeige der Künstler, die niemals war, noch jemals sein wird" (Latham, *Olbrich*, 52).

21. Wasmuth Introduction, n.p.

22. Ibid.

23. Ibid.

24. Walt Whitman, Preface to Leaves of Grass (1855), in *The Harvard Classics*, Charles W. Eliot, ed., vol. 39 (New York: P. F. Collier & Son, c. 1910), 409. For Wright and Whitman, see also Narciso Menocal, "Frank Lloyd Wright's Concept of Democracy: An American Architectural Jeremiad," in Bruce Brooks Pfeiffer and Gerald Nordland, eds., *Frank Lloyd Wright: In the Realm of Ideas* (Carbondale, Ill.: Southern Illinois University Press, 1988), 149–64, esp. 150–51.

25. Wasmuth Introduction, n.p.

26. Ibid.

27. FLW to TW, 22 April [1911], UUL.

28. Louis H. Sullivan, "The Young Man in Architecture," lecture to the second Architectural League of America Convention, June 1900, Chicago. Sullivan's lecture was published as "The Young Man in Architecture," *Inland Architect* 35 (June 1900): 38–40. Wright read a paper entitled "The Architect" at the same convention; it was reported in *The Brickbuilder* 9 (June 1900): 124–28.

Wright reiterated the theme of the importance of youth in his lecture "To the Young Man in Architecture," presented at the Chicago Art Institute in Fullerton Hall on 1 October 1930. It was one of two speeches by Wright; the second, given the following day, was "In the Realm of Ideas." They were published as Frank Lloyd Wright, *Two Lectures on Architecture* ([Chicago]: Art Institute, [1931]); reprinted in idem, *The Future of Architecture* (New York: Horizon Press, 1953).

29. FLW to TW, 6 April, 1911; FLW to TW, 22 April [1911], UUL. The developments with Wasmuth were: the first edition of the *Sonderheft* had been rejected and would therefore be sold only in Europe; and the American edition would be enlarged and superior, but no *Sonderheft* would be sold until all the monographs had been sold.

30. FLW to TW, 22 April [1911], UUL.

31. FLW, *A Testament*, 84.

32. Advertising prospectus, *Ausgeführte Bauten und Entwürfe von Frank Lloyd Wright*, n.p., n.d., TAL. The prospectus was a seven-page pamphlet. Although the document is undated and has no publisher's name, Sweeney (*Bibliography*, 19) provides 1911 as the date of the pamphlet, with Ralph Fletcher Seymour, Chicago, as publisher. Seymour would be a logical designation as publisher; he was publishing Mamah Borthwick's translations of Ellen Key's writings. The date corresponds to the period when Wright's office was at 805 Orchestra Hall, Chicago, as indicated on letterheads. Sweeney illustrated the cover as plate 3 in his *Bibliography*.

33. Confirmation of Wright's office sending out copies of the second folio of the monograph by 14 December 1911 is found in FLW to George Dittke, 17 September 1912, TAL. During the fall, financing the remodeling of his studio had continued to be a problem. Wright wired Martin in November 1911 that he was "trying to move [the] Monograph without troubling you but Oak Park [remodeling] pressing . . ." (DDM to FLW, 18 November 1911, SUNYB, quoting telegram of FLW to DDM, 13 November 1911).

34. Mamah had not gone back to Edwin Cheney, her husband. He consequently sued for divorce on the grounds of desertion. It was granted in the summer of 1911, and she resumed her maiden name of Mamah Bouton Borthwick. The case for divorce was filed 28 July, heard 3 August, and the decree given 5 August (Certificate of Evidence, filed August 5 or 6 [date is unclear] 1911, Superior Court, Cook County, Illinois). Court records indicate that the children remained in the custody of Edwin Cheney. When Mamah left in June 1909, Edwin Cheney's mother, Armilla, moved in and stayed with the Cheney children. My thanks to Anne Nissen for providing copies of the Certificate of Evidence.

35. Gill (*Many Masks*, 207) maintains that Wright's efforts to lead an "honest" life were merely attempts "to mitigate the guilt he feels at his selfishness," and that Wright's "mangled" interpretation of Key's ideas were "in philosophical terms, gibberish."

36. An elaboration of Key's ideas and their impact on Borthwick and Wright can be found in the author's "Taliesin: 'To Fashion Worlds in Little'," *Wright Studies* 1 (1991): 44–65. For the biography of Key, see Louise Nyström-Hamilton, *Ellen Key, Her Life and Work*, trans. A. E. B. Fries (New York: G. P. Putnam's Sons, 1913). Family financial problems caused her to make a living by teaching in Stockholm in 1880, and from that point on she began to lecture.

37. Ellen Key, *The Morality of Woman and Other Essays*, authorized translation from the Swedish by Mamah Bouton Borthwick (Chicago: Ralph Fletcher Seymour Co., 1911): 69.

38. Key's *The Morality of Woman and Other Essays* included the essays "The Morality of Woman," "The Woman of the Fire," and "The Conventional Woman." Borthwick's other translations of Key's books were *Love and Ethics*, authorized translation from the Swedish by Mamah Bouton Borthwick (Chicago: Ralph Fletcher Seymour Co., 1912); ibid., *The Torpedo under the Ark; "Ibsen and Women,"* authorized translation from the Swedish by Mamah Bouton Borthwick (Chicago: Ralph Fletcher Seymour Co., 1912); ibid, *The Woman Movement*, translated by Mamah Bouton Borthwick, A.M., with an introduction by Havelock Ellis (New York and London: G. P. Putnam's Sons, 1912; reprinted in *Pioneers of the Woman's Movement* (Westport, Conn.: Hyperion Press, 1976).

One of Borthwick's translations was published posthumously: Ellen Key, "Romain Rolland," trans. Mamah Borthwick, *Little Review* 2 (October 1915): 22–30.

39. FLW, *An Autobiography*, 163–64. In the 1932 edition of Wright's *Autobiography* he began the statement of principles with "SOCIOLOGICAL (A 'Tract')," 166–67. In both editions Wright added further comments on his "conclusions."

40. Theodore Turak, "Mr. Wright and Mrs. Coonley," in Richard Guy Wilson and Sidney Robinson, eds., *Modern Architecture in America: Visions and Revisions* (Ames, Iowa: Iowa State University Press, 1991), 150. Both the Coonleys came from reformist backgrounds. Turak quite accurately describes Queene Ferry Coonley (1874–1958) as an "aristocratic liberal, a reformer" (ibid.) She enjoyed the wealth and social prestige that came from the mercantile success of her father's seed business. A graduate of Vassar, she wanted to pursue teaching and social work and worked in a Chicago settlement house before marrying Avery Coonley in 1901. Like the Darwin D. Martins, both she and her husband were practitioners of Christian Science. She actually commissioned Wright, but Avery Coonley overcame his initial reluctance and gave his support to the architect. For Avery Coonley, see also Eaton, *Two Chicago Architects*, 82–86, 217–20.

41. Mrs. Coonley drew, however, a strong line at iconoclastic relationships based on love, not marriage. Nevertheless, she overlooked Wright's nonconformist behavior and remained his supporter. Queene Coonley joined with others to provide funds for Wright's corporation in 1928 (Turak, "Mr. Wright and Mrs. Coonley," 159).

42. Wright's father, William Carey Wright, was a minister as well as a musician. There were also preachers on his maternal side, the Lloyd Joneses.

43. Elaine Harrington to Karen Wilson, 27 March 1992.

44. "Wright Reveals Romance Secret," CST, 31 December 1911, p. 4. The "established order" was a favorite phrase for Wright's summation of people representing social convention.

45. "Architect Wright in New Romance with 'Mrs. Cheney'," CST, 24 December 1911, pp. 1, 4. In his pioneering biography, Twombly es-

tablished Wright's activities around December 1911 largely from news-paper accounts (*Life and Architecture*, 137–41, with notes); I have reexamined Twombly's sources and added some others. Twombly considered Wright's moral pronouncements pretentious, elitist, and supercilious. My account reexamines the documentation in a different light.

For additional references to the December defense, see *CDT*, 1 January 1912; *Chicago Record-Herald*, 29, 31 December 1911; *Wisconsin Journal*, 30 December 1911.

46. *CDT*, 28, 29, 30, 31 December, 1 January 1912; *Chicago Record-Herald*, 29, 31 December 1911; *Wisconsin Journal*, 30 December 1911; cited in Twombly, *Life and Architecture*, 138–39., n. 31.

47. "Spends Christmas Making 'Defense' of 'Spirit Hegira'," *CDT*, 26 December 1911, 1.

48. Ibid. Wright informed the newspaper that he was twenty-one and Catherine was eighteen when they had married twenty years ago.

49. Ibid.

50. Ibid.

51. Ibid.

52. Wright's initial statement insufficiently clarified his purpose to his neighbors, so he decided to prepare a second: "Wright to give 'Report for All'," *CDT*, 29 December 1911, p. 5. Concerning efforts for a divorce, arranged through Sherman Booth, see "'Family Caucus'; Plan of Wright," *CDT*, 30 December 1911, p. 16.

53. "Wright in Castle Fearless of Raid," *CDT*, 28 December 1911, p. 2.

54. Ibid.

55. Ibid.

56. Jenkin Lloyd Jones to Jane Lloyd Jones, 28 December 1911; ibid., 4 January 1912, Jane Lloyd Jones Collection, SHSW; Richard Lloyd Jones in the *Chicago Record-Herald*, 28 December 1911; in Twombly, *Life and Architecture*, 139, n. 32.

57. 3 February 1912, affidavit by Wright signed at Taliesin, Spring Green, Wisconsin, 3 February 1912, and notarized by notary public Thomas W. King. Sweeney Collection, TAL. The original exists in the Jane Lloyd Jones Collection, SHSW.

The Hillside Home School, run by Wright's aunts, had increasing financial problems and entered bankruptcy. Troubles for the Lloyd Jones sisters had already begun by 13 November 1909 when a petition for bankruptcy was made (Petition for "Discharge of Bankrupt" Ellen C. [?] Lloyd Jones, as of 3 September 1909, dated 13 November 1909. U.S. District Court, western district of Wisconsin, copy at TAL). Receivership followed in January 1910 (28 January 1910, Petition in the matter of Jane Lloyd Jones, Bankrupt, copy at TAL). Enos Lloyd Jones was appointed to transfer the stock of the corporation, including 332 shares of stock, to Sidney H. Stuart, Madison, Wisconsin.

On 24 August 1912 the stockholders of the Hillside Home School decided to sell the south half of the southwest quarter of section thirty, T8N R4E, to the State Bank of Spring Green for $5,000 (4 September 1912, mortgage Hillside Home School to State Bank of Spring Green, signed by the Lloyd Jones sisters on 26 August 1912, entered vol. 42 of Mortgages, p. 44, Iowa County Wisconsin; copy at TAL).

Three years later, the sisters conveyed to Wright for one dollar all their possessions and property, furnishings and personal property in

their rooms; all the capital stock of the Hillside Home School, except the shares owned by Mrs. Susan L. Dana of Springfield, Illinois, and C. E. Roberts of Oak Park (10 May 1915, warranty deed from Ellen C. Lloyd Jones and Jane Lloyd Jones to FLW, registered Iowa County, 20 September 1921 vol. 105 of Deeds, page 56). Wright was obliged to provide room and board for his aunts and pay them $250 per year and expenses in case of sickness. If the sisters wanted to provide for themselves outside the Home School, Wright was to pay them $600 per year.

On 4 August 1917, Wright bought the building of the Hillside Home School for $25,000; he immediately mortgaged it for $5,000 to the Bank of Wisconsin, with fulfillment of the note occurring on 7 November 1919 (vol. 100 of Deeds, p. 341; vol. 58 of Mortgages, p. 140; vol. 61 of Mortgages, p. 271, Register of Deeds, Dodgeville, Wisconsin).

58. W. R. Purdy, "A Prophet is not without Honor Save in His Own Country," *The Weekly Home News*, 28 December 1911, in Twombly, *Life and Architecture*, p. 140, and n. 34. There was also a rumor that citizens wanted the sheriff to oust Wright; he steadfastly refused ("Asks Sheriff's Aid to Oust Wright," *CDT*, 27 December 1911, p. 2).

59. "Wright Reveals Romance Secret," *CST*, 31 December 1911, p. 4.

60. In none of his correspondence that I have examined did Wright give any indication of wanting to remain in Europe on a permanent basis. After less than a year abroad, he seemed impatient and anxious to return. He stated that he had left Mamah in Berlin, which, if correct, gives more fragmentary evidence of her whereabouts. Also, he added that, when she returned, she went to Canada where her children were on vacation. There, Edward Cheney had visited and arranged a divorce.

61. "Wright Reveals Romance Secret," *CST*, 31 December 1911, p. 4. Wright may have perceived that his work was usurped, yet this claim could not be substantiated on the basis of the contract resolution between Wright and Von Holst.

62. Ibid.

63. Ibid.

64. Ibid.

65. FLW, Letter to the editor of *The Weekly Home News*, 4 January 1912, in Twombly, *Life and Architecture*, 140 n. 35.

66. *CDT*, 27, 30 December 1911, in Twombly, *Life and Architecture* 140 n. 36.

67. "The Women's Building and the Neighborhood Club," *The Weekly Home News* 16 July 1914, p. 1. Wright proposed a flat-roof building with top-lit exhibition gallery and attached side yard for children. A pitched-roof version was built. William Marlin brought the design to my attention.

68. Twombly provides citations to the various accounts of the Taliesin tragedy (*Life and Architecture*, 172 n. 28). News of the murders spread as far as New York: see "Wild Negro Chef Kills 6, Wounds 4," 16 August 1914, *NYT*, part 2, p. 12. For Wright's account of the tragedy, see FLW, *Autobiography*, 184–90. In addition to Mamah Borthwick, her two children, and the draftsman Emil Brodelle the following were murdered: the son of William Weston, the carpenter; David Lindblom, a gardener; and Thomas Brunker, a farm hand. John Lloyd Wright

recalled that he and his father were working on the decoration for the Bar Room at Midway Gardens when Wright received word of the fire (JLW to FLW, 25 May 1931, courtesy of Katie Kosut).

For Brodelle's role as a draftsman of the aerial-perspective renderings of Taliesin and the Imperial Hotel, see John Lloyd Wright to H. Allen Brooks, 22 April 1970, in Brooks, *Prairie School*, 85.

69. William Marlin to author, personal communication, 25 February 1987.

70. Twombly, *Life and Architecture*, 169. The Borthwick and Wright translation of the poem was published as Johann Wolfgang von Goethe, "A Hymn to Nature," *Little Review* 1 (February 1915): 30–32.

71. FlW, *Autobiography* (1932 ed.), 185–86.

72. For a closer look at the relationship of Wright and Borthwick, see the author's "Taliesin: 'To Fashion Worlds in Little,' " *Wright Studies* 1 (1991): 44–65.

73. Menocal, "Wright's Concept of Democracy," in *Frank Lloyd Wright: In the Realm of Ideas*, 151.

74. Thomas Carlyle, "The Hero as Poet," in *Heroes, Hero-Worship and the Heroic in History* (New York: Charles Scribner's Sons, 1898), iii. Wright owned this copy, inscribed 1901, and *Past and Present* (New York: Charles Scribner's Sons, n.d.,) inscribed "Frank Lloyd Wright, April 1908." Both are in the Collections of the Frank Lloyd Wright Home and Studio.

Chapter Five

1. FLW, Wasmuth Introduction, n.p.

2. Ibid.

3. For a synopsis of the appeal of primitivism to artists, see William Rubin, "Modernist Primitivism, an Introduction," in *Primitivism in 20th Century Art: Affinity of the Tribal and the Modern* 2 vols. I (New York: Museum of Modern Art, 1984): 1: 1–81. See also *The Spiritual in Art: Abstract Painting 1890–1985*, (New York: Abbeville Press, 1986); and Peter Selz, *German Expressionist Painting* (Berkeley: University of California Press, 1957). Primitivism appealed to artists because primitive art was perceived to be more conceptual than naturalistic art; its cultures were more sophisticated than those wedded to naturalism; its art integrated the materials of its making; and it was close to nature. Furthermore, primitive art utilized flat surfaces without relying on illusionistic effects. These factors occurred in the context of a search for artistic renewal in which history painting would have no role.

I use the term "archaic" in reference to forms characteristic of an earlier, more primitive time, or for the *prehistory* of the earliest known cultures of an area. "Ancient" refers to the *historical* period of the earliest known civilizations, particularly of the classical world, that extended to the fall of the Roman Empire in the fifth century.

4. As Wright typically reedited his writings after their publication—often directly on his own copies of his books—he later slightly altered the Wasmuth Introduction for its use in his exhibition at the Palazzo Strozzi, Florence, in 1951:

It would seem that appreciations of fundamental beauty on the part of primitive peoples is coming home to us today in another Renaissance to open our eyes so

we may cut away the dead wood and brush aside the accumulated rubbish— heaps of centuries of false adoration. This Renaissance-of-the-Primitive may mean eventual return to more simple conventions in harmony with Nature. Primarily we all need **simplifying**, though we must avoid nature-ism. Then, too, we should learn the more spiritual lessons the East has power to teach the West, so that we may build upon these basic principles the more highly developed forms our more highly developed life will need if the Machine is to be a safe tool in our hands.

The text was also published in Edgar Kaufmann, Jr., and Ben Raeburn, comps. *Frank Lloyd Wright: Writings and Buildings* (New York: Horizon Press, 1960; reprint New York: Meridian Books, 1974), 88.

5. Wright seemed to grasp intuitively the extent to which an interest in folk arts would affect the literature, music, and art of early twentieth-century modernism, in the work of Bartok and Kandinsky, among others. As he noted in the Wasmuth introduction: "here as elsewhere, the true basis for any serious study of the art of architecture is in those indigenous structures, the more humble buildings everywhere which are to architecture what folk-lore is to literature or folk-songs are to music, and with which architects are seldom concerned" (Wasmuth Introduction, n.p.).

6. For a study of Otto Wagner's interest in the exoticism of Byzantine architecture, see Ákos Moravánszky, "Byzantinismus in der Baukunst Otto Wagners als Motiv seiner Wirkung östlich von Wien," in Gustav Peichl, ed., *Die kunst des Otto Wagner* (Vienna: Akadamie der bildenden Künste, 1984), 40–45.

For a survey of recent literature on exoticism, orientalism, and primitivism in the arts, see Frederick N. Bohrer, review of *Europa und der Orient, 800-1900*, by the Martin-Gropius-Bau, and *Exotische Welten, Europäische, Phantasien*, by the Institut für Auslandsbeziehungen and the Württembergischer Kunstverein, *Art Bulletin* 73:2 (June 1991): 325–30.

7. For a view of the Rookery interior, see *M* 2:333; for Wright's comments: ibid., 333. The building was managed by his client Ed Waller and contained the business offices of Wright's clients, William Winslow and the American Luxfer Prism Company.

8. For a drawing of the Beachy House mural, see *M*, 2: 379.

9. For the mantle in the Martin living room, see *S*, 50; for views of the hall mantle, *S*, 48, 51. After examining restored textiles at TAL, Katie Kosut noted the similarity (Kosut to author, personal communication, 17 July 1990).

10. On the role of ancient Egypt in the European imagination, see Sylvia Lavin "Images and Imaginings of Ancient Egypt," *Design Book Review*, 20 (Spring 1991): 44–46.

11. While Wright traveled in Europe in 1909–10, the results of archaeological excavations were generating debates about the role of antiquity in relationship to religion. Germany's nationalistic efforts to compete with English and French excavators had produced, among its results, the controversy stirred up by Friedrich Delitzsch's *Babel und Bibel* (Leipzig: J. C. Hinrichs, 1903). A brilliant anti-Semite, Delitzsch proposed that archaeology had shown that the true Christian religion stemmed from Babylonia and was not dependent on Judaic tradition. The zeal of the period saw archaeology as a principal means in the search for Truth (*Wahrheit*), and that search was a common theme in

the contemporary debates (Mögens Trolle Larson, "Archaeology in the Nineteenth Century," lecture given at the Institute of Fine Arts, New York University, 17 March 1987).

12. R. Wittkower, *Selected Lectures*, 36.

13. Ferdinand von Feldegg, "Die Grabstätte der Familie Ludwig," *Der Architekt*, 13 (1907), p. 23, quoted in Iain Boyd Whyte, *Emil Hoppe, Marcel Kammerer, Otto Schöntal: Three Architects from the Master Class of Otto Wagner* (Cambridge: MIT Press, 1989), 65 n. 43.

14. Wilhelm Worringer, *Abstraktion und Einfühlung. Ein Beitrag zur stilpsychologie* (Neuwied: Heuser, 1907). For comments on the significance of Worringer's ideas, see David Watkin, *The Rise of Architectural History* (Chicago: University of Chicago Press, 1983), 14–16.

15. Nine editions of Jones's book had been printed by 1910. For comments on his work, see Lenore Newman, "Works by Owen Jones and Christopher Dresser in the Domino's Center for Architecture & Design," *News from Domino's Center for Architecture and Design* (Ann Arbor: Domino's Center) (Summer 1989): n.p. For an insightful discussion and analysis of Jones's plates and the changing role of ornament in modern architecture, see Thomas Beeby, "The Grammar of Ornament/Ornament as Grammar," *Via* 3 (1977): 11–29.

16. Another source for the study of Egyptian ornament was the beautiful plates of Achille C. T. E. Prisse d'Avennes, *Histoire de l'art égyptien d'après les Monuments . . .* , 2 vols. (Paris: A. Bertrand, 1878–79). It followed d'Avennes's earlier work, *Monuments égyptiens, bas-reliefs, peintures, inscription, . . .* (Paris: Didot, 1847). This monumental, two-volume double folio with atlas provided the complete repertory of Egyptian iconography in exquisite detail. Its beautiful, richly saturated chromolithograph plates ranged from carefully executed architectural plans, sections, elevations, and perspectives to column details and surface decorations. It was a principal source book for the Viennese. The library of the Vienna Academy of Fine Arts, where Wagner had his Master class, contained all these works.

17. See the author's "The Kunsthistorisches Museum: A Treasure House for the Secessionists," in the *Jahrbuch des Kunsthistorisches Museum* (in press).

18. *Egyptian Art I* 1890/91. Novotny and Dobai, *Klimt*, 219, cat. 49; 293, cat. 55.

19. For the Mycenean influences on Klimt's work, see Jaroslaw Leshkow, "The Influence of the Mycenaean Discoveries on Modern Art," M.A. thesis, Columbia University, 1968. For ancient Greece, Lisa Florman, "Gustav Klimt and the Precedent of Ancient Greece," *Art Bulletin* 72 : 2 (June 1990): 310–326.

20. See Alessandra Comini, *Gustav Klimt* (New York: George Braziller, 1975), 19, 23 n. 26; Robert Alexander of the University of Iowa brought the relationship of the relief and Klimt's painting to the attention of Comini. The rounded shapes of conventionalized mountains and stylized palms formed the background for a scene concerning the slaying of lust.

21. M. E. Warlick, "Mythic Rebirth in Gustav Klimt's Stoclet Freize: New Considerations of Its Egyptianizing Form and Content," *Art Bulletin* 74, no. 1 (March 1992): 115–34.

22. See, for example, Jože Plečnik's amusing illustration of a sphinx for *Der Architekt* 1 (1895): 15.

23. [Baedeker, Karl]. *Austria-Hungary with Excursions to Cetinje, Belgrade, and Bucharest. Handbook for Travelers by Karl Baedeker*, 11th. ed. (Leipzig: Karl Baedeker; London: T. Fisher Unwin; New York: Charles Scribner's Sons, 1911), 51. The previous edition of the guide used similar exotic descriptors, but called the building a "remarkable structure" instead of a curiosity (idem, *Austria-Hungary including Dalmatia and Bosnia. Handbook for Travelers by Karl Baedeker*. 10th. ed. (Leipzig: Karl Baedeker; London: Dulau and Co.; New York: Charles Scribner's Sons, 1905), 36.

24. FLW, *An Autobiography*, 75; Owen Jones, *The Grammar of Ornament* (London: Day and Son, 1856; rpt. ed., Portland House, 1986), 5. Wright used a reprint edition, probably the first American edition of 1880, of *The Grammar of Ornament* in the library of All Souls Church, for which his uncle, Reverend Jenkin Lloyd Jones, was pastor.

Wright recounted that Louis Sullivan mentioned "Raguenet" when quizzing Wright about the sources of his ornament studies. Wright stated he did not know the name (FLW, *An Autobiography*, 92). Wright may have confused "Raguenet," who published architectural monographs, with a reference by Sullivan to Racinet. Racinet's *L'ornement polychrome . . . plans en couleurs or et argent . . . art ancien asiatique, moyên age, renaissance, XVIIe et XVIIIe Siècles*, 2 vols. (Paris: Firmin-Didot, 188?) was the appropriate comparison with the work of Owen Jones. Like Jones's folios and those of Prisse d'Avennes, Racinet's plates were a basic nineteenth-century repository of comparative ornament and showed both continuities and diversities of ornament from one culture to another.

25. FLW, *An Autobiography*, 91–92.

26. Deneken's work was subtitled *Ein Formenschatz für das Kunstgewerbe* (Berlin : Becker, 1896). For his folio of plates Deneken utilized private collections, the Royal Arts and Crafts Museum in Berlin, and the Museum of Arts and Crafts in Hamburg.

27. Hendrik P. Berlage, excerpt from *Schweizerische Bauzeitung* 60 (14 September 1912): 148–50; (21 September 1912): 165–67, in H. Allen Brooks, ed., *Writings on Wright: Selected Comments on Frank Lloyd Wright* (Cambridge: MIT Press, 1981), 133.

28. J. H. De Groot (1865–1932), *Vormharmonie* (Amsterdam: Ahrend, 1912) and *Macmillan Encyclopedia*, s.v. "De Groot, J.H." For K. P. C. De Bazel (1869–1923), see A. W. Reinink, *K. P. C. De Bazel* (Amsterdam: J. M. Meulenhoff, 1965). For their early development, see *Nederlandse Architectuur 1880–1930: Architectura 1893–1918* (Zaandam: C. Huig, 1975). For J. L. M. Lauweriks (1864–1932), see Nic. H. M. Tummers, *J. L. Mathieu Lauweriks, zijn werk en zijn invloed op architectuur en vormgeving rond 1910: "De Hagener impuls"* (Hilversum: G. van Saane "Lectura Architectonica," 1968); and idem, *Der Hagener Impuls. J. L. M. Lauweriks, Werk und Einfluß auf Architektur und Formgebung um 1910* (Hagen: Linnepe Verlagsgesellschaft, 1972).

29. In their studies of theosophy Lauweriks and De Bazel also found geometric and proportional systems of a higher order, creating a synthesis that allowed science and art to serve religion.

30. "Frank Lloyd Wright, een modern Bouwmeester in Amerika," *De Bouwwereld* 11, no. 3 (17 January 1912): 21 (translation courtesy of Maya Moran).

31. Hendrik P. Berlage, "Art and Community," *Western Architect*

congress for art and drawing lessons in London in 1908. When she married Franz Schleiss around 1909, she changed her surname to Schleiss-Simandl. Together they founded the Gmundner Keramik.

23. *Traum und Wirklichkeit, Wien, 1870–1930*, 524–526.

24. *Katalog der internationale Kunstschau Wien 1909*, 6. Simandl also exhibited a wooden figure in a vitrine in a section on Viennese arts and crafts.

25. FLW, *The Japanese Print*, 16.

26. An extensive photographic documentation was included in Marcel Kammerer, "Die Architektur der 'Kunstschau,' *Moderne Bauformen* 7, no. 9 (1908): 361–408; it included interior views of many rooms, including Metzner's gallery, Otto Wagner's designs for a war ministry in Vienna and a new study for his Friedenspalast, the Haag. See also, *The Studio* 47 (1909): 239–42, which included as its only photograph an interior of a room arranged by Josef Hoffmann with an equestrian statue by Metzner. For additional publications about the Kunstschau, see Sekler's bibliography, *Hoffmann*, 325.

27. Wright's print collection contains etchings similar to those of Muirhead Bone who had five items in a vitrine in gallery twenty-six (*Kunstschau Wien 1909*, 47).

28. Ibid., 48

29. *The Studio* 47 (1909): 240.

30. *Kunstschau Wien 1909*, 43 and unnumbered plate.

31. Wright's designs for lamps and china were produced, but none of his designs for furniture were executed (see FLW, "Frank Lloyd Wright" *Architectural Forum* 68 [January 1938]: 86).

32. An appropriate but cursory comparison between Wright's work and that of his immediate contemporaries in Europe can be made by juxtaposing his Wasmuth monograph with the collected works of Joseph Olbrich, or the emerging efforts of Peter Behrens. See Olbrich, *Architektur von Olbrich*, and the catalogue, Buddensieg, *Industriekultur. Peter Behrens*.

33. *S*, 5, 6. An earlier version of the sculpture was made by John Van Bergen, Wright's model-maker. Wright rejected it (Elaine Harrington to Karen Wilson, 27 March 1992).

34. Flower in the crannied wall,
   I pluck you out of the crannies,
   I hold you here, root and all, in my hand,
   Little flower—but *if* I could understand
   What you are, root and all, and all in all,
   I should know what God and man is.

   (Alfred Lord Tennyson, "Flower in the Crannied Wall" [1869])

For a brilliant analysis of the sculpture, see Narciso G. Menocal's comments in "Taliesin, the Gilmore House, and *The Flower in the Crannied Wall*," *Wright Studies* 1 (1991): 70–80.

35. At the Heller House, Richard Bock's row of robed, female, contrapposto figures, holding hands, are typical of his orthodox, sugary style. The murals by Orlando Giannini (or possibly Charles Corwin) for the playroom that Wright designed for his children presented a realistic figure and a partially abstracted one: a young man sits to observe the djin, floating from the magic bottle, who appears as a frontal,

winged figure with egyptoid headdress, stylized epaulets, and an aura of golden light around his head.

36. Bock's sources for the Heller House sculpture were Wright's designs for *The House Beautiful* and the *Eve of St. Agnes* (Hallmark, *Bock*, 155–57). Wright designed the text for *The House Beautiful*, and he and William Herman Winslow printed it in 1896–97. Wright designed a title page for Keats's poem *The Eve of St. Agnes* in 1896; Winslow and another client, Chauncey L. Williams, published the poem (Sweeney, *Bibliography*, 4).

37. For an illustration, see *S*, 7. The plaster model of the relief was exhibited at the Chicago Art Institute (*S*, 102, 103).

38. For a discussion of the panel, see Quinan, *Larkin Building*, 96–100. He accurately describes (p. 96) the themes of the lobby reliefs as presenting "the virtues of work and the global aspirations of the Larkin Company."

39. *S*, 135; Quinan, *Larkin Building*, 92–96.

40. *S*, 129, 131, 140–41; *W*, pl. 33a, pl. 33b. See also Quinan, *Larkin Building*, 86–91. Hitchcock called the putti "not altogether happy" and noted that the lack of abstraction in the exterior reliefs made them less suitable to the aesthetic of the building than the carvings at the tops of the piers on the interior (Hitchcock, *Nature*, 51).

41. *S*, 37.

42. *S*, 98. Bock made the sculpture in 1897 in Wright's studio and exhibited it in 1898 (Hallmark, *Bock*, 188). The Avery Coonleys also had a copy of the sculpture in their living room (*S*, 124).

43. FLW, *Japanese Print*, 32. Wright found the antithesis of the principles of simplification in "the 'Rogers Groups,' literal replicas of incidents that as sculpture are only pitiful" (ibid.). For a discussion of Wright's collection of classical casts, see Elaine Harrington, "Classical Sculpture in the Work of Frank Lloyd Wright," *Wright Angles* 16, no. 3 (Fall 1990), n.p. Wright bought his classical sculpture from the Caproni Company in Boston (Elaine Harrington to Karen Wilson, 27 March 1992). H. H. Richardson had several of the same and similar plaster casts in his professional library; Wright placed his casts in his Oak Park office, library, and elsewhere, including the house entry, where he had a cast of a frieze of the Great Altar of Zeus at Pergamon. See Meg Klinkow, "Wright Family Life in the House Beautiful," *Wright Angles* 17, no. 3 (Summer 1991), n.p. Wright also had casts of the Heller House eaves sculpture placed above the fireplace in his studio c. 1898 (Lisa Schrenk to author, 20 February 1993).

44. For Brown's Bookstore, *S*, 104; for the Larkin Building, *S*, 132. A Winged Victory also appears in a drawing for the remodeling of C. Thaxter Shaw House, 1906 (*M*, 2:416).

45. For Wright's studio, *S*, 99; for the Coonley House, *W*, pl. LVI (b).

46. Wright's octagonal studio in Oak Park contained figurines (*S*, 106). The Avery Coonley House had a cast of a seated mother and child (*S*, 121, 125; *W*, pl. LVI [b]). Other examples of Wright's sculpture include designs for a communion rail and altar sculpture for the Bagley Company, Chicago, 1894 (*M*, 1:125, 126); the center opening of the Scoville Park Fountain, Oak Park, 1903 (*M*, 2:154); and the front facade with "sculptured stone," First National Bank of Dwight, scheme #1, end of 1904 (*M*, 2: 343).

47. An exception was the use of a Winged Victory in the living room of the Francis Little House, Northome. This project was filled with problems with the client, did not receive Wright's full attention, and was tardy in its completion. For an illustration of the sculpture, see Hitchcock, *Nature*, fig. 200b.

48. Paul Kruty, "Pleasure Garden on the Midway," *Chicago History* 16 (Fall/Winter 1987–88): 4–27; subsequently cited as Kruty, "Midway." Kruty's dissertation, "Frank Lloyd Wright and Midway Gardens" (Ph.D. diss., Princeton University, 1989), includes much material on Metzner and Simandl that appeared in my dissertation, which was completed in 1987. See the author's "Frank Lloyd Wright: The Lessons of Europe, 1910–1922" (Ph.D. diss., Columbia University), 155–86, and Kruty's discussion, 187–217.

I included a synopsis of my discussion of the connection between Metzner and Wright in a public lecture, "Frank Lloyd Wright: the Impact of Europe, 1910–1914," at the annual meeting of the Society of Architectural Historians, Chicago, 16 April 1988. Kruty's dissertation was not available during my research, and I was not able to examine his treatment until October 1991. Although he uses material I presented earlier, he comes to the conclusion that there was no sculptural program at Midway Gardens ("Frank Lloyd Wright and Midway Gardens," 215–16) Obviously, I have argued otherwise—the "corroboration" comes from Wright's letters, written theories, and drawings, as well as the analysis of the formal attributes of the sculptures themselves. My main objection to Kruty's position is that he provides no iconographic analysis of the sculpture at all. While his treatment of Midway Gardens is an important and worthwhile addition to the literature, it lacks a critical apparatus or conceptual framework in which the Midway Gardens can be adequately assessed.

49. Edward C. Waller, Jr. (1877-?), attended Oak Park High School, Pennsylvania Military College, and graduated from Yale in 1899. After serving with Roosevelt's Rough Riders in the Spanish-American War in 1898, he was involved in the Chicago real estate and loan business. He had a penchant for yachting, belonged to social clubs, and was a Republican. In 1911 he maintained an office in Chicago and lived in Wheaton, Illinois (*Who's Who in Chicago. The Book of Chicagoans*, Albert N. Marquis, ed., [Chicago: A. N. Marquis & Co., 1926], s.v. "Waller, Edward C., Jr.," 402; *Lakeside Directory* [1911], 1413.)

50. The drawing F1401.007 also identifies Oscar J. Friedman as a client.

51. William Marlin to author, personal communication, 25 February 1987.

52. FLW, *An Autobiography*, 176.

53. Kruty, "Midway," 8.

54. Ibid.

55. JLW, *My Father*, 71; ibid., 71–74, for an account of John Wright's involvement with the Midway Gardens.

56. For Wright's concept of architecture conceived thoroughly in the mind, see FLW, "The Concept and the Plan," *Architectural Record* (January, February 1928), in Kaufmann and Raeburn, *Writings and Buildings*, 221–22.

57. By February 1914, Wright had the concept of the project clearly in mind. F1401.103 has written on its lower right-hand corner, "First plan for Midway Gardens." It is composed of a large U-shaped court closed at one end with a semicircular band shell or amphitheater with polygonal bandstand, and a dining room at the other. Arcades extend below the dining room, thus forming a subsidiary courtyard similar to plan forms in the project for Harold McCormick. In this scheme the building is embedded within the block. One arcade extends at right angles to the central axis near the band shell; another arcade extends to an unidentified building. Two octagons flank each side of the dining room, and an octagon is used as the podium for the band or orchestra shell.

In a subsequent drawing, F1401.105, the spaces are identified: the polygons become "fore halls," the central area a "winter garden" with a gallery at one end and four small dining rooms, each with a fireplace, at the corners of the "winter garden." The arcade off the central form is eliminated, and two private dining rooms extend beyond the sides of the main dining complex. Balconies are located at the upper level with the inner court balcony overlooking a rectangular pool. A garden now fills much of the area between winter garden and amphitheater, which now appears to float in a water-filled basin. The arcade on the left would contain "boxes" for listening and watching; the one on the right is a dining balcony with kitchen at its end. The arcade from the shell, now called a "loggia," clearly extends to the street. Below it is an area blocked out for a hotel. At the front of the complex a long narrow pool extends between the entries on Cottage Grove Avenue.

In F1401.102 Wright experimented with an asymmetrical version of the scheme, with the complex shifted to the southwest corner of Cottage Grove Avenue and 60th Street. The symmetry of the winter garden is kept, but the band shell is turned ninety degrees and attached to the end of the northern, or left, arcade. In this scheme there would be around the winter garden a dance hall, saloon, skating rink, kitchen, casino, and a theater along the street to the east. Between the small theater and the Midway complex is a garden with picturesque, winding paths. These programmatic ideas would became absorbed into the scheme as it increased in size to occupy the block. (A perspective view of this second scheme, F1401.104, has indicated on its lower right corner in Wright's hand "First sketch of the Midway," to which was added "w/ Emil Brodelle/Midway Gardens 1913–14 H. R. H[itchcock].")

Kruty also identifies two schemes preceding the final: one completed at the end of 1913, and a second alteration to the plans made in early 1914, with the final scheme completed in February 1914 ("Midway," 10). The plan can be decomposed into a grid of squares with a module that has dimensions approximately those of a belvedere interior. The overall plan was a square with sixteen modules on a side. To accommodate the function of the program, Wright combined the square modules to make rectangles, resulting, for example, in the winter garden being four modules wide and two modules deep. The rectangles lay over the grid of squares and provided the opportunity for a rich variety of spatial experiences.

Frantic development of the design followed the resolution of the plan: working drawings were required for bidding in thirty days, and construction was to be completed within ninety days for an opening date of 1 May 1914. Wright worked on the design at Taliesin in Wisconsin; Harry Robinson, the former employee from the Oak Park studio, ran the Chicago office in Orchestra Hall. A preview of Wright's designs for Midway Gardens was seen when he exhibited his drawings and model in April 1914 at the annual exhibition of the Chicago Architectural Club.

58. See Kruty, "Midway," 5, 9.

59. FLW, *An Autobiography*, 175–84, 190–92.

60. Ibid., 176.

61. Ibid., 177.

62. Alfonso Iannelli (1888–1965) was born in Andretta, Italy, in 1888. He studied from 1903 to 1906 at Newark Technical High School with William St. John Harper and then from 1906 to 1908 at the Art Students League in New York with George B. Bridgeman and Gutzon Borglum. In 1907 he won the Saint-Gaudens Prize. Later in his career, Iannelli was head of the design department at the Art Institute of Chicago and had one-man exhibits there in 1921 and 1925. He also designed industrial objects, including a coffee maker for Sunbeam, the appliance manufacturer ("Biographical Data," Alfonso Iannelli Collection, Box 1, folder 15, CHS). For a review of his work, see Joseph Griggs, "Alfonso Iannelli, the Prairie Spirit in Sculpture," *The Prairie School Review*, 2 no. 4 (1965): 5–23.

63. Barry Byrne to Emerson Goble, 18 November 1960, Series III, Box 5, folder title "Manuscripts—Barry Byrne writings," Francis Barry Byrne Collection, CHS.

64. Hallmark, *Bock*, 267. In Bock's own account of his work at Midway Gardens, he pointed out his monolithic relief that had Mephistopheles at its center (Pierre, ed., *American Artist*, 96). It shared in the exotic and strange atmosphere sought at the Gardens. Although Bock claimed the relief was a result of his own stylistic development, the relief shows that he had incorporated Wright's ideas and Iannelli's conventionalized style. For executing the painted murals, Wright employed two teachers from the Chicago Academy of Fine Arts, John W. Norton and William P. Henderson, the latter of whom brought his student, Katherine Dudley. They were joined by the Chicago painter Jerome Blume (Kruty, "Midway," 13).

65. John Lloyd Wright informed Iannelli that the Wright office had made a design for "confetti" ornament, which the Coonleys had rejected, and he proposed a new theme: fairies, a subject in keeping with the lighthearted character intended for the building and the children's playful associations with magic (JLW to AI, 19 September 1913, telegram, AI Coll., CHS). The fairy theme recalled the magical playroom in Oak Park, designed by his father, which John and his siblings had enjoyed.

John Wright sent Iannelli a sketch of the elevation of the Coonley Playhouse, indicating precisely where the modeled figures or "oil color decoration" would go. John noted that the model of sculpture for the Coonley Playhouse should be as large as possible so that it could be exhibited at Wright's next exhibition at the Art Institute of Chicago. The area under the eaves was filled with a running frieze of clear and stained glass instead of sculpture.

John also inquired about the status of the sculpture of the "Workingmen's Group" for the Workingmen's Hotel in San Diego, which John had designed while working with Harrison Albright. Iannelli had not yet completed his execution of the sculpture (JLW to Alfonso Iannelli, [late September/October 1913], AI Coll., CHS).

66. JLW to AI, 12 February 1914, telegram, AI Coll., CHS.

67. AI to JLW, 17 August 1914, AI Coll, CHS. Orlandi's contract with Iannelli was dated 23 May 1914 and was for the sum of $1,000.

68. "Concrete—Decorative Features of Midway Gardens," *Rock Products and Building Materials* 7 (January 1915): 26. The full title of the journal is not included with the article. Clipping in "Scrapbook, 1930–1932," TAL. The article indicated that Mueller Construction Company—Wright's contractor for other major buildings—was in charge, and that Iannelli superintended the "modeling of figures and panels." The Mueller Construction Company had a special corps of workmen who had previous experience with concrete casting. The technique involved first making foundry patterns of wood and plaster. A carpentry shop provided the forms; it was equipped with a saw rig driven by a Novo gasoline engine. From the forms, molds of paper and a glue-like gelatinous substance were made. The molds were to be assembled and disassembled in pieces; some figures required two parts, and some figures required as many as eighty parts. After casting, the concrete figures were sprayed with a hose until cured.

69. FLW, *An Autobiography*, 181. Wright's allusion to Kindergarten play was an indirect reference to his experience with Froebel gifts, his favorite—but facile—explanation of how he learned the geometry of architecture. Wright was introduced to the Froebel gifts, not in kindergarten, but after 1876, when he would have been about nine. Therefore, the cognitive impact of the gifts would have been far different than that on a child of four or five. The Froebel gifts were used in training his own children, as indicated by the discovery of a square block from the set found during the restoration of Wright's Oak Park Home (Elaine Harrington to Karen Wilson, 27 March 1992) and by Catherine Baxter's interview comments with Donald Kalec, June 1975 (Frank Lloyd Wright Home and Studio Research Center Archive). For an extensive treatment of the Froebel gifts, see Jeanne S. Rubin, "The Froebel-Wright Kindergarten Connection: A New Perspective," *JSAH* 48, no. 1 (March 1989): 24–37. Studies of the Froebel blocks indicate important parallels with Wright's design process: where Wright used a grid, the Froebel system used a "net" (ibid., 30), and the transformational processes using rotation, mirroring, and translation of shapes are analogous to Wright's design process. One common thread in Froebel and Wright is the nineteenth-century development of crystallography. The rationalism of crystalline structure affected not only scientists and Froebel but architects, including J. N. L. Durand, whose writings in turn were important for Viollet-le-Duc, one of Wright's major theoretical sources. See Alofsin, letter to the editor, *JSAH* 48, no. 4 (December 1989): 414–15.

70. FLW, *The Japanese Print*, 16. See my discussion in Chapter 5.

71. FLW to AI, 26 May 1915, AI Coll., CHS.

72. The prismatic treatment of the figure with scepter was developed in F1401.005, F1401.011, F1401.013; drawings with dimensions are F1401.077 and F1401.078.

73. Kruty ("Pleasure Garden," 13) identified the Winged Sprite as the "Queen of the Garden," but I have no found documentary substantiation for this title.

74. For the figure, Cube, see F1401.002, F1401.012, F1401.044, and, for its dimensions, F1401.117.

75. For development drawings of the Sprites, see F1401.005 and F1401.077.

76. Little of the Midway Gardens sculpture remains. Three examples in Chicago include an angular sprite, later installed in the garden of the Glessner House; a curvy, free-standing, sinuous example in the collections of the Chicago Architecture Foundation; a naturalistic, slender sprite, which may have been a prototype for Sphere, in the collections of the Frank Lloyd Wright Home and Studio (Elaine Harrington to Karen Wilson, 27 March 1992). Also, an angular head of a sprite is in the collections of the Art Institute of Chicago. Other examples, including the maquettes, are in the collection of Seymour Persky, Chicago.

77. Cube and Octagon were both conventionalized on drawing F1401.079, and both appear on F1401.009. For confirmation of the locations of most of the sculptures, see AI to Grant Manson, 13 May 1957, AI Coll., CSH.

78. Iannelli's sketches for Triangle are dated 25 March and 28 March 1914. See Griggs, "Iannelli," frontispiece, and University of Chicago, College Humanities Staff, *The Midway Gardens 1914–1929; an Exhibition of the Building and the Sculpture of Alfonso Iannelli* (Chicago: University of Chicago Press, 1961), fig. 4.

79. Griggs, "Iannelli," 12.

80. Totem Pole was developed in drawings F1401.003. F1401.012, F1401.044, F1401.076. Wright explored an alternative design, adding flanking "Spindles" in F1401.014.

81. The themes of Midway Gardens conveyed the "joy" of architecture Wright mentioned in his Wasmuth Introduction.

82. The key to understanding the containers as cornucopias is their "fruit" which I identify from multicolored cubes noted on F1401.003. Kruty (*Midway Gardens*, 198) sees them as "two foaming beer steins," but, consistent with his approach of downplaying symbolic meaning for sculpture, provides no explanation of their iconography, including Wright's identification of the figures as "Totem Poles."

83. See F1401.079.

84. For Michelangelo's tomb, designed by Vasari in 1570, see *La Basilica di Santa Croce* (Florence: Bonechi Editore, 1972), 6–7.

85. For Wright's design of a title page for Keats's *The Eve of St. Agnes*, see M, 1:209, and for Wright's design of *The House Beautiful*, see M, 1:212.

86. FLW, *An Autobiography*, 181.

87. Commenting on a visit to the Gardens with his father, John Lloyd Wright wrote, "Later Dad and I sat alone in the Architect's Box, a finial at the corner—a needle of light ran up the sky. This romantic building, like the expression he bore, was the mask of a great inner love" (JLW, *My Father*, 72–73).

88. R. F. Webster, "Midway Gardens to Be Formally Opened Tonight," 27 June 1914, CDT, p. 9. The Gardens opened seven weeks after its initial projected opening date.

89. JLW to AI, 23 September 1914, AI Coll., CHS. The subsequent completion of the sculpture involved the following: by the end of July

1914, Iannelli had returned to Los Angeles to recuperate from an illness and from there sent instructions on finishing the sculpture (AI to JLW, 30 July 1914, AI Coll., CHS). Iannelli indicated that he would soon communicate with Albright about restarting work on the sculptural group for the Workingmen's Hotel; the results would be quite different from his efforts in 1912. Iannelli also reported that he had seen Lloyd Wright, who had returned to California. He recommended to John Lloyd Wright that the Sphere (the figure is identified by its geometrical attribute) casting by Orlandi should be recast because it was too much trouble to correct. Triangle, however, was acceptable and only needed retouching, which Iannelli would provide, with Orlandi's agreement, when he returned to Chicago. Additional retouching was required on all the "spindles" and the Maid of the Mud. As for the original models, he suggested that most of them be destroyed, except for a few fragments that could be removed, but John could do with them whatever he considered best. He requested that John Wright have his photographer (Henry Fuermann) take photographs of the sculpture at Iannelli's expense. Iannelli also suggested that he carve a small model of the groups that Orlandi could cast and put on a model of the building. Furthermore, he was curious how the casts of the Totem Pole came out.

90. FLW, *An Autobiography*, 214.

91. Charles W. Collins, "Tales of . . . Stately Pleasure Ground is Visited" [1914] [Chicago, Illinois], in "Scrapbook, 1930–1932," TAL. Neither the full title of the article, nor the name of the newspaper is included with the clipping. Collins visited the building when it was not quite finished.

92. Ibid.

93. "Concrete—Decorative Features of Midway Gardens," *Rock Products and Building Materials*, 26.

94. Ibid.

95. Henry Blackman Sell, "Interpretation, Not Imitation: Work of F. L. Wright," *International Studio*, 55 (May 1915): lxxix–lxxxiii. One wonders what Taft thought of Wright's sculptures when he hosted an "Artist's Night" at Midway Gardens in May 1915.

96. FLW, "In the Cause of Architecture," *Architectural Record* 35 (May): 405–13. Many of Wright's theories continued the discussion outlined in his Wasmuth monograph Introduction.

97. FLW: "Style is the external manifestation of organic integrity and decoration merely an element of styles," quoted in Sell, "Interpretation," lxxix.

98. FLW: " . . . with the legitimate use of the great modern—the machine—and in harmony with the best architectural tradition we have inherited" (ibid.).

99. For the epochal event in the arrival of modernism in America, see Milton Brown, *American Painting from the Armory Show to the Depression* (Princeton: Princeton University Press, 1955). See also Sue Ann Prince, ed., *The Old Guard and the Avant-Garde: Modernism in Chicago, 1910–1940* (Chicago: University of Chicago Press, 1990).

100. The exhibit lasted from 24 March through 16 April 1913 (Hallmark, *Bock*, 274).

101. Sell, "Interpretation," lxxxii.

102. Ibid.

103. Ibid.

104. While Sell's article prominently presented Wright's geometricized sculpture and abstract murals, the article was followed, ironically, with the announcement of the death of Karl Bitter, a friend of Richard Bock and a sculptor who also found models for his sculpture in the work of Metzner. Bitter had sought the source of modern art in archaism, but was fettered by his connections to the traditions of figural representation and never completely escaped the demands of realism. On Bitter, see James M. Dennis, *Karl Bitter: Architectural Sculptor, 1867–1915* (Madison: University of Wisconsin Press, 1967). For Bitter, his relationship to Metzner, and archaism, see Susan Rather, "Toward a New Language of Form: Karl Bitter and the Beginnings of Archaism in American Sculpture," *Winterthur Portfolio* 25, no. 1 (Spring 1990): 1–19.

105. Ultimately, the records in Wright's office indicated most importantly the work for which Iannelli was responsible and secondarily the fees that were due from contracts with the Mueller Construction Company, general contractors of Midway Gardens:

Exterior sculpture:	Cornice figures	
	Tower panels	
	subtotal	$ 500
less cancelled Tower panels		250
From Midway Gardens Company:		
	Interior sculpture:	
	Sprites	
	Entrance group	
	Spindles	
	subtotal	2000
Exterior totem poles		
	subtotal	150

The total was $2,400 of which Iannelli had been paid $2,050, leaving a balance of $350 (Harry F. Robinson to AI, 5 November 1914, AI Coll., CHS). Apparently Iannelli had written Wright's office in October for an accounting of what he was owed, and Harry Robinson replied with the accounting that indicates the extent of Iannelli's commission.

Iannelli's studio requested the payment of $350 due on 5 November as noted in a letter of 14 October from Robinson (Iannelli Studios to Harry F. Robinson, 5 November 1914, AI Coll., CHS). Iannelli explained to Robinson that the accounting was completely acceptable, and that he had written him for the accounting only as a formality to confirm the total of the contract which was required on the creditor's agreement that he had been sent.

106. AI to FLW, 21 May 1915, AI Coll., CHS. Wright initiated the exchange of letters in FLW to IA, 17 May 1915, in ibid.

107. AI to FLW, 21 May 1915, AI Coll., CHS.

108. Ibid.

109. Ibid.

110. Ibid. Wright's explanation of the matter was insufficient for Iannelli, who wrote a long and angry response (AI to FLW, 5 June 1915, AI Coll., CHS.) Iannelli maintained that he had attempted to conventionalize the figure independent of Wright, and that he deserved credit for his own efforts to actualize the sculptures. Iannelli believed his work was superior to Metzner's, and that: "Mentzner [sic] . . . has never accomplished a unified architectural expression in his sculptures even to this day, after all his years of work" (ibid.). Furthermore, Iannelli expanded the argument beyond a dispute between the two men to the issue of the "connection between artists and architects in this country, and the relative credits due them . . ." (ibid.).

Wright replied with imperious annoyance: "Your note makes me quite tired. It is so usual—the usual gratitude and misunderstanding" (FLW to IA, 18 June 1915, copy, AI Coll., CHS). Yet, he maintained that Iannelli's work had given him gratification and pleasure and that the work had received insufficient consideration.

In 1954 John Lloyd Wright wrote to Iannelli to confirm his important role at the Midway Gardens and Frank Lloyd Wright's difficulty in acknowledging Iannelli's collaboration, but on several subsequent occasions Iannelli was compelled to defend his contribution at Midway Gardens (JLW to AI, 10 June 1954; AI to Grant Manson, 13 May 1957, AI Coll., CHS).

111. FLW to AI, 18 June 1915, copy, AI Coll., CHS.

112. Iannelli never collected the balance owed to him. Insufficient as the construction budget was, Iannelli and other creditors had few prospects for collecting payment for work done at the Gardens. The Gardens were in financial distress even before they opened. John Lloyd Wright had earlier sounded an ominous note about the financial condition of the Gardens that ultimately would have dire consequences and affect Iannelli and others who were owed money for work on it (JLW to AI, 23 September 1914, AI Coll., CHS.). John reported that the Midway Company was upset with "Mr. Waller's tactics" and that the stockholders would lose their money but the creditors would be paid (ibid.) Orlandi had not been paid anything yet. Despite the financial conditions of the company, the Gardens were crowded with visitors most of the time. A lack of capital from its inception doomed the Gardens to financial ruin regardless of the crowds who thronged to it. Bankruptcy proceedings began in 1916: a meeting at the office of Butz, Von Ammon & Johnson, was announced for 13 May 1916 for the creditors of the Midway Gardens ("To the Note Holders of the Midway Gardens Company," 20 May 1916, AI Coll., CHS).

Chapter Seven

1. FLW, *A Testament*, 189.

2. FLW, *Japanese Print*, 67–68.

3. FLW, Wasmuth Introduction, n.p.

4. Ibid. Wright's use of the phrase "self-imposed limitations" is unclear; these limits could have been either the budgets of his clients or his own lack of skills.

5. Wright wrote "Machine Age Ornament" on F1401.014, a variant design of the sculpture Totem Pole.

6. Quinan, *Larkin Building*, 115. Wright's "Reply to Mr. Sturgis's Criticism" was withheld from publication in the *Architectural Record* in

deference to the death of the critic on 11 February 1909. The Larkin Company published the essay in April 1909, but it appears to have had very limited distribution.

7. FLW, *An Autobiography*, 162.

8. For the seminal work on primary forms, see Otto Antonia Graf, *Otto Wagner*, vol. 3. *Die Einheit der Kunst, Weltgeschichte der Grundformen* (Vienna and Cologne: Böhlau Verlag, 1990); subsequently cited as Graf, *Grundformen*.

9. Deneken's plate of "Star Pattern with Snow Flowers" provides a similar universal pattern: the polygonal grid with a structure capable of nearly infinite subdivision. In this example the artist chose to identify two regular polygons, one filed with dots, the other with the "snow flower." Rather than fill the space between with a third polygon, the artist suppressed the form and allowed the void to assume the shape of a six-pointed star that echoes the multipointed star that it contains. These are visual patterns that exist in polygonal designs of Islamic architecture as depicted in Owen Jones, *The Grammar of Ornament* or Racinet, *Ornement polychrome*. The polygonal grid provides the underlying structure which supports a variety of patterns that are found in a variety of cultures.

10. Graf, *Grundformen*, 66–77, for the introduction of the Isis circle.

11. Isis is depicted in one aspect as having a circle, her hieroglyph, over her head; in another aspect as assimilated with the goddess Hathor, with horns and a circle; and in a third aspect resembling the Hathor assimilation and suckling an infant pharaoh. See R. E. Witt, *Isis in the Graeco-Roman World* (Ithaca: Cornell University Press, 1971), pls. 1–3. For references contemporary with Wright's activities, see E. A. T. W. Budge, *The Gods of the Egyptians*, 2 vols. (London: n.p., 1904).

12. The rotated square may also be produced by incorporating the circle into the square and connecting the points of tangency to provide a second square rotated about the first square. Connecting the midpoints of the sides of the rotated square produces a third square which is parallel to the sides of the first square and half its area.

13. For the plan, see Graf, *Otto Wagner*, I, 26, cat. no. 33.

14. For studies concerning mysticism, abstraction, and spiritualism, see the catalogue *The Spiritual in Art: Abstract Painting 1890–1985* (New York: Abbeville Press, 1986).

15. M. E. L. Mallowan and J. Cruikshank Rose, "Excavations at Tall Arpachiyah 1933," *Iraq* 2, part 1 (April 1935), pl. I, fig. d, for stone foundations of tholoi TT7–10; fig. 3 for a site plan showing the prevalence of tholoi; and pl. II for an aerial view of the site.

16. M. E. L. Mallowan, "Excavations at Brak and Chagar Bazur," *Iraq* 9 (1947), pls. III, IV, XXX.

17. Mark A. Brandes, *Untersuchungen zur Komposition der Stiftmosaiken an der Pfeilerhalle der Schicht IVa in Uruk-Warka* (Berlin: Gebruder Mann, 1968), pl. VII.

18. For an example of half columns in front of the Pillar Terrace at Warka, see Anton Moortgat, *The Art of Ancient Mesopotamia* (London and New York: Phaidon, 1969), 163, fig. 2.

19. W. Stevenson Smith, *The Art and Architecture of Ancient Egypt*, (Harmondsworth: Penguin, 1981), 25.

20. The motifs of primary form pervade the architecture, painting, graphic arts, and craft objects of the Vienna Secession and the Wiener Werkstätte. For a visual summary of these motifs in the furniture, objects, and interiors of the Secessionists and members of the Wiener Werkstätte, see Paul and Stefan Asenbaum and Christian Witt-Dörring, *Moderne Vergangenheit 1800–1900* (Vienna: Gesellschaft bildender Künstler Österrichs, Künstlerhaus [1981]).

21. W, pls. LVIIb, XXXIIb, XXXIb, IV; pl. XXXV; and for Wolf Lake, pl. LXa, LXb.

22. See F1401.973.

23. An alternative study exists for the mural: F1401.008.

24. FLW, *Japanese Print*, 16.

25. Wright achieves his effect by making a regular set of horizontal lines spaced 12 units apart that forms a matrix with vertical lines spaced 12, 12, then 14, 14, 14, 12, 12, 14, 14, 14, 12, 12. All centers of the circles fall on at least one of the grid lines. Thus a free-floating imagery is disciplined by a grid whose vertical rhythm is A A B B B A A B B B A A, and whose horizontal rhythm is A A A A A A A A A A A.

26. FLW, *Japanese Print*, 15–16.

27. Graf, *Grundformen*, 139–40.

28. For the symbolism of the square, see Carl Jung, *Psychology and Alchemy, in Collected Works*, vol. 12 (London, 1953), and Enel, *La langue sacrée* (Paris, 1932), both of which are cited in J. E. Cirlot, *A Dictionary of Symbols*, 2nd ed. (New York: Philosophical Library, 1971). Citing M. Senard, *Le Zodiaque*, (Lausanne, 1948), Cirlot states that in the Romanesque period the square resting on a corner (a rotated square) symbolized the sun.

29. Eduard Sekler to author, personal communication, May 1987. Hoffmann and Moser were familiar with decorative configurations of squares before they saw examples by Mackintosh (Sekler, *Hoffmann*, 508 n. 37). Their method of working had led them in this direction, but much before the work of Mackintosh there was a more fundamental source available from Holland through Dutch theories of design. See Marian Bisanz-Prakken, "Das Quadrat in der Flächenkunst der Wiener Secession," *Alte und Moderne Kunst* 27, nos. 180–81 (January 1982): 39–46.

30. *Ver Sacrum* 5, no. 17 (1902), unpaginated gallery after p. 260.

31. Wright's original signature to his buildings was a square containing the upper portion of a Celtic cross; he used it, for example, at the Winslow House in 1893 and on office stationery (see F0407.024). (For a discussion of the signature, see Graf, *Die Kunst*, 1: 14–15, 45–50.) Although Wright adopted the square as a monogram, he used the circle within a square in various building designs, such as in the playroom plan of the Coonley House (Wijdeveld, *Life Work*, 14) and the Imperial Hotel, where it was the motif of the urn at the entry of the building (*IH*, fig. 31, 2–3). In plan and elevation the urns are composed of a circle within a square. When executed, the circle was carved as a sphere and the square as a framing device.

32. See Wright's signature block on F1108.001, a facade drawing for the Coonley Kindergarten, which Wright dated 1911.

33. Wright eventually adapted for his signature the practice of adding his initials and the date to the square.

34. From the first plate showing the windows of the Winslow House (pl. Ib) to the last plan for Unity Temple (pl. LXIVa), the square

82. Tw
83. See
84. See
main entry
85. Sig
Architectur
"as everyw
operates as
Willendorf
86. Ma
vol. 13 of I
pl. 4.
87. See
rich's worl
A. Becker,
pearances
88. Ibi
89. At
level in wl
tation of tl
striations.
Arthur J. 1
versity Mt
crenelated
Anu ziggu
90. Se
North Am
gan Librar
91. Se
G., in Hei
92. Tl
ustrade ar
hofer's vil
There, it t
able in th
93. C
Studio 19
94. F
stätte (Vi
95. S
96. S
angle, un
97. T
cuted (M
98. S
Rilke's p
99. T
illustrate
100.
seine wir
101.
(1899):
crum, 18

dominates. When combined with the octagon, Wright used it to generate practically all the plans of his designs.

35. See "The Cement Show," *NYT*, 4 December 1910, pt. 6, p. 11, and "Cement Show Opens To-night," *NYT*, 14 December 1910, p. 2.

36. *S*, 111.

37. See F1404.014.

38. Wright's aesthetic concept of the Machine Age, first articulated in 1901 in "The Art and Craft of the Machine," was also part of a larger cultural discourse which included such pronouncements as Paul Haviland's in the modernist journal *291*: "We are living in the age of the Machine. Man made the Machine in his own image" ([Introductory statement] *291*, nos. 7–8 [October 1915]).

39. For Wright's 1908 discussion of the "nature of materials," see *In the Cause of Architecture*, ed. Gutheim (New York: Architectural Record Books, 1975), 53–63, and the Wasmuth monograph Introduction, n.p.

40. Graf, *Grundformen*, 186.

41. By rotating a Cartesian grid, a dynamism is introduced in the composition whereby the matrix visually opposes the ground plane in a special case of triangulation. When the rotated grid is condensed, the squares become diamonds, with each unit consisting of two triangles sharing a common base.

This forms a lattice pattern that, like primary forms themselves, is seen throughout traditional cultures. As Elaine Harrington has pointed out, diamond-shaped patterns had been long used in America: at a small scale in early American homes of the seventeenth century; at a larger scale during the the Gothic revival of 1840–60; and in the American Colonial revival of 1890–1910 (Elaine Harrington to Karen Wilson, 27 March 1992). Wright had used the pattern for leading in glazing throughout his own home and in the early versions of the Oak Park studio. He also used diamond shapes in the windows of Tanyderi for his sister and in brother-in-law (c. 1901, built 1907) in a manner common to architects of the Arts and Crafts movement. It was the temporary pattern of the "decorated frieze" at the Coonley House exterior murals, and he used it as the temporary pattern for Midway Gardens facades (for the lattice at the Coonley House, see *M*, 3:7, 8).

However, when he began to use the lattice as a field, he used it more generically, as it had been used for centuries for the backgrounds of relief sculpture, for instance, on the garments worn by figures in Maya reliefs. Wright used the rotated lattice in his design for the facade of a cinema in San Diego of c. 1913–15, where it produced a eye-catching matrix (see *M*, 12:33).

42. *Meno* 81B–87A, in *Great Dialogues of Plato* (New York: New American Library, Mentor Books, 1956), 42–52.

43. Prism with patent number 28,007. See *Official Gazette*, U.S. Patent Office, vol. 81, pt. 3, no. 10.

44. Brown House, scheme no. 2, 1906 *M*, 2:463–465. The rotated square also appears as a minor motif in the facades of the house for Robie Lamp, Wright's childhood friend. In this project the square is a motif that could have been cast onto blocks. But this may have been the work of Walter Burley Griffin, who was fond of the diamond shape (see John O. Holzhueter, "Wright's Designs for Robie Lamp," in Paul Sprague, ed., *Frank Lloyd Wright and Madison: Eight Decades of Artistic*

and Social Interaction (Madison: Elvehjem Museum of Art, 1990), 13–27.

45. In a study of the plan Wright considered inserting rotated squares at each end of the first floor, but he crossed out the square at one end and left it at the other (*M*, 2:3,4).

46. For a rotated square in the ceiling of the Ward Willits House of 1901, see *M*, 1:404, and for rectilinear glass patterns, see *M*, 1:405.

47. For Wright's additive process applied to a semicircular living room, see Hiram Baldwin House, scheme #2, (*M*, 2:278).

48. Donald Kalec to author, personal communication, 3 November 1990.

49. See *M*, 12:67.

50. Graf, *Grundformen*, 186–98.

51. The second edition, of 1779, is in the Academy's library.

52. See the plan of Temple II, Tikal, Teobert Maler, *Explorations in the Department of Petén, Guatemala: Tikal*, in Memoirs, Peabody Museum of Archaeology and Ethnology 5, no. 1 (1911), 31, fig. 5. The publication was completed by A. M. Tozzer, *Preliminary Study of the Ruins of Tikal, Guatemala*, ibid., 5, no. 2 (1911).

53. The use of the square-within-a-square motif in painting and the graphic arts provides a subject unto itself. For one example, see the motif as used in Peter Janssens Elinga's (1623–82) *Room in a Dutch House*, in *Dutch and Flemish Painting from the Hermitage* (New York: Metropolitan Museum of Art, 1988), 31.

54. Graf, *Wagner*, 53–55, fig. 50.

55. Wagner used the square within a square for the articulation of cornices. Instead of relying on moldings or brackets of a traditional classical cornice, he inserted the motif under the eaves of the cornice at the Postal Savings Bank (1903–10) and under the eaves at the building on Döblergasse 4 (1911), where at the corners of the cornice he elided two squares and snipped away the corner of both the cornice and corner of the building below—an inversion (or negative) of the re-entrant corner of Schinkel. The square within a square also appeared in his Villa Wagner (1912) (ibid., 649, fig. 889) and in his design for Hotel Wien (ibid., 694, fig. 939). Wright used an analogous treatment for the cornice of the *Call* Building.

56. For the publication of Purkersdorf Sanatorium, see Sekler, *Hoffmann*, 288; *Hohe Warte* 2 (1905–6): 70; *DKuD* 18 (1906): 421–443; and *International Studio* 43 (1911): 193.

57. An excellent example of the quadrate is a glass bowl, designed by Josef Hoffmann in 1905, which is in the collection of J. and L. Lobmeyer, Vienna.

58. Elaine Harrington to Karen Wilson, 27 March 1992. The laquerware is in the collection of the Frank Lloyd Wright Home and Studio; the personal stationery in a private collection.

59. FLW, *Japanese Print*, 23. Wright wrote an essay on the Shibaraku role for the Introduction to the Chicago Arts Club, *Antique Colour Prints from the Collection of Frank Lloyd Wright*, (Chicago: Chicago Arts Club, 1917). The exhibition was held 12 November through 15 December 1917 at the Fine Arts Building, Chicago. Wright's Introduction was dated 12 October 1917.

60. For the meaning of *mon* as badge, see B. W. Robinson's review of *The Art of Surimono: privately published Japanese woodblock prints*

study; only the formal logic of the ornament will be touched on here. My investigations are based on the archival drawings and other documents at TAL.

112. The drawing is dated 15 February 1921.

113. Additional studies of ornament using the circle as the main motif include F1509.184, F1509.244, F1509.273, F1509.466, F1509.467, and F1509.545.

114. F1509.340.

115. F1509.224; F1509.445 and F1509.087; F1509.036; and F1509.361 in which the motif is nearly identical to the relief panels on the Ravine Bluffs Bridge of 1915.

116. See F1509.006 and *IH*, 84, fig. 114.

117. F1509.034 and F1509.035; F1509.032.

118. See also the simple use of multiple frames in F1509.534, F1509.465 with a strong diagonal emphasis; and F1509.228, combined with other motifs.

119. See F1509.228.

120. See also F1509.514.

121. F1409.016.

122. See Hoffmann's Purkersdorf Sanitarium (1904), in Sekler, *Hoffmann*, 67, for wall treatments similar to those in Wright's first Imperial Hotel scheme.

123. Monroe, "The Orient an Influence," 1914, p. 8.

124. See also F1409.008 in the series of studies for the first scheme.

125. See *M*, 12: 61; *M*, 4: 29, 30.

126. Josef A. Lux, "Klinger's Beethoven und die moderne Raum-Kunst," *DKuD* 10 (1902): 481, quoted in White, *Hoppe, Kammerer, Schöntal*, 17.

127. The motifs of primary forms could be seen as analogous to language itself. Otto Graf has suggested that the concept of the deep plane (*tiefe Tafel*) was important to Otto Wagner, which implies the correlative of the recessed plane in architecture to linguistic concepts (Otto Antonia Graf, personal communication to author, May 1987). This analogy can be summarized briefly in the work of Ludwig Wittgenstein, whose productive years followed the generation of the prime movers of the Secession. He grew up in Vienna during the formative years of the Secession, his father helped finance Olbrich's Secession Building, and the family maintained a salon which artists frequented (Gary Indiana, "Ludwig Wittgenstein, Architect," *Art in America* 73 no. 1 (January 1985): 121).

Wittgenstein described language in the terms of architecture: "Our language can be seen as an ancient city: a maze of little streets and squares, of old and new houses, and of houses with additions from various periods; and this surrounded by a multitude of new boroughs with straight regular streets and uniform houses" (Ludwig Wittgenstein, *Philosophical Investigations* 3d ed. [New York: Macmillan, 1958], 8e, remark 19). To understand language was to understand life itself, according to Wittgenstein, and underlying language was a logic of fundamental unity: "In what sense is logic something sublime? For there seemed to pertain to logic a peculiar depth—a universal significance. Logic lay, it seemed, at the bottom of all sciences" (ibid., p. 42e, remark 89). Depth (*Tiefe*) provided character that gave the structure of

language a universality and was found even in the misinterpretations of language. According to Wittgenstein, words had both surface and depth, a "surface grammar" and a "depth grammar."

Chapter Eight

1. FLW, *A Testament*, 111.

2. Hitchcock, *Nature of Materials*, 59–72, set the generally received attitudes about the period. With respect to the Coonley Playhouse: "In the interior more than the exterior we notice a certain heaviness or membering, which, in general, differentiates the houses of the these years from the more delicately domestic work before 1910" (p. 61). Hitchcock also commented that the small houses of the later Prairie style period were "often somewhat heavy. The projecting trellises are [the] most successful elements of detail" (caption, plates 201, 202).

3. The seminal article is Dimitri Tselos, "Exotic Influences in Frank Lloyd Wright," *Magazine of Art* 47 (April 1953):. 160–69, 184; subsequently cited as Tselos, "Exotic Influences." It was followed by idem, "Frank Lloyd Wright, Klassiker der modernen Weltarchitektur," *Universitas* (Stuttgart), (1959): 355–62; idem, "Frank Lloyd Wright and World Architecture," *JSAH* 28 (March 1969): 58–72; subsequently cited as Tselos, "World Architecture." Gabriel Weisberg addressed Maya influences on Wright in "Frank Lloyd Wright and Pre-Columbian Art—the Background for His Architecture," *Art Quarterly* 30 (Spring 1967): 40–51; subsequently cited as Weisberg, "Background." Further discussions of the exotic influences on Wright have been recapitulations of these articles; see Terry R. Kirk, "The Sources of Pre-Columbian Influences in the Architecture of Frank Lloyd Wright" (M.A. thesis, Columbia University, 1986), for an expansion of the subject and approach introduced by Tselos and Weisberg. For a popular treatment, see Marjorie Ingle, *Mayan Revival Style: Art Deco Mayan Fantasy* (Salt Lake City: Peregrine Smith Books, 1984).

4. Tselos, "World Architecture," 58–60. Vincent Scully cites Wright's own house in Oak Park of 1889 as an indirect example of the influence of Désiré Charnay's publication of 1885. Scully argues that Wright's house was derived from a shingle-style house by Bruce Price, that Price knew of Charnay's book, and therefore that Wright could have absorbed Price's interest in the Maya. Scully also describes the entry of Wright's Winslow House as the mask of the Maya rain god, Tlaloc, grafted onto a Froebel block (*Nature of Frank Lloyd Wright*, xix). However, the entry could be analyzed exclusively as a design deriving from Louis Sullivan's system of ornament and Wright's interest in Cartesian geometry. Furthermore, Scully provides no context to explain why Wright would use a Maya motif at the Winslow House.

5. FLW, "A Conversation," in *The Future of Architecture* (New York: Horizon Press, 1953; reprint ed., New York: New American Library, 1970), 38.

6. FLW, *Japanese Print*, 28.

7. John L. Stephens, *Incidents of Travel in Central America, Chiapas, & Yucatan*, 2 vols. (New York: Harper and Brothers, 1841); reprinted, 2 vols. in 1 (New Brunswick: Rutgers University Press, 1949). For some of the available sources, see Weisberg, "Background," 47–48.

For the broad range of exhibits, see also *Chicago World's Columbian Exhibition Official Catalogue*, Part 12, Anthropological Building, Midway Plaisance, and Isolated Exhibits (Chicago: W. B. Gonkey, 1893). Among the full-size casts were the arch at Labna, portions of the Temple of the Serpents, and sections of the Nunnery at Uxmal (Tselos, "Exotic Influences," 163). Maler's photographs have been unnoticed in the literature on the fair. His photographs and his site plans of Tikal in Guatemala would also have been available by 1911 in Teobert Maler, *Explorations in the Department of Petén, Guatemala: Tikal*, in Memoirs, Peabody Museum of Archaeology and Ethnology 5, no. 1 (1911). The publication was completed by A. M. Tozzer, *Preliminary Study of the Ruins of Tikal, Guatemala*, ibid., 5, no. 2 (1911).

8. Désiré Charnay, *Cités et ruines américaines, Mitla, Palenqué, Ixmal, Chichén-Itzá, Uxmal. Recueillés et photographiées par Désiré Charnay, avec un text par M. Viollet-le-Duc* (Paris: Gide, 1863), 1–104.

9. William Marlin to author, personal communication, 4 June 1991. Lloyd Wright conveyed this information to Marlin during an interview.

10. Tselos states ("Exotic Influences," 184) that the motif appears on the title page of a biography on Wright; I have not been able to confirm this after examining various editions. He may have been mistaken about its source. The motif appears as a logo and trademark on the cover and title page of *Frank Lloyd Wright on Architecture. Selected Writings 1894–1940* ed. and introduction by Frederick Gutheim (New York: Duell, Sloan, Pearce, 1941).

11. Ibid. Marlin discovered this material from correspondence in the Iannelli Archive in a private collection in Chicago.

12. Ibid.

13. Edgar L. Hewett, Introduction by W. N. Holmes, "Ancient America at the Panama-California Exposition," *Art and Archaeology* 2. no. 3 (November 1915): 64–102.

14. W. H. Holmes, Introduction, in ibid., 66.

15. Ibid., 67.

16. Among the exhibits were casts of four sculptures from Palenque; hieroglyphic inscriptions from Palenque; a column reproduced from the portal on top of the pyramid "El Castilo" (or "Temple of the Sacrifice") at Chichén Itzá; a large relief map showing the location of fifty ancient Temple cities; replicas of monoliths from Quiriguá including the Great Turtle, named by Maudslay and identified as the "greatest of all Central American Sculptures"; stele of a "Death God," a leaning shaft described as the largest known stele; "The Queen," and "The Dragon."

The frescoes by Carlos Vierrà of the School of American Archaeology, included the cities of Quiriguá (excavated in 1910 and 1916), Copan, Tikal, Palenque, Chichén Itzá, and Uxmal.

17. Hewett, "Ancient America," 99–101. The Temple of Kukulkan was also referred to as the "Temple of the Sacrifice."

18. Ibid., 78.

19. Ibid., 75.

20. For the wall murals by Orlando Giannini, see "Mural Restoration Project Uncovers Giannini Artwork," *Wright Angles*, (April–June 1986) n.p. The glass ceiling panel for the Harley Bradley House contained another example of Wright's interest in Indian motifs. See *Frank Lloyd Wright Update*, no. 26 (vol. 3, no. 6) (Summer 1991): 60.

21. William Norman Guthrie, *Offices of Mystical Religion* (New York and London: The Century Co., 1927).

22. Alice D. Fletcher, "The Hako: A Pawnee Ceremony," Part II of the *Twenty-Second Annual Report of the Bureau of American Ethnology* (Washington, D.C.: Government Printing Office, 1904).

23. Ibid., 280.

24. The sacred objects included eagle feathers of white and brown to symbolize male and female principles; these were hung on a stem painted blue to symbolize the heavens, a male principle. The pipe was painted to represent contact with the heavens (ibid., 218). "Mother Corn" was the same object that the explorer Marquette had seen in 1672 among the Illinois Indians; he called it a "calumet" (ibid., 279).

25. Guthrie, *Offices of Mystical Religion*, xix, xx.

26. Wright owned many of Guthrie's works. The following remain in Wright's archive at TAL: *The Gospel of Osiris—A Lay of the Lady Isis* (New York: Brentano's, 1916), which was signed by Guthrie to Wright, "The House of Helios" (Guthrie's Drawings and Sketches) (1926); and an undated MS, "Foreword and Godspeed (Taliesin), Story-Narrative."

27. For the only historical treatment of the project, see Mary Jane Hamilton, "The Kehl Dance Academy," in Paul Sprague, ed. *Frank Lloyd Wright and Madison: Eight Decades of Artistic and Social Interaction* (Madison: Elvehejm Museum of Art, 1990), 65–68.

28. Weisberg, "Background," 49 and figs., 5, 6, from Frederick Catherwood's illustrations for Stephens, *Incidents of Travel in Central America, Chiapas & Yucatan*.

29. F1205.001. Wright later dated the drawing "1906," but there is no evidence to support such an early date.

30. F1205.008. The date "1913" is written in the lower left of the drawing, along with Wright's signature. The completed perspective was not published until 1925, when it appeared in H. Th. Wijdeveld, ed., *The Life Work of the American Architect Frank Lloyd Wright* (Santpoort, Holland: C. A. Mees, 1925). The book was the first major update of Wright's work after the Wasmuth publications in 1910 and 1911. It is often referred to as *Wendingen* because it included a series of articles previously published by the journal of the same name. A second edition appeared as *The Work of Frank Lloyd Wright, The Life Work of the American Architect Frank Lloyd Wright with Contributions by Frank Lloyd Wright*, The Wendingen Edition (New York: Horizon Press 1965; New York: Bramhall House [1965]. Unless noted otherwise, this and subsequent citations are to the Bramhall edition; the Kehl Dance Academy perspective appears on p. 99.

Although uncredited, Weisberg's fig. 1 ("Background," 40) is from the illustration in Wijdeveld, *Life Work*.

31. Weisberg, "Background," 49.

32. For discussions of the warehouse, see Randolph C. Henning, *The A.D. German Warehouse: A Rehabilitation and Adaptive Reuse Design* (Master of Architecture thesis, University of Wisconsin, Milwaukee, 1980; Ann Arbor: University Microfilms, 1985); and Margaret H. Scott, *Frank Lloyd Wright's Warehouse in Richland Center, Wisconsin* (Richland Center: Richland County Publishers, 1984).

33. Henning, *Warehouse*, 4–9. German bought the property, which included the Hotel Badger, in 1907 and built a storage warehouse in 1912. The reason for German commissioning Wright is unclear; Wright may have bought supplies from him, or offered the design as barter for goods, but that remains speculation; no correspondence at TAL has been uncovered to establish their relationship in the 1910s. The original estimated cost for the building was $30,000 but was well over $125,000 in 1919. German lost the warehouse due to nonpayment of taxes, repurchased it the 1930s and had Wright remodel the building in 1934. German went bankrupt in May 1939 and lost the building a second time.

34. Tselos, "Exotic Influences," 163; Weisberg, "Background," 49–50; Scully, *Frank Lloyd Wright*, 24.

35. Tselos published a model of the Temple of the Frescoes in the collections of the Brooklyn Museum ("Exotic Influences," 165, fig. 11); Weisberg reproduces the Temple of Tulum citing his sources as in illustrations from Frederick Catherwood's illustrations for Stephens, *Incidents of Travel in Central America* (1841) and *Incidents of Travel in Yucatan* (1843) ("Background," 44, figs. 5, 6).

36. For the sun-god masks, compare the reconstruction of the façade (Tatiana Proskouriakoff, *An Album of Maya Architecture*, rev. ed. [Norman: University of Oklahoma Press, 1963], 93); and the masks of sun gods on Structure 5C-2nd, at the recently excavated site of Cerros, Belize, late pre-classic (Mary Ellen Miller and Linda Schele, *The Blood of Kings: Dynasty and Ritual in Maya Art*, [Fort Worth: Kimball Art Museum, 1986], 106–8, figs. II.1, II.2).

37. See F1504.012.

38. The perspective view (F1504.001) was not published until 1925 in Wijdeveld, *Life Work*. It is rendered in the same manner as the perspective for the Kehl Dance Academy, and may have been drawn for the publication, instead of for presentation to the client. See also F1504.008.

39. Tselos ("Exotic Influences," 163) has pointed to the Maya hooked tongues found at the Temple of the Three Lintels at Chichén Itzá as analogous to the warehouse brackets. The range of reliefs recalls galleries of Puuc architecture. See Mary Ellen Miller, *The Art of Mesoamerica from Olmec to Aztec* (London: Thames and Hudson, 1986), 179.

40. In analyzing the multiple references of the German warehouse we could also consider a reference to oriental culture. Because of its function as a storage depot, Wright may have also referred to the *kura*, a type of warehouse for storage. From his travels or from Morse's popular *Japanese Homes and Their Surroundings* Wright would have known of this building type as a thick-walled, fireproof structure for storing valuable possessions; its roof was immensely thick, and its roof ridge was ornamented with designs in stucco and terminated with ornamental tiles in high-relief. See Edward S. Morse, *Japanese Homes and Their Surroundings* (Boston: Ticknor and Co., 1886; reprint, New York: Dover, 1961), 33–35, 75–76; and Norman F. Carver, Jr., *Japanese Folk Houses* (Kalamazoo, Mich.: Documan Press, 1984), 53; and 75, 85, 90 for typical roof types.

41. Elaine Harrington has noted that the "arrow" design of the stained glass of Wright's house for Governor Henry J. Allen in Wich-

ita, Kansas (1917), indicates Wright's interest in American Indians along with a Japanese aesthetic found in the gold appliqué placed between brick courses (Elaine Harrington to Karen Wilson, 27 March 1992).

42. Wright's account of his relationship with Aline Barnsdall and the building of Hollyhock House is indispensable: see his *An Autobiography*, 224–33. The seminal article is Kathryn Smith, "Frank Lloyd Wright, Hollyhock House, and Olive Hill, 1914–1924," *JSAH* 38, no. 1 (March 1979): 15–33; subsequently cited as Smith, "Hollyhock House." See also Neil Levine, "Hollyhock House and the Romance of Southern California," *Art in America* 71, no. 8 (September 1983): 150–65; and idem, "Landscape into Architecture: Frank Lloyd Wright's Hollyhock House and the Romance of Southern California," *AA Files*, no. 3 (January 1983): 22–41.

43. Smith ("Hollyhock House") has published these studies as figs. 14–18. The original drawings are in the collection of the City of Los Angeles, Department of Recreation and Parks and the Municipal Art Department.

44. Tselos, "Exotic Influences," 166.

45. Scully, *Frank Lloyd Wright*, 25 and pl. 62.

46. Ingle, *Mayan Revival*, 15.

47. For Wright's use of enclosed courtyards, see the project for the Arthur W. Cutten House of 1911 and the Henry J. Allen House, Wichita, Kansas of 1917 (Wijdeveld, *Life Work*, 54; ibid., 34–35). Both rely exclusively on Wright's Prairie-period style.

48. Quoted in Smith, "Hollyhock House," 27 n. 35.

49. Smith has shown ("Hollyhock House," 26–27) that Hollyhock House demonstrated Wright's efforts to have the form of these residences respond to the character and technology of poured concrete.

50. Smith, "Hollyhock House," 27 n. 34.

51. Wijdeveld, *Life Work*, 142–43. For a brief discussion of the theater projects, see *M*, 10: 23. For a sketch of the octagon-topped scheme, F2005.01, *M*, 10; a more developed rendering is F2005.03, *M*, 10: 31. Wright designed a total of four theaters for Barnsdall, and made three models, only one of which is extant.

52. At least three models were made. The top for an octagonally-terminated version exists in the collections of the Frank Lloyd Wright Foundation at Spring Green. Wijdeveld published three versions for the square-topped scheme with various portions of the plaster model cut away (*Life Work*, 158–61). Hitchcock (*Nature of Materials*, fig. 214) published a different view of the *Life Work* illustration on p. 159.

53. Tselos, "Exotic Influences," 166; Ingle, *Mayan Revival*, 15.

54. Tselos's illustration of the theater is from Wijdeweld, *Life Work*, and the illustration of the Maya building is by the photographer V. L. Annis. The original drawing appears in *M*, 10:32.

55. The theater complex was developed as part of a series of designs and given clear definition in F2005.003, where Wright identified the central building as the theater and the pavilion on the right as a club house.

56. This corner treatment is also found in window-glass patterns for the Hollyhock House. A drawing of window-glass patterns in the collection of the Library of Congress shows patterns that could have been used in a number of Wright's earlier houses. This undated design

comes from an office Wright maintained at the Homer Laughlin Building, Room 522, Los Angeles.

57. See Smith, "Hollyhock House," 23, figs. 8–10, for Wright's further development of the theater complex and the Hollyhock House.

58. F1705.001. The drawing has written on its lower left, "Mr. Wright's original sketch at Olive Hill"; above this, Wright has added his initials and the date 1913. The date, however, is incorrect, and the existence of preliminary studies indicates that this sketch followed earlier designs. The cubic masses of the center building were flanked with two pavilions, all three of which had roofs with canted attics. Above this central building was another cubic form in whose center is a tall, pointed arch, an analogue of the triangular archway used in both Maya and Mesopotamian architecture.

59. See F1705.064 in *M*, 10:29.

60. See *M*, 10: 39, 41, 42, 44.

61. For illustrations, see Wijdeveld, *Life Work*, 158–61.

62. The sculptures are present in Wijdeveld, *Life Work*, 160 but absent in the variant model, p. 161. For the use of conventionalized sculpture at the *Call* Building, see the author's "The *Call* Building: Frank Lloyd Wright's Skyscraper for San Francisco," in *The Urban Dimension: Essays in Architectural History and Criticism* (Vienna: Böhlau Verlag, in press).

63. For an illustration of the lower portion of the model of the Barnsdall Theater, see Hitchcock, *Nature of Materials*, fig. 214. Hitchcock dates the model to 1920.

64. Wright also designed a pair of conventionalized birds for the fountain in the interior. The birds are poised as if to drink from the fountain. Barbara Elsner kindly provided the author with photographs of the exterior and interior of Bogk House, which is currently her residence.

65. For drawings of the elevation, see F1602.10, F1602.019.

66. Harriet Riddle, "The F. C. Bogk House, Milwaukee, Wisconsin," *Frank Lloyd Wright Newsletter* 2, no. 1 (1979): 1–4. Riddle's article was written in 1937. Construction began in 1917 but was hindered by a scarcity of laborers, who were becoming involved in World War I, and by Wright's absence in Japan. The walls were reinforced concrete with a brick veneer. For a brief, general description of the Bogk House, see also *M*, 4:90–210.

67. See F. C. Bogk House, elevation study, Drawing no. 887810.2 in Drawings of Frank Lloyd Wright, Collection of the Library of Congress, Division of Prints and Photographs, Library of Congress, Washington, D.C.; subsequently cited as LC.

68. Wijdeveld, *Life Work*, 97

69. Tselos, "Exotic Influences," 167, 184, and fig. 20, p. 169.

70. Esther Pasztory, *Aztec Art* (New York: Abrams, 1983), 76, 80–82, observes that the symbolic forms of Aztec culture derive from Mixteca-Puebla designs in manuscripts and polychrome pottery and predate development of Aztec art.

For the representation of winged figures in Aztec art, see the Sun Deity in Eagle Dress, a vertical drum in the collection of the Museo del Malinalco, illustrated in ibid., 273, pl. 289; and a high dignitary wearing a bird mask with wings, illustrated in Henri Stierlin, *Art of the Aztecs and Its Origins* (New York: Rizzoli, 1982), 65, pl. 42.

71. Herbert J. Spinden, *A Study of Maya Art*, vol. 6 of the Memoirs of the Peabody Museum of American Archaeology and Ethnology, Harvard University (Cambridge, Mass: Peabody Museum, 1913; reprint, New York: Dover, 1975). For Hochob, see pl. 11, fig. 2. Fig. 1, the left wing of the principal structure, also shows the sculpture. See also Gordon R. Willey, *Das Alte Amerika*, vol. 18, Propyläen Kunstgeschichte (Berlin: 1974), pl. 155.

72. In one version of the frieze (F1602.003) Wright had only large figures. In the blank areas between the large figures, he inserted the smaller figures as seen in the LC drawing "Detail of Stone Lintel . . . Bogk House" and in Wijdeveld, *Life Work*, 96.

73. The projects included an unsolicited design for a United States Embassy in Tokyo (1914) for which Wright reworked the plan and elevation of the Thaxter Shaw House; houses for Count Immu, Tokyo (1918), Viscount Inoue, Tokyo (1918), Baron Goto, Tokyo (1921), and the cinema for the Ginza, Tokyo (1918–20). Works executed based on Wright's designs included the Odawara Hotel (begun in 1917, but unfinished); Fukuhara House, Hakone, (begun in 1918, resumed in 1921, and destroyed in 1923); Imperial Hotel, Tokyo (1915–23) and the Imperial Hotel Annex (1915); Hayashi House, Tokyo (1917); Yamamura House, Ashiya, Hyogo (1918); and the Jiyu Gakuen School of the Free Spirit, Tokyo (1921–26). For brief discussions of these works, see Masami Tanigawa, *Measured Drawings: Frank Lloyd Wright in Japan* [Tokyo: Graphic Co., 1980]; and Robert Kostka, "Frank Lloyd Wright in Japan," *Prairie School Review* 3, no. 3 (1966): 5–27 and cover.

74. The ridge pole ceremony, signifying completion of the house, was held on 1 February 1924. Two units of measurement were used: the foot as a horizontal unit, and the *shaku* as a vertical unit, thus implying that Endo prepared the working drawings. See Tanigawa, *Measured Drawings*, 32, 40–49 for drawings.

75. Ingle, *Mayan Revival*, 15. The author also states, "its massing and proportions are similar to the Hollyhock House, but with the forms stacked pyramid-like."

76. See Désiré Charnay, *Les anciennes villes du nouveau monde; voyages d'exploration au Mexique et dans l'Amérique Centrale, 1857–1882* (Paris: Nachette, 1885, trans. J. Gonino and Helen S. Conant, *The Ancient Cities of the New World, being voyages and explorations in Mexico and Central America from 1857–1882* (New York: Harper and Bros., 1888), 250; Teobert Maler, *Explorations in the Department of Péten, Guatemala: Tikal*, vol. 5, no. 1 of Memoirs, Peabody Museum, Harvard University (Cambridge: Mass, 1911); A. M. Tozzer, *Preliminary Study of the Ruins of Tikal, Guatemala*. vol. 5. no. 2 of Memoirs, Peabody Museum, Harvard University (Cambridge: Mass, 1911).

77. Masami Tanigawa, "Frank Lloyd Wright, Master Living in Legend," in Sakae Ohmi and Terunobu Fujinori, eds., *Unusual Modern Architects* (Tokyo: Asahi Newspaper Publishers, 1984), 175. My thanks to Katie Kosut, who drew this material to my attention.

78. See J. Eric S. Thompson, Introduction, Spinden, *Maya Art*, Dover ed., x.

79. For a house near Lake Biwa, see Carver, *Japanese Folk Houses*, 75; for the roof style near Hiroshima, ibid., 90. For the prevalence of these traditional roof shapes in the nineteenth century, see Morse, *Japanese Homes*, especially fig. 41, p. 59, for a house near Mororan,

Yezo. Wright may have traveled very little outside Tokyo during the intensive years of work on the Imperial Hotel. But such travel was not impossible, and Wright's travels through the countryside on his first trip to Japan are established by the extensive photographic scrapbook he made that is now in the archive of the Frank Lloyd Wright Home and Studio. Numerous Japanese castles used canted stone bases as part of their fortifications, as at Nijo Castle, Kyoto.

If considered strictly as a conventionalization of natural form, the roof of the Yamamura House could be seen to recall the inclined angle of Rokko-san, an unusually treeless mountain nearby.

80. See Morse, *Japanese Homes*, fig. 43, p. 61, for a three-storied house in Rikuchiu.

81. Wright's strong interest in Japanese roof forms is confirmed by the photographs he took during his travels in Japan in 1905.

82. See F1509.021 for the Imperial Hotel lobby roof. For an illustration of the model for the cinema in the Ginza, 1918, see Hitchcock, *Nature of Materials*, fig. 215.

83. There is no evidence that Wright received a commission for this scheme prior to his design. Realizing that the Japanese were interested in motion pictures, he may have proposed the design for the Ginza in order to attract a client. Despite the unusual massing and character of the ornament, the Japanese might have seen the interior as a space similar to those in existing theaters. If Wright had found a client for the project, he could then have made necessary alterations to accommodate a cinema.

84. FLW, *Japanese Print*, 68.

85. Thus, the canting of walls recalled the precedents of earthworks in the earliest burial mounds or the earthen cores of multistory Chinese buildings. For the earthen cores of Chinese buildings, see Robert L. Thorp, "Architectural Principles in Early Imperial China: Structural Problems and Their Solutions," *Art Bulletin* 68, no. 3 (September 1986): 360–78. Even in Maya architecture, the canted roof form is so pervasive that many models can be cited, such as the Temple of the Cross at Palenque and Temple V at Tikal. See George Kubler, *The Art and Architecture of Ancient America: The Mexican, Maya and Andean Peoples* (Baltimore: Penguin, 1962), 116, fig. 30, for a comparison of roof forms among Maya buildings.

86. FLW, Wasmuth Introduction, n.p.

Chapter Nine

1. FLW, *Japanese Print*, 15–16.

2. FLW, Wasmuth Introduction, n.p.

3. See Beeby, "Grammar of Ornament," 14, for discussions of symmetry and nature, in D'Arcy Thompson, *On Growth and Form*.

4. Typical glass patterns before 1910 include the flower pattern in an oval arch, Little House, Peoria, a precursor of the Dana House (*M*, 2: 47); the Unity Temple auditorium ceiling (*M*, 2: 234); glass in the W. R. Heath House in Buffalo, 1905 (*M*, 2: 251, 252); and the Robie House, 1906–10 (*M*, 2: 358–61, 364).

5. See F0803.031.

6. See Reyner Banham, "The Wilderness Years of Frank Lloyd Wright," *Journal of the Royal Institute of British Architects* 76 (December 1969): 516 and n. 14 in which Banham cites FLW, *An Autobiography*, 255, and Finis Farr, *Frank Lloyd Wright: A Biography* (New York: Charles Scribner's Sons, 1962), 142.

7. Neil Levine, "Frank Lloyd Wright's Diagonal Planning," in Helen Searing, ed., *In Search of Modern Architecture: A Tribute to Henry-Russell Hitchcock.* (New York: Architectural History Foundation; Cambridge, Mass.: MIT Press, 1982), 245–77. Levine asserts that "Between 1910 and 1920, Wright's planning became more and more classical, emphasizing rectilinearity, closure, and formality" (250).

This view of Wright's regression, however, sidesteps several important issues. Many of Wright's earlier plans are symmetrical; Midway Gardens and the Imperial Hotel were continuations of these planning principles. Both buildings had precedents in symmetrical models, from European beer gardens for Midway, to royal Chinese palace precincts for the Imperial Hotel. And, following Wright's dictum that buildings should grow "in response to actual needs" (FLW, Wasmuth Introduction, n.p.), it is important to realize that symmetrical plans often facilitate the circulation systems of large public buildings.

Furthermore, Levine notes an exception to his argument for Wright's "regressive" planning between 1910 and 1920 when he cites the "aggressive diagonality" of Wright's design for Taliesin I in 1911 (252–53). Levine sees the building as the lone example of the period and proposes that Wright provided his clients with no other such buildings until Fallingwater in the mid-1930s. Wright's first design for the house of Sherman Booth, however, which preceded Taliesin I in 1911, had shifting axes in its planning and dramatically engaged its site. Most important, such assertions should be placed in the larger context of the development of Wright's work.

8. See Louis Sullivan, *A System of Architectural Ornament According with a Philosophy of Man's Powers*, reprint with essay by Lauren S. Weingarden (New York: Rizzoli in cooperation with The Art Institute of Chicago, 1990); citations are to the reprint edition. The first edition was published in 1924.

9. Ibid., 129, pl. 5.

10. In a drawing of a Midway Gardens window (F1401.111) Wright used the central mullion to provide a center line, but in contrast to his earlier methods, strict symmetry is broken by inverting some of the triangles and their colors on each side of the mullion. A dynamism is introduced in the Midway design by the inclusion of countervailing lines, drawn between upper left and lower right corners, that demarcate shaded triangles. Instead of bilateral symmetry dominating, the diagonal dominates in the presence of local symmetries.

11. Wright's term "Dancing Glass" appears on F1401.015. The "Dancing Glass" motif is found in a family of decorative motifs at Midway Gardens for panels, doors, and glass in drawings including F1401.016, F1401.066, F1401.067, F1401.068, F1401.069, F1401.070, F1401.071, F1401.081 and F1401.111. See also F1401.080.

12. F1401.081.

13. F1401.004.

14. For the design study of the pier, see F1401.080.

15. FLW, *An Autobiography*, 191.

16. The drawing is in the LC collection. For Wright's early use of the matrix, see the stained-glass-window sketch for Darwin D. Martin House, 1904 (M, 2:192).

17. F1509.096. The variation of theme here is a parallelism, replicated in parallelograms with one placed within another. The resulting interstitial triangles connect to a line intersecting the corner of the long parallelogram, thus creating the opposing diagonal. Planes can be raised or lowered to create visual tension. F1509.097 is a duplicate of F1509.096.

18. F1509.098.

19. F1509.464 and F1509.125.

20. See, for instance, in F1509.524 the interlacing frame details between the piers.

21. F1509.005, and a similar study, F1509.004. These designs are related to the more restrained stone overmantel relief at the Barnsdall Hollyhock House (see F.1705.027, published in M, 10:18 and M, 4: 269). The design dates of the Barnsdall House and Imperial Hotel overmantels remain to be established.

22. "Takara-No-Ma," IH, 108.

23. For the seminal article on this project, see Mary Jane Hamilton, "The Nakoma Country Club," in Paul Sprague, ed., Frank Lloyd Wright and Madison, 77–82. The developers of the suburb wanted to associate the suburb with its Indian origins, and, disregarding historical accuracy, chose the name Nakoma, a Chippewa word for "I do as I please." Associations with Indians became a theme for the golf club.

24. Ibid., 81.

25. "Unique Lodge Plan in Nakoma," Wisconsin State Journal, in Hamilton, "Nakoma Country Club," 80.

26. The Arthur E. Cutten residence was a project designed for Downers Grove, Illinois. The house for Henry J. Allen in Wichita, Kansas, was one of the most elaborate residences of the decade. The design was begun in 1916. Allen, a newspaper publisher and state governor, was an important client for Wright; their relationship and the history of Allen's house deserve further examination. For George Niedecken's involvement in furnishing Allen's house, see Niedecken, 84–87.

Chapter Ten

1. FLW, A Testament, 205.

2. FLW, Wasmuth Introduction, n.p.

3. Smith, "Postscript," 309.

4. Numerous publications appeared on the Imperial Hotel's survival. See FLW, Experimenting with Human Lives (Chicago: Ralph Fletcher Seymour, 1923), and Louis H. Sullivan, "Concerning the Imperial Hotel, Tokyo, Japan," Architectural Record 53 (April 1923): 332–52; and idem, "Reflections on the Tokyo Disaster," Architectural Record 55 (February 1924): 113–18. For other publications, see Sweeney, Annotated Bibliography, 29–30.

5. Twombly, Life and Architecture, 182.

6. FLW, An Autobiography, 260.

7. For a summary of the turmoil with Miriam Noel and Wright's meeting of Olgivanna Hinzenburg, see Twombly, Life and Architecture, 182–192.

8. For the concept of Kunstwollen, see Alois Riegl, Stilfragen (Berlin: G. Siemens, 1893).

9. For a cogent review of the Austrian movement, see Hans Ankewicz-Kleehoven, "Kunstgewerbe," in Carl Brockhausen, Österreich in Wort und Bild (Berlin, Vienna, and Leipzig: Franz Schneider Verlag, 1924), 44–47.

10. The date of the cinema project (F0517.02) has been published as "1905?" (M, 12:33), but the design could not have been made before 1913 and more likely followed the Midway Gardens sculptures in 1914–15. Wright also provided the location, San Diego, where he visited his son John in 1913. (See also San Diego cinema project in M, 2: 323, 324.)

11. F1509.024 is a revised detail of the sculpture for the promenade entrance; the drawing is dated 7 October 1921 and signed by Wright.

12. For a view of the sculpture at the roof ridge, see IH, fig. 2, pp. 2–3; fig. 9, p. 9.

13. Study for exhibition poster, LC. Executed in graphite and colored pencils, the poster announced: "Exhibition of Japanese Colour Prints and Paintings by Late Hashi Guchi Goyo and his Collection of Old Colour Prints Will be Held at Takashimaya Dept. St[ore] Kyobashi, Tokyo, Oct. 28, 29, 30. Free to All. The Ukiyoye Society of Japan."

14. For the commission of the sculpture, see Mary Jane Hamilton, "Nakoma Memorial Gateway," in Paul Sprague, ed., Wright in Madison, 83–88. The date of the commission is not addressed, but since the fate of the project was doomed by August 1926, the commission must have come before. Although never executed for their site, various casts and reproductions of the figures were subsequently made (ibid., 87).

15. Wright's personal interest in Indians was reinforced by an apocryphal story that Olgivanna and her child posed for Nakoma (ibid., 84). Hamilton's version includes Iovanna as a model, but she had not yet been born.

The interest in Indians was further confirmed by Erich Mendelsohn's account that, during his visit to Wright in 1924, Wright had the German architect dress up in Indian clothing, replete with bark shoes, staff, gloves, and tomahawk (ibid., citing H. Allen Brooks, ed., Writings on Wright, 7).

16. For Taft's sculpture, see Hamilton, "Nakoma Memorial Gateway," 86.

17. Booklet prepared for the Madison Realty Company, developers of the Nakoma suburb, quoted in ibid., 84.

18. Ibid.

19. One exception is in the 1957 project for a monument to Haroun-al-Rashid, caliph of Baghdad; the figure is conventionalized in the manner of the Nakomis sculpture. See F5751.004 and Bruce Brooks Pfeiffer, ed., Frank Lloyd Wright Drawings (New York: Abrams in association with the Frank Lloyd Wright Foundation and the Phoenix Art Museum, 1990), 163–64.

20. FLW to Erica Karawina, 15 December 1931, TAL. Karawina, an artist, wrote to Wright after hearing one of his lectures. Katie Kosut provided me with this information.

21. Taft, *Modern Tendencies in Sculpture*, 27–29.

22. Ibid., 66. Taft's attack here is on George Sieburg's decorations for the Marble Theater in Berlin. Taft's thinking also characterized a belief in certain, definable, and inevitable artistic lineages of influence: "In the lineage of art every manifestation is traceable to a definite ancestor" (73; see also 97).

23. Ibid., 63.

24. Ibid., 62.

25. For a synoptic assessment of the development of cubism, see William Rubin, *Picasso and Braque: Pioneering Cubism* (New York: Museum of Modern Art; Boston: Bulfinch Press, Little, Brown, 1989).

26. Ibid., 144. For Manship, see Harry Rand, *Paul Manship*, (Washington, D.C.: Smithsonian Institution Press, 1989; Susan Rather "The Origins of Archaism and the Early Sculpture of Paul Manship" (Ph.D. diss., University of Delaware, 1986); idem, "Toward a New Language of Form: Karl Bitter and the Beginnings of Archaism in American Sculpture," *Winterthur Portfolio* 25, no. 1 (Spring 1990): 1–19; idem, "The Past Made Modern: Archaism in American Sculpture," *Arts Magazine* 59 (November 1984): 111–19; and idem, *Archaism, Modernism, and the Art of Paul Manship* (Austin: University of Texas Press, 1992).

27. William Norman Guthrie to FLW, [18 February 1916], Guthrie Papers, Harvard University. Guthrie wrote from his church at St. Mark's In-the-Bouwerie in New York.

28. By mid-summer of 1919 Wright had translated his concept of a wood-frame construction system to a concrete prototype design for T. P. Hardy, his former client in Racine, Wisconsin. The system followed Wright's efforts throughout the teens in the American System-Built houses, developed for the Milwaukee builder Arthur Richards.

In the Hardy project Wright continued to search for a means of mechanically replicating surface pattern in addition to seeking an economical construction system for mass production. The plan for this residence was cruciform. On the first floor were a living room, a double-height dining room, and kitchen; on the second floor, a bedroom, an outside sleeping porch, and a second porch where plants could be grown. Consistent with Wright's other designs using concrete, the roof was flat.

Designed for steel-reinforced concrete and wood-framed windows, the walls would have been poured into forms, and when tied into the slabs of the floors would have created a monolithic unit. The continuity of surface resulting from the pouring process was countered by Wright's squaring of the wall surfaces into a grid. Each unit of the grid contained a screen-covered square, a "concrete separator," at a corner, which was intended to provide ventilation to the slab and a pattern to the monotonous concrete surface.

Wright considered that the system he devised had sufficient commercial potential to have Rudolph Schindler prepare drawings and to patent the design in August 1919. (FLW, Copyright Deposit, "The Monolith Home for T. P. Hardy, Racine, Wisc.") Schindler signed the copyright drawing in July 1919, and Wright submitted four sheets

of blueprints to the copyright office, which granted patent number CL I 4867R on 18 August 1919 (LC).

The project was not realized, but it had ramifications for Wright's subsequent studies in economical systems of mass production that featured the patterning of surfaces. The pouring of monolithic slabs of concrete required, however, the costs of formwork, and the technology of the process limited the surface of concrete to a uniform expression.

29. Robert Sweeney has carried out the definitive research on Wright's textile block houses. For preliminary results of his investigations, see Robert L. Sweeney and Charles M. Calvo, "Frank Lloyd Wright: The Textile Block Houses," *Space Design* 7–9, no. 240 (September 1984): 63–78.

30. Undated blueprints at LC containing seven figures demonstrating the textile block construction system. Wright is named as the "inventor" of the system, and the sheet was submitted by W. R. Litzenberg, his attorney.

31. An early study in the LC collection shows a relatively simple panel pattern: a repeat composed of an imbedded square motif, flanked above, below, and on its sides by rectangles, with squares filling in the corners. The plans of these elements had beveled edges and were to be recessed or raised.

32. The units could be assembled to span spaces in the same way as beams. Thus, individual units, which, like conventional tiles, were associated with their decoration, could be amalgamated into composite structural members, denying their conventional tectonic meaning as surface elements.

33. Tselos, "World Architecture," 67. The cylinder seal, published by Tselos as fig. 16, contained the symbol of the Lamat, which was used as a Venus-sign, or as a glyph of a twenty-day period, or both. It is also known as the Kan-cross from the classic Maya period when it was used as a symbol of the four corners of the world, and, among the Aztec, as a symbol of turquoise, water, and fertility. Tselos ("Exotic Influences," 166) also compared the ornament of Millard House to the inner court of the Zapotec palace, Mitla.

34. Ingle, *Mayan Revival*, 17.

35. Interview with Kameki Tsuchiura by C. Ford Peatross, 2 May 1991, Tokyo. My thanks to Peatross for sharing the answers to questions prepared by myself and Katie Kosut.

36. Drawing for pattern block of the Freeman House, full-scale, LC.

37. The elements of the Freeman House block form a secondary level of pattern in a way similar to Wright's study for the nine-unit pattern of the Imperial Hotel. Here, the secondary pattern arises when four units are grouped into a square to reveal an imbedded octagon and, within it, four squares, which, in turn, combine to form a square.

The difference between the pattern blocks of the Freeman House and the blocks of the Imperial Hotel is their means of fabrication and material. Wright replaced hand carving with the mechanical reproduction of modules made possible by mold-casting; concrete replaced oya stone. Also, since the assembly of the textile blocks created an opening between the surfaces, the deepest plane of the pattern could be a void—"a perforation" of the surface "where needed," as Wright indicated on the Freeman House block drawing. While concrete was more dense than the oya, these perforations physically lightened the textile block and visually enlivened it by allowing deeper contrasts of solid and void, producing a delicate, screen effect in a dense material.

38. Although the textile block system contained for Wright the means of expressing pattern and was a potentially economic system of construction, it also had the basic problem of requiring nonstandard units. Wright still had to confront the conventional architectural problems of terminations, joints, and turning corners with building elements. The unit replicated over a plane posed no problems, but when it came to an edge—at floors, ceilings, and windows—special blocks were needed.

This required difficult design solutions of a technical nature, added to the number of molds and units required, and thus increased the cost of building and complexity of construction. These problems subsequently plagued the textile block system, and later in the 1920s combined with other factors to force a simplification of the patterns and ultimately a reduction in the use of the system.

The Arizona Biltmore Hotel and cottages, designed and built in conjunction with Albert McArthur in Phoenix in 1927, was a major textile block design. Its blocks show a simplification from previous designs. By 1929, when Wright had completed design of Westhope, a residence for his cousin Richard Lloyd Jones in Tulsa, Oklahoma, the exterior block had no patterns. Without ever fully solving the technical processes, Wright eventually abandoned the textile block system, and the patterned blocks along with it, in favor of simpler construction systems that ultimately led to the varied systems of the Usonian House, a more successful model of low-cost housing.

39. Neil Levine sees these plan forms as representations of nature. For his explanation, see his "Abstraction and Representation in Modern Architecture: The International Style of Frank Lloyd Wright," *AA Files*, no. 11 (Spring 1986): 3–21.

40. Rubin, "Modern Primitivism, an Introduction," in *Primitivism in 20th Century Art*, 2–3. Rubin notes that "With the 'discovery' of African and Oceanic masks and figure sculptures by Matisse, Derain, Vlaminck, and Picasso in the years 1906–07, a strictly modernist interpretation of the term began." This change signaled a shift of artistic interest, with "primitive art" becoming identified with the tribal art of Africa, Oceania, and North American Indians and Eskimos.

41. For the incorporation of ornament and polychromy in socialist worker housing, see, for example, the Hufeisen Siedlung (Horseshoe Housing) of Bruno Taut and Martin Wagner in Britz, Berlin (1927).

42. See FLW, review of *Towards a New Architecture* by Le Corbusier, in *World Architecture* 2 (September 1928): 393–95; and for the Elizabeth Noble Apartment House (Los Angeles), see Hitchcock, *Nature*, figs, 303, 304 with captions; and *M*, 5:147–51.

43. See Lloyd Wright's design for the Sowden House in Los Angeles, in Francis S. Onderdonk, *The Ferro-Concrete Style. Reinforced Concrete in Modern Architecture, with Four Hundred Illustrations of European and American Ferro-Concrete Design* (New York: Architectural Book Publishing Co., 1928), 112–16.

44. Benjamin, "The Work of Art in the Age of Mechanical Reproduction," in *Illuminations*: 217–51, particularly 220–25.

45. Rudolf Wittkower, "Interpretation of Visual Symbols," in *Allegory and the Migration of Symbols* (Boulder: Westview Press, 1977), 186.

46. In 1985, in Wright's studio at Taliesin, I found the following volumes in the Orbus Pictus/Weltkunst-Bücherei series (ed. Paul Westheim [Berlin: Ernst Wasmuth, A.G., 1922 (?)]): vol. 5, *Asiatische Monumentalplastik*, foreword by Karl With; vol. 16, Carl Einstein, *Die Frühere Japanische Holzschnitt*; vol. 1, *Indische Baukunst*, foreword by Paul Westheim; vol. 14, *Islamische Architektur*, introduction by Sattar Kheira; vol. 8, Walter Lehmann, *Altmexicanische Kunstgeschichte, Ein Entwurf in Umrissen*; vol. 9, Otto Weber, *Die Kunst der Hethiter*. Also, included in the series was an incongruous subject, a book on the paintings of Poussin, David, and Ingres, vol. 15, *Klassizismus in Frankreich*, foreword by Paul Westheim.

Lehmann's *Altmexicanische Kunstgeschichte*, pl. 44, illustrates a column representing a feathered serpent from the Temple of the Tiger and Jaguar; it may be the plate that Tselos glimpsed when he visited Wright in the early 1950s (Tselos, "Exotic Influences," 184). Einstein's *Die Frühere Japanische Holzschnitt*, p. 39, has an illustration of the Ichikawa *mon*.

47. FLW, *A Testament*, 205.

48. FLW to DDM [1929], MS 355, Box 3, 15, ST. Internal evidence indicates the date of this letter. For an example of Bossom's interest, see Alfred C. Bossom, *An Architectural Pilgrimage in Old Mexico* (New York: Scribner's, 1924). For the romanticization of the Maya, see also an illustration of Tikal prepared by Bossom in conjunction with the 41st Annual Exhibition of the Architectural League in New York (idem, "Restoration of Ancient City of Tikal, Guatemala, *American Architect* 129, no. 2491 [20 February 1926]: 266. For further comment, see Dennis Sharp, ed., *Alfred C. Bossom's American Architecture, 1903–1926* (London: Book Art, 1984), 74.

Popular interest in the Mesoamerican, particularly the Olmec, had been stimulated by the efforts of the *National Geographic* in the 1930s to boost lagging sales by featuring stories on the charming qualities of these relatively forgotten origial Americans. Teams were sent to document the sites and sculptures, thus adding to a rebirth of general interest in early Mesoamerica.

49. FLW to DDM [c. 1927], ST.

50. FLW, *Frank Lloyd Wright on Architecture* (New York: Duell, Sloan and Pearce, 1941), 192; quoted in Walter Creese, *The Crowning of the American Landscape: Eight Great Spaces and Their Buildings* (Princeton: Princeton University Press, 1985), 267.

51. Frank Lloyd Wright and Baker Brownell, *Architecture and Modern Life*. (New York: Harper and Brothers, 1938), 17.

52. FLW to Robert J. Goldwater [editor, *Magazine of Art*], n.d., in Tselos, "World Architecture," 72.

53. FLW, *Ausgeführte und Entwürfe von Frank Lloyd Wright* (Berlin: Ernst Wasmuth, 1924).

54. Correspondence at TAL demonstrates that Wright put H. Th. Wijdeveld, who was collating the issues of Wright's work in the Dutch magazine *Wendingen*, in competition with Heinrich de Fries, who published Wright's work in Germany. See Wijdeveld, *Life Work* (1925),

and Heinrich de Fries, *Frank Lloyd Wright: Aus dem Lebenswerke eines Architekten* (Berlin: Verlag Ernst Pollak, 1926).

55. Jean Badovici, "Entretiens sur l'architecture vivante: l'art de Frank Lloyd Wright," *L'Architecture Vivante* 2 (Winter 1924): 26–27, pls. 34–35.

56. FLW, "A Conversation" [Television interview with Hugh Downs], in *The Future of Architecture*, (New York: Horizon Press, 1953; reprint, New York: New American Library, 1970), 38.

57. FLW, *Buildings, Plans, and Designs* (New York: Horizon Press, 1963), n.p.

58. Ibid.

59. Bruce Brooks Pfeiffer to author, personal communication, 8 July 1984.

60. For Wright's absorption of contemporary architecture at the turn of the century, see Vincent Scully, *Frank Lloyd Wright*, 11–15.

61. Wittkower, *Selected Lectures*, 192.

62. FLW to CRA, 26 September 1910, quoted in Crawford, "Ten Letters," 69. Wright's statement followed in a postscript.

63. Ibid.

Appendix A

1. Ralph Mueller to FLW, 9 March 1939, in Dana Hutt, "Architectural Collaboration and Frank Lloyd Wright, Case Study: Contractor Paul F. P. Mueller," typescript, 5 May 1992.

2. Ibid.

Bibliography

The literature on Frank Lloyd Wright is vast, predominantly of a secondary nature, and conveniently cited in over 2,000 entries through October 1977, in Robert Sweeney, *Frank Lloyd Wright, An Annotated Bibliography.* Only the works essential for this research, Wright's own writings, and material published after 1977 are listed here. Since much of the work for this book was based on unpublished archival sources and comprehensive monographic treatment of individual buildings was not a goal, only brief bibliographies for individual buildings are included. However, I have emphasized sources outside the standard bibliographies for subjects that I believe require further investigation, such as the origins of ornament and the flow of ideas between America and Europe just after the turn of the century.

The bibliography has been organized into four sections to facilitate reference to the authors and documents cited in the text. The first section lists the archival collections consulted. The second section includes monographic works mentioned, including dissertations. The third list includes references to essays, journals, and periodicals. The fourth list consists of the various editions of Wright's monograph and *Sonderheft,* except for commercial publications of calendars and appointment books that use the plates of the Wasmuth monograph for illustrations.

1. Manuscripts and Archival Collections

Andover-Harvard Theological Library, Harvard Divinity School, Cambridge, Mass.: William Norman Guthrie Papers.

Avery Library, Columbia University, New York: Drawings and Archives Collection.

Chicago Historical Society, Charles F. Murphy Architectural Study Center, Chicago: Francis Barry Byrne Papers, Alfonso Iannelli Papers, John Lloyd Wright Papers.

Domino's Center for Architecture and Design, Ann Arbor, Michigan: Frank Lloyd Wright Collection and the Henry Fuermann photographic archive.

Elvehjem Museum, University of Wisconsin, Madison, Wisconsin: Van Vleck Collection.

Frank Lloyd Wright Foundation, Taliesin West, Scottsdale, Arizona: Frank Lloyd Wright Archives.

Harvard University Archives, Pusey Library, Harvard University. Cambridge, Mass.: Kuno Francke Papers.

Institut für Kunstgeschichte. Akadamie der bildenden Künste (Academy of Fine Arts), Vienna, Austria: Otto Wagner Archive and Kupferstichkabinett.

Library of Congress, Architecture, Design and Engineering Collections, Prints and Photographs Division, Washington, D.C: uncatalogued drawings of the Frank Lloyd Wright Collection.

Metropolitan Museum of Art, New York: Division of Prints and Drawings.

National Archives Trust Fund Board, National Archives and Records Administration, Washington, D.C.: Index to passport applications.

Northwest Architectural Archives. University Library, University of Minnesota, St. Paul, Minnesota: William Gray Purcell Papers.

Österreichisches National Bibliothek (Austrian National Library), Vienna, Austria: Handschriftenabteilung (Manuscript Division) and Bildarchiv (Picture Archive).

Stanford University Libraries, Department of Special Collections, Palo Alto, California: Frank Lloyd Wright–Darwin D. Martin Papers, M355.

State Historical Society of Wisconsin, Madison: Iconographic Collections.

State University of New York at Buffalo, University Archives: Wright–Martin Papers, MS22, no. 86–052.

University of Utah Libraries, Manuscripts Division, Special Collections

Department, Salt Lake City, Utah: Taylor Woolley Papers, Accession No. 152.

Vienna Stadt-und Landesarchiv, Vienna, Austria: Meldezettel of the Magistratsabteilung.

2. Monographs and Dissertations

Adlon, Hedda. *Hotel Adlon, the Life and Death of a Great Hotel.* Translated by Norman Denny. New York: Horizon Press, 1960.

Akashi, Nobumichi (Shindo). *Kyu Teikoku Hoteruno Jisshoteki Kenkyu* [*Frank Lloyd Wright in Imperial Hotel*]. [Tokyo: Tokodo Shoten, 1972].

Allgemein Städtebau-Ausstellung. Literatur Verzeichnis. Berlin: Ulstein & Co. [1910?].

Alofsin, Anthony. "Frank Lloyd Wright: The Lessons of Europe, 1910–1922." Ph.D. dissertation, Columbia University, 1987.

Alofsin, Anthony, ed. *Frank Lloyd Wright: An Index to the Taliesin Correspondence.* With an introduction, "Frank Lloyd Wright as a Man of Letters," by Anthony Alofsin. 5 volumes. New York: Garland, 1988.

Anderson, Stanford O. "Peter Behrens and the New Architecture of Germany." Ph.D. dissertation, Columbia University, 1968.

Asenbaum, Paul; Asenbaum, Stefan; and Witt-Dörring, Christian. *Moderne Vergangenheit 1800–1900.* Vienna: Gesellschaft bildender Künstler Österreichs, Künstlerhaus [1981].

Asiatische Monumentalplastik. Foreword by Karl With. Vol. 5, Orbus Pictus/Weltkunst-Bücherei. Edited by Paul Westheim. Berlin: Ernst Wasmuth, A.G. [1922?].

Association of American Painters and Sculptors. *Catalogue of International Exhibition of Modern Art, at the Armory of the Sixty-Ninth Infantry.* New York: n.p., 1913.

Ausstellung amerikanischer Kunst. Königliche Akadamie der Künste in Berlin. Essay by Christian Brinton. Organized and edited by Kuno Francke. Berlin: F. Bruckmann, 1910.

Ausstellung amerikanischer Kunst. Munich: n.p., 1910.

Ausstellung Österreichischer Kunstgewerbe 1910–1911. Vienna: K. K. Österreichisches Museum für Kunst und Industrie, 1910.

Ausstellung Schwedischer Volkskunst und Hausindustrie. Vienna: K. K. Österreichisches Museum für Kunst und Industrie, 1910.

[Baedeker, Karl.] *Austria-Hungary including Dalmatia and Bosnia. Handbook for Travelers by Karl Baedeker.* 10th ed. Leipzig: Karl Baedeker; London: Dulau and Co.; New York: Charles Scribner's Sons, 1905.

———. *Austria-Hungary with Excursions to Cetinje, Belgrade, and Bucharest. Handbook for Travelers by Karl Baedeker.* 11th ed. Leipzig: Karl Baedeker; London: T. Fisher Unwin; New York: Charles Scribner's Sons, 1911.

———. *Berlin und Umgebung. Handbuch für Reisende von Karl Baedeker.* 16th ed. Leipzig: Karl Baedeker, 1910.

———. *Italy From the Alps to Naples. Handbook for Travelers by Karl Baedeker.* Leipzig: Karl Baedeker; London: T. Fisher Unwin; New York: Charles Scribner's Sons, 1909.

Banham, Reyner. *A Concrete Atlantis: U.S. Industrial Building and European Modern Architecture.* Cambridge: MIT Press, 1986.

Barney, Maginel Wright. *The Valley of the God-Almighty Joneses.* New York: Appleton-Century [1965].

Benjamin, Walter. *Illuminations.* Translated by Harry Zohn and edited by Hannah Arendt. New York: Schocken Books, 1969.

Bericht über den VIII. Internationalen Architekten-Kongress Wien 1908. Edited by Otto Wagner. Vienna: Schroll, 1909.

Berlage, Hendrik P. *Grundlagen und Entwicklung der Architektur.* Berlin: Julius Bard, 1908.

———. *Een Drietal Lezingen in Amerika Gebouden.* Rotterdam: W.L. and J. Brusse, 1912.

Beyer, Oskar, ed. *Erich Mendelsohn: Letters of an Architect.* London, New York, Toronto: Abelard-Schumann, 1967.

Bloom, Harold. *The Anxiety of Influence: A Theory of Poetry.* New York: Oxford University Press, 1973.

Bossom, Alfred C. *An Architectural Pilgrimage in Old Mexico.* New York: Scribner's, 1924.

Bradley, Arthur Granville. *Owen Glyndwr and the Last Struggle for Welsh Independence, with a Brief Sketch of Welsh History.* New York: G. P. Putnam's Sons, 1901.

Brandes, Mark A. *Untersuchungen zur Komposition der Stiftmosaiken an der Pfeilerhalle der Schicht IVa in Uruk-Warka.* Baghdadter Mitteilungen Beiheft. Berlin: Gebrüder Mann, 1968.

Brockhausen, Carl. *Österreich in Wort und Bild.* Berlin, Vienna, and Leipzig: Franz Schneider Verlag, 1924.

Brooks, H. Allen. *The Prairie School: Frank Lloyd Wright and His Midwest Contemporaries.* Toronto and Buffalo: University of Toronto Press, 1972; reprint, New York and London: W. W. Norton, 1976.

———. *Frank Lloyd Wright and the Prairie School.* New York: George Braziller in association with the Cooper-Hewitt Museum, 1984.

Brooks, H. Allen, ed. *Writings on Wright: Selected Comment on Frank Lloyd Wright.* Cambridge: MIT Press, 1981.

Brown, Milton W. *American Painting from the Armory Show to the Depression.* Princeton: Princeton University Press, 1955.

Buddensieg, Tilmann. *Industriekultur. Peter Behrens und die AEG, 1907–1914.* In collaboration with Henning Rogge, contributions by Gabriele Heidecker et al. Berlin: Mann, 1979. Translated by Iain Boyd Whyte as *Industriekultur: Peter Behrens and the AEG, 1907–1914.* Cambridge: MIT Press, 1984.

Budge, E. A. T. W. *The Gods of the Egyptians.* 2 vols. London: n.p, 1904.

Burkhardt, François; Eveno, Claude; and Podreca, Boris, eds. *Jože Plečnik, Architect: 1872–1957.* Translated by Carol Volk. Cambridge, Mass. and London: MIT Press, 1989.

Busch-Reisinger Museum. *The Busch-Reisinger Museum, Harvard University.* Introduction by Charles Haxthausen. New York: Abbeville Press, 1980.

Canina, Cav. Luigi. *L'architetettura antica descritta e Dimostrata coi Monumenti dall'Architetto.* 3 vols. Rome: n.p, 1834–44.

Carver, Norman F., Jr. *Japanese Folk Houses.* Kalamazoo: Documan Press, 1984.

Catalogue of Japanese Prints. 5 vols. in 1. London: [Sotheby], 1913.

Catalogue of a Memorial Exhibition of Japanese Color Prints from the

Collection of the Late Clarence Buckingham. Notes and introduction by Frederick W. Gookin. Chicago: Art Institute of Chicago, 1915.

Chappell, Sallie Anderson. *Barry Byrne: Architecture and Writing.* Ph.D. dissertation, Northwestern University. Ann Arbor: University Microfilms, 1975.

Chappell, Sallie Kitt, and Van Zanten, Ann. *Barry Byrne and John Lloyd Wright: Architecture and Design.* Chicago: Chicago Historical Society, 1982.

Charnay, Désiré. *Cités et ruines américaines, Mitla, Palenqué, Ixmal, Chichén-Itzá, Uxmal. Recueillés et photographieés par Désiré Charnay, avec un text par M. Viollet-le-Duc.* Paris: Gide, 1863.

———. *Les anciennes villes du nouveau monde; voyages d'exploration au Mexique et dans l'Amérique Centrale, 1857–1882.* Paris: Hachette, 1885. Translated by J. Gonino and Helen S. Conant, under the title *The Ancient Cities of the New World, being voyages and explorations in Mexico and Central America from 1857–1882.* New York: Harper and Bros., 1888.

Chicago Architecture Club 1912. Catalogue of the Twenty-fifth Annual Exhibition. Chicago: Art Institute of Chicago, 1912.

Chicago Architecture Club 1913. Catalogue of the Twenty-Sixth Annual Exhibition. Chicago: Art Institute of Chicago, 1913.

Chicago Arts Club. *Antique Colour Prints from the Collection of Frank Lloyd Wright.* [Chicago: Chicago Arts Club: 1917.]

Chicago World's Columbian Exhibition Official Catalogue. Part 10, Department of Fine Arts. Part 12, Anthropological Building, Midway Plaisance, and Isolated Exhibits. Chicago: W. B. Gonkey, 1893.

Cirlot, J. E. *A Dictionary of Symbols.* 2d ed. New York: Philosophical Library, 1971

Clair, Jean, et al. *Vienne 1880–1938, L'Apocalypse Joyeuse.* Paris: Centre Pompidou, 1986.

Clark, Robert J. "Joseph Maria Olbrich and Vienna." Ph.D. dissertation, Princeton University, 1973.

Comini, Alessandra. *Gustav Klimt.* New York: George Braziller, 1975.

Condit, Carl. *Chicago, 1910–1929, Building, Planning, and Urban Technology.* Chicago: University of Chicago Press, 1973.

Connors, Joseph. *The Robie House of Frank Lloyd Wright.* Chicago: University of Chicago Press, 1984.

Crawford, Alan. *C. R. Ashbee: Architect, Designer and Romantic Socialist.* New Haven: Yale University Press, 1985.

Creese, Walter. *The Crowning of the American Landscape: Eight Great Spaces and Their Buildings.* Princeton: Princeton University Press, 1985.

Curtis, William J. R. *Modern Architecture Since 1900.* 2d ed. Englewood Cliffs: Prentice-Hall, 1987.

Darling, Sharon S. *Chicago Furniture, Art, Craft & Industry, 1833–1983.* New York: Chicago Historical Society in association with W. W. Norton, 1984.

Das Werk von Gustav Klimt. Introductions by Hermann Bahr and Peter Altenberg. Vienna and Leipzig: Hugo Haller Kunstverlag, 1918.

de Bussierre, Sophie. *La Grande Galerie Nord. Histoire et Décor.* Petit Palais Dossier No. 3. Paris: Musées de la Ville de Paris, 1984.

De Fries, Heinrich. *Frank Lloyd Wright: Aus dem Lebenswerke eines Architekten.* Berlin: Verlag Ernst Pollak, 1926.

De Groot, J. H. *Vormharmonie.* Amsterdam: Ahrend, 1912.

Delitzsch, Friedrich. *Babel und Bibel.* Leipzig: J. C. Hinrichs, 1903.

Deneken, Friedrich. *Japanische Motive für Flächenverzierung. Ein Formenschatz für das Kunstgewerbe.* Berlin: Becker, 1896.

Dennis, James M. *Karl Bitter: Architectural Sculptor, 1867–1915.* Madison: University of Wisconsin Press, 1967.

Desgodetz, Antoine. *Les Edifices Antiques de Rome.* Paris: Chez Jean Jombert, 1682; 2d ed., 1779.

Deutsches Kunstgewerbe in St. Louis 1904. Berlin: Ernst Wasmuth, A.G., 1904.

de Wit, Wim, ed. *Louis Sullivan: The Function of Ornament.* New York and London: W. W. Norton, 1986.

Die Kunstdenkmäler Wiens. Die Profanbauten des III. IV. und V. Bezirkes. Vol. 44, Österreichische Kunsttopographie. Edited by Geza Hajos and Eckart Vancsa. Vienna: Verlag Awton Schroll, 1980.

Die Vertreibung des Geistigen aus Österreich. Zur Kulturpolitik des Nationalsozialismus. Vienna: Zentralsparkasse und Kommerzialbank and the Hochschule für angewandte Kunst, 1985.

Dolinschek, Ilse. *Die Bildhauerwerke in den Ausstellungen der Wiener Sezession von 1898–1910.* Beiträge zur Kunstwissenschaft, vol. 30. Munich: Scaneg, 1989.

The Domestic Scene (1897–1927): George M. Niedecken, Interior Architect. Edited by Milwaukee Art Museum with articles by Terrence Marvel and Cheryl Robertson. Milwaukee: The Museum, 1981.

Donnelley, Reuben, comp. *The Lakeside Annual Directory of the City of Chicago.* Chicago: Reuben Donnelley Co., 1910–14.

Eaton, Leonard. *Two Chicago Architects and Their Clients: Frank Lloyd Wright and Howard Van Doren Shaw.* Appendix by Elizabeth M. Douvan. Cambridge, Mass., and London: MIT Press, 1969.

———. *American Architecture Comes of Age.* Cambridge, Mass., and London: MIT Press, 1972.

Eberstadt, Rudolf; Möhring, Bruno; and Peterson, Richard. *Ein Programm für die Planung einer neuzeitlichen Gross-Stadt.* Berlin: Ernst Wasmuth, A.G., 1910.

Ein Dokument deutscher Kunst: Darmstadt, 1901–1976. Darmstadt: E. Roether, 1976.

Einstein, Carl. *Die Frühere Japanische Holzschnitt.* Vol. 16, Orbus Pictus/Weltkunst-Bücherei. Edited by Paul Westheim. Berlin: Ernst Wasmuth, A.G. [1922?].

Encyclopédie Photographique de l'Art. Le Musée du Louvre. Vol 1. Paris: Éditions Tel, 1935.

Evans, J. Gwenogvryn, ed. *The Book of Taliesin.* Series of Old Welsh Texts, no. 9. Leanbedrog, N. Wales, 1910 [1915].

Farr, Finis. *Frank Lloyd Wright: A Biography.* New York: Charles Scribner's Sons, 1962.

Ficke, A. Davison. *Chats on Japanese Prints.* New York: Frederick A. Stokes Co. [1915].

Fletcher, Alice D. "The Hako: A Pawnee Ceremony." Part II of the *Twenty-Second Annual Report of the Bureau of American Ethnology.* Washington, D.C.: Government Printing Office, 1904.

Fliedl, Gottfried. *Kunst und Lehre am Beginn der Moderne. Die Wiener Kunstgewerbeschule 1867–1918.* Salzburg and Vienna: Residenz Verlag, 1986.

Meehan, Patrick. *Frank Lloyd Wright: A Research Guide to Archival Sources.* New York and London: Garland, 1983.

Mellink, Machteld J., and Filip, Jan. *Frühe Stufen der Kunst.* Vol. 13, Propyläen Kunstgeschichte. Berlin: Propyläen Verlag, 1974.

Menocal, Narciso, ed. *Wright Studies.* Vol. 1, *Taliesien, 1911–1914.* Carbondale and Edwardsville: Southern Illinois University Press, 1992.

Metropolitan Museum of Art. *Dutch and Flemish Painting from the Hermitage.* New York: The Museum, 1988.

Miller, Mary Ellen. *The Art of Mesoamerica from Olmec to Aztec.* London: Thames and Hudson, 1986.

Miller, Mary Ellen, and Schele, Linda. *The Blood of Kings: Dynasty and Ritual in Maya Art.* Fort Worth: Kimball Art Museum, 1986.

Moortgat, Anton. *The Art of Ancient Mesopotamia.* London and New York: Phaidon, 1969.

Moravánszky, Ákos. *Die Architektur der Donaumonarchie 1867 bis 1918.* Berlin: Ernst and Sohn, 1988.

———. *Die Erneuerung der Baukunst. Wege zur Moderne in Mitteleuropa 1900–1940.* Salzburg and Vienna: Residenz Verlag, 1988.

Morse, Edward S. *Japanese Homes and Their Surroundings.* Boston: Ticknor and Co., 1886; reprint, New York: Dover, 1961.

Nash, D. W. *Taliesin; or, the Bard and Druids of Britain.* London: John Russell Smith, 1858.

Nebehay, Christian M. *Gustav Klimt: Dokumentation.* Vienna: Verlag der Galerie Christian M. Nebehay, 1969.

———. *Ver Sacrum, 1898–1903.* Vienna: Edition Tusch, 1975; English ed. translated by Geoffrey Watkins, New York: Rizzoli International, 1977.

Nederlandse Architectuur 1880–1930: Americana. Zaandam: C. Huig, 1975.

Nederlandse Architectuur 1880–1930: Architectura 1893–1918. Zaandam: C. Huig, 1975.

Nederlandse Architectuur. H. P. Berlage 1856–1934, Boumeester. Zaandam: C. Huig, 1975.

Neuwirth, Waltraud. *Österreichische Keramik des Jugendstils.* Munich: Prestel-Verlag, [1974].

———. *Wiener Werkstätte.* Vienna: privately printed, 1984.

Novotny, Fritz, and Dobai, Johannes. *Gustav Klimt.* Edited by Friedrich Welz. Salzburg: Verlag Galerie Welz [1967]. Boston: New York Graphic Society, 1968.

Nyström-Hamilton, Louise. *Ellen Key, Her Life and Work.* Introduction by Havelock Ellis. Translated by A. E. B. Fries. New York: G. P. Putnam's Sons, 1913.

Office of the Imperial Japanese Government Commission to the Japanese-British Exhibition [1910]. *An Illustrated Catalogue of Japanese Old Fine Arts Displayed at the Japan-British Exhibition, London, 1910.* 2 vols. Tokyo: Shimbi Shoin [1910].

Olbrich, Joseph M. *Architektur von Olbrich.* 3 vols. Berlin: Ernst Wasmuth, 1901–14; reprinted under the title *Joseph Maria Olbrich: Architecture,* with texts by Peter Haiko and Bernd Krimmel and catalogue by Renate Ulmer. New York: Rizzoli International, 1988.

———. *Neue Gärten von Olbrich. Der Farbengarten aus einem Vortrag anlässlich der XVIII Hauptversammlung Deutscher Gartenkünstler.* Berlin: Ernst Wasmuth, A.G., 1905.

Onderdonk, Francis S., Jr. *The Ferro-Concrete Style: Reinforced Concrete in Modern Architecture, with Four Hundred Illustrations of European and American Ferro-Concrete Design.* New York: Architectural Book Publishing Co., 1928.

Österreichisches Museum für angewandte Kunst, ed. *Verborgene Impressionen/Hidden Impressions. Japonismus in Wien/Japonisme in Vienna, 1870–1930.* Vienna: Österreichisches Museum für angewandte Kunst, 1990.

Pasztory, Esther. *Aztec Art.* New York: Abrams, 1983.

Pevsner, Nicholas. *Pioneers of the Modern Movement.* London: Faber and Faber, 1936; rev. ed. under the title *Pioneers of Modern Design.* Harmondsworth: Penguin Books, 1975.

Pfeiffer, Bruce Brooks, ed. *Frank Lloyd Wright Drawings.* New York: Abrams in association with the Frank Lloyd Wright Foundation and the Phoenix Art Museum, 1990.

Pfeiffer, Bruce Brooks, and Nordland, Gerald, eds. *Frank Lloyd Wright: In the Realm of Ideas.* Carbondale: Southern Illinois University Press, 1988.

Pierre, Dorothi Bock, ed. *Memoirs of an American Artist: Sculptor Richard W. Bock.* Los Angeles: C.C. Publishing Co., 1989.

Polano, Sergio, ed. *Hendrik Petrus Berlage. Complete Works.* New York: Rizzoli International, 1988.

Porada, Edith. *Corpus of Ancient Near East Seals in North American Collections.* Vol 1, *The Collection of the Pierpont Morgan Library.* Bollingen Series XIV. Washington, D.C.: Pantheon Books, 1948.

Pötzl-Malikova, Maria, ed. *Franz Metzner: ein Bildhauer der Jahrhundertwende in Berlin-Wien-Prag-Leipzig.* Munich: Adalbert Stifter-Verein and Stuck-Jugendstil-Verein, 1977.

Prelovsek, Damjan. *Josef Plečnik. Wiener Arbeiten von 1896 bis 1914.* Translated by Maria Bister and Feliks J. Bister. Vienna: Edition Tusch, 1979.

Prince, Sue Ann, ed., *The Old Guard and the Avant-Garde: Modernism in Chicago, 1910–1940.* Chicago: University of Chicago Press, 1990.

Prisse d'Avennes, Achille C. T. E. *Histoire de l'art égyptien d'après les Monuments. . . .* Text by P. Marchand de la Faye after the notes of the author. 2 vols. Paris: A. Bertrand, 1878–79.

———. *Monuments égyptiens, bas-reliefs, peintures, inscription, etc. . . . .* Paris: Didot, 1847.

Pritchard, James B. *The Ancient Near East in Pictures Relating to the Old Testament.* 2d ed. with supplement. Princeton: Princeton University Press, 1969.

Proskouriakoff, Tatiana. *An Album of Maya Architecture.* Rev. ed., Norman: University of Oklahoma Press, 1963.

Quinan, Jack. *Frank Lloyd Wright's Larkin Building: Myth and the Fact.* New York: Architectural History Foundation; Cambridge: MIT Press, 1987.

Racinet, Auguste. *L'ornement polychrome . . . plans en couleurs or et argent . . . art ancien asiatique, moyên age, renaissance, XVIIe et XVIIIe siècles.* 2 vols. Second series. Paris: Firmin-Didot [188?].

Rand, Harry. *Paul Manship*. Washington, D.C.: Smithsonian Institution Press, 1989.

Rather, Susan. "The Origins of Archaism and the Early Sculpture of Paul Manship." Ph.D. Dissertation, University of Delaware, 1986.

————. *Archaism, Modernism, and the Art of Paul Manship*. Austin: University of Texas Press, 1992.

Reichskommission. *Weltausstellung in St. Louis 1904. amtlicher Katalog*. Edited by Theodor Lewald. Berlin: George Stilke [1904].

Reinink, A. W. *K. P. C. De Bazel*. Amsterdam: J. M. Meulenhoff, 1965.

Robinson, James A. *The Life and Work of Harry Franklin Robinson, 1883–1959*. Hong Kong: Hilcross Development, 1989.

Rubin, William, ed. *Primitivism in 20th Century Art: Affinity of the Tribal and the Modern*. 2 vols. New York: Museum of Modern Art, distributed by the New York Graphics Society, 1984.

Rubin, William, comp. *Picasso and Braque: Pioneering Cubism*. New York: Museum of Modern Art; Boston: Bulfinch Press, Little, Brown, 1989.

Saliga, Pauline, ed. *Fragments of Chicago's Past* Chicago: Art Institute of Chicago, 1990.

Satzinger, Helmut. *Ägyptische Kunst in Wien*. Vienna: Kunsthistorisches Museum, n.d.

Schulze, Franz. *Mies van der Rohe, A Critical Biography*. Chicago and London: University of Chicago Press, 1985.

Scott, Margaret H. *Frank Lloyd Wright's Warehouse in Richland Center, Wisconsin*. Richland Center: Richland County Publishers, 1984.

Scott, Robert Douglas. *The Thumb of Knowledge in Legends of Finn, Sigurd, and Taliesin*. New York: [Institute of French Studies], 1930.

Scully, Vincent J., Jr. *Frank Lloyd Wright*. New York: George Braziller, 1960.

————. Foreword to *Studies and Executed Buildings by Frank Lloyd Wright*. New York: Rizzoli International, 1986.

————. *Modern Architecture*. New York: Braziller, 1961.

————. *The Architecture of the American Summer: The Flowering of the Shingle Style*. New York: Rizzoli International, 1989.

Searing, Helen, ed. *In Search of Modern Architecture: A Tribute to Henry-Russell Hitchcock*. New York: Architectural History Foundation; Cambridge: MIT Press, 1982.

Secrest, Meryle. *Frank Lloyd Wright: A Biography*. New York: Knopf, 1992.

Sekler, Eduard F. *Josef Hoffmann: The Architectural Work*. Translated by the author. Catalogue translated by John Maass. Princeton: Princeton University Press, 1985.

Selz, Peter. *German Expressionist Painting*. Berkeley: University of California Press, 1957.

Shankel, Carol. *Sallie Casey Thayer and Her Collection*. Lawrence: University of Kansas Museum of Art, 1976.

Sharp, Dennis, ed. *Alfred C. Bossom's American Architecture, 1903–1926*. London: Book Art, 1984.

Sheffler, Karl. *Die Grosstadt*. 1913.

Simon, Hans-Ulrich, ed. *Eberhard von Bodenhausen, Harry Graf Kessler: ein Briefwechsel, 1894–1918*. Marbacher Schriften no. 16. Marbach am Neckar: Deutschen Literaturarchiv, 1978.

Smith, W. Stevenson. *The Art and Architecture of Ancient Egypt*. 2d ed., rev. by William Kelly Simpson. Harmondsworth: Penguin, 1981.

Souvenir Book of the Louisiana Purchase Exposition: Day and Night Scenes. Official Publication. St. Louis: Official Photographic Co., 1904.

Spinden, Herbert J. *A Study of Maya Art. Its Subject Matter and Historical Development*. Vol. 6 of the Memoirs of the Peabody Museum of American Archaeology and Ethnology, Harvard University. Cambridge, Mass.: Peabody Museum, 1913. Reprint, with introduction and bibliography by J. Eric S. Thompson, New York: Dover, 1975.

The Spiritual in Art: Abstract Painting 1890–1985. Organized by Maurice Tuchman, Los Angeles County Museum of Art. New York: Abbeville Press, 1986.

Sprague, Paul E., ed. *Frank Lloyd Wright and Madison: Eight Decades of Artistic and Social Interaction*. Madison: Elvehjem Museum of Art, 1990.

Stephens, John L. *Incidents of Travel in Central America, Chiapas, & Yucatan*. Illustrated by Frederick Catherwood. 2 vols. New York: Harper and Bros., 1841; reprint of 12th ed. of 1856, 2 vols. in 1. Edited with introduction and notes by Richard L. Predmore. New Brunswick: Rutgers University Press, 1949.

Stierlin, Henri. *Art of the Aztecs and Its Origins*. New York: Rizzoli, 1982.

Storrer, William A. *The Architecture of Frank Lloyd Wright. A Complete Catalog*. 2d ed. Cambridge, Mass. and London: MIT Press, 1978; paperback ed., 1982.

The Studio Year-Book of Decorative Art. London: The Studio, 1907, 1909, 1910.

Sullivan, Louis. *A System of Architectural Ornament According with a Philosophy of Man's Powers*. 1924; reprint, with essay by Lauren S. Weingarden, New York: Rizzoli in cooperation with the Art Institute of Chicago, 1990.

Sweeney, Robert. *Frank Lloyd Wright: An Annotated Bibliography*. Los Angeles: Hennessey and Ingalls, 1978.

Taft, Lorado. *Modern Tendencies in Sculpture*. Chicago: Art Institute of Chicago, 1921; reprint, Freeport, N.Y.: Books for Library Press, 1970.

Tanigawa, Masami. *Measured Drawings: Frank Lloyd Wright in Japan*. [Tokyo: Graphic Co., 1980.]

Tessenow, Heinrich. *Handwerk und Kleinstadt*. Berlin: Cassirer, 1919.

Thieme, Ulrich, and Becker, Felix. *Allgemeines Lexikon der bildenden Künstler von Antike bis zur Gegenwart*. 37 vols. Vols. 16–36 edited by Hans Vollmer. Leipzig: W. Engelmann, 1907–50.

Tobler, Arthur J. *Excavations at Tepe Gawra*. 2 vols. Philadelphia: University Museum, University of Pennsylvania, 1950.

Traum und Wirklichkeit, Wien, 1870–1930. 2d ed. Vienna: Museum of the City of Vienna, 1985.

Tummers, Nic. H. M. *J. L. Mathieu Lauweriks, zijn werk en zijn nvloed op architectuur en vormgeving rond 1910: "De Hagener impuls."* Hilversum: G. van Saane "Lectura Architectonica," 1968.

————. *Der Hagener Impuls. J. L. M. Lauweriks, Werk und Einfluß auf Architektur und Formgebung um 1910*. Hagen: Linnepe Verlagsgesellschaft, 1972.

Twombly, Robert. *Frank Lloyd Wright: An Interpretive Biography.* New York: Harper and Row, 1973.
———. *Frank Lloyd Wright: His Life and His Architecture.* New York: John Wiley and Sons, 1979.
———. *Louis Sullivan, His Life and Work.* New York: Viking Penguin, 1986.
Universal Exhibition St. Louis 1904. Exhibition of Professional Schools for Arts and Crafts. Vienna: Imperial Royal Ministry for Public Instruction, 1904.
University of Chicago, College Humanities Staff. *The Midway Gardens 1914–1929; an Exhibition of the Building and the Sculpture of Alfonso Ianelli.* Chicago: University of Chicago Press, 1961.
Van Zanten, David. *Walter Burley Griffin, Selected Designs.* Palos Park, Ill.: Prairie School Press, 1970.
Vasari, Giorgio. *Lives of Seventy of the Most Eminent Painters, Sculptors and Architects.* Edited and annotated by E. H. Blashfield, E. W. Blashfield, and A. A. Hopkins. 4 vols. New York: Charles Scribner's Sons, 1907.
Vereinigung Berliner Architekten. *Anregungen zur Erlangung von Gross-Berlin . . . .* Berlin: Ernst Wasmuth, A.G., 1907.
Ver Sacrum. Special issue, *Die Wiener Secession und die Ausstellung in St. Louis* [Vienna, 1904].
Wagner, Otto. *Moderne Architektur.* 1st ed. Vienna: A. Schroll, 1896, 1898–1902; 2d ed. under the title *Modern Architecture: A Guide for His Students to This Field of Art,* introduction and translation by Harry Francis Malgrave. Santa Monica: Getty Center for the History of Art and the Humanities, 1988.
Waissenberg, Robert. *Die Wiener Secession, eine Dokumentation.* Munich and Vienna: Jugend und Volk, 1971.
Wasmuth, Ernst, ed. *Führer durch die allgemeine Städtebau-Ausstellung in Berlin in 1910.* Berlin: [Ernst Wasmuth, A.G., 1910].
Weaver, Lawrence. *Houses and Gardens of E. L. Lutyens.* London: Offices of *Country Life,* 1914; reprint, Woodbridge, Suffolk: Antique Collectors Club, 1981.
Weber, Otto. *Die Kunst der Hethiter.* Vol. 9, Orbus Pictus/Weltkunst-Bücherei. Edited by Paul Westheim. Berlin: Ernst Wasmuth, A.G. [1922?].
Whyte, Iain Boyd. *Emil Hoppe, Marcel Kammerer, Otto Schöntal: Three Architects from the Master Class of Otto Wagner.* Cambridge: MIT Press, 1989.
Wiener Jugendstil aus Privatbesitz. Vienna: Galerie Würthle, 1983.
Wijdeveld, H. Th., ed. *The Life Work of the American Architect Frank Lloyd Wright.* Santpoort, Holland: C. A. Mees, 1925; 2d ed. under the title *The Work of Frank Lloyd Wright, The Life Work of the American Architect Frank Lloyd Wright with Contributions by Frank Lloyd Wright,* The Wendingen Edition. New York: Horizon Press 1965; New York: Bramhall House [1965].
Willey, Gordon R. *Das Alte Amerika.* Vol. 18, Propyläen Kunstgeschichte. Berlin, Propyläen Verlag, 1974.
Wilson, Richard Guy, and Robinson, Sidney, eds. *Modern Architecture in America: Visions and Revisions.* Festschrift for Leonard K. Eaton. Ames: Iowa State University Press, 1991.

Witt, R. E. *Isis in the Graeco-roman World.* Ithaca: Cornell University Press, 1971.
Wittgenstein, Ludwig. *Philosophical Investigations.* Translated by G. E. M. Anscombe. 3d ed. New York: Macmillan, 1958.
Wittkower, Rudolf. *Allegory and the Migration of Symbols.* Collected Essays of Rudolf Wittkower, vol. 3. Boulder: Westview Press, 1977.
———. *Selected Lectures of Rudolf Wittkower: The Impact of Non-European Civilizations on the Art of the West.* Compiled and edited by Donald Martin Reynolds. Foreword by Margot Wittkower. Cambridge and New York: Cambridge University Press, 1989.
The World's Fair, St. Louis, U.S.A., 1904. Celebrating the Centennial of the Louisiana Purchase. St. Louis: R. A. Reid, 1902.
Worringer, Wilhelm. *Abstraktion und Einfühlung. Ein Betrag zur stil-psychologie.* Neuwied: Heuser, 1907.
Wright, Frank Lloyd. *An Autobiography.* London, New York, and Toronto: Longmans, Green, 1932.
———. *An Autobiography.* 2d ed. New York: Duell, Sloan and Pearce, 1943.
———. *An Autobiography.* 3d ed. New York: Horizon Press, 1977.
———. *Experimenting with Human Lives.* Chicago: Ralph Fletcher Seymour Co., 1923.
———. *Frank Lloyd Wright on Architecture. Selected Writings 1894–1940.* Edited and with an Introduction by Frederick Gutheim. New York: Duell, Sloan, and Pearce, 1941.
———. *The Future of Architecture.* New York: Horizon Press, 1953; reprint, New York: New American Library, 1970.
———. *Genius and the Mobocracy.* New York: Duell, Sloan and Pearce, 1949; enl. 2d ed., New York: Horizon Press, 1971.
———. *In the Cause of Architecture. Essays by Frank Lloyd Wright for Architectural Record, 1908–1952.* Edited by Frederick Gutheim. New York: Architectural Record Books, 1975.
———. *The Japanese Print: An Interpretation.* Chicago: Ralph Fletcher Seymour Co., 1912; reprint, New York: Horizon Press, 1967.
———. *A Testament.* New York: Horizon Press, 1957.
Wright, Frank Lloyd, and Brownell, Baker. *Architecture and Modern Life.* New York: Harper and Bros., 1938.
Wright, Gwendolyn. *Building the American Dream: A Social History of Housing in America.* New York: Pantheon Books, 1981.
———. *Moralism and the Model Home: Domestic Architecture and Cultural Conflict in Chicago, 1873–1913.* Chicago: University of Chicago Press, 1980.
Wright, John Lloyd. *My Father Who Is on Earth.* New York: G. P. Putnam's Sons, 1946.
Yamashita, Kwanjiuro. *The Illustrated Catalogue of Japanese Fine Art Exhibit in the Art Palace at the Louisiana Purchase Exposition, St. Louis, Mo., U.S.A..* Kobe: Publishing Department of Kwansai Shoshin Seiha Insatsu Goshi Kaisha, 1904.
Yeomans, Alfred B., ed. *City Residential Land Development: Studies in Planning; Competitive Plans for Subdividing a Typical Quarter Section of Land on the Outskirts of Chicago.* Publications of the City Club of Chicago. Chicago: University of Chicago Press [1916].
Zukowsky, John, ed. *Chicago Architecture, 1872–1922. Birth of a*

Metro-polis. Munich: Prestel Verlag and the Art Institute of Chicago, 1987.

3. Articles and Essays

Adams, Thomas, and Lutyens, Edward L. "A Recent Example of Town Planning: Kenilworth." *Architectural Review.* Town Planning Supplement No. 3, 27 (April 1910): 252–55.

Alofsin, Anthony. "Grundformen: eine Einführung in die 'versenkte Fläche' " [Detail, Ornament, and Primary Form: An Introduction to the Recessed Panel]. *Archithese, Zietschrift und Schritenreihe für Architektur* 20, no.6 (November-December 1990): 18–21.

———. "Taliesin: 'To Fashion Worlds in Little.' " *Wright Studies* 1, *Taliesin 1911–1914* (1992): 44–65.

———. "Taliesin I: A Catalogue of Drawings and Photographs." *Wright Studies* 1, *Taliesin 1911–1914* (1992): 98–141.

———. "Tempering the Ecole: Nathan Ricker at the University of Illinois and Langford Warren at Harvard." In *The History of History in American Schools of Architecture, 1865–1975*, edited by Gwendolyn Wright and Janet Parks, 73–88. Princeton: Buell Center for the Study of American Architecture and Princeton Architectural Press, 1990.

———. "The *Call* Building: Frank Lloyd Wright's Skyscraper for San Francisco." In *The Urban Dimension: Essays in Architectural History and Criticism*. Vienna: Böhlau Verlag, in press.

———. "The Kunsthistorisches Museum: A Treasure House for the Secessionists." *Jahrbuch des Kunsthistorisches Museum*. In press.

Ames, Robert Leonard. "A Western Suburban Home." *American Homes and Gardens* 9 (March 1912): 86–89.

"L'architettura Riceve F. Ll. Wright," *L'architettura* 2 (1956): 398.

Ashbee, Charles R. "Taliesin, the Home of Frank Lloyd Wright, and a Study of the Owner." *Western Architect* 19 (February 1913): 16–19.

Badovici, Jean. "Entretiens sur l'architecture vivante: l'art de Frank Lloyd Wright." *L'Architecture Vivante* 2 (Winter 1924): 26–27, pls. 34–35.

Baillie Scott, M. H. "On the Characterization of Mr. C. F. A. Voysey's Architecture." *International Studio* 22 (1907–8): 19–24.

Banham, Reyner. "The Wilderness Years of Frank Lloyd Wright." *Journal of the Royal Institute of British Architects* 76 (December 1969): 512–19.

Beeby, Thomas. "The Song of Taliesin." *Modulus* (1980–81): 2–11.

———. "The Grammar of Ornament/Ornament as Grammar." *Via* 3 (1977): 11–29.

Behrendt, Walter Curt. Review of *Frank Lloyd Wright Chicago. Achtes Sonderheft der Architekture des zwanzigsten Jahrhunderts* by Frank Lloyd Wright. In *Kunst und Künstler* 11, no. 9 (May 1913): 487.

"Beilage für Vereine. Berichte über Versammlungen und Besichtigungen." *Deutsche Bauzeitung* 44, no. 79 (1 October 1910): 641.

Bergdoll, Barry, and Richard Pommer. "Tagungen," *Kunstchronik* 42, no. 11 (October 1989): 570–74.

Berlage, Hendrik P. "Neuere amerikanische Architektur." Parts 1–3. *Schweizerische Bauzeitung* 55 (14, 21, 28 September 1912): 148–

50, 165–67, 178. Translated in Don Gifford, ed., *The Literature of Architecture: The Evolution of Architectural Theory and Practice in Nineteenth-Century America*. New York: Dutton, 1966, 606–16.

———. "Art and Community." *Western Architect* 18, no. 8 (August 1912): 85–89, with plates.

———. "Foundations and Development of Architecture." Parts 1–2. *Western Architect* 18, no. 9 (September 1912): 96–99; 18, no. 10 (October 1912): 104–8.

Billcliffe, Roger, and Virgo, Peter. "Charles Rennie Mackintosh and the Austrian Art Revival." *Burlington Magazine* 119, no. 896 (November 1977): 739–46.

Bisanz-Prakken, Marian. "Das Quadrat in der Flächenkunst der Wiener Secession." *Alte und Moderne Kunst* 27, nos. 180–81 (January 1982): 39–46.

Bletter, Rosemarie Haag. "Expressionism and the New Objectivity." *Art Journal* 43, no. 2 (1983): 108–20.

Bohrer, Frederick N. Review of *Europa und der Orient, 800-1900,* by the Martin-Gropius-Bau, and *Exotische Welten, Europäische, Phantasien,* by the Institut für Auslandsbeziehungen und Württembergischer Kunstverein. *Art Bulletin* 73, no. 2 (June 1991): 325–30.

Borthwick, Mamah Bouton, trans., "Romain Rolland," by Ellen Key. *Little Review* 2 (October 1915): 22–30.

Borthwick, Mamah, and Wright, Frank Lloyd, trans. "A Hymn to Nature," by Johann Wolfgang von Goethe. *Little Review* 1 (February 1915): 30–32.

Bossom, Alfred C. "Restoration of Ancient City of Tikal, Guatemala." *American Architect* 129, no. 2491 (20 February 1926): 266.

Brooks, H. Allan. "Frank Lloyd Wright and the Wasmuth Drawings." *Art Bulletin* 48, no. 2 (June 1966): 193–202.

Brown, Frank Chouteau. "Tendencies in Apartment House Design. Part VII. Courtyard Plans." *Architectural Record* 51 (January 1922): 63ff.

Clark, Robert J. "J. M. Olbrich: 1867–1908." *Architectural Design* 37 (December 1967): 562–72.

Collins, Christiane C. "Vienna 1900 and the Ideology of Gesamtkunstwerk." *Design Book Review* (Winter 1986): 28–33.

———. "A Visionary Discipline: Werner Hegemann and the Quest for the Pragmatic Ideal." *Center. A Journal for Architecture in America* 5 (1989): 74–85.

"Concrete—Decorative Features of Midway Gardens." *Rock Products and Building Materials* 7 (January 1915): 26.

Crawford, Alan. "Ten Letters from Frank Lloyd Wright to Charles Robert Ashbee." *Architectural History* 13 (1970): 64–76.

Creutz, Max. "Die 'Fine Arts' auf der Weltausstellung in St. Louis." *Die Kunst für Alle* 19 (1904): 568–74.

Dennis, James M., and Wenneker, Lu B. "Ornamentation and the Organic Architecture of Frank Lloyd Wright." *Art Journal* 25 (1965): 7.

"Descendants of Anna Lloyd-Jones (1839–1923)." *The Frank Lloyd Wright Newsletter* 3, no. 2 (1980): 5–7.

"Die Einweihung des Völkershlachtdenkmals in Leipzig." *Neue Freie Presse*, nos. 17656, 17657 (18 and 19 October 1913).

Engelbrecht, Lloyd C. "Henry Trost: The Prairie School in the Southwest." *Prairie School Review* 6, no. 4 (Fourth quarter 1969): 5–29.

Fletcher, Alice D. "The Hako: A Pawnee Ceremony." Part II of the *Twenty-Second Annual Report of the Bureau of American Ethnology.* Washington, D.C.: Government Printing Office, 1904.

Florman, Lisa. "Gustav Klimt and the Precedent of Ancient Greece." *Art Bulletin* 72, no. 2 (June 1990): 310–26.

"Frank Lloyd Wright, een modern Bouwmeester in Amerika." Parts 1–2. *De Bouwwereld* 11, no. 3 (17 January 1912): 2–22; no. 4 (24 January 1912): 27–29.

Frank Lloyd Wright Update, no. 26 (vol. 3, no. 6) (Summer 1991): 60.

Fred, W. "The Artist Colony at Darmstadt." *The Studio* 24 (1902): 22–30.

———. "The Work of Prof. J. N. Olbrich." *The Studio* 24 (1902): 91–100.

[W. Fred.] "The International Exhibition of Modern Decorative Art at Turin. The German Section." *The Studio* 27 (1903): 188–97.

Gendrop, Paul. "El tablero talud en la arquitectura mesoamericana." Centro de Investigaciones Arquitectonicas, Escuela National de Arquitectura. Paper presented at the 41st International Congress of Americanists (Mexico City), 1974.

Geraniotis, Roula. "The University of Illinois and German Architectural Education." *Journal of Architectural Education* 38, no. 4 (Summer 1985): 15–21.

"The Germanic Museum of Harvard University." *Harvard Alumni Bulletin* (November 1909): 257–60.

Goss, Peter. "Wright's Fiesole Studio." *The Frank Lloyd Wright Newsletter* 5, no. 1 (1982): 8.

Graf, Otto Antonia. "Instructions from Imhotep? WW—Wagner from Vienna and Wright from Chicago." In *Frank Lloyd Wright, Architectural Drawings and Decorative Art.* Essays by David Hanks, Jennifer Toher, and Otto Antonio Graf, 20–23. London: Fischer Fine Art [1985].

Green, William. "A Peerless Pair: Frederick W. Gookin and Frank Lloyd Wright and the Art Institute of Chicago's 1908 Exhibition of Japanese Prints." *Andon* 4, no. 14 (Summer 1984): 14–19.

Griggs, Joseph. "Alfonso Iannelli, the Prairie Spirit in Sculpture." *The Prairie School Review* 2, no. 4 (1965): 5–23.

Hallmark, Donald P. "Richard W. Bock: Sculptor for Frank Lloyd Wright and the Architects of the Chicago School." Master's thesis, University of Iowa, 1970.

Hamilton, Mary Jane. "The Madison Hotel." In *Frank Lloyd Wright and Madison,* edited by Paul Sprague, 57–63. Madison: Elvehjem Museum of Art, 1990.

———. "The Nakoma Country Club." In *Frank Lloyd Wright and Madison,* edited by Paul Sprague, 77–82. Madison: Elvehjem Museum of Art, 1990.

Hanks, David A. "Frank Lloyd Wright's 'The Art and Craft of the Machine'." *Frank Lloyd Wright Newsletter* 2, no. 3 (1979): 6–9.

Hanks, David A., and Tofer, Jennifer."The Decorative Designs of Frank Lloyd Wright and His European Contemporaries: 1895–1915." In *Frank Lloyd Wright, Architectural Drawings and Decorative Art.* Essays by David Hanks, Jennifer Tofer, and Otto Antonio Graf, 6–19. London: Fischer Fine Art [1985].

Harrington, Elaine. "Classical Sculpture in the Work of Frank Lloyd Wright." *Wright Angles* 16, no. 3 (Fall 1990): n.p.

———. "International Influences on Henry Hobson Richardson's Glessner House." In *Chicago Architecture, 1872–1922. Birth of a Metropolis,* edited by John Zukowsky, 189–208. Munich: Prestel Verlag and the Art Institute of Chicago, 1987.

Haviland, Paul B. Introductory statement. *291,* nos. 7–8 (October 1915).

Heath, William R. "The Office Building and What It Will Bring to the Office Force." *Larkin Idea* 6 (November 1906): 10–14.

Hewett, Edgar L. "Ancient America at the Panama-California Exposition." Introduction by W. N. Holmes. *Art and Archaeology* 2, no. 3 (November 1915): 64–102.

Hitchcock, Henry-Russell. "Frank Lloyd Wright and the 'Academic Tradition' of the Early Eighteen-Nineties." *Journal of the Warburg and Courtauld Institutes* 7 (January-June 1944): 46–63.

———. "Wright's Influence Abroad." *Parnassus* 12, no. 8 (1940): 11–15.

Hoffmann, Donald. "Frank Lloyd Wright and Viollet-le-Duc." *Journal of the Society of Architectural Historians* 28, no. 3 (October 1969): 173–83.

Holzhueter, John O. "Wright's Designs for Robie Lamp." In *Frank Lloyd Wright and Madison,* edited by Paul Sprague, 13–27. Madison: Elvehjem Museum of Art, 1990.

"House at Shackleford, Surrey: Current Architecture." *Architectural Review* 5 (December 1898–May 1899), supplemental pl. III.

"House for an Art-Lover." *American Architect and Building News* 85 (24 September 1904): 104, pl. 1500.

"House for R. H. Cazalet, Esq. Castlemorton, Worcestershire, England." *American Architect and Building News* 30 (1 November 1890): 75, pl. 775.

Hovey, Richard. "Taliesin, A Masque." Parts 1–3. *Poet-Lore, A Monthly Magazine of Letters* (Boston: Poet-Lore Co., 1896), 3, no. 1:1–14, 163–78; 8, no. 2: 63–78; 8, no. 6:292–306.

Indiana, Gary. "Ludwig Wittgenstein, Architect." *Art in America* 73, no. 1 (January 1985): 112–33.

Ingraham, Elizabeth Wright. "The Chapel in the Valley." *The Frank Lloyd Wright Newsletter* 3, no. 2 (1980): 1–4.

Johnson, Donald Leslie. "Notes on Frank Lloyd Wright's Paternal Family." *The Frank Lloyd Wright Newsletter* 3, no. 2 (1980): 5–7.

Jones, Jenkin Lloyd. "A House for a Cousin: The Richard Lloyd Jones House." *The Frank Lloyd Wright Newsletter* 2, no. 4 (1979): 1–3.

Kalas, E. B. "L'Art de Glasgow." *De La Tamise à la Sprée l'essor des industries d'art* (Rheims: n.p., 1905).

Kammerer, Marcel. "Die Architektur der 'Kunstschau'." *Moderne Bauformen* 7, no. 9 (1908): 361–408

Kaufmann, Edgar, Jr. "Centrality and Symmetry in Wright's Architecture." *Architect's Yearbook* 9 (1960): 120–31.

———. "Crisis and Creativity, Frank Lloyd Wright, 1904–1914." *Journal of the Society of Architectural Historians* 25, no. 4 (December 1966): 292–96.

———."Frank Lloyd Wright and the Fine Arts." *Perspecta* 8 (1963): 40–42.

———. "Frank Lloyd Wright: Plasticity, Continuity,and Ornament." *Journal of the Society of Architectural Historians* 37, no. 1 (March 1978): 34–39.

———. "Frank Lloyd Wright at the Metropolitan Museum." *Bulletin of the Metropolitan Museum of Art* 40 (Fall 1982): entire issue.

Kirk, Terry R. "The Sources of Pre-Columbian Influences in the Architecture of Frank Lloyd Wright." Master's thesis, Columbia University, 1986.

Klinkow, Meg. "Wright Family Life in the House Beautiful." *Wright Angles* 17, no. 3 (Summer 1991): n.p.

Kostka, Robert. "Frank Lloyd Wright in Japan." *Prairie School Review* 3, no. 3 (1966): 5–27 and cover.

Kruty, Paul. "Pleasure Garden on the Midway." *Chicago History* 16 (Fall/Winter 1987–88): 4–27.

———. "The Influence of the European Early Modern Movement on the Architecture of the Prairie School." Master of Arts Thesis, University of Wisconsin-Milwaukee, 1984.

Kuzmany, Karl M. "Die 'Kunstschau' Wien 1909." *Die Kunst für Alle* 25 (October 1909): 20–22.

Lavin, Sylvia. "Images and Imaginings of Ancient Egypt." *Design Book Review* 20 (Spring 1991): 44–46.

Levine, Neil. "Abstraction and Representation in Modern Architecture: The International Style of Frank Lloyd Wright." *AA Files*, no. 11 (Spring 1986): 3–21.

———. "Frank Lloyd Wright's Diagonal Planning." In *In Search of Modern Architecture: A Tribute to Henry-Russell Hitchcock*, edited by Helen Searing, 245–77. New York: Architectural History Foundation; Cambridge, Mass.: MIT Press, 1982.

———. "Hollyhock House and the Romance of Southern California." *Art in America* 71, no. 8 (September 1983): 150–65.

———. "Landscape into Architecture: Frank Lloyd Wright's Hollyhock House and the Romance of Southern California." *AA Files*, no. 3 (January 1983): 22–41.

———. "Frank Lloyd Wright's Own Houses and His Changing Concept of Representation." In *The Nature of Frank Lloyd Wright*, edited by Carol R. Bolon, Robert S. Nelson, and Linda Seidel, 20–69. Chicago and London: University of Chicago Press, 1988.

"Lord Chance's Estate, Surrey, England." *American Architect and Building News* 96, no. 758 (1 September 1909): plates.

Ludwig, Delton. "Frank Lloyd Wright in the Bitter Root Valley of Montana." *The Frank Lloyd Wright Newsletter* 5, no. 2 (1982): 7–16.

Lux, Josef A. "The Vienna Art Exhibit—1908." *Deutsche Kunst und Dekoration* 23 (1908–9): 33–77.

McCoy, Jerry A. "The Stockman House." *Frank Lloyd Wright Quarterly* 2, no. 3 (Summer 1991): 9–10.

Maler, Teobert. *Explorations in the Department of Petén, Guatemala: Tikal.* Vol. 5, Memoirs, Peabody Museum of Archaeology and Ethnology no. 1 (1911).

Mallowan, M. E. L. "Excavations at Brak and Chagar Bazur." *Iraq* 9 (1947).

Mallowan, M. E. L., and Rose, J. Cruikshank. "Excavations at Tall Arpachiyah 1933." *Iraq* 2, part 1 (April 1935).

Manson, Grant Carpenter. "The Wonderful World of Taliesin: My Twenty Years on Its Fringes." *Wisconsin Magazine of History* 73, no. 1 (Autumn 1989): 33–41.

Meech-Pekarik, Julia. "Frank Lloyd Wright and Japanese Prints." In *Frank Lloyd Wright at the Museum of Metropolitan Art*, 48–56. New York: The Museum, 1982. Reprint from *Metropolitan Museum of Art Bulletin* 40, no. 2 (Fall 1982).

Menocal, Narciso G. "Form and Content in Frank Lloyd Wright's *Tree of Life* Window." *Elvehjem Museum of Art Bulletin* (1983–84): 18–32.

———. "Frank Lloyd Wright and the Question of Style." *Journal of the Decorative and Propaganda Arts* 2 (Summer/Fall 1986): 4–19.

———. "Taliesin, the Gilmore House, and *The Flower In the Crannied Wall*." *Wright Studies* 1, *Taliesin 1911–1914* (1992): 70–80.

———. "Frank Lloyd Wright's Concept of Democracy: An American Architectural Jeremiad." In *Frank Lloyd Wright: In the Realm of Ideas*, edited by Bruce Brooks Pfeiffer and Gerald Norland, 149–64. Carbondale: Southern Illinois University Press, 1988.

Miller, R. Craig. "Frank Lloyd Wright and Modern Design: An Appraisal." *Frank Lloyd Wright Newsletter* 3, no. 1 (1980): 1–6.

Monroe, Harriet. "The Orient an Influence on the Architecture of Wright." *Chicago Daily Tribune*, 12 April 1914, section 8, p. 8.

Moravánszky, Ákos. "Byzantinismus in der Baukunst Otto Wagners als Motiv seiner Wirkung östlich von Wien." In *Die kunst des Otto Wagner*, edited by Gustav Peichl, 40–45. Wiener Akademie-Reihe, vol. 16. Vienna: Akadamie der bildenden Künste, 1984.

Morris, G. Ll. "Edwin L. Lutyens, Architect of Houses and Gardens." *International Studio* 36 (1908–9): 268–81.

"Mr. C. F. A. Voysey's House, 'The Orchards' Chorley Wood, Herts." *Architectural Review* 10 (July 1901): 32–38.

"Mural Restoration Project Uncovers Giannini Artwork." *Wright Angles* (April-June 1986): n.p.

Newman, Lenore. "Works by Owen Jones and Christopher Dresser in the Domino's Center for Architecture & Design." *News from Domino's Center for Architecture and Design* (Ann Arbor: Domino's Center) (Summer 1989): n.p.

Pächt, Otto. "Art Historians and Art Critics—VI: Alois Riegl." *Burlington Magazine* 105 (1963): 189.

"Portfolio of Current Architecture." *Architectural Record* 39 (February 1916): 172.

Pötzl-Malikova, Maria. "Franz Metzner und die Wiener Secession." *Alte und Moderne Kunst* 21, nos. 148/149 (1976): 30–39.

Price, C. Matlack. "Secessionist Architecture in America. Departures from Academic Traditions of Design." *Arts and Decoration* 3 (December 1912): 51–53.

Quinan, Jack. "Frank Lloyd Wright's Buffalo Clients." *The Frank Lloyd Wright Newsletter* 5, no.1 (1982): 1–3.

———. "Frank Lloyd Wright, Darwin D. Martin, and the Creation of the Martin House." *Prairie House Journal*, supplement (1987): 5–12.

Rather, Susan. "Toward a New Language of Form: Karl Bitter and the Beginnings of Archaism in American Sculpture." *Winterthur Portfolio* 25, no. 1 (Spring 1990): 1–19.

————. "The Past Made Modern: Archaism in American Sculpture," *Arts Magazine* 59 (November 1984): 111–19.

"Restored Work of Frank Lloyd Wright: Former Yamamura Residence." *Japan Architect* 394 (February 1990): 8–12.

Riddle, Harriet. "The F. C. Bogk House, Milwaukee, Wisconsin." *The Frank Lloyd Wright Newsletter* 2, no. 1 (1979): 1–4.

Robinson, B. W. Review of *The Art of Surimono: privately published Japanese woodblock prints and books in the Chester Beatty Library, Dublin*, by Roger Keys. *Burlington Magazine* 128, no. 99 (June 1986): 442.

Rubin, Jeanne S. "The Froebel-Wright Kindergarten Connection: A New Perspective," *Journal of the Society of Architectural Historians* 48, no. 1 (March 1989): 24–37.

Schliepmann, Hans. "Haus 'Rheingold' in Berlin." *Deutsche Kunst und Dekoration* 7, no. 1 (April 1907): 1–60.

Schölermann, Wilhelm. "Modern and Applied Art in Vienna." *The Studio* 16 (1899): 30–38.

Schubert, Hermann. "The Squaring of the Circle, an Historical Sketch of the Problem from Earliest Times to the Present Day." In *Annual Report of the Board of Regents of the Smithsonian Institution . . . to July 1890,* (Washington, D.C.: U.S. Government Printing Office, 1891): 97–120.

Schuyler, Montgomery. "An Architectural Pioneer: Review of the Portfolios Containing the Works of Frank Lloyd Wright." *Architectural Record* 31 (April 1912): 427–36.

Scully, Vincent, J., Jr. "Frank Lloyd Wright vs. the International Style." *Art News* 53 (March 1954): 32–35, 64–66.

————. "The Heritage of Frank Lloyd Wright." *Zodiac* 8 (1961): 8–13.

————. Introduction. In *The Nature of Frank Lloyd Wright,* edited by Carol R. Bolon, Robert S. Nelson, and Linda Seidel, xiii-xxii. Chicago and London: University of Chicago Press, 1988.

Sekler, Eduard F. "Frank Lloyd Wright zum Gedächtnis." *Der Aufbau* (Vienna) 14, no. 8 (August 1959): 303–6.

————. "Mackintosh and Vienna." *Architectural Review* 144 (December 1968): 454–56.

Sell, Harry Blackman. "Interpretation, Not Imitation: Work of F. L. Wright." *International Studio* 55 (May 1915): lxxix–lxxxiii.

Singer, Hans W. "Modern German Lithography, II—Some Karlsruhe Artists." *The Studio* 16 (1899): 164–75.

Smith, Kathryn. "Frank Lloyd Wright, Hollyhock House, and Olive Hill, 1914–1924." *Journal of the Society of Architectural Historians* 38, no. 1 (March 1979): 15–33.

————. "Frank Lloyd Wright and the Imperial Hotel: A Postscript." *Art Bulletin* 67, no. 2 (June 1985): 296–310.

Smith, Nancy K. Morris, ed. "Letters, 1903–1906, by Charles E. White, Jr., from the Studio of Frank Lloyd Wright." *Journal of Architectural Education* 25 (Fall 1971): 104–12.

"Some Designs and Executed Buildings by Frank Lloyd, Architect." *Kenchiku gaho* 8, no. 11 (November 1917): entire issue.

"Some Recent Works of C. F. A. Voysey, an English Architect." *House and Garden* 3 (1903): 254–60.

Spencer, Robert C., Jr. "The Work of Frank Lloyd Wright." *Architectural Review* (Boston) 7 (June 1900): 61–72.

Stamp, Gavin. "Lutyens' Deanery Garden: An English House for Country Life." *International Architect* 1, no. 6 (1981): 43.

Stübben, T. "Aus der Geschichte des Architekten-Vereins zu Berlin." In *Hundert Jahre Architekten Verein zu Berlin, 1824–1924,* . Berlin: Wilhelm Ernst and Son, 1924, 7–12, 20.

"The Studio-Home of Frank Lloyd Wright." *Architectural Record* 33 (January 1913): 45–54.

Sullivan, Louis H. "Concerning the Imperial Hotel, Tokyo, Japan." *Architectural Record* 53 (April 1923): 332–52.

————. "Reflections on the Tokyo Disaster." *Architectural Record* 55 (February 1924): 113–18.

————. "The Young Man in Architecture." *Inland Architect* 35 (June 1900): 38–40.

Sweeney, Robert L. "The Coonley Playhouse, Riverside, Illinois." *The Frank Lloyd Wright Newsletter* 1, no. 6 (November–December 1978): 2–4.

Sweeney, Robert L., and Calvo, Charles M. "Frank Lloyd Wright: Textile Block Houses." *Space Design* 7–9, no. 240 (September 1984): 63–78.

Tanigawa, Masami. "Frank Lloyd Wright, Master Living in Legend." In *Unusual Modern Architects,* edited by Sakae Ohmi and Terunobu Fujinori, 173–82. Tokyo: Asahi Newspaper Publishers, 1984.

Thorp, Robert L. "Architectural Principles in Early Imperial China: Structural Problems and Their Solutions." *Art Bulletin* 68, no. 3 (September 1986): 360–78.

Townsend, Horace. "Notes on Country and Suburban Houses Designed by C. F. A. Voysey." *The Studio* 16 (1899): 157–64.

Tozzer, A. M. *Preliminary Study of the Ruins of Tikal, Guatemala.* Vol. 5, Memoirs, Peabody Museum of Archaeology and Ethnology no. 2 (1911).

Tselos, Dimitri. "Exotic Influences in Frank Lloyd Wright." *Magazine of Art* 47 (April 1953): 160–69, 184.

————. "Frank Lloyd Wright, Klassiker der modernen Weltarchitektur." *Universitas* (Stuttgart), (1959): 355–62.

————. "Frank Lloyd Wright and World Architecture." *Journal of the Society of Architectural Historians* 28, no. 1 (March 1969): 58–72.

Turak, Theodore. "Mr. Wright and Mrs. Coonley." In *Modern Architecture in America: Visions and Revisions,* edited by Richard Guy Wilson and Sidney Robinson, 144–63. Ames: Iowa State University Press, 1991.

Twombly, Robert C. "Frank Lloyd Wright in Spring Green, 1911–1932." *Wisconsin Magazine of History* 51 (Spring 1968): 200–217; reprinted in *Wisconsin Stories.* Madison: State Historical Society of Wisconsin, 1980.

Vallance, Aymer. "Some Recent Work by Mr. C. F. A. Voysey." *The Studio* 31 (1904): 127–34.

Van der Rohe, Mies. "A Tribute to Frank Lloyd Wright." *College Art Journal* 6 (1946): 41–42.

Van Zanten, David. "The Walter Burley Griffin–Otto Wagner Correspondence, 1914–1915." *Chicago Architectural Journal* 6 (1987): 22–25.

"The Vienna Kunstschau Exhibition." *The Studio* 44 (1908): 308–14.

Wagner, Otto. "Modern Architecture." Parts 1–3. Abridged translation by N. Clifford Ricker. *The Brickbuilder* 10, no. 6 (June 1901): 124–28; no. 7 (July 1901): 143–47; no. 8 (August 1901): 165–71.

Warlick, M. E. "Mythic Rebirth in Gustav Klimt's Stoclet Freize: New Considerations of Its Egyptianizing Form and Content." *Art Bulletin* 74, no. 1 (March 1992): 115–34.

Webster, R. F. "Midway Gardens to Be Formally Opened Tonight." *Chicago Daily Tribune*, 27 June 1914, p. 9

Weigand, Elizabeth. "The Arts at Midway Gardens." *Inland Architect* 29, no. 4 (July/August 1985): 45–47.

Weisberg, Gabriel. "Frank Lloyd Wright and Pre-Columbian Art—the Background for His Architecture." *Art Quarterly* 30 (Spring 1967): 40–51.

White, Charles E., Jr. "Are There Two American Schools of Architecture?" *The Art World* 2, no. 2 (May 1917): 178–82.

White, Gleeson. "Some Glasgow Designers and Their Work." *The Studio* 11 (1897): 86ff.

Wilson, Richard Guy. "Chicago and the International Arts and Crafts Movements: Progressive and Conservative Tendencies." In *Chicago Architecture, 1872–1922, Birth of a Metropolis*, edited by John Zukowsky, 115–34. Munich: Prestel Verlag and Art Institute of Chicago, 1987.

"The Women's Building and the Neighborhood Club." *The Weekly Home News,* 16 July 1914, p. 1.

Wright, Frank Lloyd. "The Architect." Reported in *The Brickbuilder* 9 (June 1900): 124–28.

———. "The Art and Craft of the Machine." In *Catalogue of the Fourteenth Exhibition of the Chicago Architectural Club.* [Chicago: Architectural Club, 1901], n.p.

———. "Frank Lloyd Wright." *Architectural Forum* 68 (January 1938): entire issue.

———. "In the Cause of Architecture." *Architectural Record* 23 (March 1908): 155–221.

———. "In the Cause of Architecture, Second Paper." *Architectural Record* 35 (May 1914): 405–13.

———. "Civilization without Culture." Unpublished address to the Taliesin Fellowship, Taliesin West, 25 February 1951, transcription, TAL MS cr. 15.

———. "Daniel Hudson Burnham: An Appreciation." *Architectural Record* 23 (August 1912): 175–84.

———. Review of *Towards a New Architecture* by Le Corbusier. *World Architecture* 2 (September 1928): 393–95.

4. The Wasmuth Publications

Editions of the Monograph

Wright, Frank Lloyd. *Ausgeführte Bauten und Entwürfe von Frank Lloyd Wright.* Two folios. Berlin: Ernst Wasmuth, 1911.

———. *Ausgeführte Bauten und Entwürfe.* Edited by Goichi Takeda. 1st Japanese edition. Osaka: Seikizen-Kan-Honten, 1916.

———. *Ausgeführte Bauten und Entwürfe.* 2d German ed. Berlin: Ernst Wasmuth [1924].

———. *Buildings, Plans, and Designs.* Preface by Frank Lloyd Wright. Foreword by William W. Peters. New York: Horizon Press, 1963. Japanese edition. Translated by Tadashi Yokayama. Tokyo: A.P.A.Edita, 1976.

———. *Studies and Executed Buildings by Frank Lloyd Wright. Ausgeführte Bauten und Entwürfe von Frank Lloyd Wright.* Palos Park, Ill.: Prairie School Press, 1975.

———. *Drawings and Plans of Frank Lloyd Wright. The Early Period (1893–1909).* New York: Dover, 1983.

———. *Studies and Executed Buildings by Frank Lloyd Wright.* London: Architectural Press, 1986.

———. *Studies and Executed Buildings by Frank Lloyd Wright.* Foreword by Vincent Scully. New York: Rizzoli, 1986.

———. *Ausgeführte Bauten und Entwürfe.* Tübingen, Germany: Wasmuth Verlag, 1986.

Editions of the *Sonderheft*

———. *Frank Lloyd Wright Chicago. Achtes Sonderheft der Architektur des zwanzigsten Jahrhunderts.* European edition. Introduction by Charles Robert Ashbee, "Frank Lloyd Wright. Eine Studie zu seiner Würdigung." Berlin: Ernst Wasmuth A.-G., 1911.

———. *Frank Lloyd Wright: Ausgeführte Bauten.* American edition. Introduction by Charles Robert Ashbee, "Frank Lloyd Wright. Eine Studie zu seiner Würdigung." Berlin: Ernst Wasmuth A.-G., 1911.

———. *Frank Lloyd Wright: The Early Work.* Foreword by Edgar Kaufmann, Jr. Introduction by Charles Robert Ashbee. "Frank Lloyd Wright. A Study and an Appreciation." New York: Horizon Press, 1968 (edited American edition).

———. *Frank Lloyd Wright: The Early Work.* New York: Bramhall House, n.d. [c. 1968].

———. *The Early Work of Frank Lloyd Wright. The "Ausgeführte Bauten" of 1911.* Introduction by Grant C. Manson. New York: Dover, 1982 (original American edition).

Index

Frank Lloyd Wright; Frank Lloyd Wright: Ausgeführte Bauten; Frank Lloyd Wright, Chicago; "In the Cause of Architecture"; Japanese Print, The; Sonderheft; "Studies and Executed Buildings by Frank Lloyd Wright"

Wright, John, 139, 331n.99, 359n.65, 360n.89, 361n.112; request to study with Wagner, 339n.141
Wright, Lloyd: assistance with Wasmuth drawings, 41; in Florence with Woolley, 43; on Francke's connection with Wasmuth, 325n.14; on Hollyhock House, 241; in Paris with Wright, 46–47; photograph of, 50; upon return to United States, 336n.87; travels with Woolley, 46, 336nn. 82, 84; on Woolley, 335n.63; and Wright's American iconography, 302; on Wright's purported meeting with Brahms, 335 n.76; on Wright's purported trip to Yucatan, 223–24

Zacherl House (Vienna), 129, 130, 131, 131, 133, 176, 179
Ziggurat in Ur, 181, 183

Photo Credits

Courtesy of The Busch-Reisinger Museum, Harvard University, Cambridge, Massachusetts: 2, 4; Courtesy of Alan Crawford and Felicity Ashbee: 19; Domino's Center for Architecture and Design: 68, 218, 303; Domino's Center for Architecture and Design, Henry Fuermann, photographer: 28, 58, 59, 70, 101, 116, 118–22, 124–25, 127, 130, 279, 280–81; Hispanic Society of America: 126; Idemitsu Museum of Art, Tokyo: 100; The Metropolitan Museum of Art, all rights reserved: 63, 167; Museum of Fine Arts, Boston: 160; The Museum of Modern Art, 64, 67; Peabody Museum, Harvard University, photograph by C.I.W.: 244; Harry Ransom Humanities Research Center, University of Texas at Austin: 13, 24, 32, 48; Cervin Robinson for HABS: 78; State Historical Society of Wisconsin: 73–74, 158; University Archives, State University of New York at Buffalo: 21; University of Utah Libraries: 34, 40–45; Copyright © 1957, 1959, 1962, 1977, 1981, 1982, 1984, 1985, 1986, 1987, 1988, 1991, 1993, Frank Lloyd Wright Foundation: frontispiece, 8, 53, 55–57, 96, 102, 114–15, 117, 145, 147, 152, 168, 180–81, 193–95, 200–201, 203, 208–13, 215, 222, 234–37, 246, 248, 253–55, 257–58, 270, 272–73, 276–78, 283–87, 289, 292, 295–98, 301, 305, 308–13.